Ethics in Crime and Justice

Dilemmas and Decisions

Fourth Edition

JOYCELYN M. POLLOCK

Southwest Texas State University

THOMSON

WADSWORTH

Australia • Canada • Mexico • Singapore • Spain
United Kingdom • United States

Dedication

To Eric and Gregory, as always,
and to Violet Pollock, the "coolest" Mom one could have.

Senior Acquisitions Editor, Criminal Justice: Jay Whitney

Editorial Assistant: Paul Massicotte

Technology Project Manager: Susan DeVanna

Marketing Manager: Dory Schaeffer

Marketing Assistant: Neena Chandra

Advertising Project Manager: Stacey Purviance

Project Manager, Editorial Production: Jennie Redwitz

Print/Media Buyer: Judy Inouye

Permissions Editor: Bob Kauser

Production Service: Judy Ludowitz at Shepherd, Inc.

Copy Editor: Cheryl Ferguson

Cover Designer: Belinda Fernandez

Cover Image: S. S. Yamamoto/Photonica

Compositor: Shepherd, Inc.

Text and Cover Printer: Webcom

Printed in Canada

2 3 4 5 6 7 07 06 05 04 03

For more information about our products, contact us at:
Thomson Learning Academic Resource Center
1-800-423-0563
For permission to use material from this text, contact us by:
Phone: 1-800-730-2214
Fax: 1-800-730-2215
Web: http://www.thomsonrights.com

Library of Congress Cataloging-in-Publication Data

Pollock, Joycelyn M.
  Ethics in crime and justice: dilemmas and decisions / Joycelyn M. Pollock.— 4th ed.
    p.   cm.
  ISBN 0-534-56349-X
  I. Title.
                        2003106453

Wadsworth/Thomson Learning
10 Davis Drive
Belmont, CA 94002-3098
USA

Asia
Thomson Learning
5 Shenton Way #01-01
UIC Building
Singapore 068808

Australia/New Zealand
Thomson Learning
102 Dodds Street
Southbank, Victoria 3006
Australia

Canada
Nelson
1120 Birchmount Road
Toronto, Ontario M1K 5G4
Canada

Europe/Middle East/Africa
Thomson Learning
High Holborn House
50/51 Bedford Row
London WC1R 4LR
United Kingdom

Latin America
Thomson Learning
Seneca, 53
Colonia Polanco
11560 Mexico D.F.
Mexico

Brief Contents

Contents

Preface

The world has changed since the third edition of this book was written in 1998. The tragedy of the World Trade Center attack has forever destroyed this country's sense of invulnerability and created fear and disquiet that continues to affect people's lives. The world seems a more dangerous place. The result has been a reordering of the nation's priorities and a mammoth federalization of law enforcement. Fighting terrorism is hardly a local affair. As this book was being completed, conflict in Iraq continues. Further acts of terrorism are expected. Before September 11, 2001, the issues that might have been at the forefront of our discussion would have been racial profiling, how to address the drug problem, corruption by public or private leaders, and how to treat juvenile offenders. These issues are still important, but we must add to them a discussion of what is acceptable in war and in our fight against terrorism. Do these "ends" justify torture? Do they justify curtailing the civil liberties of resident aliens? Of citizens? I have tried to address these questions either directly or indirectly in several chapters of this edition.

Obviously, the government's response to the terrorist attack on the World Trade Center is a pervasive theme of this new edition. It was striking to me that in reading back over the arguments concerning utilitarian thinking (ends–means justifications) that had been used to discuss criminal justice procedural issues before 9/11, it was apparent that the arguments hadn't changed, but the world has. The fear engendered by terrorism is a challenge to rights-based ethics.

NEW TO THIS EDITION

Changes in this edition are, to some degree, reflective of the concerns expressed by the six reviewers who kindly offered suggestions, as well as the many people who have spoken or corresponded with me regarding the last edition. I have attempted to make the chapters more equal in length and increased the number to 14 to more closely match a typical semester. I have eliminated most of the literary perspectives since several reviewers indicated that these were not very helpful. Personally, I believe in using fiction to teach this course, and I hope that the instructor's manual that is being prepared by Wadsworth will give ideas about how to incorporate fiction into the teaching of these concepts. I have also tried to suggest movies and books in relevant chapters to be used for class projects. I have eliminated the abortion example and the Heinz dilemma from discussion in the first several chapters. Some reviewers suggested that they were less effective than other dilemmas, and I agreed.

In every edition I must balance the desire of some reviewers to lengthen the discussion of ethical systems and the philosophy of ethics against the desire of users who teach the course with a more direct focus on criminal justice issues. I have come to the conclusion that it is impossible to continue to add or expand discussions of philosophical topics such as existentialism, the social contract theory, Rawls's conceptions of justice, moral pluralism, and so on. I could, but the book would keep expanding and I could never cover these topics as well as a philosophy text and still provide current issues in criminal justice. Thus, I have cut about ten pages from the chapter on ethical systems. I apologize to those who would have preferred that chapter be expanded rather than shortened. I would encourage and expect that those who are dissatisfied with the treatment of the ethical systems will use a second book written by an ethicist who will more clearly, carefully, and comprehensively cover these issues. I have instead, in this edition, attempted to cover the current issues that exist in the criminal justice system without adding significantly to the cost or length of the book.

Other changes include some attention to juvenile issues, although I must confess that much more could be done in this area. I have, of course, added discussions of current news events when applicable, such as the Ramparts scandal in California, the Louima and Diallo cases in New York City, the Innocence Project findings of innocents on death row, racial profiling reports, scandals with private correctional institutions, and sex-offender registration laws. There are many other events that I probably have missed or chose to delete in the interest of keeping this book to a reasonable length. I continue to encourage instructors to utilize their newspaper and other media outlets to add to course content. I sometimes have students keep a journal of newspaper articles that have relevance to the course, and ask them to add their own commentary.

Academic contributions to the field of ethics continue to expand. John Crank and Michael Caldero's book on noble-cause corruption has been a very important contribution to the field of law enforcement ethics, and I have borrowed liberally from it. I have also added updated sources and added new sources in the appropriate chapters. It is always a challenge to keep abreast of all that is written since the field has expanded tremendously since the first edition of this book in 1985. I apologize in advance for missing some current sources and promise that I will include them in the next edition.

ACKNOWLEDGMENTS

I am especially grateful for the help of Tim Prenzler in Australia, who graciously shared his opinion that the book would be more valuable by enlarging the perspective to include worldwide ethical issues, and provided me with some of the work that he has done in this area. Dennis Hawkins, Roger Roundtree, and Tom Martinelli have helped in providing a reality check on some of the application chapters for criminal justice professionals. Mickey Braswell has always been my ethics guru, and I appreciate his honesty, humor, and stories. As stated before, the anonymous reviewers provided by Wadsworth have been very thorough and helpful. They are:

Cyndi Banks, *Northern Arizona University*

Tara Gray, *New Mexico State University*

Richard Kania, *University of North Carolina, Pembroke*

Lee Libby, *Washington State Community College*

Tom Mahoney, *University of California, Santa Barbara*

Julius Wachtel, *California State University, Fullerton*

Noel Pinero has been an invaluable source in his role as editor of a group "listserve" provided by the Open Society Institute in New York. Through his efforts I have been exposed to newspaper articles across the country relevant to the topics discussed in this book and the use of such articles has enriched this discussion. I thank my colleagues, and especially the chair here at Southwest Texas State University, Quint Thurman, for creating a pleasant and productive work environment and Autumn Hanna who helped with the index. Finally, I thank my family, who have allowed me to steal family time to finish this book.

1

Morality, Ethics, and Human Behavior

Key Terms

wholesight
morals
ethics
meta-ethics
normative ethics
applied ethics
professional ethics
judgments
duties
superogatories
imperfect duties
values
opinions

laws
crime
intent
knowing
age of reason
negligence
recklessness
regulations
standards
guidelines
ethical dilemmas
moral rules

Chapter Objectives

- Become familiar with the major arguments supporting the importance of studying ethics in the criminal justice field.
- Understand the vocabulary of ethics—that is, morals, ethics, values, ethical codes, ethical standards, and dilemmas.
- Understand how to analyze an ethical dilemma.
- Become sensitive to the types of ethical dilemmas faced in one's professional life.

Consider the following dilemmas: You are a police officer patrolling late at night and see a car weaving back and forth across lanes of traffic. You turn on your siren, and the car pulls over. The driver stumbles out of the car, obviously intoxicated. There is no question that the driver meets the legal definition of intoxication. He also happens to be your father. What would you do?

You are a correctional officer working the late night shift. Your sergeant and another officer from the day shift come onto the tier you are working and ask you to open up an inmate's cell. You do so, they enter the cell, and you hear a series of sounds, including grunts, cries, and moans. They exit, muttering about how the inmate has been taught a lesson. You believe that you have just been a party to an assault, but say nothing. The next night, you find out that the inmate never reported the incident, nor did any other inmates. You believe that if you come forward and report what you saw, you will be severely ostracized, that you may not even be believed (especially if the inmate doesn't back you up), and that you might lose your job. What would you do?

You are a student interning in a criminal defense lawyer's office. As part of your duties, you sit in court with the lawyer you are working with, help her with legal research, and assist in interviewing witnesses. During the course of the internship you conclude that the lawyer is, in your opinion, extremely negligent. She does not return client calls, she misses appeal deadlines, and she ignores or does not follow up on promising leads that might lead to exculpatory evidence. You are appalled that several of her clients are advised to plead guilty, even though you think that the evidence against them is weak. After bringing up these issues with her, she fires you on the spot, and tells you that all her clients are guilty anyway and she is just another "cog in the wheel" of the justice machine. What, if anything, would you do?

WHY STUDY ETHICS?

How would you decide what to do in these situations? Learning how to determine the "right thing to do" is the central purpose of this book. We make ethical decisions all the time, whether we recognize them or not. Think about some ethical choices you have been faced with in the last couple weeks. Perhaps the choice occurred at work when you were asked to cover for an employee who wanted to go home early and not report the time lost; or when a friend and co-worker took something from the store where you both worked and expected you to say nothing. Perhaps the choice occurred when a friend asked you to lie, or when you, yourself, felt compelled to tell a professor a "white lie" when asking for an extension on an assignment or a different test time.

All of us are faced with choices that can be judged under ethical standards. Furthermore, we frequently judge other people's behaviors as right or wrong. Criminal justice professionals, whether they work in law enforcement, the courts, or corrections, experience a multitude of situations where they must make choices that can be judged after the fact as right or wrong. A characteristic of every criminal justice profession is that the role entails a public trust that involves power over others. Those who have such power over others must be especially sensitive to the ethical issues that may arise in their professional lives.

Criminal justice issues are serious, difficult, and affect people's lives in fundamental ways. These are just a sample of the criminal justice issues that have ethical implications:

- Decriminalization of soft drugs
- Megan's Law and similar legislation that require sex-offender registries (perhaps spurring vigilante actions)
- A moratorium of the death penalty
- Mandatory DNA testing in death penalty cases
- Three-strikes legislation
- Racial profiling
- Law enforcement corruption (i.e., the Ramparts scandal)
- Waiver of juveniles to adult courts
- Citizen oversight committees for police departments
- The Patriot Law and other challenges to civil liberties in the wake of terrorism

The criminal justice system is often examined using political, organizational, or sociological approaches. Let us shift the lens somewhat and look at the steps in the system through an ethics perspective. Although our primary discussion concerns ethical dilemmas faced by individuals, the same analytical approach might be used to help shed light on the issues listed, as well as others.

Legislators have the power to define behavior as illegal and, therefore, punishable. They also have the power to set the amount of punishment. They do so usually from some rationale of public safety, but also employ moral definitions for deciding which behaviors should be legal and which should be illegal. For instance, there is obviously a public-safety rationale for laws against murder or armed robbery, but is there a public-safety rationale for laws that prohibit same-sex marriages? It seems that the only argument against same-sex marriages is a purely moral one. "Protection of public morality" is the rationale for a number of other laws, including abortion, sodomy between consenting adults, drug laws, gambling, and prostitution. Legislators impose the public "will" and define what is wrong. Ultimately, that definition leads to deprivations of liberties for those who do not believe in the wrongness of the action. For example, although you might not believe there is anything morally wrong with small amounts of marijuana, you act on that belief at your peril. Thus, one might question how legislators use their great discretion and how they balance the rights of all people. Chapter 5 explores these questions in more detail.

Police officers have the power to deprive people of their liberty (through arrest), they have the power to decide which individuals to investigate and perhaps target for undercover operations, and they have the power to issue a ticket or provide "mercy" and let a driver off with a warning. They serve as the interface between the awesome power of the state and the citizenry governed. In some countries, police operate as a fearsome coercive force for a controlling political body. In this country, some see police operating in a similar way; however, we do enjoy constitutional protections against untrammeled police power. In Chapters 6, 7, and 8, the ethical use of police discretion will be discussed in more detail.

Prosecutors probably face the least public scrutiny of all criminal justice professionals, which is ironic since they wield incredible power in their discretion in deciding who and how to prosecute. They decide which charges to pursue and which to drop, which cases to take to a grand jury, how to prosecute a case, whether to pursue the death penalty in homicide cases, and so on. They often make general decisions about the types of crimes to pursue, affecting police officers' enforcement decisions. They have ethical duties to pursue "justice" rather than conviction, but one might argue that, at times, their decision making may seem to be more political than just. Judges also hold incredible power, typically employed through decision making in accepting plea bargains, decisions regarding rules of evidence, and decisions about sentencing. Chapters 9 and 10 deal with the ethical issues of legal professionals in the criminal justice system.

Finally, correctional officials also have immense powers over the lives of certain citizens. Probation officers make recommendations in pre-sentence reports and violation reports that affect whether an individual goes to prison. Prison officials decide to award and take away "good time," and they make decisions regarding placing inmates into segregation—in both types of decisions, the individual's liberty is affected. Correctional officers make daily decisions that affect the life and health of the prisoners they supervise. The discretion of parole officials includes the decision to file a violation report, as well as less serious decisions regarding the parolee's life. In short, all correctional professionals have a great deal of discretion over the lives of those they control. The ethical issues of correctional professionals are discussed in Chapters 11, 12, and 13.

All the professionals discussed have several elements in common:

1. *They each have discretion, meaning the power to make a decision.* While the particular decisions are different, they all involve power over others and potential deprivation of life, liberty, or property.

2. *They each have the duty of enforcement of the law.* Although this concept is obvious with police, it is also clear that each of the professionals mentioned has a basic duty to uphold and enforce all laws; they serve the law in their professional lives.

3. *They must accept that their duty is to protect the constitutional safeguards that are the cornerstone of our legal system, specifically, due process and equal protection.* Due process protects each of us from error in a governmental deprivation of life, liberty, or property. We recognize the right of government to control and even to punish, but we have certain protections against arbitrary or inaccurate use of that power. Due process protects those interests. We also expect that government's power will be used fairly and in an unbiased manner. Equal protection should ensure that what happens to us is not determined by the color of our skin, our gender, nationality, or the religion we practice. Laws are for everyone, and the protection of the law extends to all of us. Although there is a fair amount of evidence to indicate that different treatment does exist, the ideal of equal protection is an essential element of our legal system and should be an operating principle for everyone working in this system.

4. *They are public servants.* That is, their salaries come from the public purse. Public servants possess more than a job; they have taken on special duties involving the public trust. Individuals such as legislators, public officials, police officers, judges, and prosecutors are either elected or appointed guardians of the public's interests. Arguably, they must be held to *higher* standards than those they guard or govern. Temptations are many, and often it seems we find examples of *double* standards, where public servants take advantage of their positions for special favors, rather than *higher* standards of exemplary behavior.

QUOTE

Part of what is needed [for public servants] is a public sense of what Madison meant by wisdom and good character: balanced perception and integrity. Integrity means wholeness in public and private life consisting of habits of justice, temperance, courage, compassion, honesty, fortitude, and disdain for self-pity.

Delattre, 1989b: 78–83.

Obviously, the law governs many of the decisions that public servants make, but because of the discretion that exists at every step of the criminal justice process, there is always the possibility of an unethical use of such discretion. Understanding the ethical issues involved in one's profession might help to guide such discretion and prevent abuse. Therefore, all professionals in the criminal justice field must be sensitive to ethical issues. These issues may involve their relations with citizens and others over whom they have power, their relationships with their agency, or their relationships with one another. The "Principles of Public Service Ethics" box considers how ethics should be applied by public servants.

Principles of Public Service Ethics

1. *Public service.* Public servants should treat their office as a public trust, only using the power and resources of public office to advance public interests, and not to attain personal benefit or pursue any other private interest incompatible with the public good.
2. *Objective judgment.* Public servants should employ independent objective judgment in performing their duties, deciding all matters on the merits, free from avoidable conflicts of interest and both real and apparent improper influences.
3. *Accountability.* Public servants should assure that government is conducted openly, efficiently, equitably, and honorably in a manner that permits the citizenry to make informed judgments and hold government officials accountable.
4. *Democratic leadership.* Public servants should honor and respect the principles and spirit of representative democracy and set a positive example of good citizenship by scrupulously observing the letter and spirit of laws and rules.
5. *Respectability.* Public servants should safeguard public confidence in the integrity of government by being honest, fair, caring, and respectful, and by avoiding conduct creating the appearance of impropriety or which is otherwise unbefitting a public official.

SOURCE: Josephson Institute of Ethics.

Felkenes (1987: 26) explained why the study of ethics is important for criminal justice professionals:

1. Professionals are recognized as such in part because [a] "profession" . . . normally includes a set of ethical requirements as part of its meaning. . . . Professionalism among all actors at all levels of the criminal justice system depends upon their ability to administer policy effectively in a morally and ethically responsible manner.
2. Training in critical ethics helps to develop analytical skills and reasoning abilities needed to understand the pragmatic and theoretical aspects of the criminal justice system.
3. Criminal justice professionals should be able to recognize quickly the ethical consequences of various actions, and the moral principles involved.
4. Ethical considerations are central to decisions involving discretion, force, and due process which require people to make enlightened moral judgments.
5. Ethics is germane to most management and policy decisions concerning such penal issues as rehabilitation, deterrence, and just deserts.
6. Ethical considerations are essential aspects of criminal justice research.

In answer to a similar question, Braswell (2002: 8) explains the five goals of a study of ethics:

1. Become aware and open to ethical issues.
2. Begin developing critical thinking skills.

3. Become more personally responsible.

4. Understand how the criminal justice system is engaged in a process of coercion.

5. Develop **wholesight** (which roughly means exploring with one's heart as well as one's mind).

The comprehensive nature of these two lists requires no additions. We will simply reiterate some basic points. First, we study ethics because criminal justice is uniquely involved in coercion, which means there are many and varied opportunities to abuse such power. Second, almost all criminal justice professionals are public servants and, thus, owe special duties to the public they serve. Finally, we study ethics to sensitize the student to ethical issues and provide tools to help identify and resolve the ethical dilemmas that may be faced in their professional lives.

QUOTE

Raise the salaries [of public servants], we are encouraged, and then you can expect better. I doubt it. . . . Raise the salaries if the jobs merit higher pay but not in expectation of buying integrity. Nobody sells that. People who have it give it for free.

———————

Delattre, 1989b: 78–83.

DEFINING TERMS

The words **morals** and **ethics** are often used in daily conversations. For instance, when public officials use their offices for personal profit or when politicians accept bribes from special interest groups, they are described as unethical. When an individual does a good deed, engages in charitable activities or personal sacrifice, or takes a stand against wrongdoing, we might describe that individual as a moral person. Very often, *morals* and *ethics* are used interchangeably. This makes sense because they both come from similar root meanings. The Greek word *ethos* pertains to custom (behavioral practices) or character, and *morals* is a Latin word with a similar meaning.

Morals and Ethics

Morals and *morality* refer to what is judged as good conduct. (*Immorality* refers to bad conduct.) The term *moral* is also used to describe someone who has the capacity to make value judgments and discern right from wrong (Souryal, 1992: 12). *Ethics* refers to the study and analysis of what constitutes good or bad conduct (Barry, 1985: 5; Sherman, 1981: 8).

There are several branches or schools of ethics. **Meta-ethics** is "the highly technical discipline investigating the meaning of ethical terms including a critical study of how ethical statements can be verified" (Barry, 1985: 11). **Normative ethics** and **applied ethics** are concerned with the study of what constitutes right and wrong behavior in certain situations. Normative ethics determines what people ought to do and defines moral duties. Applied ethics is the application of ethical principles to specific issues. **Professional ethics** is an even more specific type of applied ethics relating to the behavior of certain professions or groups.

To many people, ethics has come to mean the definition of particular behaviors as right and wrong within a profession. Very often, in common usage, morality is used to speak of the total person, or the sum of a person's actions in every sphere of life, and ethics is used to refer to behaviors relating to a profession, and is an analysis of behavior relevant to a certain profession. For instance, the medical profession follows the Hippocratic Oath, a declaration of rules and principles of conduct for doctors to follow in their daily practices; it dictates appropriate behavior and goals. In fact, most professions have their own set of ethical standards or canons of ethics.

Even though professional ethics typically restricts attention to areas of behavior relevant to the profession, these can be fairly inclusive and enter into what we might consider the private life of the individual. For instance, doctors are judged harshly if they engage in romantic relationships with their patients, as are professors if they become involved with students. These rules are usually included in codes of ethics for these professions. We are very much aware of how politicians' private behavior can affect their career in politics. When politicians are embroiled in controversial love affairs or are exposed as spouse abusers, these revelations have definite effects on their future. It is clear that, in some professions, anyway—typically those involving public trust such as politics, education, and the clergy—there is a thin line between one's private life and one's public life.

QUERY

- Should we be concerned with a politician who has extramarital affairs? Drinks to excess? Gambles? Uses drugs? Abuses his or her spouse? What if the person was a police officer? A judge?
- Should a police officer be sanctioned for drinking to excess in public and making a spectacle of himself or herself in a bar? Should a police officer be sanctioned for posing naked in a men's magazine, but identified as a police officer, using pieces of the uniform as "props"?
- Should a probation officer socialize in bars that his or her probationers are likely to frequent?

It does not make a great deal of difference for our purposes whether we use the formal or colloquial definitions of *morals* and *ethics*. This text is an applied ethics text, in that we will be concerned with what is defined as right and wrong behavior in the professions relevant to the criminal justice system and how people in these professions make decisions in the course of their careers. It is also a professional ethics text, because we are primarily concerned with professional ethics in criminal justice.

Making Moral Judgments

We make moral or ethical **judgments** all the time: "Abortion is wrong." "Capital punishment is just." "It is good to give to charity." "It is wrong to hit your spouse." These are all judgments of good and bad behavior. We also make choices that can be judged as right or wrong. Should you call in sick even though you aren't, to get a day in the sun? Should you give back extra change that a clerk gave you by mistake? Should you tell a friend that her husband is having an affair even though he asked you not to tell? Not all behaviors involve questions of ethics. In order to more specifically draw the boundaries of our ethical discussion, we need to know what sorts of behavioral decisions might be judged under ethical standards. Decisions that can be judged involve human acts of free will that affect others.

Act First of all, we must have some act to judge. For instance, we are concerned with the act of stealing or the act of contributing to charity, rather than an idle thought that stealing a lot of money would enable us to buy a sailboat or a vague intention to be more generous. We are not necessarily concerned with how people feel or what they think about a particular action unless it has some bearing on what they do. The intention or motive behind a particular behavior is an important component of that behavior; for instance, in ethical formalism (which we will discuss in Chapter 2) one must know the intent of an action in order to be able to judge it as moral, immoral, or neither. However, one must have some action to examine before making a moral judgment.

Only Human Acts Second, judgments of moral or ethical behavior are directed specifically to human behavior. A dog that bites is not considered immoral or evil, although we may judge careless pet owners who allow their dogs the opportunity to bite. Nor do we consider drought, famine, floods, or other natural disasters immoral, even though the death, destruction, and misery caused by these events are probably greater than that caused by all combined acts that humans have perpetrated on their victims. Behaviors of animals or events of nature cannot be judged in the same way as actions performed by human beings. The reasons we view them differently may become apparent in the next paragraph. Morality (or immorality) has been applied only to humans because of their capacity to reason. Because only humans have the capacity to be "good," which involves a voluntary, rational decision and subsequent action, only humans, of all members of the animal kingdom, have the capacity to be "bad."

Free Will In addition to limiting discussions of morality to human behavior, we also usually further restrict our discussion to behavior that stems from free will and free action. Culpability is not assigned to persons who are not sufficiently aware of the world around them to be able to decide rationally what is good or bad. The two groups traditionally exempt from responsibility in this sense are the young and the insane. Arguably, we do not judge the morality of their behavior because of a belief that they do not have the capacity to reason and therefore cannot choose to be moral or immoral. Although we may punish a two-year-old for hitting a baby, we do so to educate or socialize, not to punish, as we would an older child or adult. We incapacitate the mentally ill to protect ourselves against their violence and strange behavior, but we consider them sick, not evil. This is true even if their actual behavior is indistinguishable from that of other individuals we do punish. For example, a murder may result in a death sentence or a hospital commitment, depending on whether the person is judged to be sane or insane, responsible or not responsible. Admittedly, at times we have difficulty in deciding whether behavior originates with free will, or we do not care whether it does. This issue will be addressed in more detail later in this chapter.

QUERY

- Do you agree that a child before the legal age of reason is not morally culpable for his or her actions? Why or why not? What should the age of reason be?
- What are some situations in which the individual cannot be considered rational or, alternatively, is not acting from free will? Is the behavior that results moral or immoral?

Affects Others Finally, we usually discuss moral or immoral behavior only in those cases where the behavior significantly affects others. For instance, throwing a rock off a bridge would be neither good nor bad unless you could possibly hit or were aiming at a person below. If no one were there, your behavior is neutral; if someone were below, however, you might endanger that person's life, so your behavior would be judged as "bad." All the moral dilemmas we will discuss in this book involve at least two parties, and the decision to be made affects the other individual in every case. In reality, it is difficult to think of an action that does not affect others, however indirectly. Even self-destructive behavior is said to harm the people who love us and who would be hurt by such actions. We sense that this is an important aspect of judging morality when we hear the common rationale of those who, when caught, protest, "But nobody was hurt!" Indeed, even a hermit living alone on a desert island may engage in immoral or unethical actions. Whether he wants to be or not, the hermit is part of human society; therefore, some people would say that even he might engage in actions that could be judged immoral if they degrade or threaten the future of humankind, such as committing suicide or polluting the ocean.

One's actions toward nature might also be defined as immoral, so relevant actions include not only actions done to people, but also to animals and to nature. To abuse or exploit animals can be defined as immoral—judgments can be made against cockfighting, dog racing, laboratory experimentation on animals, and hunting. The growth of environmental ethics reflects increasing concern for the future of the planet. The rationale for environmental ethics may be that any actions that harm the environment affect all humans. It might also be justified by the belief that humankind is a part of nature—not superior to it—and part of natural law would be to protect, not exploit, the world of which we are a part.

QUERY

- Can you think of any action that does not affect other people?
- Do you believe the state should regulate behavior that arguably doesn't hurt anyone else (such as motorcycle or bicycle helmet laws)? Prostitution? Gambling?
- Do you hold someone just as accountable for acts that are reckless and acts that are deliberate?

Thus far, we know morality and ethics concern the judgment of behavior as right or wrong. Furthermore, such judgments are directed only at voluntary human behavior that affects other people, the earth, and living things. We can further restrict our inquiries regarding ethics to those behavioral decisions that are relevant to one's profession in the criminal justice system. Discussions regarding the ethics of police officers would concern issues such as whether to take gratuities, whether to cover up the wrongdoing of a fellow officer, whether to sleep on duty, whether to call in sick when one wants to play golf or go fishing, and whether to lie on an expense sheet. All of these actions affect other people. Review the "Inventory of Ethical Issues." Notice that ethical work decisions fall into major categories: effects on citizenry, effects on other employees, and effects on the organization one works for.

Inventory of Ethical Issues

The Individual and the Organization:

work ethic

petty theft

overtime abuse

gifts and gratuities

falsifying reports

misuse of sick days

personal use of supplies or equipment

personal demands interfering with work performance

The Organization and Employees:

sexual or racial harassment

discouraging honest criticism

unfair decisions

inadequate compensation

no recognition of good performance

inadequate training

unrealistic demands

The Individual and Other Employees:

backstabbing and lack of support

gossip

sexual or racial harassment

lying to cover up blame

taking credit for other's work

The Individual and the Public:

misuse of authority

inadequate performance of duty

sexual, racial, ethnic harassment

special treatment

lack of expertise in profession

Duties

Another comment we should make about behavior and morality is that philosophers distinguish between moral duties and superogatories. **Duties** refer to those actions that an individual must perform in order to be considered moral. For instance, everyone may agree that one has a duty to support one's parents if able to do so, one has a duty to obey the law (unless it is an immoral law), and a police officer has a moral and ethical duty to tell the truth on a police report. Duties are what you must do in order to be good.

Other actions, considered **superogatories,** are commendable but not required. A Good Samaritan who jumps into a river to save a drowning person, risking his or her own life to do so, has performed a superogatory action—there is no moral condemnation of those who stood on the bank, because the action was above and beyond anyone's moral duty. Of course, if one can help save a life with no great risk to oneself, then a moral duty does exist in that situation. Police officers may have an ethical duty to get involved when others do not. Consider the World Trade Center. One of the most moving images of that tragedy was that police officers and firefighters ran toward danger while most people ran away. This professional duty to put oneself in harm's way is why we revere and pay homage to these public servants. Many civilians also put themselves in harm's way, and since they had no professional duty to do so, they could be said to be performing superogatory actions.

There are also what are called **imperfect duties.** These are general values that one should uphold, but without specific application as to when or how. For instance, most ethical systems would support a general duty of generosity, but there is no specific duty demanding a certain type or manner of generosity.

Values

Values are defined as elements of desirability, worth, or importance. Values and judgments of worth are often equated with moral judgments of goodness. We see that both can be distinguished from factual judgments, which can be empirically verified. Note the difference between the factual judgments "He is lying" and "It is raining" and the value judgments of "She is a good woman" or "That was a wonderful day." The last two judgments are more similar to moral judgments in that "facts" are capable of scientific proof, whereas values and moral judgments are not.

Some writers think that value judgments and moral judgments are indistinguishable, since neither can be verified (Mackie, 1977; Margolis, 1971). Some also think that values and morals are relativistic and individual. For these people, there are no universal values; they are subjective rather than objective. Thus, they are not "truth," but, rather, something closer to opinion (Mackie, 1977: 22–24). Because they are only **opinions,** in this view, no value is more important than any other value. Others believe that not all values are equal. Values such as honesty, for instance, are always more important than values such as pleasure. Universalists would not hesitate to propose that valuing money over life, for instance, would be wrong, as would valuing pleasure over charity.

Discussions concerning values imply a choice or judgment. If, for instance, you were confronted with an opportunity to cheat on an exam, your values of academic success and honesty would be directly at odds. Values and morals are similar, but while values merely indicate *relative* importance, morals prescribe or proscribe behavior. The value of honesty is conceptually distinct from the moral rule against lying.

Individual values form value systems. All people prioritize certain things that they consider important in life. Behavior is generally consistent with values. For instance, some individuals may believe that financial success is more important than family or health. In this case, we may assume that their behavior will reflect the importance of that value and that these persons will be workaholics, spending more time at work than with family and endangering their health with long hours, stress, and lack of exercise. Others may place a higher priority on religious faith, wisdom, honesty, and/or independence than financial success or status. Most of us live our lives in rough accordance with our values. But it is also true that very often we live our lives without taking a close look at the value system that influences our behavior. See the "Exercise" box.

This discussion concerning values is fairly explicit in Messner and Rosenfeld's (1994) theory of crime. In their explanation of why the United States experiences a higher rate of violent crime than other Western countries, they propose that the American value system that emphasizes consumerism over family, honesty, or other (more honorable) values creates an environment where crime results. Success in the United States is defined almost exclusively by the accumulation of material goods, not by doing "good." Since behavior is influenced by one's value system, individuals who place material success over any other value will behave dishonestly or even violently in the pursuit of such goods.

An explicit value system is a part of every ethical system, as we will see in Chapter 2. Certain values hold special relevance to the criminal justice system. Privacy, freedom, public order, justice, duty, and loyalty are all values that will come up again in later discussions. The values of life, respect for the person, and the continued survival of society can be found in all ethical systems.

Exercise

Rank the following values in order of importance, with #1 representing the most important value to you, and so on. Now go through the list again and rank these values according to how you believe most people would rank them. Compare your answers with others as a class exercise.

Achievement	Friendship	Power
Altruism	Health	Recognition
Autonomy	Honesty	Religion
Beauty	Justice	Success
Creativity	Knowledge	Wealth
Duty	Love	Wisdom
Emotional well-being	Loyalty	
Family	Pleasure	

MORALITY AND THE LAW

Laws govern many aspects of our behavior. **Laws,** in the form of statutes and ordinances, tell us how to drive, how to operate our business, and what we can and cannot do in public and even in private. They are the formal, written rules of society. Yet they are not comprehensive in defining moral behavior. There is a law against hitting one's mother (assault) but no law against financially abandoning her, yet both are considered morally wrong. We have laws against "bad" behavior, such as burglarizing a house or embezzling from our employer, but we have very few laws prescribing "good" behavior, such as helping a victim or contributing to a charity. The exception to this would be the "Good Samaritan laws" that exist in some states and are quite common in Europe. These laws make it a crime to pass by an accident scene or witness a crime without rendering assistance.

Some actions prohibited by law are thought to be private decisions of the individual and not especially wrong or harmful. Many people object to sodomy laws and other laws regulating sexual behavior because they feel this is private behavior and outside the parameters of social control. When laws prohibit behaviors that are not universally condemned, such as laws prohibiting alcohol, drugs, and prostitution, enforcement is more subject to criticism and, not incidentally, more prone to corruption because there is a greater ability to rationalize under-enforcement or preferential treatment. Consider, for instance, the argument that organized crime grew tremendously during Prohibition and unknown numbers of law enforcement officers were corrupted by bribery and protection rackets. Some argue the same scenario is occurring again today in the drug war.

We have had laws in the past that were or are now considered immoral—for instance, the internment of Japanese Americans during World War II, "Jim Crow" laws before the Civil Rights era, and pre–Civil War laws that mandated the return of runaway slaves to their owners. An important question in the study of ethics is whether one can be a good person while obeying a bad law. Civil disobedience occurs when someone voluntarily disobeys what they consider to be an unjust or immoral law. In Chapter 4 and 5, we discuss morality and immorality in relation to the legal system.

QUERY
- Which, if any, laws do you believe legislate what should be private decisions of individuals?
- Which, if any, laws do you believe are themselves morally wrong (or support immoral behavior)?
- If one followed all laws, would that make them a moral person?

A crime is composed of three elements: an *actus reus,* a *mens rea,* (with concurrence between the two), and causation. The *actus reus* is the physical act that is defined as the **crime.** Furthermore, the act must have been the result of the defendant's own volition. If, for instance, the act was performed while sleepwalking or when the person was not fully conscious, then there was no *actus reus.* The *mens rea* is the level of culpability required for each crime in order to find guilt. The four levels of legal culpability are negligent, reckless, knowing, and intentional. Causation is when the *actus reus* creates the result prohibited or described by the law. For instance, when the defendant's blow injures or kills the victim, "proximate" cause is the law's attempt to use common sense to limit a defendant's capability. For instance, if the dependant's assault puts the victim in the hospital and then the person is killed in an accidental fire, even though death ultimately resulted from the assault, the defendant is not guilty of homicide because the assault was not the "proximate cause" of the death.

Criminal Culpability/Moral Culpability

The law recognizes different levels of responsibility by the different levels of *mens rea*. First-degree homicide, for instance, requires proof of **intent,** while second-degree homicide requires only evidence of **knowing.** Crimes that require only evidence of negligence or recklessness have less-severe punishments attached to them because the level of culpability, fault, or blame is less severe. Careless actions, such as driving while intoxicated or killing someone while playing with a loaded weapon, are judged as less "bad" than those actions performed with deliberation and intent. An individual who has weighed the consequences and knows the outcome and all the ramifications of the action and then proceeds has greater legal culpability than someone who has proceeded without such deliberation, albeit with a negligent disregard for potential or probable consequences.

It might be that one's mental state prevents the state from considering any level of guilt. If one is found "incompetent to stand trial," it means that there has been a legal determination that the individual is incapable of understanding the proceedings and assisting in his or her own defense. We have a long legal tradition of requiring the defendant to be at least minimally competent and rational and recognize different levels of culpability.

Historically, two groups have been considered "excused" from criminal culpability: the insane and juveniles. This is because of a belief that individuals in one or both of these groups are not rational—in other words, they cannot weigh the consequences of their actions and, therefore, should not be held accountable. Thus, even those found competent to stand trial may be acquitted by reason of insanity. Or they may not. We continue to imprison and even execute those who show obvious signs of mental illness, despite our legal tradition of holding only "rational" people legally culpable.

QUOTE

[An expert witness discusses Albert Fish, who killed and ate children and engaged in other bizarre practices such as sticking needles in his body, eating his own feces, and setting fire to his rectum.]

Well, a man might for nine days eat that [human] flesh and still not have a psychosis. There is no accounting for taste.

Quoted in Miller and Radelet, 1993: 7.

The Mentally Ill Miller and Radelet (1993) discuss the long history of excusing the mentally ill, a practice that dates back to medieval times. The supporting rationales for not punishing those judged insane are as follows:

1. Humanitarian reasons require mercy.
2. They can't help themselves.
3. Retributive goals are not met because they don't appreciate their suffering.
4. They can't spiritually prepare for death, so it is cruel to execute them.
5. Deterrence is not served because others identify only with premeditated acts, not those borne of insanity.
6. They can't help in their own defense, calling into question the accuracy of guilt. (1993: 2–4)

Even so, there are many examples of individuals who were not only prosecuted but convicted and executed, arguably because of the extreme nature of their crimes, rather than a belief that their actions stemmed from rational thought. Several states have passed laws that create a "guilty but insane" conviction rather than the previous acquittal "by reason of insanity." Thus, they need no legal fiction of "sanity" in order to punish. Individuals are housed in forensic facilities until (or unless) they are "cured," at which time they are transferred to penal facilities for punishment.

Juveniles The other group that has traditionally been excused from criminal culpability is juveniles. Attitudes toward the **age of reason** and when a child is said to have reached it seem to be changing. In the early twentieth century, there was a concerted effort to remove juveniles from the adult legal system and to create a legal system for juveniles that would include protection as part of its mission. The system would adhere to a *parens patriae* model (standing in the stead of a parent), rather than act purely as punisher. This different philosophy of the juvenile system was because of the belief that the juvenile acted with less rationality than the adult. Today that trend seems to be reversing itself. States have reduced the age at which a child is considered an adult, have developed procedures allowing youngsters to be remanded to adult courts for trial and sentencing, and have allowed juveniles, even though sentenced in the juvenile system, to be held in facilities for adults. The United States is one of the few countries in the world that will execute seventeen-year-olds, a distinction shared by such countries as Iran, Iraq, and Nigeria (Miller and Radelet, 1993: 8).

Part of the impetus for this harsher treatment of juveniles has been a public perception that juvenile crime is increasing and is becoming more violent. Since lawmakers respond to public pressure, public perceptions affect laws. For instance, the public perceives there is a growing risk of mass murders in schools; therefore, we have seen an incredible escalation of security procedures and zero tolerance treatment of juveniles who express hostile feelings. The reality is that victimization in schools has actually decreased in the last ten years, but this fact carries less weight than the pictures of the grieving relatives after such an event. We will discuss trends in the juvenile justice system in more detail in Chapter 5.

The insane and juveniles have traditionally been excused because they lack the rationality to weigh their actions. Some argue that there are other individuals who are not fully responsible for their actions. For instance, the myriad "abuse excuses" dominate the legal landscape today. These defenses argue that the defendant might have committed the crime, but did so under some explanatory and excusing reason, i.e. they were battered or abused, they suffered from post traumatic stress syndrome, they suffered harassment, they were under the influence of alcohol or drugs, and so on. Other reasons why the defendant might be held to be less than fully responsible for their actions might be that they were unduly influenced by music, television or movies; that they were affected by sugar or food additives, or they were driven to desperate acts by the actions of a spouse. Dershowitz (1994) argues that we have gone too far in allowing a multitude of excuses for criminal behavior; a conclusion that is somewhat ironic since, as a criminal defense attorney, he has helped introduce some of these defenses himself.

QUERY

An upper middle class professional woman found her husband at a hotel with his mistress after he had sworn to her that he had broken off the affair. She was devastated because the couple had young toddler twins and she had attempted to save her marriage through changing her appearance and de-emphasizing her career. She fought with the mistress in the hotel lobby and was dragged off the woman and pushed down by her husband. Then, in the parking lot of the hotel where the confrontation occurred, in front of many witnesses, she ran over her husband and killed him. Would you find her guilty of first degree murder, second degree, or some other crime? What punishment does she deserve?

The moral culpability of an actor is not necessarily equivalent to legal culpability, although we often use the legal terms **negligence** and **recklessness** in discussions concerning ethical judgments. These concepts are useful for us in moral judgments, yet we should not be misled that moral judgments and legal judgments are always the same. One might not be guilty of a crime and might still be considered morally culpable. Alternatively, one might be guilty of a crime and be considered morally blameless; the last dilemma at the back of this chapter involves a loving mother who killed her suffering sons. Is she legally culpable but morally blameless; both legally and morally culpable; or some other combination?

QUOTE

Laws are just like spider's webs, they will hold the weak and delicate who might be caught in their meshes, but will be torn to pieces by the rich and powerful.

Anacharsis, 600 B.C..

The more mandates and laws which are enacted. The more there will be thieves and robbers.

Lao-Tze, 600 B.C.
Quoted in Roth and Roth, 1989: 3.

There is an argument that some actions are caused by life circumstances and, therefore, are not completely voluntary. For instance, if someone came from an impoverished background and was exposed only to criminal role models, is this person responsible for his or her subsequent delinquency? Do all people truly have freedom of choice? It is illegal for a rich man or a poor man to steal a loaf of bread, but a rich man doesn't have to, nor does he have to engage in armed robbery to obtain goods. He might, however, commit tax evasion, toxic waste dumping, or embezzlement.

We are all bound by limitations (or opportunities) of birth and circumstance. If we were to analyze moral culpability on the basis of life choices, it might be that, because of their respective life positions, some people who commit serious crimes are less blameworthy than others who come from better backgrounds and commit less serious crimes. Who is more culpable, the head of a company like Enron who made millions in salary but (allegedly) committed fraud to make a few million more; or the burglar who has no job and steals your television set? You might argue that both are equally culpable. Remember, the idea of moral culpability may be quite different from legal responsibility.

Regulations, Standards, and Rules

In addition to laws, we have a vast number of **regulations** governing the activities of occupations from physician to plumber and organizations from governmental agencies to private clubs. Regulations typically come from a governmental authority and often specify sanctions for noncompliance; **standards** may come from private or public bodies and are often used as a basis for some type of accreditation; **guidelines** may come from a professional group and are usually recommendations rather than directions. Distinctions can be made among these terms, although they are often used interchangeably. These rules for behavior do not carry the formal sanctions of criminal law, but some may carry civil liabilities.

Most regulations are set by state and federal governments. For instance, the Food and Drug Administration prescribes certain procedures and rules for pharmaceutical companies to follow in developing, testing, and distributing drugs. The Environmental Protection Agency watches over industry to make sure that safe methods for disposal of hazardous wastes are implemented. The Occupational Safety and Health Agency sets safety standards for the workplace in order to avoid or reduce the number of workplace injuries.

Noncompliance with standards and regulations is not equated with immoral behavior as readily as is criminal lawbreaking. Although fines may be levied against the construction supervisor who ignores Occupational Safety and Health Agency standards or the automaker who violates standards of the Consumer Safety Board, ordinarily they are not considered criminals, even when these actions result in injury or death.

> **QUOTE**
>
> *Why do 26 dead miners amount to a "disaster," and six dead suburbanites a "mass murder"? "Murder" suggests a murderer, while "disaster" suggests the work of impersonal forces. But if over 1,000 safety violations had been found in the mine—three the day before the first explosion—was no one responsible for failing to eliminate those hazards? And if someone could have prevented the hazards and did not, does that person not bear responsibility for the deaths of 26 men? Is he less evil because he did not want them to die, although he chose to leave them in jeopardy? Is he not a murderer, perhaps even a mass murderer?*
>
> _____
>
> Reiman, cited in Scheingold, 1984: 23.

When rules or standards are violated, other relevant criminal charges may be imposed as well. For instance, if a company blatantly violates safety regulations by forcing employees to work with toxic chemicals, company officials may be charged with negligent manslaughter if a worker dies. However, this situation is extremely rare, and there is usually a great deal of difference between the sanctions related to a violation of regulations and criminal lawbreaking.

Examples of businesses or individuals in business routinely violating standards and/or regulations include the recent WorldCom, Enron, and Arthur Anderson scandals. Insider information trading on Wall Street, toxic waste dumping, and marketing of unsafe products are frequent topics in the news. Some of the individuals who are caught and punished are truly surprised that their actions could result in criminal punishment. In no way would these individuals define themselves as criminal, even after they put on a prison uniform.

In addition to guidelines and standards, professions usually have a code of ethics or set of professional rules to educate and encourage their members to perform in accordance with an ideal of behavior. These may be fairly general or fairly specific; for instance, lawyers have extensive rules, but police officers are often given the International Chiefs of Police Code of Ethics, which is only a page. Laws, standards, regulations, guidelines, and codes of ethics are all designed to control and guide behavior.

It is interesting to observe that regulations and rules for behavior often seem to expand in inverse relation to the practiced ethics of a particular profession or organization. Frequently, when a breakdown in ethical behavior is detected, there is an attempt to bring people back in line by the use of rules. However, it seems that in any profession, the most effective ethical guides are not those that specify behavior, but rather those that are consistent with and support an organizational ideal. People can find many ways of violating the spirit of an administrative rule while complying with its exact wording. There are always current examples of politicians engaged in behavior involving conflicts of interest, but without actually breaking any laws, and lawyers who get around their ethical responsibilities by complying with the letter but not the spirit of the rules. However, decision makers in organizations often feel it is necessary to give employees extensive lists of rules. In an office these may include injunctions not to take supplies, not to make personal telephone calls, and not to spend more than fifteen minutes on breaks. Enforcing rules is very different from promoting an ethical standard of honesty and integrity in the workplace. Where ethical standards are nonexistent, it is doubtful that multitudinous rules of behavior will be able to eliminate wrongdoing.

MORALITY AND BEHAVIOR

One of the most difficult things to understand about human behavior is the disjunction between moral beliefs and behavior. We all can attest to the fact that believing something is wrong does not always prevent us from doing it. Very often, in fact, we engage in acts that we believe are bad, such as lying, stealing, and cheating. In any group of people (such as a college class), a majority will have engaged in some type of wrongful act at least once.

Why do people engage in behavior they believe to be wrong? Criminology attempts to explain why people commit unlawful acts, but the larger question is, why do any of us engage in wrongful acts? Psychological experiments show that a large percentage of schoolchildren will cheat when given the opportunity to do so, even though they know it is wrong (Lickona, 1976). More recent studies show that many people will keep found wallets or purses. Theories that endorse everything from learning and role modeling to biological predisposition abound, but we still haven't answered fundamental questions of causation. Even with all the scientific and philosophical attempts to explain human action, we are left with troubling questions when we read or hear about people who kill, steal, or otherwise offend our sense of morality. Evil is still one of the great mysteries of life.

In discussions concerning these questions, basic beliefs about the nature of humankind must be considered. Are people fundamentally bad and only held in check by rules and fear of punishment? Or, are they fundamentally good and commit bad acts because of improper upbringing or events that subvert their natural goodness? Or, are there fundamentally bad and fundamentally good people who are just "born that way" for no reason?

Ironically, our society seems to define "goodness" in one way, while glorifying just the opposite. Al Capone and Jesse James are, in some ways, cultural heroes even though they were known criminals. We have also glorified business executives when their actions could be defined as exploitative, as in the movie *Wall Street*. Yet when real men engage in such behavior, we prefer to see them punished. We are dismayed by the amount of violence and crime in our society, yet the television programs that play on these themes are the most popular. We abhor lying, but politicians who tell the truth are rejected by voters. We profess to be a country that cherishes our Constitution and due-process rights, but we clap and cheer in movie theaters when "Dirty Harry" types kill the "bad guys."

Why do we idolize people who have done things we know and believe to be wrong? Some say we sublimate our wish for excitement and our greed through their exploits. Many of the ideals of success in this society involve aspects of ruthlessness and aggression—traits hard to reconcile with an ideal conception of the good person. At least in Western culture, a "good" person who upholds the ideals of honesty, charity, and selflessness is considered somewhat of a weakling. The fact that our society has mixed values regarding what is considered good and desirable is reflected both in our popular culture and in individual action.

ANALYZING ETHICAL DILEMMAS

Ethical discussions in criminal justice can be either issues or dilemmas. *Issues* are broad social questions, often concerning the government's social control mechanisms and the impact on those governed—for example, what laws to pass, what sentences to attach to certain crimes, whether to abolish the death penalty, and whether to build more prisons or use community correctional alternatives. The typical individual does not have much control over these issues. **Ethical dilemmas** are those situations in which one person must make a decision about what to do. Either the choice is unclear, or the "right" choice will be difficult because of the costs involved. Ethical dilemmas involve the individual struggling with personal decision making, whereas ethical issues are those topics wherein one might have an opinion, but rarely a chance to take a stand that has much impact (unless one happens to be a Supreme Court judge or a governor).

It should be noted, however, that there are times when one's belief regarding an ethical issue gives rise to a personal dilemma. George Ryan, the ex-governor of Illinois, declared a moratorium on the use of the death penalty in his state in 2000 when at least five individuals on death row were exonerated through the use of DNA evidence. One of his last acts as he left office at the end of 2002 was to pardon the rest of those on death row and commute their sentences to life without parole. Governor Ryan faced a difficult personnel dilemma because he was in a position to do something about his belief that the death penalty was implemented in a way that could never be just. The fact that there was strong support *and* strong opposition to his action indicates the depth of his dilemma and the seriousness of the issue. Although most of us do not have the power to commute death sentences, we can do something about our beliefs. Writing letters, petitioning our legislators, marching in demonstrations, and working to pass (or overturn) laws are all examples of acting on our moral beliefs.

Personal ethical dilemmas occur when the individual is forced to choose between two or more choices of behavior. In order to analyze such dilemmas, one must discover all relevant information. The following analytical steps might be taken in order to clarify the dilemma:

1. Review all the facts. Make sure that one has all the facts that are known—not future predictions, not suppositions, not probabilities.
2. Identify all the potential values of each party that might be relevant.

3. Identify all possible moral issues for each party involved. This is to help us see that sometimes one's own moral or ethical dilemma is caused by the actions of others. For instance, a police officer's ethical dilemma when faced with the wrongdoing of a fellow officer is a direct result of that other officer making a bad choice. It is helpful to see all the moral issues involved in order to address the central issue.

4. Decide what is the most immediate moral or ethical issue facing the individual. This is always a behavior choice, not an opinion. For example, the moral issue of whether abortion should be legalized is quite different from the moral dilemma of whether I should have an abortion if I find myself pregnant. Obviously, one affects the other, but they are conceptually very distinct.

5. Resolve the ethical or moral dilemma.

Let us use the dilemma at the beginning of this chapter of the correctional officer who must decide what to do about the possible beating he observed. First, this officer needs to make sure he has all the facts. Was the inmate hurt? Did his injuries occur during the time the two other officers were in his cell? Is the officer sure that no one reported it? Would the inmate come forward if he believed that someone would testify against the other two officers, or would he deny the assault (if there was one)? What other facts are important to know? Remember that facts are those things that can be proven; however, it does not necessarily mean that the individual facing the dilemma has the proof. Second, the officer might examine the relevant values. In this situation, one can identify duty, legality, honesty, integrity, safety, protection, loyalty, self-preservation, and trust. Are there any other values important to resolve the dilemma? The next step is to resolve the dilemma. For this step, it is helpful to work through Chapter 2 first because the way to resolve ethical dilemmas is to decide on an ethical system. If the officer was a utilitarian, he would weigh the costs and benefits for all concerned in coming forward and in staying quiet. If he followed duty-based ethics (ethical formalism), he would find the answer once he determined his duty.

In order to resolve any dilemma, think of ethical judgments as a pyramid, as indicated in Figure 1-1. The tip of the pyramid is the judgment itself. We make ethical judgments all the time. The moral rules that support such judgments make up the body of the pyramid. Suppose someone said, "Capital punishment is wrong." If one asked, "Why is capital punishment wrong?" the answer might take the form of **moral rules,** which are general rules of right and wrong or value statements. For instance, in this case, the rules cited might include: One should never take a life. One should preserve life. One should abhor violence. Two wrongs don't make a right. And so on. These rules, in turn, must be supported by ethical systems, which will be covered in the next chapter. Some rules are inconsistent with some ethical systems, however. For instance, "One must always follow the law" may be consistent with ethical formalism and inconsistent with ethics of care.

These concepts will be clearer as we work through a number of ethical systems in the next chapter. Suffice to say for now that ethical judgments always have some rationale behind them. These rationales tend to be consistent with

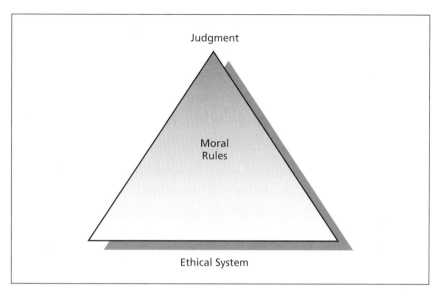

FIGURE 1–1 Ethical Judgments

traditional and historical ethical systems. In Chapter 2, we will explore some of these traditional ethical systems.

CONCLUSION

In this chapter, we defined the terms *morals* and *ethics* as both relating to standards of behavior. It was noted that not all behaviors would be subject to ethical judgments—only those that are performed by humans who are acting with free will and that affect others. Professional ethics deals only with those behaviors relevant to one's profession. We also discussed the relationship between law (and regulations) and ethics and discovered that, while there is an overlap, the two are not synonymous. Our ethical judgments (what we consider right and wrong) are made using rationales derived from historical and traditional ethical systems. These ethical systems will be described in the following chapter.

This chapter closes with some review questions to answer in class or in a journal. Ethical dilemmas are also presented to encourage the reader to practice ethical analysis. Throughout the text, ethical dilemmas will be presented that are relevant to the topics discussed in each chapter.

REVIEW QUESTIONS

1. Why should we study ethics or morals?
2. Define *morals, ethics, values, duties,* and *ethical systems.*

3. What types of behaviors are judged under ethical criteria?

4. Do laws cover all moral rules? If your answer is no, explain why.

5. What are the steps in analyzing an ethical dilemma?

ETHICAL DILEMMAS

Situation 1

Patty was a rich businessman's daughter. She had the best of everything all her life. Her future would have been college, a good marriage to a successful young man, and a life of comparative luxury, except that she was kidnapped by a small band of radical extremists who sought to overthrow the government by terror, intimidation, and robbery. After being raped, beaten, and locked in a small, dark closet for many days, continually taunted and threatened, she was told she must participate with the terrorist gang in a bank robbery; otherwise, she and her family would be killed. During the course of the robbery, she shot a bank guard. Was her action immoral? What if she had killed the guard? What if the terrorists had her mother or father, too, and told her if she didn't cooperate, they would kill her parents immediately? What would you have done in her place? [Many readers might recognize this dilemma as the Patty Hearst case. In the 1970s, the Symbionese Liberation Army, a terrorist group, kidnapped the daughter of Randolph Hearst, the tycoon of a large newspaper chain. Her subsequent capture, trial, conviction, and prison sentence has been portrayed in books and movies and provide ripe material for questions of free will and legal and moral culpability.]

Situation 2

You are taking an essay exam in a college classroom. The test is closed book and closed notes, yet you look up and see that the person sitting next to you has hidden a piece of paper filled with notes under his blue book, which he is using to answer some questions. What would you do? Would your answer change if the test was graded on a curve? What about if the student was a friend? What would you do if the student was flunking the course and was going to lose the scholarship he needed in order to stay in school?

Situation 3

You are selected for a jury in a trial of a 64-year-old mother who killed her two adult sons. The two men were institutionalized and suffered from Huntington's disease, a degenerative brain disease. They were certain to die and would endure much pain and suffering before they did. Her husband had also died from this same disease and she had nursed him through his suffering. She took a gun into the nursing home, kissed her sons goodbye, and then shot them both through the head. She was arrested for first-degree murder. The prosecutor informs you that there is no "mercy killing" defense in the law as it is written. How would you decide this case? What punishment does she deserve? [See Ellington, K. 2003, "Justice Tempered With Mercy," *Houston Chronicle,* January 30, 10A. The prosecutor took a plea of guilty to assisting suicide.]

SUGGESTED READINGS

Braswell, M., McCarthy, B., and McCarthy, B. (eds.), 2002. *Justice, Crime and Ethics,* 3rd ed. Cincinnati: Anderson.

Dershowitz, A. 1994. *The Abuse Excuse and Other Cop-Outs, Sob Stories, and Evasions of Responsibility.* Boston: Little, Brown and Company.

Leighton, P., and Reiman, J. 2001. *Criminal Justice Ethics.* Upper Saddle River, NJ: Prentice-Hall.

Miller, K., and Radelet, M. 1993. *Executing the Mentally Ill.* Newbury Park, NJ: Sage.

Muraskin, R., and Muraskin, M. 2001. *Morality and the Law.* Upper Saddle River, NJ: Prentice-Hall.

2

Determining Moral Behavior

Key Terms

- ethical system
- deontological ethical system
- teleological ethical system
- ethical formalism
- hypothetical imperatives
- utilitarianism
- act utilitarianism
- rule utilitarianism
- religious ethics
- natural law
- social contract theory

- ethics of virtue
- principle of the golden mean
- ethics of care
- egoism
- psychological egoism
- enlightened egoism
- cultural relativism
- principle of forfeiture
- situational ethics
- moral pluralism

Chapter Objectives

- Become familiar with the major ethical systems and the criticisms leveled against each.
- Understand the controversy between relativism and absolutism.
- Become familiar with how the major ethical systems have relevance to issues in criminal justice.
- Learn how to apply the major ethical systems to ethical dilemmas.

Detective Russell Poole was a Robbery-Homicide Division investigator with the Los Angeles Police Department. In 1998, he was assigned an investigation regarding an alleged beating and cover-up of Ismael Jimenez, a reputed gang member, by L.A.P.D. officers. In his investigation he uncovered a pattern of complaints of violence by the anti-gang task force in the Ramparts Division. Gang members told Poole and his partners that a number of officers harassed them, assaulted them, and pressured them to provide untraceable guns. The beating occurred because Jimenez would not provide the officers with a gun. In fact, in a search of the house of Rafael Perez, a member of the anti-gang task force, Poole found a box with a half dozen very realistic replica toy guns. He concluded that a number of the officers in the division were "vigilante cops" and requested that the investigation proceed further.

After Poole laid out what his investigation had uncovered, Bernard Parks, the L.A.P.D. chief at the time, ordered him to limit his investigation solely to the Jimenez beating. Poole prepared a 40-page report on the Jimenez case for the district attorney's office, detailing the pattern of complaints, alleged assaults, and other allegations of serious wrongdoing on the part of the Rampart officers. However, Poole's report never reached the district attorney's office because his lieutenant, enforcing the chief's orders, replaced his detailed report with a two-page report written by the lieutenant and another supervisor. Poole knew that in not providing the district attorney's office with all the information he uncovered, he could be charged with obstruction of justice, and the report provided so little information that the officer probably would not even be charged. He was then asked by his lieutenant to put his name on the report (Golab, 2000).

How did Sergeant Poole decide what was the right thing to do in this situation? He had conflicting duties and conflicting values. He knew that not signing the report might have serious consequences for his career. How would you determine the right thing to do if you were in a similar situation?

As discussed in the first chapter, if one is confronted with an ethical dilemma, it is important to first identify all relevant facts. Then one must identify relevant values. One's values of duty, friendship, loyalty, honesty, and self preservation are usually at the heart of professional ethical dilemmas. The third step is to identify the possible choices one might make. In order to resolve the dilemma, one must make a moral judgment about the right thing to do. This judgment is made with the help of basic moral rules that are embedded in ethical systems. This chapter presents descriptions of a number of ethical systems.

ETHICAL SYSTEMS

Our principles of right and wrong form a framework for the way we live our lives. But where do they come from? Before you read on, answer the following question: If you believe it is wrong to steal, why do you believe this to be so? You probably said it is because your parents taught you or because your religion forbids it or maybe because society cannot tolerate people harming one another. Your answer is an indication of your **ethical system.** Ethical systems are the source of moral beliefs. They are the underlying premises from which you make judgments. Typically, they are beyond argument. That is, although ethical decisions may become the basis of debate, the decisions are based on fundamental truths or propositions that are taken as a given by the individual employing the ethical system.

C. E. Harris (1986: 33) refers to such ethical systems as *moral theories* or *moral philosophies,* and defines them as a systematic ordering of moral principles. To be accepted as an ethical system, the system of principles must be internally consistent, must be consistent with generally held beliefs, and must possess a type of "moral common sense." Baelz (1977: 19) further described them as having the following characteristics:

1. *They are prescriptive.* Certain behavior is demanded or proscribed. They are not just abstract principles of good and bad, but rather, have substantial impact on what we do.

2. *They are authoritative.* They are not ordinarily subject to debate. Once an ethical framework has been developed, it is usually beyond question.

3. *They are logically impartial or universal.* Moral considerations arising from ethical systems are not based on favoritism: If something is considered wrong, it is wrong for everyone. Relativism has no place in an ethical framework.

4. *They are not self-serving.* They are directed toward others; what is good is good for everyone, not just the individual.

We don't consciously think of ethical systems, but we use them to make judgments. For instance, we might say that a woman who leaves her children alone to go out drinking has committed an immoral act. That would be a *moral judgment.* Moral rules that underlie this judgment might be "Children should be looked after," "One shouldn't drink to excess," or "Mothers should be good role models for their children." These basic moral rules are derived from an ethical system. The ethical judgment pyramid that was introduced in Chapter 1 (p. 23) is a visual representation of this discussion.

In this chapter we will not discuss all possible ethical systems, nor will we claim that the short descriptions here are enough to give the reader a total picture of each of the systems mentioned. A reader would be well advised to consult texts in philosophy and ethics for more detail. However, we will explore and provide brief summaries of the most often used ethical systems.

DEONTOLOGICAL AND TELEOLOGICAL ETHICAL SYSTEMS

These may be unfamiliar words, but the concepts that underlie them will be very familiar to you. A **deontological ethical system** is one that is concerned solely with the inherent nature of the act being judged. If an act is inherently good, then even if it results in bad consequences, it is still considered a good act. **Teleological systems** judge the consequences of an act. An act might look bad, but if it results in good consequences, then it can be defined as good under a teleological system. The phrase "the end justify the means" is a teleological statement. The clearest examples of these two approaches are ethical formalism (a deontological or "nonconsequentialist" system) and utilitarianism (a teleological or "consequentialist" system).

Ethical Formalism

Ethical formalism is a deontological system because the important determinant for judging whether an act is moral is not its consequence, but only the motive or intent of the actor. According to Kant, the only thing that is intrinsically good is a *good will*. If someone does an action from a good will, then even if it results in bad consequences, it can be considered a moral action. On the other hand, if someone performs some activity that looks on the surface to be altruistic, but does it with an ulterior motive—for instance, to curry favor or gain benefit—then that act is not moral. For instance, Gold, Braswell, and McCarthy (1991) offer the example of a motorist stranded by the side of the road; another driver who comes along has a decision to help or pass by. If the decision is made to stop and help, this would seem to be a good act. Not so, according to ethical formalism, unless it is done from a good will. If the helper stops because he or she expects payment, wants a return favor, or for any reason other than a good will, then the act is only neutral—not moral. Only if the help springs from a good will can we say that it is truly good.

Immanuel Kant (1724–1804) believed moral worth comes from doing one's duty (Kant, 1949). Just as there is the law of the family (father's rule), the law of the state and country, and the law of international relations, there is also a universal law of right and wrong. Morality, according to Kant, arises from the fact that humans, as rational beings, impose these laws and strictures of behavior upon themselves.

The following comprise the principles of Kant's ethical formalism (Bowie, 1985: 157):

1. *Act only on that maxim through which you can at the same time will that it should become a universal law.* In other words, for any decision of behavior to be made, examine whether that behavior would be acceptable if it were a universal law to be followed by everyone. For instance, a student might decide to cheat on a test; but for this action to be moral, the student would have to agree that everyone should be able to cheat on tests.

2. *Act in such a way that you always treat humanity, whether in your own person or that of any other, never simply as a means but always at the same time as an end.* In other words, one should not use people for one's own purposes. For instance, being friendly to someone so that you can use their car is using them as a means for one's own ends. Even otherwise moral actions, such as giving to charity or doing charitable acts for others, would be considered immoral if done for ulterior motives such as self-aggrandizement.

3. *Act as if you were, through your maxims, a lawmaking member of a kingdom of ends.* This principle directs that the individual's actions should contribute to and be consistent with universal law. Also, because we freely choose to abide by moral law and these laws are self-imposed rather than imposed from the outside, they are a reflection of the higher nature of humans.

These are absolute commands—together, they form the categorical imperative. According to Kant, **hypothetical imperatives** are commands that designate certain actions to attain certain ends. An example is, "*If* I want to be a success, *then* I must do well in college." A categorical imperative, by contrast, commands action that is necessary without any reference to intended purposes or consequences (Kant, 1949: 76):

> This imperative is categorical. It concerns not the material of the action and its intended result but the form and the principle from which it results. What is essentially good in it consists in the intention, the result being what it may. This imperative may be called the imperative of morality.

A system such as ethical formalism is considered an absolutist system—if something is wrong, it is wrong all the time, such as murder or lying. To assassinate evil tyrants like Hitler, or Idi Amin, or Saddam Hussein might be considered moral under a teleological system because of the action's consequence of ridding the world of dangerous people. However, in the deontological view, if the act and intent of killing is wrong, it is always wrong; thus, assassination must be considered immoral in all cases, regardless of the good consequences that might result. Even lying is deemed to be immoral in this system, despite some good arguments for the case that, at times, lying might be beneficial. For instance, Kant used an example that if someone asked to be hidden from an attacker in close pursuit and then the attacker asked where the potential victim was hiding, it would be immoral to lie about it. This seems wrong to many and serves to dissuade people from seeing the value of ethical formalism. However, according to Kant, lying or not lying is not the determining factor in that scenario or in any other. An individual cannot control consequences—only actions—therefore, one must act in a moral fashion without regard to potential consequences. In the example, the attacker may not kill the potential victim; the victim may still be able to get away; the attacker may be justified—the point is that no one person can control anything in life, so the only thing that makes sense is to live by the categorical imperative.

QUERY

- Are there any situations in which lying is acceptable?
- Can you think of any acts that result in bad consequences but should still be considered good acts?
- Do people do things solely for altruistic reasons, or are there always hidden motives and egoistic agendas operating?

Kant also defends his position with semantics—he distinguishes untruths from lies with the explanation that a lie is a lie only when the recipient is led to believe or has a right to believe that he or she is being told the truth. The attacker in the previous scenario or an attacker who has one "by the throat" demanding one's money has no right to expect the truth; thus, it would not be immoral to not tell this person the truth. Only if one led the attacker to believe that one were going to tell the truth and then did not would one violate the categorical imperative. In other words, Kant distinguishes untruths from lies. To not tell the truth when the attacker doesn't deserve the truth is not a lie, but if one intentionally and deliberately sets out to deceive, then that is a lie—even if it is being told to a person who doesn't deserve the truth (Kant, 1981).

This ethical framework is somewhat difficult to understand, but it follows simply from the beliefs that an individual must follow a self-imposed moral law, and that one is capable of using reason to determine right actions since one can evaluate any action using the principles just listed. The major criticism directed at ethical formalism is that it seems to be unresponsive to extreme circumstances. If something is wrong in every circumstance regardless of the good that results or the reasons for the action, then otherwise good people might be judged immoral or unethical.

Critics also argue that morality is limited to duty in this system. One might argue that duty is the baseline of morality, not the highest aspiration of it. Further, it is not always clear where one's duty lies. At times one might face a dilemma where two duties conflict with one another. Another problem with the Kantian view is the priority of motive and intent over result. It may be seriously questioned whether the intention to do good, regardless of result or perhaps with negative result, is always moral. Many would argue that the consequences of an action and the actual result must be evaluated to determine morality (Maestri, 1982: 910).

How would ethical formalism help resolve the dilemma faced by Sergeant Poole when he was asked to sign the "doctored" report for the district attorney's office? First, what was his duty? His duty was obviously to uphold the law. Did he also have a duty to obey his superiors? Did he have a duty to protect the police department from scandal? Did he have a duty to serve the public? Could he perform all these duties at the same time, or are some inconsistent with each other?

The first principle in the categorical imperative states that one must act in such a way that the behavior could be universal. Would not reporting all the relevant facts to the district attorney's office be a rule that we would want to endorse universally? Probably not. It seems that if evidence is routinely held back from prosecutors, they would not be able to do their job.

The second principle states that we must not treat others as a means to an end. It seems clear that Poole's superiors were attempting to use him to further their own interest. Would he be using someone as a means to an end by signing the shortened report? Would he be using someone as a means to an end by not signing the shortened report?

The third principle might be interpreted to mean that all of our behavior must be autonomous and freely chosen to be judged as moral or immoral. If Poole was frightened or pressured into doing something, then the action would not be moral regardless of what it was. If, for instance, he believed that the district attorney would find out and come after him for falsifying a legal document, then he might not sign it, but it would not be because of a good will, and, therefore, could not be considered a moral act.

Other writers present variations of deontological ethics that do not depend so heavily on Kant (Braswell, McCarthy, and McCarthy, 1996/2002). The core elements of any deontological ethical system are the importance placed on intention and the use of a predetermined set of principles rather than looking to the consequences of the act to determine goodness.

Utilitarianism

Utilitarianism is a teleological ethical system: what is good is determined by the consequences of the action. Jeremy Bentham (1748–1832), a major proponent of utilitarianism, believed that the morality of an action should be determined by how much it contributes to the good of the majority. According to Bentham, human nature seeks to maximize pleasure and avoid pain, and a moral system must be consistent with this natural fact.

The "utilitarian doctrine asserts that we should always act so as to produce the greatest possible ratio of good to evil for everyone concerned" (Barry, 1985: 65). That is, if you can show that an action significantly contributes to the general good, then it is good. In situations where one must decide between a good for an individual and a good for society, then society should prevail, despite the wrong being done to an individual. This is because generally the utility or good derived from that action outweighs the small amount of harm done (because the harm is done only to one, whereas the good is multiplied by the many). For instance, if it could be shown that using someone as an example would be an effective deterrent to crime, whether or not the person was actually guilty, the wrong done to that person by this unjust punishment might be outweighed by the good resulting for society. This assumes that citizens would not find out about the injustice and lose respect for the authority of the legal system, which would be a negative effect for all concerned.

> **QUOTE**
>
> *Nature has placed mankind under the governance of two sovereign masters, pain and pleasure. It is for them alone to point out what we ought to do, as well as to determine what we shall do. On the one hand, the standard of right and wrong, on the other the chain of causes and effects, are fastened to their throne. They govern us in all we do, in all we say, in all we think; every effort we can make to throw off our subjection, will serve but to demonstrate and confirm it. In words, a man may pretend to abjure their empire: but in reality he will remain subject to it all the while. The principle of utility recognizes the subjection, and assumes it for the foundation of that system.*
>
> Bentham, quoted in Borchert and Stewart, 1986: 183.

Bentham did not judge the content of utility. He considered pleasure a good whether it derived from vice, such as avarice or greed, or from virtue, such as charity and kindness. Later utilitarians, primarily John Stuart Mill (1806–1873), judged some utilities (benefits) as better than others. For instance, art offers a different utility for society than alcohol. On the other hand, who is to determine which is better? (Borchert and Stewart, 1986: 190). In fact, while the concept of weighing utilities to decide what action to take makes sense, the actual exercise is sometimes very difficult. Try it with the dilemmas at the back of each chapter.

Another difficulty related to weighing utilities is that utilitarianism presumes you can predict the consequences of your actions, but is that realistic? In the well-known "lifeboat" dilemma, five people are in a lifeboat with enough food and water only for four. It is certain that they will survive if there are only four; it is also certain that they will all perish if one does not go overboard. What should be done? Under ethical formalism, it would be unthinkable to sacrifice an innocent, even if it means that all will die. Under utilitarian ethics, it is conceivable that the murder of one might be justified to save the others. But this hypothetical points out the fallacy of the utilitarian argument. In reality, it is not known whether any will survive. The fifth might be murdered, and five minutes later, a rescue ship appears on the horizon. The fifth might be murdered, but then the remaining four are still eaten by sharks. Only in unrealistic hypothetical situations does one absolutely know the consequences of one's action. In real life, you never know if your action will result in a greater good or ultimate harm.

An important criticism of this ethical system is that there is little concern for individual rights in utilitarianism. In ethical formalism, it is presumed that each individual must be treated with respect and not be used as a means to an end. However, under utilitarianism, the rights of one individual may be sacrificed for the good of many. For instance, Winston Churchill allowed Coventry to be bombed in World War II so the Germans would not know the Allies had cracked the Germans' secret military radio code. Several hundred English people were killed in the bombing raid of Coventry: many might have been saved if they had been warned. It was a calculated loss for greater long-term gains: bringing the war to an end sooner. This could be justified under utilitarianism but never under ethical formalism. The 2003 Iraq war was justified by the argument that it will save the lives of countless American citizens from some future terrorist acts and also protect Iraq citizens from a brutal dictator, but there is no question that in order to bring about this good end, innocent Iraq citizens died. Utilitarian ethics justifies these deaths.

QUERY

In the movie, *Sophie's Choice,* a woman was forced to choose which one of her children to send to the gas chamber. If she did not decide, both would be killed. How would ethical formalism resolve this dilemma? How would utilitarianism?

Utilitarianism has two forms: act utilitarianism and rule utilitarianism. The basic difference between the two can be summarized as follows: In **act utilitarianism,** the basic utility derived from an action is alone examined. We look at the consequences of any action for all involved and weigh the units of utility accordingly. In **rule utilitarianism,** one judges that action in reference to the precedent it sets and the long-term utility of the rule set by that action.

Act utilitarianism might support stealing food when one is hungry and has no other way to eat, because the utility of survival would outweigh the loss to the store. On the other hand, rule utilitarianism would be concerned with the effect that the action would have if made into a rule for behavior: "Anytime an individual cannot afford food he or she can steal it" would result in a state of lawlessness and a general disrespect for the law. Such a rule would not result in the greatest utility for the greatest number. With rule utilitarianism, then, we are not only concerned with the immediate utility of the action, but also with the long-term utility or harm if the action were to be a rule for all similar circumstances. Note the similarity between rule utilitarianism and the first principle of the categorical imperative. In both approaches, one must judge as good only those actions that can be universalized.

Applying utilitarianism to Detective Russell Poole's dilemma, it seems clear that his superiors were engaged in damage control. They did not want a scandal, especially considering it had not been that long since the Rodney King incident. By suppressing evidence of further wrongdoing, they probably assumed that they could keep the information from the public and deal with it internally. In fact, Chief Parks fired more than 100 officers during his time as chief; however, he did so in a way that the district attorney's office was unable to prosecute any of the officers for their alleged crimes. Internal Affairs routinely used a practice of compelling testimony, without reading the officer his rights before questioning. This meant that the evidence obtained could be used to discipline the officer, but not to prosecute him or her. The result was that officers were fired, but their cases never ended up in court—nor in the paper.

If Detective Poole used utilitarian reasoning, where did the greatest benefit lie? Was there greater benefit to all concerned in opposing his superiors' attempts to suppress the investigation, or with going along with the cover-up?

Actually, the attempt to suppress the actions of the Ramparts Division officers was unsuccessful, anyway. A year after Poole refused to sign the report, Rafael Perez was prosecuted for stealing a large amount of cocaine from the evidence room. In a plea arrangement, he told investigators for the D.A.'s office the whole story of the Ramparts Division officers, leading to a biggest scandal in L.A.P.D.'s history (Golab, 2000; Boyer, 2001).

In summary, utilitarianism holds that morality must be determined by the consequences of an action. Society and the survival and benefit of all are more important than any individual. This is a functional theory of right and wrong—something is right when it benefits the continuance and good health of society. Rule utilitarianism may be closer to the principles of ethical formalism, because it looks at general universal laws; the difference between the two is that the laws themselves are judged right or wrong depending on the motives behind them under ethical formalism, whereas utilitarianism looks to the long-term consequences of the behavior prescribed by the rules to determine their morality.

OTHER ETHICAL SYSTEMS

The following ethical systems can be described as deontological or teleological as well, although utilitarianism and ethical formalism are arguably the two best representatives of the contrast. As you read through these systems, apply the definitions of teleological systems and deontological systems to determine if you can categorize each. Some, such as egoism, are easy to categorize. It is clearly teleological. The others might not be so easy.

Religion

Probably the most frequently used source of individual ethics is religion. Religion might be defined as a body of beliefs that addresses fundamental issues such as "What is life?" and "What is good and evil?" A religion also provides moral guidelines and directions on how to live one's life. For instance, Christians and Jews are taught the Ten Commandments, which prohibit certain behaviors defined as wrong. The authority of **religious ethics,** in particular Judeo-Christian ethics, stems from a willful and rational god. For believers, the authority of God's will is beyond question and there is no need for further examination because of His perfection. The only possible controversy comes from human interpretation of God's commands. Indeed, these differences in interpretation are the source of most religious strife.

QUOTE

I have set an example, that you should do as I have done to you. . . .
I give you a new commandment: love one another.
As I have loved you, you are to love one another.

John 13:15.

Religious ethics is, of course, much broader than simply Judeo-Christian ethics. Religions such as Buddhism, Confucianism, and Islam also provide a basis for ethics, since they provide explanations of how to live the "good life" and also address other philosophical issues, such as "What is reality?" Pantheistic religions, those of primitive hunter–gatherer societies, promote the belief that there is a living spirit in all things. A basic principle follows from this belief that life is important and one must have respect for all things, including trees, rivers, and animals. However, there must be a willful and rational god or god figure before there can be a judgment of right and wrong, and thus a basis for an ethical system. Those religions that do have a god figure consider that figure to be the source of principles of ethics and morality.

It is also true that of the religions we might discuss, many have similar basic moral principles. Many religions have their own version of the Ten Commandments; in this regard, Islam is not too different from Judaism, which is not too different from Christianity. The Golden Rule, "Do unto others as you would have them do unto you," is echoed in Hinduism ("Do naught to others which, if done to thee, would cause thee pain: this is the sum of duty"), in Buddhism ("In five ways should a clansman minister to his friends and familiars . . . by treating them as he treats himself"), in Confucianism ("What you do not want done to yourself, do not do unto others"), and in Judaism ("Whatsoever thou wouldest that men should not do unto thee, do not do that to them") (Reiman, 1990: 147). "Other Major World Religions" are described in the following box.

One issue in Western religious ethics is how to determine God's will. Some believe that God is inviolable and that positions on moral questions are absolute. This is a legalist position. Others believe that God's will varies according to time and place—the situationalist position. According to this position, situational factors are important in determining the rightness of a particular action. Something may be right or wrong depending on the circumstances (Borchert and Stewart, 1986: 157). For instance, lying may be wrong unless it is to protect an innocent, or stealing may be wrong unless it is to protest injustice and to help unfortunates. In fact, some would say it is impossible to have an *a priori* knowledge of God's will because that would put us above God's law, since we ourselves would be "all-knowing"; rather, for any situation, if we are prepared to receive them, we can know God's divine commands through faith and conscience.

According to Barry (1985), human beings can "know" God's will in three ways:

1. *Individual conscience.* An individual's conscience is the best source for discovering what God wants one to do. If one feels uncomfortable about a certain action, it is probably wrong.

2. *Religious authorities.* They can interpret right and wrong for us and are our best source if we are confused about certain actions.

3. *Holy scriptures.* The third way is to go directly to the Bible, Koran, or Torah as the source of God's law. Some believe that the written word of God holds the answers to all moral dilemmas (Barry, 1985: 51–54).

Islam

One of the newest yet largest religions is Islam. Like Christianity, this religion recognizes one god, Allah. Jesus and other religious figures are recognized as prophets, as is Muhammed, who is considered the last and greatest prophet. Islam has the Koran, which is taken much more literally as the word of Allah than the Bible is taken by most Christians. There is a great deal of fatalism in Islam: *Im Shallah,* meaning "If God wills it," is a prevalent theme in Moslem societies. On the other hand, there is recognition that if people choose evil, they do so freely. The five pillars of Islam are (1) repetition of the creed *(Shahada),* (2) daily prayer *(Salah),* (3) almsgiving *(Zakah),* (4) fasting *(Sawm),* and (5) pilgrimage *(Has).* One of the other features of Islam is the idea of the holy war. In this concept, the faithful who die defending Islam against infidels will be rewarded in the afterlife (Hopfe, 1983).

Buddhism

Siddhartha Gautama (Buddha) attained enlightenment and preached to others how to do the same and achieve the release from suffering. He taught that good behavior is that which follows the "middle path" between hedonistic pursuit of sensual pleasure and asceticism. Essentials of Buddhist teachings are ethical conduct, mental discipline, and wisdom. Ethical conduct is based on universal love and compassion for all living beings. Compassion and wisdom are needed in equal measures. Ethical conduct can be broken into right speech (refraining from lies, slander, enmity, and rude speech); right action (abstaining from destroying life, stealing, and dishonest dealings, and helping others lead peaceful and honorable lives); and right livelihood (abstaining from occupations that bring harm to others, such as arms dealing and killing animals). To follow the "middle path," one must abide by these guidelines (Kessler, 1992).

Confucianism

Confucius taught a humanistic social philosophy that included central concepts such as *Ren,* which is human virtue and humanity at its best, as well as the source of moral principles; *Li,* which is traditional order, ritual, or custom; *Xiao,* which is familial love; and *Yi,* which is rightness, both a virtue and a principle of behavior—that is, one should do what is right because it is right. The doctrine of the mean exemplifies one aspect of Confucianism that emphasizes a cosmic or natural order. Humans are a part of nature and are included in the scheme of life. Practicing moderation in one's life is part of this natural order and reflects a "way to Heaven" (Kessler, 1992).

Hinduism

In Hinduism, the central concept of *Karma* can be understood as consequence. Specifically, what one does in one's present life will determine what happens in a future life. The goal is to escape the eternal birth–rebirth cycle by living one's life in a moral manner so that no bad Karma will occur (Kessler, 1992). People start out life in the lowest caste, but if they live a good life, they will be reborn as members of a higher caste, until they reach the highest Brahman caste, and at that point the cycle can end. An early source for Hinduism was the Code of Manu. In this code are found the ethical ideals of Hinduism, which include pleasantness, patience, control of mind, nonstealing, purity, control of the senses, intelligence, knowledge, truthfulness, and nonirritability (Hopfe, 1983).

Strong doubts exist as to whether any of these methods are true indicators of divine command. Our consciences may be no more than the products of our psychological development, influenced by our environment. Religious authorities are, after all, only human, with human failings. Even the Bible seems to support contradictory principles.

The question of whether people can ever know God's will has been explored through the ages. Thomas Aquinas (1225–1274) believed that human reason was sufficient not only to prove the existence of God, but also to discover God's divine commands (Borchert and Stewart, 1986: 159). Others feel that reason is not sufficient to know God, and that it comes down to unquestioning belief, so reason and knowledge must always be separate from faith. These people believe that one can know whether an action is consistent with God's will only if it contributes to general happiness, because God intends for us to be happy, or when the action is done through the *holy spirit*—that is, when someone performs the action under the influence of true faith (Borchert and Stewart, 1986: 164–171).

To summarize, the religious ethics system is widely used and accepted. The authority of the god figure is the root of all morality; basic conceptions of good, evil, right, and wrong come from interpretations of the god figure's will. Many people throughout history have wrestled with the problem of determining what is right according to God, and current controversies within and between religious groups illustrate the unresolved difficulties that continue to exist.

Natural Law

In the **natural law** ethical system, there is a universal set of rights and wrongs that is similar to many religious beliefs, but there is no reference to a specific supernatural figure. Originating with the Stoics, natural law is an ethical system wherein no difference is recognized between physical laws—such as the law of gravity—and moral laws. Morality is part of the natural order of the universe. Further, this morality is the same across cultures and times. In this view, Christians simply added God as a source of law (as other religions added their own prophets and gods), but there is no intrinsic need to resort to a supernatural figure, since these universal laws exist quite apart from any religion (Maestri, 1982).

The natural law ethical system presupposes that what is good is what is natural, and what is natural is what is good. The essence of morality is what conforms to the natural world; thus, there are basic inclinations that form the core of moral principles. For instance, the preservation of one's own being is a basic, natural inclination, and thus is a basic principle of morality. Actions consistent with this natural inclination would be those that preserve one's own life, such as in self-defense, but also those that preserve or maintain the species, such as a prohibition against murder. Other inclinations are peculiar to one's species—for instance, humans are social animals; thus, sociability is a natural inclination that leads to altruism and generosity. These are natural and thus moral. The pursuit of knowledge or understanding of the universe might also be recognized as a natural inclination of humans; thus, actions that conform to this natural inclination are moral.

QUERY

- What are "natural rights"—rights that everyone has purely by virtue of being alive?
- What are the "natural" inclinations of human beings?

Souryal (1992) describes natural law as the "steward" of natural rights. This country's founders might be described as natural law theorists. In the Constitution, "natural rights" endowed by the Creator are recognized. Fishman (1994) explains, however, that Thomas Hobbes and John Locke transformed the original natural law theory that emphasized duties or obligations of humans in the natural order, to one that emphasized "natural" human rights. In order to stay true to the internal consistency and historical legacy of natural rights theory, one must balance the emphasis on rights with an emphasis on obligations. For instance, the protections of individual freedoms as natural rights is an important component of any democracy, but that democracy can exist only when citizens accept and perform their obligations of citizenship. Citizens who are not vigilant in protecting their freedoms through the political process, for instance, risk losing them. In this sense, natural law theory is somewhat similar to the duty emphasis in ethical formalism.

Hobbes's claim that self-preservation (the law of the jungle) was paramount, and Locke's view that property is a natural right, created the foundation for the **social contract theory.** According to the social contract theory, members of society originally were engaged in a "war of all against all." The "contract" is one where individuals give up the freedom to aggress against others in return for their own safety. According to Hobbes, each individual has chosen to "lay down this right to all things; and be contented with so much liberty against other men, as he would allow other men against himself" (from Hobbes, *Leviathan,* 1651, quoted in Beauchamp, 1982: 264).

Natural law theory defines good as that which is natural. The difficulty of this system is identifying what is consistent and congruent with the natural inclinations of humankind. How do we know which acts are in accordance with the natural order of things? What are the natural laws? These are the fundamental problems with this ethical system.

The Ethics of Virtue

Each of the foregoing ethical systems seeks to define, "What is good action?" The **ethics of virtue** instead asks the question, "What is a good person?" This ethical system rejects the approach that one might use reason to discover what is good. Instead, the principle is that to be good, one must do good. Virtues that a good person possesses include thriftiness, temperance, humility, industriousness, and honesty. It is a teleological system because it is concerned with acting in such a way as to achieve a good end (Prior, 1991). The specific "end" is happiness, or *eudaimonia*. However, the meaning of this word is not the same as the meaning given by utilitarians. This translation of happiness did not mean simply having pleasure, but also living a good life, reaching achievements, and attaining moral excellence.

The roots of this system are in the work of Aristotle, who defined virtues as "excellences." These qualities are what enable an individual to move toward the achievement of what it takes to be human. Aristotle distinguished intellectual virtues (wisdom, understanding) from moral virtues (generosity, self-control). The moral virtues are not sufficient for "the good life"; one must also have the intellectual virtues, primarily "practical reason."

Aristotle evidently was a learning theorist—he believed that we are, by nature, neither good nor evil but become so through training and the acquisition of habits:

> . . . the virtues are implanted in us neither by nature nor contrary to nature: we are by nature equipped with the ability to receive them and habit brings this ability to completion and fulfillment. (Aristotle, quoted in Prior, 1991: 156–157)

Habits of moral virtue are obtained through following the example of a moral *exemplar*. They are also more easily instilled when "right" or just laws also exist. Moral virtue is a state of character in which choices are consistent with the **principle of the golden mean.** This principle states that virtue is always the median between two extremes of character. For instance, liberality is the mean between prodigality and meanness, proper pride is the mean between empty vanity and undue humility, and so on (Albert, Denise, and Peterfreund, 1984). The "Catalog of Virtues" lists others.

Moral virtue comes from habit, which is why this system emphasizes character. The idea here is that one does not do good because of reason; rather, one does good because of the patterns of a lifetime. If one has a good character, she or he will do the right thing; but if one has a bad character, she or he will usu-

---

Catalog of Virtues

Area	Defect	Mean	Excess
Fear	cowardice	courage	recklessness
Pleasure	insensitivity	self-control	self-indulgence
Money	stinginess	generosity	extravagance
Honor	small-minded	high-minded	vain
Anger	apathy	gentleness	short temper
Truth	self-depreciation	truthfulness	boastfulness
Shame	shamelessness	modesty	self-hate

SOURCE: Adapted from Prior, 1991: 165.

ally choose the immoral path. In *Character and Cops: Ethics in Policing,* Edwin Delattre uses an excerpt from a police chief's biography to illustrate an individual who represents the ethics of virtue:

> One Friday, just before Christmas in 1947, Seedman helped lug into the Safe and Loft office dozens of cartons of toys that had been recovered from a hijacking case. There were dolls, teddy bears, stuffed animals of all kinds. Ray McGuire, busy overseeing the operation, suddenly looked up and saw that it was close to three o'clock. "I'm never going to get to lunch," he said. "I was going to stop at Macy's to pick up some toys for my girls." One of the detectives mentioned he had to do the same at Macy's. McGuire handed him a twenty-dollar bill. "Pick up a pair of dolls for me, will ya?" (cited in Delattre, 1989a: 41)

It never even occurred to McGuire to take any of the dolls and toys surrounding him, because that would be stealing. As Delattre writes, "The habit of not even considering greedy behavior, of not speculating about ways to profit from vice, prevents such conduct from ever occurring to us" (1989a: 41).

An ethical formalist might say that McGuire applied the categorical imperative to the situation and concluded that the action of taking a doll could not be translated into a universal law. A utilitarian formulation would have McGuire weigh the relative utilities of taking the doll or not. However, in the ethics of virtue, as Delattre indicates, if one has developed a habit of integrity, taking advantage of the situation never even occurs to that person. Under this moral system, those individuals who possess the necessary virtue will act morally, and those who don't will act immorally.

It should also be noted that some of us have some virtues and not others. There are many other virtues besides those already mentioned, including compassion, courage, conscientiousness, and devotion. Some of us may be completely honest in all of our dealings but not generous. Some may be courageous but not compassionate. Therefore, we all are moral to the extent that we possess moral virtues, but some of us are more moral than others. One difficulty is in judging the primacy of moral virtues. For instance, in professional ethics there are often conflicts that involve honesty and loyalty. If both are virtues, how does one resolve a dilemma in which one virtue must be sacrificed?

The ethics of virtue probably explains more of individual behavior than other ethical systems because most of the time, if we have developed habits of virtue, we do not even think about the possible "bad" acts we might do. For instance, most of us do not have to analyze the "rightness" or "wrongness" of stealing every time we go into a store. We do not automatically consider lying every time a circumstance arises. Most of the time, we do the right thing without thinking about it a great deal. However, when faced with a true dilemma— that is, a choice where the "right" decision is unclear—the ethics of virtue may be less helpful as an ethical system.

Alasdair MacIntyre (1991: 204), a current philosopher, defines virtues as those dispositions that will sustain us in the relevant "quest for the good, by enabling us to overcome the harms, dangers, temptations and distractions which we encounter, and which will furnish us with increasing self-knowledge and increasing knowledge of the good." In recent works, MacIntyre (1999) seems to move closer to an ethics of care approach because he discusses the need for virtue as necessary in order to care for the next generation. He sees life as one of "reciprocal indebtedness" and emphasizes "networks of relationships" and the locale of giving and receiving the benefits of virtues. This language is very similar to that of ethics of care that we will discuss next.

Detective Poole reported that he never considered putting his name on a report he knew was wrong. His superiors, co-workers, and colleagues describe him as "professional," "hard working," "loyal, productive, thorough and reliable," "diligent," "honest," and "extremely credible." He was known as a first-rate investigator and trusted by the D.A.'s office to provide thorough and credible testimony. In other words, his habits in his professional life were directly contrary to participating in a cover-up, and he didn't (Golab, 2000).

The Ethics of Care

The **ethics of care** is another ethical system that does not depend on universal rules or formulas to determine morality. The emphasis is on human relationships and needs. The ethics of care has been described as a feminine morality because women in all societies are the childbearers and consequently seem to have a greater sensitivity to issues of care. Noddings (1986: 1) points out that the "mother's voice" has been silent in Western, masculine analysis: "One is tempted to say that ethics has so far been guided by Logos, the masculine spirit, whereas the more natural and perhaps stronger approach would be through Eros, the feminine spirit."

The ethics of care is founded in the natural human response to care for a newborn child, the ill, and the hurt. Carol Gilligan's work on moral development in psychology, discussed in more detail in Chapter 3, identified a feminine approach to ethical dilemmas that focuses on relationships and needs instead of rights and universal laws. She found that in their responses to ethical dilemmas, some women were resistant to solving the dilemmas given the restraints of the exercise. They wanted to know what would happen after the fact, they wanted to know what the person felt, and they wanted to know other elements that might be deemed not relevant if one was applying a "rights-based" ethical system. These women were ranked fairly low on the moral development scale, yet Gilligan proposed that theirs was not a less-developed morality but, rather, a different morality. The most interesting feature of this approach is that while a relatively small number of women actually voiced these principles, no men did. She attributed this to the fact that in Western society, both men and women are socialized to Western ethics, which are primarily concerned with issues of rights, laws, and universalism (Gilligan, 1982).

Applying the ethics of care leads not to different solutions necessarily, but perhaps different questions. In an ethical system based on care, we would be concerned with issues of needs rather than rights. Other writers point to some

Eastern religions, such as Taoism, as illustrations of the ethics of care (Gold et al., 1991). In these religions, a rigid, formal, rule-based ethics is rejected in favor of gently leading the individual to follow a path of caring for others. In criminal justice, the ethics of care is represented to some extent by the rehabilitative ethic rather than the just-deserts model. Certainly the "restorative justice" movement is consistent with the ethics of care because of an emphasis on the motives and needs of all concerned, rather than simply retribution. In personal relationships, the ethics of care would promote empathy and treating others in a way that does not hurt them. In this view, meeting needs is more important than securing rights.

Recently, there have been several writers who have exemplified the "ethics of care" operating in criminal justice. Whether it is called feminine justice, peacemaking justice, restorative justice, or some other term, various authors are discussing alternative concepts to retribution and punishment that are distinct from treatment goals that characterized an earlier era. For instance, in a recent text Braswell and Gold (2002) discuss a concept called *peacemaking justice*. They show that the concept is derived from ancient principles, and it concerns care as well as other concepts: "Peacemaking, as evolved from ancient spiritual and wisdom traditions, has included the possibility of mercy and compassion within the framework of justice" (2002: 25). They propose that the peacemaking process is composed of three parts: "connectness," has to do with the inter-relationships we have with one another and all of us have with the earth; "caring" is similar to the concepts discussed on page 42 (they use Noddings as a source to discuss this idea that the "natural" inclination of humans is to care for one another); and "mindfulness" involves being aware of others and the world (2002: 25–37).

Egoism

Very simply, **egoism** postulates that what is good for one's survival and personal happiness is moral. The extreme of this position is that all people should operate on the assumption that they can do whatever benefits themselves. Others become the means to ensure happiness and have no meaning or rights as autonomous individuals. **Psychological egoism** is a descriptive principle rather than an ethical prescription. Psychological egoism refers to the idea that humans naturally are egoists and that it would be unnatural for them to be any other way. All species have instincts for survival, and self-preservation and self-interest are merely part of that instinct. Therefore, it is not only moral to be egoistic, but it is the only way we can be, and any other explanations of behavior are mere rationalizations.

Enlightened egoism is a slight revision of this basic principle, adding that the objective is long-term welfare. This may mean that one should treat others as we would want them to treat us to ensure cooperative relations. Even seemingly selfless and altruistic acts are consistent with egoism, since these acts benefit the individual by giving self-satisfaction. Under egoism, it would be not only impossible but also immoral for someone to perform a completely selfless act. Even those who give their lives to save others do so perhaps with the expectation of rewards in the afterlife. This system completely turns around the priorities of utilitarianism to put the individual first, before anyone else and before society as a whole. As Harris (1986: 47) puts it,

> Egoism as a moral philosophy originated in ancient Greece, but the modern emphasis on the individual in competition with other individuals has given it special prominence. The egoistic moral standard states that actions are right if and only if they produce consequences that are at least as good for the self-interest of the egoist as the consequences of any alternative action. Each egoist must personally define self-interest and propose a hierarchy of goods within that definition. Most egoists will be concerned with the fullest realization of their self-interest over a lifetime rather than during only a short period of time.

Obviously, egoism is rejected by many philosophers and laymen because it violates the basic tenets of an ethical system. Universalism is inconsistent with egoism, because to approve of all people acting in their own self-interest is not a logical or feasible position. It cannot be right for both me and you to maximize our own self-interests, because it would inevitably lead to conflict. Egoism would support exploitative actions by the strong against the weak, which seems wrong under all other ethical systems. However, psychological egoism is a relevant concept in natural law (self-preservation is natural) and utilitarianism (hedonism is a natural inclination). But if it is true that humans are *naturally* selfish and self-serving, one can also point to examples that indicate that humans are also altruistic and self-sacrificing. What is the true nature of humankind?

RELATIVISM AND ABSOLUTISM

Ethical relativism describes those moral systems in which what is good or bad changes, depending on the individual or group. The generation of the 1960s encapsulated this belief in the saying, "You do your thing and I'll do mine." What is right is determined by culture and/or individual belief; there are no universal laws.

There are two main arguments for relativism. The first is that there are so many different moral standards of behavior. According to Stace (1995: 26), "We find that there is nothing, or next to nothing, which has always and everywhere been regarded as morally good by all men." The second argument is that we do not know how to determine the absolute rules. Who is to say what is right and what is wrong?

One may look to anthropology and the rise of social science to explain the popularity of moral relativism. Over the course of studying different societies—past and present, primitive and sophisticated—anthropologists have found that there are very few universals across cultures. Even those behaviors often believed to be universally condemned, such as incest, have been institutionalized and encouraged in some societies (Kottak, 1974: 307). Basically, **cultural relativism** defines good as that which contributes to the health and survival of society. For instance, societies where women are in ample supply may endorse polygyny, and societies that have a shortage of women may accept polyandry; hunting and gathering societies that must contend with harsh environments may hold beliefs allowing for the euthanasia of burdensome elderly, whereas agricultural societies that depend on knowledge passed down through generations may revere their elderly and accord them an honored place in society.

In criminology, cultural differences in perceptions of right and wrong are important to the subcultural deviance theory of crime, wherein some deviant activity is explained by subcultural approval for that behavior. The example typically used to illustrate this is that of the Sicilian father who kills the man who raped his daughter, because to do otherwise would violate values of his subculture emphasizing personal honor and retaliation (Sellin, 1970: 187). A more recent case of subcultural differences involves a father who sold his fourteen-year-old daughter into marriage. Because he lived in Chicago, he was arrested; if he had lived in his homeland of India, he would have been conforming to accepted norms of behavior. We should also note how governments attempt to change culture through the criminal law. The cultural support in India for killing wives whose families do not provide the dowry is being slowly eroded by the current legal system that (albeit half-heartedly) investigates and punishes those responsible. Cultural relativists recognize the differences in cultures, absolutists argue that the mere existence of cultural norms does not make them moral.

QUERY

- Do you believe that there are no absolute moral truths and that morality is simply an individual's definition of right and wrong?
- If you answered yes to the question above, then are you also saying that child molesters and cannibals have the right to decide which behaviors are acceptable for them?

Although cultural relativism accepts the fact that different societies may have different moral standards, it also dictates that individuals within a culture conform to the standards of their culture. Therein lies a fundamental flaw in the relativist approach; if there are no universal norms, why should individuals be required to conform to societal or cultural norms? If their actions are not accepted today, it might be argued, they could be accepted tomorrow—if not by their society, perhaps by some other. An additional inconsistency in cultural relativism is the corresponding prohibition against interfering in another culture's norms. The argument goes as follows: since every culture is correct in its definitions of morality, another culture should not step in to change those definitions. However, if what is right is determined by which culture one happens to belong to, why then, if that culture happens to be imperialistic, would it be wrong to force cultural norms on other cultures? Cultural relativism attempts to combine an absolute (no interference) with a relativistic "truth" (there are no absolutes). This is logically inconsistent (Foot, 1982).

Cultural relativism usually concerns behaviors that are always right in one society and always wrong in another. Of course, what is more common is behavior that is judged to be wrong most of the time but acceptable in certain instances. For example, killing is wrong except possibly in self-defense and war; lying is wrong except when one lies to protect another. Occupational subcultures also support standards of behavior that are acceptable only for those within the occupation. For instance, some police officers believe that it is wrong to break the speed limit unless one happens to be a police officer—even an off-duty one.

It must be noted that even absolutist systems may accept some exceptions. The **principle of forfeiture** associated with deontological ethical systems holds that people who treat others as means to an end or take away or inhibit their freedom and well-being forfeit the right to protection of their own freedom and well-being (Harris, 1986: 136). Therefore, people who aggress first forfeit their own right to be protected from harm. This could permit self-defense (despite the moral proscription against taking life) and possibly provide justification for lying to a person who threatens harm. Critics of an absolutist system see this exception as a rationalization and a fatal weakness to the approach; in effect, moral rules are absolute *except* for those exceptions allowed by some "back-door" argument.

Relativism allows for adaptation to specific circumstances, but universalists would argue that if moral absolutes are removed, subjective moral discretion leads to egoistic rationalizations. I might believe that lying for a good cause is acceptable, but how do I determine what is a "good enough" cause to lie for; and if I can justify it for one reason, why not another, and another?

TOWARD A RESOLUTION: SITUATIONAL ETHICS

Situational ethics is often used as a synonym for *relativism;* however, if we clarify the term to include the elements discussed on page 47, it might serve as a resolution to the problems inherent in both an absolutist and a relativist approach to ethics. Recall that relativism, on one hand, is criticized because it must allow any practice to be considered "good" if it is considered good by some people; therefore, even human sacrifice and cannibalism would have to be considered moral, a thoroughly unpalatable consequence of accepting the doctrine. Absolutism, on the other hand, is also less than satisfactory because we all can think of some examples where the "rule" must be broken; even Kant declined to be purely absolutist in his argument that lying isn't really lying if told to a person who is trying to harm us. What is needed, then, is an approach that resolves both problems. Hinman (1998) resolves this debate by defining the balance between absolutism and relativism as **moral pluralism.** In his elaboration of this approach, he stops short of an "anything goes" rationale, but does recognize multicultural "truths" that affect moral perceptions.

QUOTE

All I really need to know about how to live and what to do and how to be I learned in kindergarten. Wisdom was not at the top of the graduate-school mountain, but there in the sandpile at Sunday School. These are the things I learned:
Share everything.
Play fair.
Don't hit people.
Put things back where you found them.
Clean up your own mess.
Don't take things that aren't yours.
Say you're sorry when you hurt somebody. . . .

Fulghum, Robert. *All I Really Needed to Know I Learned in Kindergarten* (New York: Villard Books, 1986): 6. Copyright © 1986, 1988 by Robert Fulghum. Reprinted by permission of Villard Books, a division of Random House, Inc.

The solution offered here, whether one calls it situational ethics, or some other term, is as follows:

1. There are basic principles of right and wrong.

2. These can be applied to ethical dilemmas and moral issues.

3. These principles may call for different results in different situations, depending on the needs, concerns, relationships, resources, weaknesses, and strengths of the individual actors.

Fletcher (1967: 26) proposes that "love" be one of the guiding principles or norms:

> The situationist enters into every decision making situation fully armed with the ethical maxims of his community and its heritage, and he treats them with respect as illuminators of his problems. Just the same he is prepared in any situation to compromise them or set them aside in the situation if love seems better served by doing so.

Situational ethics is different from relativism because absolute norms are recognized, whereas under relativism there are no norms. What are absolute norms? Natural law, the Golden Rule, and the ethics of care could help us fashion a set of moral absolutes that might be general enough to ensure universal agreement. For instance, we could start with the following propositions:

1. Treat each person with the utmost respect and care.

2. Do one's duty(ies) in such a way that one does not violate the first principle.

These principles would not have anything to say about dancing (as immoral or moral), but they would definitely condemn human sacrifice, child molestation, slavery, and a host of other practices that have been part of human society. Practices could be good in one society and bad in another—for instance, if polygamy was necessary to ensure the survival of society, it might be acceptable; if it was to serve the pleasure of some by using and treating others as mere objects, it would be immoral. Selling daughters into marriage to enrich the family would never be acceptable because that is not treating them with respect and care; however, arranged marriages might be acceptable if all parties agree and the motives are consistent with care.

To resolve the dilemma from Chapter 1 of the police officer who stops his father for DWI, one might argue that he can do his duty and still respect and care for his father. He could help his father through the arrest process, treat him with care, and make sure that he received help, if he needed it, for his drinking. Although this might not be enough to placate his father, and his father might still be angry with him, as would others, their reaction could then be analyzed: Are they treating the officer with care and respect? Is it respecting someone to expect him to ignore a lawful duty?

This system is not too different from a flexible interpretation of Kant's categorical imperative, a strict interpretation of rule-based utilitarianism, or an inclusive application of the Golden Rule. All ethical systems (except egoism) struggle with objectivity and subjectivity, along with respect for the individual and concern for society. Interestingly, situational ethics seems to be entirely consistent with the ethics of care, especially when one contrasts this ethical system with a rule-based, absolutist system. In the ethics of care, you will recall, each individual is considered in the equation of what would be the "good."

The following schemata may help to isolate the differences and similarities between these concepts:

Absolutist	*Situational*
Rationality, law, rules, duty	Emotion, mercy, discretion
Natural law, ethical formalism	Religion, ethics of care, emotivism

Utilitarianism is arguably on the legal/rule side since the absolute rule of "the greatest utility for all" is often at the expense of the individual. Interestingly, the ethics of virtue, at least Aristotle's version, might be placed on the situational side, even though Aristotle believed that "practical reason" was more important than "moral virtues." This is because he recognized in the "Golden Mean" the concept of individuality. In other words, one person's "mean" of courage might be different from another's, and this would have to be taken into account before judging behavior.

RESULTING CONCERNS

As mentioned previously, ethical systems are not moral decisions as such; rather, they provide the guidelines or principles to make moral decisions. "The Major Ethical Systems" box summarizes the key principles for these ethical systems. It can happen that moral questions are decided in different ways under the same ethical system—for instance, when facts are in dispute. When there is no agreement concerning the accepted facts in a certain case, it is confusing to bring in moral arguments before resolving the factual issues. Capital punishment is supported by some because of a belief that it is a deterrent to people who might commit murder. Others believe that capital punishment is wrong regardless of its efficacy in deterrence. Most arguments about capital punishment get confused during the factual argument about the effectiveness of deterrence. "Is capital punishment wrong or right?" is a different question from "Does capital punishment deter?" The second question might be answered through a study of facts; the former can only be answered by a moral judgment.

Another thing to consider is that none of us are perfect—we all have committed immoral or unethical acts that we know were wrong. Ethical systems help us to understand or analyze morality, but knowing them is no guarantee that we will always act morally and ethically. Very few people follow such strong moral codes that they *never* lie or *never* cause other people harm. One can condemn the act and not the person. The point is that just because some behaviors are understandable and, perhaps, excusable, does not make them moral or ethical.

Very few people consistently use just one ethical system in making moral decisions. Some of us are fundamentally utilitarian and some predominantly religious, but we may make decisions using other ethical frameworks as well. Most of us try to behave ethically most of the time. Dilemmas occur when we are confused about the right thing to do, or the right thing to do carries considerable cost. Detective Poole knew what the right thing to do was. He also knew that he would pay a price for doing it. In fact, he was transferred to a less prestigious position and denied a promotion. He was vilified and treated as a traitor by some officers when he went public with his evidence of a cover-up. Ultimately, he resigned from the Los Angeles Police Department (Golab, 2000).

CONCLUSION

In this chapter we have explored some of the major ethical systems. Ethical systems are ordered principles that define what is right or good. Each of these ethical systems answers the question, "What is good?" in a different way. Sometimes

---

The Major Ethical Systems

Ethical formalism: *What is good is that which* conforms to the categorical imperative.
Utilitarianism: *What is good is that which* results in the greatest utility for the greatest number.
Religion: *What is good is that which* conforms to God's will.
Natural law: *What is good is that which* is natural.
Ethics of virtue: *What is good is that which* conforms to the Golden Mean.
Ethics of care: *What is good is that which* meets the needs of those concerned.
Egoism: *What is good is that which* benefits me.

the same conclusion to an ethical dilemma can be reached using several different ethical systems, but sometimes using different ethical systems may result in contradictory answers to the determination of goodness. Ethical systems are more complex to apply than they are to explain. For instance, utilitarianism is fairly easy to understand, but the measurement of utility for any given act is often quite difficult. Ethical formalism says to "do one's duty," but does not help us when there are conflicting duties. The ethics of care emphasizes relationships but is quite vague in providing the steps necessary to resolve ethical dilemmas. Relativism and absolutism are contrary principles but may be reconciled using the concept of situational ethics.

REVIEW QUESTIONS

1. If you had to choose one ethical system, which one most closely conforms to your own beliefs? Be explicit.

2. Is there a universal truth relating to right and wrong, moral and immoral? If you answered yes, what are the principles of such a system?

3. Describe each of the ethical systems and provide a critique of each.

4. Discuss the arguments against and supporting relativism. Do the same for absolutism.

5. Explain the differences between situational ethics and relativism.

ETHICAL DILEMMAS

Situation 1

You are a manager of a retail store. You are given permission by the owner of the store to hire a fellow classmate to help out. One day you see the classmate take some clothing from the store. When confronted by you, the peer laughs it off and says the owner is insured, no one is hurt, and it was under $100. "Besides," says your acquaintance, "friends stick together, right?" What would you do?

Situation 2

You are in a lifeboat along with four others. You have only enough food and water to keep four alive for the several weeks you expect to be adrift until you float into a shipping lane and can be discovered and rescued. You will definitely all perish if the five of you consume the food and water. There is the suggestion that one of you should die so that the other four can live. Would you volunteer to commit suicide? Would you vote to have one go overboard if you choose by straws? Would you vote to throw overboard the weakest and most sickly of the five? If you were on a jury judging the behavior of four who did murder a fifth in order to stay alive, would you acquit them or convict them of murder?

Situation 3

You aspire to be a police officer and are about to graduate from a criminal justice department. Your best friend has just been hired by a local law enforcement agency, and you are applying as well. When you were both freshman, you were caught with marijuana in your dorm room. Although you were arrested, the charges were dismissed because it turned out that the search was illegal. On the application form, there is a question that asks if you have ever been arrested. Your friend told you that he answered no because he knew this agency did not use polygraphs as part of the hiring process. You must now decide whether to also lie on the form. If you lie, you may be found out eventually, but there is a good chance that the long-ago arrest will never come to light. If you don't lie, you will be asked to explain the circumstances of the arrest and your friend will be implicated as well. What should you do?

SUGGESTED READINGS

Braswell, M., McCarthy, B., and McCarthy, B. (eds.). 2002. *Justice, Crime, and Ethics*, 3rd ed. Cincinnati: Anderson.

Foot, P. 1982. "Moral Relativism." Pp. 152–167 in Meiland, J., and Krausz, M. (eds.), *Relativism: Cognitive and Moral*. Notre Dame: University of Notre Dame Press.

Hinman, L. 1998. *Ethics: A Pluralistic Approach to Moral Theories*. Fort Worth, TX: Harcourt Brace Publishers.

Prior, W. 1991. *From Virtue and Knowledge: An Introduction to Ancient Greek Ethics*. New York: Routledge, Kegan Paul.

Stace, W. 1995. "Ethical Relativity and Ethical Absolutism." Pp. 25–32 in Close, D., and Meier, N. (eds.), *Morality in Criminal Justice*. Belmont, CA: Wadsworth.

3

Developing Moral and Ethical Behavior

Key Terms

predeterminers

modeling

reinforcement

cognitive dissonance

Kohlberg's moral stages

Chapter Objectives

- Become familiar with the major theories regarding the development of moral behavior, especially Kohlberg's moral development theory and learning theory.
- Become familiar with Gilligan's research exploring gender differences in moral development.
- Recognize the difficulty associated with the relationship between moral beliefs and behavior.
- Become familiar with some of the applications of moral development theory to criminal offenders.
- Become familiar with some issues regarding teaching ethics in criminal justice.

In the previous chapter, we explored the question, "How does one determine what is good?" In this chapter, we will discuss, "How does one become a good person?" As we have seen, philosophers have looked to God, natural law, reason, intuition, and emotion to determine moral truths. The fundamental question about the nature of morality is whether it is subjective and of human construction, or whether it is apart from and only discoverable by humans, thus universal and objective. The fundamental question regarding the nature of humans is whether we are born good or evil, or whether we become that way through life circumstances. Philosophers and psychologists both address this question, and it is the central issue in the field of criminology. In fact, the premise of this chapter is that the study of moral development clearly overlaps the study of criminology.

QUERY

- Who has been the greatest influence on your moral development? Why? How?
- Why do you think people behave in ways that hurt other people?
- Have you ever done something you knew to be wrong? Why did you do it?
- Do criminals have the same moral beliefs as others? Do they know that stealing is wrong?
- Can we predict individuals who will perform unethical or immoral actions?

THEORIES OF MORAL DEVELOPMENT

Psychology seeks to understand why people behave the way they do. If someone is a chronic liar, why are they that way? If someone is aggressive and takes what they want regardless of other people's needs or desires, why do they behave that way? It should also be noted that *beliefs* and *actions* are related, but one does not necessarily predict the other. As stated before, just because we know something is wrong does not mean that we never do it. The most important contributions to this discussion involve biological approaches, learning theory, and moral development theories. To simplify the approaches: biological theories would propose that we are good or bad because of biological predispositions; learning theory argues that our behavior is based on the rewards we have received; and developmental theories explain that people's behavior is influenced by their intellectual and emotional stage of development; one reaches higher stages of development or not based on one's environment.

QUOTE

We all know, from what we experience with and within ourselves, that our conscious acts spring from our desires and our fears. Intuition tells us that is true also of our fellows and of the higher animals. We all try to escape pain and death, while we seek what is pleasant. We all are ruled in what we do by impulses, and these impulses are so organized that our actions in general serve for our self-preservation and that of the race. Hunger, love, pain, fear are some of those inner forces which rule the individual's instinct for self-preservation. At the same time, as social beings, we are moved in the relations with our fellow beings by such feelings as sympathy, pride, hate, need for power, pity, and so on. All these primary impulses, not easily described in words, are the springs of man's actions. All such action would cease if those powerful elemental forces were to cease stirring within us. Though our conduct seems so very different from that of the higher animals, the primary instincts are much alike in them and in us. The most evident difference springs from the important part which is played in man by a relatively strong power of imagination and by the capacity to think, aided as it is by language and other symbolical devices. Thought is the organizing factor in man, intersected between the causal primary instincts and the resulting actions. In that way imagination and intelligence enter into our existence in the part of servants of the primary instincts.

Albert Einstein, *Out of My Later Years* New York: Philosophical Library, 1950: 15. Reprinted with permission.

BIOLOGICAL THEORIES

The most controversial theories of human behavior point to biological **predeterminers.** Researchers who study the brain have discovered links between the brain and the predisposition to certain behaviors, as well as (potentially) the development of moral behavior. The frontal lobes seem to be the part of the brain implicated in feelings of empathy, shame, and moral reasoning. Individuals with frontal-lobe damage display the following characteristics (Ellis and Pontius, 1989: 6):

1. Increased impulsiveness
2. Decreased attention span
3. Difficulty in logical reasoning
4. Difficulty adjusting to new events
5. Tendency toward apathy and erratic mood shift
6. Tendency toward rude, unrestrained, tactless behavior

7. Tendency to not be able to follow instructions, even after verbalizing what is required

Researchers present a theory postulating the frontal lobe and limbic system's influence on the individual's capacity for moral reasoning:

> Our model suggests that individuals who have frontal–limbic functioning which is lateralized toward the right hemisphere will be more antisocial than those who have lateralization toward the left hemisphere. Second, those with frontal–reticular functioning that is relatively insensitive to environmental input at a given intensity will be more antisocial than those with more sensitive frontal–reticular functioning. Third, individuals whose prefrontal lobes are disinclined to carefully devise long term goals and continuously monitor and fine-tune strategies for achieving those goals will be more antisocial than persons with opposite prefrontal lobe tendencies. (Ellis and Pontius, 1989: 19)

The authors go on to discuss sex differences in brain activity. They discuss research presenting evidence that women are more inclined to empathy and sensitivity to human relationships. More than seventy studies found evidence that males are more antisocial, commit more serious types of offenses, and more often have serious childhood conduct disorders. There are also sex differences in delinquency, school performance, hyperactivity, impulsivity, and attention-deficit disorders. The authors propose that these differences are due to sex-linked brain activity, specifically in the frontal lobes and limbic regions. Males' sex hormones influence brain development prenatally and during puberty. Although there is a great deal of overlap between male and female populations in brain development and activity, there are also distinct and measurable differences; specifically, these differences may influence the brain's ability to absorb "moral messages" or act upon them.

Wilson (1993) is one of the few authors who accept some amount of biological causation in criminology. He argues that values such as sympathy, fairness, self-control, and duty are moral "senses" that are inherent in humans and arise through a combination of genetics and socialization. More detailed explications of how biology might be used to help us understand why people engage in bad behaviors is offered by Walsh (1995, 2001), who also postulates how bad behavior might be explained in evolutionary terms. The area of biological criminology is growing, but slowly. Interestingly, many social scientists are unwilling to explore biological causation, even though there are excellent treatments of the subject available, such as Fishbein's (2000) review of bio-behaviorial influences on criminality.

Learning Theory

Learning theorists believe that children learn what they are taught, including morals and values as well as behavior. In other words, right or wrong is not discovered through reasoning; rather, all humans are shaped by the world around them, and they form completely subjective opinions about morality and ethics.

This learning can take place through modeling or by reinforcement. In **modeling,** values and moral beliefs come from those one admires and aspires to identify with. If that role model happens to be a priest, one will probably develop a religious ethical system; if it happens to be a pimp or a sociopath, an egoistic ethical system may develop. If the identification is broken, moral beliefs may change. It is no surprise that when asked who has been important in their moral development, most people say their parents, since parents are the most significant people in one's life during important formative years. Although we may not hold exactly the same views and have exactly the same values as our parents, there is no doubt that they are influential in our value formation.

Another way learning theorists explain moral development is through **reinforcement.** Behaviors and beliefs that are reinforced (either through material rewards or through more subjective rewards, such as praise) are repeated and eventually become permanent. Since behavior is more easily stabilized and tends to come before permanent attitude change, it is often the case that behavior leads to the development of consistent beliefs. For example, I am rewarded for sharing (by parental praise or the ability to borrow others' toys), and eventually I develop the belief that "sharing is good." Alternatively, I might be rewarded for being selfish and bullying others to gain what I want. On the playground, other children are afraid of me, and I use their fear to demand toys or extra turns. No adults reprimand me, or they do so inconsistently, so the rewards far outweigh the negative consequences of such behavior. Eventually I may develop a "me first" and "every person for themselves is the way to live" philosophy of life.

When behavior is not consistent with beliefs, the discomfort that results is called **cognitive dissonance.** This leads to the development of attitudes to support one's behavior. The child who is told constantly to share toys and is disciplined upon refusal is learning not just the desired behavior, but also the values of cooperativeness and charity. In an adult, these values may be manifested by lending one's lawn mower to a neighbor or contributing to charities. On the other hand, if a child is never punished for aggressive behavior and instead is rewarded—for instance, by always getting the desired object—then aggressiveness and the accompanying moral principle of "might makes right" develops. If we do acts that are contrary to the beliefs that we have heard, we will either stop doing the acts or change our beliefs to reduce the dissonance.

Bandura (cited in Boyce and Jensen, 1978: 123–124) states that there is a developmental approach to teaching, keyed to what the child is capable of understanding:

> According to the social learning view, people vary in what they teach, model and reinforce with children of differing ages. At first, control is necessarily external. In attempting to discourage hazardous conduct in children who have not yet learned to talk, parents must resort to physical intervention. . . . Successful socialization requires gradual substitution of symbolic and internal controls for external sanctions and demands. . . .

According to learning theorists, even the most altruistic behaviors provide rewards for the individual. For instance, acts of charity provide rewards in the form of goodwill from others and self-satisfaction. Acts of sacrifice are rewarded in similar ways. Honesty, integrity, and fairness exist only because they have been rewarded in the past and present and are part of the behavioral repertoire of the individual. The moral principles of "honesty is right," "integrity is good," and "fairness is ethical" come after the behavior has been stabilized, not before. This theory is very different from the view that moral beliefs influence actions.

There is little room in this theory for universalism, absolutism, or the idea that a moral truth exists apart from humans that is not of their construction, but that awaits their discovery. The theory is completely humanistic in that morality is considered a creation of humans that explains and provides a rationale for learned behavior. Behavior is completely neutral; an infant can be taught any behavior desired and the moral beliefs consistent with that belief. In one experiment, children were told a hypothetical story in which an adult punished a neutral act, such as a child practicing a musical instrument. The children later defined that act as bad, despite the intrinsic neutrality of the action. This indicates the power of adult definitions and punishment in the child's moral development (Boyce and Jensen, 1978: 133–170).

Much research exists to support a learning theory of moral development. For instance, it was found that large gains in moral maturity (as measured by paper-and-pencil tests of expression of beliefs) could be achieved by direct manipulation of rewards for such beliefs. Contrary to the view that an individual comes to a realization of moral principles through cognitive development, this theory proposes that one can encourage or create moral beliefs simply by rewards (Boyce and Jensen, 1978: 143).

Developmental Theories

Developmental theories propose that individuals mature cognitively and emotionally, as well as physically, but that development might be stunted by negative environmental influences. Normal physical development can be charted by a pediatrician. We discover at the pediatrician's office whether the height and weight of our child is in the "normal curve" of development. Intellectual development is also measured by a variety of intelligence tests, and charted against a normal curve of development. We do not expect the child to understand concepts before certain developmental markers. Emotional or social development also progresses at a predictable and normal pace, although it may be more difficult to measure. Social maturity is marked by the ability to empathize with others and a willingness to compromise one's desires with other's needs. An emotionally mature person neither abandons self for others, nor puts oneself above others, but, rather, balances individual needs with other's demands.

Kohlberg's Moral Stages   The contributions of Jean Piaget and Lawrence Kohlberg have become essential to any discussion of moral development. Piaget believed that we all go through stages of cognitive, or intellectual, growth. These stages parallel moral stages of development, and together they describe a systematic way of perceiving the world. Piaget studied the rules that children develop in their play. These rules reflect the perceptions they hold of themselves and others and move from egocentrism to cooperativeness. Kohlberg carried on with Piaget's work and more fully described the stages each individual passes through in moral and cognitive development (Kohlberg, 1984; Boyce and Jensen, 1978: 87–95).

Two-year-olds do not understand the world in the same way as twenty-year-olds do. This lack of understanding also affects their moral reasoning ability. The infant lacks sensitivity toward others and has a supreme selfishness regarding his or her needs and wants. Infants are not concerned with others because they are only vaguely aware of their existence. An infant's world is confined to what is within reach of his or her hands and mouth. Even a mother is only important as the source of comfort and food. Very slowly the infant becomes aware that others also have feelings and needs. This awareness leads to empathy and the recognition of right and wrong. At later stages, abstract reasoning develops, which leads to the ability to understand more difficult moral concepts. **Kohlberg's moral stages** are shown in the box.

The following are some characteristics of these cognitive and moral stages (Hersh et al., 1979: 52):

1. *They involve qualitative differences in modes of thinking, as opposed to quantitative differences.* The child undergoes dramatic changes in perceptions; for instance, in an early stage the realization occurs that what one does has an impact on others. An infant realizes that when she pulls someone's hair, the person reacts; when she cries, someone comes; and when she performs certain behaviors, she is praised.

2. *Each stage forms a structured whole; cognitive development and moral growth are integrated.* Perceptions of the world and the corresponding moral framework are similar among all individuals at that particular stage. Simplistically, this means that a child cannot be sensitive to larger issues such as world hunger until he is able to grasp the reality of such conditions.

3. *Stages form an invariant sequence; no one bypasses any stage and not all people develop to the higher stages.* In fact, according to Kohlberg, very few individuals reach the post-conventional level; the majority reach the conventional level and stay there.

4. *Stages are hierarchical integrations.* That is, each succeeding stage encompasses and is more comprehensive and complicated than the stage that precedes it.

Kohlberg describes three levels of moral reasoning; included in each level are two stages. The levels and stages are described as follows (Barry, 1985: 14–16; Kohlberg, 1976):

Kohlberg's Moral Stages

Level A: Preconventional

Stage 1: "Right is blind obedience to rules and authority, avoiding punishment, and not doing physical harm."

Stage 2: "Right is serving one's own or others' needs and making fair deals in terms of concrete exchange."

Level B: Conventional

Stage 3: "Right is playing a good 'nice' role, being concerned about other people and their feelings, keeping loyalty and trust with partners, and being motivated to follow rules and expectations."

Stage 4: "Right is doing one's duty in society, upholding the social order, and the welfare of society or the group."

Level C: Post-Conventional

Stage 5: "Right is upholding the basic rights, values, and legal contracts of a society, even when they conflict with the concrete rules and laws of the group."

Stage 6: "Right is guided by self-chosen ethical principles of justice, equality, and respect. Laws and social agreements are usually consistent with these principles."

SOURCE: Gibbs, J., Kohlberg, L., Colby, A., and Speicher-Dubin, B. "The Domain and Development of Moral Judgment: A Theory and Method of Assessment." In Meyer, J. (ed.), *Reflections on Values Education* (Waterloo, Ontario: Wilfrid Laurier University Press, 1976): 19–20.

Level A (Preconventional Level) At the preconventional level, the person approaches a moral issue motivated purely by personal interests. The major concern is the consequences of the action for the person. For instance, young children do not share toys with others because they see no reason to do so. They derive pleasure from them, so to give them to others is not logical. Even if the toys belong to others, there is a predisposition for children to appropriate them. Parents know the tears and tantrums associated with teaching a child that toys belonging to others must be given back. Young children at play first start sharing, in fact, when they perceive benefit to themselves, such as giving someone their doll in exchange for a game or a ball, or they grudgingly share because they fear punishment from an adult if they do not.

Stage 1 has a punishment and obedience orientation. What is right is that which is praised; what is wrong is that which is punished. The child submits to an authority figure's definition and is concerned only with the consequences attached to certain behaviors, not with the behavior itself.

Stage 2 has an instrument and relativity orientation The child becomes aware of and is concerned with others' needs. What is right is still determined by self-interest, but the concept of self-interest is broadened to include others.

Relationships are important to the child, and he or she is attached to parents, siblings, and best friends, who are included in the ring of self-interest. There is also the emerging concept of fairness and a recognition that others deserve to have their needs met.

Level B (Conventional Level) At the conventional level, people perceive themselves as members of society, and living up to role responsibilities is paramount in believing oneself to be good. Children enter this level when they are capable of playing with other children according to rules. In fact, games and play are training grounds for moral development, since they teach the child that there are defined roles and rules of behavior. For instance, a game of softball becomes a microcosm of real life when a child realizes that he or she is not only acting as self, but also as a first baseman, a role that includes certain specific tasks. Before this stage, the child runs to the ball regardless of where it is hit. Thus, in a softball game with very young children playing, one may see all the players running after the ball and abandoning their bases, because they have difficulty grasping the concept of role responsibilities. Furthermore, although it would be more expeditious to trip the runners as they leave the base so they can be tagged out, the child learns that such behavior is not "fair play" and is against the rules of the game. Thus, children learn to submerge individual interest to conform to rules and role expectations.

Stage 3 has an interpersonal concordance orientation. The person performs conventionally determined good behavior to be considered a good person. The views of "significant others" are important to one's self-concept. Thus, individuals will control behavior so as to not hurt others' feelings or be thought of as bad.

Stage 4 has a law-and-order orientation The individual is concerned not just with interpersonal relationships, but also with the rules set down by society. The law becomes all-important. Even if the laws themselves are wrong, one cannot disregard them, for that would invite social chaos.

Level C (Post-Conventional Level) A person at the post-conventional level moves beyond the norms and laws of a society to determine universal good—that is, what is good for all societies. Few people reach this level, and their actions are observably different from the majority. For instance, Gandhi might be described as a person with post-conventional morality. He did not subscribe to the idea that laws must be obeyed, and he carried out peaceful noncompliance against the established law to conform to his belief in a higher order of morality. At this level of moral development, the individual assumes the responsibility of judging laws and conventions.

Stage 5 has a social contract orientation The person recognizes larger interests than current laws. This individual is able to evaluate the morality of laws in a historical context and feels an obligation to the law because of its benefits to societal survival. *The orientation of Stage 6 is universal ethical principles* The person who has reached this stage bases moral judgments on the higher abstract laws of truth, justice, and morality.

A seventh stage? Kohlberg advanced the possibility of a seventh stage, which has been described as a "soft" stage of ethical awareness with an orientation of cosmic or religious thinking. It is not a higher level of reasoning, but qualitatively different. According to Kohlberg, in this highest stage individuals have come to terms with such questions as, "Why be just in a universe that is largely unjust?" It is a different question from the definition of justice that forms the content of the other stages. In this stage, one sees oneself as part of a larger whole and humanity as only part of a larger cosmic structure. This stage focuses on *agape*—a nonexclusive love and acceptance of the cosmos and one's place in it (Kohlberg, 1983; Power and Kohlberg, 1980).

Critics of Kohlberg Some believe that Kohlberg's theory of moral development has several serious flaws. First, the stages tend to center too much on the concept of justice, ignoring other aspects of morality. Second, the stages, especially 5 and 6, may be nothing more than culturally based beliefs regarding the highest level of morality: "Kohlberg assumes that the core of morality and moral development is deontological, that it is a matter of rights and duties as prescriptions" (Levine, Kohlberg, and Hewer, 1985: 95). Justice, rules, and rights are emphasized as higher values than are caring and relationships. Others say Kohlberg emphasizes reason in moral decisions and ignores emotional factors. In response, Kohlberg and his associates assert that the theory is a measurement of "justice reasoning," not an attempt to present the "total complexity of the moral domain" (Levine, Kohlberg, and Hewer, 1985: 99).

Other studies have found significant cultural differences in the age at which children reach different stages of moral development. This criticism does not necessarily negate the validity of a stage sequence theory; however, it does call into question the specifics of movement through the stages (Boyce and Jensen, 1978). Still others criticize the lack of connection between reasoning levels and moral action in particular situations. There does not seem to be a perfect correlation between one's moral stage, as measured by the interview format of Kohlberg's research or more recently devised paper-and-pencil tests of recognition, and how one will respond when faced with a situation that offers a choice to be honest or dishonest (Lutwak and Hennesy, 1985).

Kohlberg's research can also be described as sexually biased because he interviewed boys almost exclusively in early research. Subsequent studies have found that women tend to cluster in Stage 3 because of their greater sensitivity to and emphasis on human relationships. Stage 3 is lower than the law-and-order stage, where men tend to be clustered. Unless one believes that women are generally less moral or less intellectually developed than men, this is a troubling finding and one that calls into question the hierarchical nature of the theory.

Carol Gilligan (1982, 1987), one of Kohlberg's students, researched the apparent sex difference in moral reasoning and proposed that women may possess a *different* morality from men. Most men, it seems, analyze moral decisions with a rules or justice orientation (Stage 4), whereas many women see the same moral dilemma with an orientation toward needs and relationships (Stage 3). Gilligan labels this a *care perspective*. A morality based on the care perspective would be more inclined to look at how a decision affects relationships and addresses needs, whereas the justice perspective is concerned with notions of equality, rights, and universality. This ethics of care has been described in Chapter 2 as one of the ethical frameworks.

In Gilligan's study, although both men and women raised justice and care concerns in responses to moral dilemmas, among those who focused on one or the other, men exclusively focused on justice while half of the women who exhibited a focus did so on justice concerns and the other half focused on care concerns (Gilligan, 1987). It was also found that both male and female respondents were able to switch from a justice to a care perspective (or back again) when asked to do so; thus, their orientation was more a matter of perspective than inability to see the other side. What Gilligan points out in her research is that the care perspective completely drops out when one uses only male subjects—which is what Kohlberg did in his early research for the moral stage theory. The box, "Are Women More Ethical?" examines this sex difference.

Another study of fifty college students (half men, half women) tested the subjects' orientation to three moral dilemmas, and the results were consistent with Gilligan's findings. However, the content of the dilemma evidently influenced whether care considerations would be found. The dilemmas involving interpersonal relationships were more likely to have care considerations than those without (Rothbart, Hanley, and Albert, 1986; Flanagan and Jackson, 1987). It should also be noted that other studies failed to find any differences between men and women in their responses to moral dilemmas (see reviews in Walker, 1986; Thoma, 1986).

The importance of Kohlberg's work is the link he makes between moral development and reason. This concept originated with Kant and even earlier philosophers, but Kohlberg provides a psychological analysis that sheds light on

---

Are Women More Ethical?

A recent study supports the premise that women in business are more ethical than men. A Baylor University study found that there were significant differences between females and males when asked to respond to different hypothetical scenarios, with women more often taking the ethical "high road." The study included 1,831 women and men from all fifty states who worked in professional and managerial positions. Women responded with more ethical responses to hypothetical situations involving exceeding legal pollution limits, bribery, corporate espionage, promotion practices, product safety, and executive salaries versus workers' salaries. Men responded more ethically to situations involving collusion in construction bidding and copying computer software. Researchers suggest socialization differences between men and women as a possible explanation for such differences.

How would Carol Gilligan explain the differences these researchers found?

SOURCE: Roser, M. A. 1996. "Business Study Finds Women More Ethical," *Austin American Statesman*, December 26: A1, A11.

how reason influences moral judgments. Also important in Kohlberg's work is the guidance it provides to education. According to the theory of moral stages, one can encourage movement through the stages by exposing the individual to higher-stage reasoning. The procedures for encouraging moral growth include presenting moral dilemmas and allowing the individual to support his or her position. Through exposure to higher reasoning, one sees the weaknesses and inconsistencies of lower-level reasoning (Hersh et al., 1979). Kohlberg indicates clearly what is needed for moral growth. Despite reservations about his descriptions of the moral stages, the proposed guidelines to encourage moral development seem valid and are supported by other authorities.

Kohlberg (1976) described the following as necessary for moral growth:

1. *Being in a situation where seeing things from other points of view is encouraged.* This is important because upward-stage movement is a process of getting better at reconciling conflicting perspectives on a moral problem.

2. *Engaging in logical thinking, such as reasoned argument and consideration of alternatives.* This is important because one cannot attain a given stage of moral reasoning before attaining the supporting Piagetian stage of logical reasoning.

3. *Having the responsibility to make moral decisions and to influence one's moral world.* This response is necessary for developing a sense of moral agency and for learning to apply one's moral reasoning to life's situations.

4. *Exposure to moral controversy and to conflict in moral reasoning that challenges the structure of one's present stage.* This is important for questioning one's moral beliefs and forcing a look at alternatives.

5. *Exposure to the reasoning of individuals whose thinking is one stage higher than one's own.* The importance here is in offering a new moral structure for resolving the disequilibrium caused by moral conflict.

6. *Participation in creating and maintaining a just community whose members pursue common goals and resolve conflict in accordance with the ideals of mutual respect and fairness.*

People may become stuck at a certain point in moral development for several reasons, including not having sufficiently developed cognitive skills and/or living in a social environment that does not allow for role-taking opportunities or personal growth. For instance, a child growing up in a family that repeats basic moral views with little attempt to explain or defend them will learn to be closed to other viewpoints. A child who is never given responsibility or forced to take responsibility for his or her own actions will have difficulty developing moral reasoning skills and will not advance to higher stages. Such children will be, in a sense, stunted at the Kohlberg preconventional level of an infant, constantly fed and cared for, but not allowed to discover that other people exist and must be considered. As adults, if we surround ourselves only with people who think as we do, then it is very unlikely that we will ever change our moral positions or even consider others.

Exercise

Talk to a child (four to eight years old) about a variety of moral issues—
e.g., what is bad? What is good? Give the child a moral dilemma relevant
to his or her world (make the characters children, the issue a familiar
one). How does the child respond? Can you identify any moral
principles? Can you identify which of Kohlberg's stages seems to describe
the child's reasoning?

ETHICS, BEHAVIOR, AND CRIMINALITY

Can one predict behavior from moral beliefs? Psychologists who have studied
"immoral" behavior, such as lying and cheating among adults and children,
have found it hard to predict who will perform these behaviors. There seems
to be little consistency between beliefs and behaviors.

Predicting Behavior

Some studies, however, do find beliefs and actions to be correlated. In one study,
"honesty scores" for people in three organizations were compiled from an atti-
tudinal questionnaire about beliefs. It was found that the organization with the
highest average honesty score had the least employee theft, and the organization
with the lowest average honesty score had the most employee theft (Adams,
1981). In contrast, Kohlberg cites the Hartshone and May study, which found no
correlation between different tests of honesty and behavior, and another study in
which a group of women prisoners were found to have the same rank orderings
of values as female college students. He uses these studies as support for the
proposition that one cannot measure a trait in isolation and expect to find consistency between values and action (Kohlberg and Candel, 1984: 499–503).

Recall that learning theory proposes that behavior precedes moral beliefs.
Good behavior is created by external rewards, and then one develops the beliefs
that go along with such behavior. However, there is some evidence to indicate
that compliance gained from external rewards is not stable until it becomes
internalized, which involves adaptation to existing personality structures
(Borchert and Stewart, 1986: 133–145). The question of when and why beliefs
and values are internalized is not as easy to research. Even if ethical behavior
could be ensured by providing rewards, this would not necessarily develop
"moral character" or moral principles unless beliefs are somehow internalized.

Part of the problem is the difficulty in measuring moral beliefs and the
validity of the instruments used. Kohlberg's work has been so influential in this
field that it is difficult to find any measurement of morality that does not
directly or indirectly use his stage definitions. If one attempts to examine
whether bad behavior is associated with lower-stage scores, there is the
assumption that lower-stage scores mean the person has less developed moral
reasoning. We have previously discussed Carol Gilligan's challenge of this conception, yet practically all studies that examine the correlation between behavior and belief continue to use stage scores as a measure of moral development.

Measurement of moral stages was accomplished in Kohlberg's work by interviews with subjects who were questioned using hypothetical moral dilemmas. Their responses were then rated by interviewers, with emphasis placed not necessarily on the answer given, but rather, on the reasoning for the answer. What factors were emphasized, then, were used to place the person into the proper moral stage. This procedure is time-consuming and expensive, so paper-and-pencil tests have been devised, arguably measuring the same type of reasoning but through simpler, quicker means. Much criticism is directed at these so-called "recognition" tests, which require the subject merely to recognize and identify certain moral principles and agree with them, as opposed to "production" measures, which require the subject actually to reason through a dilemma and provide some rationale, which is then analyzed. It may be that recognition measures are less reliable in predicting behavior. Gavaghan, Arnold, and Gibbs (1983) reported that while production measures were able to distinguish between a group of delinquents and nondelinquents, recognition measures could not.

Those who subscribe to a stage theory of moral development would argue that inconsistent behavior merely means that the individual has not fully incorporated the higher-level reasoning. Learning theorists, by contrast, would propose that the rewards for good behavior are weak or not immediate. For instance, individuals who believe stealing is wrong may nevertheless be tempted because of the immediacy of the reward (the coveted item). If they have internalized a strict sense of morality regarding stealing that would result in unpleasant feelings of guilt, then that immediate punishment will counteract the immediate reward. If, however, they had not been punished enough in the past (either physically or emotionally) for such action, then the guilt feelings will not occur to counteract the temptation. See the box on "Honesty," on the next page.

Teaching Ethics

Many people believe that the general morality of this nation is declining. Others point to examples abroad. Transparency International (2003) is an organization that compiles evidence of corruption from across the world and rates countries on how much corruption exists. The United States was scored in sixteenth place, as having more corruption than countries such as Finland, Denmark, New Zealand, Iceland, Singapore, Sweden, Canada, Australia, and the United Kingdom. Third-world countries such as Bangladesh, Nigeria, Uganda, Indonesia, Kenya, Cameroon, Bolivia, and Azerbaijan were rated as having the most corruption.

QUOTE

There is no end in sight to the misuse of power by those in public office—and corruption levels are perceived to be as high as ever in both the developed and developing worlds.

Peter Eigen, Chairman of Transparency International. 2001. Press Release.

Honesty

Reader's Digest conducted a nonscientific test of the public's honesty by dropping 120 wallets containing $50 and family pictures in various locales, including cities, suburbs, and small towns. They then watched who returned the wallets and who kept the wallets.

	Returned Wallet	Kept Wallet
Big Cities:		
Seattle	9	1
St. Louis	7	3
Atlanta	5	5
Suburbs:		
Los Angeles	6	4
Houston	5	5
Boston	7	3
Medium Cities:		
Greensboro, NC	7	3
Las Vegas	5	5
Dayton, OH	5	5
Small Towns:		
Meadville, PA	8	2
Concord, NH	8	2
Cheyenne, WY	8	2
Men (60)	37	23
(62% returned)		
Women (60)	43	17
(72% returned)		

SOURCE: Bennett, R. K. "How Honest Are We?" *Readers Digest* v. 146–147 (December 1995), 49–56.

In the United States of America, the William Clinton–Monica Lewinsky debacle, the Enron bankruptcy, and the Abner Louima case in New York City have created a perception that the nation is at a new low in levels of ethics and morality. One of the reasons given for this perceived decline is that we have eliminated many of the opportunities for the teaching of morals. The community is not a cohesive force any longer, the authority of religion is not as pervasive as it once was, the family is weakening as a force of socialization, and educators have abdicated their responsibility for moral instruction in favor of scientific neutrality. It was not always this way.

In most colleges in the 1800s, a course in moral philosophy was required of all graduates. This class, often taught by the college president, was designed to help the college student become a good citizen. The goal of college was not only to educate but also to help students attain the moral sensibility that would make them productive, ideal citizens. As it was taught, ethics involved not only the history of philosophical thought but also a system of beliefs and values and the skills to resolve moral or ethical dilemmas. Gradually, the general field of social science became more and more specialized. Each discipline carved out for itself an area of behavior or part of society to study, so today we have, among others, sociology, psychology, economics, history, and philosophy. The increasing empiricism of these disciplines crowded out the earlier emphasis on moral decision making. Schools affiliated with religious denominations still routinely require courses that focus on one's moral character, but such courses are, for the most part, missing in undergraduate curriculums.

QUERY

- How many students do you think have ever cheated on a test?
(In a survey of 1,139 students at 27 universities, 60 percent reporting cheating at some point in high school or college.)

Reported by Ryan, 2002, A11.

However most professional schools today (in law, medicine, and business) require at least one class in professional ethics. Typically, these classes present the opportunity to examine the ethical dilemmas that individuals may encounter as members of that profession and help students discover the best way to decide ethical issues. Usually, there is a combination of discussion and instruction. Although some class time is devoted to letting students discuss their views, certainly part of the task is to train new members in what has been determined to be correct behavior.

The alternative, of course, would be to ignore ethics in the learning phase of an occupation and let the person encounter ethical dilemmas on the job— for instance, when a prosecutor is tempted to ignore evidence to ensure an easy conviction, when a doctor must choose between two people who both need a heart transplant, or when a business executive is asked to accept a bribe to award a contract. In the rushed, pressure-filled real world, ethical decisions will be made in haste, with emotional overtones, and with peer and situational pressures heavily influencing the decision.

Such classes have gained new importance recently because of the business scandals that emerged in 2002. Evidently, there is a growing new field of ethics instruction and "ethics officers" hired by businesses to ensure that their workers behave honestly and ethically. Whether such classes are successful will depend, in large part, on whether CEOs are good students. Consider the box "Ethics Classes: Solution or Scam?" See the following page.

Administrators and managers exert the strongest influence on the ethical climate of an agency, regardless of whether ethics classes are offered. If leaders are honest, ethical, and caring, there is a good chance that those who

---

Ethics Classes: Solution or Scam?

In an editorial poking fun at the recent rise of ethics classes, Joan Ryan of the *San Francisco Chronicle* writes that Raytheon, a defense contractor, has produced a video where the company's vice president, along with Roger Ebert, the film critic, give thumbs up or down to a series of behaviors. Ryan wonders if Bert and Ernie of *Sesame Street* might have done a better job. An attempt to improve the ethics of a workforce is laudable, but the approach may be patronizing or even cynical, depending on the company's motivation. She points out that businesses that have ethics programs in place are eligible for reduced fines if they are found guilty of corporate wrongdoing. The behavior of leaders and the values of the company are more important determiners of employees' behaviors than whether or not they sat through a class. Says Ryan, ". . . the post-Enron era is much like the pre-Enron. Companies were cooking the books, faking transactions, lying to shareholders. The problem was about perpetuating a sham. Now so, too, is the solution."

SOURCE: Ryan, J. 2002. "The Appearance of Ethics," Austin American Statesman, Saturday, Nov. 16: A11.

---

work for these managers are also ethical. If administrators and/or managers are hypocritical, untruthful, and use their positions for personal gain, then workers often march in these same footsteps. If the business itself is premised on misleading the consumer and perpetrating fraud to secure higher profits, then why should business leaders expect that workers would behave any differently?

Teaching Ethics in Criminal Justice

Recall that in Chapter 1 it was proposed that because criminal justice organizations are involved with public service, there needs to be a special sensitivity to ethics on the part of criminal justice professionals. Should ethics be a part of law enforcement academies and in-service training? Should correctional, probation, and parole officers be required to complete ethics classes? Many believe that it is much more effective to present moral or ethical questions to new members of a profession before the individual is faced with "real-life" dilemmas. Of course, what often happens is that once students leave this setting they are usually told to forget what they've learned. This happens often in police academies, where cadets are taught "the book" and learn "the street" when they are paired with an older officer. This also happens when lawyers realize that the high ideals of justice they learned in law school have little to do with the bargaining and bureaucratic law of the courthouse.

People respond to the discrepancies between official and subcultural ethics in a number of ways. They may ignore, participate in, or confront activities of their peers that they feel are wrong. It is difficult to ignore actions that run contrary to one's own value system, but very often employees establish complicated rationalizations to explain why it is not their business that others around them steal, perform less than adequately, or conduct illicit business during working hours. People often do not feel it is right to confront the immoral behavior of others even when their own behavior is consistent with accepted standards of morality.

Others are able to redefine their moral beliefs to accept the type of behavior practiced and approved of in the subculture. Chapter 7 discusses how police officers develop their "moral careers," which may include many types of otherwise immoral and unethical behavior. Confronting the activities of one's peers typically involves a greater moral strength than most of us possess. One must also often sacrifice other values, such as loyalty or friendship, to confront wrongdoing.

Individuals are sometimes confronted with the choice of saying nothing and allowing corruption to continue or risk ostracism and censure from peers. The books *Serpico* (Maas, 1973) and *Prince of the City* (Daley, 1984) described two examples of police officers who chose to challenge the "blue curtain" of secrecy and testify against their fellow officers in corruption hearings. In *Prince of the City,* the officer agreed to testify only if he could protect his partners. Ultimately, he was unable to do so and had to live with the hatred, betrayal, and even suicide of past friends.

If one is interested in changing unethical behavior in an organization, the primary target might be new recruits, since those who have been engaging in unethical activities have built up comprehensive rationales for their behavior. Socio-moral reasoning opportunities could exist in classroom settings, such as academies. Learning theorists, on the other hand, might say that the most effective way to change the ethics of a profession is to make sure that behavior changes. According to learning theory principles, if one was sure to be punished for accepting bribes, lying, or performing other unethical behaviors, then the subcultural supports for such behavior and the moral apologia for it would disappear. However, only pure behaviorists would conclude that mere monitoring and application of consistent rewards and punishments would result in an ethical workforce. Others believe that although monitoring might result in a workforce that performed in an ethical manner, in order for ethical behavior to continue without monitoring, and for people to believe in principles of right and wrong, they must internalize an ethical system.

According to Sherman (1982: 17–18), the following elements are necessary for any ethics program relating to criminal justice:

1. Stimulating the "moral imagination" by posing difficult moral dilemmas
2. Encouraging the recognition of ethical issues and larger questions instead of more immediate issues such as efficiency and goals
3. Helping to develop analytical skills and the tools of ethical analysis
4. Eliciting a sense of moral obligation and personal responsibility to show why ethics should be taken seriously
5. Tolerating and resisting disagreement and ambiguity
6. Understanding the morality of coercion, which is intrinsic to criminal justice

7. Integrating technical and moral competence, especially recognizing the difference between what we are capable of doing and what we should do

8. Becoming familiar with the full range of moral issues in criminology and criminal justice

In the study of criminal justice ethics, there are many areas ripe for inquiry. Issues include the definitions of justice and crime, the appropriate use of force, the relative importance of due process over efficiency, the ethical use of technology to control the populace, the variables used to determine responsibility and punishment, the right of society to treat (or punish), and the limits that should be placed on treatment (or punishment). Furthermore, there has been a wealth of excellent material published in the last several years, so the student or interested reader should be able to find sources that explore the issues above, as well as others. Souryal and Potts (1996) propose that there is a standard body of knowledge available for those who want to become "literate" in the study of criminal justice ethics. In the box titled "Cultural Literacy in Criminal Justice" Souryal and Potts's sources are presented. The interested student would be well served to use this list to start a study of ethics.

Morality, Criminology, and Offender Populations

Even though criminology is directly concerned with crime—behavior that is usually judged as immoral—it typically avoids moral definitions. Deviance is a sociological concept, and crime is defined simply as unlawful behavior. Of course it may not be true that criminal acts are always immoral behaviors. Radical criminologists raise important points in their discussion of how certain behaviors are defined as criminal and who is allowed to do the defining. However, most criminal behavior—stealing, killing, assaulting, bribing, and so on—can also be defined as immoral or unethical. The field of psychology offers

---

Cultural Literacy in Criminal Justice

The Philosophy of Ethics

Adler, M. (1978). *Aristotle for Everybody: Difficult Thought Made Easy*
Albert, E., Denise, T., and Peterfruend, S. (1988). *Great Traditions of Ethics*
Bloom, A. (1987). *The Closing of the American Mind*
Borchert, D., and Stewart, D. (1986). *Exploring Ethics*
Campbell, K. (1986). *A Stoic Philosophy of Life*
Keyes, C.D. (1978). *Four Types of Value Destruction: A Search for the Good Through Ethical Analysis of Everyday Experience*
Lavine, T. Z. (1984). *From Socrates to Sartre: The Philosophic Quest*
Porter, B. (1988). *Reasons for Living: A Basic Ethics*
Thiroux, J. (1990). *Ethics: Theory and Practice*
Warmington, E., and Rouse, P. (1984). *Great Dialogues of Plato*

Cultural Literacy in Criminal Justice (continued)

Moral Rules and Moral Judgment

Brink, D. (1989). *Moral Realism of the Foundations of Ethics*
Carson, T. (1984). *The State of Morality*
Cooper, N. (1981). *The Diversity of Moral Thinking*
Fishkin, J. (1984). *Beyond Subjective Morality: Ethical Reasoning and Political Philosophy*
Gert, B. (1970). *The Moral Rules*
Goldman, A. (1988). *Moral Knowledge*
Kekes, J. (1989). *Moral Tradition and Individuality*
Lee, K. (1985). *A New Basis for Moral Philosophy*
Singer, P. (1979). *Practical Ethics*

Justice Theories

Cohen, R. (1986). *Justice: Views from the Social Sciences*
Dworkin, R. (1977). *Taking Rights Seriously*
Feinberg, J., and Cross, H. (1980). *Philosophy of Law*
Hobbes, T. (1968). *Leviathan*
Hochischild, J. (1981). *What Is Fair? American Beliefs About Distributive Justice*
Lycos, K. (1987). *Plato on Justice and Power*
MacIntyre, A. (1988). *Whose Justice? Which Rationality?*
Rawls, J. (1971). *A Theory of Justice*
Reiman, J. (1990). *Justice and Modern Moral Philosophy*

Ethics of Public Service

Beauchamp, T. (1975). *Ethics and Public Policy*
Bok, S. (1978). *Lying: Moral Choice in Public and Private Life*
Cleveland, H. (1985). *The Knowledge Executive: Leadership in an Information Society*
Dubin, R. (1974). *Human Relations in Administration*
Elliston, F., and Bowie, N. (1982). *Ethics, Public Policy and Criminal Justice*
Herzberg, F. (1976). *The Managerial Choice: To Be Efficient and to Be Human*
Nettler, G. (1982). *Lying, Cheating, Stealing*
Regan, T., and Van DeVeer, D. (1982). *And Justice for All: New Introductory Essays in Ethics and Public Policy*
Rohr, J. (1978). *Ethics for Bureaucrats: An Essay on Law and Values*
Williams, J. D. (1980). *Public Administration: The People's Business*

Ethics of Criminal Justice Agencies

Braswell, M., McCarthy, B., and McCarthy, B. (1991). *Justice, Crime and Ethics*
Delattre, E. (1989). *Character and Cops: Ethics in Policing*
Fleisher, M. (1989). *Warehousing Violence*
Heffernan, W., and Stroup, T. (1985). *Police Ethics: Hard Choices in Law Enforcement*
Lozoff, B., and Braswell, M. (1989). *Inner Corrections: Finding Peace and Peace Making*
Pollock-Byrne, J. (1989). *Ethics in Crime and Justice: Dilemmas and Decisions*
Schmalleger, F. (1990). *Ethics in Criminal Justice*

Souryal, S. (1992). *Ethics in Criminal Justice: In Search of the Truth*
Travis, L., Schwartz, M., and Clear, T. (1983). *Corrections: An Issues Approach*
Whitehead, J. (1989). *Burnout in Probation and Corrections*

SOURCE: Souryal, S., and Potts, D. "What Am I Supposed to Fall Back On? Cultural Literacy in Criminal Justice Ethics." *Journal of Criminal Justice Education* 4 (1996): 15–41. Reprinted with permission of S. Souryal and the Academy of Criminal Justice Sciences.

theories of moral development, and the fields of sociology and criminology propose theories of deviance and criminality. Interestingly, only recently have there been attempts to merge the two.

Two current attempts to explain criminality seem to indicate that theorists are moving back to developmental rather than social force theories of delinquency and crime. Tonry, Ohlin, and Farrington (1991) report on a long-term study of delinquency in which a cohort sample will be followed from birth to age twenty-five. Variables associated with delinquency are being studied. They include sex (males are more likely to be delinquent), low verbal intelligence, hyperactivity, unpopularity among peers, family history of crime and delinquency, discordant families (marital instability and harsh and erratic disciplinary practices), economic adversity, and living in a socially disorganized community.

The authors cite three major theoretical perspectives that address the origins of delinquency—temperament, attachment, and social learning. After exploring the relative merits of these approaches, the authors postulate that temperament and attachment are interrelated in that the personality of the child may affect parental interaction, which, in turn, affects attachment. Alternatively, parents themselves may be poor or inconsistent caregivers, in which case attachment will be weak. Not rejecting any of the three perspectives, the researchers state that while parental child-rearing methods (attachment) may affect age of onset of delinquency, peer influence (social learning) may affect continuation or intensity of delinquency. These and many other hypotheses are being tested, but the general findings of the study thus far are that attachment and parental discipline are extremely important factors in delinquency.

Parental practices, such as the use of affection and inductive discipline rather than power assertion or the withdrawal of affection, have also been identified as important in moral development in adolescents (Leahy, 1981). Whether the association of parental practices and moral development (as measured by paper-and-pencil tests) operates in the same way that parental practices influence delinquent behavior is a separate question.

These approaches reject the subcultural deviance theory that delinquent or criminal behavior is learned in a subcultural group along with a different moral code that justifies such behavior. Rather, they view deviance as the absence of learning, or incomplete socialization. When the individual does not develop self-control or internal standards of behavior, he or she will not make correct decisions when faced with opportunities to indulge in immediate gratification. Thus, criminals do not have different moral codes; rather, they know what is right, but simply are unwilling to conform their behavior to it because they were not taught to do so at a very early stage of development. These theories are consistent with learning theory, although biological research sheds light on the interplay between family socialization and biological predispositions.

One should note that such theories ignore the importance and influence of socioeconomic factors on crime causation. It may be that such factors determine not the existence of antisocial (immoral) behaviors, but rather, the form that such behaviors will take. Individuals who are born into poor families and experience the parenting styles that are associated with antisocial development may end up committing street crime, while children who are born into middle-class and upper-middle-class families and experience similar parenting styles will ultimately engage in "suite crime" (white-collar crime) because of the different opportunity structures between the two groups of children.

If the current science of criminology has avoided questions of morality, there was no such hesitation in early corrections. Historically, criminality and sin were associated, and correctional practitioners were primarily concerned with reformation in a religious sense. Hence, early prisons were built to help the individual achieve redemption. There was a heavy dose of moral instruction in corrections; those who were said to lead dissolute and immoral lives were also targeted for reform. Society approved of official attempts to intervene in individuals' lives to help them become moral and productive citizens. For instance, the juvenile court system was given the mission to reform and educate youth (primarily those from immigrant groups) in a manner consistent with societal beliefs (Platt, 1977).

The orientation of corrections in the latter part of this century (1950s–1970s) became more scientific than religious, and intervention adopted the aim of psychological readjustment rather than personal redemption. After the end of the rehabilitative ideal (1960–1970s), however, the rationale for corrections and punishment seemed to return to a moral orientation. Interestingly, "faith-based" correctional programs are experiencing a resurgence, with the support of the White House. Religious instruction and correctional programs that utilize a religious orientation have emerged as options for correctional administrators seeking programs. Critics argue that public finances should not be used for such programs because the First Amendment prohibits state endorsement of any religion, but President George Bush evidently disagrees and heartily supports such programs.

Advocates of deterrence versus advocates for treatment set up arguments using distinctly moral terms and asking such questions as, "Does society have the right to treat/punish?" and, "What are the limits of punishment/treatment?" The "just deserts" position, covered in Chapter 11, is probably the clearest example of a moral perspective in criminal justice literature.

In the last twenty years or so, there have been various attempts to introduce offenders to "moral education." Hickey and Scharf (1980), who studied under Kohlberg, undertook an early attempt to apply moral development theory to corrections in their creation of a therapeutic community in a Connecticut prison. Eventually they had "just communities" for both men and women that were run according to principles of fairness, justice, and rights. Prisoners were exposed to moral analysis in discussions and group meetings. Increases in stage scores were measured as averaging one-and-one-half stages after prisoners had lived in the just community.

It appears that simply offering moral discussion groups may also result in an increase in stage scores. Gibbs and his colleagues (1984) report on another intervention involving sixty incarcerated juvenile delinquents. Sociomoral reasoning improved significantly after eight weeks of discussion groups using moral dilemmas. Whereas 87.5 percent of the treatment group moved from Stage 2 to Stage 3, only 14.3 percent of the control group moved to Stage 3.

Wiley (1988) reported on a more modest application of moral development education in the Texas Department of Corrections. She reports that teacher style influenced gains in moral development scores. Specifically, inmate–students in prison classrooms where the teacher employed an interactive style (challenging and allowing active participation) showed significant gains in post-tests of moral development, unlike those inmate–students in classrooms where the teaching style was authoritarian and teacher-centered. Interestingly, the course content was less important. These were not moral development classes, but standard social science classes.

Arbuthnot and Gordon (1988) review findings from several studies that show that interventions with delinquents and adult offenders using sociomoral reasoning result in stage score improvement and also behavioral change. In one program for delinquents, for instance, subjects were monitored for one year, and significant differences in post-experimental problem behaviors existed between the experimental group and the control group. These authors also discuss some reasons why sociomoral reasoning development programs are not prevalent in corrections; specifically, they point to the need for organizational support, consistent organizational goals, the continuing need for expert consultation, an onsite champion of the program, and the careful selection and training of staff, among other factors.

Arbuthnot (1984) also discusses the interplay of environment and sociomoral reasoning programs. He points out that some prisoners find no rewards for expressing higher-stage reasoning, much less acting upon such reasoning. Therefore, any gains made in reasoning through an intervention such as a moral analysis discussion group would be unlikely to result in changes in behavior unless the environment was more supportive of higher stages. It seems fairly clear that for such programs to work in prison, an isolated living situation must be created to insulate participants from the negative environment of the prison. Also, if the intervention is in the community, attention must be given to the social environment of the participants. If there are no social supports for stage improvements, the gains may not be expressed in behavioral choices. Arbuthnot's discussion, then, combines Kohlberg's stage theory with a type of reinforcement theory.

More recently, moral reasoning programs have been used with sex offenders (Buttell, 2002). It was found that sex offenders tested at significantly lower moral stage development than a control sample. Pearson (2002), in a recent review of cognitive programs, including moral reasoning programs, concluded that such programs did decrease recidivism when compared to control groups.

CONCLUSION

Philosophers, religious scholars, biologists, psychologists, sociologists, and criminologists have all tried to explain why people do bad things. The three approaches we explored in this chapter were biological theory, learning theory, and developmental theory. Those who study biological predispositions do not propose biological determinism, only that certain traits or biological characteristics may influence one's behavior. Learning theory argues that people learn morals through rewards. It is relativistic in that it postulates human learning as neutral. There is no one true moral theory to discover; rather, the individual will adopt whatever moral theory has been rewarded. Kohlberg's theory proposes a hierarchy of moral stages, with the highest stage holding the most perfect moral principles. However, not everyone has the cognitive capacity or the proper exposure to discover these principles. According to Kohlberg, in the higher stages of moral development, ethical relativism must give way to universalism, and all those who reach the highest stages have discovered the true moral principles that are absolute and exist apart from humanity.

If one believes that morals are simply what humans chose to define as such, then one might be more inclined to a learning theory perspective. If one believes that morals exist naturally and humans only discover their existence through reasoning ability, one might be more inclined to accept the developmental stage theory of moral development. However, the approaches to moral development presented in this chapter are not necessarily mutually exclusive. One can believe in biological influences along with learning theory or developmental theory. One might agree with stage theory with the understanding that at lower stages, rewards are necessary to elicit moral behaviors (e.g., rewarding young children for sharing). One might support learning theory but also accept the notion that when we are intellectually mature, our reasoning abilities mediate simple rewards. Thus, while small children might be fooled into thinking that practicing the piano is bad because someone was punished for it in a story, no older child or adult would be taken in by such a trick; and, individuals in a totalitarian society may continue to believe in democratic ideals (through reasoning) regardless of punishments they may receive for such beliefs.

REVIEW QUESTIONS

1. Provide your own answer to the question, "Why do people do bad things?"
2. Briefly explain how biological approaches might explain antisocial behavior.
3. Discuss learning theory as it applies to moral development. What problems do critics see with this theory?
4. Explain Kohlberg's moral development theory. What problems do critics see with his theory?
5. How does one measure moral beliefs? What are the problems with such measurements?
6. What are the elements necessary for teaching ethics?
7. Describe some applications of moral training in corrections.

ETHICAL DILEMMAS

Situation 1

You are a rookie police officer and are riding with a Field Training Officer (FTO). During your shift the FTO stops at a convenience store and quickly drinks four beers in the back room of the store. He is visibly affected by the beers and the smell of alcohol is very noticeable. What should you do?

Situation 2

You are a criminal justice student interning at a police department. One of the tasks you learn at the department is how to look up individuals' criminal histories on the computer. You are telling your friends about your experiences, and they want you to look up their names to see what, if anything, is listed for them. You are pretty much left alone to do your work at the police department and it would be an easy matter to look up anyone. What would you tell your friends?

Situation 3

You are a senior getting close to graduation and have taken too many classes your last semester. You find yourself getting behind in classes and not doing well on tests. One of the classes requires a thirty-page term paper and you simply do not have the time to complete the paper by the due date. While you are on the Internet one day you see that term papers can be purchased on any topic. You ordinarily would do your own work, but the time pressure of this last semester is such that you see no other way. Do you purchase the paper and turn it in as your own?

SUGGESTED READINGS

Arbuthnot, J. 1984. "Moral Reasoning Development Programmes in Prison: Cognitive—Developmental and Critical Reasoning Approaches." *Journal of Moral Education* 13(2): 112–123.

Gavaghan, M., Arnold, K., and Gibbs, J. 1983. "Moral Judgment in Delinquents and Nondelinquents: Recognition Versus Production Measures." *The Journal of Psychology* 114: 267–274.

Gilligan, C. 1982. *In a Different Voice: Psychological Theory and Women's Development.* Cambridge, MA: Harvard University Press.

Hickey, J., and Scharf, P. 1980. *Toward a Just Correctional System.* San Francisco: Jossey-Bass.

Kohlberg, L., and Power, C. 1984. "Moral Development, Religious Thinking and the Question of a 7th Stage." pp. 311–372 in Kohlberg, L. (ed.), *The Psychology of Moral Development.* New York: Harper & Row.

4

Justice and the Law

Origins of the Concept of Justice

Components of Justice
Distributive Justice
Corrective Justice

Paradigms of Law
The Consensus Paradigm
The Conflict Paradigm

Conclusion

Review Questions

Ethical Dilemmas

Suggested Readings

Key Terms

justice
distributive justice
corrective justice
commutative justice
fairness
equality
impartiality
natural right
substantive justice
procedural justice
retributive justice

due process
exclusionary rule
consensus paradigm
conflict paradigm
mechanical solidarity
repressive law
organic solidarity
restitutive law
pluralist paradigm
social contract

Chapter Objectives

- Understand the origins and components of the concept of justice.
- Understand the paradigms of law.

What is justice? How is justice related to law? Professionals in the criminal justice system serve and promote the interests of law and justice, and this chapter explores these concepts. An underlying theme will be that the ends of law and justice are different—perhaps even, at times, contradictory. Although law is often defined as *the administration of justice,* it may very well be the case that law forces consequences that many might conclude are "unjust." Legal rights might be different than moral rights, rights might be different than needs, and needs may not be protected under either the law or justice.

Definitions of justice include the concepts of fairness, equality, impartiality, and appropriate rewards or punishments. According to Lucas (1980: 3), justice "differs from benevolence, generosity, gratitude, friendship, and compassion." It is not something for which we should feel grateful, but rather, something upon which we have a right to insist. Justice should not be confused with "good." Some actions may be considered good, but not necessarily just—for instance, the recipients of charity, benevolence, and forgiveness do not have a right to these things; therefore, it is not an injustice to withhold them. Justice concerns rights and interests more often than needs. Although the idea of need is important in some discussions of justice, it is not the only component or even the primary one. It is important to understand that what is just and what is good are not necessarily the same. See the "Definitions of Justice" box.

People can often be described as displaying unique combinations of generosity and selfishness; fairness and self-interest. Some writers insist that the need for justice arises from the nature of human beings and the fact that they are not naturally generous, open-hearted, or fair. On one hand, if we behaved all the time in accordance with those virtues, we would have no need for justice. On the other hand, if humans were always to act in selfish, grasping, and unfair ways, then we would be unable to follow the rules and principles of jus-

---

Definitions of Justice

- "The maintenance or administration of what is just, especially by the impartial adjustment of conflicting claims or the assignment of merited rewards or punishments"
- "The administration of law; especially the establishment or determination of rights according to the rules of law or equity"
- "The quality of being just, impartial or fair"
- "The principle or ideal of just dealing or right action"

SOURCE: *Webster's Ninth New Collegiate Dictionary* (Springfield, MA: Merriam-Webster, 1984).

tice. Therefore, we uphold and cherish the concept of justice in our society because it is the mediator between people's essential selfishness and generosity; in other words, it is the result of a logical and rational acceptance of the concept of fairness in human relations. David Hume, a philosopher, said that "Justice does not dictate a perfect world, but one in which people live up to agreements and are treated fairly" (cited in Feinberg and Gross, 1977: 75). Galston (1980: 282) described justice as follows:

> more than voluntary agreement, [but] . . . less than perfect community. It allows us to retain our separate existences and our self-regard; it does not ask us to share the pleasures, pains, and sentiments of others. Justice is intelligent self-regard, modified, by the requirements of rational consistency.

ORIGINS OF THE CONCEPT OF JUSTICE

Justice originates in the Greek word *dike,* which is associated with the concept of everything staying in its assigned place or natural role (Feinberg and Gross, 1977: i). This idea is closely associated with the definitions of justice given by Plato and Aristotle. Even today, some writers describe justice as "the demand for order: everything in its proper place or relation" (Feibleman, 1985: 23).

According to Plato, justice consists of maintaining the societal status quo. Justice is one of four civic virtues, the others being wisdom, temperance, and courage (Feibleman, 1985: 173). In an ordered state, everyone performs his or her role and does not interfere with others. Each person's role is the one for which the individual is best fitted by nature; thus, *natural law* is upheld. Moreover, it is in everyone's self-interest to have this ordered existence continue because it provides the means to the good life—appropriate human happiness. Plato's society is a *class system,* based on innate abilities, rather than a *caste system,* which differentiates people purely by accidents of birth.

Aristotle believed that justice exists in the law and that the law is "the unwritten custom of all or the majority of men which draws a distinction between what is honorable and what is base" (Feibleman, 1985: 174). Aristotle distinguished *distributive justice* from *rectificatory justice. Rectificatory justice,* or *commutative justice,* concerns business deals where unfair advantage or undeserved harm has occurred. Justice demands remedies or compensations to the injured party.

Distributive justice concerns what measurement should be used to allocate society's resources. Aristotle believed in the idea of proportionality along with equality. In Aristotle's conception of justice, the lack of freedom and opportunity for some people—slaves and women, for instance—did not conflict with justice, as long as the individual was in the role in which, by nature, he or she belonged. In other words, unequal people should get unequal shares.

COMPONENTS OF JUSTICE

Justice can be separated into distributive, corrective, and commutative justice (Feinberg and Gross, 1977: 53). **Distributive justice** is concerned with the allocation of the goods and burdens of society to its respective members. Rewards and benefits from society include wealth, education, entitlement programs, and health care. Because some people get less than others, it may be that these goods are not distributed fairly. Burdens and responsibilities must also be distributed among the members of society; for instance, decisions must be made about who should fight in war, who should take care of the elderly and infirm, who should pay taxes, and how much each should pay. The difficulties in deciding how to divide these goods and burdens and what each person deserves are the subject in any discussion of distributive justice.

Corrective justice concerns the determination and methods of punishments. Again, the concept of *desert* emerges. In corrective justice, we speak of offenders getting what they deserve, but this time the desert is punishment rather than goods. The difficulty, of course, is in determining what is a *just desert* for a specific crime.

Finally, **commutative justice** is associated with transactions and interchanges where one person feels unfairly treated. The process of determining a fair resolution—for example, when one is cheated in a business deal, or when a contract is not completed—calls into play the concepts of commutative justice. The method for determining a fair and just resolution to the conflict depends on particular concepts such as rights and interests.

A continuing theme in any discussion of justice—whether distributive, corrective, or commutative justice—is the concept of **fairness.** Parents ordinarily give each child the same allowance unless differences between the children, such as age or duties, warrant different amounts. In fact, children are sensitive to issues of fairness long before they grasp more abstract ideas of justice. No doubt every parent has heard the plaintive cry "It's not fair—Johnny got more than I did" or "It's not fair—she always gets to sit in the front seat!" What children are sensing is unequal and, therefore, unfair treatment. The concept of fairness is inextricably tied to equality and impartiality.

Another theme of justice is the concept of **equality.** There is a predisposition to demand equity or equal shares for all. (In contrast to the concept of equal shares is the idea of needs or deserts; in other words, we should get what we need or, alternatively, what we deserve by status, merit, or other reasons.) The concept of equality is also present in retributive justice in the belief that similar cases should be treated equally—for instance, all individuals who commit a similar crime should be similarly punished. (Again, the alternative argument is that sometimes it serves the purpose of justice to treat similar crimes differently because of mediating or aggravating circumstances.)

Are there ever any situations where people are truly equal? If we want to distribute opportunities equally to equals, how would we measure equality? Do we assume that everyone starts off with the same skills, backgrounds, and family circumstances, or must we not take into account individual differences, societal goals, and a host of other factors in decisions such as whether to employ affirmative action plans, individualized sentences, and receipt of social services?

The concept of **impartiality** is at the core of our system of criminal justice. Our symbol of justice represents, with her blindfold, impartiality toward special groups and, with her scales, proportionally just punishments. Impartiality implies fair and equal treatment of all without discrimination and bias. It is hard to reconcile the ideal of "blind justice" with the individualized justice of the "treatment ethic" because one can hardly look at individual circumstance if one is blind toward the particulars of the case. Indeed, most would argue, individual differences and culpabilities should be taken into consideration—if not during a finding of guilt or innocence, then at least when sentencing occurs. The blindfold may signify no special treatment for the rich or the powerful, but then it must also signify no special consideration for the young, the misled, or those operating under extraordinary circumstances. These issues will be addressed again in the next chapter.

QUERY

Do you believe that who you are makes a difference in today's system of justice? Give examples.

Distributive Justice

The concept of the appropriate and just allocation of society's goods and interests is one of the central themes in all discussions of justice. According to one writer, justice always involves *rightful possession* (Galston, 1980: 117–119). The goods that one might possess include economic goods (income or property), opportunities for development (education or citizenship), and recognition (honor or status). It is only in a condition of scarcity that a problem arises with the allocation of goods. Two valid claims to possession are *need* and *desert*. The principles of justice involve the application of these claims to specific entitlements.

Different writers have presented various proposals for deciding issues of entitlement. Lucas (1980: 164–165) lists several different distribution theories. They involve distributions based on need, merit, performance, ability, rank, station, worth, work, agreements, requirements of the common good, valuation of services, and legal entitlement. Despite differences, all schemes include some concept of need and merit (also see Raphael, 1980: 90). The box "After the Cash Rains Down in Miami, Finders Remain Quiet Keepers," illustrates how some people's concept of what one deserves is sometimes related to need rather than merit.

The difficulty lies in determining the weight of each of the factors in a just allocation of benefits. The various theories can be categorized as egalitarian, Marxist, libertarian, or utilitarian, depending on the factors that are emphasized (Beauchamp, 1982). Egalitarian theories start with the basic premise of equality or equal shares for all. Marxist theories place need above desert or entitlement. Libertarian theories promote freedom from interference by government

---

After Cash Rains Down in Miami, Finders Remain Quiet Keepers

MIAMI—Police went from door to door through one of Miami's poorest neighborhoods Thursday, asking people to admit they scooped up some of the half million dollars that spilled from a Brinks truck and, if they did, to give it back.

Residents generally responded with a good laugh.

"Nobody's going to tell them," said Debbie, a resident of Overtown who, like most, would only give her first name.

"This is a once-in-a-lifetime thing," added another resident named George. "This couldn't happen to a more *deserving* neighborhood."

Thousands of dollars in coins, bills and food stamps rained down on the street Wednesday morning after an armored Brinks truck carrying $3.7 million overturned on an Interstate 95 overpass.

People swarmed over the area, digging money out of the dirt and scooping it off the street, stuffing bags, boxes and pockets before police took charge. An estimated $500,000 vanished.

Thursday, police knocked on seventy-five doors urging people to turn in the money, no questions asked, before a two-day grace period ends at noon Saturday. Nobody did.

After the grace period expires, police plan to seek television news videotape to aid them in identifying money grabbers. Those caught with more than $1,000 could face grand theft charges.

Which, if any, system supports the individual's justification that he or she "deserved" the stolen money?

SOURCE: Associated Press. Reported in *Austin American-Statesman,* 10 Jan. 1997: A7. Emphasis added. Reprinted with permission of the Associated Press.

---

in social and economic spheres; therefore, merit, entitlement, and productive contributions are given weight over need or equal shares. Utilitarian theories attempt to maximize benefits for individuals and society in a mixed emphasis on entitlements and needs.

QUERY

Determine the fair salary for these professions and occupations. Propose an average salary, balancing such factors as seniority and education.

Nurse: Electrician:
Elementary schoolteacher: Sanitation worker:
Police officer: Prison guard:
College professor: Software engineer:
City council member: Lawyer:
Secretary: Judge:

Now compare your responses to those of others. Is there general consensus on salaries for these positions? Compare your responses to published figures (you can find this information in a library or the career center of your university).

How do the theories apply to the wide disparities in salaries found in this country? For instance, a professional athlete's salary is sometimes one hundred times greater than a police officer's salary. A few CEOs make $10 million a year—or at least they did in the 1990s when the stock market seemed as if it would go up forever. Perhaps shareholders will no longer approve such outrageous salaries today. Which distribution principle justifies such extreme discrepancies? Libertarian theories would shrug at such disparity; Marxist theories would not. Obviously, few would agree that workers in all jobs and all professions should be paid the same amount of money. First, not many people would be willing to put up with the long hours and many years of schooling needed in some professions if there were no incentives. Second, some types of jobs demand a greater degree of responsibility and involve greater stress than others. However, we can readily see that some remuneration is entirely out of proportion to an analysis of worth. For instance, it is hard to see how any corporate executive could deserve $10 million for one year's work. The same argument applies to athletes, rock musicians, and actors.

If we are primarily concerned with performance and ability, why do we not pay individual workers in the same job category differently if one works harder than the other? Although some production jobs pay according to how much is produced (the piecework payment method), most of us are paid according to a step-grade position, earning roughly what others in the same position earn. Which is the fairer system of payment? What about people who produce less on the piecework system because they are helping their coworkers or taking more time to produce higher quality products? Is it fair for them to earn less? If all work were paid according to production, how would one pay secretaries, teachers, or customer service workers, whose production is more difficult to measure? How would one pay police officers—by the number of arrests?

QUERY

You are on a promotion committee to recommend to the chief of police a candidate for a captain's position. All are lieutenants and have received similar scores in the objective tests available for the position. The candidates:

1. A thirty-nine-year-old woman who has been with the police department for nine years. She has obtained a college degree and a master's degree by going to school at night. She has spent relatively little time in her career on the street (moving quickly to juvenile, community service, and DARE positions).
2. A forty-six-year-old white male who has also had experience in command positions in the army before joining the police force. He has fifteen years of experience—all in patrol positions—and has a college degree.
3. A forty-year-old Hispanic male with ten years of experience. He has been very active with the community; several community groups have endorsed him, and they demand that there be Hispanic representation on the command staff. He also has strong support among Hispanic officers, serving as their association president. He has a two-year college degree.

Who would you endorse? Why? If you need more information, what type of information would you want?

Marxist distribution systems propose that we pay people according to need. This sounds fair in one sense because people would get only what they needed to survive at some predetermined level. In that case, a person with two children would earn more than a person with no children. In the past, this was the argument used by employers to explain why they would favor men over women in hiring, promotions, and pay increases—because men had families to support and women did not. Two arguments were used against this type of discriminatory treatment; the first was that women deserve as much as men if they are of equal ability and performance; the second was that women also, more often than not, have to support families. These two arguments emphasize different principles of justice. The first is based on an equal-deserts argument; the second rests on an equal-needs argument.

Although race- and gender-based discrepancies in wages and hiring patterns are becoming a thing of the past, there are still continuing issues of fairness in employment rights. One such issue is family or pregnancy leave. The principle of justice that is being used to support the right to take leave (whether it be the unpaid leave mandated by Congress or paid leave) is not worth, merit, ability, or performance; rather, it is need. Does justice dictate an employee's right to family leave? This is not equal treatment (since we're discriminating against people who do not fit any category of the family leave bill, but desire leave for other reasons). In fact, this may be a question of *goodness* rather than *justice*. That is, it is a social good (good for society, good for the individual), but it is not a right. On the other hand, some people insist that there is a **natural right** to productive employment and also the ability to have a family; therefore, there is a state duty to provide adequate, affordable child care for workers and leave for pregnancy and sickness.

Just distribution of other goods in society is also problematic. Welfare is one example of this difficulty. The principle of need is the rationale we use to take from the financially solvent, through taxes, and give to those who have little or nothing. There is always some resentment over this redistribution because of the belief that some people choose not to work and take advantage of welfare. If there are such people, justice may dictate that they be dropped from welfare rolls.

Another "good" that society distributes to its members is opportunity. Many people would argue that education (at least at the university level) is a privilege that should be reserved for those few who have the ability and the drive to succeed. However, the educational system of this country is fundamentally democratic. Not only do we have guaranteed, in fact compulsory, education at elementary and secondary levels; we also have open admission to some universities. Moreover, remedial courses are available to help those without the skills to meet college standards. In fact, massive amounts of time and money are devoted to helping some students improve their skills and ultimately graduate from college.

There is also a compelling argument that although the *ideal* of education is democratic, the *reality* is that because of unequal tax bases, school districts are incredibly unequal and distribute the opportunity of education unequally. Although some school districts have swimming pools, computers in every classroom, and teachers with specialized education, other school districts make do with donated textbooks and buildings that are poorly heated and ventilated. State legislation in Texas attempted to equalize school districts' funding by "taking away" from well-off school districts and giving the money to poor districts. This so-called "Robin Hood" law raises the ire of parents who move to districts with high taxes for the express purpose of providing an excellent education for their children. The current Republican majority in the Texas legislature is planning a challenge to the law in 2003, and it is possible that a new scheme of school funding will emerge.

Affirmative action attempts to provide opportunities to groups that historically have been discriminated against—blacks, women, Hispanics. Now those groups that have been favored in the past—white males—feel that they are the new victims of discrimination. Some feel that taking affirmative steps to increase opportunities for minority groups has simply transferred unfair treatment to another group. What is acceptable to overcome previous discrimination?

Unfortunately, a promise to hire "the best person for the job" is not enough, because historical and institutionalized discrimination may take many years to overcome. For instance, some claim that under-funded schools produce students who are less qualified, and then these individuals are denied jobs based on their lack of abilities. To assume that one is eliminating discrimination by hiring on the basis of individual abilities does not solve the problem of blocked access; it merely perpetuates it in a more subtle way. The Supreme Court has ruled against affirmative action attempts, such as race-based criteria in law school and university admissions. States are also passing legislation to bar hiring decisions, promotions, and admission to state schools based on race. The same "equal protection" argument used to pass civil rights legislation in the 1960s is now being used to dismantle these programs. What effect such decisions will have on access to the opportunity of education remains to be seen. Some predict that the progress we have seen in educational and economic success for historically blocked minority groups will be negated.

This controversy only points out the extreme difficulty of determining a just distribution of goods. The fact that everyone is not equal, in terms of ability, performance, motivation, need, or any other measure, is easy enough to agree on. Very few people would argue that everyone in every position should receive the same salary, get the same education, and achieve the same status in society. On the other hand, to acknowledge inequality puts us in the position of distributing goods and other interests on the basis of other criteria, and it is here that problems arise. When injustice occurs, we sense it on the basis of fairness. We feel somehow that it is not fair that there are starving children and conspicuous wealth in the same country or the same world. We sense unfairness when people work hard yet still struggle to get along on poverty wages, while star actors or athletes make millions of dollars largely through luck or for contributions to societal welfare that seem trivial.

John Rawls's theory of justice is perhaps the best known current conception of justice. He elegantly combines utilitarian and rights-based concepts in his conception of a system of justice. Basically, he proposes an equal distribution unless a different distribution would benefit the disadvantaged. Rawls believes that any inequalities of society should be to the benefit of those who are least advantaged (Rawls, 1971: 15). He proposes the following (cited in Kaplan, 1976: 114):

1. Each person is to have an equal right to the most extensive total system of basic liberties compatible with a similar system of liberty for all.

2. Social and economic inequalities are to be arranged so that they are both reasonably expected to be to everyone's advantage; and attached to positions and offices open to all (except when inequality is to the advantage of those least well-off).

Rawls uses a heuristic device that he calls the *veil of ignorance* to explain the idea that people will develop fair principles of distribution only if they are ignorant of their position in society, since they may just as easily be "have-nots" as "haves" (Rawls, 1971: 12). Thus, justice and fairness are in everyone's rational self-interest since, under the veil of ignorance, one's own situation is unknown, and the best and most rational distribution is the one most equal to all.

Critics argue that the veil of ignorance is not sufficient to counteract humanity's basic selfishness: given the chance, people would still seek to maximize their own gain, even if doing so involved a risk (Kaplan, 1976: 199). Critics also argue that Rawls's preference toward those least well-off is contrary to the good of society. Rawls states that "all social values—liberty and opportunity, income and wealth and the bases of self-respect—are to be distributed equally unless an unequal distribution of any, or all, of these values is to the advantage of the least favored" (quoted in Sterba, 1980: 32). (See "Sterba's Distribution System.") Critics believe that this preference is ultimately dysfunctional for society, since if those least well-off have the advantages of society preferentially, there will be no incentive for others to excel. Some also argue that Rawls is wrong to ignore desert in his distribution of goods (Galston, 1980: 3).

Sterba's Distribution System

1. **Principle of Need.** Each person is guaranteed the primary social goods that are necessary to meet the normal costs of satisfying his or her basic needs in the society in which he or she lives.
2. **Principle of Appropriation and Exchange.** Additional primary goods are to be distributed on the basis of private appropriation and voluntary agreement and exchange.
3. **Principle of Minimal Contribution.** A minimal contribution to society is required of those who are capable of contributing when social and economic resources are insufficient to provide the guaranteed minimum to everyone in society without requiring that contribution or when the incentive to contribute to society would otherwise be adversely affected, so that persons would not maximize their contribution to society.
4. **Principle of Saving.** The rate of saving for each generation should represent its fair contribution toward realizing and maintaining a society in which all the members can fully enjoy the benefit of its just institution.

SOURCE: Adapted from Sterba (1980: 55).

Let us now turn to how these theories of distributive justice relate to the ethical systems discussed in Chapter 2. The ethics of care is consistent with a Marxist theory of justice, since both emphasize need. Utilitarian theories try to maximize societal good, so some balance of need and merit would be necessary to provide the incentive to produce. Ethical formalism is solely concerned with rights; thus, issues of societal good or others' needs may not be as important as the individual's rights (however those might be defined). Rawls's theory is both utilitarian and Kantian since it demands a basic level of individual rights but also attempts to establish a preference toward those who have less, for the good of all society. How one resolves these questions concerning distributive justice relates to the discussion of corrective or punitive justice, which will be discussed in the next section.

Corrective Justice

As mentioned before, corrective justice is concerned with dispensing punishment. As with distributive justice, the concepts of equality and desert, fairness and impartiality are important. Two components of corrective justice should be differentiated. **Substantive justice** involves the concept of just deserts, or how one determines a fair punishment for a particular offense; **procedural justice** concerns the steps we must take before administering punishment.

Substantive Justice What is a fair punishment for the crime of murder? Many believe the only just punishment is death, since that is the only punishment of a degree equal to the harm caused by the offender. Others might say life imprisonment is equitable and fair. One's beliefs about what is fair punishment are usually related to one's perception of the seriousness of the crime. More serious crimes deserve moreserious punishments.

Since the beginning of codified law, just punishment has been perceived as punishment set in relation to the degree of harm incurred. This was a natural outcome of the early, remedial forms of justice, which provided remedies for wrongs. For instance, the response to a theft of a slave or the killing of a horse involved compensation. The only just solution was the return or replacement of the slave or horse. This remedial or compensatory system of justice contrasts with a punishment system: the first system forces the offender to provide compensation to the victim or the victim's family, and the second apportions punishment based on the degree of seriousness of the crime suffered by the victim. They both involve a measurement of the harm, but in the first case, measurement is taken to adequately compensate the victim, and in the second it is to punish the offender. In a punishment-based system, the victim is a peripheral figure. The state, rather than the victim, becomes the central figure—serving both as victim and as punisher (Karmen, 1984). Two *philosophies* of corrective justice can be identified: retributive justice and utilitarian justice. In the box "Exercise," also decide what punishments should be given to each offender. Then share you answers with others. Do you agree or disagree?

Exercise

Rank the following crimes in order of seriousness, with 1 being the most serious and 14 being the least serious. Compare your rank orderings with those of others.

sexual assault (with force)
embezzlement of $15,000
shoplifting ($15,000)
robbery of $15,000
toxic waste dumping
  (unknown damage)
perjury
solicitation of murder

death caused by drunken driving
tax evasion—$15,000
assault (broken bones)
sexual molestation (no penetration)
murder (during barroom brawl)
drug possession (marijuana)
murder in heat of passion

Retributive Justice The concept of **retributive justice** is one of balance. The criminal must suffer pain or loss proportional to what the victim was forced to suffer. In an extreme form, this retribution takes the form of *lex talionis,* a vengeance-oriented justice concerned with equal retaliation ("an eye for an eye; tooth for a tooth"). A milder form is *lex salica,* which allows compensation; the harm can be repaired by payment or atonement (Allen and Simonsen, 1986: 4). A life for a life might be easy to measure, but most cases involve other forms of harm. In other types of victimizations, how does one determine the amount of physical or mental pain suffered by the victim, or financial loss such as lost income or future loss? And if the offender cannot pay back financial losses, how does one equate imprisonment with fines or restitution?

Historically, corporal and capital punishment were used for both property crime and violent crime. With the development of the penitentiary system in the early 1800s, punishment became equated with terms of imprisonment rather than amounts of physical pain. In fact, the greater ease of measuring out prison sentences probably contributed to these sentences' success and rapid acceptance. One might sentence an offender to one, two, or five years, depending on the seriousness of the crime. Not only was imprisonment considered more humane than corporal punishment; it was also incapacitating, allowing the offender to reflect on his crime and repent. Further, it did not elicit sympathy for the offender from the populace.

However, a term of imprisonment is much harder to equate to a particular crime. While one can intuitively understand the natural balance of a life for a life, $10 for $10, or even a beating for an assault, it is much harder to argue that a burglary of $100 is equal to a year in prison or that an assault is equal to a term of two years. A year in prison is hard to define. Research on prison adjustment indicates that a year means different things to different people. For some, it might be no more than mildly inconvenient; for others, it might lead to suicide or mental illness (Toch, 1977).

QUERY

- If you were being punished for a crime, would you rather receive a year in prison or fifty lashes?
- Why do we not use corporal punishment for criminal offenders? Do you think we should?

In addition to retribution, imprisonment was tied to reform of the criminal offender. Reform or rehabilitation may be a laudable goal, but it has no place in a retributive scheme of justice. Retributive punishment is based on balancing the victim's harm with the offender's pain or suffering. Treatment involves no such balance; therefore, there is no retributive rationale for its existence. Philosophical support for treatment of criminal offenders is found in utilitarianism. Retributive justice is not a simple equation, since other factors are taken into account in addition to the seriousness of the crime. For instance, *mens rea* (intent) has long been considered a necessary element in determining culpability. Those who are incapable of rational thought—the insane, the very young—are said to be incapable of committing wrong morally or legally; therefore, to punish them would be an injustice under a retributive framework. Other situations might prove to involve partial responsibility—for example, the presence of compulsion, coercion, or irresistible impulse. In these cases, most people feel that justice is not compromised by a lesser amount of punishment, even though the harm to the victim is obviously the same as if the offender had acted deliberately and intentionally. In this sense, we see that the amount of punishment is not solely measured by the amount of harm to the victim but involves characteristics of the offender as well.

Just punishment may also involve considering the participation of the victim. Victim precipitation may lessen the culpability of the offender. Other factors also play a part in determining punishment, some of which would not be consistent with retributive justice. In earlier systems of justice, the status of the victim was important in determining the level of harm and, thus, the punishment. Nobles were more important than freemen, who were more important than slaves. Men were more important than women. Punishment for offenders was weighted according to these designations of the worth of the victim. Although we have no formal system for weighting punishment in this way and have rejected the worth of the victim as a rationale for punishment (except in a few cases, such as assaulting a police officer), many feel that our justice system still follows this practice informally. People argue that harsher sentences are given when the victim is white than when the victim is black and when the victim is rich as opposed to poor. In a similar manner, many argue that the justice system discriminates unfairly and unjustly against characteristics of the offender. Many believe that offenders receive harsher sentences because of their race, background, or income.

Whether or not these charges are true, it is important to recognize that earlier systems of justice, including the Greek and Roman, approved of and rationalized such discriminations as perfectly fair and just. Our system of justice has rejected these discriminations even while holding on to others—specifically, intent, partial responsibility, and, to some extent, victim precipitation. It is difficult, if not impossible, for everyone to agree upon a fair and equitable measurement of punishment when one allows for exceptions, mediating factors, and partial responsibility. That is why there is so little agreement on what is fair punishment. Even when two defendants are involved in a single crime, our system of justice can support different punishments under a retributive rationale.

In Rawls's theory of justice, retributive punishment is limited in the following way (quoted in Hickey and Scharf, 1980: 168):

> . . . the liberties of a person . . . may only be reduced, compared with the liberties of other people, when it is for the good of the least advantaged, considered from the "veil of ignorance" assumption of not knowing what role one will occupy.

This statement means that only when punishment can be shown to benefit the least advantaged (the victim) can it be justified; when the advantage changes (when the victim has been repaid), then punishment must cease. Hickey and Scharf (1980: 169) point out that this limitation is similar to that proposed by Norval Morris:

1. We must punish only to the extent that the loss of liberty would be agreeable were one not to know whether one were to be the criminal, the victim, or a member of the general public, and

2. The loss of liberty must be justified as the minimal loss consistent with the maintenance of the same liberty among others.

In both these propositions, the moral limit of punishment is reached when what is done to the criminal equals the extent of his or her forfeiture, as determined by the crime.

One other issue that must be addressed here is the concept of *mercy*. Seemingly inconsistent with any definition of retributive justice, mercy is, nevertheless, always associated with the concept. From the very beginnings of law, there has also been the element of forgiveness. Even tribal societies had special allowances and clemencies for offenders, usually granted by the king or chief. For instance, the concept of *sanctuary* allowed a person respite from punishment as long as she or he was within the confines of church grounds. Benefit of clergy, dispensation, and even probation are examples of mercy by the court. However, it must be made clear that mercy is different from just deserts. If, on the one hand, because of circumstances of the crime, of the criminal, or of the victim, the offender deserves little or no punishment, then that is what he or she deserves, and it is not mercy to give a suspended sentence or probation. On the other hand, if an offender truly deserves a period of imprisonment and the court forgives the offense and releases the offender with only a warning, then the individual has been granted mercy.

Murphy (1985, 1995) proposes that retributive emotions derive from self-respect, that it is a healthy response to an injury to feel angry, resentful, and, yes, even vengeful. However, it is also acceptable to forgive and extend mercy to one's assailant, if the forgiveness extends not from a lack of self-respect, but rather from a moral system. For instance, he points out that many religions include the concept of "turning the other cheek" and extending mercy to enemies. Mercy is appropriate when the offender is divorced in some way from her or his offense. One way to a separation is true repentance.

Murphy (1985: 10) summarizes the points of mercy as follows:

1. It is an autonomous moral virtue (separate from justice).
2. It is a virtue that tempers or "seasons" justice—something that one adds to justice in order to dilute it and to make it stronger.
3. It is never owed to anyone as a right or a matter of desert or justice.
4. As a moral virtue, it derives its value at least in part from the fact that it flows from love or compassion while not losing sight of the importance of justice.
5. It requires a generally retributive outlook on punishment and responsibility.

Therefore, mercy is related to justice but is not necessarily a part of it. It is connected with a change in the offender—typically, there must be repentance—and it is connected with a quality of the victim—some form of compassion, charity, or benevolence. Other questions of mercy remain, however. Who has the right to extend mercy? At times, victims or the families of victims are upset with a sentencing judge because of the lenient sentence administered to the offender. Should victims be the only ones who have the right to give the gift of mercy?

Utilitarian Justice We have been discussing retributive justice as a rationale for and means to determine punishment. However, other rationales also support punishment. The alternative to retribution is utilitarianism. Whereas the goal of a retributive framework of justice is to restore a natural balance by righting a wrong or neutralizing criminal gain with an equal amount of loss or pain, the goal of utilitarian justice is to benefit society by administering punishment to deter offenders from future crime.

Caesare Beccaria (1738–1794) and Jeremy Bentham (1748–1832) provide a utilitarian rationale for proportionality in punishment. Punishment should be based on the seriousness of the crime: the more serious the crime (or the greater the reward the crime offered the criminal), the more serious and severe the punishment should be. A utilitarian framework of justice would determine punishment on the basis of deterrence.

Bentham's *hedonistic calculus,* for instance, is concerned with measuring the gain of the crime so that the amount of threatened pain could be set to deter people from committing that crime; the goal is deterrence, not balance. Measurement is important in both retributive and utilitarian rationales of justice. In a retributive system, we measure to determine the proportional amount of punishment to right the wrong; in a utilitarian system, we measure to determine the amount of punishment needed to deter. We see that under the utilitarian framework, there is no necessity for perfect balance. In fact, one must threaten a slightly higher degree of pain or punishment than the gain or pleasure that comes from the criminal act; otherwise, there would be no deterrent value in the punishment.

In some cases, retributive notions of justice and utilitarian notions of justice may conflict. If a criminal is sure to commit more crime, the utilitarian could justify holding him in prison as a means of incapacitation, but to hold him past the time "equal" to his crime would be seen as an injustice under a retributive system. Treatment, as mentioned before, is acceptable under a utilitarian justice system and irrelevant and unsupported by a retributive one. Deterrence is the primary determinant of justice under a utilitarian system, but desert is the only determinant of a retributive system of justice.

Procedural Justice We turn now to the procedure of administering punishment—our legal system. *Justice* and *law* are not synonymous; most writers describe law as objective and justice as subjective. Law includes the procedures and rules used to determine punishment or resolve disputes. It is a system of rules for human relations—the "whole field of the principles laid down, the decisions reached in accordance with them, and the procedures whereby the principles are applied to individual cases" (Raphael, 1980: 74). There is, then, a differentiation between justice and law. Justice is the concept of fairness; law is a system of rules.

The law is an imperfect system. Fuller (1969: 39) explores the weaknesses of law and describes ways that the procedure of law may fail to achieve justice. Possible failures include a failure to achieve rules at all, so that every decision must be made on its own; a failure to publicize rules; retroactive application of law, which abuses the concept of justice; the existence of contradictory rules; too-frequent changes in rules; and a lack of consistency between the rules and their actual administration. These failures weaken the law's ability to resolve disputes or control conflict in an objective and fair manner.

Some argue that because of the legal system's inability to determine what is just, justice derives not from the application of legal rules but from deciding each case on its merits without regard to rule or precedent. Early equity courts in England were developed because there was dissatisfaction with the King's (legal) courts' emphasis on rules and precedent that, in some cases, frustrated the ends of justice. Wasserman argues that legal precedent is an unsatisfactory way of determining justice because the particularity of each case is important. However, individual, intuitive decisions are no better, since justice then becomes "unsteady" and "wavering" (cited in Feinberg and Gross, 1977: 28–34). Some have argued that property and interest cases can be decided by legal rule but cases involving conflicts of human conduct cannot. Even this bifurcation is criticized, however, since the most straightforward contract disagreements may involve human action, misinterpretation, and interest (Wasserman, in Feinberg and Gross, 1977: 34).

We are left to assume that although a system of law is necessary for the ordered existence of society, it is not necessarily helpful in determining what is just. In fact, "moral rights" may differ from "legal rights," and "legal interests" may not be moral. Although, it should be noted that rules very often specify the procedures and steps necessary in judicial decision making. If these rules and procedures are broken, we believe that an injustice has occurred.

In our system of justice, **due process** exemplifies procedural justice. Our constitutional rights of due process require careful inquiry and investigation before punishment or forfeiture of any protected right can be carried out by the state. One has the right to due process whenever the state seeks to deprive an individual of protected rights of life, liberty, or property. Due process is the sequence of steps taken by the state that is designed to eliminate or at least minimize error. Procedural protections such as a neutral hearing body, trial by a jury of peers, cross-examination, presentation of evidence, and representation by counsel do not eliminate deprivation or punishment, but they do result in more accurate and just deprivations and punishments. Thus, if due process has been violated—by use of a coerced confession, tainted evidence, or improper police procedure—an injustice has occurred. The injustice does not arise because the offender does not deserve to be punished, but because the state does not deserve to do the punishing, having relied on unfair procedures.

QUERY

1. An eighty-seven-year-old man living in Chicago is exposed as a soldier who took part in killing hundreds of Jewish concentration camp victims. U.S. extradition procedures are followed to the letter, and he is extradited to Israel to stand trial. Israeli law determines that courts in Israel have jurisdiction over Nazi war crimes. Israeli legal procedure is followed without error, and he is convicted of war crimes and sentenced to death.
2. Federal law enforcement agents determine that a citizen of another country participated in a drug cartel that sold drugs in the United States. A small group of agents goes to the foreign country, kidnaps the offender, drugs him, and brings him back to the United States to stand trial. Upon challenge, the government agents explain that, although these actions would have been unconstitutional and illegal against a citizen of the United States in this country, since they were conducted on foreign soil against a non-U.S. citizen, they were not illegal.

What do you think? Analyze the case under procedural justice and substantive justice.

Some point out that procedural justice is recognized only for certain groups—specifically, "all persons born or naturalized in the United States. . . ." Illegal aliens and others seemingly have no rights recognized by the Constitution. This allows practices such as the incarceration of the Cuban "Marielitos" without any form of due process at all. Some of these refugees were imprisoned for more than a decade in federal prisons without any finding of guilt, harm, or reason. Jimmy Carter, in 1993, discussed their imprisonment (quoted in Hamm, 1995: 39):

> Every nation that grossly violates human rights justifies it by claiming they are acting within their laws. The way we are doing it now is the same kind of human rights violation that we'd vehemently condemn if it was perpetrated in another country.

Today, we are holding those suspected of terrorist ties without charges and without any procedural protections that might allow them to prove in a fair and neutral hearing that those ties do not exist. The argument to support their detention is that they have violated immigration laws, for instance, they have overstayed their visas. Instead of deportation, however, hundreds, if not thousands, have been incarcerated while investigations continue.

Is the right to be free from governmental deprivation of liberty without some finding of guilt a *natural* right that every government must recognize for all people, or a *legal* right that can be written into existence, written out of existence, and defined in whatever way a government chooses, depending on a perceived threat?

The **exclusionary rule** is supposed to ensure that the state follows the correct procedures before exacting punishment by excluding illegal evidence from the trial. There is debate as to whether the exclusionary rule is a mere legal protective device created by the court or a natural inherent right embed-

---

United States Constitution, Fourteenth Amendment

§1. All persons born or naturalized in the United States, and subject to the jurisdiction thereof, are citizens of the United States and of the state wherein they reside. No state shall make or enforce any law which shall abridge the privileges or immunities of citizens of the United States; nor shall any state deprive any person of life, liberty, or property, without due process of law; nor deny to any person within its jurisdiction the equal protection of the laws.

---

ded in the Constitution. The exclusionary rule has been subject to a great deal of criticism because it is perceived as a rule that lets criminals go free.

A utilitarian framework might support punishment even if the procedural rules were broken, since the net utility of punishment might outweigh the violation of due process (see the "14th Amendment" box). On the other hand, even a utilitarian may argue against punishment when the procedural protections have been broken if the damage to general respect for the law is greater than the deterrent utility of punishment. In fact, one of the rationales for the exclusionary rule is that it serves as a judicial "slap" to police departments and a deterrent against improper investigation procedures. This is clearly a utilitarian argument. Under a retributive system of punishment, it would seem that justice is violated whether one is punished or not if procedural justice is violated. If we allow the offender to go free because of the error, then the crime has not been balanced by punishment. If we punish the offender, we violate our system of procedural justice and protection of individual rights.

Supreme Court decisions have shown reduced support for the exclusionary rule. Exceptions have been created that some say threaten to undermine the rule itself. For instance, the *inevitable discovery exception* allows the tainted evidence if it would have been discovered without the improper procedure (*Nix v. Williams,* 104 S.Ct. 250 [1984]). The *good faith exception* was recognized by the Court in a case where the law enforcement officers thought they had a legal warrant even though the warrant and therefore their search was actually unlawful (*United States v. Leon,* 104 S.Ct. 3405 [1984]). Another exception to the exclusionary rule was recognized in *New York v. Quarles* (104 S.Ct. 2626 [1984]). In this case, since the officer's goal was public safety and not collection of evidence, his failure to give Miranda warnings did not result in excluding the evidence he obtained by questioning a suspect without Miranda warnings.

The majority displayed distinctly utilitarian reasoning in their cost/benefit arguments to support the holdings of the previously mentioned cases. It may be that the Supreme Court will become reluctant to uphold sanctions against any but the most extreme misconduct by police and use a *shocking to the conscience test* rather than a test that measures the violation to procedural rights. In

Shakespeare, *The Merchant of Venice*
Portia (Act IV, Scene i)

The quality of mercy is not strained;
It droppeth as the gentle rain from heaven
Upon the place beneath. It is twice blest;
It blesseth him that gives and him that takes.
'Tis mightiest in the mightiest; it becomes
The throned monarch better than his crown.
His scepter shows the force of temporal power,
The attribute to awe and majesty,
Wherein doth sit the dread and fear of kings;
But mercy is above this scept'red sway;
It is enthroned in the hearts of kings;
It is an attribute to God himself,
And earthly power doth then show likest God's
When mercy seasons justice. Therefore, Jew,
Though justice be thy plea, consider this,
That, in the course of justice, none of us
Should see salvation. We do pray for mercy,
And that same prayer doth teach us all to render
The deeds of mercy. I have spoke thus much
To mitigate the justice of thy plea,
Which if thou follow, this strict court of Venice
Must needs give sentence 'gainst the merchant there.

The Merchant of Venice employs many of the issues we discuss in this chapter. Here the plea for mercy emphasizes the relationship between justice and mercy. Shylock's demand for law (his pound of flesh) and the unwillingness of the court to deny it illustrate how law sometimes has little to do with justice. Then Portia's surprise argument—that because Shylock's contract mentioned only flesh and not blood, no blood could be spilled—is a perfect illustration of the law's slavish devotion to rule over substance. As a legal trick, this interpretation of a contract has not been improved upon yet, in fiction or reality.

SOURCE: *William Shakespeare: The Complete Works* (Baltimore: Penguin Books, 1969).

the shocking to the conscience test, police behavior is evaluated against substantive rights to be free from outrageous governmental action, such as torture, forced blood samples or surgery, or, in the case most closely associated with the test, forced regurgitation (*Rochin v. California*, 343 U.S. 165 [1952]).

We have been discussing legal procedures for determining punishment, but in some cases legal procedures may be followed completely and injustice still occur. For instance, it is unlikely that anyone would argue that Nelson Mandela, when he was imprisoned in South Africa, or Andre Sakharov, a Soviet dissident, received just punishment even though the legal procedures of their respective countries might have been followed scrupulously. These are clear examples that illustrate the difference between "procedural" justice and "substantive" justice.

QUERY

- Let's assume that in a civil dispute, one side has a very strong claim and would almost surely win in court, yet because the attorney missed a filing deadline, the judge throws out the case. Do you believe this is fair?
- Consider the case of an individual who befriends an elderly person, takes care of him, and provides him comfort in his old age even at the sacrifice of personal time and expense. When the elderly person dies, however, a distant relative who expressed the view that it wasn't her duty to take care of her relative inherits substantial assets. Is this fair? Is this just? If the law (which would typically uphold the inheritance absent any special elements such as contract or payment for personal services) does not support any recognition of the friend's non-legal "rights" to any portion of the inheritance, what theory of justice might support it?
- In a death penalty case, new evidence emerged that supported the defendant's allegations of innocence, but the evidence was uncovered after the deadline for filing an appeal. Should the execution go forward?

PARADIGMS OF LAW

The law serves as a written embodiment of society's ethics and morals. It is said to be declarative as well as active—it declares correct behavior and serves as a tool for enforcement. Law is both a prohibition and a promise. It cautions against certain types of behavior and warns of the consequences for ignoring the warning. Natural law refers to the belief that some law is inherent in the natural world and can be discovered by reason. A corollary of this thought is that some behavior is intrinsically wrong *(mala in se)*. In contrast, positive law refers to those laws written and enforced by society. This type of law is of human construction and therefore fallible (Mackie, 1977: 232).

We can trace the history of law back to very early codes, such as the Code of Hammurabi (c. 2000 B.C.), which mixed secular and religious proscriptions of behavior. These codes also standardized punishments and atonements for wrongdoing. Early codes of law did not differentiate between what we might call public wrongs and private wrongs. As mentioned before, two different areas of law can be distinguished today: criminal law is said to be punitive, whereas civil law is reparative. The first punishes while the second seeks to redress wrong or loss. Of the two, criminal law is more closely associated with the moral standards of society, yet it is by no means comprehensive in its coverage of behavior. Nor is there unanimous agreement about what it should or does cover.

Two basic paradigms aid our understanding of the function of law in society. According to Rich (1978: 1), a paradigm is a "fundamental image of the subject matter within a science. . . . It subsumes, defines, and interrelates the exemplars, theories, and methods/tools that exist within it." The **consensus paradigm** views society as a community consisting of like-minded individuals who agree on goals important for ultimate survival. This view is functionalist because it sees law as an aid to the growth and/or survival of society.

Under the **conflict paradigm,** society is perceived as being made up of competing and conflicting interests. According to this view, governance is based on power; if some win, others lose, and those who hold power in society promote self-interest, not a "greater good."

A less extreme view than the conflict paradigm is *pluralism*. Although sharing the perception that society is made up of competing interests, pluralism describes more than two basic interest groups and also recognizes that the power balance may shift when interest groups form or coalitions emerge. These power shifts occur as part of the dynamics of societal change.

The Consensus Paradigm

According to the consensus paradigm, law serves as a tool of unification. Emile Durkheim (1858–1917) wrote that there are two types of law: the *repressive,* criminal law that enforces universal norms, and the *restitutive,* civil law that developed because of the division of labor in society and resulting social interests. In Durkheim's view, criminal law exists as a manifestation of consensual norms: "We must not say that an action shocks the common conscience because it is criminal, but rather that it is criminal because it shocks the common conscience" (Durkheim, 1969: 21). What this statement means is that we define an action as criminal because the majority of the populace holds the opinion that it is wrong. This "common" or "collective" conscience is referred to as **mechanical solidarity.** Each individual's moral beliefs are indistinguishable from the whole. The function of **repressive law** is the maintenance of social cohesion. Law contributes to the collective conscience by providing an example of deviance.

Although Durkheim recognized individual differences, he believed these differences, resulting from the division of labor in society, only made the individual more dependent on society as a part of a whole. His concept of **organic solidarity** draws the analogy of individuals in society as parts of an organism: all doing different things, but as parts of a whole. Individuals exist, but they are tied inextricably to society and its common conscience. **Restitutive law** is said to mediate those differences that may come about because of the division of labor. Even here the law serves an integrative function.

The consensus view would point to evidence that we all agree, for the most part, on what behaviors are wrong and the relative seriousness of different types of wrongful behavior. In criminology, the consensus view is represented by classical thinkers such as Bentham and Beccaria, who relied on the accepted definitions of crime in their day, without questioning the validity of these definitions, only their implementation. Although the Positivists virtually ignored societal definitions of crime, Garofalo (1852–1932), a legal anthropologist, had an idea of natural law that might be considered a consensus concept. As defined earlier, natural law is the view that certain behaviors are so inherently heinous that they go against nature; therefore, there are natural proscriptions against such behavior that transcend individual societies or time periods (Kramer, 1982: 36).

We have recent evidence that there is at least some consensus in people's definitions of what constitutes criminal behavior; studies have shown that not only do individuals in this culture tend to agree on the relative seriousness of different kinds of crime, but there is also substantial agreement cross-culturally as well (Nettler, 1978: 215). In the consensus paradigm, law is representative. It is a compilation of the do's and don'ts that we all agree on. Furthermore, law reinforces social cohesion. It emphasizes our "we-ness" by illustrating deviance. Finally, law is value-neutral—that is, it resolves conflicts in an objective and neutral manner.

The Conflict Paradigm

A second paradigm of law and society is the conflict paradigm. Rather than perceiving law as representative, this perspective sees law as a tool of power holders that they use for their own purposes, which are to maintain and control the status quo. In the conflict paradigm, law is perceived as restrictive or repressive, rather than representative, and as an instrument of special interests. Basically, there are three points to the conflict paradigm: first, criminal definitions are relative; second, those who control major social institutions determine how crime is defined; third, the definition of crime is fundamentally a tool of power (Sheley, 1985: 1). Richard Quinney (1969: 17) describes the conflict paradigm as follows:

QUOTE

By formulating criminal law (including legislative statutes, administrative rulings, and judicial decisions), some segments of society protect and perpetuate their own interests. Criminal definitions exist, therefore, because some segments of society are in conflict with others. By formulating criminal definitions, these segments are able to control the behavior of persons in other segments. It follows that the greater the conflict in interests between segments of a society, the greater the probability that the power segments will formulate criminal definitions.

Quinney's description of conflict theory draws heavily on Marxist definitions of power and power holders in capitalism. Quinney (1974: 15–16) outlines the following points as making up the conflict paradigm:

1. American society is based on an advanced capitalistic society.
2. The state is organized to serve the interests of the dominant economic class. . . .
3. Criminal law is an instrument of the state and ruling class to maintain and perpetuate the existing social and economic order.
4. Crime control in capitalist society is accomplished through a variety of institutions and agencies established and administered by a governmental elite. . . .

5. The contradictions of advanced capitalism . . . require that the
   subordinate classes remain oppressed by whatever means necessary. . . .

6. Only with the collapse of capitalist society and the creation of a new
   society . . . will there be a solution to the crime problem.

Advocates of the conflict paradigm would point to laws against only certain types of gambling or against the use of only certain types of drugs as evidence that the ruling class punishes only the activities of other classes. In other words, cultural differences in behavior exist, but only the activities of certain groups (the powerless) are labeled deviant. For instance, numbers running is always illegal, yet some states have legalized horseracing, dog racing, and/or casinos. Heroin and cocaine are illegal, Valium and alcohol are not. An even better example of differential definitions and enforcement is that federal drug laws impose more severe sanctions on crack cocaine than on powder cocaine. Many believe it is not merely a coincidence that crack cocaine is more likely to be the drug of choice for minorities (being cheaper), whereas powder cocaine is associated with Caucasians and social elites. Conflict theorists believe that laws are written to protect and benefit the powerful groups in society and their interests.

Recall Jeffrey Reiman's description of the difference between reporting a mining accident and a multiple murder. Despite the same result (dead victims), the mining company would probably not be prosecuted or receive very minor punishments for its role in the death of the miners. For the conflict theorist, this would be an example of how law has been written differentially to serve the interests of the power holders. The definition of what is criminal often excludes corporate behavior, such as price fixing, toxic waste dumping, and monopolistic trade practices, because these behaviors, although just as harmful to the public good as street crime, are engaged in by those who have the power to define criminality. The regulation of business, instead of the criminalization of harmful business practices, is seen as arising from the ability of those in power positions to redefine their activities to their own advantage. Even though the Occupational Safety Board, the Food and Drug Administration, the Federal Aeronautics Administration, and other similar governmental agencies are charged with the task of enforcing regulations governing business activities in their respective areas, no one seriously believes that the level of enforcement or labeling is as serious as in criminal law. Relationships between the watched and the watchdog agencies are frequently incestuous: heads of business are often named to governmental agencies, and employees of these agencies may move to the business sector they previously regulated.

Some draw parallels between corporate crimes and organized crime, or at least describe them as occurring in the same spectrum of behavior (Krisberg, 1975: 35). Certainly it is fairly well documented that large and small corporations engage in dishonest and even criminal practices. One study reported that from a sample of businesses, 60 percent reported enforcement activity in response to one of the following violations: restraint of trade, financial manipulation, misrepresentation in advertising, income tax evasion, unsafe working conditions, unsafe food or drug distribution, illegal rebates, foreign payoffs, unfair labor practices, illegal political contributions, and environmental pollution (Clinard et al., 1985: 205). Even the highly publicized indictments of a few Enron and Worldcom officials rapidly gave way to silence. How many of the officials involved in wrongdoing will ever be punished remains to be seen.

In criminology, the conflict view was represented by early theorists such as Bonger (1876–1940), a Marxist sociologist who explained that crime causation is a result of economic power differential, and that power holders are able to label some behavior as criminal. During the 1960s, a small number of criminologists attempted to redefine criminals as political prisoners, based on their views that the state used criminal definitions to control minority groups (Reasons, 1973). Labeling theorists also questioned the criminal justice system's definitions by pointing out that only some offenders are formally labeled and treated as deviant.

The conflict theory is represented by theorists such as Platt, the Schwendingers, Krisberg, Quinney, Taylor, Walton, and Young and Chambliss (Kramer, 1982: 41). The conflict theorists explain that the myth of justice and equality under the law serves to protect the interests of the ruling class, because as long as there is a perception of fairness, fundamental questions about the distribution of goods will not be raised: "The combination of formal legal equality and extreme economic inequality is the hallmark of the liberal state" (Krisberg, 1975: 49). Law functions to depoliticize even the most obviously political actions of the oppressed by defining these actions as crime, but its greatest power is to hide the basic injustice of society itself.

Definitions are shaped by our paradigms of law. The Los Angeles riots of 1992 were sparked by the acquittal of four police officers who were videotaped beating Rodney King, a motorist who had outstanding arrest warrants for traffic violations. The riots were described by some as political action. According to this view, minorities who were frustrated by economic hopelessness and angered by the criminal justice system's oppressive and brutal treatment retaliated in like form. In this view, the riots were political statements against oppression. Alternatively, others described the same actions as blatant and simple criminality. In this perspective, violent individuals merely took advantage of the incident to exhibit their individual deviance. Conflict theorists would support the first definition, and consensus theorists would support the second.

Distinct from the conflict paradigm is the **pluralist paradigm.** In this view, law is seen as arising from interest groups, but power is more complicated than the bifurcated system described by the Marxist tradition. Roscoe Pound defines the following as interests protected by power holders: security against actions that threaten the social group, security of social institutions, security of morals, conservation of national resources, general progress, and individual life. Power is exercised in the political order, the economic order, the religious order, the kinship order, the educational order, and the public order. Law and social control constitute the public order, and powerful interests affect the law by influencing the writing of laws and the enforcement of written laws (Quinney, 1974).

Pluralism views law as influenced by interest groups that are in flux. Some interests may be at odds with other interests, or certainly the interpretation of

---

Exercise

Discuss how the conflict and consensus paradigms would interpret the following:

- Decriminalization of marijuana for medical purposes
- The passage of "hate crimes" legislation
- State "ethics laws" that criminalize some practices of state legislators
- Recent Supreme Court decisions invalidating the use of race in admissions procedures in universities and in competitions for state scholarships
- Laws prohibiting racial profiling in police stops

---

them may be. For instance, conservation of natural resources is a basic interest necessary to the survival of society, but it may be interpreted by lumber companies as allowing them to harvest trees in national forests as long as they replant or, alternatively, by conservation groups as mandating more wilderness areas. According to the pluralist paradigm, laws are written by the group whose voice is more powerful at any particular time.

Interest groups hold power, but their power may shrink or grow depending on various factors. Coalitions and shared interests may shift the balance of power. The definition of crime may change, depending on which interest groups have the power to define criminal behavior and what is currently perceived to be in the best interests of the most powerful groups.

We might consider the **social contract** as combining some of the concepts of the conflict and consensus paradigms. According to the social contract theory, members of society originally were engaged in a "war of all against all"—a conflict perspective of human nature. In a rational response to the dysfunctional nature of such conflict, individuals freely gave up some of their liberties in return for protection—in essence, a consensus perspective of the legal system. According to Hobbes, each individual has chosen to "lay down this right to all things; and be contented with so much liberty against other men, as he would allow other men against himself" (from Hobbes, *Leviathan,* 1651, quoted in Beauchamp, 1982: 264). Law is viewed as a mutual contract and voluntary transfer of rights for the benefit of all.

CONCLUSION

In this chapter, we have defined justice and discussed the relationship of justice and the law. Whereas justice is a philosophical concept concerned with rights and needs, law is the administration of justice. Justice can be further differentiated into distributive justice and corrective justice. Corrective justice is the central concern of the criminal justice system and can be further divided into substantive and procedural issues. Substantive justice is concerned with the fairness of what we do to offenders; procedural justice is concerned with the procedures that must be undertaken before punishment is to occur. Paradigms of law help us understand that there are different perceptions regarding the function of law in society. Although some view law as enforcing the will of the majority, others see law as a tool of oppression by those in power.

REVIEW QUESTIONS

1. Explain how Aristotle and Plato associated status with justice. What is the case today?
2. Discuss the differences among the various theories of distributive justice.
3. Define rectificatory justice, commutative justice, and corrective justice.
4. Discuss the differences between substantive justice and procedural justice.
5. What is the retributive argument for punishment? What is the utilitarian argument for punishment?
6. Discuss the conflict paradigm and the consensus paradigm. How is pluralism distinguished from conflict theory?
7. Explain how people distinguish between law and justice.

ETHICAL DILEMMAS

Situation 1

Two individuals are being sentenced for the exact same crime of burglary. You are the judge. One of the individuals is a twenty-year-old who has not been in trouble before and participated only because the other individual was his friend. The second person has a history of juvenile delinquency and is now twenty-five. Would you sentence them differently? How do you justify your decision?

Situation 2

In your apartment building there lives a young man who appears to be of Middle Eastern descent. You notice that other young men often visit him and they come and go at odd hours of the day and night. You engage in a conversation with him one day and during the course of that conversation he states that, "The United States deserved what happened to them on September 11 because of their imperialistic actions across the world and their support for the oppression of the Palestinian people." You feel it is your duty to report him to the local police, and they appear to be interested in your report. One day you observe him taken away in handcuffs, and you never see him again. Several weeks later, his apartment is vacant; you do not know what happened to his belongings. Would you attempt to find out what happened to him? Do you feel you should investigate further?

Situation 3

You are serving on a jury for a murder trial. The evidence presented at trial was largely circumstantial and, in your mind, equivocal. During closing, the prosecutor argued that you must find the defendant guilty because he confessed to the crime. The defense attorney immediately objected and the judge sternly instructed you to disregard the prosecutor's statement. While you do not know exactly what happened, you suspect that the confession was excluded because of a some procedural error. Would you be able to ignore the prosecutor's statement in your deliberations? Should you? Would you tell the judge if the jury members discussed the statement and appeared to be influenced by it?

SUGGESTED READINGS

Cole, D. 1999. *No Equal Justice.* New York City: The Free Press.

Hamm, M. 1995. *The Abandoned Ones.* Boston: Northeastern University Press.

Murphie, J. 1988. "Forgiveness, Mercy, and the Retributive Emotions." *Criminal Justice Ethics* 7(2): 3–15.

Rawls, J. 1971. *A Theory of Justice.* Cambridge, MA: Belknap Press.

5

Further Issues
in Retributive Justice

Law and Social Control
Legal Paternalism
Legal Moralism

Criminal and Moral Culpability
Punishing the Mentally Ill
Punishing Juveniles
Punishing White Collar Criminals

Victims' Rights
Victim Precipitation
Restorative Justice

Immoral Laws and the Moral Person
The Criminal Justice Professional
Balancing Law and Justice

Conclusion

Review Questions

Ethical Dilemmas

Suggested Readings

Key Terms

paternalism
legal moralism
culpability
victimology
victim-compensation programs

victim precipitation
restorative justice
civil disobedience
street justice

Chapter Objectives

- Explore some of the rationales for and limits of law.
- Further distinguish between moral culpability and legal culpability.
- Consider the issues of "special groups" in the criminal justice system.
- Understand the relationship between morality and law.

In the last chapter we reviewed philosophical and political theories of law. In this chapter we concentrate specifically on retributive or corrective law and further discuss some issues concerning why certain acts are defined as criminal, and the issues involved in how we punish those who break such laws.

LAW AND SOCIAL CONTROL

One can view law as a tool of behavior change (Hornum and Stavish, 1978: 148). In this theory, law is seen as a tool of social engineering and a way of changing behavior to a desired state (Aubert, 1969: 11). Law may influence behavior directly by prohibiting or mandating certain behavior, or indirectly by influencing social institutions such as family or education that, in turn, influence behavior (Dror, 1969: 93). Thus, law controls behavior by providing sanctions but also, perhaps even more importantly, by teaching people what behaviors are acceptable and what behaviors are intolerable.

The social contract theory explains that law is a contract—each individual gives up some liberties and, in return, is protected from others who have their liberties restricted as well. But how much liberty should be restricted, and what behaviors should be prohibited? Rough formulas or guidelines indicate that the law should interfere as little as possible in natural liberties and should step in only when the liberty in question injures or impinges on the interests of another.

How far should the law go in managing citizens' behavior? Obviously, we agree on laws that restrict behavior blatantly harmful to innocent victims; but, there is no agreement on, for instance, laws related to property owners who protect themselves by lethal force. Should a lethal trap set for a burglar be defined as murder or self-protection?

The fear of AIDS generated debate over the limits of government intervention. Some people wanted AIDS victims to be registered and to be prohibited from many jobs and types of participation in the public sector. Some wanted mandatory testing of certain occupational groups. Others believed that these proposed laws were discriminatory and served only to further stigmatize the sufferers. The balance between individual freedom and government control is reached with difficulty when fear and misunderstanding about the potential for danger fuel emotions. More recently, such debate has quieted because of more information concerning methods of transmission and containment. The fear over the SARS virus generated the same type of conflict as governments employed their quarantine powers in an effort to control the spread of this disease in the spring of 2003.

Then there are those behaviors that are defined and redefined as criminal over time. For instance, abortion has been ignored, outlawed, and then decriminalized. It is entirely possible that in the future it may be redefined once again as criminal. There has also been a cycle of defining certain drugs as criminal, decriminalizing them, and then redefining them as criminal, depending on which interest groups can influence the general definitions of society. In the following sections, we discuss in more detail two rationales for laws—legal paternalism and legal moralism.

Legal Paternalism

Many of our laws are *paternalistic*—they try to protect people from their own behavior. Examples include seat belt laws, motorcycle helmet laws, speed limits, drug laws, licensing laws, alcohol consumption and sale laws, smoking prohibitions, and laws limiting certain types of sexual behavior. The strict libertarian view would hold that the government has no business interfering in a person's decisions about these behaviors as long as they don't negatively affect others. The opposing view is that as long as a person is a member of society (and everyone is), he or she has a value to that society, and society is therefore compelled to protect the person with or without his or her cooperation.

It may also be true that there are no harmful or potentially harmful behaviors to oneself that do not also hurt others, however indirectly, so society is protecting others when it controls each individual. Speeding drivers may crash into someone else, drug addicts may commit crimes to support their habit, and gamblers may neglect their families and cause expense to the state, and so on. You may remember that in Chapter 1 we limited moral judgments to behavior that influences another. The justification of paternalistic laws depends on the view that very little of what we do does not affect others, however indirectly.

Some believe that government can justify **paternalism** only with certain restrictions (Thompson, 1980). First, a paternalistic law is appropriate only if the decision-making ability of the person is somehow impaired, by lack of knowledge or something else. An example would be child labor laws or laws that restrict the sale and consumption of alcohol by children. In both cases, there is a presumption that children do not understand the dangers of such behavior and, therefore, need protection. The second rule of paternalism is that the restriction should be as limited as possible. For example, DUI laws define the point of legal intoxication as when one's ability to drive safely is impaired, not simply after any alcohol consumption at all. When mountain passes close, they are reopened as soon as it is relatively safe to cross them. Laws exist that ban the sale of cigarettes to minors, but cigarettes are still available to adults—who supposedly have reached a level of maturity to understand the dangers associated with smoking. Finally, the third rule regarding paternalism states that the laws should seek only to prevent a serious and irreversible error: a death from DUI, an accident on an icy road, and so on. These rules try to create a balance between an individual's liberty and government control (Thompson, 1980).

Paternalistic laws can be supported by an ethics of care. Remember that in this framework, morality is viewed as integral to a system of relationships. The individual is seen as having ties to society and to every other member of society. Relationships involve responsibilities as well as rights. We can expect the minimum level of care necessary for survival from society under the ethics of care. However, the corollary is that society also can care for us by restricting harmful behaviors. Rights are less important in this framework; therefore, to ask whether society has a right to intervene or an individual has a right to a liberty is not relevant to the discussion. Utilitarianism would also support paternalistic laws because of the net utility to society that results from protecting each of its members.

Other ethical systems may not so clearly support paternalistic laws. Individual rights are perhaps more important under ethical formalism than the other ethical systems; individuals must be treated with respect and as ends in themselves. This view results in recognizing the rights of individuals to engage in careless or even harmful behavior as long as it is consistent with the universalism principle of the categorical imperative. In other words, people may have the moral right to engage in self-destructive or careless behavior as long as they do not hurt others. Of course, the opposing argument would be that all behaviors prohibited by paternalistic laws have the potential to affect others indirectly.

QUERY

Do you agree with laws that prohibit gambling? Drinking while driving? Underage drinking? Prostitution? Liquor violations? Drugs? Helmet laws for bicycles or motorcycles? Leash laws? Seat belts? Smoking in public places? Underage drinking or smoking laws? Can you think of any paternalistic laws not mentioned above?

Legal Moralism

The law also acts as the moral agent of society, some say in areas where there is no moral agreement. Some sexual behaviors, gambling, drug use, pornography, and even suicide and euthanasia are defined as wrong and prohibited. The laws against these behaviors may be based on principles of harm or paternalism, but they also exist to reinforce society's definitions of moral behavior.

For example, consensual sexual behavior between adults arguably harms no one, yet the Georgia state law prohibiting sodomy was upheld by the Supreme Court in *Bowers v. Hardwick* (106 S.Ct. 2841 [1986]). What harm is the state preventing by prohibiting this consensual behavior? The answer may be harm to community standards of morality. Pornography (at least that involving consenting adults) is defined as obscene, and it is prohibited arguably because of moral standards, not harmful effect. One governmental commission concluded that pornography contributed to sex crimes (Attorney General's Commission on Pornography, 1986), but this commission's findings contradicted an earlier commission's report created by President Lyndon Johnson, which found that pornography did not contribute substantially to sex crimes (Report of the Commission on Obscenity and Pornography, 1970).

Hence, we have a factual issue as to whether pornography is harmful. Yet even if pornography does not prove to be harmful to others, legal moralism endorses the government's right to prohibit the sale and purchase of pornographic materials. Under **legal moralism,** it is prohibited simply because it is wrong. Recently, the issue became even more complicated with the increasing use of the Internet and the ease with which individuals may obtain pornographic materials from anywhere in the world.

If we accept the fact that laws are the embodiment of society's morals, then legal moralism as a justification for laws would be less controversial, but in our society, there is by no means agreement that the government represents the people's view. Personal actions such as homosexuality and the use of pornography can be judged using the ethical systems discussed in Chapter 2, but it should also be recognized that whether an action is moral or immoral is a different question from whether there should be laws and governmental sanctions regarding the behavior. The box "Justifications for Law" spells out various reasons that laws are enacted.

In some cases, individuals may agree that a particular action is immoral but at the same time may not believe that the government should have any power to restrict an individual's choice. Some proponents of choice regarding abortion take great care to distinguish the difference between pro-choice and pro-abortion. To them, one does not have to approve of abortion to believe that it is wrong for government to interfere in the private decision of the individual to use the procedure. Similarly, some who advocate decriminalization of drugs do so because of cost effectiveness or libertarian reasons, not because they approve of drug use. As mentioned in the last chapter, we do not have a system in which the law completely overlaps with the moral code, and some would argue that it would be impossible in a society as heterogeneous as ours for this to occur.

Justifications for Law

1. *The harm principle:* to prevent harm to persons other than the actor when probably no other means are equally effective.
2. *The offense principle:* to prevent serious offense to persons other than the actor.
3. *Legal paternalism:* to prevent harm—physical, psychological, or economic—to the actor.
4. *Legal moralism:* to prohibit conduct that is inherently immoral.
5. *Benefit to others:* when the prohibition of the action provides some benefit to other than the actor.

SOURCE: Feinberg, cited in Feibleman, 1985: xiii.

Hate crime legislation gives us another example of a law that might be rationalized under legal moralism, although it could also be supported by a harm principle. In challenges to hate crime legislation, appellate courts have typically drawn a line between action and speech. That is, if a person commits an act that is already a crime, such as vandalism, assault, stalking, or harassment, and does so because of an expressed hatred for the victim's membership in a protected class, then the act can be punished as a "hate crime." However, if the only act prohibited by the hate crime legislation is speech, then the law violates the First Amendment's protection of free speech. Even though we abhor the message, we must protect the right of the person to express it, unless they also engage in a "legal harm." The interesting question, however, is why do we feel it necessary to create a new law instead of using the existing act-based law (such as vandalism). The reason might be because the true rationale for hate crime is legal moralism—we believe it important to enforce our moral code that hating others because of their race or sexual orientation is wrong.

QUERY

Should offenders who vandalize, assault, or kill people purely based on the victim's identity as a member of a racial group be punished more severely than a "garden-variety" criminal? What about if the target victim was a homosexual? What about if the target victim was a member of a religion, such as Islam?

Some propose that only those actions that violate some universal standard of morality, as opposed to merely a conventional standard, should be criminalized. This *limited legal moralism* would prevent the situation of some groups forcing their moral code on others. Of course this begs the question of what behaviors would meet this universal standard. Even child pornographers argue that their behavior is unfairly condemned by a conventional, rather than a universal, morality. The vast profits that are made by producing and distributing child pornography indicate that by no means a small minority are involved; does this mean that it is simply a matter of choice and not morals that should influence whether children should be seen as objects of sexual gratification? What would Immanuel Kant say about child pornography? What would Jeremy Bentham say about it?

In conclusion, we must allow for the possibility that some laws that are justified under legal moralism may not necessarily conform to our own personal views of good and bad. Many criminal justice practitioners also feel that some of the so-called gray areas of crime are not very serious, so it is not surprising that one sees discretion operating in enforcement patterns. Police will routinely ignore prostitution, for instance, until the public complains; they will routinely let petty drug offenders go, rather than take the trouble to book them; and they may let gamblers go with a warning if no publicity is attached to the arrest. Police use discretion in this way partly because these behaviors are not universally condemned.

QUERY

Analyze pornography, gambling, homosexuality, and drug use under the ethical systems discussed in Chapter 2. What other laws have limited Americans' (or certain groups') freedoms? Can they be justified under any ethical rationale?

CRIMINAL AND MORAL CULPABILITY

In the last chapter we discussed some **culpability** issues concerning corrective or retributive justice. Punishment should be administered fairly, but does fairness entail strict equality in sentencing, or does fairness require some recognition of the particular elements of the crime and the criminal? We also discussed, in Chapter 1, how moral culpability depends on rationality. One cannot be held accountable for one's actions morally if one is not rational, and the two groups that have historically been seen as irrational are the mentally ill and the young. We uphold this distinction in our legal system as well, but there are indications that the historical and traditional exceptions for these two groups are eroding.

Punishing the Mentally Ill

What would cause someone to kidnap an innocent woman, rape her, kill her, and mutilate her body by cutting out her vagina and eating it? For Arthur Shawcross, condemned to 250 years in prison in Rochester, New York, it may have been the sexual abuse by his mother that he endured as a child; or it may have been a cyst and scarring in the frontal lobes of his brain that was revealed in an MRI, but never shared with the jury during his trial. He killed two children and served fifteen years for that crime, he committed gruesome rapes and killings while serving in Vietnam, and he confessed to the grisly murders of eleven women in Rochester, New York, but the jury found him sane (Lewis, 1998). How is this possible? It seems that the murderers who are most clearly quite insane are those who we are most likely to label as sane. Why?

Probably the reason is that many believe such people must be punished for their crimes, and only by finding them sane will they be sure to be executed or serve life without parole. Or, perhaps, there is such a revulsion and fear over their acts that we experience a primitive urge to kill them. Yet holding the mentally ill responsible for their behavior runs contrary to our conception of rational culpability. In many states, in order to find a defendant insane, the jury must find that the person did not know what he or she was doing, or did not know it was wrong. The *McNaughten rule* was formed in the mid-nineteenth century. It forces psychiatrists to explain the defendants' behavior to the jury solely on the question of whether they knew right from wrong. Compulsion, or diminished capacity, is not recognized in this definition.

Dorothy Lewis (1998) is a psychiatrist that has examined dozens of murderers on death rows across the country, including Arthur Shawcross, Ted Bundy, and Mark Chapman. She describes how the violent killers she has diagnosed were physically abused, deprived, and sexually brutalized as children; many had suffered severe head trauma and, in all likelihood, were brain injured. The neurological injuries and psychiatric illnesses of these killers is evidence that they were not in control, or in some cases not even aware of their own actions at the time they committed their crimes. Yet, time after time, despite testimony to the contrary, juries find them sane.

Andrea Yates was convicted in Houston, Texas, in 2002 and sentenced to forty years in prison. She was a 36-year-old mother of five children, ranging in age from six months to seven years. One day when her husband was at work, she systematically took each child into the bathroom and drowned them. Her lawyers presented evidence that she was under psychiatric care for postpartum depression, she most probably suffered from postpartum psychosis, she had been institutionalized because of depression and suicide ideation, and that an earlier diagnosis by a doctor indicated that she should not have any more children because her syndrome seemed to be worsening with each pregnancy. In a deep depression after the birth of her last child, she came to believe that she was a terrible mother and that some great harm would befall the children if she did not commit them to God's care. After she killed them, she called the police.

Many people argue that the death penalty surely must be for someone like Andrea Yates, who killed five helpless children. Yet, is it possible to imagine that a mother, who by all accounts, was a loving mother when she wasn't suffering from depression or psychosis, could commit such a horrible act rationally? Does one rationally kill one's children and then call the police? A small number of people proposed the ridiculous argument that she was "tired of being a mother" and killed them because she was sure she would be acquitted; however, most people struggled to resolve concepts of culpability and justice in this case. The jury hedged their bets. They did not acquit her by reason of insanity, therefore, they declared her sane; but they gave her forty years instead of the death penalty. If she rationally and sanely killed her five children, why was she not executed? If she was not rational and insane, why did the jury not acquit her? In Texas, she would have been sent to a mental facility and could have lived the rest of her life in confinement if doctors diagnosed her as a continuing threat.

Other cases pose difficult questions concerning what we should do when individuals do violent acts. We are only beginning to understand how brain functioning and life experiences are dynamically related to each other and influence behavior. Children who are raised in abusive homes and endure constant stress have reduced serotonin levels, a brain chemical that tends to inhibit aggressive impulses. Over time, chronic stress can literally change the brain; thus, it should come as no surprise when we discover that those on death row have almost always endured severe abuse as children. Ironically, the law does allow some reduction of culpability under a diminished capacity argument for "passion" crimes (killing an unfaithful spouse), arguably because the "reasonable" person might also be tempted to commit the violent act. However, most of us are clearly unable to empathize with those who do the most horrific crimes. Thus, they are found to be "sane" and receive our most severe punishments.

Related to the issue of punishing the mentally ill is the issue of punishing the mentally handicapped. The Supreme Court has determined it is unconstitutional to execute the mentally handicapped, but, again, juries can ignore the evidence and sentence individuals to death who might not understand how they got there, or perhaps even what is happening to them. Lewis (1998) relates a case of a death row inmate whose mental impairment was so severe that it was unlikely he knew what was about to happen to him, and there was strong evidence to indicate that he had been incapable of even assisting in his own defense. He was executed.

QUOTE

His final meal proved to be a textbook example of how damage to certain parts of the frontal lobes affects planning. . . . this man set aside his dessert— pecan pie—so that he could have a midnight snack after his execution. In theory, prisoners cannot be executed if they do not understand what is happening to them or why. So much for theory.

Lewis, D. 1998. *Guilty by Reason of Insanity.* New York: Ivy Books, p. 93.

Punishing Juveniles

Nathaniel Brazill brought a gun to school and shot a well-liked teacher in the face, killing him. He was thirteen. The jury was asked to decide if he committed premeditated murder. Is a thirteen-year-old capable of "cold blooded murder?" Throughout most of this country's history, we have excused juveniles from their crimes because of a belief that their immaturity prevented them from engaging in the calm, rational deliberation that is required for criminal (and moral) culpability. It is the same reasoning that supports laws that prevent juveniles from drinking alcohol or buying cigarettes, voting, or serving in the military. Others argue that thirteen-year-olds know right from wrong and should be held accountable for their actions. If you feel that a thirteen-year-old murderer is responsible enough for his or her own behavior to serve a life sentence or even be executed, would you also agree that a thirteen-year-old is old enough to know whether to smoke or drink? Quit school if he feels like it? Serve in the military? If you answered yes to the life sentence, but no to the smoking or military, how do you explain the contradiction? Brazill's jury found him guilty of second-degree murder, and he will serve twenty-five years to life. His earliest release date would be when he is thirty-nine, but at that point he will have spent twenty-five years in an adult prison—in effect, raised by convicts.

Lionel Tate was twelve years old when he killed a six-year-old by breaking her neck, imitating what he saw while watching pro wrestlers. His attorneys argued that he had not meant to hurt her and was just playing. It seems very possible that he did not mean to hurt the girl, and prosecutors must have thought so too, since they offered him a sentence of three years in a juvenile facility, one year of house arrest, and ten years of probation. However, because he was a juvenile, his mother made the decision to refuse the plea bargain and go to trial. The jury found him guilty of first-degree murder, and he was sentenced to a mandatory term of life without parole (CNN.com, 2001). Lionel Tate has now become the poster child for a re-examination of how we treat juvenile offenders. Even the prosecutor in that case is now advocating a less harsh sentence for juveniles convicted of murder (Riddle, 2001).

In the 1990s, many states enacted new laws or changed existing laws to increase the controls and sanctions over juveniles. Some of these laws included curfew laws, parental responsibility laws, anti-gang laws, juvenile boot camps, gun laws, removing laws that seal juvenile records, and laws that allow transfer of juveniles to adult court (Bartollas and Miller, 2001: 7). The move to treat juvenile criminals more harshly has been fueled by the Columbine and other shootings, by the serious crimes committed by gang members, and by the pervasive view that juvenile crime is growing and the juvenile justice system is too lenient. Juvenile offenders are increasingly being waived through and prosecuted in the adult court system, and sent to adult prisons. In 2001, Florida had 572 juveniles in adult prisons, Connecticut had 505, New York had 316, Texas had 272, and California had 163 (Riddle, 2001).

Observers note that there have been cyclical periods of repressive and treatment-oriented movements for juveniles from the beginning of our nation's court systems. What distinguishes the juvenile system from the adult legal system is that it supposedly addresses the needs of those who are abused or neglected, as well as those who have committed acts that would be crimes if committed by adults. Many juveniles, of course, fit into both groups. Up until the 1970s, children who were taken into care for "their own good" were sometimes housed with adjudicated offenders. In the 1970s, this practice was ruled unconstitutional, and some due-process rights of juveniles were recognized in a series of court cases that forced the system to behave, in some ways, more like the adult system (Bartollas and Miller, 2001). However, differences were still recognized. Juveniles do not need all of the protections afforded adult criminals, supposedly, because the system's mission is to do what is best for them.

Before waiver to adult court, juveniles must be determined to be *competent*. This legal concept means that juveniles are mature enough to know what is happening, to be able to judge the consequences of the decisions they make, and be able to assist in their defense. This determination expects that juveniles understand right from wrong, but it does not require that juveniles understand why they did what they did, or that they be able to control their actions.

Some cases begin when juveniles are interrogated by police. Although some states require that juveniles have counsel or parents present, other states have no such requirement, or the juvenile is allowed to waive that right (Bartollas and Lewis, 2001: 74). Advocates for juveniles argue that they are simply unable to protect their own interests and are vulnerable to manipulation and intimidation by police officers. This issue has received recent coverage when the juveniles charged with the notorious 1989 Central Park jogger rape case appeared to be exonerated by the confession of another serial rapist and murderer and DNA evidence that linked him alone to the crime. Lawyers for the boys (now men) argue that their confessions were coerced by police. Since adults have been known to confess to crimes they did not commit, it is not difficult to understand why fourteen-year-olds might, as well.

There are many who believe that juvenile crime is becoming increasingly violent and that kids are literally "getting away with murder." This perception has been nurtured by the media's attention to a few notorious cases, the emphasis on gang activity in both fiction and news, and the idea that juvenile crime is increasing. According to 1998 crime figures, however, violent crime arrests of juveniles decreased by 8 percent and property crime arrests decreased by 11 percent between 1994 and 1998 (U.C.R. 1998). Juvenile crime has continued to decrease since 1998, and in 2001 it was reported that the murder rate was at a 15-year low, and the burglary and robbery rate was at a 20-year low (OJJDP, 2001). It appears that even though some continue to advocate harsh legislation, for juveniles, juvenile crime continues to decline.

There are also serious concerns by observers that the juvenile justice system discriminates on the basis of race. African-American and other minority youth are much more likely to be formally processed and end up in juvenile or adult facilities than whites. Poor kids are also more likely to be taken into the system. Part of this is because of lack of family support. Those juveniles who have families who are willing and likely to work with justice officials are more likely to be referred to community programs rather than institutionalization.

There are no easy answers for what to do with intractable juveniles. In some cases, kids sent to juvenile institutions are raped and abused by other kids. They, in turn, become more violent; and so are sent, after a more serious crime, to adult facilities, where they once again become prey for adult predators. It is highly doubtful that they will emerge as anything but bitter and damaged. Hate and rage are often the only emotions young offenders are familiar with.

QUOTE

. . . *juvenile institutionalization is for many youngsters a dehumanizing, brutal, and criminogenic experience. Exploitation has reached epidemic proportions in some training schools, where the weak give up everything, including their bodies, to the strong. Some youngsters come out of institutions psychologically devastated; others emerge much more committed to crime as a way of life and further alienated from conventional values and institutions than before they stay.*

Bartollas and Miller, 2001: 426.

Punishing White-Collar Criminals

In 2001 the public discovered that the Firestone tires used on the Ford Explorer were vulnerable to blowing out in high temperatures at a high rate of speed, causing rollovers. More than 100 fatal accidents were tied to tire blowouts. When this fact came to light, the media also reported that both the tire company and Ford Motor company knew about the tire's weakness and continued to use the tires on new Explorers. Angry consumers were even more enraged when they discovered that Ford had voluntarily replaced the tires and stopped using them on Ford vehicles sold overseas, but not in the United States. Ford eventually replaced 13 million tires at a reputed cost of $3 billion. A costly lesson, surely. But the financial loss was less costly than going to prison for knowingly exposing an unsuspecting public to a preventable risk.

Should Ford executives who knew of the test results have been held criminally culpable for their decision to continue to sell vehicles with the faulty tires? The case was similar to the infamous Ford Pinto case back in the 1970s, when it was discovered that there had been corporate knowledge that the gas tank would be more vulnerable to explosions, but a decision had been made that it was less costly to defend wrongful death suits than it would be to re-engineer the automobile. Ford executives were charged with negligent manslaughter, but were ultimately acquitted of criminal wrongdoing.

The difficulty in attaching criminal culpability to corporate criminals is that it is usually unclear who has responsibility for the decision that might form the offense. Thus, in a decision to continue marketing an unsafe product, no one person emerges as the clear culprit and everyone has an excuse as to why it was not his or her responsibility to do anything. Obviously such acts are not the same as taking a gun into a convenience store and shooting a clerk in the course of a robbery. On the other hand, if we accept as fact that some robbers end up killing their victim unintentionally, is the corporate criminal any less morally culpable when participating in actions where deaths are weighed against profits and factored into the bottom line?

Fraud and other forms of white-collar crime are simpler. There is criminal intent and, therefore, more likely to be criminal prosecutions. The Enron executives who knew that their accounting practices were fraudulent and engaged in them to hide corporate losses and to obtain high bonuses for themselves were no different than criminals who use stolen credit cards or run a "scam" on an elderly victim. Yet some argue that the white-collar criminals do not "deserve" prison. Why? What is a just sentence for someone who engages in price-fixing, insider trading or other violations of the SEC, gouging, or other forms of corporate crime? What is a fair punishment for someone who dumps toxic waste because it is too expensive to dispose of properly and a community suffers high rates of cancer because of it?

In these cases, there is a perception that the individual is less "guilty" than a so-called street criminal. We seem to be much less forgiving toward poor burglars than rich embezzlers. Further, a sentence of prison seems somehow more punitive for them, and, indeed, it may be. Should that make a difference in the determination of punishment? If we do take into consideration that prison is a harsher sentence for an upper-class executive, then is that not somehow punishing the poor burglar for being poor?

VICTIM'S RIGHTS

In ancient codes of law, the focus was on compensating the victim. This focus changed to the state and punishment in English common law around the time of the Magna Carta (1215). Eventually, two systems of law developed, one to deal with private wrongs (civil law) and one to deal with public wrongs (criminal law). The two may overlap—a rape victim may sue her attacker in civil court concomitantly with a state prosecution; for example, the family of Nicole Simpson sued O. J. Simpson for wrongful death after he was acquitted in a criminal trial of the murder. This does not create double jeopardy, and because rules of evidence and standards of proof are different, one may be acquitted in a criminal trial and still be held responsible civilly. The legal theory of the state as opponent is that the harm done in any crime is only incidentally to an individual. The more important harm is the crime against the state, even though it is the individual victim who is injured.

Victimology has emerged as a separate discipline in criminology, and this focus may help to provide a better balance between state harm and individual harm. For instance, victims' rights bills provide various protections and rights to victims of crime. Although it is popular for politicians to campaign with a pro-victim, crime-control agenda, their message usually panders to the voting public's fears rather than sheds light on a complex social problem where there are at times no distinct lines between victims and offenders. The media also contributes to public fear and to the stereotype of the white middle-class victim and the lower-class minority criminal.

Actually, minority groups and the poor are much more likely to be victimized than the middle class. Most victims and offenders come from the same neighborhood. Criminals are often victims themselves of past or current crimes. Moreover, there are many more victims than those defined as such by the system. Customers of inner-city supermarkets that charge higher prices because they know their customers do not have transportation to shop competitively are victims of economic exploitation. There are victims of retail credit schemes in which furniture rental stores rent and repossess a single piece of furniture several times for multiple profits. There are victims of employers who pay less than minimum wage or suddenly do not pay at all because they know the employees will not protest—either because they are illegal aliens or because they desperately need the job. Finally, there are victims of slum landlords, who must pay rent or be evicted even though the apartment has a multitude of health and safety hazards. These victims are rarely considered part of the "crime problem."

The media might be most responsible for creating a false perception of crime. Whereas violence occupies up to three-quarters of all television news time, it is a small percentage of actual crime (Elias, 1986: 43). The constant barrage of murders, rapes, and robberies in television drama contributes to the public's general fear of crime, as does the local news media's sensationalistic treatment of such crimes even while ignoring more pervasive social problems. In fact, an individual is more likely to die of pneumonia, cancer, heart disease, household fires, auto crashes, or suicide than of homicide (Elias, 1986: 43). This is not to say that violent crime is not a problem, but there is disproportionate emphasis on violence relative to other types of victimization, and there is a tendency to present every criminal event as a case of pure innocence versus pure evil. See "In the News" for a further look at the media's role.

In the real world, most victims suffer relatively small losses but receive virtually no help at all from the system. Police do not respond at all to many burglary calls because there are so many calls and so little the police can do about them. Assault calls may be handled informally and cavalierly when the combatants are acquaintances or relatives. Victims rarely have much to do with the system unless a suspect is arrested, a rare occurrence in many categories of crime. When there is a prosecution, the victim might feel used by the system, because the goal is to get a conviction, not to provide aid or compensation. The prosecutor is more interested in how the jury will perceive the victim than how much the victim lost or suffered from the crime.

In the News

In 1997, two news stories raise questions of media ethics:

In one case, the terrible sexual abuse and murder of a child in a prominent family in Colorado created a media frenzy before police were able to identify any suspects. One tabloid published crime scene photos of the body, shocking even some hardened newspaper professionals by the insensitivity and gratuitousness of the graphic nature of the photos, not to mention the issue of how the photos were obtained. Should crime scene photos of murders be published? Should those who provided them be prosecuted?

In a Dallas case, two prominent athletes were accused of raping a young woman at gunpoint. The police department immediately held a news conference, and papers across the country and world reported the allegations, along with the past legal troubles of one of the athletes. The woman then recanted, and police and prosecutors charged her with providing a false report. Now some members of the media propose that they were "victims" of her false allegations, also claiming that the police department was at fault for having a news conference that they were bound to report. The athletes and their lawyers demanded that the media report the recantation with the same enthusiasm the initial allegations were reported. Should the police department hold news con-ferences when their only evidence is a victim's allegation? Should the media withhold the accused party's name in a rape charge as they do the rape victim's, at least until they have probable cause?

In the last twenty years, there has been a "rediscovery" of victims' rights (see the "Texas Crime Victims' Bill of Rights"). Many states have enacted victims' rights bills that enumerate various rights that victims have under the law. These rights may include being present at trial (circumventing procedural rules that exclude victim witnesses from the courtroom during other testimony), being notified of any hearing dates and plea-bargain arrangements, submitting a victim-impact statement to be considered during the sentencing decision, and being treated courteously and compassionately by all law enforcement and justice system personnel. Some of these bills have created victim-witness programs in police departments or prosecutors' offices that attend to the needs of victim witnesses. Duties of program personnel might include keeping victims informed of their case, providing information, accompanying victims in court, and helping them fill out victim-compensation forms.

Victim-compensation programs have been created in many states. These programs provide compensation for certain types of crime when the victim is without insurance or other means of reimbursement. Funding comes either through court costs paid into a general fund by all criminal offenders or through the state's general funds. Usually only violent crimes and not property crimes are targeted by such programs. However, they can provide help with such expenses as lost wages, hospital and doctor bills, and even burial expenses, whether or not the offender is arrested. Restitution programs are much more common today than they have been, and these programs do target property victims as well as victims of violent crime. However, restitution programs help only victims of criminals who are caught, and that, unfortunately, is not likely for crimes such as burglary or larceny.

Victims have a right to be treated fairly by the system. All people should be accorded the same level of service and treatment, regardless of who they are. The "bag lady" should receive the same care as the mayor if both are mugged. Victims should also receive the same consideration in any punishment decision. The amount of punishment inflicted on an offender should not be based on the economic or social status of the victim, any more than it should be based on the economic or social status of the offender.

Other issues are not so simple. For instance, should the victim have equal say in the amount of punishment? What if the prosecutor believes that a plea bargain of probation is sufficient punishment, considering the crime and the costs of a trial, but the victim demands imprisonment? Should a burglary victim have the right to veto a plea bargain? What about an assault victim? Some argue, in fact, that we have gone too far in catering to victims' rights and that the system is now oriented toward victim satisfaction, rather than justice (Stickels, 2003).

We spoke of mercy before; would not some argue that the state does not have the power to grant mercy, only the victim? These questions also relate to the decision to parole. Many states now have procedures whereby the victim or the victim's family has the right to address the parole board when the criminal's parole date comes up. Should these victims have the right to veto parole when the board would have otherwise paroled the criminal? We characterize

Texas Crime Victims' Bill of Rights

A victim of a violent crime is (1) someone who has suffered bodily injury or death or who is the victim of sexual assault, kidnapping or aggravated robbery, (2) the close relative (spouse, parent, or adult brother, sister or child) of a deceased victim, or (3) the guardian of a victim. As a victim of violent crime, close relative of a deceased victim or guardian of a victim, you have the following rights:

1. The right to receive from law enforcement agencies adequate protection from harm and threats of harm arising from cooperation with prosecution efforts.
2. The right to have the magistrate take the safety of the victim or his family into consideration as an element in fixing the amount of bail for the accused.
3. The right, if requested, to be informed of relevant court proceedings and to be informed if those court proceedings have been canceled or rescheduled prior to the event.
4. The right to be informed, when requested by a peace officer concerning the defendant's right to bail and the procedures in criminal investigations and by the district attorney's office concerning the general procedures in the criminal justice system, including general procedures in guilty plea negotiations and arrangements, restitution, and the appeals and parole process.
5. The right to provide pertinent information to a probation department conducting a pre-sentencing investigation concerning the impact of the offense on the victim and his family by testimony, written statement, or any other manner prior to any sentencing of the offender.
6. The right to receive information regarding compensation to victims of crime as provided by Subchapter B, Chapter 56, including information related to the costs that may be compensated under the Act and the amounts of compensation, eligibility for compensation, and procedures for application for compensation under that Act, the payment for a medical examination under Article 56.06 of this code for a victim of a sexual assault, and when requested, to referral to available social service agencies that may offer additional assistance.
7. The right to be informed, upon request, of parole procedures, to participate in the parole process, to be notified, if requested, of parole proceedings concerning the defendant in the victim's case, to provide to the Board of Pardons and Paroles for inclusion in the defendant's file information to be considered by the Board prior to the parole of any defendant convicted of any crime subject to this Act, and to be notified, if requested, of the defendant's release.
8. The right to be provided with a waiting area, separate or secure from other witnesses, including the offender and relatives of the offender, before testifying in any proceeding concerning the offender, if a separate waiting area is not available, other safeguards should be taken to minimize the victim's contact with the offender and the offender's relatives and witnesses, before and during court proceedings.
9. The right to prompt return of any property of the victim that is held by a law enforcement agency or the attorney for the state as evidence when the property is no longer required for that purpose, and

---

Texas Crime Victims' Bill of Rights (continued)

10. The right to have the attorney for the state notify the employer of the victim, if requested, of the necessity of the victim's cooperation and testimony in a proceeding that may necessitate the absence of the victim from work for good cause, and

11. (a) The right to counseling, on request, regarding acquired immune deficiency syndrome (AIDS) and human immunodeficiency virus (HIV) infection and testing for acquired immune deficiency syndrome, human immunodeficiency virus (HIV) infection, antibodies to HIV, or infection with any other probably causative agent of AIDS, if the offense is an offense under Section 21.11(a)(1), 22.011, or 22.021, Penal Code.

    (b) A victim is entitled to the right to be present at all public court proceedings related to the offense, subject to the approval of the judge in the case.

    (c) The office of the attorney representing the state, and the sheriff, police, and other law enforcement agencies shall ensure to the extent practicable that a victim, guardian of a victim, or close relative of a deceased victim is afforded the rights granted by Subsection (a) of this article and, on request, an explanation of those rights.

    (d) A judge, attorney for the state, peace officer, or law enforcement agency is not liable for a failure or inability to provide a right enumerated in this article. The failure or inability of any person to provide a right or service enumerated in this article may not be used by a defendant in a criminal case as a ground for appeal, a ground to set aside the conviction or sentence, or a ground in a habeas corpus petition. A victim, guardian or a victim, or close relative of a deceased victim does not have standing to participate as a party in a criminal proceeding or to contest the disposition of any charge.

SOURCE: Texas Code of Criminal Procedure, Art. 56.02.

---

the victim's feelings of vengeance as personal revenge and the state's as retribution or justice, with the implication that one is bad and the other is good. In fact, victims who "take the law into their own hands" become criminals themselves. But why is the state's determination of sufficient punishment any better than the victim's? Supposedly, it is because the state has the power to objectively and rationally determine the correct measurement, but if there are other variables at work, such as goals of efficiency and convenience, then where is the objective measurement of punishment? Favoritism, bribery, and incompetence may also affect outcomes. Obviously, in these cases neither the victim nor the offender receives justice.

Some mistrust the current interest in victims' rights and believe that this recent concern is really a cynical manipulation of victim witnesses to advance the goal of making them better witnesses for the state. Also, because the definition of the victim continues to be narrow and limited to stereotypes, obfuscation about who are victims continues. This serves to blind those most at risk to the realities of their own victimization and to protect those who victimize in ways other than street crimes, such as white-collar and social crimes (Elias, 1986).

Victim Precipitation

Victim precipitation refers to the victim's role in the criminal event. Some people fear that this examination has the potential to blame the victim for the crime rather than the offender. Nevertheless, some research indicates that the victim plays a significant part in some types of crime (Karmen, 1984: 78). Retributive justice would consider instances where the victim "caused" victimization by enraging or threatening the offender, or precipitated victimization by engaging in careless or dangerous behavior. This does not mean that individuals who go out late at night deserve to be robbed or that women who are out alone drinking deserve to be raped.

Victim precipitation refers to those situations where, for instance, batterers taunt their victims to shoot them and they do. In this case, the batterer is ostensibly the victim because he has been shot, but an examination of his conduct would reveal that the so-called offender is also a victim and that the batterer's own behavior largely contributed to his victimization. In barroom brawls, pure luck often determines who becomes the injured and who becomes the offender. In these situations, the victim actually participates in the criminal event. We might allow for partial culpability, since the responsibility for the crime must be shared by both the offender and the victim.

The point is that the media and the justice system seem to conspire to paint a picture where there are perfectly innocent victims and purely evil offenders. The real world doesn't work that way. That may be the case with some crime, but more often, the offender may also be a victim, and the victim might not be purely innocent. It does not mean the justice cannot be served, but it does mean that there are no simply answers.

Restorative Justice

Our current system of justice is oriented completely to the offender. What would a system be like if the emphasis was on the victim's rights, needs, and compensation? In a system with a primary emphasis on the victim rather than the offender, money would be spent on victim services rather than prisons. It would be victims who received job skills training, not offenders. Some of the money that now goes to law enforcement and corrections would be channeled to compensation programs for victims of personal and property crimes. Victims would be helped even if their offenders were not caught. The major goal would not be punishment, but service. Offenders would be peripheral figures; they would be required to pay restitution to victims, and punishment would occur only if they did not fulfill their obligation to their victims. Could such a system work? Would such a system provide better justice?

Although the *restorative justice movement* does not propose quite this radical restructuring it does dramatically redesign the justice system and offers a new alternative to retributive justice. **Restorative justice** is a term used to describe a number of programs that seek to move compensation back to center stage in the justice system, rather than retribution. Programs that require the offender to confront the victim and provide compensation, and programs that place the victim in the middle of the process of deciding what to do about the offender can be categorized under the restorative justice rubric. The propositions of the movement are as follows:

1. Justice requires restoring victims, offenders, and communities who have been injured by crime.
2. Victims, offenders, and communities should have the opportunity to be a fully active part of the justice process.
3. Government should restore order, but the community should establish peace (Van Ness and Strong, 1997).

This approach has also been called a *peacemaking approach* and is quite consistent with the ethics of care, the ethics of virtue, and probably utilitarian ethics (Braswell, et. al., 2002). Although it does have some critics (Dzur and Wertheimer, 2002), it seems to offer an alternative to retributive justice that might benefit both offender and victim.

QUOTE

I have by degrees given up my faith in the rule of law. It is not only that the relatively absolute power we give lawgivers and law enforcers tends to corrupt these power holders absolutely. It is that imposing a pre-existing law or rule on someone literally amounts to letting one's prejudices override one's capacity to hear the many and various explanations and desires parties have.

Pepinsky, H. 1999: 64.

IMMORAL LAWS
AND THE MORAL PERSON

In the section discussing legal moralism, we discussed laws that prohibit behaviors that are judged as immoral, at least by some part of the population. In this section, we will look at laws and governmental edicts that are themselves immoral. Examples might include the laws of the Spanish Inquisition permitting large numbers of people to be tortured and killed for having different religious beliefs from the crown, or the laws of Nazi Germany demanding that Jews give themselves up to be transported to concentration camps and often death. Examples in this country might include the internment laws during World War II that forced American citizens of Japanese descent to give up land and property and be confined in internment camps until the end of the war, or the segregationist laws that once forced blacks to use different building entries and water fountains. These laws are now thought of as immoral, but they were not at the time.

The most common example of immoral laws are those that deprive certain groups of liberty or treat some groups differently, either giving them more or fewer rights and privileges than other groups. Most ethical systems would condemn such laws, and an objective ethical analysis would probably prevent the passage of such laws in the first place.

The example of Japanese American internment can be used to illustrate how one might use the ethical systems to judge a specific law. The religious ethical framework would probably not provide moral support for the action because it runs contrary to some basic Christian principles, such as "Do unto others as you would have them do unto you." Ethical formalism could not be used to support this particular law because it runs counter to the categorical imperative that each person must be treated as an end rather than as a means, and to the universalism principle. The principle of forfeiture could not justify the action since these were innocent individuals, many of whom were fiercely loyal to the United States. The only ethical framework that might be used to support the morality of this law is utilitarianism. We must be able to show that the total utility derived from internment outweighed the negative effect it had on the Japanese Americans who lost their land and liberty. Did it save the country from a Japanese invasion? Did it allow other Americans to sleep better at night? Did the benefits outweigh the harm to Japanese Americans?

Are there any laws today that might be considered immoral? After the World Trade Center attack, there was some discussion of deporting all those of Middle Eastern origin, regardless of their immigration status. This idea was rejected, perhaps partly because moral hindsight has shown that the Japanese internment was a flawed response to the fear created by World War II. We have, however, rounded up thousands of illegal aliens and are holding them without due process protections. How does this action compare with internment?

In other countries the legal climate has allowed torture and death squads to be used against political dissidents. If you lived in a South American country and knew of assassinations by government police and nighttime kidnappings and disappearances, would you follow a law that required you to turn in political subversives? If you lived in a troubled country in Europe, such as Bosnia, would you support a law that dispossessed a rival faction of their property? These issues are at the heart of our next discussion.

Can one be a moral person while enforcing or obeying an immoral law? Martin Luther King, Jr., Gandhi, and Thoreau agreed with St. Augustine that "an unjust law is no law at all." There is a well-known story about Henry David Thoreau, jailed for nonpayment of what he considered unfair taxes. When asked by a friend "What are you doing in jail?" Thoreau responded: "What are you doing out of jail?" The point of the story is that if a law is wrong, a moral person is honor-bound to disobey that law (see "Civil Disobedience").

If moral people disobeyed laws, what would happen to the stability of society? Another story concerns Socrates. About to be punished for the crime of teaching youth radical ideas, he had the opportunity to escape and in fact was begged by his friends to leave the country, yet he accepted the drink of hemlock willingly because of a fundamental respect for the laws of his country.

If we agree with the proposition that an unjust law is no law at all, we may set up a situation in which all citizens follow or disobey laws at will, depending on their own conscience. If one held a relativist view of morality, specifically the belief that one can intuit morals or decide morality on an individual basis, then two people holding different moral positions could both be right even though one position might be inconsistent with the law. An absolutist view holds that there is only one universal truth, which would mean that if one knew a law to be wrong based on this universal truth, then that person would be morally obliged to disobey the law. Evidently, either position could support civil disobedience.

QUOTE

Under a government which imprisons any unjustly, the true place for a just man is also a prison. . . .

Thoreau, quoted in Fink, 1977: 109.

[T]here are two types of laws[:] just and unjust. I would be the first to advocate obeying just laws. One has not only a legal but a moral responsibility to obey just laws. Conversely, one has a moral responsibility to disobey unjust laws.

Martin Luther King, Jr., quoted in Barry, 1985: ii.

Civil disobedience is the voluntary disobedience of established laws based on one's moral beliefs. Rawls (1971) defines it as a public, nonviolent, conscientious, yet political act contrary to law and usually done with the aim of bringing about a change in the law or policies of the government. Many great social thinkers and leaders have advocated breaking certain laws thought to be wrong.

Philosophers believe that the moral person follows a higher law of behavior that usually, but not necessarily, conforms to human law. However, it is an exceptional person who willfully and publicly disobeys laws he or she believes

---

Civil Disobedience

1. It must be nonviolent in form and actuality.
2. No other means of remedying the evil should be available.
3. Those who resort to civil disobedience must accept the legal sanctions and punishments imposed by law.
4. A major moral issue must be at stake.
5. When intelligent men [sic] of good will differ on complex moral issues, discussion is more appropriate than action.
6. There must be some reason for the time, place and target selected.
7. One should adhere to "historical time."

SOURCE: Hook, quoted in Fink, 1977: 126–127.

to be wrong. Psychological experiments show us that it is difficult for individuals to resist authority, even when they know that they are being asked to do something wrong. The Milgram experiments are often used to show how easily one can command blind obedience to authority. In these experiments, subjects were told to administer shocks to individuals hooked up to electrical equipment as part of a learning experiment (Milgram, 1963).

Unbeknownst to the subjects, the "victims" were really associates of the experimenter and only faked painful reactions when the subjects thought they were administering shocks. In one instance, the subject and "victim" were separated, and the subject heard only cries of pain and exclamations of distress, then silence, indicating that the "victim" was unconscious. Even when the subjects thought they were harming the "victims," they continued to administer shocks because the experimenter directed them to do so and reminded them of their duty (Milgram, 1963).

Although it is always with caution that one applies laboratory results to the real world, history shows that individual submission to authority, even immoral authority, is not uncommon. Those who turned in Jewish neighbors to Nazis or those who participated in massacres of Native Americans in this country were only following the law or instructions from a superior authority. To determine what laws are unjust, King used the following guidelines: "A just law is one that is consistent with morality. An unjust law is any that degrades human personality or compels a minority to obey something the majority does not adhere to or is a law that the minority had no part in making" (quoted in Barry, 1985: 3).

To explore this issue further, one could refer to the two paradigms of conflict and consensus discussed in the previous chapter. The consensus view of society would probably provide a stronger argument for the position of following laws whether one agrees with them or not. However, the conflict and pluralist perspectives hold that laws may be tools of power and are not necessarily the embodiment of the will of the people; therefore, individuals may legitimately disagree with immoral laws and have a duty to disobey them. From another perspective, Kohlberg might propose that only individuals who have reached higher stages of morality would think to challenge conventional definitions of right and wrong.

There is a widespread belief that law is synonymous with morality and that as long as one remains inside the law, one can be considered a moral person. Callahan (1982: 64) points out the following:

> We live in a society where the borderline between law and ethics often becomes blurred. For many, morality is simply doing that which the law requires; a fear of punishment is the only motivation for behavior in some minimally acceptable way.

Obviously, Callahan is concerned with the false perception of law as a total representation of morals. Most of us struggle to achieve goodness using the definitions of the society we live in; very few reach beyond accepted definitions to meet a higher standard of morality. Luckily, most of us have little need to—or do we?

> ### QUOTE
>
> *What there was, from the start, was the great silence, which appears in every civilized country that passively accepts the inevitability of violence, and then the fear that suddenly befalls it. That silence which can transform any nation into an accomplice. The silence which existed in Germany, when even many well-intentioned individuals assumed that everything would return to normal once Hitler finished with the Communists and Jews. Or when the Russians assumed that everything would return to normal once Stalin eliminated the Trotskyites. Initially, this was the conviction in Argentina. Then came fear. And after the fear, indifference. "Nothing happens to someone who stays out of politics." Such silence begins in the channels of communication. Certain political leaders, institutions, and priests attempt to denounce what is happening, but are unable to establish contact with the population. The silence begins with a strong odor. People sniff the suicides, but it eludes them. The silence finds another ally: solitude. People fear suicides as they fear madmen. And the person who wants to fight senses his solitude and is frightened.*
>
> ---
>
> Jacobo Timerman, *Prisoner Without a Name, Cell Without a Number,* trans. Toby Talbot (New York: Knopf, 1981): 51. Reprinted with permission of Alfred A. Knopf, Inc.

Remember that civil disobedience occurs when the individual truly believes the law to be wrong and therefore believes the enforcement of or obedience to it would also be wrong. We are not referring to chronic lawbreaking because of immediate rewards. Indeed, most criminals have a fairly conventional sense of morality. They agree with the laws, even though they break them. Even those gray-area laws that involve disagreement over the "wrongness" of the behavior are not proper grounds for disobedience unless one believes that the government is immorally oppressing certain people.

The Criminal Justice Professional

For the criminal justice professional who must uphold the law, this discussion of law and morality is not just academic. Line staff often face questions of individual morality versus obedience and loyalty. The My Lai incident has almost passed out of this nation's consciousness, but at the time there was a great debate over whether soldiers should follow their superiors' orders blindly or make an independent assessment of the morality of the action. In this case, several officers were prosecuted by a military court for killing women and children in a village during the war in Vietnam without any evidence that they were a threat to the unit's safety.

The officers' defense was that their superiors gave the orders to take the village without regard to whether the inhabitants were civilians or guerrillas. The rationale was that often there wasn't time to establish whether a civilian was friendly or not and that, in any event, civilians often carried grenades and otherwise harmed American troops.

There was heated public discussion in support of and against the soldiers' actions. Movies such as *Platoon* provide dramatic fictional accounts of other actions ordered by officers and the dilemmas of soldiers who knew such actions

re unethical and illegal. Is an individual excused from personal moral deci-
n making when following orders, or should one disobey orders that one
believes to be illegal or immoral? The Nuremburg war trials held individuals
personally accountable when they committed war crimes (defined as actions that
violated the Geneva Convention); whether they were following orders or not.

A soldier's dilemma is not all that different from a police officer's. At times
police officers may receive orders that they know to be illegal and/or unethical. The hierarchical nature of police work is very similar to the military, which
makes the analogy even more striking. Does the police officer (or any other
criminal justice professional) have the duty to make moral decisions and use
personal moral judgment, or is obedience to superiors mandatory?

Each individual is faced with moral choices in the course of her or his
career. Some of these choices are easy to make. However, some of the hardest
decisions involve going against superiors or colleagues. Even if the behavior is
obviously illegal, it is difficult to challenge authority; and when the accepted
pattern of behavior has the law on its side, very few of us take an individual
stand against the law or practice.

⚜ QUERY

- If a police officer received orders to storm a hostage situation and there was
  certainty that many would be killed and there were other alternatives
  available, should he follow superiors' orders or refuse on the basis of his
  moral judgment?
- If a police officer was told to pick up an individual on minor charges
  repeatedly as a form of harassment to get the individual to serve as an
  informant, should she agree to do so or refuse?
- If an undercover officer was told to get the evidence "at any cost" even if it
  meant using drugs or sex to gain the trust of dealers, what should the
  officer do?
- If a prosecutor was trying a case and the judge was obviously biased against
  the accused and allowed many errors to occur that resulted in a violation of
  due process, should the prosecutor be thankful for good luck and accept an
  easy conviction or make a stand against the judge's actions?

Balancing Law and Justice

Legislators' passing of a law is only the first step in social control. In order for
the law to be effective, it must be enforced by law enforcement and violators
must be prosecuted and punished. We know that the discretion present in each
step of the criminal justice system creates a situation in which written laws do
not necessarily represent the reality of enforcement. Police departments create
prostitution crackdowns, traffic ticket "blizzards," drug sweeps, and pornography raids with more or less cyclical patterns, sometimes in response to political pressure, sometimes not. The enforcement is, for the most part, independent
of legislative intent. In this sense, police are *de facto* definers of the law.

If we see laws as an "ought" in societal definitions of misbehavior, then
enforcement policies must be viewed as the "is" of what is tolerated and what

is not. Many laws on the books are routinely ignored and forgotten, especially in the area of private behavior. One might ask why such laws are not thrown out as irrelevant to the times in which we live. The reason they continue to exist is that no politician is going to champion removal of "ought" laws because it would seem that he or she was in favor of the behavior that the law defines as immoral. Therefore, in some states there are still laws against private sexual behavior, "blue" laws restricting business activity or the sale of liquor, and so on. On the other hand, some argue that to have laws that are ignored endangers the credibility of the entire legal system.

Studies indicate that most corruption and graft come from those gray areas of crimes such as prostitution, gambling, and drugs. It is easy to explain the emergence of unethical behavior by criminal justice professionals in these areas since such crimes do not have the same moral sentiments behind them as do "serious crimes," such as murder and child molestation. Many police officers who would have no problem letting a prostitute go free will risk their lives to catch a child killer. Part of this discretionary enforcement comes from a personal perception of the immorality of the behavior and also a perception of society's tolerance or intolerance of such behavior.

Individual officers often administer what has been called **street justice.** For instance, when a store owner has a legal right to prosecute a shoplifter, but the shoplifter is 87 years old, poor, and shoplifting food so she can eat, the police officer might try to convince the store owner not to prosecute in an attempt to soften the harshness of the law. Prosecutors may "lose" evidence in a subjective judgment that a criminal defendant doesn't need to be prosecuted. Alternatively, police may differentially enforce the law against those whom they consider "assholes," and prosecutors may ask for continuances to keep a defendant in jail, knowing that the case will ultimately be dismissed. The trouble with street justice and de facto justice is that once law is ignored in favor of individual application of subjective justice, individual definitions on what is "fair" and "just" may be arbitrary and capricious.

Spader (1984) discusses discretion and the rule of law as *a golden zigzag* between fundamental values. In this discussion, discretion has positive and negative elements, as does the rule of law. Of course, the ideal is to use discretion wisely in pursuit of ethical goals. See "Spader's Rule of Law Versus Rule of Man."

Criminal justice professionals can be seen as mediating the harshness and inflexibility of law in the application of street justice; however, it is also recognized that the same discretion that allows them to perform benevolent acts allows them to act in arbitrary and oppressive ways as well. The moral commitment that professionals have toward the laws they are supposed to uphold influences their actions. Soldiers are more loyal when they believe in the morality of the war. Police are more determined when they believe in the laws they are enforcing. Prosecutors and defense attorneys are more committed to due process when they believe in it. Correctional officials are less likely to allow prisoners to corrupt them when they have a strong sense of their goals. And all criminal justice professionals are more likely to operate in an ethical manner when they believe in the validity and justness of the system that

Spader's Rule of Law Versus Rule of Man

Rule of Law (Positives)	*Rule of Man* (Positives)
equal protection, evenhandedness, due process, fairness, rationality, notice, visibility, predictability, centralized limits on power, universality	individualization, flexibility, mercy, compassion, equity, creativity, adaptability, informality, efficiency
(Negatives)	(Negatives)
inflexibility, harshness, rigidity, mandatory legalism, technicalities, red tape, blind formalism, inefficiency	disparity, inconsistency, arbitrary and capricious abuse, uncertainty, invisibility, uncontrolled provincialism

SOURCE: Adapted from D. Spader, "Rule of Law v. Rule of Man: The Search for the Golden Zigzag Between Conflicting Fundamental Values." *Journal of Criminal Justice* 12 (1984): 379–394.

employs them. In the following chapters we will look more closely at some of the ethical decisions that criminal justice practitioners are forced to make and the moral dilemmas that confront them.

CONCLUSION

In this chapter we have explored a few additional issues in the relationship between justice and the law. We first looked at the two major justifications for laws, and then examined issues of culpability. Certain groups were identified that had special issues of culpability, such as the mentally ill, juveniles, and white-collar criminals. We also explored the relationship between victims and offenders, and noted that the trend toward victims' rights could focus solely on retribution or it could move toward a restorative justice approach that carries the potential of leaving the victim more fully compensated than retributive justice models. We looked at the issues concerning civil disobedience. Can one be a moral person and obey an immoral law? What makes a law immoral? We also explored the role of the criminal justice professional. Our final discussion of how criminal justice professionals balance law and justice begins the application of these ethical issues to the criminal justice professional.

REVIEW QUESTIONS

1. What are some justifications for law?

2. What are the arguments for and against paternalistic laws?

3. What is the McNaughton rule?

4. What are some recent laws passed to control crime by juveniles.

5. What are victims' bills of rights?

6. Explain victim precipitation.

7. Define and give examples of civil disobedience. What are the principles?

ETHICAL DILEMMAS

Situation 1

You ride a motorcycle, and you think it is much more enjoyable to ride without a helmet. You also believe your vision and hearing are better without one. Your state has just passed a helmet law, and you have already received two warnings. What will you do? What if your child was riding on the motorcycle? Do you think your position would be any different if you had any previous accidents and had been hurt?

Situation 2

You are asked to enforce a law that you believe to be wrong. For instance, you are supposed to protect a member of the Ku Klux Klan during a speech when your feelings are directly contrary to the views expressed by this individual, and you don't believe he should have the right to speak. What would you do? What would you do if you were told to deliberately perform your job in such a way as to ensure that the speaker be injured by a hostile crowd?

Situation 3

You are a D.A. and are prosecuting a burglary case. The defendant is willing to plead guilty in return for a sentence of probation, and you feel that this is a fair punishment because your evidence may not support a conviction. However, the victims are upset and want to see the offender receive prison time. They insist that you try the case. What should you do?

SUGGESTED READINGS

Arrigo, B. 1999. *Social Justice/Criminal Justice*. Belmon, CA: Wadsworth.

Crank, J. 2002. *Imagining Justice*. Cincinatti, OH; Anderson Publishing Co.

Van Ness, D. and K. Heetderks Strong. 1997. *Restoring Justice*. Cincinnati, OH: Anderson Publishing Company.

6

The Ethics
of Social Control

Key Terms

public servants
authority
power
persuasion
force

group think
discretion
discrimination
duty
zero tolerance policy

Chapter Objectives

- Understand the role of law enforcement in a democracy, including the use of authority, power, force, and persuasion.
- Compare the formal ethics of law enforcement with the values of the subculture.
- Explore the limits of discretion and corresponding duties for law enforcement officers.

The images of the Rodney King beating are indelibly imprinted on the psyche of the American public. In this one violent encounter, many of the elements discussed in this chapter are reflected:

- The "signification" of some citizens as criminal and deserving of greater police scrutiny;

- The P.O.P.O. ("pissing off a police officer") doctrine that describes how affronts to police authority often end in unethical uses of force;

- The quick resort to violence in a department that encouraged aggressive "crime control" police performance;

- The subcultural and organizational support and/or tolerance for such violence (evidenced by the computer messages that joked about it afterward);

- The initial easy acceptance of police and media definitions that justified such violence against some types of citizens (specifically, early reports indicating that Rodney King was a criminal, that he was a drug user, with the implication, therefore, that he deserved what happened to him); and, finally,

- The presence of societal divisions based on race and socioeconomic circumstance that shaped the perception of the justice.

Arguably, the Simi Valley jury acquitted the officers because white, middle-class citizens must (and do) see their police force as good; therefore, they couldn't believe that kind of incident could exist and the "good guys" could be bad. The guilty verdict in Los Angeles County was also predictable because, in this world, doubt permeates public attitudes toward police—doubt that they tell the truth and doubt that they don't beat people.

Other cases also indicate there is a crisis of credibility with at least some police departments in this country. The O. J. Simpson trial was as much a trial of police credibility as it was the guilt or innocence of the defendant. It indicated in a dramatic way what happens when doubt replaces trust in police performance, and when police testimony is received with suspicion rather than credence. The credibility of L.A.P.D. officers was under attack again after the Ramparts Division scandal. The highly publicized finding that some officers manufactured evidence, planted guns on suspects, and lied on the witness stand has inflicted a grievous harm to the credibility of all L.A.P.D. police officers. Other cities are not exempt. The Amadou Diallo case in New York City was moved to Albany, arguably so that the police officer defendants who shot an unarmed Diallo could obtain a fair trial. And perhaps it was fair, but African Americans in New York City, who have been subjected to what they perceive as a consistent pattern of oppression and brutality by some New York City police officers will never be convinced of this definition of justice.

THE POLICE ROLE IN SOCIETY

Crime Fighter or Public Servant?

We take a critical look at law enforcement in this and the next two chapters. It is important to keep in mind as we discuss issues of law enforcement ethics that the majority of officers are honest and ethical and spend their careers simply trying to do a good job. These men and women usually do not appear in newspapers or on the evening news, but they pay the price for the few who do through decreased pubic confidence and even public scorn. We are concerned with individual deviance in these chapters, but even more so with institutionalized tolerance of such deviance, and the perceptions, world views, and values that shape and influence such tolerance. Honest and ethical officers shirk their responsibility when they allow their fellow officers to act above the law. Even more troubling is when those officers who do expose wrongdoing are isolated and ridiculed, or receive even worse forms of peer sanctions. Why do police—who supposedly are the law's agents—flaunt the law when fellow officers are involved?

Harsh scrutiny is often directed at police actions; officers feel that they are treated unfairly by the public and the media. However, there is a very important reason for such scrutiny—the police represent the "thin blue line" between disorder and order, between the "war of all against all" and law. No other criminal justice professional comes under so much constant and public scrutiny, but then, no other criminal justice professional wields so much discretion in so many situations. The scrutiny is understandable when one realizes that police are power personified. They often have the choice to arrest or not to arrest, to mediate or to charge, and in decisions to use deadly force, they even hold the power of life and death. Authority, force, discretion—these elements are inherent in the role of a law enforcement officer. Murphy and Moran (1981) describe police power in the accompanying quote.

QUOTE

[N]o other public figure, or indeed any other human being, possesses greater authority over personal destiny. A jury, after a lengthy court trial and painful deliberation, may find a defendant guilty of murder and recommend the death penalty; the judge may respond by invoking the death penalty after more painful deliberation within his own conscience; and, finally, then the state may actually carry out that execution—perhaps after a dozen or so years of experiencing one appeal after another exhausted. But the police officer, in one split second, without the benefit of law school or judicial roles or legal appeals, acting as judge, jury and executioner may accomplish the same final result.

SOURCE: Murphy and Moran, 1981: 291.

We will approach law enforcement with an underlying premise that what drives individual decisions on the part of law enforcement officers and society's reactions to them derives from a perception of their mission. If one views police as a *crime control force,* certain presumptions follow: first, that criminals are the "enemy" and fundamentally different from "good" people; second, that police are the "army" that fights the enemy, using any means necessary to control, capture, and punish them; finally, that "good" people accept and understand that police are in a "war" and must be allowed deference in their decision making because they—not us—are the experts and only they "know the enemy."

If one views police as **public servants,** other presumptions follow: first, that criminals are not a distinct group, that they shop, pay taxes, have kids and parents, and often are one's next-door neighbor; second, that police have limited ability to affect crime rates one way or the other since crime is a complex social phenomenon and, in fact, the history of law enforcement originates in order maintenance, not crime control; finally, that police as "public servants" serve *all* people, including criminals. In effect, there is no "enemy" or, if there is, then "the enemy is us."

Police perception of their role as crime fighters will lead to certain decisions in their use of force, their definition of duty, their use of deception and coercion, and other decisions. Public perception of the police role as crime fighters leads to a willingness to accept certain definitions and justifications of behavior: that drug addicts are crazed, that individuals beaten must have deserved it, that all defendants must be guilty, and so on. Typically, there is public outrage only when police accidentally violate the rights of the "good" guys, instead of the "bad" guys. When a white person is the target of police brutality, when the victim of deadly force turns out to be a middle-class insurance agent, or when the public is confronted with police officers brutalizing someone on the evening news, then the easy rationalization that people get what they deserve comes into question.

Alternatively, a perception of the police role as public servant implies a much more restrictive view of the use of force and the rejection of a utilitarian—"the ends (of crime control) justify the means"—decision-making approach in favor of an approach more protective of due process and equal protection. This would be a rights-based conception of social control. Law enforcement, above all, protects the rights of all citizens and, only in this way, escapes the taint of its historical role of tool of oppression for the powerful.

This discussion is based on Herbert Packer's (1968) model of law enforcement. He described a crime control orientation as operating under the following principles:

- Repression of criminal conduct is the most important function.
- Failure of law enforcement means the breakdown of order.
- Criminal process is the positive guarantor of social freedom.
- Efficiency is a top priority.
- Emphasis is on speed and finality.
- A conveyor belt is the model for the system.
- There is a presumption of guilt.

The due process model, on the other hand, operates on these principles:

- There is a possibility of error.
- Finality is not a priority.
- There is insistence on prevention and elimination of mistakes.
- Efficiency is rejected if it involves short cuts.
- Protection of process is as important as protection of innocents.
- The coercive power of the state is always subject to abuse.

The addition to Packer's original model that is proposed here is that, besides the emphasis on rights in the second model, law enforcement is also perceived as "owned" by all people, and, therefore, the public servant role is foremost. These two models are better understood if we take a brief look at the history of law enforcement in this country.

Kappeler, Sluder, and Alpert (1994: 41) discuss the early origins of law enforcement in this country as a model of service. Police were involved in social service activities: they ran soup kitchens, provided lodging for indigents, and spurred moral reform movements against cigarettes and alcohol. Of course, early law enforcement was also involved in social control and employed utilitarian violence—that is, they acted as the force for power holders in society and were union busters and political-machine enforcers. Such force was used frequently against immigrants and the poor.

There was also frequent graft and other forms of corruption in early police departments. Crank (2003: 70), for instance, discusses how police were involved in local political machines. They stuffed ballot boxes and coerced votes. Their graft was widely tolerated because of their meager salaries. In the 1940s, the Kefauver Committee revealed that Philadelphia police overlooked prostitution, gambling, and other forms of vice in exchange for $3,000 to $4,000 a month per precinct (Fogelson, 1977: 172).

The move toward police "professionalism," starting in the 1920s was spurred by several factors, one of which was to improve the image of police as *objective* enforcers of the law rather than enforcers for whoever happened to be in power. In effect, there was a real or perceived shift of police loyalty from political bosses to the law itself (Kappeler, 1994: 49; Fogelson, 1977). Part of this transformation involved the idea that police were crime fighters, professional soldiers in the war on crime—a concept that implies objectivity, professional expertise, and specialized training. This role deemphasized the social service role and ultimately led to policing characterized by detachment from the community being policed instead of integration in that community. In this new role, police were proactive, rather than simply reactive to public demands (Payne, 2002; Crank and Caldero, 2000).

Today, we can see the legacy of both the political enforcer role and the public service role, even though the professionalism model has been well-established for more than 50 years. Law enforcement is still involved whenever there are strikes or labor disputes. Its objective today is protection and enforcement of the law, rather than strike busting; however, some might argue this point. The clearest current example of this image, perhaps, was in December of 1999 when massive protests of the World Trade Organization set off the Seattle Riots. Police were both praised for their restraint and criticized for excessive violence in their use of rubber bullets, tear gas, and concussion grenades to disperse large groups of protesters and bystanders. The handling of the protests was described as swings of underreaction, which allowed protesters to damage downtown businesses, and overreaction, which enveloped bystanders and office workers in the techniques of crowd dispersal.

The early role of social service can be seen resurrected in the community policing movement, which involves having officers develop closer relationships with community leaders to help them solve some of the social problems that are believed to be associated with the development of disorder and lead to crime. Therefore, police officers may be involved in cleaning up parks, getting the city to raze abandoned houses, cleaning up graffiti, helping to start youth programs, and so on. The elements of community policing include the following:

- A move away from a position of anonymity to direct engagement with the community, which will give officers greater information about neighborhood problems;

- Freeing the officer from emergency response to engage in pro-active crime prevention.

- More visible operations that increase police accountability.

- Decentralized operations that lead to greater familiarity with specific. neighborhoods.

- Encouraging officers to see citizens as partners.

- Moving decision-making and discretion downward to patrol officers who know the neighborhood best.

- Encouraging citizens to take more initiative in preventing and solving crimes. (National Institute of Justice, 1992: 3)

Patrol officers' resistance to community policing models may make sense if one views neighborhood policing as trading in the "crime fighter" role for a much less esteemed "social worker" role.

It is important to understand that both the crime fighter and public servant role have the potential and capacity for wrongdoing. The professional crime fighter may trample rights in the interest of efficiency in catching criminals, and community police officers may be too eager to do the bidding of community members in controlling those who upset the "order" of the community (by overenforcement of noise ordinances or loitering laws). The point cannot be overemphasized that police officers have a type of power that very few groups possess. In the next section we will more carefully examine police power.

AUTHORITY AND POWER

Klockars (1984) describes police control as comprising the following elements: authority, power, persuasion, and force. **Authority** is the unquestionable entitlement to be obeyed that comes from fulfilling a specific role. Neither persuasion nor force is needed to achieve domination when one possesses authority. Police officers are usually obeyed simply when they tell a citizen to do something. We do what they tell us because of their uniform. A teacher has a type of authority in the classroom, and parents have authority over their own children (but not over others).

Power is similar to authority in that it is inherent in the role, and the individual merely draws upon it, but it is different from authority in that power implies that there might be resistance to overcome. It also implies that if there is resistance then it will be crushed—power is the means to achieve domination. Police power is symbolized by the baton, the handcuffs, and the power of arrest.

Persuasion may also be used in response to resistance but seeks to overcome it "by mobilizing signs, symbols, words, and arguments that induce in the mind of the person persuaded the belief that he or she ought to comply." Although those who have power don't need to use persuasion, they often do, in order to avoid the use of force.

Finally, **force** is different from the previous three means of control in that it is physical, whereas the other three are exercised through mental domination and control. When force is used, "the will of the person coerced is irrelevant" (Klockars, 1984: 532). Police show their ability to use force when they use their arrest power, or when they physically restrain and subdue an individual. Force is ultimately behind every position of authority.

Police exercise four different types of domination, from unquestioned authority to physical force. Why does law enforcement have the right to employ these types of control? "We give it to them" is the easy answer. Police power is a governmental right invested in federal, state, and local law-enforcement agencies. It means that these organizations, unlike almost any other except perhaps the military, have the right to control citizens' movements to the point of using physical and even deadly force to do so.

Cohen and Feldberg (1991) develop a careful analysis of and justification for police power and propose that it stems from the social contract. As discussed in an earlier chapter, Thomas Hobbes (1588–1679) and John Locke (1632–1704) created the concept of the social contract to explain why people have given up liberties in civilized societies. According to this theory, each citizen gives up complete liberty in return for societal protection against others. Complete freedom is given up in return for guaranteed protection. Police power is part of this *quid pro quo*—we give the police power to protect us, but we also recognize that this power can be used against us.

There are corollary principles to this general idea. First, each of us should be able to feel protected. If not, then we are not gaining anything from the social contract and may decide to renegotiate the contract by regaining some of the liberties given up. For instance, vigilante movements arise when the populace feels that they are not protected by formal agents of social control. Second, since the deprivations of freedoms are limited to those necessary to ensure protection against others, police power is circumscribed to what is necessary to meet the agreed-upon purpose. If police exceed this threshold, then the public rightly objects. Third, police ethics are inextricably linked to their purpose. If the social contract is the basis of their power, it is also the basis of their ethics. Cohen and Feldberg (1991) propose five ethical standards that can be derived from the social contract: fair access, public trust, safety and security, teamwork, and objectivity.

Delattre (1989) approaches police authority and power from a slightly different point of view. Delattre asserts that police, as public servants, need those qualities one desires in any public servant. He quotes James Madison, who stated that wisdom, good character, balanced perception, and integrity are essential to any public servant. Only if the person entrusted with public power has these qualities can we be assured that there will be no abuse of such authority and power: "Granting authority without expecting public servants to live up to it would be unfair to everyone they are expected to serve" (Delattre, 1989b: 79). In this proposition, the right to authority lies in the character of the person—if one has those virtues necessary to be a public servant, one has the right to use the authority invested in the role; if one does not have those virtues, then one should not be in that position to begin with.

Is it simply a matter of individual character, or can the organization train officers to use their authority ethically and wisely? How can the organization maximize the possibility of ethical action and minimize any abuses in the exercise of the four types of control? Formal codes of ethics for police agencies attempt to provide such guidance.

FORMAL ETHICS FOR POLICE OFFICERS

It is not uncommon to have a value system or a code of ethics to educate and guide the behavior of those who work within an organization; some organizations have both. An organizational value system identifies the mission and the important objectives of the organization. Just as individual values influence one's ethics, an organizational value system influences the ethics of the organization's members. For example, if a person's highest value is wealth, integrity may be sacrificed to achieve it; in a similar way, if the value system of an organization promotes profits over all else, customer satisfaction and quality may be sacrificed. A police department with a value system emphasizing crime control may allocate resources differently from one with a value system promoting community-oriented policing. Officers in these two departments may be rewarded differently, and the formal culture of the agency will encourage different behavior patterns.

A code of ethics is more specific to the behavior of the individual officer. A professional code of ethics addresses the unique issues and discretionary practices of that profession. Davis (1991) explains that there are three distinct kinds of codes: the first is an aspiration or ideal describing the perfect professional, the second provides principles or guidelines that relate to the value system of the organization, and the third provides mandatory rules of conduct that can serve as the basis of discipline. The code of ethics promulgated by the International Association of Chiefs of Police, which will be discussed shortly, is the first kind of code. It is an aspiration or ideal that describes the perfect police officer. All police departments also have an oath of office that is a shorthand version of the value system or code of ethics. For instance, in a typical oath of office, duties are described that relate to service to the community and the sacred trust it entails for the officer.

The Law Enforcement Code of Ethics

The International Association of Chiefs of Police promulgated the Law Enforcement Code of Ethics and The Canons of Police Ethics (see the boxes on pages 141 and 142), and many departments have used these or adapted them to their own situations. Even though the code has been widely adopted, there is some question as to its relevance to individual police officers (Felkenes, 1984; Johnson and Copus, 1981: 59–65).

One argument is that the code specifies such perfect behavior that it is irrelevant to the realities of most officers. The wide disparity between the code and actual behavior is detrimental to the validity and credibility of the code. For instance, Davis, referring to the code provision, "I will never act officiously or permit personal feelings, prejudices, animosities or friendships to influence my decisions," writes that "any officer who takes this mandatory language seriously will quickly learn that he cannot do what the code seems to require. He will then either have to quit the force or consign its mandates to Code Heaven" (Davis, 1991: 18). Others argue that the code is vague, confusing, and impractical (Felkenes, 1984: 212).

The opposing argument is that the code is valuable specifically because it provides an ideal for officers to aspire to. The code is a goal to work toward, not an average of all behaviors. It would be hard to be proud of a professional code that instructed an officer to be unbiased and objective *unless* there were personal reasons to favor one party or another, to be courageous *unless* personal danger were involved, or to be honest in thought and deed *unless* it didn't served egoistic purposes. Since the code describes the highest standard of policing, all officers can improve because no officer is perfect. However, Davis (1991) contends that an aspirational code cannot be used to judge or discipline behavior that falls short of it. This comment is no doubt true; that purpose is served by departmental policies and rule books, which are more objective and enforceable. A code is far more valuable as a motivator than as a discipline device, a symbol rather than a stick.

The principle of justice or *fairness* is the single most dominant theme in the law enforcement code. Police officers must uphold the law regardless of the offender's identity. They must not single out special groups for different treatment. Police officers must not use their authority and power to take advantage

---

Law Enforcement Code of Ethics

As a Law Enforcement Officer my fundamental duty is to serve mankind; to safeguard lives and property; to protect the innocent against deception, the weak against oppression or intimidation, and the peaceful against violence or disorder; and to respect the Constitutional Rights of all men to liberty, equality and justice.

I will keep my private life unsullied as an example to all; maintain courageous calm in the face of danger, scorn, or ridicule; develop self-restraint; and be constantly mindful of the welfare of others. Honest in thought and deed in both my personal and official life, I will be exemplary in obeying the laws of the land and the regulations of my department. Whatever I see or hear of a confidential nature or that is confided to me in my official capacity will be kept ever secret unless revelation is necessary in the performance of my duty.

I will never act officiously or permit personal feelings, prejudices, animosities or friendships to influence my decisions. With no compromise for crime and with relentless prosecution of criminals, I will enforce the law courteously and appropriately without fear or favor, malice or ill will, never employing unnecessary force or violence and never accepting gratuities.

I recognize the badge of my office as a symbol of public faith, and I accept it as a public trust to be held so long as I am true to the ethics of the police service. I will constantly strive to achieve these objectives and ideals, dedicating myself before God to my chosen profession . . . law enforcement.

SOURCE: Copyright by the International Association of Chiefs of Police. Reprinted by permission.

---

of people. They must avoid gratuities because these give the appearance of special treatment.

A second theme is that of *service*. Police officers exist to serve the community. Still another theme is the *importance of the law:* police are protectors of the Constitution and must not go beyond it or substitute rules of their own. Because the law is so important, police not only must be concerned with law-breakers, but also their own behavior must be totally within the bounds set for them by the law. In investigation, capture, and collection of evidence, their conduct must conform to the dictates of law.

The final theme is one of *behavior:* Police, at all times, must uphold a standard of behavior consistent with their public position. This involves a higher standard of behavior in their professional and personal lives than that expected from the general public (Bossard, 1981: 31).

These elements, the emphasis on service, justice for all groups, and higher standards for police behavior, are consistent with the *public servant paradigm* more so than the *crime fighter paradigm*. In fact, this may be why the code is perceived as vague and confusing, since the code promotes a public servant ideal, but police are, for the most part, taught and rewarded for the crime fighter stance.

Why is professional ethics important to law enforcement? First of all, ethics contributes to the image of law enforcement as a profession. Sykes (1989) writes that a profession includes a body of specialized, internationally recognized knowledge, a pre-professional education and continuing education, legal

Canons of Police Ethics

Article 1. Primary Responsibility of Job
The primary responsibility of the police service, and of the individual officer, is the protection of the people of the United States through the upholding of their laws; chief among these is the Constitution of the United States and its amendments. The law enforcement officer always respects the whole of the community and its legally expressed will and is never the arm of any political party and clique.

Article 2. Limitations of Authority
The first duty of a law enforcement officer, as upholder of the law, is to know its bounds upon him in enforcing it. Because he represents the legal will of the community, be it local, state, or federal, he must be aware of the limitations and proscriptions which the people, through law, have placed upon him. He must recognize the genius of the American system of government which gives no man, groups of men or institution absolute power, and he must insure that he, as a prime defender of the system, does not pervert its character.

Article 3. Duty to Be Familiar with the Law and with Responsibilities of Self and Other Public Officials
The law enforcement officer shall assiduously apply himself to the study of the principles of the laws which he is sworn to uphold. He will make certain of his responsibilities in the particulars of their enforcement, seeking aid from his superiors in matters of technicality or principles when these are not clear to him; he will make special effort to fully understand his relationship to other public officials, including other law enforcement agencies, particularly on matters of jurisdiction, both geographically and substantively.

Article 4. Utilization of Proper Means to Gain Proper Ends
The law enforcement officer shall be mindful of his responsibility to pay strict heed to the selection of means in discharging the duties of his office. Violations of laws or disregard for public safety and property on the part of the officer are intrinsically wrong; they are self-defeating in that they instill in the public mind a like disposition. The employment of illegal means, no matter how worthy the end, is certain to encourage disrespect for the law and its officer. If the law is to be honored, it must first be honored by those who enforce it.

Article 5. Cooperation with Public Officials in the Discharge of Their Authorized Duties
The law enforcement officer shall cooperate fully with other public officials in the discharge of authorized duties, regardless of party affiliation or personal prejudice. He shall be meticulous in assuring himself of the propriety, under the law, of such actions and shall guard against the use of his office or person, whether knowingly, or unknowingly, in any improper or illegal action. In any situation open to question, he shall seek authority from his superior officer, giving him a full report of the proposed service or action.

Article 6. Private Conduct
The law enforcement officer shall be mindful of his special identification by the public as an upholder of the law. Laxity of conduct or manner in private life, expressing either disrespect for the law or seeking to gain special privilege, cannot but reflect upon the police officer and the police service. The community and the service require that the law enforcement officer lead the life of a decent and honorable man. Following the career of a policeman gives

Canons of Police Ethics (continued)

no man special perquisites. It does give the satisfaction of safeguarding the American republic. The officer who reflects upon this tradition will not degrade it. Rather, he will so conduct his private life that the public will regard him as an example of stability, fidelity, and morality.

Article 7. Conduct Toward the Public
The law enforcement officer, mindful of his responsibility to the whole community, shall deal with individuals of the community in a manner such as will inspire confidence and trust. Thus, he will be neither overbearing nor subservient, as the individual citizen has neither an obligation to stand in awe of him nor a right to command him. The officer will give service where he can, and require compliance with the law. He will do neither from personal preference or prejudice but only as a duly appointed officer of the law discharging his sworn obligation.

Article 8. Conduct in Arresting and Dealing with Violators
The law enforcement officer shall use his powers of arrest in accordance with the law and with due regard to the right of the citizen concerned. His office gives him no right to prosecute the violator nor to mete out punishment for the offense. He shall, at all times, have a clear appreciation of his responsibilities and limitations regarding detention of the violator; he shall conduct himself in such a manner as will minimize the possibility of having to use force. To this end he shall cultivate a dedication to the service of the people and the equitable upholding of their laws whether in the handling of law violators or in dealing with the law abiding.

Article 9. Gifts and Favors
The law enforcement officer, representing government, bears the heavy responsibility of maintaining, in his own conduct, the honor and integrity of all governmental institutions. He shall, therefore, guard against placing himself in a position which any person can reasonably assume that special consideration is being given. Thus, he should be firm in refusing gifts, favors, or gratuities, large or small, which can, in the public mind, be interpreted as capable of influencing his judgment in the discharge of his duties.

Article 10. Presentation of Evidence
The law enforcement officer shall be concerned equally in the prosecution of the wrong doer and the defense of the innocent. He shall ascertain what constitutes evidence and shall present such evidence impartially and without malice. In so doing, he will ignore social, political, and other distinctions among the persons involved, strengthening the tradition of the reliability and integrity of an officer's word.

Article 11. Attitude Toward Profession
The law enforcement officer shall regard the discharge of his duties as a public trust and recognize his responsibility as a public servant. By diligent study and sincere attention to self-improvement he shall strive to make the best possible application of science to the solution of crime and, in the field of human relationships, strive for effective leadership and public influence in matters affecting public safety. He shall appreciate the importance and responsibility of his office, hold police work to be an honorable profession rendering valuable service to his community and the country.

SOURCE: Copyright by the International Association of Chiefs of Police. Reprinted by permission.

autonomy to exercise discretionary judgment, lateral movement, and author-ized self-regulation. According to some authors, since law enforcement is miss-ing certain of these elements, it cannot be defined as a profession.

Whether or not officers have "legal autonomy to exercise discretionary judg-ment" is perhaps the most important debate in this discussion. One argument is that officers have much less discretion to make decisions than is thought since they must abide by the law; however, others point out that officers are allowed the lat-itude to decide whether to write tickets and whether to handle neighbor disputes with formal arrest or informal threat. Sykes (1989) argues that because law enforcement is an example of a classic bureaucratic organization, with rules, super-visors, and many lines of authority, these reduce discretion and, therefore, the ele-ments necessary to meet a definition of a profession are missing. An alternative argument is that the nature of law enforcement involves problem solving; every situation is unique and must be handled differently, and "cookbook" approaches to law enforcement rarely work. These characteristics support the concept of the field as a profession.

One might also suspect that the discussion holds more interest for academics than for the officer on the street. Whatever one calls the job, it requires a certain set of skills, and some amount of discretion. Officers make decisions regarding the calls they respond to in very different ways. Ideally, a set of ethics will help the officer make these decisions in a lawful, humane, and fair manner. A code of ethics also helps engender self-respect in individual officers; self-pride comes from knowing that one has conducted oneself in a proper and appropriate manner.

Further, a code of ethics contributes to mutual respect among police offi-cers and helps in the development of an *esprit de corps,* and common goal. Agreement on methods, means, and aims is important to these feelings. As with any profession, an agreed-upon code of ethics is a unifying element. A code can help define law enforcement as a profession, since it indicates a willingness to uphold certain standards of behavior and promotes the goal of public service, an essential element of any profession.

The Police Subculture and Formal Ethics

Through a number of sources an image of the police and the police value sys-tem emerges that is very different from the value system prescribed by formal ethics. Research has found police officers to be generally cynical, isolated, alienated, defensive, distrustful, dogmatic, authoritarian, and having a poor self-image (Johnson and Copus, 1981: 52).

Scheingold (1984) describes the factors that lead to the extreme nature of the police subculture. They include the fact that police typically form a homogenous social group, they have a uniquely stressful work environment, and they partici-pate in a basically closed social system. Historically, police in the United States have come from the white middle and lower classes; they are similar racially, cul-turally, and economically. Because of these similarities, police feel themselves to be more similar to one another than to the public they encounter as a part of their job. Homogenous social groups lead to **group think;** everyone agrees with the group value or belief because to do otherwise would ostracize the individual. Police are further set apart by their work life. The job of a police officer entails a great deal of stress caused by danger and unpleasant experiences. Again, this results in the feeling that police are special and different from everyone else. Finally, because of strange working hours and social stigmatism, their social life tends to be totally involved with other police officers. This leads to closed viewpoints and legitimization of subcultural values (Scheingold, 1984: 97–100).

Themes and Value Systems Van Maanen (1978), in an early exploration of the police culture, discussed how police operate under a typology of the people with whom they come into contact. The individual who does not recognize their authority is "the asshole." Other names for this type of person include creep, animal, mope, rough, jerk-off, clown, or wise-guy, but the idea is the same—that some individuals are troublemakers, not necessarily because they have broken the law, but, rather, because they do not recognize police authority (1978: 227).

Van Maanen (1978: 226) observed that " . . . certain classes in society— for example, the young, the black, the militant, the homosexual—are . . . 'fixed' by the police as a sort of permanent asshole grouping." He argued that the professionalism movement of law enforcement might widen the distance between the police and the community they served, and further allow them to be "moral entrepreneurs" who were even more likely to define some groups as "bad" simply because they did not conform to some pre-conceived standards of behavior (1978: 236).

Sherman (1982: 10–19) also has described some common themes running through police attitudes. First, loyalty to colleagues is essential; second, the public, or most of it, is the enemy (echoing, to some extent, van Maanen's research). Further, he explains that the values of police officers include the use of force, discretion, and a protective use of the truth. This is further examined in the box "Police Values."

QUOTE

Some guys need a beating. In the street or the back of the precinct, there's a guy who needs a beating. And you got to do it. If you don't do it, the next situation that a cop runs into this character, it's going to be bad. It's hard for people to understand or believe that. But the fact of the matter is, if this guy runs into a cop, gets into a fistfight and really beats the shit out of him, he believes he can beat up all cops, if you arrest him without working him out. He's got to know that the next time he does this, he's going to get his ass kicked in. So I have no problem with that. Neither did any cop I've ever known have any problem with that. As long as you don't do it in public, as long as the guy really needs it, and as long as you don't carry it too far. . . .

Police Values

1. **Discretion A:** Decisions about whether to enforce the law, in any but the most serious cases, should be guided by both what the law says and who the suspect is. Attitude, demeanor, cooperativeness, and even race, age and social class are all important considerations in deciding how to treat people generally, and whether or not to arrest suspects in particular.

2. **Discretion B:** Disrespect for police authority is a serious offense that should always be punished with an arrest or the use of force. The offense known as "contempt of cop" or P.O.P.O. (pissing off a police officer) cannot be ignored. Even when the party has committed no violation of the law, a police officer should find a safe way to impose punishment, including an arrest on fake charges.

3. **Force:** Police officers should never hesitate to use physical or deadly force against people who "deserve it," or where it can be an effective way of solving a crime. Only the potential punishments by superior officers, civil litigation, citizen complaints, and so forth should limit the use of force when the situation calls for it. When you can get away with it, use all the force that society should use on people like that—force and punishment which bleeding-heart judges are too soft to impose.

4. **Due Process:** Due process is only a means of protecting criminals at the expense of the law abiding and should be ignored whenever it is safe to do so. Illegal searches and wiretaps, interrogation without advising suspects of their Miranda rights, and if need be (as in the much admired movie, *Dirty Harry*), even physical pain to coerce a confession are all acceptable methods for accomplishing the goal the public wants the police to accomplish: fighting crime. The rules against doing those things merely handcuff the police, making it more difficult for them to do their job.

5. **Truth:** Lying and deception are an essential part of the police job, and even perjury should be used if it is necessary to protect yourself or get a conviction on a "bad guy." Violations of due process cannot be admitted to prosecutors or in court, so perjury (in the serious five per cent of cases that ever go to trial) is necessary and therefore proper. Lying to drug pushers about wanting to buy drugs, to prostitutes about wanting to buy sex, or to congressmen about wanting to buy influence is the only way, and therefore a proper way, to investigate these crimes without victims. Deceiving muggers into thinking you are an easy mark and deceiving burglars into thinking you are a fence are proper because there are not many other ways of catching predatory criminals in the act.

6. **Time:** You cannot go fast enough to chase a car thief or traffic violator, nor slow enough to get to a "garbage" call; and when there are no calls for service, your time is your own. Hot pursuits are necessary because anyone who tries to escape from the police is challenging police authority, no matter how trivial the initial offense. But calls to nonserious or social-work problems like domestic disputes or kids making noise are unimportant, so you can stop to get coffee on the way or even stop at the cleaner's if you like. And when there are no calls, you can sleep, visit friends, study, or do anything else you can get away with, especially on the midnight shift, when you can get away with a lot.

Police Values (continued)

7. **Rewards:** Police do very dangerous work for low wages, so it is proper to take any extra rewards the public want to give them, like free meals, Christmas gifts, or even regular monthly payments (in some cities) for special treatment. The general rule is: Take any reward that doesn't change what you would do anyway, such as eating a meal, but don't take money that would affect your job, like not giving traffic tickets. In many cities, however, especially in the recent past, the rule has been to take even those rewards that do affect your decisions, as long as they are related only to minor offenses—traffic, gambling, prostitution, but not murder.

8. **Loyalty:** The paramount duty is to protect your fellow officers at all costs, as they would protect you, even though you may have to risk your own career or your own life to do it. If your colleagues make a mistake, take a bribe, seriously hurt somebody illegally, or get into other kinds of trouble, you should do everything you can to protect them in the ensuing investigation. If your colleagues are routinely breaking rules, you should never tell supervisors, reporters, or outside investigators about it. If you don't like it, quit—or get transferred to the police academy. But never, ever, blow the whistle.

SOURCE: Reprinted by permission from Sherman, L. "Learning Police Ethics." *Criminal Justice Ethics* 1(1) (1982): 10–19. Copyright 1982 by the John Jay College of Criminal Justice.

Scheingold (1984) has emphasized three dominant characteristics of the police subculture. First is the idea of cynicism. Police view all citizens with suspicion. Everyone is a possible problem, but especially those who fit a type, specifically, van Maanen's "asshole." Recruits learn this way of looking at others from older officers. Cynicism spills over to their relations with everyone, since they have found that friends expect favors and special treatment, and since police routinely witness negative behavior from almost all citizens. Their work life leads them to the conclusion that all people are weak, corrupt, and/or dangerous.

The second value is related to the use of force. The police subculture embraces force for all situations wherein a threat is perceived. Threats may be interpreted as threats against the officer's authority rather than the physical person, so anyone with an "attitude problem" is thought to deserve a lesson in humility. Force is both expressive and instrumental. It is a clear symbol of the police officer's authority and legitimate dominance in any interaction with the public, and it is also believed to be the most effective method of control. It cuts across all social and economic barriers and is the most effective tool for keeping people in line and getting them to do what is required without argument.

Finally, there is the idea that police are victims themselves. They are victims of public misunderstanding and scorn, of low wages and vindictive administrators. This feeling of victimization sets police apart from others and rationalizes a different set of rules for them (Scheingold, 1984: 100–104).

Crank and Caldero (2000) also discuss values of police. They report on research that shows police officers place less emphasis on independence and more emphasis on obedience. Crank (1998) discusses a number of "themes" of policing. These themes are not values *per se,* but rather, elements of police work and/or shared perceptions of police officers. The themes include coercive territorial control, force, illicit coercion, importance of guns, suspicion, danger, uncertainty, "maintaining the edge," seduction of excitement, and, crime (he argues police learn how to be criminals from expertise gained through policing), solidarity, and masculinity.

The Cop Code Many authors present versions of the informal "code of conduct" that new officers are taught through informal socialization. Muir (1977: 191) described some elements of the informal police code: "You cover your men: don't let any officer take a job alone," "Keep a cool head," and "Don't backdoor it," a prohibition against certain gratuities.

Reuss-Ianni (1983: 14) presents a very inclusive list:

- Watch out for your partner first and then the rest of the guys working that tour.
- Don't give up another cop.
- Show balls.
- Be aggressive when you have to, but don't be too eager.
- Don't get involved in anything in another guy's sector.
- Hold up your end of the work.
- If you get caught off base, don't implicate anybody else.
- Make sure the other guys know if another cop is dangerous or "crazy."
- Don't trust a new guy until you have checked him out.
- Don't tell anybody else more than they have to know; it could be bad for you and it could be bad for them.
- Don't talk too much or too little.
- Don't leave work for the next tour.

Code rules specific toward management include:

- Protect your ass.
- Don't make waves.
- Don't give them too much activity.
- Keep out of the way of any boss from outside your precinct.
- Don't look for favors just for yourself.
- Don't take on the patrol sergeant by yourself.
- Know your bosses.
- Don't do the bosses' work for them.
- Don't trust bosses to look out for your interest.

Loyalty One of the most consistent observations of the police subculture is that police have a fierce loyalty to other police officers. This loyalty is grounded in an "us versus them" attitude of police, that places all others even management, outside the group. Brown also describes police loyalty as arising from a fundamental distrust of superiors and bureaucratic administration (Brown, 1981: 82). Muir explains loyalty by reference to the complicity that develops when police engage in individual rule breaking; once a police officer has violated a standard or rule, he or she is bound to remain silent regarding others' violations, even if they are more serious (Muir, 1977: 67, 72).

This loyalty has a dark side. As Crank (1998: 203) put it:

> Aspects of police work that encourage police solidarity—social isolation, intense in-group dependence, the suspicions cops have of the public and the distrust they have of administrative brass, the powerful currents of safety and dependence on other officers in times of danger—become veils behind which corruption and illegal behavior can flourish.

A Different Culture? Scheingold (1984: 97) describes the police subculture as no more than an extreme of the dominant American culture; it closely resembles a conservative political perspective:

> If the police subculture is ultimately shaped by American cultural values, does it really make sense to talk about a separate subculture among American police officers? My answer is that the police subculture is not so much separate as an *in extremis* version of the underlying American culture. When Americans in general become preoccupied with crime, we also move in punitive directions, but our preoccupation with crime tends to be abstract and episodic. . . . The real difference between police officers and the rest of us is that coping with crime is their full-time job. There is, in short, reason to believe that they and we share the same values but that the police are distanced from us primarily by the nature of their work.

In other words, we all agree with certain elements of the police value system; if the general public is less extreme in its views, it is only because we have not had a steady diet of dealing with crime and criminal behavior as have the police. Furthermore, citizens are not too upset when the civil rights of "criminal types" are violated, only when police misbehavior is directed at "good" people.

The subculture and the values described above may be breaking down among police departments today. Several factors contribute to the possible weakening of the subculture. The increasing diversity of police recruits has eliminated the social homogeneity of the work force. Many diverse groups are now represented in police departments, including African Americans, Hispanics, women, and the college-educated, even if only in token numbers. These different groups bring elements of their own cultural backgrounds and value systems into the police environment.

Also, police unions with their increasing power formalize relationships between the line staff and the administration, and subcultural methods for coping with perceived administrative unfairness are becoming more formal than informal. Increasingly, individual officers, especially those who come from other backgrounds not tied in as strongly to police tradition, may challenge the informal system rather than ignore or go along with obvious misconduct or corruption. Finally, civil litigation has increased the risk of covering for another officer. Although police officers may lie to Internal Affairs or even on a witness stand to save a fellow officer from sanctions, they are less likely to do so when large monetary damages may be leveled against them because of negligence and perjury.

It is still safe to say that the police, like any occupational group, maintain an informal subterranean value system that guides and provides a rationale for decision making. This value system is more influential than the police rule book or code of ethics.

DISCRETION, DISCRIMINATION, AND DUTY

Discretion can be defined as the ability to choose between two or more courses of behavior. Law enforcement professionals have a great deal of discretion regarding when to enforce a law, how to enforce it, how to handle disputes, when to use force, and so on. Every day is filled with decisions—some minor, some major. **Discrimination** occurs when discretion allows a decision maker to treat a group or individual differently from others for no justifiable reason. **Duty** can be defined as the responsibilities that are attached to a specific role.

Discretion is by no means limited to law enforcement. In each of the subsequent chapters, we will see that discretion is an important element in the criminal justice practitioner's role and plays a part in the creation of ethical dilemmas. Discretion in criminal justice has been attacked as contributing to injustice. McAnany (1981) chronicles disillusionment with discretion, citing such works as Davis's *Discretionary Justice* (1973) and the American Friends Service Committee's *Struggle for Justice* (1971). An argument might be made that solutions that attempt to establish guidelines for discretion are unsatisfactory since the suggested rules and standards either limit decision making to mechanistic applications of given rules or provide only rhetorical ideals with little or no enforcement capability.

Discretion

Discretion is a necessary element in law enforcement, but the need for discretion also leads to a greater dependence on individual ethical codes in place of rules and laws. Patrol officers are the most visible members of the police force and have a duty to patrol, monitor, and intervene in matters of crime, conflict, accident, and welfare. Investigators are primarily concerned with collecting evidence to be used in court. The ethical decisions that these two groups encounter are sometimes different. Patrol officers may have to make decisions relevant to defining crime and initiating the formal legal process. Undercover officers must make decisions regarding informants, deception, and target selection. Managers and administrators have discretion in their decision-making role over their subordinates (Bossard, 1981: 25; Cohen, 1985). We should also

note that since most police departments in this country are small, many officers fulfill two or more functions, so their discretion crosses the boundaries
designated above.

Patrol officers possess a great deal of discretion in defining criminal behavior and deciding what to do about it. When police stop people for minor traffic violations, they can write tickets or give warnings. When they pick up
teenagers for drinking or other delinquent acts, they can bring them in for formal processing or take them home. After stopping a fight on the street, they
can arrest both parties or allow the combatants to work out their problems. In
many day-to-day decisions, police hold a great deal of decision-making power
over people's lives, because of their power to decide when to enforce the law.

One study found that police do not make arrests in 43 percent of all felony
cases and 52 percent of all misdemeanor cases (Williams, 1984: 4). The amount
of discretion and how it is used depend on the style of policing characteristic
of a certain area. For instance, the *legalistic* style of policing is described as the
least amenable to discretionary enforcement. In the *watchman* style, police
define situations as threatening or serious depending on the groups or individuals involved, and act accordingly. The *caretaker* style treats citizens differently, depending on their relative power and position in society (Wilson, 1976).

Brown describes four types of police officers, each with a different application of discretion: the *old style crime fighter*, who is concerned only with action
that might be considered crime control; the *clean beat officer*, who seeks to control all behavior in his jurisdiction; the *service style*, who emphasizes public
order and peace officer tasks; and the *professional style*, who is the epitome of
bureaucratic, by-the-book policing (Brown, 1981: 224).

Muir describes these four types: the *professional*, who balances coercion
with compassion; the *reciprocating officer*, who allows citizens to solve problems
and may engage in deals to keep the peace; the *enforcer*, who uses coercion
exclusively; and the *avoider*, who either cannot handle the power he or she must
use or fears it and so avoids situations where he or she may be challenged
(Muir, 1977: 145). Each of these descriptions is obviously more detailed than
our binary description of the crime control versus public servant model. However, all of these descriptions illustrate that different beliefs about their mission
and their role in society will affect officers' decisions.

The nature of policing necessarily involves some amount of discretion.
Cohen (1985; 1983) describes discretion as balancing justice for the individual
against justice for the group and points out that full enforcement would be
unfair at times to individuals. Even courts have seemed to support police discretion over full enforcement (Williams, 1984: 26). However, this opens the
door for unethical decisions. The power to make a decision regarding arrest
creates the power to make that decision using unethical criteria, such as not
arresting someone in return for a bribe (Brown, 1981: 160).

The Commission on Accreditation for Law Enforcement Agencies
promulgates standards, and one of the standards states that law enforcement
agencies should have "A written directive [that] defines the authority, guidelines, and circumstances where sworn personnel may exercise alternatives to
arrest. . . ." (CALEA, 1994).

Besides standard directives, perhaps another effective way to encourage using discretion in an ethical manner is to delineate ethical versus unethical criteria for decision making. For example, the decision to ticket a motorist stopped for speeding or to let him or her go with a warning can be made using ethical or unethical criteria. Ethical criteria might include:

the number of miles over the speed limit,

the amount of danger posed by the speeding (school zone or open road?),

the excuse used (emergency or late to work?), and probably others.

Unethical criteria might include:

sexual attraction (or not),

the identity of the motorist (fellow police officer, political figure, entertainment figure),

the race of the motorist,

the offer of a bribe, and so on.

Other factors are less clear: Is the fact of a quota an ethical or unethical criterion? What about attitude? Many officers explain that a person might get a ticket, even for a minor violation, if she or he displays a hostile or unrepentant attitude. Is this merely an egoistic use of power on the part of an officer or a utilitarian use of the ticket as a tool for social learning? After all, if the individual does not display any remorse, there is no assurance that the person won't commit the same violation as soon as the officer is out of sight.

Above the Law? Many officers defend the use of professional courtesy to other officers stopped for speeding. Justifications for different treatment are diverse and creative. For instance, some honest justifications are purely egoistic: "If I do it for him, he will do it for me one day." Other justifications are under the guise of utilitarianism: "It's best for all of us not to get tickets, and the public isn't hurt because we are trained to drive faster." If the officer would let another person go with a warning in the same situation, it is not an unethical use of discretion. However, if *every other person* would have received a ticket, but the officer did not issue one only because the motorist was a fellow officer, then that is a violation of the code of ethics (" . . . enforce the law . . . without fear or favor"). It is a violation of deontological universalism as well as utilitarianism: Under deontological ethics, it is the officer's duty to enforce the law; under utilitarianism, the fact that the speeding officer can cause an accident just as easily as a civilian motorist means that the utility for society is greater if the ticket is issued, because it might make the officer slow down. (See "Sorry, No Breaks!" for a unique example of zero favoritism.)

Discretion and Dilemmas Discretion also comes into play when the officer is faced with situations with no good solutions. Many officers agonize over family disturbance calls where there are allegations of abuse, or when one family member wants the police to remove another family member; other calls involve elderly persons who want police to do something about the "hood-

---

Sorry, No Breaks!

According to the *New York Times* (December 8, 1995), Game Warden Joseph Dedrick of Caroline County, Virginia, is not the type of person to let someone go with a simple warning. Dedrick, on his day off (November 21), apparently went quail hunting and was lucky enough to bag one bird. Upon telling a friend about it, though, he was informed that quail season did not open until November 27, and the friend produced a game department brochure as proof. Mr. Dedrick, who has been a game warden for 27 years, immediately called his lieutenant and said: "We're going to have to get a warrant on me." Dedrick charged himself with a misdemeanor (hunting out of season), for which a judge could fine him $25.00 to $1,000.00.

SOURCE: "Sorry, No Breaks!" *The Ethics Roll Call* 3(1) (1996): 2. Reprinted with permission.

---

lums" in the neighborhood, homeless people with small children who are turned away from full shelters, and victims of crime who are left without sufficient resources to survive. In response to all of these calls, officers must decide what course of action to take and can decide to do nothing at all.

Most ethical dilemmas that police officers face derive from their powers of discretion. These ethical dilemmas are part and parcel of the job. Muir describes moral dilemmas of the police officer as frequent and unavoidable, not academic, always unpopular with some groups, usually resolved quickly, dealt with alone, and involving complex criteria (Muir, 1977: 211).

Discrimination

When individuals have discretion, it is possible that individual prejudices and perceptions of groups such as women, minorities, and homosexuals influence decisionmaking. Officers' views of the world affect the way they do their job. If this view includes prejudicial attitudes toward groups, it may be that action is affected and those groups may not receive the same protections as "good" citizens. The point is not that police officers are more prejudiced than the rest of us; it is that their special position creates the possibility that their prejudices could cause a citizen to receive less protection from the law than other citizens would:

> Essentially, when police act on personal prejudices while performing their jobs, they discriminate in the allocation of either services or enforcement of the law. Discrimination often takes the form of either to enforce the law differentially or to withhold the protections and benefits of the law (Kappeler, Sluder, and Alpert, 1994: 175).

Sexual Orientation Kappeler, Sluder, and Alpert (1994: 176–184) discuss the case of Konerak Sinthasomphone—one of Jeffrey Dahmer's victims—as an example of police bias and discriminatory treatment of homosexuals and racial minorities. Sinthasomphone was the Laotian boy who was found wandering the street, incoherent, naked, and bleeding from the rectum. He had escaped from Dahmer's apartment after he had been drugged, tortured, and sexually abused. Two African-American women called the police; when the police arrived, the women tried to tell them that Sinthasomphone was an injured boy and that Dahmer was the one who hurt him. Despite the women's attempts, police officers on the scene helped Dahmer take Sinthasomphone back to his apartment and waved away emergency medical technicians who were starting to examine him. If they had, they would have discovered the holes that Dahmer had already drilled into his skull and the acid that he had poured into the holes. Dismissing the incident as a "homosexual thing," the officers left Sinthasomphone with Dahmer, who strangled him shortly after they left.

This case is not about a mistake in judgment on the part of police officers. Their conduct represents a pattern of enforcement that allots police protection based on membership in certain categorical groups. If the Laotian boy had been white, if he had been a she, if Dahmer had been a minority member instead of a Caucasian, if the two women who requested assistance had not been African American, we might have seen a different response. Even more telling was the fact that even though the police chief suspended the officers involved, they were supported by the police union and were ultimately reinstated with back pay. No further sanctions were taken against them. See the box "Dimensions of Police Discrimination" for other examples.

Race There is a pervasive sense among minority groups in this country that law enforcement is fundamentally racist (Cole, 1999; Walker, Spohn and DeLone, 2000). Some argue that this perception is based in reality. Crank (1998) is one researcher who argues that racial bias is "endemic" in police departments. Studies show that civil rights complaints against police are positively correlated to the percentage of minorities in the population, as well as income differential (Holmes, 2000).

Lower-class African Americans have significantly more negative interactions with police. More than twice as many report disrespectful language or swearing by police officers in surveys (Weitzer, 1999). Interestingly, middle-class African Americans express more negative attitudes toward police behaviors such as racial profiling than do lower-class African Americans. One speculation for this finding is that those who live in bad neighborhoods and experience the danger and inconvenience of prevalent criminality allow police more latitude to control those who "have it coming to them" (Weitzer, 1999: 838). In the "In the News" on page 156 one egregious case of police misconduct is highlighted. Although one officer is largely responsible for this travesty of justice it should not be forgotten that the system itself failed those who were innocent of wrongdoing.

Racial profiling occurs when a police officer utilizes a "profile" to stop a suspected drug dealer (or other criminal). The problem is that the so-called profile is based largely on race. When a young, black man is seen, for instance, driving a newer model, expensive car, police officers' suspicions arise and the young man is subjected to a "pretext stop." Police use some minor traffic offense to stop the individual and, in the course of the stop, look for other evidence of wrongdoing.

Dimensions of Police Discrimination

Administrators/Managers

Internal

Refusing to place female officers in "dangerous" assignments

Placing minority employees in undesirable assignments

Making promotion decisions on the basis of race/ethnicity or other factors not related to the ability to perform the job

Refusing to commend officers for exceptional performance on the basis of such factors as race/ethnicity, gender, age

Segregating in assignment's by assigning only African-American officers to work together as partners or Caucasian officers to work together as partners

Failing to take corrective action when subordinates discriminate against co-workers

External

Making selection decisions on the basis of such factors as race/ethnicity, gender, political, or religious affiliation

Refusing to respond to complaints by minority citizens or neighborhoods predominantly populated by minorities

Using police resources and personnel to harass certain segments of the community (e.g., businesses, community groups)

By practice or custom, failing to provide police services to minority segments of the community (e.g., homosexuals, ethnic groups, religious groups)

Failing to take corrective action when officers discriminate against citizens

Officers

Internal

Intimidating minority officers by threatening not to back them up on calls

Making racist or sexist comments in the presence of minority officers

Writing graffiti or posting offensive pictures on lockers belonging to minority officers

Engaging in sexual harassment

External

Not trying to solve crimes where minorities are victims

Harassing youths, college students, or other groups

Hassling businesses frequented by minorities

Not responding to, or purposefully delaying responding to, calls in minority neighborhoods

Using racial slurs or derogatory language when dealing with Hispanic citizens

SOURCE: Adapted by permission of Waveland Press, Inc. From V. Kappeler, R. Sluder, and G. Alpert *Forces of Deviance: Understanding the Dark Side of Policing,* 1st ed. (Prospect Heights, IL: Waveland Press, 1994): 173.

In the News

Tulia, Texas, has gained an international reputation, but it is not a cause for pride for Texans. In this small Texas town, the local police department hired an investigator to gather evidence for arresting drug dealers. This investigator, who, it turned out, had been fired by other law enforcement agencies and had outstanding misdemeanor warrants against him in another county, collected his evidence, which resulted in 46 indictments. In 1999, 43 people were arrested. No drugs or weapons were found during the surprise arrests, but so far, all charged have been found guilty and the sentences of those convicted exceed 431 years.

What makes this an issue? The reason is that almost all 43 persons arrested were African American, and the few whites who were arrested were married or dating African Americans. In fact, the arrests were a substantial percentage (about 10%) of the small total of African Americans in the town. The convictions were handed down by white juries who accepted the investigator's word that those arrested had sold him drugs, even though there was little evidence beyond his word. In some cases, he could not even recognize the person charged as the one who sold drugs to him. In at least one case, defense witnesses placed the accused in another state when the so-called sale was supposed to have occurred. Even though the charges were all sales worth less than $200, the sentences handed down averaged 90 years. The NAACP and out-of-state lawyers mounted a campaign to overturn these convictions, without much help from the Texas Attorney General's office, nor the Department of Justice. They have been successful in getting a district court judge to recommend to the Texas Court of Criminal Appeals that all convictions be overturned. Because it may take up to two years for the cases to reach the Court of Criminal Appeals, legislation was written and signed by Governor Perry, that resulted in the immediate release of those incarcerated on the perjured testimony of this undercover officer. Tom Coleman, the undercover officer who is at the center of this scandal, is now facing charges of perjury.

SOURCES: Talvi, 2002; Herbert, 2002, Robinson 2003, Hockstader 2003, Herbert 2003.

The trouble is that some young black men are stopped frequently, sometimes several times a week. This can only be perceived as harassment, and those who are subject to it are rightly indignant.

Crank (2003: 242) reports that in New Jersey, 73 percent of police stops were of African Americans even though they made up only 14 percent of all motorists. In Volusa County, Florida, 70 percent of stops and 80 percent of searches after stops were directed toward African Americans or Latino, though these groups made up only 5 percent of drivers.

A utilitarian argument for racial profiling would be that the "end" of drug interdiction justifies the "means" of harassing and inconveniencing the group. However, it appears that the end is not very well served. The hit rate for finding drugs is lower for African Americans than it is for other racial groups (Cole, D., and J. Lamberth, 2001).

QUERY

In Austin, Texas, in 2002 an off-duty officer observed a very new truck being driven by two young, African-American boys. He stopped the truck for a broken taillight and the boys ran. He caught them and found cocaine in the truck, which was stolen. In an investigation of his actions, he stated that he "didn't think black kids would be driving that kind of truck." He was fired. Do you think he should have been? In this case, the officer took his case to arbitration and the departmental explanation was that he was not fired for racial profiling, but, rather he was fired for lying and insubordination.

Plohetski, 2002.

African Americans are not the only minorities who suffer from differential enforcement patterns. Perhaps some of the most egregious cases of discriminatory law enforcement occurs on this nation's borders. Crank (2003) and Huspek, Martinez, and Jiminez (2001) discuss the excessive force that is used against Latinos in controlling the flow of illegal aliens across the border. It was reported to researchers that Immigration and Naturalization Officers routinely violated the human rights of aliens and deported them before they could report actions of officers.

According to Huspek, Martinez, and Jiminez (2001: 185), there are a "substantial number" of brutal or harassing incidents on the border by INS officers toward legal and illegal residents. In their study of incidents over a three-year period, they found that such abuses are a routine occurrence, and that there is a pattern to them and identifiable logic. Of the 204 persons who participated in their study, 43 percent reported seeing physical brutality, and 12 percent reported being victimized by sexual or physical abuse (2001: 187). For example:

> In January 1996, Roman Gonzalez Garcia, after stopping and being handcuffed near the San Ysidro Port of Entry, was pulled up by the handcuffs while at the same time an agent stomped on his ankle with his entire weight, breaking the ankle. Near Campo in August 1995, after Rogelio Hernandez was stopped by Border Patrol agents, his head, hip, and testicles were injured as he was pulled out of his car window by the hair and arm. Agents then threw him to the ground, jumped on his back with their knees, beat him with batons, and held his face in the dirt, almost smothering him (2001: 187).

Many of those reporting incidents were legal residents of the U.S. though of Mexican origin. They had passports thrown away, official documents torn up, and told they should go back to Mexico. They then had to wait in Mexico until family members could replace documents and help them get back across the border. White citizens have been threatened when they questioned the actions of INS agents (2001: 193). Huspek, Martinez, and Jiminez (2001: 185) argue that agents act this way because they are encouraged by a "rhetoric of fear" and tacit acceptance of any means necessary to reduce or discourage illegal immigration.

Duty

How would one characterize the duties of a police officer? Is enforcing the law the only duty of an officer? It is now clearly established that most of police work is *order maintenance*. Police are called into situations that do not involve crime control and are often termed social-work calls. Many police officers do not feel that these are legitimate calls for their time and either give them superficial attention or do not respond at all. Brown calls the skill police develop in avoiding these calls *engineering* (Brown, 1981: 142).

Police may respond to a domestic dispute and find a wife not seriously injured, but bruised, upset, and without money or resources to help herself or her children. The officer may ascertain that departmental policy or law does not dictate any action and the woman is afraid to press charges, so the officer can leave with a clear conscience that official duties have been completed. However, the officer could take the woman to a shelter or otherwise help her get out of a bad situation. What is the ethical choice? It is difficult to determine the extent of the officer's responsibility in cases where there is no offender to arrest or law to enforce.

Police response to domestic violence calls has historically been noninterference, with the perception that domestic violence was not a crime-control matter unless it involved injury amounting to felony assault, so women who were battered received different treatment depending on whether their batterer was their intimate partner or a stranger and whether the crime was determined to be a felony or a misdemeanor. This situation is personified most dramatically by *Thurman v. City of Torrington,* 595 F. Supp. 1521 (D. Conn. 1984), which involved a woman who was beaten, stomped, and stabbed by her ex-husband on the front steps of her mother's house while a police officer sat in a car and watched. Obviously, there are few cases that are as dramatic as *Thurman*. Also, there are many other complicating factors to domestic violence, so how to intervene is not always a simple matter.

Nevertheless, it must be recognized that part of the problem was a perception on the part of police that domestic violence was somehow different from stranger violence, and deserving of less intervention. A crime-control approach supports such discrimination; a public service model probably would not. Mandatory arrest policies were supposed to protect victims of domestic violence by forcing police to take action by arresting the perpetrator. What seems to have happened, however, is a greater likelihood that both victim and offender are arrested when there is evidence that both exchanged blows. Police officers simply may refuse to sort out what happened. Thus, a crime control response may have backfired for those who attempted to make the system respond to victims.

The formal code of ethics gives no clear guidelines on how much consideration police should give a citizen in distress. The caretaker style of policing found in small cities and suburbs, where police departments are community oriented, emphasizes service and encourages police assistance to victims or citizens who need it. Matthews and Marshall (1981) discuss the lack of departmental support for any action beyond the minimal obligations of duty. Those officers who become personally involved or commit the resources of the department beyond the necessary requirements are not rewarded, but viewed as troublemakers. Structural support for this ethical action does not exist. Officers who attempt to do what they believe is right often are on their own, risking formal or informal censure.

Referring again to our two paradigms of police as crime fighters or public servants, it is apparent that the de-emphasis on service and, indeed, sanctions for performing some service functions are due to the police and public's view of police as crime fighters first and foremost. The approach of neighborhood policing changes these parameters considerably and renews the historical emphasis on peacekeeping and community integration functions, yet community policing never caught the imagination of a majority of officers, even while enjoying support and promotion from national organizations such as the Department of Justice. Today, since federal support seems to be waning, we suspect that it is a model that will continue to decline in popularity.

In situations involving questions of duty, there are three questions to ask. First, what must police do under the law? Second, what does departmental policy dictate? Third, what do individual ethics dictate? A very altruistic, involved style of interaction where the police officer would be compelled to help the victims in any way possible is supported by the ethics of care, the ethics of virtue, utilitarianism, religious ethics, and ethical formalism. But a more self-protective standard, where the actions mandated would be only those necessary to maintain a self-image consistent with the police role as crime fighter, might also be justified using utilitarianism or ethical formalism.

If police became personally involved in every case and went out of their way to help all victims, they would probably exhaust their emotional reserves in a very short time. As a matter of survival, police develop an emotional barrier between themselves and the victims they encounter. It is virtually impossible to observe suffering on a consistent basis if one does not protect oneself in such a way. Unfortunately, the result is often perceived as callousness, and because of the extreme personal resources needed to remain sensitive to individual pain, emotional deadening may result in unethical behavior toward individual victims.

When asked to share ethical dilemmas, police officers often raise the concept of duty. Officers are faced with the choice of responding to certain situations or not, leading to tempting opportunities to ignore duty. In the cases in the accompanying box, the officer's clear duty is to serve the public, but shirking that duty does not seem to be an egregious lapse of ethics. On the other hand, these mundane, some might say trivial, decisions are faced by all officers, and their repeated decisions in such situations form the fabric of their moral character. How officers use their discretion—to file a report or not, to answer a call or not, to stop and investigate or not—is just as relevant to an evaluation of ethics as the decision to accept a gratuity or report the use of excessive force, issues that will be dealt with in the next chapter.

> **QUERY**
>
> - It is ten minutes to off-duty time. You see an accident. Do you work the accident even though you want to go home, or do you avoid the accident by sneaking around it?
> - You have received the same 911 call at the same location at least twenty times. Each time, it has been unfounded. You have just been dispatched to that 911 again. Should you check it or just clear it as unfounded without driving by?

In the types of instances previously mentioned, officers must decide how much to get involved in any particular incident. Another issue of duty is raised by the nature of police work and how easy it is for officers to abuse their freedoms. Officers may report they are on a call, when in reality they are doing nothing or performing personal tasks such as shopping or standing in line at the post office. Some officers have been known to attend college classes during duty hours by informing the dispatcher that they are out on a call. Officers may turn in overtime slips for surveillance when, in fact, they were at home. They may misrepresent the times they started and finished the day. Finally, the way court appearances can be used to increase one's monthly salary is part of the socialization of every rookie.

> **QUERY**
>
> - If a young boy, upset over a lost bicycle, approaches two police officers during their dinner, what do the strict guidelines of their job dictate? What is the ethical thing to do? Should they immediately interrupt their dinner and go search for the missing bicycle? Should they take a report to make the boy feel better, knowing they won't or can't do anything about it? Should they tell the boy to go away because they've had a hard night and are looking forward to a hot meal? Does it make a difference if police officers are not paid for their dinner hour?
> - If police encounter travelers who have been robbed during their passage through the city, should they leave such victims on the street to fend for themselves? Should they take them to a mission? Should they take up a collection to help them on their way?
> - If police respond to a burglary and find that the victim is desperately poor and the theft has left them without the resources to pay their rent, buy food, or keep the electricity on, what is their ethical duty? Once they have taken the report, can they leave with a clear conscience that their job has been done?

That these actions are wrong is not in question, and it is also true that they are not qualitatively different than the minor and not so minor egoistic actions of those in other occupations and professions: office workers leave early or call in sick to go to a ball game; salespeople call in to say that they are out making sales calls when, in fact, they are heading home for a quiet afternoon nap; businesspeople declare imaginary expenses on travel vouchers. Police officers, like all employees, rationalize these behaviors in a variety of ways, such as by pointing out their low pay or the fact that they sometimes do "police work" when off duty. The general acceptance of such behavior leads to an environment where each individual sets personal limits on the extent to which he or she will deviate from formal ethics. Even those who stop at minor transgressions must cover their actions by lying, which is another layer of deception added to the first.

Another issue to consider is how an officer should resolve the dilemma when his or her own values conflict with a direct order. We have previously discussed the concept of civil disobedience—the act of resisting an immoral law. Do police have a duty to enforce laws they do not agree with or do they have a larger duty to perform in a way that is consistent with their own moral code.

QUERY

A New York City police officer refused a direct order to arrest a homeless man who was found sleeping in a private garage. He disagreed with the "zero tolerance" policy that has been enforced against the homeless, and involves sealing off all the places they might find shelter and arresting those who are left on the street. The officer was suspended for 30 days and his career doesn't look promising since Raymond Kelley, the police commissioner, had this to say about the officer's decision: "You have to be able to follow the directions of a supervisor. Being a police officer is not for everybody. And perhaps this officer feels he's not suited for the job."
Do you think the officer should have obeyed the order he disagreed with? Do you believe he should have been punished?

J. Getlin, "Officer Refuses to Arrest Homeless," *Austin American Statesman* (Nov. 30, 2002): A8.

CRIME FIGHTER *AND* PUBLIC SERVANT?

Police hear mixed messages from the public regarding certain types of crime. They are asked to enforce laws against gambling, pornography, and prostitution, but not too stringently. They are expected to enforce laws against drunk driving but also to be tolerant of individuals who aren't really "criminal." They are expected to uphold laws regarding assault, unless it is a family or interpersonal dispute that the disputants want to settle privately. In other words, we want the police to enforce the law unless they enforce it against us.

We also ask the police to take care of social problems such as the homeless, even if they have to step outside the law to do so. Extralegal means are acceptable as long as they are not used against us. Citizens who want police to move the transients out of a park or get the crack dealers off of the corner aren't concerned with the fact that the police might not have the legal authority to do so. If a little "informal" justice is needed to accomplish the task, then that is fine with some people. Yet when we accept and encourage such extralegal power in some situations, then we shouldn't be surprised when it is used in other situations as well.

The police role as enforcer in a pluralistic society is problematic. The justification for police power is that police represent the public: "The police officer can only validly use coercive force when he or she in fact represents the body politic" (Malloy, 1982: 12). But if the police do not represent all groups, then their authority is defined as oppressive. It should be no surprise that police were seen as an invading army in the ghettos of the 1960s. They were not seen as representing the interests of the people who were the target of their force. The Los Angeles riots after the acquittal of the officers who were charged with beating Rodney King illustrate the tension between minority communities and police departments. More recent disturbances have occurred in other cities, sparked by perceived police abuses.

Police take their cue from the community they serve. If they serve a community that emphasizes "crime control" over individual rights or other values, then we will see the results of that message in the way laws are enforced. A recent example of a crime control approach is William Bratton's **zero tolerance policy,** implemented when he was police chief of New York City. Police officers were instructed to take an aggressive stance against street people and minor criminals, especially those who roamed the downtown Manhattan business area and subway system.

The dramatic decline in crime enjoyed by New York City was touted as the result of the zero tolerance policy. When you arrest the little criminals, so goes the theory, the big criminals will go away. From 1993 to 1997, felony complaints dropped by 44.3 percent, murder and nonnegligent homicide dropped 62 percent, forcible rape dropped 12.4 percent, robbery 48 percent, and burglary 45 percent (Greene, 1999: 176). Critics argue that New York's success might have something to do with the 40 percent increase in sworn officers that also occurred during this time. Further, the decline of crime was felt all over the country, not just New York City. For instance, San Diego's crime rate declined by almost as much as New York's crime rate, and San Diego did not increase the number of sworn officers (Greene, 1999).

The most problematic issue regarding zero tolerance is the effect it has on police–community relations. Citizen complaints against police have gone up 75 percent in the four-year period between 1995 and 1999 (Greene, 1999: 176). Even downtown merchants, who were thrilled with the effects of the crackdown when the Times Square area was described as "safe for tourists" again, are now feeling the effects of the pervasive police influence. Some complain that police are harassing them by enforcing trivial ordinances (such as placement and size of window signs or sidewalk sales). Some New Yorkers complain that the crackdown has altered what made New York what is was, such as sidewalk vendors hawking everything from hot dogs to sunglasses. The most serious charge is that the policy and approach have led to some police officers employing an "anything goes" philosophy, leading to such extreme cases as the Abner Louima assault and Amadou Diallo shooting. Interestingly, William Bratton is now attempting to implement his "zero tolerance" approach in Los Angeles, a city where there is already serious tension between the minority community and police department (LeDuff, 2002).

Whereas the formal code of ethics emphasizes the public servant role of law enforcement, the informal subculture emphasizes the crime fighter role.

The public, too, probably expects the police to live up to the crime fighter role, but they also expect more. They expect the police to be problem solvers and supermen (and women). From noisy neighbors to incest, we expect the police to have the answers to our problems: to be the one-stop shop for solving problems.

The surprising thing is that they do so well at this impossible task. At least one study shows that a majority of respondents hold favorable attitudes toward police—79 percent agreed that police were responsive; 75 percent agreed that they do a good job maintaining order, 84 percent agreed that they care about the safety of residents, and 82 percent agreed that they do a good job protecting people from crime. Interestingly, although confidence ratings are higher among whites than minorities, the difference was not significant in this study. In fact, the difference in community attitude toward police had more to do with where one lived. Those who lived in disorganized (and most likely crime-ridden) communities held less positive attitudes toward police (Cao, Frank, and Cullen, 1996). This is not a surprising finding, and offers an interesting question: Do the individuals in the disorganized communities have more negative attitudes toward police because they experience greater fear of crime; or do they hold more negative attitudes because they are more likely to be the recipients of extralegal force on the part of police who are challenged to control such crime?

CONCLUSION

In this chapter we have explored ethics and law enforcement. We looked at the influence of the police subculture on ethical behavior and the subculture's opposition to formal ethical standards. We explored reasons for the lack of consistency between the two. The mission and role of police as crime-control fighters or as public servants is a pervasive theme when discussing a range of issues, including how police use their discretion, the types of dilemmas they face, and the inconsistency between the formal code and informal subculture. Arguably, police utilize their discretionary power to enforce societal desires for order and crime control. The pressure for order and crime control may lead to the use of illegal means to achieve these goals.

REVIEW QUESTIONS

1. Discuss the elements of the formal code of ethics and contrast them with the values of the police subculture.

2. Present the criticisms leveled against the use of any code of ethics for police officers.

3. Define *discretion,* give examples of discretion, and discuss unethical and ethical criteria for the use of discretion.

4. Evaluate the charge that police departments enforce the law in a discriminatory manner. What evidence supports such a charge? What evidence contradicts the charge?

5. Discuss the two perceptions of the police officer—crime fighter or public servant. Consider various police practices and innovations as supporting one or the other role.

ETHICAL DILEMMAS

Situation 1

As a patrol officer, you are only doing your job when you stop a car for running a red light. Unfortunately, the driver of the car happens to be the mayor. You give her a ticket anyway, but the next morning you get called into the captain's office and told in no uncertain terms that you screwed up, for there is an informal policy extending "courtesy" to city politicians. Several nights later, you observe the mayor's car weaving erratically across lanes and speeding. What would you do? What if the driver were a fellow police officer? What if it were a high school friend?

Situation 2

There is a well-known minor criminal in your district. Everyone is aware that he is engaged in a variety of crimes, including burglary, fencing, and drug dealing. However you have been unable to make a case against him. Now he is the victim of a crime—he has been assaulted and robbed at gunpoint. How would you treat his case?

Situation 3

You are completing an internship with a local police agency. The officers you ride with are great and let you come along on everything they do. One day the officer you are riding with takes you along on a drug raid. You are invited to come in when the house is secure and you observe six young men sitting on two sofas in the living room. The officers are ransacking the house and asking the young men where they have hidden the drugs. Four of the youth are African American and two are white. One of the officers walks behind the sofa where the African Americans are sitting and hits each one hard on the side of the head as he walks past. He ignores the two white boys sitting on the other sofa. You are shocked by his actions, but know that if you say anything, your chance of being hired by this agency would be very small. You desperately want a good recommendation from the officers you ride with. What would you do?

SUGGESTED READINGS

Barker, T., and Carter, D. 1991. *Police Deviance.* Cincinnati, OH: Anderson Press.

Cole, D. 1999. *No Equal Justice.* New York: The Free Press.

Dunham, R., and Alpert, G. 1997. *Critical Issues in Policing,* 3rd ed. Prospect Heights, IL: Waveland Press.

Heffernan, W., and Stroup, T. 1985. *Police Ethics: Hard Choices in Law Enforcement.* New York: John Jay Press.

Kappeler, V., Sluder, R., and Alpert, G. 1994. *Forces of Deviance: Understanding the Dark Side of Policing.* Prospect Heights, IL: Waveland Press

Kleinig, J. (ed.). 1996. *Handled with Discretion.* Lanham, MD: Rowman & Littlefield.

Perez, D., and J. Moore. 2002. *Police Ethics: A Matter of Character.* Cincinnati, OH: Copperhouse/Atomic Dog Publishing.

Prenzler, T., and J. Ransley. 2002. *Police Reform: Building Integrity.* Sydney, Australia: Hawkins Press.

Walker, S., C. Spohn, and M. DeLone. 2000. *The Color of Justice.* Belmont, CA: Wadsworth Publ. Co.

7

Corruption and the "Code"

Key Terms

grass eaters
meat eaters
gratuities
graft

baksheesh
code of silence
bad-apple argument

Chapter Objectives

- Become aware of the range of law enforcement deviance, including graft, gratuities and excessive force.
- Understand the dilemma of divided loyalties.
- Understand the explanations offered for law enforcement deviance.

Unfortunately, examples of corruption and graft in law enforcement agencies are not difficult to find. Examples of widespread corruption have been uncovered by various committees and investigative bodies, since the very beginnings of organized police departments (Barker and Carter, 1994; Murphy and Moran, 1981: 87). One study reported that by officers' own accounts, 39 percent of their number engaged in brutality, 22 percent perjured themselves, 31 percent had sex on duty, 8 percent drank on duty, and 39 percent slept on duty (Barker and Carter, 1994). Barker (1983) reported that between 9 and 31 percent of officers who had been employed for eleven months or less reported observing corrupt practices.

Unfortunately, the perception that police are corrupt is widespread in some cities. In a New York City poll, 93 percent of those polled believed that police were "corrupt" (Kraus, 1994). Moore (1997) reports, interestingly, that the public still has high opinions of police, even when they also believe they are dishonest. Souryal also chronicles the extent of police deviance (1992: 300), as do many other authors who will be cited in this chapter.

Most misdeeds of police officers are only marginally different from the unethical behaviors of other professions—for instance, doctors may prescribe unneeded surgery or experiment with unknown drugs, businesspeople may cheat on their expense accounts, lawyers sometimes overcharge clients, and contract bidders and purchase agents might offer and accept bribes. It is an unfortunate fact of life that people in any profession or occupation will find ways to exploit their position for personal gain. This is not to excuse these actions but, rather, to show that police are no more deviant than other professional groups. In all of these occupational areas, most people attempt to uphold the profession's code of ethics and their own personal moral code. However, there are those who violate the ethical code in medium to minor ways, and then a very few who exploit their position blatantly and perform extremely unethical behaviors. Why do some police officers abuse their position? Deviant behavior is largely a matter of abuse of authority, force, or discretionary power.

TYPES OF CORRUPTION

Corruption, graft, theft, and accepting bribes and gratuities are all examples of unethical law enforcement practices. Cohen refers to these behaviors as exploitation, defined as "acting on opportunities, created by virtue of one's authority, for personal gain at the expense of the public one is authorized to serve" (1986: 23).

In 1973, the Knapp Commission detailed its findings of corruption within the New York City Police Department. The terms **grass eaters** and **meat eaters** were used to describe New York City police officers who used their position to engage in corrupt practices. Taking bribes, gratuities, and unsolicited protection money was the extent of the corruption engaged in by *grass eaters,* who were fairly passive in their deviant practices. *Meat eaters,* on the other hand, participated in shakedowns, "shopped" at burglary scenes, and engaged in more active deviant practices. The Mollen Commission, investigating New York City Police Department corruption twenty years later in 1993, concluded that meat eaters were engaged in a qualitatively different kind of corruption in more recent times. More than just cooperating with criminals, the corrupt cops were active criminals themselves, selling drugs, robbing drug dealers, and operating burglary rings.

The distinction between passive and active corruption is a helpful one. However, another distinction that should be made is between crime and ethical transgressions. It is an insult to law enforcement officers when such actions described above are discussed as if they were ethical dilemmas in the same category as whether to avoid responding to a fender-bender call or whether to call in sick so you can go fishing. Stealing, robbing, and selling drugs are crimes. Officers who engage in such act are criminals who happen to wear uniforms.

Gratuities

Gratuities are items of value received by an individual because of his or her role or position, rather than because of a personal relationship with the giver. The widespread practice of free coffee in convenience stores, or half-price or free meals in restaurants, or half-price dry cleaning, and so on, are all examples of gratuities. Frequently, businesspeople offer gratuities, such as half-price meals, as a token of sincere appreciation for the police officers' work. Although the formal code of ethics prohibits accepting gratuities, many officers feel there is nothing wrong with businesses giving "freebies" to a police officer. Many officers believe that these are small rewards indeed for the difficulties they endure in police work.

What do others think? Prenzler (1995: 21) collected 398 responses from patrons of sporting clubs in Brisbane, Queensland concerning their attitude toward police gratuities. Only 4 percent of this group expressed unqualified support; 55 percent believed that police should not accept them; and, 35 percent said that it was acceptable only under certain circumstances. However, when presented with hypothetical examples, two-thirds of respondents agreed it was acceptable for police to take coffee, and about one-quarter approved of Christmas gifts. The majority were still opposed to large gifts and regular gifts. Seventy-six percent were opposed to regular free coffee, cold drinks, or discounted meals when on duty. Very few of Prenzler's respondents agreed with the commonly used arguments for acceptance of gratuities: that they build community relations (15 percent); that they give businesses police protection (8 percent), that every occupation has its perks (6 percent), or that they compensate police for poor pay (6 percent). It is unknown whether these responses from Australia are similar to what would be gathered here. In criminal justice classrooms, it is common to find fairly strong support for minor gratuities, but this may not be true if one polled other groups.

One author writes that gratuities "erode public confidence in law enforcement and undermine our quest for professionalism" (Stefanic, 1981: 63). How do gratuities undermine public confidence? Cohen believes that gratuities are dangerous because what might start without intent on the part of the officer may become a patterned expectation. It is the taking in an official capacity that is wrong, since the social contract is violated when citizens give up their liberty to exploit only to be exploited, in turn, by the enforcement agency that prevents them from engaging in similar behavior (Cohen, 1986: 26). To push this argument to the extreme, there doesn't seem to be much difference between someone coming into an inner-city store and demanding "protection money" (to avoid torching and vandalism) and a police officer coming in expecting liquor or other goods "for cost." How does the store owner know that his silent alarm will receive the same response speed if he is not grateful and generous to police officers?

Kania, on the other hand, writes that police "should be encouraged to accept freely offered minor gratuities and . . . such gratuities should be perceived as the building blocks of positive social relationships between our police and the public" (1988: 37). He rejects the slippery slope argument (that taking gratuities leads to future, more serious, deviance) and the unjust enrichment argument (that the only honest remuneration for police officers is the paycheck), proposing that gratuities actually help cement relations between the police department and the public.

Officers who stay and drink coffee with store owners and businesspeople are better informed than those officers who don't, according to Kania. A gift, freely given, ties the giver and receiver together in a bond of social reciprocity. This should not be viewed negatively but rather as part of a community-oriented policing concept. He also points out that those who offer gratuities tend to be more frequent users of police services, justifying more payment than the average citizen. The only problem, according to Kania, is when the intent of the giver is to give in exchange for some future service, and not as reward for past services rendered. Another problematic situation would be when the intent of the taker is not to receive unsolicited but appreciated gifts, but rather to use the position of police officer to extort goods from business owners. Finally, if the giver expected special treatment, and the officer has the intent to perform the special service, then that would be an unethical exchange as well. See the "Relationship of Giver and Police" box on the next page for more details.

Another issue that Kania alludes to but doesn't clearly articulate is that a pattern of gratuities changes what would have been a formal relationship into a personal, informal one. This moves the storekeeper-giver into a role more similar to a friend, relative, or fellow officer, in which case there are personal loyalty issues involved when the law needs to be administered. In the same way that an officer encounters an ethical dilemma when a best friend is

Relationship of Giver and Police

Name	Giver's Perception	Police Perception
Ethical		
True reward	gratitude for contribution or heroic deed	accepted with acknowledgment of significance
True gift	expression of gratitude for pattern of police service	accepted without further obligation
True gratuity	expression of wish that legitimate police services will be continued	accepted in spirit of continuing reciprocal obligation
Unethical Only for Police		
Uncalled debt	expression of wish that legitimate police services will be continued	accepted in credit for future legal, quasilegal, or illegal favors
Ethical Only for Police		
Bad investment	offered to receive future legal advantages, secure favors, gain special status	accepted in spirit of continuing reciprocal obligation
Unethical and Illegal		
An understanding	offered to receive future legal advantages, secure favors, gain special status	accepted in credit for future legal, quasilegal, or illegal favors
A bribe	offered to exempt illegal actions or omissions from police action	accepted to overlook or ignore ongoing illegal activities
An arrangement	offered to exempt ongoing illegal actions or omissions from police action	accepted to overlook or ignore ongoing illegal activities
A shakedown	paid unwillingly to secure protection from police enforcement action	demanded to overlook or ignore present or future illegal activities

SOURCE: Adapted from R. Kania, 1988, "Should We Tell the Police to Say "yes" to Gratuities?" *Criminal Justice Ethics*, 7, 2: 37–49. Used with permission of The Institute for Criminal Justice Ethics and the author.

stopped for speeding, the officer who stops a store owner who has been providing him or her with free coffee for the past year may also experience divided loyalties. They have become, if not friends, at least personally involved with each other to the extent that one's formal duty becomes complicated by the personal relationship.

Where should one draw the line between harmless rewards and inappropriate gifts? Is a discount on a meal OK, but not a free meal? Is a meal OK, but not any other item, such as groceries or tires or car stereos? Do the store or restaurant owners expect anything for their money, such as more frequent patrols or overlooking sales of alcohol to underage juveniles? Should they expect different treatment from officers than the treatment given to those who do not offer gratuities? For instance, suppose an officer is told by a convenience store owner that he can help himself to anything in the store—free coffee, candy, cigarettes, chips, magazines, and such. In the same conversation, the store owner asks the officer for his personal pager number "in case something happens and I need to get in contact with you." Is this a gift or an exchange? Should the officer accept the free merchandise?

Many merchants give free or discount food to officers because they like to have police around, especially late at night. The question then become the one asked frequently by citizens: Why are two or three police cars always at a certain restaurant? Police argue that they deserve to take their breaks wherever they want within their patrol area. If it happens that they choose the same place, that shouldn't be a concern of the public. However, an impression of unequal protection occurs when officers make a habit of eating at certain restaurants or congregating at certain convenience stores.

Free meals or even coffee may influence the pattern of police patrol and thus may be wrong because some citizens are not receiving equal protection. What happens when all surrounding businesses give gratuities to officers and a new business moves in? Do officers come to expect special favors? Do merchants feel pressured to offer them? Many nightclubs allow off-duty officers to enter without paying cover charges. Does this lead to resentment and a feeling of discrimination by paying customers? Does it lead to the officers' thinking that they are special and different from everyone else? Other examples of gratuities are when police accept movie tickets, tickets to ball games and other events, free dry cleaning, and free or discounted merchandise.

The extent of gratuities varies from city to city. In cities where rules against gratuities are loosely enforced, "dragging the sack" may be developed to an art form by some police officers who go out of their way to collect free meals and other gifts. One story is told of a large midwestern city where officers from various divisions were upset because the merchants from some areas provided Christmas gifts, such as liquor, food, cigarettes, and other merchandise, while merchants in other divisions either gave nothing or gave less attractive gifts. The commander, finally tired of the bickering, ordered that no individual officer could receive any gifts and instead sent a patrol car to all the merchants in every district. Laden with all the things the merchants would have given to individual officers, the patrol car returned; the commander then parceled out the gifts to the whole department based on rank and seniority.

Officers in some departments are known for their skill in soliciting free food and liquor for after-hours parties. In the same vein, officers solicit merchants for free food and beverages for charity events sponsored by police such as youth softball leagues. The first situation is similar to individual officers receiving gratuities, but the second situation is harder to criticize. Officers bring up the seeming hypocrisy of a departmental prohibition against individual officers accepting gratuities, yet at the same time an administrative policy may exist of actively soliciting and receiving donations from merchants for departmental events, such as pastries, coffee, or more expensive catering items.

QUERY

Indicate which of the following—if offered freely with no *apparent* exchange expected—are ethically acceptable.

free coffee	only on duty	on or off duty
free gum, candy, etc.	only on duty	on or off duty
half-price meal	only on duty	on or off duty
free meal	only on duty	on or off duty
free dry cleaning	only for uniform	unrestricted
free admission to clubs	n/a	off duty
free lottery tickets	only on duty	on or off duty
free television set or other expensive merchandise		

If you decided that free coffee, meals, and other items were acceptable because they didn't cost much, how do you explain the fact that, over time, the cost of the coffee or meals consumed by police officers would equal that of the more expensive items?

It might be instructive to look at other occupations. Do judges or college professors receive any types of gratuities? Obviously, any attempt to give these professionals gifts would be perceived as an attempt to influence their decisions in matters involving the gift giver. Professional ethics always discourages gifts or gratuities when the profession involves discretionary judgments about a clientele. Professors cannot receive gifts from students and expect to maintain the appearance of neutrality.

Judges are usually very careful to avoid the appearance that they have received anything of value from the participants in any proceeding. If there is any chance of a conflict of interest, if the judge is compromised by a relationship with or knowledge of the participants, then he or she is supposed to pass the case on to a neutral colleague. A revelation that a gift from either side was accepted by the judge would probably result in a mistrial, successful appeal, and the judge being removed by the commission on judicial conduct. The system of electing judges is heavily criticized with the use of such terms as "justice for sale," since judges typically rely on attorneys for campaign contributions and these same attorneys practice in the judges' courts. The receipt of gifts or campaign contributions by politicians is a frequent news item because of the belief that such gifts are buying votes or influence.

When members of Congress receive large amounts of money from special-interest groups, when companies routinely distribute complimentary gifts to members of Congress, or when a lobbyist takes politicians on an expensive fact-finding junket, there is the appearance of impropriety. Although they would argue that these gifts do no harm and are only tokens of esteem, there is a strong suspicion that such practices are not in the public interest because the politicians who received gifts will be influenced.

However, it does not seem unusual or particularly unethical for a doctor, a lawyer, a mechanic, or a mail carrier to receive gifts from grateful clients. Whether gifts are unethical relates to whether one's occupation or profession involves judgments that affect the gift givers. The police obviously have discretionary authority and make judgments that affect store owners and other gift givers. This may explain why some feel it is wrong for police to accept gifts or favors. It also explains why so many people do not see anything wrong with the practice, since police officers may not make decisions affecting the store owner as often as they simply provide a service, such as responding to a burglary or disturbance call.

An important distinction that might help the discussion is the difference between a *gift* and *gratuity*. A gift is something that is clearly given with no strings attached. An example might be when a citizen pays for a police officer's meal without telling the officer, so that when the officer gets ready to pay, the bill is already taken care of. Many officers have had this experience. In this case, because the police officer did not know of the reward (because the gift giver did not make the gift known), no judgment can be affected.

The ethical systems from Chapter 2 can be used to examine the ethics of gratuities. Religious ethics is not much help; no clear guidelines can be gleaned from religious proscriptions of behavior. Ethical formalism is more useful since the categorical imperative when applied to gratuities would indicate that we must be comfortable with a universal law allowing all businesses to give all police officers certain favors or gratuities, such as free meals, free merchandise, or special consideration. However, such a blanket endorsement of this behavior would probably not be desirable. The second principle of ethical formalism indicates that each should treat every other with respect as an individual and not as a means to an end. In this regard, we would have to condemn gratuities in those cases where the giver or receiver had improper motives according to Kania's typology. If the business owner was expecting anything in return, if only the friendship of the officer involved, then he would be using the police officer as a means to his own end and would thus be violating the second principle of ethical formalism.

If utilitarian ethics were used, one would have to weigh the relative good or utility of the interaction. On one hand, harmless gratuities may create good feelings in the community toward the officers and among the officers toward the community (Kania's "cementing the bonds" argument). On the other hand, gratuities often lead to perceptions of unfairness by shopkeepers who feel discriminated against, by police who feel that they deserve rewards and don't get them, and so on. In fact, the overall negative results of gratuities, even "harmless" ones, might lead a utilitarian to conclude that gratuities are unethical.

There would be some differences in the argument if one used act utilitarianism versus rule utilitarianism. Act utilitarianism would be more likely to allow some gratuities and not others. Each individual act would be judged on its own merits—a cup of coffee or a meal from a well-meaning citizen to a police officer who was unlikely to take advantage of the generosity would be acceptable, but gratuities given with the intent to elicit special favors would not. Rule utilitarianism would look to the long-term utility of the rule created by the precedent of the action. In this perspective, even the most innocuous of gratuities may be deemed unethical because of the precedent set by the rule and the long-term disutility for society of that type of behavior.

An ethics of care approach would be concerned with the content of the relationship. If the relationship between the giver and the receiver was already established, a gift between the two would not be seen as harmful. If there was no relationship—that is, if the store owner gave the gratuity to anyone in a blue uniform—then there may be cause for concern. A preexisting relationship would create ties between the two parties so that one would want to help the other with or without the gift. Kania's theory of social networking is appropriate to apply here. If there is no existing relationship, then the gratuity may indicate an exchange relationship that is based on rights and duties, not care. Does the gift or gratuity harm the relationship or turn it into an exchange relationship? Officers can usually recite stories of store owners who gave gifts with an expressed purpose of goodwill, only to remind the officers of their generosity at the point where a judgment was made against them, such as a traffic ticket or parking violation. In this situation, the type of relationship isn't clear until "the bill is due."

Macintyre and Prenzler (1999) conducted a survey of officers to see if they would be influenced by gratuities. They asked officers what they would do if a café owner that gave them free coffee and meals was stopped for a traffic violation. The researchers found that supervisory officers were more likely to give a ticket than rookies. Although only 15 percent would not write the ticket and would continue to go back for meals, an additional 41 percent would also not write the ticket, but would give him a warning and not go back for free meals. The remaining officers would write the owner a ticket.

The ethics of virtue would be concerned with the individual qualities or virtues of the officer. A virtuous officer could take free coffee and not let it affect his or her judgment. According to this perspective, no gift or gratuity would bias the judgment of the virtuous officer. On the other hand, if the officer does not possess those qualities of virtue, such as honesty, integrity, and fairness, then even free coffee may lead to special treatment. Further, these officers would seek out gifts and gratuities and abuse their authority by pursuing them.

An egoistic framework provides easy justification for the taking or giving of gratuities. It obviously makes police officers feel good to receive such favors, especially if they feel that they deserve them or that the favors are a measure of esteem or appreciation. Even if the person giving the gift had ulterior motives, the police officer could accept and be ethically justified in doing so under the egoistic ethical framework if the officer gained more from the transaction than he or she lost. In other words, if one could keep a positive self-image intact and obtain the gratuity at the same time, then one would be justified in doing so, and it would be a moral action. Let us not forget, however, that the egoistic ethical system is discounted by a majority of philosophers.

Graft

Graft refers to any exploitation of one's role, such as accepting bribes or protection money. Graft also occurs when officers receive kickbacks from tow truck drivers, defense attorneys, or bail bondsmen for recommending them.

Muir (1977) described a small-town police department as relatively free from corruption, but widespread patronage and petty bribery occurred because of the functional and beneficial aspects of this type of graft. For instance, a "security" firm was more or less given carte blanche to operate in legal and illegal ways to control burglaries in particular areas of the city. The police also overlooked gambling, after-hours liquor violations, and other minor infractions in exchange for information and cooperation. This behavior was seen as useful; in fact, it would be very difficult to convince the involved police officers that the behavior was at all wrong or unethical. In larger cities, the prevalence of corruption is more extreme.

The Knapp Commission documented examples of a wide range of graft, including taking bribes for changing testimony or "forgetting," or phrasing answers in a way that would aid the defense (Manning and Redlinger, 1991). Most scandals involve a wide range of behaviors, and many of them fall into the area of graft (see, for example, the box "Suburb's Cops Charged with Taking Bribes").

Sexual Harassment and Assault

It is a sad reality that a few police officers use their position of authority to extort sex from female citizens (no reported cases of female police officers

---

Suburb's Cops Charged with Taking Bribes

CHICAGO—The impoverished suburb of Ford Heights paid its officers as little as $6 an hour. To supplement their income, federal prosecutors say, six current and former officers took bribes from drug dealers, sometimes tipping them to the movements of other police agencies.

"You get what you pay for," said U.S. Attorney Jim Burns, who announced the bribery, extortion, and racketeering charges Thursday against most of the town's police force, including a former chief.

Ford Heights is one of the nation's poorest areas, with an average household income of about $14,000 in 1990. Police pay starts at about $6 an hour and tops out at $20,000 annually.

Burns said former chief Jack Davis, who was arrested in July, helped distribute drugs and that about twenty dealers regularly paid bribes to officers so they could sell crack cocaine, powdered cocaine, and heroin in a wide-open market.

The indictments leave the crime-plagued southeast Chicago suburb of 4,200 with three full-time police officers, a third of its usual strength.

"I'm not going to stand here and tell you the whole force was corrupt," Burns said. "It was not."

Do you believe that "you get what you pay for . . . " is a good explanation of police deviance?

SOURCE: *Austin American-Statesman,* (Oct. 11, 1996): A16. Reprinted with permission of the Associated Press.

extorting sex from male victims is known to this author). The other category of sexual misconduct is sexual harassment of female police officers.

Amnesty International has documented widespread mistreatment of women by police across the world. In the United States, Kraska and Kappeler (1995) looked at a sample of 124 cases of police sexual misconduct, including 37 sexual assaults by on-duty officers. These authors challenged earlier studies that indicated sexual misconduct of officers occurred most often when women traded sexual favors for lenient treatment. This study's authors concluded that norms in a police department that ignored or condoned the exchange of sex for favored treatment opened the door to officers who used more aggressive tactics to coerce sex from citizens.

Kraska and Kappeler (1995: 93) propose a continuum of sexual invasion that ranges from some type of invasion of privacy to sexual assault. This range of behavior includes viewing a victim's photos or videos for prurient purposes, field strip searches, custodial strip searches, illegal detentions, deception to gain sex, provision of services for sex, sexual harassment, sexual contact, sexual assault, and rape. Even the most innocuous of contacts between female citizens and officers where officers might ask a woman he has stopped for a date involve issues of power and coercion. The authors report that police in their study described how they routinely went "bimbo hunting," which involved sexual harassment of women out drinking (1995: 104).

A department is often aware of an officer's pattern of sexual harassment and does nothing about it. This is an obvious lapse of supervision that is unfair to the public and also costs money. Kraska and Kappeler (1995) report that police lost 69 percent of the civil rights suits brought by the victim of sexual misconduct. The defense of officers is usually that if sex occurred, it was consensual. The problem is that when officers meet women in their official capacity (either as victims, witnesses, defendants or suspects), the power differential makes consent extremely problematic.

QUERY

In one year, four Dallas police were accused of rape. All cases were taken to Grand Jury for rape indictments, but were reduced to "official oppression" because they were missing the element of "use of force."
Do you feel that officers must use physical force to coerce sex from victims before a charge of sexual assault is warranted?

Kraska and Kappeler, 1995: 105.

In one research study, it was found that 70 percent of female officers reported being sexually harassed by other police officers (Kraska and Kappeler, 1995: 92). The "macho" culture of policing exists despite the fact that women have been integrated into patrol since the early 1970s. This "locker room" culture supported the devaluation and objectification of women. Although female officers do not encounter the virulent harassment and hostility that was present in the

1970s when patrol forces were first integrated, it is fair to say that there is some remnants of that culture still in force today. Sexual harassment is a violation of policy and against the law; it is also unethical. None of the ethical systems from Chapter 2 would support coercing co-workers for sex or creating a hostile work environment. The defense is that it is innocent "kidding" or honest infatuation, but universalism is a good check on this type of behavior. Would the perpetrator want his daughter or sister subjected to the behavior?

Other Crimes

The "Buddy Boys" in New York were able to operate almost openly in a precinct rife with lesser forms of corruption. Ultimately, thirteen officers in a precinct of only a little over two hundred were indicted for crimes ranging from drug use to drug sales and armed robbery. The Buddy Boys graduated from stealing cash and drugs from drug dealers during official arrests to planned thefts where they would, sometimes on duty, target crack houses or apartments and break in and steal drugs, cash, and other valuables. In at least one such instance, customers came to buy drugs, and the officers obliged by selling drugs through the door. They had relatively nothing to fear from their victims because the individuals targeted were minority drug dealers. Their victims could hardly report a robbery, and if other police in the precinct had any idea about what was going on, they evidently did little to investigate. The situation finally was exposed when Internal Affairs (I.A.D.) investigators caught two of the individual officers accepting protection money and forced them to wear "wires" to help gather evidence on the others. Ultimately, the police commissioner transferred all officers in the precinct to other divisions (Kappeler, Sluder, and Alpert, 1994).

Michael Dowd, another New York City police officer, testified to the Mollen Commission in 1993 that he and other officers accepted money for protecting illegal drug operations, used drugs and alcohol while on duty, robbed crime victims and drug dealers of money and drugs, and even robbed corpses of their valuables (Kappeler, Sluder, and Alpert, 1994: 201–202). An NBC *Turning Point* special titled "The Tarnished Badge" described how the I.A.D. officer who attempted to investigate Dowd was, first, given no assistance or encouragement and then was sanctioned by his superiors for his dogged persistence in exposing Dowd's criminal behavior. Dowd was exposed and, ultimately, indicted and prosecuted only after police officers in a suburban city videotaped Dowd buying drugs (in uniform and in a police car).

New York City has experienced police scandals with depressing regularity, with widescale investigations and exposes occurring in 1894, 1913, 1932 (the Wickersham Commission), 1949 (the Kefauver Commission), 1972 (the Knapp Commission), and 1993 (the Mollen Commission). The most recent scandal was the Abner Louima case in 1998 (Rothlein, 1999). But New York City is definitely not alone. The "Miami River Rats" also committed armed robberies of drug deals, collecting the cash and the drugs. These robberies by a small group of police officers eventually led to at least one homicide (Dorschner, 1989; also see Rothlein, 1999; Crank and Caldero, 2000: 162). A New Orleans police officer is in a federal prison today because he used a police radio to order a hit on a woman who was going to testify against him and others in a corruption trial. Luckily, he was being monitored by federal agents who decoded the thinly disguised assassination attempt (Human Rights Watch, 1998).

Many other large cities have their own historical cycles of corruption and exposure (Kappeler, Sluder, and Alpert, 1994: 197). In 1998, forty-four Cleveland cops were indicted for providing protection for cocaine shipments. Chicago has also had its share of corruption scandals. In 1996, seven Chicago cops were indicted for conspiracy to commit robbery and extortion for shaking down undercover agents they thought were drug dealers (Crank and Caldero, 2000). In 2001, a former chief of detectives pled guilty to running a jewel-theft ring for more than a decade. This detective used police computers to follow the path of traveling jewelry sales representatives in order to target them (Fountain, 2001). Other Chicago police officers have been accused of shaking down Polish immigrants and robbing suspected drug dealers (who turned out to be F.B.I. agents). This group of officers evidently joined forces with a street gang in order to control the cocaine trade. Brutality charges and other corruption charges have also been recently leveled against Chicago officers (Babwin, 2001).

Drugs are the root of several different kinds of deviance. The range of behaviors where drugs are involved include using drugs on duty, buying drugs, selling drugs, providing protection to drug dealers, robbing drug dealers, stealing from drug dealers, and using drugs to pay informants. Carter (1999) discusses the extent of on-duty use; he cites previous research that found up to 20 percent of officers in one city used marijuana and other drugs while on duty.

Carter (1999: 316) also discusses the phenomena of police officers who go undercover and become socialized to the drug culture. They may adapt norms conducive to drug taking. Elements of police work that lead to drug use include the exposure to a criminal element, relative freedom from supervision, and the uncontrolled availability of contraband. The large amounts of money present in the drug trade and the perception that it is "just drug money" lead to some officers stealing evidence or robbing drug dealers. Carter (1999: 321) concludes that there are some mechanisms that can be used to control drug corruption, including leadership by the chief, management and supervision, supervisory training, organizational control and information management, internal auditing of the use of informants, internal affairs, drug enforcement units having audit controls, turnover of staff, better evidence handling, early warning systems, training, and discipline.

Several books, such as *Serpico* (Maas, 1973) and *Prince of the City* (Daley, 1984), detail the pervasiveness of this type of behavior in some departments and the relative ease with which individual officers may develop rationales to justify greater and greater infractions. For instance, the main character in *Prince of the City* progresses from relatively minor rule breaking to fairly serious infractions and unethical conduct, such as supplying drugs to an addicted informant, without having to make major decisions regarding his morality. It is only when the totality of his actions becomes apparent that he realizes the extent of his deviance.

A WORLDWIDE PROBLEM

Police corruption does not just occur in the United States. Across the world there are instances of many different types of corruption. **Baksheesh** is a euphemism for graft and is endemic in many developing countries. Officials, including law enforcement officers, expect *baksheesh* to do the job they are supposed to do, or, alternatively, they extort money in exchange for not doing their job. "It is just the way it is," is the explanation for why such corruption exists. In all countries, corruption includes corruption of authority, kickbacks, opportunistic theft, shakedowns, protection of illegal activity, the fix, and internal payoffs.

Tim Prenzler and his colleagues have tracked and analyzed police corruption in Australia. In Queensland, the Fitzgerald Inquiry in 1989 found a network of vertical corruption reaching to the commissioner and widespread misconduct, including fabrication of evidence and assaults on suspects. Ultimately, the police commissioner was jailed for fourteen years on charges of corrupt payments from gambling and prostitution rackets. It was a huge scandal and eventually resulted in legislation pertaining to freedom of information and whistleblower protection. In addition, an independent watchdog agency—the Criminal Justice Commission—was created (Prenzler, Harrison and Ede, 1996: 5; Prenzler and Ransley, 2002; Fitzgerald, 1989).

A similar investigation was conducted of the New South Wales police department in 1997. The Wood Commission Report (Wood, 1997) described instances of fabrication of evidence, theft, armed robberies, sale of drug evidence, sale of information, and the existence of a protection racket. An informant, Detective Trevor Haken, eventually named more than two hundred police and civilians as involved in corrupt activities (Prenzler, Harrison and Ede, 1996).

In South Africa there is a culture of policing that encourages extreme means to extract confessions. Police have been videotaped beating car thieves, and Johannesburg officers have been videotaped kicking suspects in the face and putting out a lit cigarette on the face of one of the suspects. There have also been allegations that police dogs have been used to attack suspects (Mores, 2002). Other countries have had police scandals, as well. In 1998, twenty-three police officers went on trial in Perpignan, France, on charges of corruption. The alleged activities included bribes, pocketing traffic fines, selling confiscated alcohol, and stealing from stolen vehicles (Mores, 2002).

In China, the vice minister of public security, Li Jizou, was arrested on charges of illegally importing thousands of cars. More than 11,000 Chinese police were punished for corruption in 1998. Mexico has a reputation for corruption within its national and local police forces. In 1996, 4,400 officers were dismissed allegedly for drug smuggling/corruption (Mores, 2002). In a unique sting operation, the new minister of the interior of Russia rented a Mercedes-Benz and drove across Russia in 1997. He was stopped twenty-two times by traffic officers and he offered each a bribe. Twenty-one of the twenty-two times the bribe was offered, the officers accepted. In 1997, 1,000 police officers in St. Petersburg were fired for corruption (Mores, 2002: 25).

The Brixton disorders refer to a series of riots in the United Kingdom arising from tension between police and the minority community. They led to the Scarman Inquiry in 1981. Police were accused of mishandling the investigation of the racial killing of Stephen Lawrence in 1993. This situation elevated racial tensions and resulted in an inquiry that severely criticized the London police force, which was called "institutionally racist" (Neyroud and Beckley, 2001: 9).

In Holland, the Van Traa Commission in 1996–1998 looked into how covert drug operations led to corrupt conspiracies between police and drug informants (Neyroud and Beckley, 2001: 12). In Belgium, the Marc Dutroux case led to a crisis in public confidence of police. Dutroux was convicted of raping five young girls, but served only three years of a thirteen-year sentence. Shortly after his release in 1996, young girls started disappearing in Belgium. What was discovered later was that he would kidnap them or pay an associate to kidnap them and then hold the girl in a basement cell or in one of his several houses. The evidence indicates that some of the girls were sold into the sex trade in Poland, but several bodies were dug up—buried in the backyard of his house. Two eight-year-olds evidently starved to death during a four-month period when he was in jail on theft charges. Officers, following informants' tips, were in Dutroux' house several times, even when there were captives in the basement. Finally, the basement cells were discovered and two young girls were saved. At best, police showed incredible incompetence, at worst collusion, since there were allegations that high officials in the police department were involved in Dutroux' child pornography ring. The case led to mass demonstrations and the resignation of the minister of justice (Neyroud and Beckley, 2001: 12).

Transparency International charts corruption worldwide, ranking ninety-one countries. This agency defines corruption as abuse of public office (including police) for private gain (e.g., bribe taking). The countries with the highest scores for honesty included Finland, Denmark, New Zealand, and Sweden. Some of the poorest countries had very low scores, such as Azerbaijan, Bolivia, Kenya, Uganda, and Bangladesh. Finland is a country that evidently has a very low level of police corruption. It is reported that only about 10 percent of all citizen complaints about officials are about law enforcement officers (Laitinen, 2002). Although most of our discussion involves corruption in the United States, it is obviously the case that the issues and explanations presented here apply to other countries as well.

EXCESSIVE FORCE

Police have an uncontested right to use force when necessary to apprehend and/or subdue a suspect of a crime. When their use of force exceeds that necessary to accomplish their lawful purpose, or when their purpose is not lawful apprehension or self-defense, but rather, personal retaliation or coercion, then the use of force is unethical and illegal.

The use of force by Los Angeles police against Rodney King mentioned before is an example of force used for instrumental or expressive ends, depending on who you believe. This case represents a situation in which policy, law, and ethics present different answers to this question: "Did the officers do anything wrong?" The legal question of unlawful use of force is contingent on whether the Los Angeles Police Department's use-of-force policy was legal and whether the officers conformed to departmental policy. The policy stated that the officers could use escalating and proportional force to a suspect's "offensive" behavior. The reason that two use-of-force experts—one for the prosecution and one for the defense—disagreed was that the policy, like many other policies in policing, depends on the ethical use of discretion. The defense use-of-force expert analyzed the video and identified offensive movements in every attempt to rise and in every arm movement. The prosecution expert (who wrote the departmental policy), testified that a suspect lying on the ground is not in a position to present offensive movements to officers. If an officer perceives offensiveness in every movement of every suspect, the policy justifies his or her use of force.

QUOTE

Police brutality is one of the most serious, enduring, and divisive human rights violations in the United States. The problem is nationwide, and its nature is institutionalized. For these reasons, the U.S. government—as well as state and city governments, which have an obligation to respect the international human rights standards by which the United States is bound—deserve to be held accountable by international human rights bodies and international public opinion.

Human Rights Watch, 1998: 1.

In other applications of the policy, one can see that it leaves a great deal of room for choice and that, in most cases, an officer's perceptions of the ethical use of force will become as powerful, if not more so, than the policy itself. If an officer gets shot at, the policy obviously would justify use of force, but if the officer decides that he or she is safe enough behind his or her patrol car to talk the suspect out of shooting again and into giving up the weapon, then the use-of-force policy would support that nonviolent response as well. If an officer is hit in the face by a drunk, the policy would support use of force since the drunk obviously performed an offensive action; however, the officer who accepts the fact that the drunk is irrational, allows for it, and simply puts the person in the back of the patrol car (in effect, giving him a "free punch") is also supported by the policy. In other words, the policy can be used to justify all but the most blatant abuse of police power, or not, depending on the interpretation of the individual officer.

Thus, in the Rodney King incident, an initial act of passing a police vehicle and leading officers in a high-speed chase (although the actual speed of such chase was subject to dispute) led to the involvement of twelve police cars, one helicopter, and up to twenty-seven officers. The incident resulted in King being struck at least fifty-six times, with eleven skull fractures, a broken cheekbone, a fractured eye socket, a broken ankle, missing teeth, kidney damage, external burns, and permanent brain damage (Kappeler, Sluder, and Alpert, 1994: 146).

After the incident, officers justified their actions by the explanation that King was on PCP (he was not, and in fact his alcohol level was .075), impervious to pain, and wild. These claims were repeated in the newspapers and can be interpreted as the attempt to fit the use of force into a pattern that the public could understand and accept. In fact, police use of force probably became an incident in this case only because of the videotape. In other circumstances, it would hardly have rated a small newspaper article. The media typically become interested in police use of force when the victim cannot be fit into the stereotype of the "dangerous criminal": when he is a middle-class insurance agent (in the Miami case that sparked riots), Andrew Young's son (in an incident involving the Washington, D.C., police), or a high-school athlete who would have been on his way to Yale on an academic/athletic scholarship. More examples are in the box "Use of Force."

How do victims of excessive force come to the attention of police? Often it is by challenging police authority—passing a patrol car, asking questions, challenging the stop, or intervening in the arrest of another (Kappeler, Sluder, and Alpert, 1994: 159). In Klockars's description of types of police power (authority, power, persuasion, and force), force is brought into play when one's authority is challenged. Thus, individuals who question or refuse to recognize police authority become vulnerable to the use of force. Such use of force may be perfectly legal—officers have the right to tackle a fleeing suspect, or hit back when they are defending themselves. Illegal or excessive force is when the officer goes beyond what is necessary to effect a lawful arrest, or has no lawful reason to use force at all. For instance, gratuitous violence in response to verbal insults is excessive force, as is beating a suspect who is handcuffed and helpless.

Use of Force

A police officer pointed a gun at a nine-year-old's head and threatened to pull the trigger. The child was not a suspect trying to evade the officers or posing any other threat.

McDonald v. Haskins, 966 F.2d 292 (7th Cir. 1992)

Two men on a motorcycle accidentally brushed the bumper of a DEA car. One DEA agent got out and began a physical altercation with the driver of the motorcycle. When the passenger intervened, both agents beat him and yelled anti-homosexual epithets. When the driver asked why they were beating the other man, he was beaten as well.

Anderson v. Branen, 17 F.3d 552, rehearing denied 27 F.3d 29 (2nd Dis. 1994)

An individual was met by police officers in the hallway of his apartment building who were there looking for a person who was making fraudulent calls. They shoved him against the wall, threatened him, struck him, and dragged him down the stairs.

Goetz v. Cappelen, 946 F.2d 511 (7th Cir. 1991).

Culture of Force

The use of force in response to perceived challenges to police authority is highly resistant to change, even in the presence of public scrutiny and management pressure. Even with the notoriety of the Rodney King episode and the extreme public reaction to the spectacle of police use of force, several incidents involving other officers' abusive behavior toward motorists occurred shortly afterward. It might be that this pattern is so ingrained in some police department cultures that it remains relatively unaffected.

The Los Angeles Police Department (L.A.P.D) seems to have the type of culture that tolerates, perhaps even encourages, a high level of violence. Rothlein (1999) writes that the Christopher Commission reported that L.A.P.D. management was responsible, to some extent, for the brutality exhibited by the Rodney King incident in that there was an apparent failure to punish or control those who had repeated citizen complaints of violence. Further, there was a culture that encouraged the use of force, and there was an ineffective citizen complaint system, with no civilian oversight. In other words, leadership did not exist that actively discouraged the excessive use of force.

Skolnick and Fyfe (1993) also discuss the culture of L.A.P.D. as one where the use of violence was tolerated, even encouraged. The result has been civil rights cases—in 1990, for instance, Los Angeles paid out more than $11 million in civil rights cases for excessive force violations (Skolnick and Fyfe, 1993: 3).

Some officers seem to get involved in use-of-force situations repeatedly, while others, even with similar patrol neighborhoods, rarely get involved in such altercations. Thus, even if every use of force meets the guidelines of the policy, there are lingering questions as to why some officers seem to need to enforce the policy more often than others and why some interpret actions more often as offensive. According to Souryal (1992: 242), the report by the Independent Commission of the Los Angeles Police Department (1991) reveals that the top 5 percent of officers ranked by number of reports of the use of force accounted for more than 20 percent of all reports, and that of approximately 1,800 officers who had been reported for excessive use of force from 1986 to 1990, most had only one or two allegations, but forty-four had six or more, sixteen had eight or more, and one had sixteen allegations. Breaking up departments into elite units seems to encourage "swashbuckling behavior." Skolnick and Fyfe (1993: 191) describe one case where an L.A.P.D. elite squad, acting on a tip, totally destroyed a citizen's home, including breaking toilets, ripping sofas, and spray-painting "L.A.P.D. Rules!" on the wall of the house.

All information regarding police use of force is controlled by police, including the number of incidents, the taking of reports, and the amount of information recorded. The ability to access this information is limited, even in cases dealing with a challenge to the officer's use of force. The official version of any event is that force was necessary because of dangerous offensive actions. This interpretation is often supported by other police, and there is usually little evidence to the contrary (unless there is a videotape). The victim is often an unsavory character who would be a poor choice for sympathy, and supporting witnesses may have their credibility questioned.

Los Angeles is not the only city that has been in the news because of allegations of excessive force. Kappeler, Sluder, and Alpert (1994: 222) report that Washington, D.C., was widely known for incidents of brutality, including the one against Andrew Young's eighteen-year-old son. Yet of twenty-one cases in which the Civilian Complaint Review Board recommended adverse actions against officers for use of force, the police chief took action in only five.

The Human Rights Watch (1998) identified serious problems in Atlanta, Boston, Chicago, Detroit, Indianapolis, Los Angeles, Minneapolis, New Orleans, New York, Philadelphia, Portland, Providence, San Francisco, and Washington, D.C. The report cited police leadership and the "blue wall of secrecy" as serious barriers to reducing police violence. According to this report, the mechanisms for handling police offenders ensure that violence will continue. In most cases where a citizen alleges excessive force, there is no discipline and the case is closed as unfounded. If there is a civil suit and the plaintiff wins, the city pays, and, again, the officer may not even be disciplined.

One study is cited concerning the fate of police officers named in one hundred civil lawsuits between 1986 and 1991 in twenty-two states in which juries ordered $100,000 or more. It was found that only eight of these officers were disciplined (Human Rights Watch, 1998: 82; also see Payne, 2002). Many cities do not employ early warning systems. Further, there is a tendency to block or derail internal affairs investigations, and there is strong and active resistance to civilian review boards.

The most common explanations for police officer use of force are similar to those used to explain correctional officer use of excessive force—that force is the only thing "these people" understand or that "officers are only human" and consequently get mad or frightened or angry, just like anyone else would in that situation. The weakness of such arguments is obvious. If other people get mad and use force, it is called assault and battery and they are arrested and prosecuted. Even if the only thing "these people" understand is force, it removes the differences that we like to think exist between us and "them" to use reactive force against them.

QUOTE

I saw one guy arrested once for speeding and the police officer lost his temper. Of course, this highway patrolman brought it on himself, because he was bad-mouthing the guy. Finally—he's a man, too—the guy lost his temper and spit on the highway patrolman. Right on the side of a U.S. highway on a Sunday afternoon, the highway patrolman wrestled the guy down, took a handful of hair and held his head down in the dirt and started packing the guy's mouth full of sand. The guy was choking and spitting and this patrolman was shoving sand in his mouth. "I'll teach you to spit at a trooper, boy." Those were his exact words. I'm standing in the background, watching the cars go by, slowing down to stare at this event. It looked bad.

Mark Baker, *Cops* (New York: Pocket Books, 1985): 139–140. Reprinted with the permission of Simon & Schuster from *Cops: Their Lives in Their Own Words* by Mark Baker. Copyright © 1985 by Mark Baker.

The assault on Abner Louima by Justin Volpe of the New York City Police Department shocked the nation. What was the truly amazing thing about this criminal act is that it occurred in a police station with at least one officer reportedly assisting, but with a whole squad room right outside the door. According to Volpe's testimony, Louima was brought up to the squad room and taken into the bathroom for the purpose of beating him; in fact, the broken broom handle was put in the bathroom for that purpose. This evidently didn't raise any red flags to officers at the booking desk or other officers. How could this have happened in a police station? The fact that Louima was a minority, the fact that Volpe believed he had been hit in the head by Louima, and the fact that the blue curtain of secrecy is still intact in many police departments seem to be insufficient answers to this question.

QUOTE

Two months ago, I was sentenced to thirty years in prison. Part of reclaiming my life is to tell the truth about what happened that night.

Ex-officer Justin Volpe, in court testimony, reported by Feuer, 2000.

Deadly Force

There is nothing more divisive in a minority community than a police shooting that appears to be unjustified. Cities are quite different in their shooting policies, and their rates of civilian deaths. There can also be quite a change within one city. The District of Columbia, for instance, went from thirty-two police shootings (with twelve deaths) in 1998, to only seventeen in 2001 (with three deaths) (Murphy, 2002). The fact that the D.C. police department was under a court monitor might have something to do with the fairly dramatic decline of shootings.

Skolnick and Fyfe (1993: 235) describe New York City's shooting policy and argue that the policy may be instrumental in why the N.Y.P.D. has such a low shooting rate. There is an automatic investigation every time shots are fired, the investigation is conducted by the Firearms Discharge Review Board, and there are multiple layers of report writing and investigation before the officer is cleared. The authors also note that N.Y.P.D. officers also experience a lower rate of being shot than other cities, so the stringent policy has not seemed to affect their safety.

Chevigny (1995) also discusses New York's shooting policy and compares it to the situation in Los Angeles. In L.A., police shoot more people in proportion to the size of their force than any other major U.S. police department. Between 1965 and 1993, one squad (The Special Investigations Section) shot fifty-five people killing twenty-eight, yet only one officer was shot during that time, and he was shot by a police gun. Skolnick and Fyfe (1993) and Chevigny (1995) discuss how L.A.P.D. officers in this major crimes task force allowed criminals under surveillance to carry out robberies and then the officers engaged in shootouts after the fact (also see Payne, 2002: 31).

In a couple of incidents, there was some evidence to indicate that the offenders were shot unnecessarily, although no charges against police were ever filed (Skolnick and Fyfe, 1993). For instance, one group of suspects were followed to a McDonald's and police watched while they prepared themselves and carried guns inside after closing hours. The terrified clerk called in a robbery, and patrol officers responded to the 911 call, but were waived away. The squad then allowed the robbers to come out of the drive-in and get in their cars, where they were surrounded. Three out of the four were shot to death. Evidence indicated that the robbers' guns were locked in the trunk of another car (Chevigny, 1995; Payne, 2002).

Even New York, however, has had its share of deaths that have raised tensions. Amadou Diallo allegedly resembled a rapist, and when he ignored police orders to show his hands and continued to unlock apartment building door to go inside, he was shot at forty-one times by officers in the Special Crimes Unit of N.Y.P.D. The case threatened to spark riots in the city, especially when the police officers' trial was moved to Albany and the officers were acquitted. A wrongful death suit by the family is pending. New York City paid $40 million in 1999 alone for civil rights claims. That year the number of complaints increased by 10 percent and was the largest in a decade. Nelson (2000) chronicles a long list of personal stories of harassment, brutality, illegal arrests, and coerced confessions. Her conclusion is that in the minority community, at least, there are reasons to fear police.

The use of excessive force is probably not as pervasive in this country today as it was even twenty years ago. However, there is concern that it is hard to know what occurs because the data are not readily available and individual victims often do not come forward or, if they do, are not taken seriously. It seems that there are always a few officers in every department who are truly abusers of power, but the other officers and an organizational culture protect these officers from sanctions. The more common ethical issue concerning the use of force is that of the officer who observes an unlawful use of force by another officer. This issue is addressed in the next section.

LOYALTY AND WHISTLE BLOWING

One of the most difficult ethical dilemmas that officers confront is when faced with the wrongdoing of another officer. Informing or testifying against one's peers has always been negatively perceived by any group, whether that group be lawyers, doctors, students, prisoners, or police officers. The **code of silence** discussed in relation to police work is present in other occupations and groups as well. Why do we look away or do not come forward when our peers do wrong?

> ### QUOTE
>
> *The problem is that the atmosphere does not yet exist in which honest police officers can act without fear of ridicule or reprisal from fellow officers . . .*
>
> ---
>
> Frank Serpico, Knapp Commission, 1971, as reported in Hentoff, 1999.
>
> *Cops don't tell on cops . . . "[I]f a cop decided to tell on me, his career's ruined . . . [H]e's going to be labeled as a rat.*
>
> ---
>
> Police officer witness, Mollen Commission, 1994; as reported in Walker, 2001.

There are special problems involved, however, when police officers protect each other. One of the greatest harms of cover-ups is the harm that is inflicted upon a police officer's credibility. Sykes (1996) describes a civil case wherein a jury awarded $15.9 million in damages after a case of police brutality. Jurors simply did not believe the police version of the events, and a videotape supported the plaintiff's allegations that excessive force was used. The "cost" of police cover-ups eventually becomes public distrust of police testimony.

As mentioned previously, perhaps the O. J. Simpson trial has become the classic example of what happens when a jury loses confidence in police testimony. Prosecutors can ordinarily rely on a jury to take police testimony as fact and even favor police testimony over nonpolice witnesses. When police testimony is given no greater weight than any other witness—indeed, when jury members believe that police are prone to lie on the stand—then the justice system itself is at risk.

> ### QUOTE
>
> *At the trial, it just really angered me that deputies could identify suspects from booking photos, people they never knew, and describe in detail what actions people did that night, people they hardly ever saw. And yet throughout the entire trial I don't think there was ever one deputy who was able to identify their fellow deputies or any of the actions that their fellow deputies did that night.*
>
> ---
>
> Reported in G. Sykes, "How Much Is Our Credibility Worth?" *The Ethics Roll Call* 3(1) (1996): 5.

Teleological Arguments

Recall that teleological rationales are those that argue the end justifies the means. Egoism may support not coming forward because it may not be in one's best interest. We don't want to get involved; we don't want to face the scorn of others; we feel it's not our job to come forward when there are others who are supposed to look out for and punish wrongdoing; or we don't want to alienate the peer who committed the wrong by reporting him or her. These are all egoistic reasons for not coming forward.

There are also utilitarian reasons to keep quiet about observed wrongdoing. For instance, it may be that some activities labeled corrupt actually may further the ends of justice and that complete adherence to regulations would undermine detection and enforcement. Also, the loss of a skilled police officer, even though that officer may be moderately corrupt, is a loss to society. It may be that one believes the harm to the police department as a whole is greater in exposing the deviance of one officer than the harm to society created by what that officer is doing, or there is greater utility in stopping the officer without making it public.

However, there are also teleological arguments for *coming forward*. Egoism may dictate that an individual needs to come forward to protect himself from being accused of wrongdoing. The police officer may also endure such a crisis of conscience or fear of being punished that she can only attain peace of mind by "coming clean." Utilitarian arguments for coming forward exist as well. It may be that the harm that occurs from letting the individual carry on his misdeeds or not forcing the individual to a public punishment is greater than the harm that would occur from the scandal of public exposure. This is especially true if one is forced to either tell the truth or lie; in this case, the harm to police credibility must be taken into account.

Deontological Arguments

Deontological arguments can also be used to support not exposing other officers, or for coming forward. Arguments against informing include the idea that discretion and secrecy are obligations one assumes by joining a police force, and that it would be unjust to subject an otherwise good and heroic police officer to the punishment of exposure. Arguments for coming forward include the fact that a police officer has a sworn duty to uphold the law. Also, one cannot remain silent in one situation unless one could approve of silence in all situations (Kant's categorical imperative), and one must do one's duty, which involves telling the truth when under an oath (Wren, 1985: 32–33).

Loyalty

The previous arguments are what Wren (1985) calls external moral arguments, which he contrasts with internal arguments, such as loyalty. When one considers whether to come forward about the wrongdoing of others, external moral philosophies, such as the utilitarian "it is best for everyone" rationale, are rarely articulated. What often is the prime motivator for truth telling is personal integrity. Yet the individual often feels great anguish and self-doubt over turning in or testifying against friends and colleagues, and that is understandable since "a person's character is defined by his commitments, the more basic of which reveal to a person what his life is all about and give him a reason for going on" (Wren, 1985: 35). Loyalty is a difficult concept that others have written about extensively; it can be a vehicle of ethical and unethical behavior (Fletcher, 1993).

Loyalty in police work is explained by the fact that police depend on one another, sometimes in life-or-death situations. Loyalty to one's fellows is part of the *esprit de corps* of policing and is an absolutely essential element of a healthy department. Ewin (1990) writes that something is wrong if a police officer doesn't feel loyalty to fellow officers. Loyalty is a personal relationship, not a judgment. Therefore, loyalty is uncalculating—we do not extend loyalty in a rational way or based on contingencies. Loyalty to groups or persons is emotional, grounded in affection rather than reflection.

Ewin (1990: 13) also points out that loyalty always refers to a preference for one group over another:

> Loyalty always involves some exclusion: one is loyal to X rather than to Y, with Y thus being excluded. At times, the reverse can also be true: that a group of people is excluded (whether or not they are properly excluded) can make them feel a common cause in response to what they see as oppression and can result in the growth of loyalty amongst them. That loyalty provoked by a dislike and perhaps distrust of the other group, is likely to be marked by behavior that ignores legitimate interests and concerns of the other group.

The application to policing is obvious. If police feel isolated from the community, their loyalty is to other police officers and not to the community at large. If they feel oppressed by and distrust the police administration, they would draw together against the "common enemy." To address abuses of loyalty, one would not want to attack the loyalty itself because it is necessary for the health of the organization. Rather, one would want to extend the loyalty beyond other officers to the department, and to the community. Permeability rather than isolation promotes community loyalty, just as the movement toward professionalism promotes loyalty to the principles of ethical policing as opposed to individuals in a particular department.

Wren believes that police departments can resolve the dilemma of the individual officer who knows of wrongdoing by making the consequences more palatable—that is, by having a fair system of investigation and punishment, by instituting helping programs for those with alcohol and drug problems, and by using more moderate punishments than dismissal or public exposure for other sorts of misbehavior. This is consistent with the ethics of care, which is concerned with needs and relationships. If the relationship can be saved and the need for honesty and change met, then that is the best alternative to the dilemma of exposing wrongdoing or not.

Delattre (1989a) handles the problem differently but comes to somewhat similar conclusions. He turns to Aristotle to support the idea that when a friend becomes a scoundrel, the moral individual cannot stand by and do nothing. Rather, one has a moral duty to bring the wrongdoing to the friend's attention and urge her or him to change. If the friend will not, then she or he is more scoundrel than friend, and the individual's duty shifts to those who might be victimized by the officer's behavior. One sees here not the ethics of care, but a combination of virtue-based and deontological duty-based ethics.

Souryal (1996b, 1999b) discusses loyalty to superior or to fellow police as misplaced. He argues that there are several kinds of loyalty: personal loyalty, institutional loyalty, and integrated loyalty (which relates to the ideal values of the profession). Loyalty to superiors is traced back to *divine right*—the idea that persons were indistinguishable from their office (1996b: 48). Today, however, we are governed by laws, not kings, and such loyalty should be properly placed in our laws and our values, rather than an individual. Souryal (1996b) notes that personal loyalties often lead to unethical actions, and that loyalty to values or organizations is more appropriate. One might argue that even loyalty to a police organization may be misplaced if it leads to lying to protect the organization against scandal.

The informal practice of punishing individuals who come forward is an especially distressing aspect of loyalty. For the individual who tears the blue curtain of secrecy, sanctions can be extreme. A typical example of retaliation is reported in a San Antonio newspaper concerning an officer in the San Antonio police department who arrested a sergeant for driving while intoxicated. Even though the officer previously averaged fewer than two complaints a year during his eleven years at the police department, after he arrested the sergeant, he received nine complaints resulting in a total of eighty-six days of suspension. He also experienced the following: he encountered hang-up calls on his unlisted home telephone, his belongings were stolen, his car was towed away from the police parking lot twice, officers refused to sit next to him, and officers did not respond to his requests for back-up. Witnesses also reported that they overheard officers discussing what other forms of retaliation to take against him. The sergeant who was arrested for drunken driving was released before being taken to a magistrate, contrary to departmental policy, and received no disciplinary sanctions (Casey, 1996).

Daisy Boria was a N.Y.P.D. cop who testified in a way that contradicted others in the death of Anthony Baez. In this case, a police officer allegedly used excessive force by applying a chokehold, which killed Baez, a young African-American man. Boria testified that Baez was motionless on the ground when she and her partner arrived, which contradicted the testimony of her partner and the officer who killed Baez that he was struggling. She reported that after she testified, she received death threats, did not receive back-up when she called for it, and her supervisors routinely checked her locker for bombs. She quit the N.Y.P.D. and is now living in the Midwest (Hentoff, 1999).

Those who terrorize their fellow officers evidently believe that a violation of trust has occurred that justifies the harassment. Skolnick and Fyfe (1993: 110) argue that the danger to officers who violate the blue curtain is overstated, and that the more common reason that officers have difficulty coming forward is that everyone is doing something wrong and risks exposure (Skolnick and Fyfe 1993: 132). Daisy Boria might not agree. However often it happens, there are no ethical justifications for such actions, except for perhaps egoism.

Unfortunately, in many cases, such as the one described above, administrators participate in and thereby encourage a continuation of the practice. When administrators and managers encourage or promote cover-ups, then the individual officer who exposes wrongdoing is truly alone. Such administrative support tends to be misguided utilitarianism: There is the belief that scandal is so harmful to the organization that it must be avoided, even if one has to cover it up to do so. Of course there may also be egoistic reasons for administrators cover-ups: they may be implicated or blamed. We will address this issues more fully in the next chapter.

QUOTE

Texas Whistleblower Act, 1983

(a) A state or local governmental entity may not suspend or terminate the employment of, or take other adverse personnel action against, a public employee who in good faith reports a violation of law by the employing governmental entity or another public employee to an appropriate law enforcement authority.

(b) In this section, a report is made to an appropriate law enforcement authority if the authority is a part of a state or local governmental entity or of the federal government that the employee in good faith believes is authorized to: regulate under or enforce the law alleged to be violated in the report; or (2) investigate or prosecute a violation of criminal law.

EXPLANATIONS OF DEVIANCE

Explanations of corruption can be described as individual, institutional (or organizational), and systemic (or societal). Individual explanations, such as the *rotten apple* idea, assume that the individual officer has deviant inclinations before he or she even enters the police department and merely exploits the position. Sloppy recruiting and the development of a police personality are also individual explanations of deviance. Institutional (or organizational) explanations point to organizational problems (low managerial visibility, low public visibility, and peer group secrecy, among others). Institutional explanations also include looking at the police role in the criminal justice system (as the front-line interface with criminals), the tension between the use of discretion and bureaucraticism, and the role of commanders in spreading corruption. A systemic (or societal) explanation of police deviance focuses on the relationship between the police and the public (Johnston, 1995).

Individual Explanations

The most common explanation of police officer corruption is the **bad-apple argument**—that the officer alone was deviant and that it was simply a mistake to hire him or her. This argument has been extended to describe *bad bushels* when groups of officers band together to commit deviant acts. The point of this argument is that there is nothing wrong with the barrel—deviance is individual, not endemic.

Sherman (1982) explained that deviant officers go through what he called a "moral career," as they pass through various stages of rationalization to more serious misdeeds in a graduated and systematic way. Once an individual is able to get past the first "moral crisis," it becomes less difficult to rationalize new and more unethical behaviors. The previous behaviors serve as an underpinning to a different ethical standard, since one must explain and justify one's own behaviors to preserve psychological well-being (Sherman, 1982).

When one accepts gradations of behavior, the line between right and wrong can more easily be moved further and further away from an absolute standard of morality. Many believe, for instance, that gratuities are only the first step in a spiral downward: "For police, the passage from free coffee at the all-night diner and Christmas gifts to participation in drug-dealing and organized burglary is normally a slow if steady one" (Malloy, 1982: 33). Malloy describes a passage from "perks" to "shopping" to premeditated theft (1982: 36).

Others dispute the view that after the first cup of coffee, every police officer inevitably ends up performing more serious ethical violations. Many police officers have clear personal guidelines on what is acceptable and not acceptable. Whereas many, perhaps even the majority, of police see nothing wrong with accepting minor gratuities, few police would accept outright cash, and fewer still would condone thefts and bribes. The problematic element is that the gradations between what is acceptable or not can vary from officer to officer and department to department.

Sherman also believes in the importance of a signification factor, or labeling an individual action acceptable under a personal rationale (Sherman, 1985a: 253). Police routinely deal with the seamier side of society—not only drug addicts and muggers, but middle-class people who are involved in dishonesty and corruption. The constant displays of lying, hiding, cheating, and theft create cynicism, and this, in turn, may develop into a vulnerability to temptation.

The following are some rationales that might easily be used by police to justify unethical behavior (Murphy and Moran, 1981: 93):

- The public thinks every cop is a crook—so why try to be honest?

- The money is out there—if I don't take it, someone else will.

- I'm only taking what's rightfully mine; if the city paid me a decent wage, I wouldn't have to get it on my own.

- I can use it—it's for a good cause—my son needs an operation, or dental work, or tuition for medical school, or a new bicycle. . . .

Given constant exposure to others' misdeeds, peer pressure, and vague ideas of right and wrong in these situations, the question is not why some officers engage in corrupt practices but rather, why more don't. Although research indicates the lack of evidence for an affinity argument to explain police corruption—that is, deviant individuals being attracted to police work—an affiliation theory is persuasive, arguing that police learn from one another.

Organizational Explanations

The Miami River Cops' scandal involved officers committing armed robberies of drug dealers, Some argue, it was caused by the rapid hiring of minorities during an affirmative-action drive without proper background checks; disaffection by white, mid-level supervisors who basically did not do their job of supervision, instead merely counting the days to retirement; ethnic divisions in the department; and the pervasive influence of politics in the department, which disrupted internal discipline mechanisms (Dorschner, 1989). These concepts are largely organizational explanations of police corruption. Murphy and Caplan (1989) argue that there are situational elements that "breed corruption," including lax community standards over certain types of behavior (gambling, prostitution), hesitation of the chief to enforce rules and discipline officers, tolerance by fellow officers, unguided police discretion and incompetence, and a lack of support from prosecutors and the courts (or corruption at that stage of the system as well). Most of these explanations fall into an organizational category as well.

Crank and Caldero's (2000) "noble cause" explanation of some types of deviance whereby officers lie or commit other unethical acts to catch criminals is an organizational explanation, as is any description of deviance that includes the aspect of subcultural support. Whenever one explains deviance as being supported by the organizational culture—whether that be the "formal culture" or the "informal culture," it falls into this category.

Societal Explanations

Rationalizations used by some police when they take bribes or protection money from prostitutes or drug dealers are made easier by the public's less-than-firm stance toward certain areas of vice—e.g., to accept protection money from a prostitute may be rationalized by the relative lack of concern the public shows for this type of lawbreaking. The same argument could be made about gambling or even drugs. We often formally expect the police to enforce laws while we informally encourage them to ignore the same laws. Signification occurs here as well. Although gambling carries connotations of the mob and organized crime, or numbers runners in the ghettos of our big cities, we typically don't think of church bingo or the friendly football pool down at Joe's Bar. If police were to enforce gambling laws against the stereotypical criminal, the public would support the action, but if the enforcement took place against upstanding citizens, there would be an outraged response. "Police Arrest Grandma Bingo Players!" would be the headline.

The solution is a choice: Either accept police discretion to enforce, which in most cases will be used against the poor, minorities, and stereotypically criminal among us, or change the law and make it perfectly clear by statute that some gambling is OK and other types of gambling are not. Since the political feasibility of the latter solution is fairly limited—most politicians would not be eager to champion decriminalization of prostitution, drugs, or other types of vice—police are expected to make the distinction between "good" people and "bad." Good people should be excused, ignored, or, at worst, scolded for their involvement, and bad people should be investigated, caught, and punished—for example, the practice until recently of arresting prostitutes and letting "johns" go home, or ignoring campus crime while enforcement efforts target inner-city neighborhoods. The other possibility, of course, is that some police decide that a hypocritical public won't mind a few gambling operations, or a certain number of prostitutes plying their trade, or even a few drug dealers, so they might as well accept protection money. As long as the public supports certain types of illegal activities by patronage, it is no surprise that some police officers are able to rationalize nonenforcement. Also, as long as the public relays a message that crime control is more important than individual liberties and rights, then we should not be surprised when police act on that message.

CONCLUSION

In this chapter we reviewed the range of deviant behaviors in law enforcement. There are types of deviance that are purely for self-interest, and then there is deviance that stems from "noble cause" corruption—that type will be discussed in the next chapter. One of the most serious forms of deviance is the use of excessive force. The major reason given for excessive force is it is a response to the challenge of authority. Even those officers who do not engage in deviance may feel compelled to protect those who do. The reason for the *blue curtain of secrecy* in law enforcement is largely due to loyalty, and that concept was explored. Other reasons for law enforcement deviance can be categorized into individual explanations, organizational explanations, and societal explanations.

REVIEW QUESTIONS

1. List and describe various forms of law enforcement deviance.
2. What are the arguments for the acceptance of gratuities? What are the arguments against them?
3. Provide examples of law enforcement corruption in other countries.
4. What are reasons for protecting one's fellow officers by not telling the truth or coming forward and exposing their wrongdoing? What are arguments against such deception?
5. What are the individual, organizational, and societal level explanations for police officer deviance?

ETHICAL DILEMMAS

Situation 1

You are a rookie police officer on your first patrol. The older, experienced officer tells you that the restaurant on the corner likes to have you guys around, so they always give free meals. Your partner orders steak, potatoes, and all the trimmings. What are you going to do? What if it were just coffee at a convenience store? What if the owner refused to take your money at the cash register?

Situation 2

You are a rookie police officer who responds to a call for officer assistance. Arriving at the scene, you see a ring of officers surrounding a suspect who is down on his knees. You don't know what happened before you arrived, but you see a sergeant use a tazer on the suspect and you see two or three officers step in and take turns hitting the suspect with their nightsticks about the head and shoulders. This goes on for several minutes as you stand in the back of the circle. No one says anything that would indicate that this is not appropriate behavior. What would you do? What would you do later when asked to testify that you observed the suspect make "threatening" gestures to the officers involved?

Situation 3

There is an officer in your division who is known as a "rat" because he testified against his partner in a criminal trial and a civil suit. The partner evidently hit a handcuffed suspect in the head several times in anger and the man sustained brain injuries and is now a paraplegic. Although none of the officers you know support the excessive use of force, they also were appalled that this officer did not back up his partner's story. After all, punishing the officer wasn't going to make the victim any better. Now no one will ride with this guy, and no one responds to his calls for back-ups. There have been incidents such as a dead rat being found in his locker, and the extra uniform in his locker was set on fire. One day you are parking your car and see your buddies in the employee parking lot moving away from his car—they admit they just slashed his tires. Each officer is being called into the Captain's office to state whether they know anything about this latest incident. Your turn is coming. What are you going to do?

SUGGESTED READINGS

Barker, T., and Carter, D. 1991. *Police Deviance.* Cincinnati, OH: Anderson Press.

Dunham, R., and Alpert, G. 1997. *Critical Issues in Policing,* 2nd ed. Prospect Heights, IL: Waveland Press.

Heffernan, W., and Stroup, T. 1985. *Police Ethics: Hard Choices in Law Enforcement.* New York: John Jay Press.

Human Rights Watch. 1998. *Shielded from Justice: Police Brutality and Accountability in the United States.*

Kappeler, V., Sluder, R., and Alpert, G. 1994. *Forces of Deviance: Understanding the Dark Side of Policing.* Prospect Heights, IL: Waveland Press.

Nelson, J. (ed.) 2000. Police Brutality. NY: W. W. Norton and Co.

8

Ethics and Law Enforcement Practices

Noble-Cause Corruption

Investigation
The Use of Undercover Officers
The Use of Informants
Justifications for Undercover Operations

Interrogation

Management Issues
Change Efforts
Ethical Leadership

Different Question/Different Answers?

Conclusion

Review Questions

Ethical Dilemmas

Suggested Readings

Key Terms

noble-cause corruption
informants
principle of double effect
Dirty Harry problem

integrity testing
internal affairs model
civilian review model
rights-based model

Chapter Objectives

- Understand the ethical issues involved in investigation practices, such as the use of undercover officers, informants, and other types of deception.
- Understand the ethical issues involved in interrogation. Distinguish between physical and mental coercion and understand the arguments for and against these methods of interrogation.
- Understand the methods employed to reduce or minimize corruption among police officers, and the importance of ethical leadership.
- Be aware of the current challenges to law enforcement and be able to articulate any new answers to old questions about the use of deception or other means of investigation.

The last chapter discussed a range of corrupt practices by some law enforcement officers. It is important to note that only a small percentage of officers in most police departments ever engage in any of the practices we discussed, except, perhaps the acceptance of gratuities. In this chapter, we discuss more common practices of law enforcement, specifically, those activities engaged in during investigation and interrogation of crimes. The central question of this chapter is, "How far should law enforcement officers go to catch a criminal?" The answer will depend on whether you subscribe to a crime control or a public servant model of law enforcement, and whether you subscribe to a utilitarian or an ethical formalism ethical system.

NOBLE-CAUSE CORRUPTION

In 1983, Klockars presented us with the question of whether one could still be a good person if bad means were used to arrive at a good end. In the Dirty Harry problem, he asked whether it was ethically acceptable for a police officer to inflict pain on a suspect in order to acquire information that would save an innocent victim (with due credit to Clint Eastwood). We will explore that question more carefully in the interrogation section later, but use it now to begin our discussion of what has been termed **noble-cause corruption.** The argument of those who discuss noble-cause corruption is that officers sometimes (maybe even frequently) employ unethical means to catch criminals because they believe it is right to do so. This is an example of the utilitarian viewpoint— "the ends justify the means."

Crank and Caldero (2000), for instance, argue that such practices as testilying and coercion are not caused by selfishness but by *ends-oriented thinking.* The noble cause of police officers is "a profound moral commitment to make the world a safer place to live" (2000: 9). Officers will do what it takes to get an offender off the street, even if it is a "magic pencil" (2000: 71)— meaning making up facts on affidavits to justify illegal searches or to establish probable cause for arrests. They behave this way because we hire those who have values that support such actions and train and socialize them to internalize these values even more deeply, and then put them in situations where their values dictate doing whatever it takes to "make the world safe" (2000: 88).

Further, police are not the only actors who subscribe to noble-cause values. Crime lab investigators and prosecutors also engage in short cuts and magic pencils in order to convict the perceived guilty. Prosecutors have been known to suppress evidence and allow perjured testimony, so it is not only police officers who feel compelled to break the law in order to further the noble cause of crime control (Crank and Caldero, 2000: 134).

How pervasive is this tendency? Studies show that about 60 percent of rookies support mild lies to achieve a conviction (Crank and Caldero, 2000: 157). Recall that Barker and Carter (1996) reported that officers surveyed reported that about a quarter of officers perjured themselves. *Dropsy* testimony occurs when officers report that a drug suspect dropped the drugs and ran. This is convenient because it puts the drugs in plain sight and justifies the subsequent arrest. The trouble is that *dropsy* testimony rose exponentially after the Supreme Court ruled that street pat-downs for evidence required probable cause. In reality, we simply do not know the extent of the type and pervasiveness of noble-cause actions.

· Other authors argue vehemently that noble-cause corruption is a dangerous concept because it gives credence to illegal behavior on the part of officers. Alderson (1998: 68), for instance, protests that:

> noble-cause corruption . . . is a euphemism for perjury, which is a
> serious crime. . . . In ethical police terms justice is not divisible in this
> way into means and ends, and the peddlers of this perversion of justice
> are guilty of the immorality of the totalitarian police state, and their
> views stand to be roundly condemned.

However, it may be that he misunderstands those who present the noble-cause concepts. Crank and Caldero (2000), for instance, seem to be saying that noble cause is the underlying rationale of much of officers' unethical behaviors, and, therefore, efforts to control corruption must take cognizance of this reason in order to be effective. If selfishness and personal gain are not the motives for misdeeds, then monitoring and punishments may not work. The culture of police is not supportive of egoistic criminality, but it is supportive of "catching the criminal—whatever it takes." If we want to change this attitude, then we need to address it directly.

Further, they seem to argue that such an attitude must change because we are increasingly living in a world where pluralism is the reality and the values of the police organization may not be reflective of the citizenry they police. We will return to this concept in the final section of this chapter, but first, the following sections explore some of the law enforcement practices utilized to investigate and prosecute criminals.

INVESTIGATION

The goal of investigative law enforcement is to collect evidence in order to identify and successfully prosecute the criminal. There are different issues involved in reactive investigations versus proactive investigations. In reactive investigations, a crime has already occurred and the police sift through clues to determine the perpetrator. When police and other investigators develop an early prejudice concerning who they believe is the guilty party, evidence is looked at less objectively, and there is a temptation to engage in noble-cause corruption in order to convict.

One example of this was the scandal concerning the FBI crime lab. Several news reports reported charges that FBI lab examiners had compromised cases by completing shoddy work and misrepresenting their findings. The description of the motivation of examiners was that they were not objective scientists, but rather co-conspirators with police, who were motivated and even pressured to find support for police theories regarding the guilty party. This led to overstating their findings on the witness stand and covering up tests that were done improperly. A whistleblower exposed these practices and was suspended for his efforts (Sniffen, 1997). Ultimately, thirteen examiners were implicated, although only two were even formally censured (Serrano and Ostrow, 2000). See the accompanying box.

Recently criticism has been leveled at the Justice Department which responded to the scandal by directing prosecutors to go through their cases to examine whether any were jeopardized by examiner wrongdoing. Prosecutors, it is argued, are not the most objective actors to make this determination since it is not in their best interest to find such cases. The result has been that even though prosecutors are supposed to share exculpatory evidence with defense attorneys, in many cases, the defense was not told of the potential problems with the FBI lab findings. Several defendants have sued to overturn their convictions (Serrano and Ostrow, 2000). Recently the Houston crime lab has been the target of investigation. Shoddy lab practices and possible perjury by examiners has forced the District Attorney's office to re-examine over one hundred cases. Similar charges have been leveled at the Fort Worth crime lab (Axtman, 2003). See the accompanying box, "FBI Suspends Agent Whose Charges Led to Critical Report."

In proactive police investigations, there is a more active role on the part of police. Drug distribution networks, pornography rings, and fences of stolen property all tend to be investigated through methods that involve undercover work and informants. This is because such crimes often do not result in victims coming forward or crimes being reported. It may be that deception is a necessary element in this type of investigation.

According to one author, "Deception is considered by police—and courts as well—to be as natural to detecting as pouncing is to a cat" (Skolnick, 1982: 40). Offenses involving drugs, vice, and stolen property are covert activities that are not easily detected. Klockars (1984) discusses "blue lies and police placebos." In his description of the types of lies police routinely use he differentiates

---

FBI Suspends Agent Whose Charges Led to Critical Report

A newpaper article covered the story of the FBI suspending a scientist agent whose charges led to a still-secret Justice Department report critical of some FBI crime lab workers. A Republican senator was quoted as saying, "[the suspension] appears to be a reprisal." Several others were transferred out of the FBI also took action regarding other employees criticized in the secret report, said officials who spoke on condition of anonymity. Three or four employees were transferred out of the FBI lab, but not suspended. Evidently, the inspector general hired a panel of outside scientists to evaluate the work the lab after Whitehurst alleged in late 1995 that the lab mishandled evidence and testified with "a pro-prosecution bias." He alleged that misconduct may have trained crime lab work or testimony on several high profile federal cases.

SOURCE: M.Sniffen, *Austin American-Statesman* (Jan. 28, 1997): A5.

"placebos" as being in the best interest of those being lied to—for example, lying to the mentally ill that police will take care of laser beams from Mars, lying to people that police will keep an eye out for them, or not telling a person how a loved one was killed. The motive is benign, the effect relatively harmless. *Blue lies* are those used to control the person or make the job easier in situations where force could be used—for example, to make an arrest easier, an officer will lie about where the suspect is being taken, or to get someone out of a bar, the officer will say that she only wants to talk.

Barker and Carter (1994) also propose a typology of lies, including accepted lies, tolerated lies, and deviant lies. Accepted lies are those used during undercover investigations, sting operations, and so on. These lies must meet the following standards:

- They must be in furtherance of a legitimate organizational purpose.

- There must be a clear relationship between the need to deceive and the accomplishment of an organizational purpose.

- The nature of the deception must be one wherein officers and the management structure acknowledge that deception will better serve the public interest than the truth.

- The ethical standing of the deception and the issues of law appear to be collateral concerns.

Tolerated lies, according to Barker and Carter, are those that are "necessary evils," such as lying about selective enforcement. Police may routinely profess to enforce certain laws (such as prostitution) while, in reality, use a selective manner of enforcement. Lies during interrogation or threats to troublemakers that they will be arrested if they don't cease their troublemaking are also tolerated lies.

Deviant lies are those used in the courtroom to make a case or to cover up wrongdoing. One might argue with Barker and Carter, however, that there is some evidence to indicate that for some police organizations or certain isolated examples of rogue divisions, lies to make a case are so prevalent that they must be categorized as tolerated lies rather than deviant lies.

Investigations often involve the use of informants, decoys, and undercover officers. One possible result of these procedures is entrapment. In legal terms, entrapment occurs when an otherwise innocent person commits an illegal act because of police encouragement or enticement. Two approaches have been used to determine whether entrapment has occurred. The subjective approach looks at the defendant's background, character, and predisposition toward crime. The objective approach examines the government's participation and whether it has exceeded accepted legal standards. For instance, if the state provided an "essential element" that made the crime possible, or if there was extensive and coercive pressure on the defendant to engage in the actions, then a court might rule that entrapment had occurred (Kamisar, LeFave, and Israel, 1980: 510). See "A Case of Entrapment?"

Stitt and James (1985) criticize the subjective test: it allows the police to entrap people with criminal records who might not otherwise have been tempted; it allows hearsay and rumor to establish predisposition; it forces the individual charged to admit factual guilt, which may stigmatize him or her; it provides a free rein for police discretion in choice of targets; and it degrades the criminal justice system by allowing the police to use misrepresentation and deceit. On the other hand, supporters say that the subjective test allows police to go after those most likely to harm society. The objective test would punish the police and let the criminal go free, forcing police to perjure themselves to save a case (Stitt and James, 1985: 133–136).

Legal standards, as we have discussed earlier, are very often useful guidelines for determining ethical standards, but not always. For instance, one might disagree with legal standards as being too restrictive if one believed that police should be able to do anything necessary to trap criminals. Alternatively, legal guidelines may not be sufficient to eliminate what some consider unethical behavior. For example, do you agree that an undercover officer should pose as a client in a methadone clinic and pretend to befriend other clients, then ask

---

A Case of Entrapment?

When police raided an X-rated mail-order house, they found Keith Jacobsen's name and address, as well as the information that he had ordered two magazines: *Bare Boys I* and *Bare Boys II,* neither of which had been determined to be obscene material by any court. They created a fictitious company called "The American Hedonist Society" and sent Jacobson a membership application and questionnaire. He joined and indicated an interest in preteen sexual material. In other mailings over the course of three years, the government represented itself as "Midlands Data Research," "Hartland Institute for a New Tomorrow," and Carl Long, an individual interested in erotic material. Finally, a mailing from the government posing as the "Far Eastern Trading Company, Ltd." resulted in an order from Jacobson for *Boys Who Love.* He was arrested by federal agents after he accepted receipt.

SOURCE: Adapted from G. Dix, "When Government Deception Goes Too Far," *Texas Lawyer* 7(31) (1991): 12–13.

them to "hook him up" with a drug dealer? If they do it, they will be guilty of a crime. What if the undercover officer targeted someone for eleven months, continually begging and pleading with the target to sell him drugs, until finally, simply to get rid of him, the target did so and was promptly arrested? Does this violate the subjective test of entrapment? (Remember that a methadone client would be considered predisposed to drug crimes.) Is it ethical?

One might look at the methods police use for selecting an individual target. Earlier we discussed discretion in police work. Selection of targets on any other basis than reasonable suspicion is a questionable use of discretion. Members of Congress convicted of bribery in the Abscam operation in 1980 alleged improper conduct in the FBI's selection of targets; and, Marian Barry, the ex-Mayor of the District of Columbia, alleged he was "set up" because of his race after he was videotaped using drugs with a girlfriend in a hotel room in 1990. How targets are selected is a serious question; arguably, the selection should be based on reasonable suspicion. However, Sherman (1985b) reports that "tips" are notoriously inaccurate as a reason to focus on a certain person.

Police operations that provide opportunities for crime change the police role from discovering who has committed a crime to one of discovering who might commit a crime if given a chance (Elliston and Feldberg, 1985: 137). For instance, a fake deer placed by the side of the road is used to entice overeager hunters, who are then arrested for violating hunting laws. Police officer decoys are dressed as drunks and pretend to pass out on sidewalks with money sticking out of their pocket. Undercover officers, posing as criminals, entice doctors to prescribe unneeded medications that are controlled substances, such as Percoset and Oxycontin. Are only bad people tempted? This role expansion is arguably dangerous, undesirable, and inconsistent with the social contract basis of policing.

Police also undertake various stings in which they set up fencing operations to buy stolen goods. This action has been criticized as contributing to burglary. The opposing argument is that burglaries would occur regardless and that the good of catching criminals outweighs the negative possibility that burglars steal because they know the fence (police) will take their goods. Both of these arguments exist under a utilitarian framework. So even when using the same ethical system, a particular action may be supported as ethical or unethical. Other stings are even more creative, such as sending party invitations to those with outstanding warrants, or staging a murder and then arresting those (with outstanding warrants) who come out to see what is happening. The utility of such stings is undeniable. The only argument against them is that the government deception appears unseemly; it is also possible that such actions may undermine public confidence in the police when they are telling the truth.

Journalists who unwittingly assist police by believing and publishing a false story also criticize this type of deception. There are a number of ethical issues in the relationship between the police and the media. Should the police intentionally lie to the media for a valuable end? An example might be lying about the stage of an investigation or about the travel path of a public figure for security reasons. In the 2002 Washington, D.C., sniper case, the media and the police had an extremely close relationship and the police were especially sensitive to media issues (i.e., how the media could be used to encourage tips), but also how it might create public panic. There were some who believed the media were fed "red herrings," such as the importance of the white van, in order to divert the snipers' suspicions regarding how the police investigation was going.

Should the media have complete power to publish or report crime activities regardless of the negative effect on the level of public fear or the possibility of receiving an unbiased trial? Should the media become so involved in hostage situations that they become the news rather than just the reporters of it? The situation involving David Koresh and his cult of Branch Davidians in Waco, Texas, in the spring of 1993 raised a number of questions concerning the relationship between the police and the media. For instance, the media were banished to a distance far away from the cult compound. Is this an acceptable use of police power, or does it infringe on the public's right to know? Could police have ethically used the media to deceive Koresh into giving up by feeding the media false information in response to his stated wish for a sign? Should the media have been better informed during the course of the final assault?

These questions can all be analyzed using the ethical systems already described. Regarding the bombing at the 1996 Summer Olympics in Atlanta, should the FBI have disclosed to the public that Richard Jewell was its prime suspect and given the press background information that led to the massive publicity and exposure of his life? The FBI's statements indicated a level of certainty regarding his guilt that turned out to be unsubstantiated. Jewell's experience resulted in a public letter of apology from the FBI and a lawsuit against the FBI and the television networks and the newspapers that violated his privacy, illustrating one reason that law enforcement might not want to be so forthcoming on the progress of investigations (FBI, 1996).

The Use of Undercover Officers

Undercover officers may play drug dealers, prostitutes, johns, crime bosses, friends, and, perhaps, lovers in order to collect evidence of crime. They have to observe or even participate in illegal activities to protect their cover. Undercover work is said to be a difficult role for the individual officer, who may play the part so well that he or she loses his or her previous identity. If the cover involves illegal or immoral action, the individual may have to sacrifice personal integrity to get an arrest. Marx cites examples of officers who have become addicted to drugs or alcohol and destroyed their marriages or careers because of undercover assignments (1985a: 109).

Kim Wozencraft (1990), an ex-undercover narcotics officer, has written a novel in which two undercover officers use drugs and become friends with some of the pushers they are collecting evidence against, and although officials in the federal Drug Enforcement Agency (DEA), as well as local law enforcement, know that undercover officers sometimes use and even become addicted to drugs during the course of an investigation, they ignore or cover up such behavior in order to get successful convictions. Although the work is fiction, one suspects that at least some of the experiences that Wozencraft portrays are taken from reality.

Policemen routinely pretend they are johns, and policewomen dress up as prostitutes. Those community members who live in neighborhoods plagued with street prostitution may applaud any police efforts to clean up their streets. But do we want our police officers to engage in this type of activity? One important element of this debate is the type of relationship involved in the police deception. The two extremes of intimacy are, on one hand, a brief buy–bust incident where the officer pretends to be a drug pusher and buys from a street dealer, and moments later an arrest is effected. At the other extreme would be a situation in which an undercover officer pretends to be romantically involved with a target of an investigation to maintain his or her cover. The second situation violates our sense of privacy to a much greater degree, yet there have been instances of detectives engaging in such relationships to gain confessions or other information.

In one particular case, a private detective (not a police detective) engaged in this type of relationship over a period of months and even agreed to an engagement of marriage with the suspect in order to get a confession on tape (Schoeman, 1986: 21). In another case, an officer acted as a friend to a target of an investigation, to the extent of looking after his child and living in his house for six months. The purpose of the investigation was to get any evidence on the man so that the topless bar he owned could be shut down. Eventually, the officer found some white powder on a desk in the home that tested positive for cocaine, and a conviction was secured. The Supreme Court denied a writ of certiorari in this case (*United States v. Baldwin,* 621 F.2d 251 [1980]). Many people do not see anything wrong with deceiving the criminal who is ultimately convicted, but what about others involved? In the above case, what does one say to the child who found out a trusted friend had been living a lie?

One of the reasons that some disagree with deceptive practices involving personal relationships is that they betray trust, an essential element of social life. As Schoeman (1985: 144) explains, intimate relationships are different from public exchanges and should be protected:

> Intimacy involves bringing another person within one's soul or being, not for any independently personal or instrumental objective, but for the sake of the other person or for the sake of the bond and attachment between the persons. . . . There is an expression of vulnerability and unenforceable trust within intimate relationships not present in business or social relationships. . . . Exploitation of trust and intimacy is also degrading to all persons who have respect for intimate relationships. Intimate relationships involve potential transformations of moral duties. Morally, an intimate relationship may take precedence over a concern for social well-being generally.

Note that he is probably arguing from an ethics of care position. In this ethical system, the relationship of two people is more important than rights, duties, or laws. There is no forfeiture of rights in the ethics of care positions; thus, one can't say the suspect deserves to be deceived. The harm to the relationship goes in both directions. In cases where a personal relationship has developed, if the target is hurt by the deception, so too is the deceiver.

Schoeman goes on to suggest some guidelines to be used when police interact with others in a deceptive manner. First, he believes that no interaction should go on longer than twenty-four hours without a warrant with probable cause. During this twenty-four-hour period, the officer may not enter any private area, even if invited, unless it is specifically to undertake some illegal activity. Second, although an undercover officer may engage in business and social relationships deceptively during the course of an investigation, he or she may not engage in intimate relationships. Finally, any evidence obtained in violation of the first two principles should be excluded from criminal trials against the targets (1985: 140).

Police would obviously criticize these suggestions. First, if there is probable cause, an arrest is possible, so why engage in a dangerous undercover operation? Second, almost all undercover operations last more than twenty-four hours. Finally, requiring a warrant is often unworkable, given how undercover operations develop. The question remains: How can police best minimize the harm yet still obtain some utility from the action? This balancing is characteristic of utilitarian ethics.

Do police engage in investigative deception because it is the best way to investigate drug sales, prostitution, organized crime, or illegal alien smuggling; or is it simply the easiest way? Is it necessary in undercover work, especially in the area of vice, to employ deception and techniques that might be considered entrapment? If the goal of police is crime control, then there is a clear inclination to use utilitarian rationales to justify deception as a means to an end. If the goal of police is public service, such activities are arguably harder to justify.

Marx (1985a: 106–107) proposes that before engaging in undercover operations, police investigators should ask the following questions:

1. How serious is the crime being investigated?
2. How clear is the definition of the crime—that is, would the target know that what he or she is doing is clearly illegal?
3. Are there any alternatives to deceptive practices?
4. Is the undercover operation consistent with the spirit as well as the letter of the law?
5. Is it public knowledge that the police may engage in such practices, and is the decision to do so, a result of democratic decision making?
6. Is the goal prosecution, as opposed to general intelligence gathering or harassment?
7. Is there a likelihood that the crime would occur regardless of the government's involvement?
8. Are there reasonable grounds to suspect the target?
9. Will the practice prevent a serious crime from occurring?

The Use of Informants

Informants are individuals who are not police officers, but that assist police by providing information about criminal activity, acting as the part of buyer in drug sales, or otherwise "setting up" a criminal act so that police may gather evidence against the target. Informants perform such services for some reward—either money, or to get charges dropped or reduced, or in some documented case, for drugs supplied by an officer. They may do it for retaliatory purposes. Informants typically are not middle-class, upstanding-citizen types. They have or are probably engaged in criminal activities themselves. Police use informants who often continue to commit crime while helping police. The following describes an informant who had police protection withdrawn (Scheingold, 1984: 122):

> The problem is that by the time Detective Tumulty decided to bury Carranza, the informant had already committed, by his own count, two hundred crimes, and he had confessed over one hundred of them to the police. It is not surprising that business persons victimized by Carranza were not particularly pleased when they learned the police had failed to prosecute him.

More recently, it has come to light that the F.B.I. has protected informers even after they have committed murders. John Connolly, an FBI agent, was convicted of obstruction of justice and is now serving a ten year prison sentence for protecting two organized crime figures, now implicated in eighteen murders, during the time they worked for the FBI. Other agents have admitted that they "bend the rules" in order to keep information sources. Critics argue that FBI agents should not make decisions regarding which crimes are more or less important: "Is a federal official entitled to make that decision-that one person's life is more valuable than another's?"(Donn, 2003: A16).

The federal witness protection plan has provided new identities for some witnesses *after* they have accumulated bad debts or otherwise victimized an unwary public. The rationale for informant protection is that greater benefit is derived from using them to catch other criminals than their punishment would bring. This also extends to overlooking any minor crime that they engage in during the period of time they provide information, or afterward if that is part of the deal (Marx, 1985a: 109).However, the ethical soundness of this judgment may be seriously questioned.

Police use informants partly to avoid problems that undercover police officers would encounter if they attempted to accomplish the task, but also because informants are under fewer restrictions. As Marx reports,

> Informers and, to an even greater extent, middlemen, are much less formally accountable than are sworn law officers and are not as constrained by legal or departmental restrictions. As an experienced undercover agent candidly put it, "unwitting informers are desirable precisely because they can do what we can't—legally entrap."

An incident in Houston where an informant was killed in a drug buy brought to light the many ethical issues raised by using informants. This individual came to the police to help them identify pushers. He was married and had small children. He engaged in drug deals, and after they occurred, the police would arrest the drug sellers. In one such incident, the informant was in a motel room with the pushers and was evidently identified as an informant and killed before police could enter the room. The informant was not wearing a wire, and he had no weapon or means of protecting himself. Unlike the families of undercover police officers killed in the line of duty, his family is without benefits of compensation for his death (*Houston Post,* Jan. 24, 1993: A20). Some observers question the use of civilians in such dangerous operations. One might, however, point out the fact that this informant freely volunteered his services, unlike some informants, who are threatened with prosecution if they do not cooperate.

Another problem with informants is that sometimes their reliability is highly questionable. Their rewards, whatever those might be, are contingent upon delivering some evidence of crime to law enforcement. In some cases, this evidence may be purely manufactured. In Dallas, an informant was used to buy drugs from suspected drug dealers, who were then arrested and convicted using his testimony. When the supposed cocaine that he allegedly bought from those arrested was tested, it turned out to be powdered plasterboard. In fact, in several cases of the same informant, there were no drugs. Defendants, in the meantime, had spent months in jail protesting their innocence before charges were dropped. It was concluded by police and prosecutors that this informant had planted the cocaine substitute on innocent men with no relationship to drugs. Why? He had been paid $200,000 since 2000 for helping Dallas police make drug arrests (Curry, 2002).

Sometimes officers are tempted to manufacture informants. When writing affidavits for search warrants, officers may utilize information supplied by a "confidential informant" without having to name the informant. All the officer need do is state that the informant has given good information in the past and that it would be dangerous to reveal his or her identity. This boilerplate language is routinely accepted and so information is used to establish probable cause that cannot be verified or challenged. Sutton (1991) argues that some officers are tempted to use imaginary confidential informants to allow the use of otherwise illegally obtained or simply manufactured evidence. Barker and Carter (1999) report on a tragic case of this occurring in which an officer made up evidence from a so-called informant in order to get a search warrant. In the search, an officer was killed and the lie was exposed.

Some officers openly admit that they could not do their job without informants. There are other arguments, however, that the perceived value of informants is overstated. In a British study, the Home Office concluded that informants were cost effective. However, other analysts argued that the study did not factor in other issues, such as tolerating continued crime (by informants), and informants who create crime in order to report it (Dunningham and Norris, 1999).

Some develop close working relationships with informants, while others maintain that you can't trust them no matter how long you've known them. There are disturbing questions one might ask about using private citizens to engage in dangerous operations. It may be true that narcotics investigations are difficult, if not impossible, without the use of informants. If so, then guidelines and standards are needed to govern the use of informants. The Commission on Accreditation for Law Enforcement Agencies [CALEA] has developed such standards.

Justifications for Undercover Operations

There are arguments both for and against the use of undercover operations and informants (see box on page 210). Marx (1985b; 1991) argues that they might actually create more crime. They also may lead to unintended crime and danger. For instance, he mentioned situations where decoys have been attacked, undercover officers have been robbed, undercover officers have been killed by other officers who mistook them for criminals, and policewomen acting as prostitutes have been attacked. The use of informants sometimes leads to retaliatory assaults against them. There have even been scenarios where agents from one law enforcement agency pretended to buy drugs from drug dealers who turned out to also be undercover police from another agency (Marx, 1991). Although rare, one wonders how many resources have been expended for these futile charades. Undercover operations have been criticized for the following reasons (Marx, 1992: 117–118):

1. They may generate a market for the purchase or sale of illegal goods and services.
2. They may generate the idea for the crime.
3. They may generate the motive.
4. They may provide a missing resource.
5. They may entail coercion or intimidation of a person otherwise not predisposed to commit the offense.
6. They may generate a covert opportunity structure for illegal actions on the part of the undercover agent or informant.
7. They may lead to retaliatory violence against informers.
8. They may stimulate a variety of crimes on the part of those who are not targets of the undercover operation (for example, impersonation of a police officer, crimes committed against undercover officers).

Ethical systems may or may not support undercover operations. The **principle of double effect** holds that when one does an action to achieve a good end and an inevitable but unintended effect is negative, then the action might be justified. We might justify police action in this way if the unethical consequence, such as the deception of an innocent, was not the intended consequence of the action and the goal was an ethical one. However, deceiving the suspect could not be justified under the principle of double effect because that is an intended effect, not an unintended effect.

> ## QUOTE
>
> *They were just looking at me. I couldn't even look these guys in the eyes. Here's guys I hung out with, guys I broke bread with. I really came to like some of them. And they liked me, trusted me. One guy comes up to me and says, "How could you do this, Ben? You're my friend. How could you do this?" He was sixty some years old. He was like anybody's grandfather, a nice guy, but he dealt in stolen securities. That's what we locked him up for. He put a heavy guilt trip on me. I couldn't look at him. I had to put my head down. . . . Undercover is a very strange way to do police work, because you identify with them, the bad guys. It's a strange feeling to be trusted by someone and then betray them.*
>
> ---
>
> Mark Baker, *Cops* (New York: Pocket Books, 1985): 139–140. Reprinted with the permission of Simon & Schuster from Cops: Their Lives in Their Own Words by Mark Baker. Copyright © 1985 by Mark Baker.

Religious ethics would probably condemn many kinds of police actions because of the deceptions involved. Ethical formalism would probably also condemn such actions because one could not justify them under the categorical imperative. Further, innocent family members being used as a means to a conviction of an offender would also violate the categorical imperative. Utilitarian ethics would justify police deception and deceptive techniques if one could make the argument that catching criminals provides greater benefit to society than allowing them to go free by refusing to engage in such practices. Act utilitarianism would probably support deceptive practices, but rule utilitarianism might not, because the actions, although beneficial under certain circumstances, might in the long run undermine and threaten our system of law. Finally, egoism might or might not justify such actions depending on the particular officer involved and what his or her maximum gain and loss was determined to be.

Under act utilitarianism, one would measure the harm of the criminal activity against the methods used to control it. Deceptive practices, then, might be justified in the case of drug offenses but not for business misdeeds or for finding a murderer but not for trapping a prostitute, and so on. The difficulty of this line of reasoning, of course, is agreeing on a standard of seriousness. I might decide that drugs are serious enough to justify otherwise unethical practices, but you might not. Pornography and prostitution may be serious enough to some to justify unethical practices, but to others only murder or violent crime would justify the practices.

Cohen (1991) proposes a test to determine the ethical justification for police practices. His focus is the use of coercive power to stop and search, but we might apply the same test to analyze undercover or other deceptive practices. First, the end must be justified as a good—for instance, conviction of a serious criminal rather than general intelligence gathering. Second, the means must be a plausible way to achieve the end—for example, choosing a target with no reasonable suspicion is not a plausible way to reduce any type of crime. Third, there must be no better alternative means to achieve the same end: no less-intrusive means or methods of collecting evidence exist. Finally,

Justifications for and Arguments Against Undercover Work

For:

1. Citizens grant to government the right to use means which they individually forsake.
2. Undercover work is ethical when its targets are persons who freely choose to commit crimes which they know may call forth deceptive police practices.
3. Undercover work is ethical when used for a good and important end.
4. Undercover work is ethical when there are reasonably specific grounds to suspect that a serious crime is planned or has been carried out
5. Undercover work is ethical when it is directed against persons whom there are reasonable grounds to suspect.
6. When citizens use questionable means, government agents are justified in using equivalent means.

7. Special risks justify special of precautions.
8. Undercover work is ethical when it is the best means.
9. Enforce the law equally.

10. Convict the guilty.

11. An investigation should be as nonintrusive and noncoercive as possible.
12. Undercover work is ethical when it is undertaken with the intention of eventually being made public and literally judged in court.
13. Undercover work is ethical when it is carried out by persons of upright character in accountable organizations.

Against:

1. Truth telling is moral; lying is immoral.

2. The government should not make deals with criminals.

3. The government should neither participate in, nor be a party to crime, nor break laws in order to enforce them.
4. The government through its actions should reduce, not increase crime.

5. The government should not create an intention to commit a crime which is impossible to carry out.
6. The government should neither tempt the weak, nor offer temptation indiscriminately, nor offer unrealistically attractive temptations.
7. Do no harm to the innocent.

8. Respect the sanctity of private places.
9. Respect the sanctity of intimate relations.
10. Respect the right to freedom expression and action.
11. The government should not do by stealth what it is prohibited from doing openly.

the means must not undermine some other equal or greater end; that is, if the method results in loss of trust or faith in the legal system, it fails the test.

Many people see nothing wrong—certainly nothing illegal—in using any methods necessary to catch criminals. But we are concerned with methods in use before individuals are found guilty. Can an innocent person, such as you, be entrapped into crime? Perhaps not, but are we comfortable in a society where the person who offers you drugs or sex or a cheap way to hook into cable turns out to be an undercover police officer? Are we content to assume that our telephone may be tapped or our best friend could be reporting our conversations to someone else? When we encounter police behavior in these areas, very often the practices have been used to catch a person whom we realize, after the fact, had engaged in wrongdoing, so we feel that police are justified in performing in slightly unethical ways. What protectors of due process and critics of police investigation practices help us to remember is that those practices, if not curbed, may just as easily be used on the innocent as well as on the guilty.

It is clear that norms support police deception during the investigative phase. If their norms support deception during investigation, it is not surprising that some officers may protect themselves with deception when their methods are legally questioned. In fact, one of the problems with deceptive practices is that they may lead to more deception to cover up illegal methods. For instance, Skolnick (1982) argues that weak or nonexistent standards during the investigation phase of policing lead directly to lying on the witness stand because that is sometimes the only way an officer can save his or her case.

It is unlikely that these investigative techniques will ever be eliminated; perhaps they should not be, since they are effective in catching a number of people who should be punished. Even if one has doubts about the ethics of these practices, it is entirely possible that there is no other way to accomplish the goal of crime control. However one decides these difficult questions, there are no easy answers. Also, it is important to realize that although for us these questions are academic, for thousands of police officers they are very real.

INTERROGATION

Deception often takes a different form in the interrogation phase of a case. Several court cases document the use of mental coercion, either through threat or promise. The use of the *father confessor approach* (a sympathetic paternal figure for the defendant to confide to) or *Mutt and Jeff partners* (a "nice guy" and a seemingly brutal, threatening officer) are other ways to induce confessions and/or obtain information (Kamisar, LeFave, and Israel, 1980: 54).

Skolnick and Leo (1992) present a typology of deceptive interrogation techniques. The following is a brief summary of their descriptions of these practices:

- Calling the questioning an interview rather than an interrogation by questioning in a noncustodial setting and telling the suspect that he is free to leave, thus eliminating the need for Miranda warnings

- Presenting Miranda warnings in a way designed to negate their effect, by mumbling or by using a tone suggesting that the offender better not exercise the rights delineated or that they are unnecessary

- Misrepresenting the nature or seriousness of the offense by, for instance, not telling the suspect that the victim had died

- Using manipulative appeals to conscience through role playing or other means

- Misrepresenting the moral seriousness of the offense—for instance, by pretending that the rape victim "deserved" to be raped to get a confession

- Using promises of lesser sentences or nonprosecution beyond the power of the police to offer

- Misrepresenting identity by pretending to be lawyers or priests

- Using fabricated evidence such as polygraph results or fingerprint findings that don't really exist

Skolnick (1982) writes that because physical means of coercion are no longer used—the infamous third degree—mental deception is the only means left for police officers to gain information or confessions from suspects. How does one get a killer to admit to where she left the murder weapon? If police are imaginative, they may be able to get the defendant to confess by encouraging her to think about what would happen if children found the gun. Or police might discover the location of a body by convincing the killer after he had refused to talk to police that the victim deserves a Christian burial (see *Brewer v. Williams,* 430 U.S. 387, 97 S.Ct. 1232, 51 L.Ed.2d 424 [1977]). Courts have ruled that police who use these methods are unconstitutionally infringing on the defendant's right to counsel because the conversations, even if not direct questioning, constitute an interrogation. However, other cases that involve attempts to obtain information before counsel has been appointed have been approved by the Court. Whether police have a legal right to deceive a suspect is not the same question as whether it is ethical, and, if so, what are the limits of such deception?

Skolnick's argument is that deception is used because physical coercion cannot be. It is true, of course, that the use of physical force to obtain a conviction is illegal. Most countries, in fact, have eliminated torture and formally condemn the practice. Unfortunately, some countries still endorse physical coercion as acceptable police practice. Amnesty International documents abuses in Chile, Argentina, and many other countries around the world. It is important to note that very often in these situations police are used as the means of control by the dominant political power. Therefore, they operate not under the law, as the code of ethics dictates, but above the law. Codes of ethics, adopted by many police departments that have recognized the danger of police power being misused, are very clear in directing police to abide by the law and not allow themselves to be used by people or political parties (Bossard, 1981).

This discussion has been renewed, however, because of terrorism and the Afghanistan military engagement. There have been allegations that the U.S. military handed over Al Queda captives to countries where torture was legally possible, and then participated in the interrogations in order to acquire information about Osama Bin Laden and future operations. If this is true, does the nature of the threat justify the return to physical coercion? U.S. officials admit to the use of techniques such as with holding medical attention, deprivation of food and water, sleep and light deprivation and other means short of physical torture against A1 Queda leaders (Van Natta, 2003). Are such methods morally justified?

Many would argue that whatever information is gained from an individual who is physically coerced into confessing or giving information is not worth the sacrifice of moral standards. The original legal proscriptions against torture, however, come not from an ethical rationale, but from a legal rationale that torture makes a confession unreliable. Tortured victims might confess to stop their suffering; thus, the court would not get truthful information.

Klockars (1983) describes the inevitability of certain unethical or immoral police behaviors as the **Dirty Harry problem,** after the movie character who did not let the law get in his way when pursuing criminals. In Klockars's view, using immoral means to reach a desired moral end is an irresolvable problem because there are situations where one knows the "dirty act" will result in a good end, there are no other means to achieve the good end, and the "dirty act" will not be in vain. Klockars's example of this type of problem, taken from a movie, is a situation where a captured criminal refuses to tell the location of a kidnapped victim. Because the victim is sure to die without help, the police officer (played by Clint Eastwood) tortures the criminal by stepping on his injured leg until he admits the location.

Obviously, this is an immoral act, but Klockars's point is that there is no solution to the situation. If the police officer behaved in a professional manner, the victim was sure to die; if he behaved in an immoral manner, there was a chance he could save a life. This is a dominant theme in detective and police fiction. Klockars's conclusion is that by engaging in "dirty" means for good ends, the officer has tainted his innocence and must be punished, because there is always a danger that dirty means will be redefined by those who use them as neutral or even good. Police may lose their sense of moral proportion if the action is not punished, even though the individual police officer involved may have no other way out of the moral dilemma.

Delattre (1989a) also discusses the use of coercive power. He disagrees with Klockars that the officer must inevitably be tainted in the Dirty Harry situation. Delattre points out that if one chooses physical coercion, regardless of temptation, this leads to perjury and lying about the activity and perhaps other tactics to ensure that the offender does not go free due to the illegal behavior of the police officer. However, he also excuses the actions of those who succumb to temptation in extreme situations and perform an illegal act (Delattre, 1986a: 211):

> Police officials are not tainted by refusing to step onto the slope of illegal action, neither are officials of demonstrated probity necessarily tainted by a last-ditch illegal step. Such an act may be unjustifiable by an unconditional principle, but it also may be excusable. . . . Still less does it follow that those who commit such acts are bad, that their character is besmirched, or that their honor is tainted.

One might argue that if officers commit an illegal and unethical act, it is hard for their character not to be affected or their honor tainted. To understand an action (in this case an act that results from anger or frustration) is not to excuse it. Delattre presents a virtue-based ethical system and evidently believes that an officer can have all the virtues of a good officer and still commit a bad action—in this case, the illegal use of force. His point that one act of violence does not necessarily mean that the officer is unethical in other ways is well taken. In fact, we usually reserve the terms *ethical* and *unethical* for actions rather than persons. The reaction of the officer to his or her mistake is the true test of character. Does the officer cover up and/or ask his or her partner to cover up the action? Does the officer lie to protect himself or herself? Or does the officer admit wrongdoing and accept the consequences?

Klockars's underlying point is more subtle: We all are guilty in a sense by expecting certain ones among us to do the dirty work and then condemning them for their actions. In times of war, and when dealing with other threats, the populace often wants results without wanting to know tactics. What percentage of the population cared that the CIA attempted to assassinate Fidel Castro or that the attorney general's office during the Kennedy years used questionable tactics and violated the due process rights of Cosa Nostra members targeted in the campaign against organized crime? How many of us truly want to know about the clandestine operations of Special Forces in Afghanistan or Iraq? Klockars points out the position of those who perform despicable acts that benefit the rest of us; we are comfortable in our ignorance and comfortable in our judgments, as long as we don't have to look too closely at our own role in the events. Police (and other law enforcement), in effect, become our *sin eaters* of early folklore; they are the shady characters on the fringe of society who absorb evil so that the rest of us may remain pure—shunned and avoided, these persons and their value are taken for granted.

It is certainly much easier to justify mental coercion than physical coercion and intimidation, but their justifications are the same—that is, it is an effective and perhaps necessary means to get needed information from a resisting subject. The criticism against them is also the same. Mental coercion may also result in untruths. Recently, several convictions have been overturned because new evidence proves that those convicted were innocent, yet they confessed. Why would someone confess to a crime he didn't commit?

A suspect might confess because he is a fourteen-year-old juvenile who was mentally overpowered by police using pressure and feeding him information from the crime. This is alleged to have happened in the Central Park jogger "wilding" case. In this case, the five Black and Hispanic youths who were convicted in 1990 of the beating and rape of a female stockbroker may be innocent after all, since Matias Reyes has confessed, stating that he acted alone in the crime. D.N.A. evidence supports his contention that he raped the victim (Tanner, 2002; Getlin, 2002).

Suspects might confess because police use intimidation and fear tactics to extract a confession. This is allegedly what happened in an Austin case where two men were found guilty and sentenced to death for a robbery-murder. One of them confessed and implicated the other. Now, twelve years later, it appears that the crime was actually committed by another man who wrote the District Attorney with his confession. D.N.A. evidence has also confirmed his guilt. The convicted man who confessed alleges that he did so because the police officer who interrogated him threatened that if he did not confess, Mexican police would arrest his mother and they could not guarantee her safety. They told him he would receive the death penalty if he didn't confess (Hafetz, 2002).

Although such events sound like something from television drama rather than reality, they evidently do happen. In Illinois, Governor Ryan eventually commuted the death sentences of everyone on death row. He did so because of disgust and suspicion arising from the method of finding those on death row guilty. Thirteen death penalty cases were overturned when evidence indicated the convicted might be innocent, or at the very least, did not receive due process. Five of those thirteen were from Chicago, and evidence indicated that the convictions were obtained through coerced confessions and manufactured evidence by the Chicago police investigators (Babwin, 2001).

Muir discusses the necessity for the use of coercion: A good police officer, he writes, "has to resolve the contradiction of achieving just ends with coercive means" (Muir, 1977: 3). According to Muir, the successful police officer is able to balance willingness to use coercion with an understanding of humankind, which includes such traits as empathy and sympathy toward the weaknesses of human nature. If officers overemphasize coercion, they become cynical and brutal; if they overemphasize understanding, they become ineffectual:

> Under certain conditions, a youthful policeman was likely to come upon solutions to the paradoxes of coercive power which enabled him to accept the use of coercion as legitimate. However, if his solution to his moral problems required him to blind himself to the tragedy of the human condition, then he became an enforcer. Under other circumstances, a young policeman's choice of responses to paradox left him in conflict about the morality of coercion. Then he would be transfixed by feelings of guilt, would tend to evade situations which aroused those feelings, and would develop a perspective to justify his evasions. This kind of officer became either a reciprocator or an avoider. Finally some young officers found ways to exercise coercion legitimately without having to deny their "common sense of the oneness of the human condition." These men became professionals (Muir, 1977: 24).

MANAGEMENT ISSUES

Malloy (1982: 37–40) offers some possible solutions to police corruption: increase the salary of police, eliminate unenforceable laws, establish civilian review boards, and improve training. One might add this solution: improve leadership. Metz (1990) suggests several ways that police administrators can encourage ethical conduct among officers. He suggests setting realistic goals and objectives for the department and providing ethical leadership, a written code of ethics, a whistleblowing procedure that ensures fair treatment of all parties, and training in law enforcement ethics. In this last section, we will explore some of the approaches that have been taken to nurture and encourage ethical behavior among police officers.

Change Efforts

How does one minimize or eliminate existing corruption in a police department? Because so much of police work is unpredictable and encounters such a wide range of situations, it is impossible to fashion rules for all possible occurrences. What should take the place of extensive rules are strong ethical standards. However, the internalization of these standards by individual police officers is at best tenuous; the informal police subculture is the most obvious threat to the internalization of ethical standards.

However, the particular organizational values do influence the individual officer. Klockars et al. (2000) used surveys to ask 3,235 officers in thirty U.S. police agencies to rank the corruptness of eleven hypotheticals. They ranked some as fairly nonserious: covering up a DUI accident and taking free meals. Others were ranked as more serious: excessive force, taking free drinks, and taking kickbacks. The most serious rankings were reserved for stealing from a found wallet, taking a money bribe, and stealing a watch from a crime scene. There was quite a degree of variability between agencies. Agencies where officers had belief systems that ranked all behaviors as more serious also reported that their agency would inflict harsher discipline on all conduct (Klockars, 2000: 8). One might conclude from this that law enforcement administrators can affect the value systems of officers through appropriate discipline.

Crank and Caldero (2000: 159; also see Crank, 1998: 230) argue that even the formal organizational values impose pressures that may lead to noble cause corruption. Aspirations for promotion, "implicit quotas for arrests, directives from administrators, self-esteem, [and] moral ideological commitments" all put pressure on the individual officer to lie or otherwise subvert the formal values of law enforcement, and lead to violation of suspects' rights or other unethical behaviors.

Education and Training Education has been promoted as necessary if police are to continue to be professional. However, education itself is certainly not a panacea, and, in fact, some of the officers with the worst examples of unethical behavior either had college degrees or scored above average on the academic tests to qualify for hiring. Nevertheless, study results often show that educated officers have positive qualities. Some of the differences may raise more questions; for instance, if educated officers are more likely to believe it is acceptable to ignore the law, does this mean that they are *more* likely than officers without college degrees to use arbitrary and discriminatory criteria in their enforcement? If educated officers believe that officers can depart from standard operating procedures, are they harder to supervise and more likely to substitute individualistic definitions of justice rather than perform a service function and let the process control the outcome?

Ethics training in the academy, as well as offering in-service courses, is common and recommended for all police departments today. However, what these courses might be able to accomplish is questionable. Reuss-Ianni (1983) describes how, after the Knapp Commission uncovered wide-ranging corruption in the N.Y.P.D., ethical awareness workshops were begun. Unfortunately, they have not stopped the periodic corruption scandals that have occurred since.

Many ethics courses use a moral reasoning approach, much as this book does, where various scenarios are examined in light of ethical perspectives, such as utilitarianism, to determine the right course of behavior. Implicit in this approach is the assumption that once officers know what is right, they will make the right decision. This may or may not be true.

A different perspective is offered by Delattre (1989a) and Delaney (1990) that emphasizes the importance of character. In Chapter 2 we discussed the ethics of virtue, which answers the question, "How does one live a good life?" with "Developing and forming good habits of character." This is the approach that Delattre and Delaney apply to police ethics. If one has a bad character, ethical analysis is irrelevant because that individual will continue to behave in conformance to his or her traits of avarice, deceptiveness, cowardice, and so on. An individual who has good character possesses those virtues that are necessary for moral and ethical decision making. Training may help one by reinforcing appropriate values, but one's character is already formed. What are the virtues necessary for a good police officer? Delattre discusses justice, courage, temperance, and compassion. Delaney discusses sagacity, sincerity, and persistence.

This approach would seem to negate the relevance of any attempts to improve the ethics of officers, since character is fairly well formed by the time one is an adult. Yet we might say that ethics training at this point serves to delineate those situations that might not be recognized as questions of ethics. Also, discussions of such dilemmas point out egoistic rationalizations for unethical behavior, making them harder to use by those who would try. Other training options may concentrate on only one ethical system, such as utilitarianism, or involve a more balanced treatment of other ethical systems. All must resolve the issues of relativism versus absolutism, duty versus personal needs, and minor transgressions versus major transgressions.

Martinelli (2000) offers a different rationale for having an ethics training course. He proposes a course that is grounded in the actual discipline cases of each law enforcement agency. He argues that some of the law enforcement code provisions are ambiguous to officers and need explanations—such as keeping one's private life "unsullied." Officers may not realize that they can receive departmental sanctions for their behavior in their private life. Further, case law indicates that if some attempts are not made to instruct officers in appropriate behaviors, and if agencies and city councils continue to rubber stamp the violation of civil rights that some officers commit, then the agencies themselves will be held responsible. For instance, if there is a pattern of abuse in a discipline record and the officer then commits another violation, the city and police department will probably lose a wrongful death suit or civil suit. There have also been instances, where a "failure to train" argument has successfully established liability. "Police Watch" law firms in major cities have a proven track record in winning multimillion-dollar lawsuits against departments and cities. Thus, if for no other reason than to avoid financial liability, administrators should institute training in this area.

Integrity Testing New York City has utilized **integrity testing** since the late 1970s, after the Knapp Commission exposed widespread corruption. *Field associates* were recruited straight from academies to investigate suspected officers (Reuss-Ianni, 1983: 80). This attempt to "police the police" involves setting up a situation where the officer might commit a wrongful act. For instance, an officer responds to a report of an open door to an apartment, and when he checks it out, he sees money in plain sight. The scene is being monitored, however, to see if he takes it. There are also tests whereby a wallet is turned in to see if officers would take money (Marx 1991). It is reported that almost thirty percent of officers have failed to turn in the wallet (Prenzler and Ronken, 2001: 322). After the Mollen Commission in the mid-1990s, the integrity testing program has been expanded. Prenzler and Ronken (2001a: 322) report that such "integrity tests" may be getting better results today. Of three hundred fifty-five tests involving seven hundred sixty-two officers, no criminal failures were reported, and only forty-five procedural failures were reported.

Prenzler and Ronken (2001a) discuss integrity testing in police departments in Australia and around the world. They discuss how the London Metropolitan Police instituted random integrity testing in 1998. In their study of Australia, they discovered that only two reporting police agencies used *targeted* integrity testing and none used random integrity testing. In New South Wales, integrity testing resulted in 37 percent failing. Only 27 percent passed, and the rest were referred for further investigation or discontinued (2001a: 327).

Needless to say, most police officers have very negative attitudes about integrity testing. Spokesmen argue that "testing raises serious issues regarding privacy, deception, entrapment, provocation and the legal rights of individuals" (Prenzler and Ronken, 2001a: 323–324). There is a widespread belief that it is unfair and overly intrusive and detrimental to morale. It is interesting to compare integrity testing with undercover operations. The planted wallet is similar to the buy–bust operation, and the use of field associates is similar to undercover operations.

Officers hate the idea that an officer who pretends to be a friend may, instead, be someone who is trying to obtain evidence that they are doing wrong. The argument for undercover work is that if someone isn't doing anything wrong, there is nothing to fear. However, field associates create a sense of betrayal and lack of trust, regardless of whether someone is involved in wrongdoing or not. It is the same argument, of course, that is used to criticize undercover operations. Specifically, critics argue that the use of undercover operations may undermine the fabric of social relations by reducing a level of trust.

Civilian Review or Complaint Boards There seems to be a growing belief that police departments have proven themselves to be incapable of policing themselves, and that what is needed is some outside oversight. Civilian Review Boards have been created in several cities to monitor and review the investigation and discipline of officers who have complaints filed against them. There are many models that exist for the idea of civilian review, and no one model has been reported to be more effective or better than any other. Prenzler and Ronken (2001b) argue that it is difficult to analyze the success of such bodies because a high level of complaints may mean that there is greater trust in the process rather than a spike in misconduct. The various models of misconduct review are described as follows:

The **internal affairs model** is where the police investigate themselves and utilize an internal discipline system. This is widely seen as ineffective. Citizens are discouraged from reporting; police are seen as ineffective; and, the approach seems to be not to bring out corruption or misconduct but rather to hide it. For instance, in one Toronto study, 70 percent of people who filed complaints were not confident with the process, and only 14 percent felt their complaint was handled fairly (Prenzler and Ronken, 2001b: 180). Perhaps they had reason for their suspicions; see "A Case of 'Kill the Messenger'?"

The **civilian review model** is an agency that may audit complaints and investigations. The board may also respond to appeals and act in an advisory role in investigations. Police still investigate and conduct the discipline proceeding. The Police Complaints Authority in the United Kingdom is one example of this model.

Compromise models also exist that may have an external board, for instance, but without any powers of subpoena or oversight (Prenzler and Ronken, 2001b). Walker (2001) also reviews the range of civilian review models, but does not find that any one model seems to be better than any other.

Prenzler and Ronken (2001b) report that external review models have about the same substantiation rate as do I.A.D. models—about 10 percent of all complaints filed. The major criticism of such models centers on the idea

---

A Case of "Kill the Messenger"?

It was reported in the news that a volunteer for the local television station pretended to be a citizen who wanted to file a complaint against an officer in the small town of Santa Fe (35 miles southwest of Houston). A hidden camera recorded the incident, which was then played on television stations. What viewers saw was a sergeant who refused to give him a complaint form, argued with him, then followed him outside. The sergeant then arrested the "complainant" on a charge of walking on the wrong side of the sidewalk! The sergeant was suspended, but the damage done to public trust will not be resolved so easily.

SOURCE: Associated Press, "Police Sergeant Is Suspended after Arresting TV Volunteer" *Austin American-Statesman*, (May 10, 2000), B8.

that they are not truly independent, police still conduct the investigations and sometimes even sit on the board. Prenzler (2000) argues the "capture" theory is operative in civilian review models. This occurs when the regulatory or investigative body is "co-opted" by investigated agency through informal relationships.

Other Methods Hunter (1999) proposed several means to minimize or reduce misconduct among police, including decertification of officers who commit serious misconduct, community policing programs, college, enhanced discipline, civilian review, and better training. In his survey of police officers in Florida, he found that officers believed strict and fair discipline was the best response and deterrent to misconduct. They also identified clear policies, superior performance of supervisors, and peer review boards. It was clear that, according to officers, leadership had everything to do with an ethical police force—95 percent felt that supervisors should be moral examples and 70 percent felt that unethical supervisors contributed to problem. Less than half (42 percent), however, agreed with a citizen review board.

Mores (2002) also discusses a range of methods to deter corruption, including proper recruitment, economic incentives, community-oriented policing, greater accountability, rotation of assignments, the use of informants, the use of surveillance techniques, and prosecution of offenders. Prenzler and Ransley (2002) present the most exhaustive list, also found in the 1997 Wood Report, written after an investigation of widespread corruption in The New South Wales police department. The list of "Methods to Reduce Police Corruption" is reproduced in the accompanying box on the next page.

Ethical Leadership

Crank (1998: 187) and others note that there is a pervasive sense among rank-and-file police that administrators are not to be trusted: "Officers protect each other, not only against the public, but against police administrators frequently seen to be capricious and out of touch." The classic work in this regard is Reuss-Ianni's (1983) study of a New York City precinct in the late 1970s. She described the "two cultures" of policing—street cops and management cops. She observed that law enforcement managers were classic bureaucrats who made decisions based on modern management principles. This contrasted with the street cop subculture that still had remnants of quasi-familial relationships in which "loyalties and commitments took precedence over the rule book" (1983: 4). The result of this conflict between the two value systems was alienation of the street cop.

Despite the gulf between management and line staff, most people agree that employee behavior is influenced more directly by the behavior of superiors rather than by the stated directives or ethics of the organization. Executives engaged in price fixing and overcharging should not be surprised that their employees steal company supplies or time. One cannot espouse ethical ideals, act unethically, and then expect employees to act ethically. Thus, regardless of formal ethical codes, police are influenced by the standards of behavior they

---

Methods to Reduce Police Corruption

Internal affairs units

Independent civilian oversight agencies

Overt recording devices (videocameras in cars)

Covert high technology surveillance

Targeted integrity testing

Randomized integrity testing

Drug and alcohol testing

Quality assurance test (customer service monitors)

Internal informants

Complaints profiling

Supervisor accountability

Integrity reviews

Mandatory reporting

Whistleblower protection

Compulsory rotation in corruption-prone sections

Asset and financial reviews

Surveys of police

Surveys of public

Personnel diversification

Comprehensive ethics training

Inquisitorial methods (fact-finding rather than due-process emphasis)

Complaint resolution

Monitoring and regulation of police procedures (of informants)

Decriminalizing vice

Risk analysis (to see what areas are vulnerable to corruption)

SOURCE: J. Wood, *Royal Commission into the New South Wales Police Service: Final Report* (Government Printer, 1997).

---

observe in their superiors. One might note that most large-scale police corruption that has been exposed has implicated very high-level-officials. Alternatively, police departments that have remained relatively free of corruption have administrators who practice ethical behavior on a day-to-day basis.

Administrators have their own unique ethical dilemmas to face. Budget allocations, the use of drug testing, affirmative action, sexual harassment, and decisions about corrupt officers all present ethical dilemmas for administrators and supervisors. For instance, some supervisors face problems when they are promoted from the ranks and have friends who now become their subordinates. Such friends may expect special consideration, leaving the supervisor to decide how to respond to such expectations. Supervisors also report ethical dilemmas over how they should allocate resources, such as a new patrol car or overtime. Should seniority take precedence over competence? Should friendship take precedence over seniority?

Another issue is what should be done with officers who have drug or alcohol problems. If the administrator decides to counsel or suggest treatment without any change in duty status and the officer endangers the life of someone or actually harms a citizen or other officer due to the problem, is the administrator to blame? In many situations where police leaders must make decisions, lives, property, or liberty can be at stake. It is extremely important for supervisors and administrators to understand the impact their decisions and their behavior have on everyone in the organization.

Even if leaders are not involved in corruption directly, encouraging or participating in the harassment and ostracism that is directed at those who expose wrongdoers supports an organizational culture where officers may be afraid to come forward when they know of wrongdoing. Another situation may be where there is a perception that favored cliques do not receive punishment for behaviors that others would receive punishment for; this climate destroys the trust in police leadership that is essential to ensure good communication from the rank and file.

Reuss-Ianni (1983: 51) describes a trial of a cop who killed a prisoner in custody and the code of silence that was eventually broken down when other cops testified that they had lied in their reports and to the grand jury. The officers felt victimized by the press and betrayed by a management culture who, they felt, "threw them to the wolves." What is interesting about this event is that it occurred in 1976. Now, almost thirty years later, one suspects the same dynamics apply. For instance, in the Abner Louima case a couple of officers committed a brutal crime, other cops covered it up until outside pressure became too great, then the code of silence broke down and officers were forced to testify against each other. The general effect was perhaps similar to what Reuss-Ianni described—the rank and file perceived lack of support from management when they were forced to testify against each other. What is important is that even after thirty years, the police officer who violated the law is still protected, and those who expose him (or her) are still perceived as the enemy.

It seems, however, that management is just as likely as peer officers to cover up wrongdoing of officers. Only when the scandal cannot be contained does management "throw officers to the wolves." Unless there is a scandal, corruption is swept under the rug and individual officers may receive little or no discipline. For instance, Crank and Caldero (2000: 114) report that in hundred civil lawsuits in twenty-two states during the time period between 1986 and 1991, the awards paid out by cities and police departments totaled $92 million, but of the 185 officers involved, only eight were disciplined. In fact, seventeen were promoted. It may be that noble-cause corruption is ignored by management and self-interest corruption is identified and sanctioned, but that does not seem to be the case when exploring case studies like New York and Los Angeles. In fact, it seems that what starts out, perhaps, as noble cause corruption leads to a perception that one is above the law and self interest corruption soon follows. See "A Tale of Two Cities."

A Tale of Two Cities

New York
The Investigator:

Sgt. John Tromboli was stymied in his attempt to investigate and expose the actions of Michael Dowd, an obviously crooked cop whose lifestyle far exceeded a cop's pay. For five years he had been trying to get enough evidence on Dowd to file charges, but was routinely turned down by his superiors for extra resources and for permission for wire taps and other means of investigation. He believed that his superiors were trying to shut down his investigation. Dowd was finally arrested by Suffolk County police when he was videotaped conducting narcotics transactions in uniform and in a police car. I.A.D. routinely did not share information with the prosecutor's office on crooked cops. Instead, information on corrupt officers would be hidden in a "tickler file" that was never made public.

The Scandal:

The Mollen Commission in New York was formed in 1992 by Mayor David Dinkins to investigate the allegations of corruption. The practices of Dowd and a number of other officers were exposed. They included drug dealing, theft from corpses, robberies of drug dealers, setting up rival drug dealers for arrest and prosecution, protection rackets, and other misconduct. In the highly publicized hearings, officers were pressured to testify against others, and indictments and punishments were handed down. The hearings prompted Judge Mollen to comment that the Knapp Commission found that officers were in league with criminals, but that today, officers have become the criminals themselves.

Los Angeles
The Investigator:

Detective Russell Poole, a Robbery-Homicide Division investigator, uncovered a pattern of complaints of violence by the anti-gang task force in the Ramparts Division when investigating an alleged beating of a gang member in a police squad room. He concluded that a number of the officers in the division were "vigilante cops" and requested that the investigation proceed further, but Chief Parks ordered him to limit his investigation solely to the Jimenez beating. His superiors replaced a forty-page report he had prepared for the prosecutor's office with a two-page report that did not give any information about the possibility that there might be a pattern of corruption on the part of Ramparts officers. A year later, the Ramparts scandal exploded. Poole quit the force.

The Scandal:

The Ramparts Scandal refers to the pubic disclosure of a wide range of corrupt activities by an anti-gang unit task force in the Ramparts Division of the L.A.P.D (C.R.A.S.H.—Community Resources Against Street Hoodlums). Investigators from the prosecutor's office discovered the pattern of corruption when they made a deal with Rafael Perez, a Ramparts officer who had stolen cocaine from the evidence room. The scandal eventually led to dozens of criminal cases being voided because the prosecutor's office could not depend on the truthfulness of officers' testimony. Evidence indicated that the officers lied, planted evidence, beat suspects, and shot unarmed suspects in a time period between 1995 and 1998. They also evidently held parties to celebrate shooting,

continued

A Tale of Two Cities (continued)

gave out plaques when one killed a gang member, and spread ketchup at a
crime scene to imitate blood.

Hundreds of cases had to be reviewed by staff in the prosecutor's office to
evaluate whether there was a possibility of manufactured evidence. At least one
gang member's conviction was overturned when Rafael Perez, the officer who
implicated all others, confessed under oath that they had shot the man and
then planted a gun on him and testified that he had shot at them first. The
suspect has been released from prison, but is paralyzed and in a wheelchair.
Some evidence indicates at least ninety-nine people were framed by Ramparts
officers. Prosecutors were also quoted in the paper as saying, "You can't trust
the L.A.P.D. anymore." Mayor Richard Riordan reported to the press that the
city would have to use $100 million of tobacco settlements to cover anticipated
lawsuits. Eleven officers were fired and forty convictions were overturned.

The L.A.P.D. responded with an internal management audit that admitted
that there was a lapse of supervision and oversight. The report concludes that
the corruption was caused by a few individuals whose wrongdoing had a
"contagion effect." This report (conducted just eight years after the
Christopher Commission presented a scathing commentary concerning
management and ethos of L.A.P.D.) suggested an outside civilian oversight
committee. It might be out of the department's hands at this point since they
are now under a Court monitor.

**Why were police investigators blocked in their effort to uncover corruption? In
what ways is the pattern of corruption similar in New York and Los Angeles?
Do you see any differences?**

SOURCES: Rothlein, 1999; Winters, 1995; Glover and Lait, 2000; Lait and Glover, 2000; Jablon, 2000;
Sterngold, 2000; Deutsch, 2001; Golab, 2000.

DIFFERENT QUESTIONS/
DIFFERENT ANSWERS?

Our theme in these chapters was that the police role in society is either crime
fighter or public servant. One's view of the fundamental mission of police affects
each of the issues discussed. If *crime control* is the primary mission, then utilitarian
reasoning is employed to analyze police tactics. For instance, Cohen (1987: 53)
uses a utilitarian approach in the following justification for police action:

1. The end must itself be good.

2. The means must be a plausible way to achieve the end.

3. There must be no alternative, better means to achieve the same end.

4. The means must not undermine some other equal or greater end.

Crank and Caldero (2000: 9) state, "We argue for a means–oriented ethic
of negotiated order that will prepare police for America's future." Their idea is
that noble-cause corruption stems from a utilitarian view of crime control as
the fundamental mission of police, but that in today's multicultural reality,
police will have to negotiate an "end" that takes into account the needs of all

groups in society. This is still, however, fundamentally a utilitarian view of policing. The point is that a crime control model may subvert law, policy or human rights if utilitarian reasoning justifies it. In other words, the end, if important enough, will justify any means.

If *public service* is the primary mission, then the values and ethos of law enforcement would focus on human rights, and the fundamental duty of police is to protect those rights. Kappeler, Sluder, and Alpert (1994: 243) present the U.S. Department of Justice recommendations for the values of a police department as the following:

- Preserve and advance the principles of democracy.
- Place the highest value on preserving human life.
- Prevent crime as the number-one operational priority.
- Involve the community in delivering police services.
- Belief in accountability to the community served.
- Commit to professionalism in all aspects of operations.
- Maintain the highest standards of integrity.

A **rights-based model** of policing recognizes the police as servants to the public good. Although crime control is important, protection of civil liberties is the fundamental mission. There is a suspicion of state power in this approach and a fear that police will be used to oppress the powerless. The way to avoid this is to place protection of rights as the central theme of policing, rather than crime control, because the definition of crime may be subverted for political ends.

This concept is more prevalent in Europe and the United Nations Code of Conduct for Law Enforcement Officials is a good example of this premise: "In the performance of their duty, law enforcement officials shall respect and protect human dignity and maintain and uphold the human rights of all persons" (Article 2, reported in Kleinig, 1999). Neyroud and Beckley (2001: 62) describe Police Standards in the United Kingdom as reflecting an emphasis on human rights. Standards include the following provisions:

- To fulfill the duties imposed on them by the law
- To respect human dignity and uphold human rights
- To act with integrity, dignity, and impartiality
- To use force only when strictly necessary and then proportionately
- To maintain confidentiality
- Not to use torture or ill-treatment
- To protect the health of those in their custody
- Not to commit any act of corruption
- To respect the law and the code of conduct and oppose violations of them
- To be personally liable for their acts

This discussion has become incredibly more pressing in the face of terrorist threats. The trend of community or neighborhood policing that sought to forge links between law enforcement and the community they served has now slowed, and indications are that federal support for such programs is being withdrawn. In the place of community policing, one sees troubling tendencies to nationalize police forces, reduce civil liberties, and encourage zero tolerance. The nationalization of police has been resisted because of the origins of this country and the legacy of distrust of centralized power, yet, today, it seems more of a possibility (Stuntz, 2002).

The "end" of catching terrorists is incredibly more persuasive than the "end" of catching garden-variety criminals. Thus, while racial profiling has been legally and ethically condemned as a violation of rights when used to catch drug dealers, it has been resurrected as an appropriate and justified response to catching terrorists. Our Supreme Court has held that privacy is more important than catching criminals, so wiretaps have been used sparingly and with judicial oversight; but, the prevention of terrorist attacks has changed this balance between the end and means—many are willing to give up their privacy rights in order for government to protect them from terrorism.

Some, however, argue that it is a false argument to weigh privacy or any civil liberties against security. Alderson (1998: 23), writing before the attack on the World Trade Center, presents a prescient argument against the "end" of security as a justification for taking away liberties:

> I acknowledge that liberty is diminished when people feel afraid to exercise it, but to stress security to unnecessary extremes at the price of fundamental freedoms plays into the hands of would-be high police despots. Such despots are quick to exploit fear in order to secure unlimited power.

Alderson argues that "A police devoid of a sense and a spirit of justice is inimical to the healthy progress of democracy" (1998: 67). He addressed terrorism directly: "It is important for police to maintain their high ethical standards when facing terrorism, and for their leaders to inspire resistance to any degeneration into counter-terrorism terror" (1998: 71).

Since European police have had a longer history of dealing with terrorism, it is interesting that the trend there evidently has been to move toward a rights-based model of policing. British police, for instance, have had their share of noble-cause corruption in dealing with Irish terrorists, Spain has dealt with Basque terrorists, and so on. What may be the case is that "the end justifies the means" thinking by law enforcers leads inevitably to violations of civil liberties and fear, and this official oppression always leads to more bitterness and disenfranchisement, and, ultimately, more unrest and terror.

CONCLUSION

We began these chapters on law enforcement and will also close them with the images of the use of force by the Los Angeles police. Some of us remember earlier images from the 1960s, wherein law enforcement officers appeared on newscasts beating and using attack dogs against peaceful civil rights demonstrators. One might argue that those negative images of the 1960s led to greater professionalism, better training, and racial and sexual integration of police departments in the 1970s and 1980s. The Rodney King incident and the scrutiny that resulted had led to positive results in that is has fostered a groundswell of attention on "police ethics," including a national outcry against racial profiling and discriminatory enforcement. Today, we face the greatest challenge of law enforcement in recent memory with the threat of terrorism. The enemy is more fearsome, the stakes are higher, and the fear is stronger. How that may affect the ethics of law enforcement remains to be seen.

REVIEW QUESTIONS

1. Discuss the justifications and criticisms of undercover operations.
2. Explain the Dirty Harry problem.
3. Discuss possible change efforts to reduce or eliminate various forms of police misbehavior.
4. Discuss the rights-based concept of policing versus a utilitarian crime control model, and explain how each would resolve questions of use of deception and invasive investigative techniques.

ETHICAL DILEMMAS

Situation 1

While on the witness stand you answer all the prosecutor's and defense attorney's questions. You complete your testimony and exit the courtroom, knowing that you have specific knowledge that may help the defense attorney's case. You have answered all questions truthfully, but the specific question needed to help the defense was not asked. What should you do?

Situation 2

You are a police officer testifying in a drug case. You have already testified that you engaged in a buy–bust operation and the defendant was identified by an undercover officer as the one who sold him a small quantity of drugs. You testified that you chased the suspect down an alley and apprehended him. Immediately before you caught up with him, he threw down a number of glassine envelopes filled with what turned out to be cocaine. The prosecutor finished his direct examination and now the defense attorney has begun cross-examining you. He asked if you had the suspect in your sight the entire time between when you identified him as the one who sold to the undercover and when you put the handcuffs on him. Your arrest report didn't mention it, but there were a couple of seconds where you slipped as you went around the corner of the alley and fell down. During that short time the suspect had proceeded a considerable distance down the alley. You do not think there was anyone else around and you are as sure as you possibly can be that it was your suspect who dropped the bags, but you know that if you testify to this incident truthfully, the defense attorney might be able to argue successfully that the bags were not dropped by the suspect and get him acquitted of the much more serious possession with intent to distribute charge. What should you do?

Situation 3

You are a federal agent and have been investigating a major drug ring for a long time. One of your informants is fairly highly placed within this ring and has been providing you with good information. You were able to "turn" him because he faces a murder charge—there is probable cause that he shot and killed a co-worker during an argument about five years ago, before he became involved in the drug ring. You have been holding the murder charge over his head to get him to cooperate and have been able, with the help of the U.S. District Attorney's office, to keep the local prosecutor from filing an information and arresting him. The local prosecutor is upset because the family wants some resolution in the case. You believe that the information he is able to provide you will result in charges of major drug sales and racketeering on several of the top smugglers, putting a dent in the drug trade for your region. At the same time, you understand that you are constantly risking the possibility that he may escape prosecution by leaving the country, and that you are blocking the justice that the family of the murdered victim deserve. What would you do?

SUGGESTED READINGS

Alderson, J. 1998. *Principled Policing: Protecting the Public with Integrity.* Winchester, MA: Waterside Press.

Crank, J. 2003. *Imagining Justice.* Cincinnati, OH: Anderson Publishing Co.

Crank, J., and M. Caldero. 2000. *Police Ethics: The Corruption of Noble Cause.* Cincinnati, OH: Anderson Publishing Co.

Klockars, C., and S. Mastrofski. 1991. *Thinking About Police.* New York: McGraw-Hill.

Lynch, G. (ed). 1999. *Human Dignity and the Police: Ethics and Integrity in Police Work.* Springfield, IL: Charles C. Thomas.

Prenzler, T., and J. Ransley. 2002. *Police Reform: Building Integrity.* Sydney, Australia: Hawkins Press.

Walker, S. 2001. *Police Accountability: The Role of Citizen Oversight.* Belmont, CA: Wadsworth Publishing Co.

9

Ethics and Legal Professionals

Key Terms

bureaucratic justice
wedding-cake illustration
appeal

shadow jury
situational model
systems model

Chapter Objectives

- Become familiar with the source of legal ethics.
- Understand the various perceptions of judicial processing.
- Understand the concept of attorney as a moral agent or as a legal agent.
- Learn the variety of ethical issues faced by defense attorneys.

Just as the Rodney King incident directed public scrutiny toward the ethics of law enforcement, the O. J. Simpson trial acted as a catalyst for scrutiny of the criminal court system in this country. And in the same way that the King incident has been used to illustrate how racial prejudice, distrust, and class conflict affect law enforcement procedures, the Simpson case illustrates how these same issues carry over to judicial processing and influence the administration of justice.

Many people refer to the criminal justice system as the criminal *injustice* system because of a perception that practices in this nation's courtrooms do not necessarily conform to the ideals of justice. As mentioned in previous chapters, justice is a goal that is not necessarily synonymous with law, and a legal system may not always be capable of achieving moral justice. The basic elements of a justice system are an impartial fact-finding process and a fair and equitable resolution. The ethical and moral duties of those who work within the system are typically consistent with the concept of justice. However, day-to-day practices are sometimes inconsistent with the pursuit of justice, and perhaps even violate principles of law.

FIRST, LET'S KILL ALL THE LAWYERS . . .

Public perceptions of lawyers indicate that the public has little confidence in their ability to live up to ideals of equity, fairness, and justice. In a 2001 Gallup survey, lawyers were rated as "less ethical" and "less honest" than police officers, doctors, auto mechanics, and stockbrokers. Only labor union leaders, insurance salespeople, and car salespeople (among a few others) had lower ratings than did lawyers. Only 18 percent of those polled agreed that lawyers' ethics and honesty were high or very high (Gallup, 2001).

In the 1980s, the law scandal was the savings and loan fiasco, in which the greed and corruption of those in the banking industry were ably assisted by the industry's attorneys, and the taxpayers picked up the bill for the bankrupt institutions and outstanding loans. The scandal in the 1990s was the William Clinton–Monica Lewinsky investigation, with opinions mixed as to which set of lawyers were more embarrassing—those who could coach the president that oral sex wasn't technically "sexual relations" or Kenneth Starr and his assistants, who spent millions of dollars in an investigation that centered on semen stains. This new century brought us the debacle of WorldCom and Enron and, again, lawyers have played a central role, along with business executives and accountants. Apparently, even lawyers don't think much of their profession. In a 1992 California bar poll, 70 percent of lawyers would choose another career if they could and 75 percent would not want their children to be lawyers (Glendon, 1994: 85).

The perception of the lawyer as an amoral "hired gun" is in sharp contrast to the ideal of the lawyer as an officer of the court, sworn to uphold the ideals of justice declared sacrosanct under our system of law. Interestingly, or perhaps not surprisingly, our government is made up largely of lawyers: a large percentage of elected officials are lawyers, twenty-three out of forty-one presidents have been lawyers, and thirteen out of the eighteen members of President Clinton's cabinet were lawyers (Glendon, 1994: 12). Our nation's leaders and historical heroes have just as likely been lawyers (Abraham Lincoln, for example) as generals, and our nation's consciousness is permeated with the belief in law and legal vindication.

We continue to have mixed perceptions of lawyers. On the one hand, the public tends to agree with a stereotype of lawyers as amoral, motivated by money, and with no conscience or concern for morality; on the other hand, the first response to any perception of wrong is to find a legal advocate and sue, with the belief that a lawyer will right any wrong and solve any problem. Continuing attempts for tort reform illustrate these two views: those who advocate tort reform argue that lawyers are making millions by harassing businesses and medical professionals with needless lawsuits; those against tort reform argue that without lawyers to guard the interests of consumers, businesses, including H.M.O.'s, would continue to foist unsafe products upon and provide poor service to an unsuspecting and powerless public.

QUOTE

Lawyers are upset. They have discovered what they believe to be an alarming new trend: people don't like them. The American Bar Association recently appointed a special panel to investigate the legal profession's bad image. The California State Bar has commissioned a survey to find out why so many people dislike lawyers . . . . We wish to reassure lawyers. This wave of anti-lawyer feeling is nothing new. People have always hated you.

A. Roth and J. Roth, *Devil's Advocates: The Unnatural History of Lawyers* (Berkeley, CA: Nolo Press, 1989): i.

History indicates that the ethics of those associated with the legal process have always been suspect. Plato and Aristotle condemned the advocate because of his ability to make the truth appear false and the guilty appear innocent. This early distrust continued throughout history; early colonial lawyers were distrusted and even punished for practicing law. For many years, lawyers could not charge a fee for their services because the mercenary aspect of the profession was condemned (Papke, 1986: 32). Gradually, lawyers and the profession itself were accepted, but suspicion and controversy continued in the area of fees and qualifications. Partly to counteract public antipathy, lawyers formed their own organization, the American Bar Association (A.B.A.), in 1878. Shortly afterward, this professional organization established the first ethical guidelines for lawyers.

Perhaps the best explanation for the long-standing distrust of lawyers is that they typically represent trouble. No one needs a lawyer unless he or she feels a wrong has been done to them or a person needs to be defended. The ability of lawyers to argue either side raises a level of distrust. We would prefer a passionate advocate rather than a paid advocate. In the next section, we explore basic perceptions that influence a lawyer's advocacy in our criminal justice system.

Finally, let us not forget the full context of the opening quote of this section, widely used as a negative stab at lawyers. From a Shakespeare play, the quote is from a despot, who, before making a grab for power, argued the first thing he must do was kill all the lawyers, because it was lawyers who were the guardians of law. However, it should also be pointed out that the reason the existing power holders were attacked was because they used the law to oppress the powerless. And so it is today. The law can be either a tool of oppression or a sword of justice, but, lawyers are always the ones who wield its power.

PERCEPTIONS OF JUDICIAL PROCESSING

As mentioned before, the ideal of the justice system is that two advocates of equal ability will engage in a pursuit of truth, guided by a neutral fact finder. The truth is supposed to emerge from the contest. Actual practices in our justice system are very different. Various descriptions profess to offer a more realistic picture of the system. One approach is to look at judicial processing as a game. In this chapter, each player has a certain role to perform, with rules and responsibilities. "Hidden agendas" (covert motivations and goals) exist. The adversarial system pits the defense attorney against the prosecutor, and the judge may be considered the umpire in this contest. The judge sets down the rules and, unless there is a jury, decides who wins the contest.

Does the "best" opponent always win? If a powerful and rich defendant is able to hire the best criminal lawyer in the country, complete with several assistants and investigators, the prosecutor (who is typically overworked and understaffed) is overwhelmed. Of course, this is the exception, and more commonly a defendant must rely on an overworked and probably inexperienced public defender or an attorney who can make criminal law profitable only by high caseloads and quick turnover. In these instances, the defense is outmatched by a prosecutor in a public office with greater access to evidence and investigative assistance. Heffernan and Kleinig (2000) provide a number of discussions concerning how poverty affects a wide range of judicial processing decisions. It is hard to refute the notion that one's socioeconomic status doesn't affect one's experience in the justice system.

A variation of game theory is offered by Blumberg (1969), who refers to the practice of law as a confidence game because both prosecutor and defense attorney conspire to appear as something they are not—adversaries in a do-or-die situation. What is more commonly the case is that the prosecutor and the defense attorney will still be working together when the client is gone; thus, their primary allegiance is not to the client, but to themselves. For defense attorneys this may involve either making the case appear more difficult than it is in order to justify their fee or, if the client has no resources, arbitrarily concluding a case that has merit. Attorneys may use their power for reasons other than the client's interest; in the following example cited by Blumberg (1969: 329), all actors cooperate in the conspiracy against the client:

> [Judges] . . . will adjourn the case of an accused in jail awaiting plea or sentence if the attorney requests such action. While explicitly this may be done for some innocuous and seemingly valid reason, the tacit purpose is that pressure is being applied by the attorney for the collection of his fee, which he knows will probably not be forthcoming if the case is concluded.

The game here is to make the client believe that the advocacy system is working for him or her whereas, in reality, it is being used against his or her interest. Other examples include attorneys asking for continuances because of a missing witness—"Mr. Green"—which, in reality, means simply that the attorney hasn't been paid yet and wants the court to exert pressure by keeping the client in jail or continuing the pending criminal case until payment is rendered. For this charade to be successful, all players in the system must cooperate; evidently, in many situations they do.

Great shows of anger and emotion in the courtroom help clients believe they are getting something for their money, but such performances are belied by the jocular relationship sometimes apparent between the defense attorney and the prosecutor shortly after trial or between courtroom sessions. In fact, many defense attorneys are ex-prosecutors. This is, in some respects, helpful to their clients because they know the way the prosecutor's office works and what a reasonable plea offer would be. But one also must assume that the prosecutorial experience of these attorneys has shaped their perceptions of clients and what would be considered fair punishment. Moreover, their continuing relationships with prosecutors overlap into their social and personal lives, so it is not surprising that allegiances are more often all lawyers against civilians, rather than defense versus prosecution.

Other authors have also used the analogy of a confidence game to describe the interaction among prosecutors, defense attorneys, and clients. For example, Scheingold (1984: 155) writes the following:

> [T]he practice of defense law is all too often a "confidence game" in which the lawyers are "double agents" who give the appearance of assiduous defense of their clients but whose real loyalty is to the criminal courts. The defendant, from this perspective, is only an episode in the attorney's enduring relationships with the prosecutors and judges whose goodwill is essential to a successful career in the defense bar.

Another perspective describes our courts as administering **bureaucratic justice.** Each case is seen as only one of many for the professionals who work in the system. The goal of the system—namely, bureaucratic efficiency—becomes more important than the original goal of justice. Also, because each case is part of a workload, decision making takes on more complications. For instance, a defense lawyer may be less inclined to fight very hard for a "loser" client if he or she wants a favor for another client later in the week. The prosecutor may decide not to charge a guilty person in order to get him or her to testify against someone else. In this sense, each case is not separately tried and judged, but is linked to others and processed as part of a workload.

The bureaucratic system of justice is seen as developing procedures and policies that, although not intentionally discriminatory, may contribute to a perception of unfairness. For instance, a major element in bureaucratic justice is the presumption of guilt, whereas the ideal of our justice system is a presumption of innocence. District attorneys, judges, and even defense attorneys approach each case presuming guilt and place a priority on achieving the most expeditious resolution of the case. This is the basic rationale behind plea bargaining, whether it is recognized or not: the defendant is presumed to be guilty, and the negotiation is to achieve a guilty plea while bargaining for the best possible sentence—the lowest possible is the goal of the defense while the highest possible is the goal of the prosecutor. Plea bargaining is consistent with the bureaucratic justice system because it is the most efficient way of getting maximum punishment for minimum work.

Descriptions of bureaucratic justice such as the following (Scheingold, 1984: 158) allow for the fact that efficiency is tempered with other values and priorities:

> . . . the coercive thrust of the presumption of guilt is softened
> somewhat by the operational morality of fairness that leads the
> participants to make certain that defendants get neither more or less
> than is coming to them—that defendants, in other words, get their due.

Scheingold is referring to the practices of judges, prosecutors, and defense attorneys who adapt the system to their personal standards of justice. This is exemplified by a judge who determines that an individual offender is a threat to society and so overlooks errors during trial to make sure that the individual ends up in prison. On the other hand, a person who is legally guilty might get a break because it is determined that he is a decent guy who made a mistake rather than a "crook." Moreover, in almost all cases there may be general consensus on both sides about what is fair punishment for any given offender. Defense attorneys who argue for unrealistically low sentences do so in a desultory and uncommitted fashion, knowing that the prosecutor would not and could not offer such a sentence. Prosecutors put up very little argument when defense attorneys ask for sentences that fit office guidelines. Instead of describing the justice system as one that practices the presumption of innocence and takes careful steps to determine guilt, what may be more realistic is to view it as a system wherein all participants assume guilt, take superficial steps to arrive at the punishment phase, and operate under a value system that allocates punishment and mercy to offenders according to an informal consensus of fairness. It should be noted that there has been increased influence from victims in this process so that today what is fair may also be determined by the victim's wishes. Prosecutors may not agree to a plea bargain if the victim actively opposes it. Only in cases where the victim does not take an active part does the bureaucratic system operate unfettered (Stickels, 2003).

One other perception of the criminal justice system is that of Samuel Walker's (1985) **wedding-cake illustration,** based on a model proposed by Lawrence Friedman and Robert Percival. In this scheme, the largest portion of criminal cases form the bottom layers of the cake, and the few "serious" cases form the top layer. The top layer is most dramatically represented by cases such as the murder trial of O. J. Simpson. In this highly publicized case, the defendant had an extremely skilled (and highly paid) team of attorneys as well as trial consultants, investigators, and public relations specialists. Los Angeles County paid millions to keep up with its own team of attorneys, experts, and investigators. The criminal processing and trial proceeded with admirable speed. Each side worked incredibly hard and used an arsenal of tactics (that were then critiqued by armchair experts each evening). The case itself was used in law school evidence classes because of the wealth of material present in pretrial discovery, exclusionary motions, jury selection, and the like.

The bottom of the cake is represented by the thousands of cases that are processed every year in which defendants may only meet with an attorney once or twice immediately before agreeing to a plea arrangement. It is no wonder that many believe that justice is for sale in this country, with lawyers as the panderers. Since the public is exposed only to the top of the wedding cake, it develops a highly distorted perception of the system. The majority of the American public is perhaps disgusted with the multitude of evidentiary rules and the Byzantine process of the trial itself. However, these concerns may be valid only for a very small portion of criminal cases.

According to Walker's wedding-cake analysis, the courtroom work group is believed to share definitions of seriousness and operate as a unit to keep the dynamics of the courtroom static, despite changes that are forced upon it. Changes such as the exclusionary rule, determinate sentencing, and other recent legislation have had surprisingly little impact on court outcomes because of a shared perception of serious crime and appropriate punishment. The vast majority of crime is considered trivial, and the processing of these cases involves very little energy or attention from system actors (Walker, 1985).

Dershowitz's view of the criminal justice system (see the Quote) is probably, as Dershowitz admits himself, a bit overstated, but it is a slightly different illustration of the courtroom work group or bureaucratic justice system in operation. The major ethical problem with this (if it does represent reality) is that innocence, truth, and due process are perceived as inconvenient and expendable.

> **QUOTE**
>
> *. . . Here are some of the key rules of the justice game:*
> *Rule I: Almost all criminal defendants are, in fact, guilty.*
> *Rule II: All criminal defense lawyers, prosecutors and judges understand and believe Rule I.*
> *Rule III: It is easier to convict guilty defendants by violating the Constitution than by complying with it, and in some cases it is impossible to convict guilty defendants without violating the Constitution.*
> *Rule IV: Almost all police lie about whether they violated the Constitution in order to convict guilty defendants.*
> *Rule V: All prosecutors, judges, and defense attorneys are aware of Rule IV.*
> *Rule VI: Many prosecutors implicitly encourage police to lie about whether they violated the Constitution in order to convict guilty defendants.*
> *Rule VII: All judges are aware of Rule VI.*
> *Rule VIII: Most trial judges pretend to believe police officers who they know are lying.*
> *Rule IX: All appellate judges are aware of Rule VIII, yet many pretend to believe the trial judges who pretend to believe the lying police officers.*
> *Rule X: Most judges disbelieve defendants about whether their constitutional rights have been violated, even if they are telling the truth.*
> *Rule XI: Most judges and prosecutors would not knowingly convict a defendant who they believe to be innocent of the crime charged (or a closely related crime).*
> *Rule XII: Rule XI does not apply to members of organized crime, drug dealers, career criminals, or potential informers.*
> *Rule XIII: Nobody really wants justice.*
>
> ----------
>
> Alan Dershowitz, *The Best Defense* (New York: Vintage Books, 1982): xxi.

ETHICAL ISSUES FOR LEGAL PROFESSIONALS

A profession, as defined in Chapter 6, involves a specialized body of knowledge, commitment to the social good, the ability to regulate itself, and high social status (Davis and Elliston, 1986: 13). The presence of ethical standards is essential to the definition of a profession. More importantly, membership in a profession implies a special set of rules, different from those applied to everyone else. Very often these rules may involve a higher standard of behavior, but they may also involve greater privileges or the right to act in a different way from everyone else by virtue of that membership. Formal ethical standards for lawyers and judges were originally promulgated by the American Bar Association in the Model Code of Professional Responsibility. The original canons, adapted from the Alabama Bar Association Code of 1887, were adopted by the ABA in 1908 and have been revised frequently since then. Several years ago, the ABA switched its endorsement of the Model Code as the general guide for ethical behavior to the Model Rules of Professional Responsibility. The Model Rules continue to be revised periodically, responding to changing sensibilities and emerging issues. The latest two revisions were in 2000 and 2002.

Today's Model Rules cover many aspects of the lawyer's profession, including such areas as client–lawyer relationships, the lawyer as counselor, the lawyer as advocate, transactions with others, public service, and maintaining the integrity of the profession. Ethical issues in criminal law may involve courtroom behavior, perjury, conflicts of interest, use of the media, investigation efforts, use of immunity, discovery and the sharing of evidence, relationships with opposing attorneys, and plea bargaining.

To enforce these ethical rules, the ABA has a standing committee on ethical responsibility to offer formal and informal opinions when charges of impropriety have been made. Also, each state bar association has the power to sanction offending attorneys by private or public censure or recommend to the court suspension of their privilege to practice law. Thus, the rules promulgated by the state bar have essentially the power of law behind them. The bar associations also have the power to grant entry into the profession since one must ordinarily belong to the bar association of a particular state to practice law there. Bar associations judge competence by testing the applicant's knowledge, but they also judge moral worthiness by background checks of individuals. The purpose of these restrictive admission procedures is to protect the public image of the legal profession by rejecting unscrupulous or dishonest individuals or those unfit to practice for other reasons. However, many feel that if bar associations were serious about protecting the profession, they would also continue to monitor the behavior and moral standing of current members with the same care they seem to take in the initial decision regarding entry (Elliston, 1986: 53).

A practicing attorney is investigated only when complaints have been lodged against him or her. The investigative bodies have been described as decentralized, informal, and secret. They do little for dissatisfied clients since typical client complaints involve incompetence—a vague and ill-defined term (Mark and Cathcart, 1986: 72). One study of client satisfaction found that the biggest complaint against attorneys was that too little time was given the client by the lawyer or that the lawyer was inaccessible (Arafat and McCahery, 1978: 205). Neither of these complaints is likely to receive a disciplinary ruling by an ethics committee. Many bar disciplinary committees are hopelessly understaffed and overburdened with complaints. Complaints may take years to investigate, and, in the meantime, if prospective clients call, they will be told only that the attorney is in good standing and has no substantiated complaints. In a recent study of attorney discipline by an organization for legal reform, it was reported that only 3 percent of investigations by state disciplinary committees result in public sanctions; only 1 percent end in disbarment (*San Antonio Express News,* 2002).

Individuals with complaints against their lawyers in the civil arena receive little enough satisfaction, however, criminal defendants are arguably even less likely to have anyone care or rectify incompetence or unethical behavior on the part of their attorney. "You get what you pay for" may be true to an extent, but even that phrase does not truly represent the possibility of a family mortgaging its home, signing over cars, and emptying its bank account for an attorney who promises to represent a family member against a criminal charge and then find that the attorney will not answer calls, doesn't appear in court, or is unprepared and forgets to file necessary motions.

Law schools have been criticized for being singularly uninterested in fostering any type of moral conscience in graduating students. Law schools purport to be in the practice of reshaping law students so that when they emerge "thinking like a lawyer," they have mastered a type of thinking that is concerned with detail and logical analysis. Others argue this is done at the expense of being sensitive to morality and larger social issues.

QUOTE

. . . law school is no place for human beings who care about other human beings. . . .

G. Spence, *With Justice for None* (New York: Penguin, 1989): 45.

Gerry Spence, a flamboyant defense attorney, boasts of receiving low grades in law school—an indication, he believes, that he did not "sell out" to the mindset of bottom-line winning and profit above all else that is representative of law school indoctrination (Spence, 1989). Stover (1989) writes how public interest values decline during law school. The reason for this decline seemingly has to do with the low value placed on public-interest issues by the law school curriculum, which also treats ethical and normative concerns as irrelevant or trivial compared to the "bar courses" such as contract law and torts.

Even though all law schools today require professional responsibility courses, morality and ethics are often made light of, even in those courses, where there are stories (humorous and otherwise) of how to get around the ethical and legal mandates. For instance, in the discovery phase of a lawsuit, the legal rule that requires an attorney to turn over documents requested by the other side (that are not otherwise privileged), can be circumvented by burying important documents in 600 boxes of paperwork.

There has been greater attention to ethics in recent years. Bar exams have a special section devoted to the Model Rules and the state's own professional responsibility code, but these tests are often hyper-technical, testing the minutiae of the rules, rather than the spirit of practicing law ethically and honestly. Most states also require continuing legal education credit hours in the area of ethics. However, similar to our earlier discussion of police officers, classroom ethics training that encourages one set of behaviors is often contradicted and disparaged by the professional subculture. If this is the case, then such training might not be very effective.

The Attorney–Client Relationship

Many of the Model Rules involve the special relationship the attorney has with the client. The separation of professional and personal responsibility poses difficult issues. Many lawyers feel that loyalty to the client is paramount to their duties as a professional. This loyalty surpasses and eclipses individual and private decision making, and the special relationship said to exist between lawyer and client justifies decisions that might otherwise be deemed unacceptable.

An extreme position is that the attorney is no more than the *legal agent* of the client. The lawyer is neither immoral nor moral, but merely a legal tool. This position is represented by the statement "I am a lawyer, first and foremost." A more moderate position is that the loyalty to the client presents a special relationship between client and lawyer, similar to that between mother and child or with trusted friend. This protected relationship justifies fewer actions than the one described above. The lawyer is expected to dissuade the client from taking unethical or immoral actions, but loyalty would preclude putting anyone's interests above the clients. The third position is that the lawyer is a *moral agent* who has to adhere to his or her own moral code. The client's interests come first only as long as they do not conflict with the lawyer's morality and ethical code. If there is a conflict, then the lawyer follows his or her conscience.

Some reject perspectives that discount the lawyer's responsibility as an individual to make his or her own moral decisions. Lawyers are perceived as the legal *and* moral agents of their clients, rather than merely legal agents. Their personal responsibility to avoid wrongdoing precludes involving themselves in their clients' wrongdoing (Postema, 1986: 168). This position is represented by the statement, "I am a person first, lawyer second."

Legal Agent versus Moral Agent? Elliott Cohen (1991), an advocate of the moral agent position, believes that to be purely a legal advocate is inconsistent with being a morally good person in several ways. For instance, the virtue of justice would be inconsistent with a zealous advocate who would maximize the chance of his or her client's winning, regardless of the fairness of the outcome. A pure legal agent would sacrifice values of truthfulness, moral courage, benevolence, trustworthiness, and moral autonomy. Only if the attorney is a moral agent, as well as a legal advocate, can there be any possibility of the attorney's maintaining individual morality.

Cohen (1991: 135–136) suggests some principles that attorneys must follow to be considered moral:

1. Treat others as ends in themselves and not as mere means to winning cases.
2. Treat clients and other professional relations who are relatively similar in a similar fashion.
3. Do not deliberately engage in behavior apt to deceive the court as to the truth.
4. Be willing, if necessary, to make reasonable personal sacrifices—of time, money, popularity, and so on—for what you justifiably believe to be a morally good cause.
5. Do not give money to, or accept money from, clients for wrongful purposes or in wrongful amounts.
6. Avoid harming others in the process of representing your client.

7. Be loyal to your client and do not betray his confidences.

8. Make your own moral decisions to the best of your ability and act consistently upon them.

The rationale for these principles seems to be an amalgamation of ethical formalism, utilitarianism, and other ethical frameworks. Some of these principles may seem impossible to uphold and may be subject to bitter criticism on the part of practicing attorneys. For instance, how does one avoid harming others when one is an advocate for one side in a contest? There are losers and winners in civil contests as well as in criminal law, and lawyers must take responsibility for the fact that sometimes the loser is harmed in financial or emotional ways.

Recently, Cohen's position has been attacked as naïve and wrong on several counts. Memory and Rose (2002: 29) argue against Cohen's proposed principle that a lawyer "may refuse to aid or participate in conduct that he sincerely believes, after careful reflection on the relevant facts, to be unjust or otherwise morally wrong notwithstanding his obligation to seek the lawful objectives of his client." They believe that lawyers can be effective and morally good at the same time, and argue that rules in place already prevent unscrupulous acts. For instance, Model Rule 3.3 prohibits lying. It states that lawyers may not make false statements of materials facts or law, cannot fail to disclose a material fact to a tribunal when disclosure is necessary to avoid assisting a criminal or fraudulent act by the client, fail to disclose legal authority that is directly adverse to one's client's interest, or offer evidence that one knows to be false. According to the authors, this rule and others prevent attorneys from sacrificing truth even when zealously pursuing clients' interests.

Memory and Rose (2002) argue that decisions regarding justice and morality are so subjective that it is impossible for them to be subject to judgment and that rules are developing in ways that will avoid cases of abuse by a more objective application of judgments. If lawyers acted as moral agents, the result would be the loss of the client's trust in lawyers, since the lawyer would be able to substitute his or her individual morality for the clients.

Cohen (2002: 23), in a rebuttal article, uses the ethics of care as underpinning for his continued defense of the moral agent idea:

> morality concerns concrete interpersonal relationships that can be understood only by people who have compassion and empathy for the predicaments of other people. . . . Morally virtuous lawyers (moral agents) possess such affective aspects of emotional development, but it is precisely such a dimension that must be lacking from the pure legal advocate who must get used to working injury upon others without having any strong feelings of guilt, sorrow, or regret.

He points out some inconsistencies in their article, such as their point that rules prohibit falsehoods, but require that lawyers keep quiet even when third parties will be financially harmed because of illegal actions taken by their client. His larger point, however, is that rules cannot define a moral person:

"Rules do not, however, exhaust the moral and ethical considerations that should inform a lawyer, for no worthwhile human activity can be completely defined by legal rules" (2002: 34).

In general, Cohen and Memory and Rose seem to be in agreement on the most egregious misconduct of lawyers; their disagreement comes from the value they place on rules versus individual responsibility for moral judgments. In an earlier chapter, the point was made that rules have never been able to substitute for moral decision making on the part of individual actors. This is more consistent with Cohen's position than that of Memory and Rose. Cohen's argument is essentially that training and socialization into the "culture of law" creates the legal agent role and encourages a type of "noble cause corruption" discussed in Chapter 8. In this profession, the "noble cause" is winning. In a culture that supports "ends" thinking (winning) over "means," rules are no more likely to control misconduct by lawyers than they do police officers.

QUOTE

About half the practice of a decent lawyer consists in telling would-be clients that they are damned fools and should stop.

Reported in M. Glendon, *A Nation Under Lawyers* (New York: Farrar, Straus and Giroux, 1994): 76, 75.

You're an attorney. It's your duty to lie, conceal and distort everything, and slander everybody.

J. Giradeaux, *The Madwoman of Chaillot* (adapted by Maurice Valency) (New York: Random House, Inc., 1949): Act Two.

Which of these quotes represents a legal agent statement? Which represents a moral agent statement?

A Higher Standard of Behavior?

In Chapter 6 we discussed the concept of police officers, as public servants, being held to a higher standard of conduct than those they serve. This same principle applies to attorneys. The Model Code of Professional Responsibility for lawyers dictates that they should be "temperate and dignified" and "refrain from all illegal and morally reprehensible conduct." The Model Rules expect that "a lawyer's conduct should conform to the requirements of the law, both in professional service to clients and in the lawyer's business and personal affairs." These are prescriptions similar to those found in the Law Enforcement Code of Ethics. Both groups of professionals are expected to uphold a higher standard of behavior than the general public. They provide protection and help enforce the rules and provide a model of behavior for the rest of us. Since both professions have a special place in society's attempt to control individual behavior, it is not unreasonable to expect a higher standard of behavior to apply.

However, some allege that instead of a *higher* standard, lawyers (like some police officers) allow themselves a *double* standard. Lying is lying unless it is done by a lawyer, and then it is just doing one's duty, or a "misstatement of fact." Glendon (1994), in a highly critical overview of the legal profession, proposes that the legal profession has changed in very dramatic ways, not all of which have been for the better. Although the practice of law was once governed by rules of ethics and etiquette and lawyers acted like gentlemen (literally, since the profession was for the most part closed to women, minorities, and the lower class), it has become open to those excluded groups in the last twenty-five years, but it has also become a world of "no rules" or, more accurately, only one rule: "Winning is everything."

The Use of Discretion

Recall that discretion is the ability to make a decision and exists at each stage of the criminal justice system. Professionals at each stage have the opportunity to use their discretion wisely and ethically, or, alternatively, they may use their discretion in an unethical manner. In the courts, prosecutors have discretion to pursue prosecution or not, defense attorneys have discretion to accept or refuse cases and choose trial tactics, and judges have discretion to make rulings on evidence and other trial procedures, as well as decide on convictions and sentences.

One view of law is that it is neutral and objective and that formal rules of law are used in decision making (Pinkele and Louthan, 1985: 9). The reality, however, is that lawmakers, law enforcers, and lawgivers have a great deal of discretion in making and interpreting the law. Law is political in that it is responsive to power interests. Far from being absolute or objective, the law is a dynamic, ever-changing symbol of political will. Just as lawmaking and interpretation are influenced by political will and power groups, individual lawgivers and those who work in the system also have a great deal of discretion in interpreting and enforcing the law. The Supreme Court, as the ultimate authority of law in this country, decides constitutionality, and these interpretations are far from neutral, despite the myth of objective decision making. This is the reason that selection of Supreme Court justices (as well as all federal judges) is such a hard-fought political contest. Ideological positions do make a difference, and no one is fooled that a black robe removes bias.

If we accept that discretion is an operating reality in the justice system, then we must ask in what ways legal professionals use this discretion. If individual value systems replace absolute rules or laws, then these value systems may be ethical or unethical. For instance, a judge may base a decision on fairness, or the judge may base the decision on prejudicial beliefs (e.g., that blacks are more criminal so they deserve longer sentences, or that women are not dangerous so they should get probation). There may be many other situations where one's biases and prejudices are not so easily identified.

Judges' rulings on evidentiary matters are supposed to be based on rules of evidence, but sometimes there is room for interpretation and individual discretion. Again, some judges use this discretion appropriately and make decisions in a best effort to conform to the spirit of the evidentiary rule, but other judges use arbitrary or unfair criteria, such as personal dislike of an attorney, disagreement with the rule, a desire for one side or the other to win the case, or, as in the case of at least one particular judge, awarding favorable rulings to each attorney by turns with no regard to the merit of each objection.

Defense attorneys and prosecutors also have a great deal of discretion in the decisions they must make. Prosecutors must decide whether to charge, and what to charge. They must decide trial strategy and what to offer in a plea bargain. Defense attorneys do not have the discretion to accept the plea against their client's wishes, but they have a great deal of power in persuading their client to take a plea or not; deciding what the chances of winning at trial are, and whether to use affirmative defenses.

How does one know whether one is using discretion ethically or unethically? The best approach is to follow the law or legal rule and go outside established law only if there is an egregious violation of some higher standard of justice. However, when the rule or the law appears, on its face, to result in some serious miscarriage of justice, then perhaps ethical systems can be applied to judge alternative courses of action. This is similar to Cohen's moral agent idea.

It should also be noted that discretionary decisions at the trial level can be reexamined through the process of **appeal.** Appeals are part of due process in that they serve as a check on the decision making of trial judges. Supposedly, any gross errors will be corrected; any extremely unethical actions will result in a new trial. However, appeals are not conducted in all cases, and even in cases that are appealed, many errors go unnoticed and uncorrected. For instance, courtroom behavior is seldom noticed or corrected unless it extremely and blatantly violates constitutional rights. Further, it is possible—and indeed, probable—that politics and other considerations affect appellate decisions.

The remainder of this chapter and the next chapter will explore the use of discretion in the courts by looking at the role responsibilities of the major actors in the system—the defense attorney, the prosecutor, and the judge. Obviously, these actors work with a criminal code that is handed down to them by the legislature. The formation of laws and the factors and compromises that go into a law's creation or revision constitute a subject matter that will be left to others. We will address the ethical questions that arise in the *implementation,* rather than the *creation,* of law.

ETHICAL ISSUES FOR DEFENSE ATTORNEYS

The role of the defense attorney is to protect the due-process rights of the defendant. Due process is supposed to minimize mistakes in judicial proceedings that might result in a deprivation of life, liberty, or property. Due-process rights, including notice, neutral fact finders, cross-examination, and presentation of evidence and witnesses, are supposed to minimize the risk of error. The defense attorney is there to ensure that these rights are protected—for instance, during interrogation to make sure no coercion is used, at lineup to make sure it is fair and unbiased, and during trial to ensure adequate cross-examination and presentation of evidence. This pure role of advocate is contradictory to the reality that the defense attorney must, if he or she is to work with the other actors in the court system, accommodate their needs as well as those of clients.

Defense attorneys are always in the position of balancing the rights of individual clients against overall effectiveness. Extreme attempts to protect one client's rights will influence the defense attorney's effectiveness for all clients. Furthermore, defense attorneys must balance the needs and problems of the client against their ethical responsibilities to the system and profession. Individual rights are balanced by other considerations.

Except for a few high-powered "stars" across the country, defense attorneys have a fairly negative reputation in the legal community, as well as with the general public. They are seen as incompetent or unable to compete on the higher rungs of the status ladder of law (those higher rungs being corporate, tax, and international law). Alternatively or additionally, they are seen as "shady" or "money grubbers" who get the guilty off by sleazy tactics. In fiction, defense attorneys are presented as either fearless crusaders who always manage to defend innocent clients (usually against unethical prosecutors) or as sleazy deal makers who are either too burned out or selfish to care about their clients. The reality, of course, fits none of these portrayals. Kittel (1990) finds that the majority of defense attorneys would not change their career given an opportunity to do so, and that most chose their career because they were interested in the trial work it offered or for public policy reasons, as opposed to the common myth that criminal defense attorneys enter that field because they couldn't make it anywhere else.

As stated earlier, many defense attorneys started out as prosecutors. This sometimes causes problems when they have trouble making the transition from "good guy battling evil" to the more subtle role of defender of due process. Often those one represents are not people that one can feel proud to be helping. If the attorney cannot make the transition from prosecution to defense and feel comfortable in the role, then it is difficult to do a zealous defense (Cohen, 2001).

As mentioned earlier, the system tends to operate under a presumption of guilt. Indeed, defense attorneys are often in the position of defending clients they know are guilty. The rationale for defending a guilty person is that a person deserves due process before a finding of guilt and punishment. Before punishment can be morally imposed, a fair procedure must ensure that the punishment is appropriate. To ensure appropriate punishment, a set of fact-finding procedures is necessary, and the defense attorney's role is to make sure that the rules are followed. If defense attorneys are doing their job, then we can all be comfortable with a conviction. If they do not do their job, then we have no system of justice, and none of us is safe from wrongful prosecution and the awesome power of the state to investigate, prosecute and punish. Due process protects us all by making the criminal justice system prove wrongdoing "beyond a reasonable doubt." The person who makes sure no shortcuts are taken is the defense attorney.

QUERY

Defense attorney David Smith of Greensboro, N.C., accepted a capital appeal. Smith, a highly respected former ex-U.S. attorney, admitted that he "sabotaged" the appeal of his client because "I decided that Mr. Tucker deserved to die, and I would not do anything to prevent his execution." He went through a moral crisis afterward and confessed to the state bar what he did. The appellate court extended the deadline.
You are on a state bar disciplinary committee; would you vote to disbar him?

Rimer, 2000.

In the early 1990s the ABA promulgated its Standards for Criminal Justice. "The Defense Function," Chapter 4, covers a multitude of issues, such as these:

- The function of defense counsel
- Punctuality, public statements
- Duty to the administration of justice
- Access and the lawyer–client relationship
- Duty to investigate
- Control and direction of litigation
- Plea bargaining
- Trial conduct
- Appeal

These standards are much more specific than the Law Enforcement Code of Ethics. Instead of being aspirational, the standards are specific guidelines for behavior. In this section, we will explore only a few of the many different ethical issues that confront defense attorneys in their representation of clients.

Responsibility to the Client

The basic duty defense counsel owes to the administration of justice and as an officer of the court is to serve as the accused's counselor and advocate with courage and devotion and to render effective, quality representation (Standard 4-1.2(b)).

Defense attorneys are always in the position of balancing the rights of the individual client against overall effectiveness. Extreme attempts to protect these rights will reduce the defense attorney's effectiveness for other clients. Furthermore, defense attorneys must balance the needs and problems of the client against their ethical responsibilities to the system and profession.

A lawyer is supposed to provide legal assistance to clients without regard for personal preference or interest. A lawyer is not allowed to withdraw from a case simply because he or she no longer wishes to represent the client. Only if the legal action is for harassment or malicious purposes, if continued employment will result in a violation of a disciplinary rule, if discharged by a client or if a mental or physical condition renders effective counsel impossible can a lawyer be withdrawn. In other cases, a judge may grant permission to withdraw when the client insists upon illegal or unethical actions, is uncooperative and does not follow the attorney's advice, or otherwise makes effective counsel difficult. In general, judges are loathe to allow a defendant to proceed with a *pro se* defense (by oneself) because of the risk that the conviction will be overturned on appeal.

QUERY

Would you be able to zealously defend Timothy McVeigh (convicted in the Oklahoma City bombing of a federal building)? Why or why not? Would you be able to defend a terrorist caught and tried for the World Trade Center bombing?

Legal ethics mandate that people with unpopular causes and individuals who are obviously guilty still deserve counsel, and it is the ethical duty of an attorney to provide such counsel. In fact, although many people condemn attorneys, and especially the American Civil Liberties Union's attorneys, for defending such groups as the American Nazi Party or the Ku Klux Klan or individuals such as Charles Manson or notorious drug dealers, clearly they could not do otherwise under the ethical principles of their profession.

Some lawyers have no problem at all with defending "unworthy" clients. Drug cases are becoming well known as lawyers' pork barrels. Many lawyers have made millions of dollars defending major drug smugglers and dealers. In effect, they share in the wealth generated by illegal drugs. Is it ethical to accept any client able to pay large and continuing bills? It is commonly believed that any time a criminal defendant can and will pay, a lawyer can always be found to take the case to trial and conduct innumerable appeals, no matter the likelihood of winning.

The Racketeer Influenced and Corrupt Organizations Statute (18 U.S.C. Sections 1961–68), usually referred to as RICO, has been used to confiscate drug money, including fees already paid to attorneys. Defense attorneys object strenuously to this practice, protesting that it endangers fair representation for drug defendants because attorneys may not be willing to defend these clients when there is a possibility that their fees will be confiscated. Some prosecutors, it should be noted, have gone a step further and are starting to prosecute attorneys themselves if there is evidence that an attorney is engaged in a continuing conspiracy to further a criminal enterprise by his or her association with the client. This use of the RICO statute is extremely controversial, as are other uses of it that will be discussed later.

Many people are firmly convinced that the quality of legal representation is directly related to how much money the defendant can pay. When people can make bail and hire private attorneys, do they receive better justice? Do defense attorneys exert more effort for clients who pay well than they do for court-appointed clients? Obviously, professional ethics would dictate equal consideration, but individual values also affect behavior. If an attorney felt confident that his or her court-appointed clients received at least adequate representation, then could one not justify a more zealous defense for a paying client? Where adequate representation is vaguely and poorly defined, this question is problematic.

QUOTE

[A]n advocate in the discharge of his duty, knows but one person in all the world, and that person is his client. To save that client by all means and expedients, and at all hazards and costs to other persons, and, among them, to himself, is his first and only duty, and in performing this duty he must not regard the alarm, the torments, the destruction which he may bring upon others.

Lord Brougham, 1820. Quoted in M. Glendon, *A Nation Under Lawyers* (New York: Farrar, Straus and Giroux, 1994): 40.

Confidentiality

Defense counsel should not reveal information relating to representation of a client unless the client consents after consultation, except for disclosures that are impliedly authorized in order to carry out the representation and except that defense counsel may reveal such information to the extent he or she reasonably believes necessary to prevent the client from committing a criminal act that defense counsel believes is likely to result in imminent death or substantial bodily harm (Standard 4-3.7(d)).

The attorney–client privilege refers to the inability of authorities to compel an attorney (through subpoena or threat of contempt) to disclose confidential information regarding his or her client. The ethical duty of confidentiality prohibits an attorney from disclosing to any person, or using for one's own gain, information about one's client obtained through the attorney–client relationship. The confidentiality protection is said to be inherent in the fiduciary relationship between the client and the attorney, but more important is that the client must be able to expect and receive the full and complete assistance of his or her lawyer. If a client feels compelled to withhold negative and incriminatory information, he or she will not be able to receive such assistance; thus, the lawyer must be perceived as a completely confidential agent of the client. Parallels to the attorney–client relationship are relationships between husband and wife, and the priest–penitent relationship. In these cases the relationship creates a legal entity that approximates a single interest rather than two, so a break in confidentiality would violate the Fifth Amendment protection against self-incrimination (Schoeman, 1982: 260).

The only situations wherein a lawyer can ethically reveal confidences of a client are when the client consents, when disclosure is required by law or court order, when the intention of the client is to commit a crime and the information is necessary to prevent the crime, or when one needs to defend oneself or employees against an accusation of wrongful conduct. As mentioned before, the Model Rules have supplanted the Code of Professional Responsibility as the national model for legal ethics. One of the most debated portions was the part of this rule that specifies that an attorney may violate a client's confidence only to prevent a future crime involving imminent death or grievous bodily harm. The older code allowed disclosure to prevent *any* crime. Many states have refused to adopt the restrictive rule, or have enlarged it to include any crime. This argument has been renewed in the wake of Enron. Proponents of enlarging the scope of the rule argue that such a rule would have prevented Enron lawyers from participating in the scheme to defraud stockholders by hiding the true level of debt.

Neither the restricted or inclusive rule regarding disclosing a client's future crime applied to the Garrow incident (described in the accompanying box "Too Confidential?"), so the lawyers felt ethically bound to withhold the location of two bodies from the family of the victims. Harris (1986) evaluated the actions of Garrow's two lawyers under the utilitarian ethical framework and

---

Too Confidential?

In July 1973, Robert Garrow, a 38-year-old mechanic from Syracuse, New York, killed four persons, apparently at random. The four were camping in the Adirondack Mountains. In early August, following a vigorous manhunt, he was captured by state police and indicted for the murder of a student from Schenectady. At the time of the arrest, no evidence connected Garrow to the other deaths. . . . The court appointed two Syracuse lawyers, Francis R. Belge and Frank H. Armani, to defend Garrow.

Some weeks later, during discussions with his two lawyers, Garrow told them that he had raped and killed a woman in a mine shaft. Belge and Armani located the mine shaft and the body of the Illinois woman but did not take their discovery to the police. The body was finally discovered four months later by two children playing in the mine. In September, the lawyers found the second body by following Garrow's directions. This discovery, too, went unreported; the girl's body was uncovered by a student in December. . . . Belge and Armani maintained their silence until the following June. Then, to try to show that he was insane, Garrow made statements from the witness stand that implicated him in the other three murders. At a press conference the next day, Belge and Armani outlined for the first time the sequence of events.

The local community was outraged. The lawyers, however, believed they had honored the letter and spirit of their professional duty in a tough case. "We both, knowing how the parents feel, wanted to advise them where the bodies were," Belge said, "but since it was a privileged communication, we could not reveal any information that was given to us in confidence."

Their silence was based on the legal code that admonishes the lawyer to "preserve the confidence and secrets of a client." The lawyer–client "privilege" against disclosure of confidences is one of the oldest and most ironclad in the law. If the defendant has no duty to confess his guilt or complicity in a crime, it can make no sense to assert that his lawyer has such a duty. Otherwise, the argument goes, the accused will tell his lawyer at best a deficient version of the facts, and the lawyer cannot as effectively defend the client. This argument frequently seems unconvincing; it certainly did to the people of Syracuse.

SOURCE: Harris, C. 1986: *Applying Moral Theories.* Belmont, CA: Wadsworth: 114–115. Reprinted with permission of Wadsworth Publishing Company.

decided that they did the right thing because it is ethically acceptable for lawyers to break client confidentiality only in cases in which a death or crime could be prevented by disclosure. This rule is justified by utilitarianism because it is believed that society benefits in the long run from the presence of the attorney–client confidence. Therefore, this confidence should be sacrificed only when it endangers a life.

Religious ethics might condemn the attorneys' actions because with-holding the location of the bodies was a form of deception. On the other hand, in the Catholic religion, a similar ethical dilemma might arise if some-one confessed to a priest. It would be impossible for the priest to betray that confession no matter what the circumstances. Ethical formalism is also diffi-cult to reconcile with the lawyers' actions. First of all, under the categorical imperative, the lawyers' actions must be such that we would be willing for all others to engage in similar behavior under like circumstances. Could one will that it become universal law for attorneys to keep such information secret? What if you were the parents who did not know the whereabouts of their daughter, or even if she was alive or dead? It is hard to imagine that they would be willing to agree with this universal law. On the other hand, if one was the criminal, or one's son or daughter was the criminal, one would not want a lawyer to betray confidences that would hurt his case. If one were a lawyer, it is imagined that he or she would want a rule that encouraged a client to be truthful in order to provide an adequate defense. Ethical formal-ism is also concerned with duty; it is obvious that the duty of an attorney is always to protect the interests of his or her client. As with the utilitarian for-mulation, we might differentiate between circumstances of future crimes and circumstances of past crimes.

The ethics of care would be concerned with the needs of both the client and the parents in the case described. It would perhaps resolve the issue in a less absolutist fashion than the other rationales. For instance, when discussing this case in a college classroom, many students immediately decide that they would call in the location of the bodies anonymously, thereby relieving the parents' anxiety and also protecting, to some extent, the confidential com-munication. This compromise is unsupported by an absolute view of confi-dentiality since it endangers the client (perhaps he would not even be charged with the crimes if the bodies were never found). However, it does protect the relationship of the attorney and the client and still meets the needs of the parents.

It should be noted that the rule of confidentiality does not apply to phys-ical evidence. Anything that is discoverable in the possession of a client is equally discoverable if in the possession of an attorney. Therefore, an attorney must hand over files or other incriminating evidence subject to a valid search warrant, motion, or subpoena. If the attorney is merely told where these items may be found, he or she is not obliged to tell the authorities where they are. For instance, if a client tells an attorney a murder weapon is in a certain loca-tion, the attorney cannot divulge that information to authorities. However, if the client drops a murder weapon in the attorney's lap, he or she runs the risk of being charged with a felony if it is hidden or withheld from the police. If the attorney is told where a murder weapon is and goes to check, that information is still protected; however, if the attorney takes the weapon back to his or her office, or moves it in any way, then the attorney may be subjected to felony charges of obstruction of justice, or evidence tampering.

A defense attorney's ethics may also be compromised when a client insists on taking the stand to commit perjury. Disciplinary rules specifically forbid the lawyer from allowing perjury to take place; if it happens before the attorney realizes the intent of the client, the defense must not use or refer to the perjured testimony (Freedman, 1986; Kleinig, 1986). The quandary is that if the attorney shows his disbelief or discredits the client, then this behavior violates the ethical mandate of a zealous defense, and to inform the court of the perjury violates the ethical rule of confidentiality.

Pellicotti (1990) explains that an attorney should first try to dissuade the client from committing perjury. If the client persists in plans to lie, the attorney then has an ethical duty to withdraw from the case, and there is some authority that the attorney should disclose to the court that the client plans to lie. Withdrawal is problematic since it will usually jeopardize a case, and disclosure is even more problematic since, arguably, it affects the judgment of the hearing judge. An attorney may refuse to call witnesses who plan to lie, but if the defendant's testimony will be perjured, it is, arguably, a violation of his or her rights for the attorney not to allow the defendant to take the stand.

Nix v. Whiteside (475 U.S. 157, 89 L.Ed.2d 123 [1986]) held that it did not violate the defendant's Sixth Amendment right to counsel for the attorney to refuse to help the defendant commit perjury. In this murder case, the defendant told his lawyer that he had not seen a gun in the victim's hand. At a later point, he told his attorney that if he didn't testify that he saw a gun, he would be "dead" (lose the case). The attorney told him that if he testified falsely, he would have to impeach him and would seek to withdraw from the case. The defendant testified truthfully, was found guilty, and then appealed based on ineffective counsel. The court found that the right to counsel did not include the right to an attorney who would suborn perjury.

Pellicotti (1990) describes the *passive* role and the *active* role of an attorney with a client who commits perjury. In the passive role, the attorney asks no questions during direct examination that would elicit untruthful answers, and may make a statement that the client is taking the stand against the advice of an attorney. The attorney does not refer to perjured testimony during summation or any arguments. The active role allows for the attorney to disclose to the court the fact of the perjured testimony. There is no great weight of authority to commend either approach, leaving attorneys in a difficult ethical dilemma. The best defense of some attorneys is not to know about the lie in the first place.

If the attorney is not sure the client would be committing perjury, then there is no legal duty to disclose; in fact, the weight of authority indicates that the attorney with doubts should proceed with the testimony—any disclosure of such doubts is improper and unethical. Thus, some attorneys tell their client,

"Before you say anything, I need to tell you that I cannot participate in perjury and if I know for a fact that you plan to lie, I cannot put you on the stand," or ask their client, "What do I need to know that is damaging to this case?" rather than if the client is guilty of the crime. Further, many attorneys argue that all defendants lie about everything and you can't believe them anyway. If this is true, then some attorneys may conclude that there are always doubts and this allows an easy justification for allowing the defendant to say anything on the stand.

Conflicts of Interest

Defense counsel should not permit his or her professional judgment or obligations to be affected by his or her own political, business, property, or personal interests (Standard 4-3.5(a)).

Attorneys are specifically prohibited from engaging in representations that would compromise their loyalty to their clients. Specifically, attorneys must not represent clients who may have interests that conflict with those of the attorney—for instance, an attorney may not represent a client who owns a company that is a rival to one in which the attorney has an interest. The attorney also must not represent two clients who may have opposing interests—for instance, co-defendants in a criminal case, since very often one will testify against the other. The attorney would find it impossible in such situation to represent each individual fairly. Disciplinary rules even prohibit two lawyers from a single firm from representing clients with conflicting interests. In some informal and formal decisions from ethics committees, this rule has even been used to prohibit legal aid or public defender offices from defending co-defendants, although this is a fairly routine practice (American Bar Association, 1986).

United States v. Schwarz, F. 3d (2d Cir. 2002), decided February 28, 2002, is a case involving one of the three police officers convicted in the brutal assault on Abner Louima. In the initial trial of Justin Volpe and Charles Schwarz, Volpe reached a plea agreement and the jury was not told of its terms. The trial continued against Schwarz, who was found guilty. In this appeal, Schwarz argued that his attorneys had a conflict of interest since they also represented the Policemen's Benevolent Association and Louima was suing the union for covering up the assault. Even though during the trial he waived the potential conflict of interest in writing, the appellate court reversed Schwarz's conviction because of a finding that the conflict of interest was not waivable.

Charles Schwarz was represented by Worth and London, two attorneys who were paid by the Policeman's Benevolent Association (P.B.A.). Six months after being retained, Worth and London created a new law firm and secured a two-year, $10 million retainer agreement as the new law firm for the P.B.A., payable in installments. When the government attorneys raised the issue of a conflict of interest, Schwarz waived any conflict of interest, and the trial judge ruled it was acceptable to proceed.

The conflict stems from the fact that the P.B.A. was being sued by Louima, thus the lawyers had dual duties—to the P.B.A. and to the individual defendants. These dual duties conflicted because the lawsuit argued there was a conspiracy between the P.B.A. and the criminal defendants to injure Louima and cover it up. Schwarz's defense could have been that there was another officer in the bathroom with Volpe, but it wasn't him; yet his attorney did not bring that fact out in court and, instead, argued to the jury that Louima was lying when he testified that there was another officer in the bathroom. The attorney's conflict was that if he showed there was another officer in the bathroom with Volpe to help Schwartz, then that would support Louima's civil suit against the P.B.A. The jury didn't believe the argument that no one assisted Volpe in the assault on Louima, and convicted Schwartz. The appellate court ruled that Worth and London were operating with an unwaivable conflict of interest and Schwarz' conviction was overturned and a new trial ordered.

Although attorneys may not ethically accept clients with conflicting interests, there is no guidance on the more abstract problem that all criminal clients in a caseload have conflicting interests if their cases are looked upon as part of a workload rather than considered separately. Many defense attorneys make a living by taking cases from people with very modest means or taking court-appointed cases with the fee set by the court. The defense attorney then becomes a "fast-food lawyer," depending on volume and speed to make a profit. What happens here, of course, is that quality may get sacrificed along the way. When lawyers pick up clients in the hallways of courtrooms and from bail bondsmen's referrals, the goal is to arrange bail, get a plea bargain, and move on to the next case. Rarely do these cases even come to trial.

The vast majority of cases in the criminal justice system are settled by a plea bargain. The defense attorney's goal in plea bargaining is to get the best possible deal for the client—probation or the shortest prison sentence that the prosecutor is willing to give for a guilty plea. The defense attorney is aware that he or she cannot aggressively push every case without endangering the ongoing relationship with the prosecutor. A courtroom appearance may be an isolated event for the client, but for the defense attorney and prosecutor, it is an ongoing, weekly ritual—only the names of the defendants change. Because of the nature of the continuing relationship, the defense attorney must weigh present needs against future gains. If the defense becomes known as unwilling to play ball, reduced effectiveness may hurt future clients.

Another conflict of interest may occur if the attorney desires to represent the client's interests in selling literary or media rights. Standard 4-3.4 specifically forbids entering into such an agreement before the case is complete. The temptations are obvious—if the attorney hopes to acquire financial rewards from a share of profits, his or her professional judgment on how best to defend the client may be clouded. Whether putting off signing such an agreement until the case is complete removes the possibility of unethical decisions is debatable. In the O. J. Simpson trial, it appears that every major player wrote a book about the trial. One wonders if trial tactics and speeches aren't evaluated, at least in passing, on how they will appear in a later first-person narrative or movie screenplay. The potential for biased judgments is obvious—for instance, if an attorney has a client who has committed a particularly spectacular crime, there is the potential for celebrity status only if the case comes to trial, so a plea bargain—even if it is in the best interest of the client may be less carefully considered by the attorney.

Zealous Defense

Defense counsel, in common with all members of the bar, is subject to standards of conduct stated in statutes, rules, decisions of courts, and codes, canons, or other standards of professional conduct. Defense counsel has no duty to execute any directive of the accused which does not comport with law or such standards. Defense counsel is the professional representative of the accused, not the accused's alter ego (Standard 4-1.2(e)).

Few would challenge the idea that all people deserve to have their due-process rights protected. However, what many people find unsettling is the zeal with which some defense attorneys approach the courtroom contest. How diligent should the defense be in protecting the defendant's rights? A conflict may arise between providing an effective defense and maintaining professional ethics and individual morality. Lawyers should represent clients zealously within the bounds of the law, but the law is sometimes vague and difficult to determine. Some actions are simply forbidden. The lawyer may not engage in motions or actions to intentionally and maliciously harm others, knowingly advance unwarranted claims or defenses, conceal or fail to disclose that which he or she is required by law to reveal, knowingly use perjured testimony or false evidence, knowingly make a false statement of law or fact, participate in the creation or preservation of evidence when he or she knows or it is obvious that the evidence is false, counsel the client in conduct that is illegal, or engage in other illegal conduct. The attorney is also expected to maintain a professional and courteous relationship with the opposing attorneys, litigants, and witnesses and to refrain from disparaging statements or badgering conduct. The defense attorney must not intimidate or otherwise influence the jury or trier of fact or use the media for these same purposes.

Despite these ethical rules, practices such as withholding evidence, manufacturing evidence, witness badgering, and defamation of victims' characters are sometimes used as tactics in the defense arsenal. For instance, the practice of bringing out the sexual history of rape victims is done purely to paint her as a victim who deserved or asked for her rape. Even though rape–shield laws exist that prohibit most exposés of sexual history, attorneys still attempt to bring in such evidence. Destroying the credibility of honest witnesses is considered good advocacy. For instance, if a witness accurately testifies to what he or she saw, a good attorney may still cast doubt in the jurors' minds by bringing out evidence of the use of glasses, mistakes of judgment, and other facts that tend to obfuscate and undercut the credibility of the witness. Attorneys will do this even when they know that the witness is telling the truth. A zealous defense demands the questioning of the credibility of a prosecution witness.

In some cases defense attorneys go to extreme lengths to change the course of testimony, such as bribing witnesses, allowing their client to intimidate a witness, instructing their client to destroy physical evidence or to manufacture an alibi and then commit perjury. In Chapter 7, criminal behavior on the part of law enforcement officers was discussed as abhorrent but rare, and this is also the case with blatantly criminal behavior on the part of attorneys. Most ethical conflicts occur over more subtle questions of how far one should go to provide a zealous defense.

It is sometimes difficult to determine when a defense attorney's treatment of a witness is badgering as opposed to energetic cross-examination, or when exploring a witness's background is a character assassination as opposed to a careful examination of credibility. Some attorneys focus attacks on opposing counsel—female attorneys report that opposing male attorneys attempt to infantalize, patronize, or sexualize them in front of the judge and jury as a trial tactic to destroy their credibility. Young attorneys encounter treatment by opposing counsel—with such comments as "what my young colleague here has evidently not learned yet . . . ."—designed to provide the jury with the view that the older attorney is more wise, honest, or mature than the younger attorney. Personal attacks on credibility and more subtle attempts to influence juries' perceptions of opposing counsel may also occur—such as talking during opposing counsel's opening or closing; rolling one's eyes in response to a statement or question; and making other verbal or physical gestures indicating disbelief, amusement, or disdain. These tactics are obviously not in the same category as bribing witnesses or manufacturing evidence, but are they ethical?

Defense attorneys may sacrifice integrity or friendships for the sake of a case. For instance, in one trial, a defense attorney and a prosecutor were getting ready to try a barroom murder case. The prosecutor was able to present only one eyewitness to the shooting—the bartender. No one else in the bar was willing to testify that they saw anything. The prosecutor had other circumstantial evidence of the defendant's guilt, but the eyewitness was crucial. Unfortunately, the bartender had a ten-year-old murder conviction—a fact that would reduce his credibility in the jury's eyes. This fact could be brought out by the defense under the rules of evidence; however, the prosecutor could petition the court to have the fact suppressed and have a good chance of succeeding since it bore no relevance to the case and would be prejudicial. In this instance, however, she had forgotten to file the appropriate motion. Just before the trial was about to start, the prosecutor asked the defense attorney if he was going to bring out this fact on his cross-examination of the bartender. If he planned to do so, the prosecutor would have asked for a continuance and filed a motion to have it suppressed, or at least brought it out on direct to reduce its impact. He told her specifically and clearly that he had no intention of using that information or questioning the witness about it since it was so long ago and irrelevant to the case. When the direct examination of this witness was over and the defense attorney started his cross-examination, his very first question was "Isn't it true that you were convicted of murder in 19—?" Although the prosecutor may have committed an error in judgment by trusting the defense attorney, the defense attorney deliberately misled the prosecutor as to his intentions—he lied.

When asked about his actions, the defense attorney explained that it "just slipped out" and complained that the prosecutor took these things "too seriously." This behavior is an example of a lie used for short-term gain, an egoistic rationalization, and a view of due process as a game since when an opponent is offended by the lie, she is taking things "too seriously." In this case, the defense attorney may have lost more than he gained by the trick; a conviction was achieved in spite of the witness's background, and the attorney found that previously helpful and cooperative prosecutors were suddenly unwilling to agree to continuances, closed their files to him even though it was generally an "open file" office, and in other ways treated him as untrustworthy, which indeed he was.

A recent innovation in trial tactics is the development of "scientific" jury selection. Attorneys often contend that a trial has already been won or lost once the jury has been selected. Whether or not this is true, attorneys are becoming increasingly sophisticated in their methods of choosing which members of a jury panel would make good jurors. A good juror is defined not as one who is unbiased and fair, but as someone who is predisposed to be sympathetic to that attorney's case. The ability to use these methods is limited only by one's budget.

Some lawyers, such as the famed "Racehorse" Haynes of Houston, have used methods such as surveying a large sample of the population in the community where the case is to be tried to discover how certain demographic groups feel about issues relevant to the case so that these findings can be used when the jury is selected. Other attorneys hire jury experts, psychologists who sit with the attorney and, through a combination of nonverbal and verbal clues, identify those jury panel members who are predisposed to believe the case presented by the attorney.

Another method uses a **shadow jury**—a panel of people selected by the defense attorney to represent the actual jury that sits through the trial and provides feedback to the attorney on the evidence being presented during the trial. This allows the attorney to adjust his or her trial tactics in response. Some of these methods were used in the William Kennedy Smith rape trial in Florida, which resulted in an acquittal. More recently, they were used by the defense "dream team" in the O. J. Simpson case. Attorneys have always used intuition and less sophisticated means to decide which jury members to exclude, but these newer tactics are questioned by some as too contrary to the basic idea that a trial is supposed to start with an unbiased jury (Smith and Meyer, 1987). The accompanying box further discusses the presence of trail consultants.

Can our ethical systems help to determine what actions are ethically justified in defending a client zealously? Utilitarianism and egoism would probably allow a greater range of actions, depending on the particular interests or rewards represented by the case. Ethical formalism and religion might restrict the actions of a defense attorney to those allowed by a strict interpretation of the Model Rules.

Aronson (1977: 59–63) discusses two methods for resolving ethical dilemmas. The first is called the **situational model,** wherein lawyers weigh the priorities in each case and decide each case on the particular factors present. This is similar to our explanation of situational ethics. For instance, client confidentiality may be sacrificed when others' interests are at stake, but be paramount

Are Trial Consultants Good for Justice?

The O. J. Simpson murder trial introduced millions of Americans to a relatively new figure in the nation's courts: the trial consultant. These professionals—many of whom work in fields such as psychology, communications and marketing—help lawyers pick juries and develop trial strategies. Curiosity about them accelerated when a jury acquitted Simpson after deliberating less than four hours. But consultant-picked juries have produced other surprising results:

- William Kennedy Smith was acquitted of rape charges in 1991 in Florida.
- Lyle and Erik Menendez, who admitted killing their parents, were spared by separate hung juries in L.A. in 1994. (They were convicted in a second trial.)

With such high-profile verdicts, the public could reasonably ask how consultants are affecting our court system. What role do they play in the search for truth and justice? To lawyers, it is a matter of figuring out why jurors exposed to the same evidence reach different conclusions.

"Clearly, it must be due to pre-existing attitudes," says Shari Diamond of the American Bar Foundation. "In scientific jury selection, the consultant helps identify which backgrounds will be associated with favorable or unfavorable reactions."

What They Do

Consultants provide services ranging from witness preparation to mock trials, juror profiles, and phone surveys on public attitudes about a case. They may use "shadow juries," people selected to mirror the real jury, who are asked their impressions about the trial. They also may offer advice on things like effective posture, clothing choice, and tone of voice.

One powerful tactic is to use "focus groups," informal talk sessions, to find out opinions about a case. Jo-Ellan Dimitrius, the Simpson team's consultant, says the defense thought of using the videotaped testimony of a neighbor's maid. "We changed that after we played the tape to focus groups and found she was off the charts of believability," Dimitrius says.

Consultants work on an estimated 6,000 trials a year, mostly civil cases. The American Society of Trial Consultants, a professional organization, has more than 400 members. Most are independent, but some are employed by companies like DecisionQuest, FTI Corp., and National Jury Project.

Top consultants charge upwards of $150 an hour. Dimitrius customarily gets $300 an hour but lowered her rate for Simpson. "If we had charged the full rate for what we did, it would have been at least a $500,000 deal," she says.

Picking a Jury

Part of a consultant's job may be to help lawyers screen potential jurors. In the Simpson trial, candidates were asked to fill out a 78-page list of questions devised by Judge Ito, defense and prosecution attorneys and Jo-Ellan Dimitrius. (Don Vinson, the prosecution's consultant, was not involved.) Actual questions included: "What TV shows do you watch? Do you think police are trustworthy? Do you attend church?"

This information is then used to screen jurors. . . . The argument is that clever consultants can use the preemptory challenge to stack juries or "dumb them down," arriving at the least sophisticated or educated group.

Simpson's acquittal brought heated arguments that consultants know ways to stack juries. "Lawyers will argue that this is all part of an adversarial system," says Stephen J. Adler, author of *The Jury: Disorder in the Courts.* "But it doesn't have to work that way. It might serve the public better to remove preemptory challenges and take strategy out of jury selection. I think that would be a step toward getting truth and justice."

"Given the time, money and energy spent [on the Simpson trial]," Adler adds, "there might have been more confidence in the decision of a jury chosen not by consultants but by picking twelve names out of a hat."

SOURCE: B. Gavzer, *Parade* Magazine (January. 5, 1997): 20. Copyright © 1997. Reprinted with permission of the author and publisher.

in other considerations. The **systems model,** on the other hand, would be a more absolute or legalistic model in that behavior would always be considered wrong or right depending on the ethical rule guiding the definition. Obviously, these two systems of decision making bear a great deal of resemblance to the situational ethics and absolutist models discussed in Chapter 2.

CONCLUSION

In this chapter we have examined the source of legal ethics and the reasons that the public seems to have such a poor opinion of the ethics of legal professionals. One might expect that the public's respect and trust for legal professionals, as guardians of the justice system, would be high, but that is not the case. Part of the reason is the ability to take "either side" in a controversy. Also, the advocacy role that attorneys embrace at times justifies "means" that appear to be and even may be ethically questionable.

Observers have made analogies that compare the practice of law to a game, with one side winning and the other side losing depending on the skill of the players. In the practice of criminal law, one side is represented by the defense attorney, and the other is represented by the prosecutor. There are similar duties for both parties, but there are also crucial differences in the duties and ethical responsibilities of these professionals. In the next chapter, we will continue our discussion by exploring the ethics of prosecutors and judges.

REVIEW QUESTIONS

1. What are the three models of judicial processing described in this chapter?
2. What are the advantages of and problems with plea bargaining?
3. Describe the moral agent, legal agent, and special relationship views of the attorney–client relationship.
4. What is the source of formal ethics for attorneys? Describe the history of the origin of these ethics.
5. Describe at least three issues related to the defense attorney's ethical obligations.

ETHICAL DILEMMAS

Situation 1

Your first big case is a multiple murder. As defense attorney for Sy Kopath, you have come to the realization that he really did break into a couple's home and torture and kill them in the course of robbing them of jewelry and other valuables. He has even confessed to you that he did it. However, you are also aware that the police did not read him his Miranda warning and that he was coerced into giving a confession without your presence. What should you do? Would your answer be different if you believed that he was innocent or didn't know for sure either way?

Situation 2

You are completing an internship at a defense attorney's office during your senior year in college. You plan to enter law school after graduation and pursue a career as an attorney, although you have not yet decided what type of law to practice. Your duties as an intern are to assist the private practitioner you work for in a variety of tasks, including interviewing clients and witnesses, organizing case files, running errands, and photocopying. A case that you are helping with involves a defendant charged with armed robbery. One day while you are at the office, the defendant comes in and gives you a package for the attorney. In it you find a gun. You believe, but do not know for a fact, that the gun is the one used in the armed robbery. When the attorney returns, he instructs you to return the package to the defendant. What should you do? What should the attorney do?

Situation 3

You are an attorney and are aware of a colleague who could be considered grossly incompetent. He drinks and often appears in court intoxicated. He ignores his cases and does not file appropriate motions before deadlines expire. Any person who is unlucky enough to have him as a court-appointed attorney usually ends up with a conviction and a heavy sentence because he does not seem to care what happens to his clients and rarely advises going to trial. When he does take a case to trial, he is unprepared and unprofessional in the courtroom. You hear many complaints from defendants about his demeanor, competence, and ethics. Everyone—defense attorneys, prosecutors, and judges alike—knows this person and his failings, yet nothing is done. Should you do something? What?

SUGGESTED READINGS

Glendon, M. 1994. *A Nation Under Lawyers.* New York: Farrar, Straus and Giroux.

Radelet, M., H. Bedau, and C. Putnam. 1992. *In Spite of Innocence.* Boston: Northeastern University Press.

Rhode, D. 2001. *In the Interests of Justice: Reforming the Legal Profession.* New Haven, CT: Oxford University Press.

Spence, G. 1989. *With Justice for None.* New York: Penguin.

Zitrin, R., and C. Langford. 1999. *The Moral Compass of the American Lawyer.* New York: Ballantine Books.

10

Special Issues for Prosecutors and Judges

Ethical Issues for Prosecutors
Use of Discretion
Conflicts of Interest
Plea Bargaining
Media Relations
Expert Witnesses
Zealous Prosecution
Prosecutorial Misconduct

Ethical Issues for Judges
Ethical Guidelines
Use of Discretion
Judicial Misconduct

Conclusion

Review Questions

Ethical Dilemmas

Suggested Readings

Key Terms

halo effect
innocence project
blue curtain of secrecy

Chapter Objectives

- Understand how the role of prosecutors is qualitatively different from the role of defense attorneys.
- Understand the responsibilities and challenges of judges in the criminal justice system.

In the last chapter we explored the ethics of the defense attorney. As a pure advocate, the defense attorney's duty is to pursue a client's interest. As long as he or she does not run afoul of the law or ethical mandates, the client's defense is the sole objective. Prosecutors and other court actors have a more inclusive mission. Prosecutors do not serve an individual client; rather, their client is the system or society itself. Pursuit of justice rather than pursuit of the best interest of the client characterizes the aims of prosecutors and judges.

ETHICAL ISSUES FOR PROSECUTORS

As the second line of decision makers in the system, prosecutors have extremely broad powers of discretion. The prosecutor acts like a strainer—he or she collects some cases for formal prosecution while eliminating a great many others. Because of limited resources, the difficulty of enforcing outdated or unsupported laws, and weak cases, prosecution of every case is impossible. It might be inappropriate in some situations to impose criminal sanctions, even when laws have been broken, because these particular laws are trivial or lacking in public support. Early diversion of such cases saves taxpayers money and saves individuals trouble and expense.

To guide discretion, there are ethical standards relating specifically to the role of the prosecutor. Chapter 3 of the A.B.A. Standards for Criminal Justice covers the prosecution function. These standards cover topics similar to those for defense attorneys, but they also make special note of the unique role of the prosecutor as a representative of the court system and the state (Douglass, 1981).

Use of Discretion

A prosecutor should not institute . . . criminal charges . . . not supported by probable cause. (Standard 3-3.9(a)).

The prosecutor must seek justice, not merely a conviction. Toward this end, prosecutors must share evidence, exercise restraint in the use of their power, represent the public interest, and give the accused the benefit of reasonable doubt. Disciplinary rules are more specific. They forbid the prosecutor from pursuing charges when there is no probable cause and mandate timely disclosure to defense counsel of evidence, especially exculpatory evidence or evidence that might mitigate guilt or reduce the punishment. Ethical issues of the prosecutor are similar to those of the defense attorney in that they are seen as opposing players; however, prosecutors have a qualitatively different role because of their discretionary power in the decision-making process. It is their discretion in charging that moves someone along or diverts the person from the system. Prosecutors' role as an officer of the court then puts them in a very powerful position and, as such, may result in different ethical questions.

One court has described the prosecutor's functions in the following way (*State v. Moynahan,* 164 Conn. 560, 325 A.2d 199, 206; cert. denied, 414 U.S. 976 [1973]):

> As a representative of the people of the state, [the prosecutor] is under a duty not solely to obtain convictions but, more importantly, (1) to determine that there is reasonable ground to proceed with a criminal charge [citation omitted]; (2) to see that impartial justice is done the guilty as well as the innocent; and (3) to ensure that all evidence tending to aid in the ascertaining of the truth be laid before the court, whether it be consistent with the contention of the prosecution that the accused is guilty.

Despite these ideals of prosecutorial duty, an unstated influence over prosecutorial discretion is that prosecutors want to and must (to be considered successful) win. Their choice of cases is influenced by this. Law enforcement considerations also influence prosecutorial action. If there is a bargain to be struck with an informant, if a lesser charge will result in testimony or information that could lead to further convictions, then this is considered in decision making. Finally, the pressure of public opinion is a factor to consider. Prosecutors might pursue cases they would otherwise have dropped if there is a great deal of public interest in the case.

However, prosecutors might not pursue cases that have no stakeholders of importance. For instance, victims who have mental impairments may not make the best witnesses and there may be less chance of getting a conviction. In one such case, five women with developmental disabilities had been raped and terrorized by the owner of a licensed home they lived in. The prosecutor declined to pursue charges under the rationale "that any women with a developmental disability would have zero credibility in court." Only when the licensing authority secured additional testimony, revoked the license of owner, and publicly exposed the situation did the prosecutor press charges (Hook, 2001).

The decision to prosecute is influenced by political and public pressures, the chance for conviction, the severity of the crime, a "gut" feeling of guilt or innocence, prison overcrowding, and the weight of evidence. The prosecutorial role is to seek justice, but justice doesn't mean the same thing to everyone and certainly does not mean prosecuting everyone to the fullest extent of the law. Whether to charge is one of the most important decisions of the criminal justice process. The decision should be fair, neutral, and accomplished with due process, but this is an ideal that is sometimes supplanted by other considerations.

Prosecutors don't usually use their charging power for intimidation or harassment, but other factors may be involved in the decision to charge. For instance, a prosecutor might have a particular interest in a type of crime such as child abuse or drugs that results in the prosecutor pursuing these cases more intensely. Public pressure over a particular crime may impel the prosecutor to charge somebody quickly. Public perception might also influence a prosecutor not to charge. Prosecutors in state capitols often have "public integrity" units that prosecute wrongdoing on the part of public officials. Prosecutors might charge at election time for political purposes, or they might be falsely accused of such political considerations when they do charge politicians with public integrity violations.

A special case of discretion and charging is the decision to pursue a capital homicide conviction. Prosecutors have the power to decide whether to seek the death penalty or a prison term. It is clear that the decision to seek the death penalty is not made uniformly across jurisdictions. In Texas, for instance, there is wide disparity in the number of cases in which the death penalty is sought. The Harris County (Houston) district attorney seeks the death penalty in a disproportionately greater number of cases than other jurisdictions. One of the biggest considerations is cost. Because capital trials are very expensive, counties that have bigger budgets are more likely to seek the death penalty. They have the resources and staff to handle the cases (Hall, 2002). Obviously these considerations have nothing to do with justice, and it should cause concern that criteria other than severity of the crime or future dangerousness affects whether an offender ultimately receives the death penalty.

The decision not to charge is also open to ethical scrutiny. To give one defendant accused of brutal crime immunity to gain testimony against others is efficient, but is it consistent with justice? To not charge businesspeople because they are good citizens is highly questionable, as is not charging because the individual is a relative of a powerful figure. In some situations, prosecutors do not charge because of an outpouring of public sympathy or support for the accused, perhaps because of the type of crime or identity of the victim. Prosecutors who do not charge in these cases may attribute the reason to lack of evidence or the unlikelihood of obtaining a conviction, but their political popularity probably also has something to do with their decision.

Various studies have attempted to describe prosecutors' decision making; one cites office policy as an important influence. *Legal sufficiency* is an office policy that weeds out those cases in which the evidence is not strong enough to support further action. *System efficiency* is an office policy with goals of efficiency and accountability; all decisions are made with these goals in mind, so many cases result in dismissals. Another policy is *defendant rehabilitation,* which emphasizes diversion and other rehabilitation tools rather than punitive goals. Finally, *trial sufficiency* is an office policy that encourages a charge that can be sustained through trial (Jacoby, Mellon, and Smith, 1980).

Another study looked at the prosecutor as operating in an exchange system. The relationship between the prosecutor and the police was described as one of give-and-take. Prosecutors balance police need or wishes against their own vulnerability. The prosecutor makes personal judgments as to which police officers can be trusted. Exchange also takes place between the prosecutor's office and the courts. When the jails become overcrowded, more recommendations may be made for deferred adjudication and probation; when dockets back up, charges may be dropped. Finally, exchange takes place between defense attorneys and prosecutors, especially since many defense attorneys have previously served as prosecutors and may be personally familiar with the procedures and even personalities in the prosecutor's office (Cole, 1970).

QUERY

A prosecutor was working with police in a stand-off between a triple murderer and police. When the murderer demanded to talk to a public defender, the police did not want to have a public defender get involved so the prosecutor pretended to be one. He spoke with the suspect on the telephone and lied about his name and being a pubic defender; the man then surrendered to police. He was sanctioned by the state bar for misrepresentation and was put on probation and required to take twenty hours of continuing legal education in ethics, pass the Multistate Professional Responsibility Examination and be supervised by another attorney.
Do you think he did the right thing? Why or Why not?

Tarnoff, 2001.

On one hand, discretion is considered essential to the prosecutorial function of promoting individualized justice and softening the impersonal effects of the law. On the other hand, the presence of discretion is the reason why the legal system is considered unfair and biased toward certain groups of people or individuals. Even though we would not want to eliminate prosecutorial discretion, it could be guided by regulations or internal guidelines. For instance, an office policy might include a procedure for providing written reasons for dropping charges, and this procedure would respond to charges of unbridled discretion.

Conflicts of Interest

A prosecutor should avoid a conflict of interest with respect to his or her official duties (Standard 3.1-3(a)).

Part-time prosecutors present a host of ethical issues. A Bureau of Justice Statistics bulletin (1992) reported that 47 percent of prosecutors held their jobs as a part-time occupation (Dawson, 1992: 1). Obviously, this poses the possibility of a conflict of interest. It may happen that a part-time prosecutor has a private practice, and situations may occur where the duty to a private client runs counter to the duty of the prosecutor's duty to the public. In some cases, it may be that a client becomes a defendant, necessitating the prosecutor to hire a special prosecutor. Even when there are no direct conflicts of interest, the pressure of time always poses a conflict. The division of time between the private practice, where income is correlated with hard work, and prosecuting cases, where income is fixed no matter how many hours are spent, may result in a less energetic prosecutorial function than one might wish.

It is well known that the prosecutor's job is a good stepping stone to politics, and many use it as such. In these cases, one has to wonder whether cases are taken on the basis of merit or on their ability to place the prosecutor in the public eye and help his or her career. Winning also becomes more important. It should be noted that in populous counties, there are many assistant district attorneys (A.D.A.s); only the district attorney is elected. For instance, in Harris County, Texas, there are more than 200 A.D.A.s. Many work in the prosecutor's office for a number of years and then move into the private sector. The reason has largely to do with money. Assistant district attorneys make an average of $40,000 to $60,000, but in private practice they could make much more than that (Cohen, 2001). The question then becomes, Does the career plan to work for a defense firm affect their prosecutorial decision making?

QUOTE

"I don't see any other honorable way I could do it."
(County attorney who explained why he rescinded a plea bargain deal he had offered to a state senator and a state representative charged with illegal lobbying after he accepted an offer to join a law firm that received a yearly retainer from the senator. The law firm hired him to be its ethics advisor and improve its image after one of its partners was convicted of bribery for paying money to city council members in return for lucrative tax collection work.)
Do you feel that pulling the deal off the table to let his successor decide whether to re-offer the plea takes care of the conflict of interest in this case?

Copelin, 2003.

The RICO statute has increasingly been used as a tool to confiscate property and money associated with organized criminal activity. Once this tactic was approved by the courts, a veritable flood of prosecutions began that were designed, it seems, primarily to obtain cash, boats, houses, and other property of drug dealers. Making decisions based on the potential for what can be confiscated rather than culpability of offenders is a very real and dangerous development in this type of prosecution.

The origin of civil forfeiture was in the Comprehensive Drug Abuse and Control Act of 1970 and the Organized Crime Control Act of 1970. Both of these laws allowed mechanisms for the government to seize assets gained through illegal means. Eventually, the types of assets vulnerable to seizure were expanded, including those assets *intended* to be used as well as those gained by or used in illegal activities. All states have passed similar asset-forfeiture laws. The "take" from asset forfeiture increased from $27.2 million in 1985 to $874 million in 1992 (Jenson and Gerber, 1996). Since the early 1990s, the amount of federal forfeiture proceeds shared with state and local law enforcement is $2.5 billion! (Hartman, 2001)

There are a number of problematic issues with asset forfeiture. The exclusionary rule does not apply to civil forfeiture proceedings, so some allege that police are now pursuing assets instead of criminals, because in a civil proceeding the defendant does not receive legal aid. A civil forfeiture hearing can take place without any criminal prosecution and without the presence of the alleged criminal. Unlike a criminal trial, in asset forfeiture, it had been the case that the government needed only to show probable cause, and then the burden of proof shifted to the individual to prove his or her innocence. This changed when President Clinton signed into law the Civil Asset Forfeiture Reform Act, which shifted the burden of proof from the claimant to the government (Worral, 2001). Now at least the presumption of innocence has been put back into place.

Perhaps one of the most troubling aspects of civil forfeiture is that third parties are often those most hurt by the loss. For example, spouses or parents of a suspected drug dealer may lose their home. In one of the most widely publicized forfeiture cases, a man solicited a prostitute; the state instituted proceedings and was successful in seizing the car he was driving when he solicited the prostitute—which was, in fact, his wife's car! This case received so much press because the Supreme Court ruled that no constitutional violation occurred with the forfeiture, even though his wife had nothing to do with the criminal activity. Another case that received a great deal of media attention was a man who lost his very expensive motorboat when one marijuana cigarette was found on it.

It seems to be the case that these and other uses of asset forfeiture have spurred reforms and court decisions that are curtailing its use to some extent. The Supreme Court has ruled that the Eighth Amendment prohibiting excessive fines did apply to civil forfeiture; therefore, the government must regulate its forfeiture to some standard of proportionality with the crime. Another case indicated that the accused must be provided notice and some type of adversarial hearing before assets can be seized unless there are "exigent" circumstances (Jensen and Gerber, 1996). It is very clear, however, that asset forfeiture has become an almost indispensable source of revenue for law enforcement and the courts (Worral, 2001).

Plea Bargaining

A prosecutor should not knowingly make false statements or representations as to fact or law in the course of plea discussions with defense counsel or the accused (Standard 3–4.1(c)).

As discussed earlier, there are serious ethical concerns over the practice of plea bargaining. Most conclude that plea bargaining, even if not exactly "right," is certainly efficient and probably inevitable. Even in those jurisdictions that have moved to determinate sentencing, what has happened is that plea bargaining has become charge bargaining instead of sentence bargaining.

Should we measure the morality of an action by its efficiency? This efficiency argument is similar to that used to defend some deceptive investigative practices of police. If the goals of the system are crime control or bureaucratic efficiency, then plea bargaining makes sense. If the goals of the system are the protection of individual rights and the protection of due process, then plea bargaining is much harder to justify under a utilitarian argument, or any other. Obviously, plea bargaining would fail under the categorical imperative, since the individual is treated as a means in the argument that plea bargaining is good for the system.

Arguments given in defense of plea bargaining include the heavy case-loads, limited resources, legislative over-criminalization, individualized justice, and legal problems of cases (legal errors that would result in mistrials or dropped charges if the client didn't plead) (Knudten, 1978: 275). If we concede that plea bargaining can be justified, there are remaining ethical problems over specific practices relating to plea bargaining. Should prosecutors overcharge—that is, charge at a higher degree of severity or press more charges than could possibly be sustained by evidence—so that they can bargain down? Should prosecutors mislead defense attorneys about the amount of evidence or the kind of evidence they have or about the sentence they can offer to obtain a guilty plea? Only 36 percent of chief prosecutors reported that explicit criteria for plea bargains were in place in 1990 (Bureau of Justice Statistics, 1992). Guidelines providing a range of years for certain types of charges would help the individual prosecutors maintain some level of consistency in a particular jurisdiction.

Gershman (1991) documents prosecutors engaged in false promises, fraud, misrepresentation of conditions, deals without benefit of counsel, package deals, and threats during plea bargaining. Critics contend that prosecutors hold all the cards in plea bargaining. Defense attorneys can take what is offered (perhaps without knowing the nature of the evidence against the client) or argue, but most of the time arguing with a plea-bargain offer does not do the client much good and does the attorney even less.

In an earlier chapter, the evidently false confession obtained by N.Y.P.D. detectives from the "Central Park–jogger rapists" was discussed. The fact is, however, that in New York, prosecutors are involved at a very early stage of investigation; thus, there was a prosecutor who evaluated that confession knowing full well the circumstances, and used it to secure a conviction. If there is any blame to be distributed regarding coercive tactics leading to a miscarriage of justice, then the prosecutors involved also deserve some portion of it.

Media Relations

The prosecutor has an important relationship with the press. The media can be enemy or friend, depending on how charismatic or forthcoming the prosecutor is in interviews. Sometimes cases are said to be "tried in the papers," with the defense attorney and the prosecutor staging verbal sparring matches for public consumption. Prosecutors may react to cases and judges' decisions in the paper, criticizing the decision or the sentence and, in the process, denigrating the dignity of the system. More often, the defense attempts to sway the press to a sympathetic view of the offense, which is easier to accomplish during prosecutorial silence.

ABA Model Rule 3.6(b) is a prohibition against out-of-court statements that a reasonable person should expect would have a substantial likelihood of materially prejudicing a proceeding. Prosecutors are probably not as inclined to use the media to try a case as defense attorneys, but when they do make statements, it is possible there is more damage done. Defense attorneys might be *expected* to make statements to exonerate their client and disparage the state's case, but prosecutor's statements have a greater ring of authority. The rule specifies that no statements should be given involving any of the following topics:

- The character, credibility, reputation, or criminal record of a party, suspect, or witness
- The identity of a witness
- The expected testimony of a party or witness
- The performance or results of any test or examination
- The refusal of any party to submit to such tests or examinations
- The identity or nature of physical evidence
- Inadmissible information
- The possibility of a guilty plea
- The existence or contents of a confession or admission
- The defendant's refusal to make a statement
- An opinion about the guilt or innocence of the defendant or suspect
- A statement that the defendant has been charged with a crime unless it is in the context that a charge does not mean the party is guilty.

The following facts may be disclosed:

- The general nature of the claim or charge
- Any information in a public record
- The fact that the matter is being investigated and the scope of the investigation
- The schedule of litigation
- A request for assistance in obtaining information
- A warning of danger
- The identity, residence, occupation, and family status of accused
- Information to enable the accused's capture (if at large)
- The fact, time, and place of arrest
- The identity of investigating and arresting officers.

One wonders, when reading the papers and listening to television news reports, if prosecutors and defense attorneys have ever read these rules. Certainly in high-profile cases they seem to be ignored.

Expert Witnesses

A prosecutor who engages an expert for an opinion should respect the independence of the expert and should not seek to dictate the formation of the expert's opinion on the subject (Standard 3–3.3(a)).

Expert witnesses, who can receive a fee, are often accused of compromising their integrity for money or notoriety. The use of expert witnesses has risen in recent years. Psychiatrists often testify as to the mental competency or legal insanity of an accused. For many years, forensic experts have testified regarding factual issues of evidence ranging from ballistics to blood spatter. Today, criminologists and other social scientists may be asked to testify on such topics as victimization in prison, statistical evidence of sentencing discrimination, the effectiveness of predictive instruments for prison riots and other disturbances, risk assessment for individual offenders, mental health services in prison, patterns of criminality, the battered-woman syndrome, and so on (see Anderson and Winfree, 1987).

When the expert is honest in his or her presentation as to the limitations and potential bias of the material, no ethical issues arise. However, expert witnesses may testify in a realm beyond fact or make testimony appear factual when some questions are not clearly answerable. Because of the **halo effect**—essentially, when a person with expertise or status in one area is given deference in all areas—an expert witness may endow a statement or conclusion with more legitimacy than it may warrant. When expert witnesses take the stand, they run the risk of having their credibility attacked by the opposing side. Credibility is obviously much easier to attack when a witness has attempted to present theory or supposition as fact or conclusion, either for ideological reasons or because of pressure from zealous attorneys.

Those who always appear on one side or the other may also lose their credibility. For instance, a doctor who is used often by prosecutors in one jurisdiction during capital sentencing hearings has become known as "Dr. Death" because he always determines that the defendant poses a future risk to society, which is one of the necessary elements for the death penalty. Although this doctor is well known to both prosecutors and defense attorneys by reputation, juries would not be expected to know of his predilection for finding future dangerousness and would take his testimony at face value unless the defense attorney brings this information out during cross-examination.

Competing expert witnesses who present entirely different "facts" to the jury create an atmosphere of cynicism and distrust. There is a tendency to believe that expert witnesses are neutral and "teach" the facts to the jury, but recent cases have brought to light that expert witnesses might be incompetent in their methodology or interpretation, might testify to certain facts for political or other reasons, or might simply enjoy the notoriety of testifying. Since much of expert testimony concerns scientific principles that are incomprehensible to laypeople, the potential for being misled by an expert witness is magnified. (See the accompanying box, "FBI Lab Alters Findings.")

Recently, there have been questions raised as to the accuracy of the chemical composition tests the FBI labs use to match bullets. This method has been used in thousands of cases to tie suspects to the bullet retrieved at the crime scene. The theory is that the chemical composition of bullets in a single production batch is similar and that bullets from a single batch are different from other batches. Bullets owned by the suspect are compared to the crime-scene

---

FBI Lab Alters Findings

A series of articles in major newspapers brought to light an investigation and report concerning the FBI's vaunted crime laboratory. Evidently, the investigation was initiated by a senior chemist—Frederic Whitehurst—who alleged that chemists were sometimes pressured to change their findings to support the prosecution's case, and in other cases supervisors even changed lab reports. One of the many cases implicated in allegations of altered lab findings is the Oklahoma City bombing. Whitehurst also alleges that he was suspended and transferred for speaking out. The Justice Department's Office of the Inspector General is investigating the allegations.

SOURCE: R. Serrano, "FBI Agents Allegedly Pushed Lab Workers to Alter Findings," *Austin American-Statesman* (Jan. 30, 1997): A3.

---

bullet and the expert testifies as to whether the crime-scene bullet came from the suspect's box of remaining bullets. Emerging scientific evidence challenges the method since tests indicate that there is a large margin of error—chemical compositions between batches are more similar than believed; and the chemical composition within a batch can vary quite a bit depending on a number of factors. These findings are problematic because ballistics experts from the FBI lab and other labs have testified in a way that greatly overstates the importance of the chemical matches. It is possible that some people have been wrongly convicted because of this evidence (Piller and Mejia, 2003).

Recently, the Houston police crime lab has come under fire for lax procedures and inaccurate testimony. At least one man has already been exonerated by a retest of the DNA evidence that convicted him. Unfortunately, he has already served several years in prison. There are troubling indications that he is only the tip of the iceberg, and the Harris County D.A.'s office has begun a review of dozens of case files where the offender may have been convicted on faulty lab evidence. Criticism includes poorly trained technicians, lax procedures, shoddy records, overstated testimony, and inability to do certain tests such as separate DNA when there were mixed samples. The lab has been closed and case reviews have begun. Seven of the cases up for review are death-row inmates, and since Harris County has sent more defendants to death row than any other county in Texas, some of those convicted through tainted evidence may have already been executed (Liptak, 2003; Axtman, 2003)

Television shows such as *C.S.I.* and *Crossing Jordan* contribute to the mystique of crime scene investigators as scientific Sherlock Holmes who use physics, chemistry, and biology to catch criminals. The fact of the matter, however, is that some so-called expert testimony is simply *junk science*. A Justice Department study of 240 crime labs found hair comparison error rates ranging from 28 percent to 68 percent. Dental comparison rates are not much better. In fact, hair comparison testimony is so suspect that it is outlawed in Michigan and Illinois, but not in other states. Arson investigation is called an "inchoate science" because empirical testing shows that most of it may be guesswork and imagination (Hall, 2002). DNA testing has also been called into question (Anderson, 1989). Defense attorneys that are incompetent, unqualified, or unprepared do not object to improper evidence. Sometimes it is not their fault because they must justify every dollar they spend on indigent defense to the county judge. This means that the state's expert witnesses may go unrebutted by contradicting experts (Hall, 2002). The use of expert witnesses can present ethical problems when the witness is used in a dishonest fashion. Obviously, to pay an expert for his or her time is not unethical, but to shop for experts until one is found who benefits the case may be unethical, since the credibility of the witness is suspect.

Another difficulty is presented when either side obtains an expert who develops a conclusion or set of findings that would help the other side. Ethical rules do not prohibit an attorney in a civil matter from merely disregarding the information, without notice to the opponent that there is information that could benefit his or her case. However, prosecutors operate under a special set of ethics because their goal is justice, not pure advocacy. Any exculpatory information is supposed to be shared with the defense; this obviously includes test results and may also include expert witness findings.

The use of DNA evidence has risen dramatically in recent years. Based on the scientific principle that no two individuals possess the same DNA (deoxyribonucleic acid), a DNA "fingerprint" is analyzed from organic matter such as semen, blood, hair, or skin. Whereas a blood test can identify an individual only as being a member of a group (e.g., all those with blood type A positive), DNA testing can determine, with a small margin of error, whether two samples come from the same individual. It has been described as the greatest breakthrough in scientific evidence since fingerprinting, but there are problems with its use. Careless laboratory procedures render results useless, and there are no enforced guidelines or criteria for forensic laboratories conducting DNA tests. Without vigorous investigation and examination of lab results from the opposing counsel, incorrect DNA test results or poorly interpreted results may be entered as evidence and used to determine guilt or innocence.

Zealous Prosecution

The duty of the prosecutor is to seek justice, not merely to convict (Standard 3-1.2(c)).

Just as the defense attorney is at times overly zealous in defense of clients, prosecutors may be overly ambitious in order to attain a conviction. The prosecutor, in preparing a case, is putting together a puzzle—each fact or bit of evidence is a piece of that puzzle. Any piece of evidence that doesn't fit the puzzle is sometimes conveniently ignored. The problem is that this type of evidence may be exculpatory, and the prosecutor has a duty to provide it to the defense.

The prosecutor is trying just as hard as the defense to put together a strong case. Tactics such as using witnesses with less than credible reasons for testifying, preparing witnesses (both in appearance and testimony), and "shopping" for experts are prosecutorial tools as well as defense tools. Witnesses are not supposed to be paid, but their expenses can be reimbursed, and this often is incentive enough for witnesses to say what they think the prosecutor wants to hear. Further, one tool in the prosecutor's arsenal that the defense attorney does not have is that prosecutors can make deals to reduce charges in return for favorable testimony. There are many offenders in prison because of co-defendant's testimony against them that was "bought" by a reduced charge or sentence. These practices are not illegal, but whether or not they are ethical is a different question.

QUERY

Are the following actions of a prosecutor legal? Are they ethical?

- Authorizing the arrest of one brother for drugs, even though the prosecutor knows the charge would be thrown out but the young man would lose a scholarship to college, in order to have leverage so that he would give evidence against his brother.
- Announcing a suspect of a drive by shooting to the media so that the offender is in danger from the rival gang members, and then offering protective custody only if the man will plead guilty.
- Authorizing the arrest of a 10-year-old boy who confessed to a crime, even though there was no serious possibility that he was guilty, in order to pressure a relative to confess.

Prosecutors want to win, and there are very few checks or monitors on their behavior. The result is that noble-cause corruption occurs when prosecutors do anything it takes to win a case. This can take the form of persistent references to illegal evidence, leading witnesses, nondisclosure of evidence to the defense, appeals to emotions, games and tricks, and so on. One prosecutor admitted that early in his career he sometimes made faces at the defendant while his back was to the jury and the defense attorney wasn't looking. The jury saw the defendant glowering and looking angry for no discernible reason, which led to a negative perception of his sanity, temper, or both. Of course, the defense attorney may be engaged in the same type of actions, so the contest between them becomes who has better "tricks" rather than who has the better case.

In some cases, prosecutors, along with police, deliberately ignore evidence, destroy exculpatory evidence, lie about evidence, or do not share exculpatory evidence with the defense. Radelet, Bedau, and Putnam (1992) gathered together dozens of capital cases where innocent defendants were convicted of crimes they did not commit. Some were sentenced to death. False convictions can occur because of incompetent defense counsel and unethical and illegal practices on the part of prosecutors and police. A recent case illustrates the problem: Delma Banks was convicted based on testimony of a police inform-ant and a long-time drug offender who was promised a shorter sentence and coached to provide details of the crime scene. Neither of these facts was brought out at trial. Further, the jury pool was race-coded by prosecutors and all African-American jurors were excluded. Recent reanalysis of forensics indi-cates that the victim was possibly killed when Banks was out of town. Despite these new findings, the Court of Criminal Appeals and the Board of Pardons and Paroles have refused to stay the execution. The Supreme Court has recently accepted a writ of certiorari and granted a stay of execution, evidently refusing to ignore the very distinct possibility that an innocent man was to be executed (Pasztor, 2003).

QUOTE

"The questions presented in Mr. Banks' petition directly implicate the integrity of the administration of death penalty in this country . . . The prosecutors in this case concealed important impeachment material from the defense."

From a brief filed by former F.B.I. Director William Sessions, along with two former federal judges and a former federal prosecutor, asking the court to halt the execution and re-open the case of Delma Banks. Source: Pasztor, D. 2003. Lawyer, ex-judges Fear Texas About to Kill an Innocent Man. *Austin American-Statesman* (March 6, 2003), A1, A11.

Clarence Brandley was a high school janitor in a small Texas town near Houston. In 1980, a young woman on a visiting girls' volleyball team disappeared while her team was practicing. The school was empty except for five janitors and the volleyball team. A search uncovered the girl's body in the school auditorium; it was later determined that she had been raped and strangled. Clarence Brandley and another janitor found the body and were the first to be interrogated by police. Brandley was black; the other janitor was white. The police officer who interrogated them reportedly said, "One of you two is going to hang for this." Then he said to Brandley, "Since you're the nigger, you're elected."

Police and prosecutors then evidently began a concerted effort to get Brandley convicted:

- Evidence that might have been helpful to the defense was "lost" (such as Caucasian hairs near the girl's vagina that were never tested and compared to those of the other janitors).

- Witnesses were coerced into sticking to stories that inculpated Brandley (one of the janitors reported that he had been threatened with jail if he didn't promote the story supporting Brandley's guilt).

- Witnesses who came forward with contrary evidence were ignored and sent away (the father-in-law of one of the janitors who later became a prime suspect told the prosecutor that this man had told him where the girl's clothes would be found two days before police actually found them).

- Defense attorneys were not told of witnesses (such as a woman who came to the prosecutor after the second trial and stated that her common-law husband had confessed a murder to her and ran away the same night the girl's body had been found).

This woman's husband had worked as a janitor at the school, had been fired a month previous to the murder, but had also been seen at the school the day of the murder. What defense attorneys eventually discovered was that in all probability this man and another janitor had abducted and murdered the girl. The other janitors had seen the girl with these two men (not Brandley) but had lied during the two trials. Here are the words of an appellate judge who ruled on the motion for a new trial:

> In the thirty years that this court has presided over matters in the judicial system, no case has presented a more shocking scenario of the effects of racial prejudice . . . and public officials who for whatever motives lost sight of what is right and just. . . . The court unequivocally concludes that the color of Clarence Brandley's skin was a substantial factor which pervaded all aspects of the State's capital prosecution against him. (quoted in Radelet, Bedau, and Putnam, 1992: 134)

Yet, even after this finding, it took another *two years* for the Texas Court of Criminal Appeals to rule that Brandley deserved a new trial. Clarence Brandley served nine years on death row before his defense attorneys finally obtained his freedom. He was at one point six days away from execution. Others have been executed, and only afterward did evidence or perpetrators' confessions exonerate the accused and expose the prosecution's misconduct that led to the miscarriage of justice (Radelet, Bedau, and Putnam, 1992).

Whereas some of the cases described by Radelet, Bedau, and Putnam involved pure and extreme racial prejudice, probably a more common factor in misguided prosecution is a more subtle form of racism—one shared by many in the criminal justice system—a prejudgment of the guilt of the accused, especially if he is a black man. There is a pervasive stereotypical belief that all defendants are guilty, and most defendants are black. This thought pattern shapes and distorts decision making on the part of prosecutors who sift and use evidence in a way to support their predetermined beliefs.

In Boston, Charles Stuart murdered his wife, threw her body into the river, and then faked a mugging. He described a fictional black assailant who robbed him and murdered his pregnant wife. Susan Smith also described a fictional black assailant who abducted and killed her children, after she drowned them by driving her car into the lake with the children strapped in their car seats. Is it a coincidence that both chose African-American men as their fictional criminals, or did Stuart and Smith consciously or unconsciously rely on our common stereotypes of criminals? Even though these cases did not result in a false finding of guilt for some innocent man, they could have. If Radelet, Bedau, and Putnam's facts are accurate, such miscarriages of justice have occurred and are probably continuing to occur.

When police or prosecutors allow their biases and prejudices to influence their decision making, evidence is lost or ignored, witnesses are discounted and disbelieved, tests aren't conducted, and true perpetrators literally "get away with murder" if there is a convenient suspect who looks guilty. This is an ever-present and pervasive reality in our justice system and probably accounts for why there is such a divergence in the perceptions of blacks and whites regarding the fairness of the system. For instance, in a Gallup poll, 71 percent of whites said murder charges against O. J. Simpson were probably or definitely true, but only 28 percent of African Americans agreed (reported in Mitchell and Banks, 1996: J7). Is this a reflection of a different way of measuring evidence or a different perception of trust in law enforcement and legal professionals' ability to collect and interpret evidence? Is the lack of trust warranted?

Unfortunately, the answer to that question is probably yes. As mentioned in an earlier chapter, in a study conducted by the Columbia Law School, 68 percent of all death verdicts handed down between 1973 and 1995 were reversed due to serious errors. The errors involved defense lawyers' incompetence, but also police and prosecutors suppressing exculpatory evidence or engaging in other types of professional misconduct. Almost 10 percent of the cases sent back for retrial resulted in not-guilty verdicts. The study concluded that the high rate of errors occurred because of the indiscriminate use of the death penalty and factors such as race, politics, and poorly performing law-enforcement systems (Columbia Law School, 2000). Justice Sandra Day O'Connor, in a speech, admitted that since 1973, ninety death row inmates have been exonerated of the crimes for which they were convicted because of the use of DNA evidence (Memory and Rose, 2002: 67).

In Arizona, between 1974 and 2001, 7 of the 220 death-row inmates have been freed and 12 have had sentences reduced from death to time in prison ranging from 10 to 35 years. Some Arizona lawyers are now suggesting an **innocence project** to review all death-penalty cases, similar to the national projects. Arizona does have a law that sets no deadline for post-appeal DNA. testing; thus, inmates like Larry Youngblood of Tucson, who spent 10½ years in prison for conviction of sexual molestation, was freed when DNA tests showed he wasn't guilty (Sowers, 2001).

In Texas, since 1976, 927 people have been sentenced to death, 285 have been executed, and 188 have had sentences reduced—most for violations of procedure, but some because of fundamental errors or misconduct, such as withholding exculpatory evidence. Twelve have been set free because their convictions were reversed, and the state declined to retry or they were acquitted on retrial (Hall, 2002: 124).

Prosecutorial Misconduct

When prosecutors forget that their mission is to protect due process, not obtain a conviction at all costs, misconduct can occur. The types of misconduct range from fairly nonserious lapses of ethical rules to commission of criminal acts (such as hiding evidence). The following paragraphs offer some of the possible rules that are violated when prosecutors forget their mission.

Communications with Defendants When a criminal defendant is represented by an attorney, the prosecutor should not attempt any communication with him or her outside the presence of the defense attorney. The attorney's presence is designed to eliminate the possibility of improper or intimidating behavior, illegal deals, and improper interrogation or plea-bargain offers.

Ex Parte Communications with the Judge Prosecutors and judges work together on a daily basis. There is a prohibition on attorneys and judges discussing a case outside the presence of the other attorney; but because of working conditions, this is much more likely to apply to prosecutors than to defense attorneys. The reason for the rule is fairness. It is not fair for the judge to hear one side without the other side there to defend its point of view. This rule applies to casual conversations as well as more formal interchanges or offerings of information.

Duty to Correct False Testimony Similar to a defense attorney's quandary when a witness commits perjury, a prosecutor must also take steps to avoid allowing false testimony to stand. In point of fact, the prosecutor's role is the easier one because there are no conflicting duties to protect a client; therefore, when a prosecution witness perjures himself or herself, the prosecutor has an affirmative duty to bring it to the attention of the court.

Failure to Disclose Evidence Perhaps the most common charge leveled against prosecutors, failure to disclose evidence, stems from a duty to reveal exculpatory evidence to the defense (if the defense files a "Brady motion" requesting such evidence). Because the rule indicates that only evidence that is "likely to lead to a different outcome" is subject to this discovery requirement, some prosecutors who withhold evidence argue that "It wasn't important" or "I didn't believe it." These rationalizations ignore a basic difference between their role and the role of the defense attorney. Whereas the defense attorney's only mission is the defense of his or her client, the prosecutor's role is to seek justice. This means that all evidence should be brought forward and shared so that "truth shall prevail."

Examples Examples of prosecutorial misconduct typically involve ignoring the procedural protections of due process. When prosecutors are too zealous in their attempts to obtain a conviction, their role as officer of the court is ignored and they become judge and jury. A *Chicago Tribune* investigation found that since 1963, 381 defendants across the country have had a homicide conviction thrown out because prosecutors concealed exculpatory evidence or presented evidence they knew to be false. Of the 381, 67 had been sentenced to death and were exonerated by DNA evidence or independent investigations. Nearly 30 of the 67 on death row were freed, but they served between five and twenty-six years before their convictions were reversed (Armstrong and Possley, 2002). The prosecutorial misconduct included the following:

- Concealed evidence that discredited their star witnesses, pointed to other suspects, or supported defendants' claim of self defense
- Suppressed evidence that the murder occurred when the defendant had an alibi, or where the murder occurred
- Depicted red paint as blood

- Portrayed hog blood as human
- Suppressed statements of eyewitnesses that offenders were white when prosecuting two black men
- Received a knife from a crime scene from police, but hid it and when defendant argued that he killed after he had been stabbed with knife; taunted defense for the absence of a knife to prove their theory
- Hid knife when there was self-defense argument (another case)
- Hid a victim's gun when the defendant argued self-defense
- Hid an iron pipe the victim had used to attack defendant
- Hid blood-spatter expert's report that supported defendant's version of events
- Withheld evidence suggesting police informant had framed defendant
- Concealed evidence indicating their chief witness was the killer, not the defendant (Armstrong and Possley, 2002)

Sanctions There are very few controls on the behavior of prosecutors in the courtroom. Voters have some control over who becomes a prosecutor, but once in office most prosecutors stay in the good graces of a voting public unless there is a major scandal or an energetic competitor. In cities, most work is conducted by assistant prosecutors who are hired rather than elected. Misconduct in the courtroom is sometimes orally sanctioned by trial judges. Perhaps an appellate decision may overturn a conviction, but prosecutors are rarely punished even when cases are overturned.

Gershman (1991) writes that prosecutors misbehave because it works and they can get away with it. Because misconduct is scrutinized only when the defense attorney makes an objection and then files an appeal (and even then the appellate court may rule that it was a harmless error), there is a great deal of incentive to use improper tactics in the courtroom. The main reason they engage in misconduct is because they want to win and there is very little chance of being punished.

The Supreme Court has ruled that prosecutors cannot be subject to civil suits against them even in cases of egregious rule breaking. The most important fact uncovered in the *Chicago Tribune* investigation was that not one of the prosecutors was convicted of a crime, and none were even disbarred. Some became judges, district attorneys, and one became a congressman! (Armstrong and Possley, 2002) See the accompanying box "In Texas: No Innocents on Death Row?"

ETHICAL ISSUES FOR JUDGES

Perhaps the most popular symbol of justice is the judge in his or her black robe. Judges are expected to be impartial, knowledgeable, and authoritative. They guide the prosecutor, defense attorney, and all the other actors in the trial process from beginning to end, helping to maintain the integrity of the proceeding. This is the ideal, but judges are human, with human failings.

In Texas: No Innocents on Death Row?

Randall Dale Adams was the subject of *The Thin Blue Line,* a documentary about his case. He was convicted in 1976 of killing a Dallas police officer who stopped the car driven by David Harris. Harris said Adams was the gunman, Adams said he wasn't even in the car. The state relied on an eyewitness who had picked someone else out of lineup and Harris, a sixteen-year-old with a long juvenile record. Harris eventually confessed he killed the officer alone.

Clarence Brandley was the subject of a *60 Minutes* investigation that eventually led to his release. He was convicted of a 1980 rape and murder of a high school cheerleader. Police intimidated witnesses who had evidence that another had committed the crime, and the prosecutor lost evidence that could have proven his innocence. His conviction was overturned and he was eventually freed.

Ricardo Guerra was convicted in 1982 of killing a police officer. Shots were fired from another's gun and both the officer and the gun owner were killed. All evidence pointed to the dead man as the shooter, but prosecutors and police pursued a conviction against Guerra, hiding evidence pointing to the other suspect and bullying witnesses to lie. His conviction was overturned in 1997, and a federal court called police misconduct outrageous.

Kerry Max Cook was convicted of sexually mutilating and killing a woman in 1977. His sentence was overturned in 1997 because the prosecution withheld evidence. DNA proved semen stains on the victim's underwear belonged to her married boyfriend.

Federico Macias was convicted in 1984 of killing an El Paso couple. His defense attorney never called alibi witnesses. *Pro bono* appeal lawyers found witnesses, raised doubts, and the federal court overturned his conviction in 1992. The grand jury refused to re-indict.

SOURCE: M. Hall, "Death Isn't Fair." *Texas Monthly* (December 2002): 124–167.

Ethical Guidelines

To help guide judges in their duties, the Model Code of Judicial Conduct was developed by the American Bar Association (latest revision 2000). This Code identifies the ethical considerations unique to judges. The primary theme of judicial ethics is impartiality. If we trust the judge to give objective rulings, then we must be confident that his or her objectivity isn't marred by any type of bias.

Judges should not let their personal prejudices influence their decisions. To avoid this possibility, the ABA's ethical rules specify that each judge should try to avoid all appearance of bias as well as actual bias. Judges must be careful to avoid financial involvements or personal relationships that may threaten objectivity. We expect judges, like police officers and prosecutors, to conform to higher standards of behavior than the rest of us. Therefore, any hint of scandal in their private lives also calls into question their professional ethics. The obvious rationale is that judges who have less-admirable personal values cannot judge others objectively, and those judges who are less than honest in their financial dealings do not have a right to sit in judgment of others.

There are a number of problematic issues in the perceived objectivity of judges. For instance, in those states where judges are elected, the judges must solicit campaign contributions. These monies are most often obtained from attorneys, and it is not at all unusual for judges to accept money from attorneys who practice before them. In fact, quite often, the judge's campaign manager is a practicing attorney. Does this not provide at least the appearance of impropriety? This situation is exacerbated in jurisdictions that use court appointments as the method for indigent representation. In these jurisdictions, judges hand out appointments to the same attorneys who give money back in the form of campaign contributions, or have other ties to the judge. In one jurisdiction, it was discovered that a female attorney, in her first year out of law school, received appointments totaling more than $100,000 from a family court judge with whom she had a personal relationship (Harper, 1992: A9). Obviously, the appearance, if not the actuality, of bias is present in such a situation.

The practice of awarding indigent cases to one's friends or for reasons other than qualifications may not only be unethical, but may have serious consequences for the defendant. In a Texas Bar Report called "Muting Gideon's Trumpet" (2000), it was reported that many capital cases were appointed to friends of judges and to lawyers who were known for speeding cases through the system. Some lawyers who received appointment had been disciplined by the state bar. The 2001 Fair Defense Act of Texas requires counties to appoint qualified attorneys and pay fair fees, but the fact is that indigent defense, when run on the appointment system, creates a potential for abuse.

Use of Discretion

Judges' discretion occurs in two major areas: interpretation of the law and sentencing. The first area is in the interpretation of the law in court cases. For instance, a judge might be called upon to assess the legality of evidence and make rulings on the various objections raised by both the prosecutors and the defense attorneys. A judge also writes the extremely important instructions to the jury. These are crucial because they set up the legal questions and definitions of the case.

Judges must rule on the legality of evidence; they may make a decision to exclude a confession or a piece of evidence because of the way it was obtained and by so doing allow the guilty to go free. The exclusionary rule has generated a storm of controversy since it could result in a guilty party avoiding punishment because of an error committed by the police. The basis for the exclusionary rule is that one cannot accept a conviction based on tainted evidence. The ideals of justice reject such a conviction because accepting tainted evidence, even if obtained against a guilty party, is a short step away from accepting any type of evidence, no matter how illegal, and thus poses a threat to the whole concept of due process. The conviction is so violative of due process that it is ruled void.

A more practical argument for the exclusionary rule is that if we want police officers to behavior in a legal manner, then we must have heavy sanctions against illegalities. Arguably, if convictions are lost due to illegal evidence collection, police will reform their behavior. Actual practice provides little support for this argument, though. Police have learned how to get around the exclusionary rule, and, in any event, cases lost on appeal are so far removed from the day-to-day decision making of the police that they have little effect on police behavior.

Court decisions have also created several exceptions to the exclusionary rule. Judges can now rule that the evidence be allowed because of public safety, good faith, or inevitable discovery exceptions. Those who decide to exclude evidence and set aside convictions do so by disregarding short-term effects for more abstract principles—specifically, the protection of due process.

Do the ethical frameworks justify allowing a guilty person to go free because of "tainted" evidence? Religious ethics don't give us much help unless we decide that this ethical system would support vengeance and thus would permit the judge to ignore the exclusionary rule in order to punish a criminal. On the other hand, religious ethics might also support letting the criminal go free to answer to an ultimate higher authority, since human judgment was in this case imperfect. Egoism would support the decision to let a criminal go free or not, depending on the effect it would have on the judge's well-being. The categorical imperative would support the exclusionary rule, on one hand, because one would not want a universal rule accepting tainted evidence. On the other hand, one would have to agree to retry all criminals, regardless of the severity of the crime, whenever the evidence was tainted, despite the possibility of further crime or harm to individuals. Act utilitarianism would support ignoring the exclusionary rule if the crime was especially serious or if there was a good chance the offender would not be retried successfully. The utility derived from ignoring the rule would outweigh the good. However, rule utilitarianism could be used to support the exclusionary rule, since the long-term effect of allowing illegal police behavior would be more serious than letting one criminal go free.

QUERY

Should the confession of a suspect that he attempted to reach for a police officer's gun be admitted into evidence against him in an excessive-force civil suit against Oxnard Police Department and the officer who shot the suspect five times, paralyzing and blinding him?

"I am dying! What are you doing to me?" screamed Martinez as officers persistently interrogated him. They indicated that he would receive help only after he talked and continued to question him in the ambulance and emergency room. No Miranda warning was given.

The city argues that because Martinez was never charged with a crime, no Miranda warnings were needed. Plaintiff argues that since he wasn't given a Miranda warning, the confession must be considered coerced, and to protect the integrity of the court it cannot be used.

What do you think? Should police be able to use the confession of a man who was in great pain and thought he was dying, after telling him that he would get medical treatment only after he talked?

Associated Press, 2002.

The judge is called upon to decide many and various questions through-out a trial. Of course, he or she is guided by the law and legal precedent, but in most cases each decision involves a substantial element of subjectivity. Judges have the power to make it difficult for either the prosecutor or the defense attorney through their pattern of rulings on objections, evidence admitted, and even personal attitude toward an attorney, which is always noted by the jury and is influential in their decision.

There are multiple layers of discretion in our judicial system. Supposedly, even after a judge might have made a biased or incorrect decision during trial, such decisions can be dealt with on appeal. The problem is that the appellate system is, in some states, heavily influenced by politics, or is hyper-technical. The Court of Criminal Appeals in Texas has shifted from being known as a group of liberal Democrats who overturned many cases to a group of conservative Republicans who do not find error even in the most egregious of situations.

For instance, the Calvin Burdine "sleeping lawyer" case received national attention when the Court of Criminal Appeals held that Burdine did not deserve a new trial because there was no showing that the lawyer slept dur-ing *crucial* parts of the trial. Roy Criner challenged his conviction and ninety-nine-year sentence for rape because of a DNA test that showed the sperm in the victim was not Criner's. The trial judge ordered a new trial, the state appealed, and the Court of Criminal Appeals in a five-to-three decision denied the new evidence, arguing that it didn't establish innocence, since he could have used a condom or not ejaculated. In another case, a defendant who confessed because police threatened to have Mexican police harm his relatives was denied a new trial because the Court ruled it was "harmless error" (Hall, 2002). Despite the belief that simply applying the rules will lead to the right conclusion or decision, the reality is that judges and justices are simply human with very real biases influencing their decision making. The suspicion that appellate court judges decide where they want to end up and make up the argument to get there is one that is hard to deny after careful analysis.

The other type of appellate decision making that we might scrutinize is when there is a complete absence of "equity" thinking (basic fairness) in place of hypertechnical application of rules. Cases that are denied because a dead-line was missed, or appeals denied because they are not drawn up in the cor-rect fashion, are examples of this application of discretion. For example, in the case of Delma Banks, discussed earlier, lawyers were denied a clemency hear-ing from the state Board of Pardons and Paroles despite the fact that there was new forensic evidence that Banks was out of town when the murder occurred and that one of the chief prosecution witnesses was coached and the transcript of the coaching was deliberately withheld from the defense for close to nine-teen years and only finally surrendered when ordered by a federal district judge. The reason the Board denied the petition? It was filed one week late (Pasztor, 2003).

> **QUOTE**
>
> *"The question before the court . . . is the validity of the judgment, not the correctness of the judgment . . ."*
>
> *Quote from state lawyer arguing against releasing Jeffrey David Cox, who was serving life plus a fifty-year sentence for kidnapping and murder, a crime he didn't commit. Evidence from the F.B.I. and the arrest of another suspect proved his innocence.*
>
> ——————
>
> *Washington Post,* 2001 "And in Virginia" (editorial) retrieved 11/12/2001 from
> http://www/washingtonpost.com/wp-dyn/articles/A12860-2001Nov11.html

Sentencing The second area of judicial discretion is in sentencing. The following makes clear the small amount of training judges receive for this awesome responsibility (Johnson, 1982: 20):

> Few judges have the benefit of judicial training sessions prior to embarking upon the often bewildering and frequently frustrating task of pursuing that vague, if not indefinable, entity so commonly known as justice. . . . Thus, it is not uncommon for the new judge, relying upon a philosophy often formulated hastily, to be placed in the unenviable position of pronouncing a sentence upon another human being without any special preparation.

Judges' decisions are scrutinized by public watchdog groups and appellate-level courts. In fact, one wonders if judges aren't overly influenced in their sentencing by the current clamor for strict punishments. However, if judges are supposed to enact community sentiment, perhaps it is proper for them to reflect its influence. Is there one just punishment for a certain type of offender, or does the definition of what is just depend on community opinion of the crime, the criminal, and the time? Look at the scenarios in the accompanying box and decide "How Would You Rule?"

Evidence indicates that the decision making of judges is actually based on personal standards, since no consistency seems to appear between the decisions of individual judges in the same community. One study found that two judges in Louisiana had remarkably different records on numbers of convictions. The two also differed in their patterns of sentencing (Pinkele and Louthan, 1985: 58). Hofer et. al. (1999) point out that most sentencing disparity in the federal system before sentencing guidelines came into effect occurred because of different patterns exhibited by individual judges. They cite studies that found, for instance, that judges' sentences were influenced by whether they had been prosecutors and by their religion.

The other extreme is when judges have no discretion in sentencing. Federal sentencing guidelines instruct the judge as to the sentence that must be imposed unless there is a proven mitigating or aggravating factor(s) in the case. Hofer et al. (1999) examined the effect of guidelines on federal sentencing disparity and

How Would You Rule?

Assume you are a judge with the appropriate jurisdiction to decide the following:

1. You are a judge who must decide whether to allow the jury to consider a lower level of homicide for Andrea Yates. She drowned all five of her children in the bathtub and then called police. Although the jury makes the factual judgment, the judge decides if, as a matter of law, there is enough evidence to consider a lower charge.

2. You are an appellate judge and must decide whether to set aside a conviction of a woman who murdered an infant. The defense alleges that the sheriff violated attorney–client privilege by obtaining a warrant to seize a map drawn by the convicted woman showing where the baby was buried. She drew the map for her lawyer and, as such, legal experts contend it should be protected under the attorney–client privilege. The trial judge granted the warrant because of testimony by the sheriff and his deputies that they believed the baby might still be alive and they needed the map to find him, but evidence presented to you indicates that all law enforcement officials involved believed that the baby was dead and only wanted the map to help convict the offender. There is overwhelming evidence of guilt, and a new trial would subject the parents to continued reminders of their loss. What would you do?

3. You must decide whether a particular piece of artwork is obscene. The artist has painted a series of sex scenes, including bondage, sadomasochism, bestiality, and necrophilia, interspersed with painting of nude children at play. She states that her art has redeeming social qualities because it is a statement of the many faces of humanity. The series of paintings is being displayed in a public gallery supported by city and federal funds. The district attorney has filed for an injunction to close the show due to obscenity. How would you rule? How did you decide?

concluded that they had a small but significant effect on reducing disparity. However, there were some areas that were resistant, including regional differences in drug sentencing.

The federal sentencing guidelines have received a great deal of criticism because of the draconian sentences applied to drug crimes. Once again, we see a potential racial bias: crack cocaine receives a sentence that is one hundred times longer than that given for powder cocaine. Although the argument is that crack cocaine is more associated with other crimes and there are good reasons for distinguishing the two, there is a widespread belief that the disparity is simply racism in action, since African Americans are much more likely to be convicted of crack crimes and whites for power cocaine (Hofer, et al., 1999). Some federal judges have been so appalled by the sentences that they have refused to sentence or even quit, rather than impose the mandated sentences.

Judicial Misconduct

Examples of judicial misconduct are fairly rare, perhaps because judges' behavior is more shielded than other actors in the system. Operation Greylord in Chicago is probably the most well-known exposé of widescale judicial corruption. This investigation resulted in convictions of thirty-one attorneys and eight judges for bribery. Judges accepted bribes to "fix" cases, meaning to rule in favor of the attorney offering the bribe. Not unlike law enforcement's **blue curtain of secrecy,** not one attorney came forward to expose this system of corruption, even though it was fairly well known what was occurring (Weber, 1987: 60).

Judges' neutrality is questioned when they voice strong opinions in issues or cases. Talking to the media used to be rare, but now many judges find a venue to express their views, take a stand, and act as advocate. Many question this role for judges, and judges have needed to recuse themselves when they have indicated to news media that they already had opinions on a case before it was concluded.

Some question judges' motives in allowing cameras in the courtroom— personal vanity rather than the interests of justice could be an issue. There seems to be real concern that judges and lawyers play to the camera, perhaps to the detriment of the swift resolution of the case. Recently a judge in Houston, Texas, wanted to allow a television camera in the jury room. The argument is that the public should be allowed to see this most secret of tribunals; the argument against it is that jury members need that privacy in order to conduct their business in a fair and impartial manner. If cameras recorded who said what, they might feel constrained not to say anything and not to vote their conscience.

QUERY

- Do you believe that cameras should be allowed to record jury deliberations?
- Do you believe that congressional hearings should be able to investigate a judicial candidate's beliefs about abortion, affirmative action, and other issues and use such findings to decide whether or not to confirm?
- Do you believe a judge can ever be purely impartial in a case?

Judges' relationships with other actors in the system are always suspect. For instance, the fact that Judge Ito in the O. J. Simpson case was married to a homicide detective caused many to question whether he could be objective when the defense planned to attack the credibility of police procedure. However, since many of those who work in the justice system develop friendships, socialize, and sometimes marry others in the system, to recuse oneself from every case that involved some overlapping acquaintances or relations would be impossible for many judges.

Courtroom decorum is established by the judge, and if he or she displays an irreverent or self-aggrandizing attitude, or flaunts the law, his or her behavior degrades the entire judicial process. Some judges seem to be overly influenced by their power—as was the case of one district court judge who instructed courtroom workers to address him as "God." Most courtroom gossip includes the idiosyncrasies of some judges, like the judge who was reputed to keep a gun

---

A Judicial "Raspberry"

A judge was removed from office for conduct ranging from "giving the finger" to a defendant who came to court late to making a sound commonly referred to as a "raspberry" in response to a defendant's testimony.

SOURCE: *Spruance v. Commission on Judicial Qualifications,* 13 Cal. 3d 778 {1975}.

A judge was removed from office for beginning proceedings in the absence of tardy counsel, questioning witnesses himself, excusing himself from the bench for periods of time and instructing the attorneys to carry on without him, and pressuring the district attorney's office to drop charges pending against friends and relatives.

SOURCE: *Gonzalez v. Commission on Judicial Performance,* 188 Cal. Rptr. 880 {1983}.

---

under his robes and pointed it at tardy attorneys, the judge who arrested citizens in the hall outside his courtroom for creating a public disturbance because they were talking during a court session, the judge who ordered a woman arrested for contempt when she wrote a scathing letter to a newspaper regarding his competence, the judge who sentenced a man to probation for killing his wife (excusing such behavior in open court with a statement indicating that the nagging victim deserved it), or the judge who signed an order of execution with a smiley face. These individuals illustrate that putting on a black robe doesn't necessarily give one the wisdom of Solomon (see "A Judicial 'Raspberry' ").

Other forms of unethical behavior are less blatant. Judges have a duty to conclude judicial processing with reasonable punctuality. However, there are widespread delays in processing, and part of the reason is the lack of energy with which some judges pursue their dockets. In the same jurisdiction, and with a balanced assignment of cases, it is not unusual for one judge to have only a couple dozen pending cases and another judge to have literally hundreds. The reason is that judges routinely allow numerous continuances; set trial dates far into the future, start the docket call at 10:00 A.M. and conclude the day's work at 3:00 P.M., and in other ways take a desultory approach to swift justice.

We must be careful not to paint with too broad a brush. The most egregious examples of unethical behavior such as taking bribes or trampling the due-process rights of defendants are performed by only a few judges, in the same way that extreme behaviors are committed by only a small percentage of police officers, defense attorneys, and prosecutors.

CONCLUSION

According to the basic tenets of our law, the accused is innocent up to the point of conviction. Prosecutors, judges, and defense attorneys are all "officers of the court" and as such are sworn to uphold the highest principles of our law, including this basic assumption of innocence. However, in the day-to-day operations of courthouse politics and bureaucracy, the rights of individuals may compete with the goal of efficient processing.

The presence and use of discretion in the criminal justice system are pervasive, and decision makers are often influenced by individual values and ethics that prompt them to stray from the parameters of structured laws and rules. Thus, it is crucial that these professionals remember and believe in the basic tenets of due process and be ever vigilant against the influence of prejudice or bias in the application of law toward the pursuit of justice.

REVIEW QUESTIONS

1. Describe at least three issues related to the prosecutor's ethical obligations.
2. Describe at least three issues related to the judge's ethical obligations.
3. What are the problems with expert witnesses?
4. Using moral and ethical criteria, analyze some recent innovations designed to improve crime prevention. Some possibilities to consider are such things as preventive detention, neighborhood justice centers that mediate rather than find guilt or innocence, the use of a waiver to adult court for violent juvenile offenders, increased sentences for gang-related or drug-related crimes, and criminalization of nonpayment of child support.
5. Using ethical and moral criteria, evaluate recent courtroom practices. Examples include the use of videotaped testimony, allowing television cameras into the courtroom and jury room, and victim statements during sentencing.
6. Watch a movie that presents a legal dilemma (e.g., *Criminal Law, Penalty Phase, Presumed Innocent, The Witness*) and analyze the dilemmas of using one of the ethical frameworks described in this book.

ETHICAL DILEMMAS

Situation 1

You are a deputy prosecutor and have to decide whether to charge a defendant with possession and sale of a controlled substance. You know you have a good case because the guy sold to the local junior high school and many of the kids are willing to testify. The police are pressuring you to make a deal because he has promised to inform on other dealers in the area if you don't prosecute. What should you do?

Situation 2

You are a judge who must sentence two defendants. One insisted on a jury trial and, through his defense attorney, dragged the case on for months with delays and motions. He was finally convicted by a jury. The other individual was his co-defendant, and he pleaded guilty. Apparently, they were equally responsible for the burglary. How will you sentence them?

Situation 3

You are a member of a jury. The case is a child molestation case in which the defendant is accused of a series of molestations in his neighborhood. You have been advised by the judge not to discuss the case with anyone outside the courtroom and especially not to anyone on either side of the case. Going down in the elevator after the fourth day of the trial, you overhear the prosecutor talking to one of the police officer witnesses. They are discussing the fact that the man has a previous arrest for child molestation but that it has not been allowed in by the judge as being too prejudicial to the jury. You were pretty sure the guy was guilty before, but now you definitely believe he is guilty. You also know that if you tell the judge what you have heard, it will probably result in a mistrial. What would you do?

Situation 4

You are a prosecutor in a jurisdiction that does not use the grand jury system. An elderly man has administered a lethal dose of sleeping tablets to his wife, who was suffering from Alzheimer's disease. He calmly turned himself in to the police department, and the case is on the front page of the paper. It is entirely up to you whether to charge him with murder. What would you do? What criteria did you use to arrive at your decision?

SUGGESTED READINGS

Dwyer, J., P. Neufeld, and B. Scheck. 2001. *Actual Innocence: When Justice Goes Wrong and How to Make it Right.* New York City: Signet Books.

Gershman, B. 1990. *Prosecutorial Misconduct.* New York: Clark Boardman.

Radelet, M., H. Bedau, and C. Putnam. 1992. *In Spite of Innocence.* Boston: Northeastern University Press.

Spence, G. 1989. *With Justice for None.* New York: Penguin.

11

The Ethics of Punishment and Corrections

Key Terms

punishment
treatment
retribution
prevention
expiation
three strikes laws
justice model
just deserts model

new rehabilitationists
specific deterrence
general deterrence
incapacitation
cruel and unusual punishment
stigmatizing shaming
reintegrative shaming

Chapter Objectives

- Understand the definitions of punishment and treatment and their rationales.
- Learn how the ethical frameworks justify punishment.
- Become familiar with the arguments for and against capital punishment.
- Understand the role that discretion, authority, and power play in corrections.
- Explore the ethical issues involved with privatization of corrections.

After someone has been found guilty of a criminal offense, an array of possible sanctions and treatments are possible. A suspended sentence or probation with restitution or community service as conditions may be required. If the crime is serious, the offender dangerous, or both, incarceration for a period of time is a possibility. During incarceration, the wrongdoer may be required to participate in treatment programs ranging from self-help groups such as Alcoholics Anonymous to psychosurgery. The ultimate punishment the state can impose, of course, is death.

According to one author (Leiser, 1986: 198), five elements are essential to the definition of **punishment:**

1. There are at least two persons—one who inflicts the punishment and one who is punished.

2. The person who inflicts the punishment causes a certain harm to occur to the person who is being punished.

3. The person who inflicts the punishment has been authorized, under a system of rules or laws, to harm the person who is punished in the particular way in which he or she does.

4. The person who is being punished has been judged by a representative of that authority to have done what he or she is forbidden to do or to have failed to do what he or she is required to do by some relevant rule or law.

5. The harm that is inflicted upon the person who is being punished is specifically for the act or omission mentioned in Condition 4.

We need also to define **treatment.** According to correctional terminology, *treatment* may be anything used to induce behavioral change. The goal is to eliminate dysfunctional or deviant behavior and to encourage productive and normal behavior patterns. In prison, treatment includes diagnosis, classification, therapy of all sorts, education, religious activity, vocational training, and self-help groups.

The infliction of punishment and even treatment is usually limited by some rationale or guideline. For instance, von Hirsch (1976: 5) presents the following restrictive guidelines:

1. The liberty of each individual is to be protected so long as it is consistent with the liberty of others.

2. The state is obligated to observe strict parsimony in intervening in criminals' lives.

3. The state must justify each intrusion.

4. The requirements of justice ought to constrain the pursuit of crime prevention (that is, deterrence and rehabilitation).

In this chapter, we will first explore the various rationales for punishment, briefly discuss capital punishment in particular, and discuss private corrections. In the next chapter, we will examine ethical issues related to institutional corrections. In Chapter 13, we will discuss ethical issues relevant to community corrections.

RATIONALES FOR PUNISHMENT
AND CORRECTIONS

Does society have the right to punish or correct miscreants? If it does, where does that right come from? The rationale for punishment and corrections comes from the social contract. In the same way that the social contract forms the basis for police power, it also provides a rationale for further control in the form of punishment and corrections. Recall that, according to this theory, we avoid social chaos by giving the state the power to control us. In this way we protect ourselves from being victimized by others by giving up our liberty to aggress against others. If we do step outside the bounds, the state has the right to control and punish us for our transgressions. Concurrently, the state is limited in the amount of control it can exert over individuals. To be consistent with the social contract, the state should exert its power only to accomplish the protection purpose; any further interventions in civil liberties are unwarranted.

Corrections pursues a mixture of goals, including retribution, reform, incapacitation, deterrence, and rehabilitation. The long-standing argument between proponents of punishment and proponents of treatment reveals a system without a clear mandate or rationale for action. Garland (1990) writes that even the state's goal of punishment is problematic because it is marked with inconsistencies between the intent and the implementation. The moral contradictions are that it seeks to uphold freedom by means of its deprivation and it punishes private violence by inflicting state violence.

Can treatment and punishment occur at the same time? Or, as many critics argue, is the treatment ethic simply empty rhetoric? Since the emergence of penitentiaries in this country, we can see recurring cycles of emphasis — reform is replaced with retribution and then swings back again. In our current punitive cycle, we have virtually abandoned rehabilitation as a goal. Can a punishment system in which the definition of "just" punishment is relative and changes with time ever be an ethical or moral one? We simply do not seem to agree on what an individual offender deserves; therefore, specific punishments for similar crimes vary according to time, place, persons involved, and other factors.

An important question to ask is, "Who are we punishing?" Studies show that only a very small minority of individuals who commit crimes end up in prison; furthermore, we may assume that those numbers are not representative of the larger population. Those in our jails and prisons are there not only because they committed crimes, but also because they are poor, members of a minority group, or powerless. Certain types of criminals tend to avoid the more punitive sanctions of the corrections system. For instance, businesses routinely bilk consumers out of billions of dollars annually and chalk up the punitive fines incurred to operating expenses, yet it would not be uncommon in some jurisdictions for a shoplifter to be sent to prison. Streams and land are routinely polluted by industrial waste, but again, punitive fines are the typical sanctions, and these cannot begin to restore what has been taken away in the flagrant pursuit of financial profit. In fact, such costs are typically passed on to the consumers, so, taxpayers suffer the crime and then also pay the fine. Very seldom do we see executives responsible for company policy go to prison.

White-collar criminals routinely receive fines, probation, or short stays in halfway houses whereas so-called street criminals receive prison sentences. In the Enron and WorldCom scandals, there were some very public arrests and promises of prosecutions, but in the subsequent months, we have not seen any of the initial actors actually prosecuted. By the time the legal system finally completes the process, it is doubtful that anyone will see the inside of a prison, and if they do, it will probably be a short stay in a minimum-security federal prison. Many people question the justification of punishment when its imposition is so influenced by factors other than guilt.

Long ago, criminals were viewed as sinners with no ability to change their behavior, so punishment and incapacitation were seen as the only logical ways to respond to crime. Bentham (1748–1833) and Beccaria (1738–1794) viewed the criminal as rational and as having free will, and therefore saw the threat of punishment as a deterrent. Neoclassicists such as Quetelet (1796–1894) and Guerry (1802–1866) recognized that the insane and juveniles could not be held entirely responsible for their actions and therefore believed that they should not be punished. The insane and the young were treated differently because they were considered moral infants, not possessing the sense to refrain from wrongdoing. Then the positivist school influenced thinking to the extent that all criminal acts were believed to be merely symptoms of an underlying pathology. The passage from the 1870 Prison Congress exemplifies this view.

QUOTE

A criminal is a man who has suffered under a disease evinced by the perpetration of a crime, and who may reasonably be held to be under the dominion of such disease until his conduct has afforded very strong presumption not only that he is free from its immediate influence, but that the chances of its recurrence have become exceedingly remote.

From the 1870 Prison Congress, quoted in Mitford, 1971: 104.

The treatment programs created in the last one hundred years or so operate under the assumption that we can do something to offenders to reduce their criminal activity. That "something" may involve treating a psychological problem, such as a sociopathic or paranoid personality; addressing social problems, such as alcoholism or addiction; or resolving more pragmatic problems, such as chronic unemployment, with vocational training and job placement. Obviously, the perception of the criminal influences the rationale for correction and punishment.

The two major justifications for punishment and treatment are **retribution** and **prevention.** The retributive rationale postulates that punishment is an end in itself, whereas the preventive approach views punishment as a means rather than an end and embraces other responses to crime. The retributive rationale is probably more consistent with a view of the criminal as rational, and the prevention rationale, with certain exceptions, is more consistent with the view of the criminal as somehow less responsible for his or her behavior.

Retribution

As mentioned before, the social contract provides the rationale for punishment. As long as one is a member of society, one has implicitly agreed to society's rules and right to punish. One criticism of the social contract theory is that it is completely contingent on a consensus perspective of society. That is, the members of society are assumed to share the same goals, beliefs, and power. The ideal state is one of agreement, which is seen as entirely possible. All people benefit from the social contract because they get to keep what they've got, with the assumption that what they've got is fairly equally distributed. The conflict perspective views society as made up of a number of conflicting groups; when one wins, the other loses, because their interests can never be the same. Obviously, the social contract theory is difficult to reconcile with a conflict perspective. For some people, no advantages are received from the sacrifice of liberties. If someone perceives himself or herself as disenfranchised from society, does the right to punish still exist? Can we still use the social contract as the rationale for punishment?

The retributive rationale for punishment is consistent with the social contract theory. Simply stated, the retributive rationale is that the individual offender must be punished because he or she deserves it. Mackie (1982: 4) describes three specific types of retribution. The first, negative retribution, dictates that one who is not guilty must not be punished for a crime; the second, positive retribution, demands that one who is guilty ought to be punished; and the third, permissive retribution, says that one who is guilty may be punished. This formulation states that retribution may support punishment but may also limit punishment. There are limits as to as who may be punished (only those who commit crimes) and restrictions on the amount of punishment (only that sufficient to balance the wrong). Further, this formulation implies that punishment need not be administered in all cases. The exceptions, although not discussed by Mackie, may involve the concepts of mercy or diminished responsibility.

Our system of justice was created to take the place of private vengeance. We do not allow victims to seek their own revenge but, rather, replace *hot vengeance* with *cool justice,* dispassionate in its determination and distribution. The social contract supports the notion that it is intrinsically right for the state, rather than the victim's family, to execute a killer. The state has taken over the necessary task of punishment to ensure the survival of society by preventing private vengeance. Intentionally inflicting pain on another is an evil, but not if it meets the definitional elements of punishment.

Another retributivist justification for punishment is that it is the only way the individual can achieve salvation. In fact, we owe the offender punishment because only through suffering can atonement occur, and only through atonement or **expiation** can the offender achieve a state of grace. Some would strongly object to this interpretation of religious ethics and argue that Christianity, while supportive of just punishment, does not necessarily support suffering as the only way to achieve a state of grace: there must be repentance, and there is also room for forgiveness. One other view consistent with retribution is that punishment balances the advantage gained by a wrongdoer. The criminal act distorts the balance and parity of social relationships, and only a punishment or similar deprivation can restore the natural balance that existed before the criminal act.

QUERY

Carla Faye Tucker was executed by the state of Texas in 1998. Her crime was a gruesome double murder. Many people across the world, including the pope, argued that she should be spared the death penalty because (a) she was a born-again Christian, (b) she was truly repentant, or (c) she committed her crime in a drug-and alcohol-induced haze and was an abused child whose mother introduced her to prostitution at the age of 12.

Do you believe the Board of Pardons and Paroles and Governor George W. Bush should have commuted her sentence to life in prison? If not, what sort of person should the power of commutation be used for?

The question of whether to punish the crime or the criminal is long-standing and important in any discussion of retributive punishment. Jeremy Bentham believed that each criminal offense deserves a measure of punishment calculated to balance the potential pleasure or profit of the criminal offense. However, the neo-classicists allowed some characteristics of the offender to influence the punishment decision. This debate continues today with those who argue for determinate sentencing over indeterminate sentencing. Determinate sentencing punishes the offense, with the length of the sentence determined by the seriousness of the crime. Indeterminate sentencing, in contrast, allows judges a great deal of discretion so that they can tailor the punishment to fit the individual offender. A young offender might get a second chance because he has the potential to change; a woman might receive probation instead of prison because she has an infant to take care of; a habitual criminal might be the unhappy recipient of an increased sentence because he is considered unsalvageable. This type of individualized justice is inconsistent with a retributive rationale since punishment is based on *who* the criminal is rather than on *what* the crime was.

Habitual offender laws, or the so-called **three-strikes laws,** punish according to the individual offender because the offender receives a longer term (perhaps even a life sentence) because of prior crimes, for which he or she has already been punished. The policy implications of the three-strikes laws are still very much in debate, but the Supreme Court has ruled in the past that habitual-felon laws are constitutional and in March of 2003 ruled that the California three-strikes law was not unconstitutionally disproportionate when used for a nonviolent third felony (see the accompanying box).

What is an appropriate amount of punishment? This is a difficult question, even for the retributivist. The difference between a year in prison and two years in prison is measurable only by the number of days on the calendar, not by how it is experienced by different people. Should this be considered during sentencing? Punishment of any kind affects individuals differently. For instance, a whipping may be worse than death for someone with a low tolerance for pain, better than prison for someone with a great need for freedom, and perhaps even pleasurable for someone who enjoys physical pain. Prison may be experienced as an inconvenience for some and such a traumatic experience for others that it may induce suicide. Our current system of justice seldom recognizes these individual vulnerabilities or sensitivities to various punishments.

Three-Strikes Law

Ewing v. California **challenged Ewing's twenty-five-to-life sentence for stealing golf clubs. The Supreme Court upheld California's right to impose the sentence under their three-strikes law.**

Ewing's sentence is justified by the state's public-safety interest in incapacitating and deterring recidivist felons, and amply supported by his own long, serious criminal record. Ewing has been convicted of numerous misdemeanor and felony offenses, served nine separate terms of incarceration, and committed most of his crimes while on probation or parole. His prior "strikes" were serious felonies including robbery and three residential burglaries. To be sure, Ewing's sentence is a long one. But it reflects a rational legislative judgment, entitled to deference, that offenders who have committed serious or violent felonies and who continue to commit felonies must be incapacitated.
Justice O'Connor from *Ewing v. California* (March 2003)

Ewing's sentence is, at a minimum, two to three times the length of sentences that other jurisdictions would impose in similar circumstances. That sentence itself is sufficiently long to require a typical offender to spend virtually all the remainder of his active life in prison. These and the other factors that I have discussed, along with the questions that I have asked along the way, should help to identify "gross disproportionality" in a fairly objective way at the outer bounds of sentencing.
Justice Breyer (dissenting) from *Ewing v. California* (March 2003)

Sentencing studies routinely show that little or no agreement exists regarding the type or amount of punishment appropriate for a wrongdoer. Disparity in sentencing is such a problem that many reforms are aimed at reducing or even eliminating judges' discretion. Yet when legislators take on the task themselves by setting determinate sentences, their decisions are arrived at by obscure methods, probably more influenced by political pressure and compromise than from the application of fair and equitable standards. The basic premise of retribution is that offenders deserve punishment. If we are retributivists, we feel the balance is restored when they have suffered as much as their victims.

QUERY

Kathy Boudin, a 1960s activist who participated in a 1981 Brinks truck robbery in which a guard and two police officers were killed, went before the parole board in 2001. She had spent more than 20 years in prison. In those years, she developed an AIDS education program that has been adopted by prisons nationwide, she earned a master's degree in education, has been instrumental in the parenting program of the prison, and won a 1999 PEN award for poetry. She did not personally shoot any of the victims but did participate in the robbery. The relatives have petitioned to keep her in prison.

Do you think she should be paroled? If not, is there anything else she can do to make up for her crime and earn parole?

Haughney, C. "Former Activist's Bid for Parole Opposed," *Washington Post* online, retrieved August 23, 2001, from *http://washingtonpost.com/wp-dyn/articles/A42020-2001Aug21.html*. (Parole was denied.)

The **justice model** and the **just deserts model** are both retributive rationales for punishment (Fogel, 1975; Fogel and Hudson, 1981). Early advocates of the *justice model* describe the perspective as including concepts relating to the nature of humankind, the function of law, and the right of society to punish. This model, described more fully in the accompanying box, may be seen as part of a backlash against the abuse of discretion that characterized the rehabilitative era of the 1970s; it promotes a degree of predictability and equality in sentencing by reverting back to earlier retributive goals of punishment and restricting the state's right to use treatment as a criterion for release.

The *just deserts model* is also retributive and bases punishment on "commensurate deserts" (von Hirsch, 1976: xxvi). As the spokesman for this view, von Hirsch (1985: 138) disagrees with deterrence and punishment theorists who feel that retributive and deterrent or incapacitative goals can be combined. However, von Hirsch does approve of a system of punishment that incorporates incapacitative features in judging the weight of a crime by its recidivism potential. Offenders who commit similar crimes are punished equally, but the rank ordering of crimes is determined by recidivistic potential. This system, categorical incapacitation, combines deserts and prevention but in a way that, according to von Hirsch, is not unjust to the individual offender (von Hirsch, 1985: 150). Von Hirsch continues to disagree with the **new rehabilitationists,** who he feels

---

The Justice Model

1. The criminal law is the "command of the sovereign."
2. The threat of punishment is necessary to implement the law.
3. The powerful manipulate the chief motivators of human behavior—fear and hope—through rewards and punishments to retain power.
4. Socialization of individuals, however imperfect, occurs in response to the commands and expectations of the ruling social–political power.
5. The criminal law protects the dominant prescribed morality (a system of rules said to be in the common and best interest of all), reflecting the enforcement aspect of the failure of socialization.
6. In an absence of any absolute system of justice or "Natural Law," no accurate etiologic theory of crime is possible, nor is the definition of crime itself historically stable.
7. Although free will may not exist perfectly, the criminal law is largely based upon its presumed vitality and forms the only foundation for penal sanctions.
8. A prison sentence represents a punishment sanctioned by a legislative body and meted out through the official legal system against a person adjudged responsible for his behavior. Although a purpose of such punishment may be deterrence or rehabilitation, more specifically, such punishment is the deprivation of liberty for a fixed period of time.
9. When corrections becomes mired in the dismal swamp of preaching, exhorting, and treating it becomes dysfunctional as an agency of justice. Correctional agencies should engage prisoners as the law otherwise dictates; as responsible, volitional, and aspiring human beings, and not conceive of them as patients.

SOURCE: Fogel, D., and Hudson, J. *Justice as Fairness* (Cincinnati, OH: Anderson, 1981): vii. Reprinted with permission.

---

are trying to resurrect a rehabilitative ethic with the rationale that humane conditions during incapacitation require some treatment options. Von Hirsch believes that while treatment options may be offered within the same categories of punishments, they should never be substituted for punishment itself or be part of the equation (von Hirsch and Maher, 1992).

Garland (1990) offers a different view. He believes that if social control is what is desired, then the emphasis should be placed on ways of accomplishing that purpose other than punishment after the fact. If we had a system that was better at socializing and integrating its citizens—he calls this a system of social justice and moral education—then we would not have to worry so much about punishing them. The punishment that was still necessary would be viewed as morally expressive rather than instrumental, and would be retributive rather than attempt prevention goals.

Prevention

Three common justifications or rationales for punishment can all be subsumed under a general heading of prevention. Prevention assumes that something should be done to the offender to prevent future criminal activity. The three possible methods of prevention are deterrence, incapacitation, and treatment. Each of these goals is based on certain assumptions that must be considered in addition to the relevant moral questions—for instance, it is a factual question as to whether people can be deterred from crime, but it is a moral question as to what we should do to an individual to ensure deterrence.

Deterrence Specific deterrence is what is done to offenders to prevent them from deciding to commit another offense. **General deterrence** is what is done to an offender to prevent others from deciding to engage in wrongful behavior. The first teaches through punishment; the second teaches by example.

Our right to deter an individual offender is rooted in the same rationale used to support retribution. By virtue of membership in society, individuals submit themselves to society's controls. If we feel that someone's actions are damaging, we will try various means to persuade him or her to cease that activity. The implicit assumption of a deterrence philosophy is that in the absence of controls, society would revert back to a jungle-like, dangerous "war of all against all;" we need the police and official punishments to keep us all in line. Under this rationale, the true nature of humankind is perceived to be predatory and held in check only by external controls. Deterrence advocates support deterrence as a justification of punishment. In recent years, general deterrence has given way to specific deterrence because empirical support for the efficacy of general deterrence is lacking (von Hirsch, 1985).

QUOTE

1. *Those who violate others' rights deserve punishment.*
2. *However, there is a countervailing moral obligation to not deliberately add to the amount of human suffering, and punishment creates suffering.*
3. *Deterrence results in preventing more misery than it creates, thus justifying punishment.*

Adapted from von Hirsch, 1976: 54.

The rationale of specific deterrence depends on the effectiveness of punishment in deterring future behavior. Unfortunately, it is very difficult to find any studies that show that anything we do to the offender, whether under the heading of punishment or treatment, has any predictable effect on subsequent behavior. Arguments are made that this ineffectiveness is due to implementation problems; in other words, punishment doesn't deter because it is inconsistent, uncertain, and slow. If punishment was applied more consistently and with more swiftness, the argument goes, then we would see a deterrent effect.

The amount of punishment needed for deterrence is even more problematic if we seek to deter others. First, it becomes much harder to justify. If we know that a term of imprisonment either will not deter an offender or is much more than what would be needed to deter an individual but is the amount needed to deter others, it is questionable whether this further punishment can be justified. A clear example of this situation is the so-called passion murderer who probably does not need specific deterrence because the chance of killing again is slim. However, he or she is usually given a long sentence to make it clear that killing will not be tolerated. (There is, of course, also a good retributive rationale for the long sentence.) Under deterrence theory, the offender is only a tool to teach a lesson to the rest of us. The sociologist Emile Durkheim believed that the value of criminals is in establishing the parameters of acceptable behavior. By their punishments, we can define ourselves as good and resolve to stay that way.

If one's goal is purely general deterrence, there does not necessarily need to be an original crime. Consider a futuristic society wherein the evening news routinely shows or describes the punishments received by a variety of criminals. The crime—or the punishment, for that matter—does not have to be real to be effective. If punishing innocent people for crimes they *might* do were just as effective as punishing criminal offenders, this action might satisfy the ends of deterrence but would obviously not be acceptable under any system of ethics, except perhaps act utilitarianism.

Actually, what the public hears about sentences bears little resemblance to what the individual offender actually serves, except perhaps in states that have determinate sentencing laws. Although the public is becoming more sophisticated in this regard, not many know that when the judge sentences an offender to fifteen years in prison, with good time, time served, and parole, the actual prison time may be much less. Actual time served seems to be an inconsistent phenomenon having more to do with prison overcrowding, politics, and availability of prison cells rather than some standard of justice.

Incapacitation Another purpose of punishment is to prevent further crime through **incapacitation.** Strictly speaking, incapacitation does not fit the classical definition of punishment, since the purpose is not to inflict pain but only to hold an offender until there is no risk of further crime. The major issue concerning incapacitation is prediction. Unfortunately, our ability to predict is no better for incapacitative purposes than it is for deterrence purposes. Two possible mistakes may be made releasing an offender who commits further crimes and *not* releasing an offender who would not.

Carrying the goal of incapacitation to its logical conclusion, one would not have to commit a crime at all to be declared potentially dangerous and subject to incapacitation. We now incarcerate career criminals, not for their last offense but for what they might do in the future. We justify habitual-felon laws by the prediction that these criminals will continue to commit crime. Some argue that a small group of offenders commit a disproportionate share of crime, and those individuals can be identified by predictive elements such as the following: prior conviction for the crime they are in prison for, having been incarcerated for more than 50 percent of the last two years, a conviction before the age of sixteen, time in juvenile detention, heroin or barbiturate use in the preceding two years, heroin or barbiturate use as a juvenile, and having been employed less than 50 percent of the last two years (Greenwood, 1982). See the box, "Court Allows Judges to Consider Acquittals in Boosting Sentences."

Court Allows Judges to Consider Acquittals in Boosting Sentences

This newspaper article covered a Supreme Court decision where the justices ruled 7–2 that trial judges may stiffen prison terms of convicted defendants by considering charges on which they were acquitted. The author said, "Many judges and legal scholars consider such a result unjust. One Supreme Court dissenter, John Paul Stevens, called it 'perverse.' The other dissenter, Anthony Kennedy, said the decision 'does raise concerns about undercutting the verdict of acquittal.'" The decision was supported by the Clinton administration. And the tough-on-crime court majority found nothing legally wrong with using acquittals to enhance punishment.

Is the court ruling consistent with retributivism? Remember that in retributivism, one is punished for the offense, rather than for individual characteristics of culpability.

SOURCE: Epstein, A. (Knight-Ridder Washington Bureau). *Austin American-Statesman*, January 7, 1997: A4.

Selective incapacitation is a policy of incarcerating these individuals for longer periods of time than other criminals. More recent studies indicate that actually our ability to predict who would commit further crime is very poor. Auerhahn (1999) points out that the original study by Peter Greenwood had a 48 percent error rate. Replications have error rates as high as 55 percent. This means that more than half of the time a prediction is made that the offender would re-offend, that prediction is wrong. She concludes that until our prediction methods appreciably improve, there are grave ethical issues in using the selective incapacitation concept to lengthen sentences.

The three-strike laws are a type of selective incapacitation. These laws are defended under an incapacitative rationale because it is argued that these individuals are more likely to commit future crime and so they should be held for long periods of time. More than half of all states now have some type of three-strikes or habitual-offender laws, but only a few states have used their laws to any great extent (King and Mauer, 2001). California has the dubious honor of incarcerating the most offenders under its three-strikes law (40,511 as of 2001).

Critics argue that for both practical and ethical reasons, the California three-strikes sentence is bad policy. It incarcerates those past their crime-prone age years, it incarcerates nonviolent offenders for very long periods of time, and it is so expensive that it draws resources away from other social needs, such as schools. Further, it is unfairly disproportionate to the crime. Some offenders have committed fairly minor third felonies and received twenty-five years to life (King and Mauer, 2001, Zimring, Hawkins and Kamin, 2001). Another troubling aspect of three-strikes laws is that African Americans tend to be disproportionately affected (Cole, 1999). The Supreme Court considered a challenge to California's three-strikes law in its 2002 term (*Lockyer v. Andrade*, No. 01-1127) after the Ninth Circuit in California ruled that the law violated the Eighth amendment. The Ninth Circuit ruled that it was grossly disproportional to sentence nonviolent, fairly minor third felons to twenty-five years to life. However, the Supreme Court ruled in March 2003 that it was not grossly disproportionate and deferred to the state's authority in setting punishments. It is clear that if three-strikes laws are overturned, it will have to be through state constitutional rights, not federal.

Treatment If we can find justification for the right to punish, can we also find justification for treatment? Treatment can be considered as one type of specific deterrence because it is an attempt to prevent future crime by changing the criminal offender. Treatment is considered to be beneficial to the individual offender, as well as to society. It is a very different approach from the moral rejection implicit in retributive punishment. Treatment implies acceptance rather than rejection, support rather than hatred. However, the control over the individual is just as great as with punishment; some people, in fact, would say it is greater.

What is treatment? We sometimes consider anything experienced after the point of sentencing to be treatment, including education, prison discipline, and religious services. Can treatment be experimental? Must it be effective to be considered treatment? A court was obliged to define treatment in *Knecht v. Gillman,* 488 F.2d 1136 (1973). Inmates challenged the state's right to use apomorphine, a drug that induces extreme nausea and a feeling of imminent death, as a form of aversive conditioning. In its holding, the court stated that calling something treatment did not remove it from Eighth Amendment scrutiny. In other words, merely labeling some infliction of pain as treatment would not necessarily justify it. *Treatment* was further defined as that which constitutes accepted and standard practice and which could reasonably result in "cure." More recently, the court had occasion to consider whether prison officials could administer antipsychotic drugs against the will of the prisoner. Despite arguments that even prisoners had an inherent right to be free from such intrusive control, the court held in *Washington v. Harper,* 494 US 210 (1990), that an inmate's right to refuse such medication did not outweigh the state's need to administer such drugs if there was a showing that the inmate posed a security risk.

What we think needs to be cured is another issue. Recall the discussion of whether our society could be characterized by consensus or conflict. Treating a deviant may be justifiable if one believes that society is basically homogeneous in its values and beliefs, but viewed from a conflict perspective, treatment may look more like brainwashing and a coercive use of power. Civil libertarians would point out that it is no accident that political dissidents in totalitarian states are often handled as if they have mental problems and are treated with mind-altering drugs and other brainwashing regimens. The greater intrusiveness inherent in treating the mind is sometimes considered worse than punishment.

According to some experts, treatment can be effective only if it is voluntary—others disagree. It is true that much of the treatment inmates and other correctional clients participate in is either implicitly or directly coerced. Providing treatment for those who want it is one thing; requiring those who are resistant to participate in psychotherapy, group therapy, religious activities, or chemotherapy is quite another. It is not justifiable under a retributivist ethical system; is it consistent with a prevention perspective?

ETHICAL FRAMEWORKS
FOR CORRECTIONS

The various rationales for punishment just described are well established, and most can be found in many texts. The ethical systems that were introduced in Chapter 2 are less commonly discussed in corrections texts, but they form the underlying philosophical rationale for the goals or missions of retribution and prevention (including deterrence, incapacitation, and treatment). Ethical formalism and utilitarianism receive a disproportional amount of attention here, but the reader is urged to apply the other ethical systems as well.

Utilitarianism

Utilitarianism is often used to support the last three rationales of punishment: deterrence, incapacitation, and treatment. According to utilitarianism, punishing or treating the criminal offender benefits society, and this benefit outweighs the negative effect on the individual offender. This is a teleological argument because the morality of the punishment is determined by the consequences derived—reduced crime. Jeremy Bentham was the major proponent of the utilitarian theory of punishment and established basic guidelines for its use. Bentham believed that punishment works when it is applied rationally to rational people, but is not acceptable when the person did not make a rational decision to commit the crime, such as when the law forbidding the action was passed after the act occurred, the law was unknown, the person was acting under compulsion, or the person was an infant, insane, or intoxicated (Bentham, 1970; also see Beccaria, 1977). The utility of the punishment would be lost in these cases; therefore, punishment could not be justified (Borchert and Stewart, 1986: 317).

"Bentham's Rules of Punishment" are in the accompanying box. All of Bentham's rules ensure that punishments are acceptable to the utilitarian framework. The basic formula provides that the utility of punishment to society outweighs the negative of the punishment itself. Utilitarian theory also supports treatment and incapacitation if they can be shown to benefit society. If, for instance, treatment and punishment had equal amounts of utility for society, treatment would be the more ethical choice because it has a less negative effect on the individual. Likewise, if incapacitation and punishment are equally effective in protecting and providing utility to society, then the choice with the least negative utility would be the ethical one.

Bentham's Rules of Punishment

1. The value of the punishment must not be less, in any case, than what is sufficient to outweigh that of the profit of the offense.
2. The greater the mischief of the offense, the greater is the expense it may be worth while to be at, in the way of punishment.
3. When two offenses come in competition, the punishment for the greater offense must be sufficient to induce a man to prefer the less.
4. The punishment should be adjusted in such manner to each particular offense, that for every part of the mischief there may be a motive to restrain the offender from giving birth to it.
5. The punishment ought in no case to be more than what is necessary to bring it into conformity with the rules here given.
6. That the quantity of punishment actually inflicted on each individual offender may correspond to the quantity intended for similar offenders in general, the several circumstances influencing sensibility ought always to be taken into the account.
7. That the value of the punishment may outweigh the profit of the offense, it must be increased in point of magnitude, in proportion as it falls short in point of certainty.
8. Punishment must be further increased in point of magnitude, in proportion as it falls short of proximity.
9. When the act is conclusively indicative of a habit, such an increase must be given to the punishment as may enable it to outweigh the profit, not only of the individual offense, but of such other like offenses as are likely to have been committed with impunity by the same offender.
10. When a punishment, which in point of quality is particularly well calculated to answer its intention, cannot exist in less than a certain quantity, it may sometimes be of issue, for the sake of employing it, to stretch a little beyond that quantity which, on other accounts, would be strictly necessary.
11. In particular, this may be the case where the punishment proposed is of such a nature as to be particularly well calculated to answer the purpose of a moral lesson.
12. In adjusting the quantum of punishment, the circumstances by which all punishment may be rendered unprofitable ought to be attended to.
13. Among provisions designated to perfect the proportion between punishments and offenses, if any occur which by their own particular good effects would not make up for the harm they would do by adding to the intricacy of the code, they should be omitted.

SOURCE: Bentham, 1843/1970.

Ethical Formalism

Contrast the utilitarian views toward punishment discussed in the previous section with Kant's (see the accompanying Quote). Ethical formalism clearly supports a retributive view of punishment. It is deontological because it is not concerned with the consequences of the punishment or treatment, only its inherent morality. It would support the idea that a criminal is owed punishment because to do otherwise would not be according him or her equal respect as a human. However, the punishment should not be used as a means to any other end but retribution. Treatment is not supported by ethical formalism because it uses the offender as a means to protect society.

QUOTE

Juridical punishment . . . can be inflicted on a criminal, never just as instrumental to the achievement of some other good for the criminal himself or for the civil society, but only because he has committed a crime; for a man may never be used just as a means to the end of another person. . . . Penal law is a categorical imperative, and woe to him who crawls through the serpentine maze of utilitarian theory in order to find an excuse, in some advantage to someone, for releasing the criminal from punishment or any degree of it, in line with the pharasaical proverb "it is better that one man die than that a whole people perish"; for if justice perishes, there is no more value in man living on the earth. . . . What mode and degree of punishment, then, is the principle and standard of public justice? Nothing but the principle of equality. . . . Thus, whatever undeserved evil you inflict on another person, you inflict on yourself. . . .

Kant, quoted in Borchert and Stewart, 1986: 322.

Several arguments support this retributive rationale. First, Mackie (1982) discusses the universal aspects of punishment: the urge to react in a hostile manner to harm is an element inherent in human nature; therefore, one might say that punishment is a natural law. Another supporting argument is found in the principle of forfeiture, which postulates that when one intrudes on an innocent person's rights, one forfeits a proportional amount of one's own rights. By restraining or hurting a victim in some way, the aggressor forfeits his or her own liberty; in other words, he or she forfeits the right to be free from punishment (Bedau, 1982).

Ethics of Care

The ethics of care would probably not support punishment unless it was essential to help the offender become a better person. This ethical system defines good as that which meets everyone's needs — victim and offender alike. The rationale that most closely approximates the ethics of care is an entirely different one from retribution or prevention — it is restorative justice, which we will discuss more fully in Chapter 13.

Several authors have discussed the ethics of care in relation to the justice and corrections system. For instance, Heidensohn (1986) and Daly (1989) discuss differences in the perception of justice from a care perspective versus a retributive perspective. They discuss these as female and male perceptions, respectively. The female care perspective emphasizes needs, motives, and relationships. The corrections system, ideally, should be supported by a caring ethic because it takes into account offender needs. Community corrections, especially, emphasizes the relationship of the offender to the community. In this perspective, one should help the offender to become a better person, because that is what a caring and committed relationship would entail.

Retributive punishment and deterrence are not consistent with the ethics of care. However, some say that retribution and a care ethic are not, nor should they be considered, dichotomous. Restorative justice might be considered the merger of the two in that this approach views the offender as responsible for the wrong committed but the responsibility is satisfied by reparation to the victim rather than by punishment and pain.

Rawlsian Ethics

John Rawls presents an alternative to utilitarianism and retributivism. Rawls's defense of punishment starts with Kant's proposition that no one should be treated as a means, and with the idea that each should have an "equal right to the most extensive basic liberty compatible with a similar liberty to others." According to Rawls, a loss of rights should take place only when it is consistent with the best interests of the least advantaged. Rules regarding punishment would be as follows (cited in Hickey and Scharf, 1980: 169):

1. We must punish only to the extent that the loss of liberty would be agreeable were one not to know whether one were to be the criminal, the victim, or a member of the general public [the veil of ignorance].
2. The loss of liberty must be justified as the minimum loss consistent with the maintenance of the same liberty among others.

Furthermore, when the advantage shifts—when the offender instead of the victim or society becomes the one with the least advantage—then punishment must cease. This theory leaves a lot of unanswered questions. For instance, if victims were chosen carefully (i.e., only those who would not suffer financially or emotionally), and the criminal came from an impoverished background; then the criminal would still be at a disadvantage and, thus, not morally accountable for his or her actions. On the other hand, Rawls's system does seem to be consistent with the idea that the criminal act creates an imbalance between offender and victim, and that punishment should be concerned with regaining that balance. The utilitarian thread in this proposition is that by having this check-and-balance system in the determination of punishment, all of society is benefited.

PUNISHMENT

We have discarded many punishments that were acceptable in earlier times, such as flogging, hanging, banishment, branding, cutting off limbs, drawing and quartering, and pillories and stocks. Although we still believe society has the right to punish, what we do in the name of punishment has changed substantially. As a society, we became gradually uncomfortable with inflicting physically painful punishments on offenders, and as these punishments were discarded, imprisonment was used as the substitute. Inside prison, we have only relatively recently abandoned physical punishments as a method of control (at least formally).

Humane Punishment

The Eighth Amendment protects all Americans from **cruel and unusual punishment.** Although what is "cruel and unusual" is vague, several tests have been used to define the terms, such as the following, discussed in *Furman v. Georgia,* 408 U.S. 238, 92 S.Ct. 2726, 33 L.Ed.2d 346 (1972):

1. *Unusual* (by frequency): Those punishments that are rarely, if ever used thus become unusual if used against one individual or a group. They become arbitrary punishments because the decision to use them is so infrequent.

2. *Evolving standards of decency:* Civilization is evolving and punishments considered acceptable in the nineteenth century are no longer acceptable in the twentieth century.

3. *Shock the conscience:* A yardstick for all punishment is to test it against the public conscience. If people are naturally repelled by the punishment, then it must be cruel and unusual by definition.

4. *Excessive or disproportionate:* Any punishment that is excessive to its purpose or disproportionately administered is considered wrong.

5. *Unnecessary:* Again, we are looking at the purpose of the punishment in relation to what is done. If the purpose of punishment to deter crime, then we should only administer an amount necessary to do so. If the purpose is to protect and the offender presents no danger, then prison should not be used.

These tests have eliminated the use of the whip and the branding iron, yet some say that we may have done nothing to move toward humane punishment and that, in fact, we may have moved away from it. Graeme Newman points out the possibility that corporal punishment, at least the less drastic kinds such as whipping, is actually less harmful than a prison sentence. In fact, physical punishment may be more of a deterrent and yet less damaging to a person's future. After all, a whipping takes perhaps days or weeks to get over, but a prison sentence may last years and affect all future earnings (Newman, 1978: 270).

QUERY

- Would you rather spend a year in prison or receive a severe whipping?
- Would you rather spend a year in prison or receive five years of probation with very severe restrictions?
- Would you rather spend a year in prison or pay a $30,000 fine?

A criminal offender may be sentenced to probation instead of prison. A fine or other conditions of probation may be attached. For instance, a probationer may be required to perform community service, pay court costs, pay restitution to the victim, find employment, submit to drug tests and complete drug counseling, or conform to any number of other conditions. Some recent examples of conditions include those convicted of driving while intoxicated (DWI) being required to have an instrument that measures their blood alcohol level attached to their car, the use of electronic monitoring instruments, and, in one case, being forced to donate blood to a blood bank.

So-called "shaming" conditions include DWI offenders having special license plates that indicate to other drivers that the driver has been convicted of DWI, probation officers putting signs up in the yard or nailing them to the door of convicted sex offenders warning people that a sex offender lives there, announcing to one's church congregation one's criminal conviction and asking for forgiveness, and taking out an advertisement in the town newspaper for the same purpose. These conditions are rarely challenged in court because the offender would usually prefer them to a prison sentence. However, there is some question as to the legal authority for such conditions (Book, 1999).

We could also examine them in light of the ethical systems above. One real question concerning the "shaming" conditions is the effect such conditions have on family members of offenders and whether these conditions constitute a type of extralegal punishment for them without any due-process procedures of trial and conviction. Braithwaite (2000), Karp (1998), and others, distinguish between **stigmatizing shaming** and **reintegrative shaming.** While the first is a rejection of the individual and has negative effects, the second is only a rejection of the person's behavior and creates a healthier relationship between the individual and his community. We will revisit these concepts in Chapter 13 when we discuss restorative justice.

QUERY

- If you knew for certain that prison did not deter, would you still be in favor of its use? Why?
- If we could predict future criminals, would you be willing to incapacitate them before they commit a crime in order to protect society?
- Should we have guidelines for what we do in the name of treatment? What should they be?

Capital Punishment

What sets capital punishment apart from all other punishments is its quality of irrevocability. This type of punishment leaves no way to correct a mistake. For this reason, some believe that no mortal should have the power to inflict capital punishment, because there is no way to guarantee that mistakes won't be made. Certainly, Radelet, Bedau, and Putnam's (1992) collection of cases concerning innocent people who were executed in error, and the other investigations that have also documented errors in the prosecutions in capital cases, support this viewpoint.

The Bureau of Justice Statistics (2002) reports that the sixty-six prisoners executed in 2001 were nineteen fewer than those executed in 2000. Most had been under the sentence of death for an average of eleven years and ten months. Only three were women. Most (48) were white. At the end of 2001, about 3,581 prisoners were on death row. California had the largest number on death row with 603, followed by Texas with 453, and Florida with 372. Our rate of sentencing offenders to death is evidently at a twenty-year low. In the year 2000, 214 were given the death penalty, which is lower than the 272 who received the penalty in 1999 (Corrections Digest, 2002).

The major ethical positions that can support the death penalty are utilitarianism and retribution. Because of controversy over the factual issues involved, utilitarian arguments are used both to defend and condemn capital punishment. If we believe, as do retentionists, that capital punishment is just because it deters people, then we must show proof that it does indeed deter. The abolitionists present evidence that it does not.

Arguments for the retention of the death penalty include considerations of justice and considerations of social utility. Considerations of justice involve the retributivist, deontological view that the moral order is upset by the commission of an offense, and the disorder can only be rectified by punishment equal in intensity to the seriousness of the offense. Utilitarians view the evil of capital punishment as far outweighed by the future benefits that will accrue to society. However, Walker (1985: 79) summarizes the evidence marshaled on both sides of the deterrence question and finds very little support for the proposition that executions are useful deterrents. Further explorations of the issue also conclude that there is little reason to believe that capital punishment has any deterrent effect (Kronenwerter, 1993).

Abolitionists emphasize the "inherent worth and dignity of each individual." The taking of a human life is judged a morally unacceptable practice and is believed to be nothing more than vengeance (Mappes, 1982: 83–87). In fact, executions may even create a net negative effect on society, because although criminals may receive what they deserve, society is negatively affected by the brutalizing image of execution. This view would be one consistent with the idea that "violence begets violence," and, far from showing societal intolerance toward murder, capital punishment is seen as actually cheapening human life and encouraging blood lust (Bedau, 1991).

Religious ethics have been used both to support and condemn capital punishment. The Old Testament law supporting the taking of "an eye for an eye" is used by retentionists whereas the commandment "Thou shalt not kill" is used by the abolitionists. Kania (1999) presented a comprehensive religious justification for capital punishment, along with a social contract justification. The ethical justification of capital punishment presents serious and probably irresolvable problems. It is a telling commentary that for as long as society has used capital punishment to punish wrongdoing, critics have defined it as immoral (Johnson, 1991).

Questions also arise about the methods and procedures of capital punishment. Should all murderers be subject to capital punishment, or are some murders less serious than others? Should we allow defenses of age, mental state, or reason? If we do apply capital punishment differentially, doesn't this open the door to bias and misuse? Evidence indicates that capital punishment has been used arbitrarily and discriminatorily in this country. Minorities are more likely to be executed when their victims are white; in Georgia, black offenders charged with killing a white were 4.3 times more likely to be sentenced to death than those charged with killing a black. Yet the Supreme Court has stated that evidence of statistically disproportional administration is not enough to invalidate the death penalty (*McClesky v. Kemp*, 481 U.S. 279 [1987]).

Because our justice system is based on rationality, executions of the mentally ill and the mentally retarded have been vehemently criticized. The Supreme Court has ruled that executing the mentally ill is cruel and unusual (*Ford v. Wainwright*, 477 U.S. 399 [1986]). Miller and Radelet (1993) present a detailed account of the *Ford* case, describing the mental deterioration of Ford and the long ordeal of appeals before the Supreme Court finally ruled. They also point out the ethical issues involved when psychiatrists, other medical professionals, and psychologists participate in procedures that involve certifying someone as *death ready* and then assist in the administration of the chosen method of execution. There are deep and divisive views in these professions regarding the seeming inconsistency between identifying oneself as a helping professional and then helping someone be put to death.

In *Penry v. Lynaugh*, 107 S.Ct. 2934 [1989], the Supreme Court ruled that evidence of mental retardation should be presented to the jury to consider mitigation of the sentence. The *Penry* case involved a man who had committed a brutal rape and murder but who had an IQ that was just barely above the level that would ordinarily result in institutionalization. After the Supreme Court ruled that the state of Texas could execute someone who was mentally retarded, but that the trial judge must allow evidence of mental retardation to be provided to the jury in consideration of mitigation, a retrial resulted in a second death sentence from the new jury.

In June 2002, the Supreme Court finally decided that it was cruel and unusual to execute a retarded person. In *Atkins v. Virginia*, the court held that a man with an I.Q. of 59 could not be put to death, finding that the evolution of decency and public opinion supported such a decision. The dissent, comprising the most conservative of the Justices (Rehnquist, Scalia, and Thomas) argued that there was no common consensus regarding executing the mentally retarded and that it was not violative of the Eighth Amendment.

Another issue is whether capital punishment should be used for juveniles. The Supreme Court has refused to hear an appeal from Kevin Nigel Stanford arguing that his death sentence was unconstitutional because he committed his crime at the age of seventeen. The argument is that youth may excuse one from being held responsible to the same extent that an older person would be. This country is one of a very few that have laws allowing the execution of juveniles, and some argue that it puts the United States in violation of International Human Rights treaties (Criminal Justice Newsletter, 2002).

Although one would assume that the offender must have had to kill someone to receive a death sentence, that is not the case. In *Tison v. Arizona,* 481 U.S. 137 (1987), the Court ruled that crime partners in a felony that resulted in a death could be executed even if they did not kill the victim and they did not intend a death to occur. The Tison brothers had no criminal records, but they helped their father escape from an Arizona prison. During the escape, their father and a fellow escaped convict killed a family after kidnapping them for their car. The brothers did not participate, but by this point were felons themselves because of their role in the escape. A massive search ensued, and they were separated from their father, who eventually ended up dying of exposure in the desert. One wonders if the fact that he escaped his punishment was the reason that the brothers were then tried for capital murder. Responding to their appeal, the Supreme Court affirmed the state's right to execute for felony murder—where crime partners become responsible for any murder that occurs in the course of a felony they participate in, regardless of their role in killing.

Unless the Supreme Court revises its current position, which seems unlikely, the legality of executions is not in question, even though the procedures used to arrive at the decision to execute may continue to be challenged. However, the morality of capital punishment is still very much a topic of debate, and it elicits strong feelings on the part of many people. As discussed earlier, ex-Governor Ryan of Illinois, deeply disgusted with the number of errors in the legal process leading to a death sentence, commuted all death sentences in his state as one of his last acts as Governor. Whether his act is a portent of things to come remains to be seen.

PRIVATE CORRECTIONS

In much of the foregoing discussion, we described punishment as a uniquely state function. However, the state may delegate the authority to punish. Private prisons are built and then leased to the state or, in some cases, actually run by the private corporation, which bills the state for the service. Many have objected to the profit motive being introduced into corrections and point to a number of ethical issues raised by private "profiteers." First, there are potential abuses of the bidding process, as in any situation where the government contracts with a company for services or products. Money may change hands to ensure that one organization receives the contract, companies may make informal agreements to "rig" the bids, and other potentially corrupt practices may go on. Legal as well as ethical issues abound when private and public motives are mixed.

In the building phase, private corporations may cut corners and construct buildings without meeting proper standards for safety. Managing the institution also raises the possibility that a private contractor will attempt to maximize profits by ignoring minimum standards of health and safety and will, if necessary, bribe inspectors or monitors to overlook the deficiencies. It has certainly happened in other areas, such as nursing homes, that those who contract with the state government and receive state monies reap large profits by subjecting clients to inhumane conditions.

King, Mauer, and Huling (2003) analyzed the effect of prison building on rural communities. In the last twenty years, the majority of new prisons were built in rural counties, and many of those were private correctional institutions. The new prison was sold to the county as an economic boom, and counties that were experiencing economic downturns and anemic economies sometimes competed to have the prison built in their county. Actually, an economic analysis showed that the county received a very minimal economic benefit when the prison was built. The construction contracts were not directed to local companies, but, rather, went to companies who had the experience, qualifications, and history with building institutions, and correctional workers were often imported from outside the county. What happened in some cases was that, in return for tax breaks and sometimes even free land, counties got very little. One might argue that it is unethical for the planners of these prisons to promise benefits that have never emerged from the building of a prison.

In a more general sense, some feel that punishment and profit are never compatible, and historically linking the two has led to a variety of abuses (such as the contract labor system in the South). Although the decision to use private corporations is made by legislators, correctional administrators are faced with a variety of ethical dilemmas because of it, such as whether to support the idea, whether to accept a part-time position as a consultant to a private corporation when one has decision-making authority over issues that concern the corporation, whether to take anything of value from the corporation (from a free lunch to a "grant" for personal study), and whether to allow one corporation to have insider information in order to prepare a more favorable bid.

On the other hand, private corporations report that some state systems subject them to endless and picayune rules and continually audit them to the point that it appears that state prison officials are trying to find noncompliance in order to return the "action" to state actors. There is probably some truth that some corrections department officials are not happy to have legislators approve the use of private contractors and would like to see them fail.

Private prisons hold about 5 percent of all prison beds in the country (Parenti, 1999: 218). Correctional corporations such as Corrections Corporation of America and Wackenhut have their stock traded on the New York Stock Exchange. Corrections Corporation of America is the largest player in the private prison industry, holding a little more than half of all private prison beds (over 60,000 beds in the United States alone). In late 1998, it merged into the Prison Realty Trust (PRT), an accounting move that allowed the entity to be exempt from tax liability as long as it distributed 95 percent of its earnings to its stockholders (Geis, Mobley and Shichor, 1999). There are troubling connections between C.C.A. founders and executives and Tennessee politicians. Researchers have tracked campaign contributions from C.C.A. in states where they received lucrative contracts (Mobley and Geis, 2002).

QUOTE

Sorry to be late clueing you to this great new money-making opportunity, but there may still be time to get in on the seminar that will show you how to imprison people for fun and profit. . . . If you're looking for something really reliable, what better to invest in than human misbehavior? It has been a sure thing since Cain and Abel.

Columnist Tom Teepen, 1996.

In 2001, C.C.A.'s stock lost 93 percent of its 2000 value (Greene, 2001: 26). This financial meltdown is partly caused by a decline of crime and prisoners, and partly fueled by a rash of scandals that have plagued C.C.A.'s prison facilities. Account after account of escapes, violence, under-trained officers, and understaffing have plagued C.C.A. for several years (Parenti, 1999: 219).

The C.C.A. also has been the target of a loosely organized, global organization of students and reformers that seek to persuade college campuses to drop their contracts with Sodexho Marriott Services, a corporation that owned about 48 percent of C.C.A. stock. Students, upset that their money was being used to fund a corporation that "violat[ed] the human rights of prisoners and prison employees by sacrificing health and safety to improve the corporate bottom-line," have been successful in getting several large campuses to drop their contracts with Sodexho (Pranis, 2001). The giant corporation has bowed to their threat and sold its shares in C.C.A. (Ward, 2001).

Wackenhut has more than 25,000 beds at several dozen facilities across the country and is considered Number 2 among the private prison providers. It holds 11,000 prison beds internationally (57 percent of the international market of private prisons) (Austin and Irwin, 2001: 66; Perez, 2001). It also runs mental health facilities and addiction treatment centers. Since going public in 1994, Wackenhut's stock price has increased by 800 percent. Wackenhut has also had a series of incidents reported in its facilities that have affected its reputation and financial standing (Greene, 2001). Lawsuits and investigations in states concern the use of tear gas (Louisiana), failing to prevent sexual abuse (Texas), paying $3 million to a member of the state's prison policy panel (Florida), and a murder rate that is much higher than the state-run institutions (New Mexico) (Solomon, 1999; Fecteau, 1999).

In addition to the big two, there are more than a dozen smaller companies across the nation that compete for the private prison bids put out by the states. Replete with allegations of bribes, sweetheart deals, and other forms of corruption, some critics contend that the private prison industry seems to be characterized by crooks on both sides of the bars. A New York scandal is simmering with allegations that a private corrections company paid money to several New York politicians in return for favors in seeking state contracts. Some of the campaign contributions evidently came in the name of workers who said they were not responsible for the contribution. There are also allegations that some legislators received free transportation from the prison company for travel from New York City to Albany, and that the company forced employees to work on the campaigns of certain politicians, including former mayor David Dinkins. In fact, the lead whistleblower in the case was fired when he refused to work on a politician's campaign (Levy, 2003 a & b).

Proponents argue that private corrections can save the state money. Arguments include the idea that private corporations are more efficient, they can build faster with less cost and less red tape, and they have economies of scale (i.e., that they can obtain savings because of their size). It may be true that private prisons can be built faster because private corporations are not bound by restrictions placed on government. For instance, a state would most likely have to go to voters to pass a bond in order to build new prisons; however, they can contract with a private provider without voter approval. States and local governments are bound by a myriad of bidding and siting restrictions, unlike private corporations. However, in a Government Accounting Office meta-analysis, it was concluded that private and public institutions cost about the same (GAO, 1996). Any profits realized by a private entity being "leaner and meaner" is offset by the profit margin private companies maintain, and a regulatory system the state must put in place to make sure contract specifications are adhered to.

Some studies have concluded that private prisons produce results equal to state institutions for less cost. Bourge (2002) describes Segal and Moore's study that examined 28 governmental and institutional studies comparing public and private facilities, and found that 22 of the private prisons showed cost savings of 5 to 15 percent. They concluded that there is "significant evidence" that private facilities can provide comparable quality to state institutions. However, critics argue that studies that ignore higher assault rates in private prisons and other indices of quality of service and only look at costs, are flawed.

One of the emerging problems is that low wages prevent the hiring of qualified staff. In one situation, a private corrections company, Capital Correctional Resources, was forced to defend the actions of its officers who were videotaped using stun guns and dogs to brutalize inmates. It was later discovered that two of the officers had been fired from the state system for brutality (Langford, 1997). Generally, private corrections pay officers a lower salary than the state, and so officers often transfer to state departments after they are trained. Turnover is high in both private corrections and state corrections.

There have been issues concerning the evaluators, as well. The evaluation by Segal and Moore, for instance, was funded by a libertarian think tank that arguably would be inclined to promote private enterprise over government involvement (Bourge, 2002). The biggest scandal in private prison evaluation research concerned Charles Thomas, a University of Florida professor who published many articles and books as "objective" evaluations of private prisons. Thomas testified before Congress and state legislatures considering private prison contracts. He consistently promoted the effectiveness and efficiency of private prisons, arguably as an independent, objective evaluator. His objectivity was called into question, however, when it was discovered that he was a highly paid consultant of C.C.A. and owned over $500,000 in C.C.A. stock. He was sanctioned by the State of Florida for violating their conflict of interest laws in 1999, yet continues to write articles on private prisons and provides evaluations that tout their effectiveness (Geis, Mobley and Shichor, 1999; Mobley and Geis, 2002).

Ogle (1999) argues that private correctional facilities operate in a Catch 22 where organizational imperatives are contradictory. On the one hand is the corporate imperative of profit, on the other is the public service imperative of legitimacy. The two conflict when the most profitable way to run a prison conflicts with the perceived "just" or "humane" way to run a prison. When the private corporation is pursuing profit, it uses adaptations such as compromise and avoidance techniques, or defiance and manipulation techniques to circumvent governmental mandates for services and contract fulfillment.

A more abstract and subtle criticism of private corrections is that if someone is making money from incarcerating offenders, where is the incentive to correct them? If recidivism were to somehow mysteriously plummet; corporations would show reduced profits and stockholders would lose money. The financial incentive to incarcerate more people for longer periods of time, arguably ensures that we will never see a reduction of imprisonment, as long as privatization continues to grow. Of course, private corrections officials scoff at the above scenario. They point out that their piece of the "corrections pie" is quite small in comparison to the states, that they are closely monitored by staff officials who are unhappy with sharing any amount of resources with them, and there is plenty of opportunity to expand in other states and even in other countries without somehow conspiring to keep offenders in prison solely for some profit motive.

CONCLUSION

In this chapter we have looked at some of the ethical rationales for punishment. What we do to offenders is influenced by our views on such things as free will and determinism, the capacity for individual change, and the basic nature of humankind. Punishment has always been used against those who hurt other members of society and thus might be considered consistent with natural law. However, the limits of punishment have been more changeable and have been subject to the laws and mores of each historical era. Today, our punishments primarily consist of imprisonment or some form of restricted liberty, such as probation or parole. The death penalty continues to be used; however, the controversy surrounding it continues as well.

We have seen a trend where the state delegates its authority to sentence. Serious questions have arisen over this practice. Some argue that the profit motive is incompatible with the awesome power of the state to deprive individuals of liberty in the name of punishment.

REVIEW QUESTIONS

1. Discuss the major rationales of punishment.
2. Now defend the rationales of punishment through the use of the ethical systems.
3. Support three-strike laws through a retributive rationale and then through a utilitarian rationale.
4. State your belief on the use of capital punishment and the reasons for your position. Now take the opposite side and give the reasons for this view.
5. What are some ethical problems with treatment?
6. Support or criticize the use of private corrections and give your reasons.

ETHICAL DILEMMAS

Situation 1

A legislator has proposed a sweeping new crime and punishment bill with the following provisions for punishment. Decide each issue as if you were being asked to vote on it:

- Mandatory life term with no parole for any crime involving a weapon
- Corporal punishment (using an electrical apparatus that inflicts a shock) for all personal violent crimes
- Mandatory five-year prison sentences for those convicted of DWI
- Public executions
- Abolition of probation, to be replaced with fines and prison sentences for those who are not able to pay are or unwilling to do so

Situation 2

Another legislator has suggested an alternate plan with the following provisions. Vote on these:

- Decriminalization of all drug crimes
- Mandated treatment programs for all offenders who were intoxicated by alcohol or other drugs at the time of the crime
- Restructuring the sentencing statutes to make no sentence longer than five years, except for homicide and attempted homicide
- Implementation of a restitution program for all victims whereby offenders stay in the community, work and pay the victim back for the losses and/or injuries they received

Situation 3

Your state is one of the few that allows relatives of homicide victims to witness the execution of the perpetrator. Your brother was killed in a robbery, and the murderer is about to be executed. You receive a letter advising you of the execution date and your right to be present. Would you go?

SUGGESTED READINGS

Bedau, H. 1991. "How to Argue About the Death Penalty." *Israel Law Review* 25, 466–480.

Kania, R. 1999. "The Ethics of the Death Penalty." *The Justice Professional* 12: 145–157.

Kronenwerter, M. 1993. *Capital Punishment: A Reference Handbook.* Santa Barbara, CA: ABC-CLIO.

12

Ethics for Correctional Professionals

Key Terms

correctional officer

pluralistic ignorance

reciprocity

human service model

hostile work environment

Chapter Objectives

- Become familiar with the ethical issues for correctional officers and treatment professionals.
- Understand some of the unique ethical issues for correctional managers and administrators.

In the last chapter, we examined the rationales for punishment and corrections. In this and the next chapter, we turn our attention to the ethical issues of correctional professionals. As with law enforcement officers and court professionals, discretion is an important topic when discussing the ethics of working in corrections.

CORRECTIONAL PROFESSIONALS

Institutional correctional personnel can be divided into two groups: (1) correctional officers and their supervisors, and (2) treatment professionals, a group that would include educators, counselors, psychologists, and all others connected with programming. These groups have different jobs and different ethical questions. In this book we devote a disproportionate amount of attention to prison officers, primarily because most of the available information concerns prison personnel. A number of ethical issues that treatment personnel may be faced with are similar to those experienced in a more general way by all treatment professionals, so available sources dealing with ethics in the helping professions would also be applicable to those who work in the corrections field (see, for instance, Corey, Corey, and Callanan, 1988).

We have previously discussed how discretion plays a role in each phase of the criminal justice system. In corrections, discretion is involved when a correctional officer decides to write a disciplinary ticket or merely delivers a verbal reprimand; this is similar to the discretion police have that allows them the decision to arrest. Discretion is also involved when the disciplinary committee makes a decision to punish an inmate for an infraction: the punishment can be as serious as increasing sentence length through loss of good time, or as minor as a temporary loss of privileges. What punishment may be administered depends on state law and Supreme Court decisions related to prisoners' rights, but also largely on the discretion of disciplinary committees. This type of discretion is similar to the discretion of the prosecutor and judge in a criminal trial.

Correctional psychiatrists, psychologists, and counselors have a responsibility to the correctional client. Like the defense attorney, they must use discretion to balance the client's needs against the larger needs of the system or institution. Their role may actually involve more ambiguity than the defense lawyer's because there is some question as to whether they owe their primary allegiance to the offender or to society.

Hence, we see that similarities exist between correctional personnel and the other professionals in the criminal justice system. As always, when the power of discretion is present, the potential for abuse is also present. Professional ethics should guide individual decision makers in their use of discretion, but, as with law enforcement and legal professionals, adherence to a code of ethics is influenced by the occupational subculture and institutional values. Formal ethics for correctional personnel will be discussed in more detail shortly.

Correctional officers (C.O.s) are similar to police officers in that their uniform represents the authority of the institution quite apart from any personal power of the person wearing it. Some C.O.s are uncomfortable with this authority and do not know how to handle it. Some C.O.s revel in it and misperceive the bounds of authority given to them as a representative of the state. The following statement is a perceptive observation of how some C.O.s misuse the authority they have (Kauffman, 1988: 50):

> [Some officers] don't understand what authority is and what bounds you have within that authority. . . . I think everyone interprets it to meet their own image of themself. "I'm a corrections officer [slams table]! You sit here! [Slam!] You sit there!" Rather than "I'm a person who has limited authority. So, you know, I'm sorry gentlemen, but you can't sit there. You are going to have to sit over there. That's just the rules," and explaining or something like that the reason why.

This officer obviously recognized that the uniform bestows the authority of rational and reasonable control, not unbridled domination. The power of the C.O. is limited. In actuality, it is impossible to depend on the authority of the uniform to get tasks accomplished, and one must find personal resources—respect and authority stemming from one's personal reputation—in order to gain cooperation from inmates. Some officers who perceive themselves as powerless in relation to the administration, the courts, and society in general may react to this perceived powerlessness by misusing their little bit of power over inmates. They may abuse their position by humiliating or abusing those in their control.

Thus, in ways somewhat similar to those of police officers, correctional officers have power over offenders. They have the full range of coercive control, including loss of liberty through physical force if necessary. Their power may be misused; a blatant example would be an officer who beats an inmate, or a psychologist who coerces sex from an inmate. These are abuses of power and the possibility for them exists because of the powerlessness of the offender relative to the correctional professional. Sensitivity to ethical issues involves the recognition and respect that one has for this element of the profession.

CORRECTIONAL OFFICERS

During the rehabilitative era of the 1970s, professional security staff in corrections exchanged their old label of *guard* for a new one—**correctional officer.** However, the slang terms used to describe these individuals, such as *hack, screw,* and *turnkey,* have been more resistant to change. Although increasing professionalism and greater knowledge acquisition now characterize the individuals in this occupation, correctional officers, by any name, are still perceived as operating under punitive goals. Crouch (1995) examined how changing goals in the 1970s and 1980s created role conflict and ambiguity for the correctional officer. Along with greater rights for inmates, this era brought danger, loss of control, stress, racial and sexual integration, and deviant behavior among officers. Other factors that have changed the role of the guard include unionization, professionalism, and bureaucratization (Crouch, 1995; Silberman, 1995; and Johnson, 1996/2002).

The American Correctional Association's Code of Ethics outlines formal ethics for correctional professionals (see the accompanying box). The original code was adopted in 1975 and was revised in 1990. The changes between the 1975 version and the 1990 version included changing male pronouns to gender-neutral language. The other consistent change was all references to the offender as *client* were deleted in favor of the use of the term *individual* or *person*. This change may be interpreted as moderating the influence of the treatment ethic and medical model in corrections. The changes made in 1994 were fairly minor. There exist many similarities between this code and the Law Enforcement Code presented in Chapter 6. For instance, integrity, respect for, and protection of individual rights, and service to the public are emphasized in both codes, as are the importance and sanctity of the law. Also, the prohibition against exploiting professional authority for personal gain is stressed in both codes.

Another similarity between this code and the Law Enforcement Code is the disparity that sometimes exists between the ideal behavior it describes and what actually occurs. The A.C.A. Code of Ethics describes the ideal behavior of correctional staff; however, as was discussed in Chapter 6, subcultural values may be inconsistent with and subvert formal ethical codes. This is also the case with correctional personnel. Although the ethical code clearly calls for fair and objective treatment, integrity, and high standards of performance, the actual practices of some correctional staff may be quite different.

In an interesting discussion of implementing an ethics program for correctional officers, Barrier, et al. (1999) described how officers presented the elements of what they felt were important in an ethics code:

- Acting professionally
- Showing respect for inmates and workers
- Maintaining honesty and integrity
- Being consistent
- Acting impartially
- Being assertive but not aggressive
- Confronting bad behavior but reinforcing good behavior
- Standardizing rule enforcement
- Respecting others
- Practicing the golden rule
- Encouraging teamwork
- Using professional language

American Correctional Association Code of Ethics

Preamble

The American Correctional Association expects of its members unfailing honesty, respect for the dignity and individuality of human beings and a commitment to professional and compassionate service. To this end, we subscribe to the following principles.

Members shall respect and protect the civil and legal rights of all individuals.

Members shall treat every professional situation with concern for the welfare of the individuals involved and with no intent to personal gain.

Members shall maintain relationships with colleagues to promote mutual respect within the profession and improve the quality of service.

Members shall make public criticism of their colleagues or their agencies only when warranted, verifiable, and constructive.

Members shall respect the importance of all disciplines within the criminal justice system and work to improve cooperation with each segment.

Members shall honor the public's right to information and share information with the public to the extent permitted by law subject to individual's right to privacy.

Members shall respect and protect the right of the public to be safeguarded from criminal activity.

Members shall refrain from using their positions to secure personal privileges or advantages.

Members shall refrain from allowing personal interest to impair objectivity in the performance of duty while acting in an official capacity.

Members shall refrain from entering into any formal or informal activity or agreement which presents a conflict of interest or is inconsistent with the conscientious performance of duties.

Members shall refrain from accepting any gifts, service, or favor that is or appears to be improper or implies an obligation inconsistent with the free and objective exercise of professional duties.

Members shall clearly differentiate between personal views/statements and views/statements/positions made on behalf of the agency or Association.

Members shall report to appropriate authorities any corrupt or unethical behaviors in which there is sufficient evidence to justify review.

Members shall refrain from discriminating against any individual because of race, gender, creed, national origin, religious affiliation, age, disability, or any other type of prohibited discrimination.

Members shall preserve the integrity of private information; they shall refrain from seeking information on individuals beyond that which is necessary to implement responsibilities and perform their duties; members shall refrain from revealing nonpublic information unless expressly authorized to do so.

Members shall make all appointments, promotions, and dismissals in accordance with established civil service rules, applicable contract agreements, and individual merit, rather than furtherance of personal interests.

Members shall respect, promote, and contribute to a work place that is safe, healthy, and free of harassment in any form.

Adopted August 1975 at the 105th Congress of Correction
Revised August 1990 at the 120th Congress of Correction
Revised August 1994 at the 124th Congress of Correction
Reprinted with permission of the American Correctional Association, Lanham, MD.

- Not abusing sick leave
- Telling inmates the truth
- Admitting mistakes

These elements are similar to those expressed in the law enforcement code of ethics and are consistent with the ethical frameworks.

The Correctional Officer Subculture

The subculture of the correctional officer has never been as extensively described as the police subculture, but some elements are similar. First of all, the inmate may be considered the enemy, along with superiors and society in general. Moreover, the acceptance of the use of force, the preference toward redefining job roles to meet only minimum requirements, and the willingness to use deceit to cover up wrongdoing are evident in both subcultures (Johnson, 1996; Crouch, 1980; Grossi and Berg, 1991).

Kauffman (1988: 85–112), in an excellent study of the officers' world, notes the following norms of the correctional officer subculture:

1. *Always go to the aid of another officer.* Similar to law enforcement, the necessity of interdependence ensures that this is a strong and pervasive norm in the correctional officer subculture. Kauffman describes a "slam" in Walpole Prison as when the officer slams a heavy cell door, which reverberates throughout the prison building, bringing a dozen officers to his or her aid in minutes—an obvious parallel to the "officer down" call in law enforcement.

2. *Don't lug drugs.* This prohibition is to ensure the safety of other officers, as is the even stronger prohibition against bringing in weapons for inmates. The following norm against "ratting" on a fellow officer may except informing on an officer who is a known offender of this lugging norm.

3. *Don't rat.* In similar ways to the law enforcement subcultural code and, ironically, the inmate code, correctional officers also hate those who inform on their peers. Kauffman notes two subordinate norms: never rat out an officer to an inmate, and never cooperate in an investigation or, worse yet, testify against a fellow officer in regard to that officer's treatment of inmates.

4. *Never make a fellow officer look bad in front of inmates.* This applies regardless of what the officer did, since it jeopardizes the officer's effectiveness and undercuts the appearance of officer solidarity.

5. *Always support an officer in a dispute with an inmate.* Similar to the previous provision, this prescribes behavior—not only should one not criticize a fellow officer, but one should support him or her against any inmate.

6. *Always support officer sanctions against inmates.* This is a specific version of the previous provision. This includes the use of illegal physical force as well as legal sanctions.

7. *Don't be a white hat.* This prohibition is directed at any behavior, attitude, or expressed opinion that could be interpreted as sympathetic toward inmates. Kauffman also notes that it is often violated and does not have the strong subcultural sanctions that accompany some of the other norms.

8. *Maintain officer solidarity against all outside groups.* Similar to police officers, correctional officers feel denigrated and despised by society at large. This norm reinforces officer solidarity by making any other group, including the media, administration, or public the out-group.

9. *Show positive concern for fellow officers.* This norm promotes goodwill toward other officers. Two examples are, never leave another officer a problem, which means don't leave unfinished business at the end of your shift for the next officer to handle; and help your fellow officers with problems outside the institution, meaning lending money to injured or sick officers or helping out in other ways.

Kauffman notes that this code may vary from institution to institution, depending on such factors as permeability, the administration, the level of violence from inmates, architecture, and the demographic profile of officers. Distrust of outsiders, dissatisfaction, and alienation are elements of both the police and the correctional officer subcultures. In both professions, the individuals must work with sometimes-unpleasant people who make it clear that the practitioner is not liked or appreciated. Further, there is public antipathy (either real or perceived) toward the profession, which increases the social distance between criminal justice professionals and all others outside the profession. In addition, the working hours, the nature of the job, and the unwillingness to talk about the job to others outside the profession intensify the isolation that workers feel. One additional point to be made about the occupational subculture is that both law enforcement and corrections have been changed by the entry of minorities, the college educated, and women into the ranks.

It should also be pointed out that some researchers feel that some of the values embedded in the correctional officer subculture may not be shared by most officers—a concept referred to as **pluralistic ignorance.** This refers to the idea that a few outspoken and visible members shape the perception that all group members have toward the characteristics of the majority. In a prison, this may mean that a few officers endorse and publicize subcultural values, whereas the majority, who are silent, privately believe in different values (Johnson, 1996: 130). Kauffman found this to be true in attitudes toward the use of force and toward the value of treatment. Individually, officers expressed more positive attitudes than they believed to be typical of the subculture (1988: 179). This situation is probably true of the police subculture as well.

Relationships with Inmates

One would assume that the general relationship between officers and inmates is one of hatred. That is not necessarily the case. As Martin (1993), a prisoner-writer, points out, the posturing and vocalization from either side come from a small number, with the majority of inmates and officers living in an uneasy state of truce, hoping that no one goes over the line on either side. Those officers who engage in unethical activities can go in one direction or another—there are officers who become too friendly with inmates, and there are officers who conduct campaigns of harassment or terror against inmates.

QUOTE

Some convicts hate all prison guards. They perceive them as the physical manifestation of their own misery and misfortune. The uniform becomes the man, and they no longer see an individual behind it. . . . Many guards react in kind. The hatred is returned with the full force of authority. These two factions become the real movers and shakers in the prison world. They aren't a majority in either camp, but the strength of their hatred makes its presence known to all.

Martin, D. *Committing Journalism: The Prison Writings of Red Hog* (New York: Norton, 1993): 94–95. Originally published in the *San Francisco Chronicle.*

The majority of both guards and inmates prefer to live in peace, and understand that they need to treat each other with some modicum of respect to get along. Unfortunately, both feel they must take sides when conflict occurs. Even though prisoners have come to the aid of officers in physical confrontations, in general, inmates must support their fellow inmates and guards must support their fellow guards, regardless of how little support the individual deserves. Thus, a brutal guard may be protected by his fellows and a racist guard will not be informally or formally sanctioned. Likewise, an assaultive inmate will not be kept in check by his peer group, unless his actions are perceived to hurt their interests.

One serious threat to an officer's ethics and professionalism occurs when relationships with inmates become personal. Gresham Sykes discussed the issue of **reciprocity** in supervision: officers become dependent on inmates for important task completion and the smooth management of the tier; in return, C.O.s may overlook inmate infractions and allow a certain degree of favoritism to enter their supervision style (cited in Crouch, 1980: 239).

One example of a type of reciprocal relationship that may lead to unethical actions is that between an officer and an informant. Hassine (1996: 119), an ex-prisoner, relates that the widespread use of informants created several negative elements in the prison where he was housed, including pervasive tension and distrust within the inmate population, particularly between parole violators and long-termers, because parole violators were more likely to snitch to obtain favorable treatment in their short stay. Officers elevated snitches to higher-status positions through granting favored jobs and privileges. The practice did not reduce drugs in prison, according to Hassine, because informers informed only on some drug dealers and not others. Marquart and Roebuck (1986) also discuss the practice of giving special privileges in return for informing. According to these officers, prisons were, for the most part, managed on information supplied by snitches.

When C.O.s become personally involved with inmates, their professional judgment is compromised. Involvement is possible because of proximity and close contact over a period of time, combined with shared feelings of victimization by the administration. Officers may start to feel they have more in common with inmates than with the administration, especially now that officers are more likely to come from urban areas, from minority groups, and are more demographically similar to the inmates they supervise. Identification and friendship may lead to unethical conduct, such as ignoring infractions or doing illegal favors for an inmate. McCarthy (1991) writes of this exchange relationship as an incentive for further corruption. He also points out that lack of training, low visibility, and unfettered discretion also contributes to a variety of corrupt behaviors.

The subcultural norms against sympathizing with or becoming too friendly with inmates, as described by Kauffman (1988), may be seen as a preventative to avoid this identification with inmates. An officer who is too close to inmates is not to be trusted. The subculture minimizes this possibility by a view of inmates as animalistic and not worth human sympathy. Kauffman also notes that inmates themselves make it difficult for C.O.s to continue to hold sympathetic or friendly views. In her study, new officers were continually harassed by inmates until the neutral or positive views they held at entry were replaced with negative views. She described Walpole in the 1970s as overrun with rats and roaches, with excrement smeared on the walls and garbage ankle-deep on the floors—inmates wouldn't clean up, and officers could not. Extreme inmate-on-inmate violence, including mutilations and torture, was commonplace, and officers feared being thrown from the tiers, being knifed in the back, or being hit in the head by soup cans or other heavy objects thrown from the tiers above. This description obviously is not representative of most prisons, then or now, but the elements of inmate hostility, fear, and hopelessness are characteristic of all prisons to some degree.

Just as officers may act in unethical ways when they like an inmate, officers have the power to make life difficult for the inmate they do not like. These extralegal harassments and punishments may include "forgetting" to send an inmate to an appointment, making an inmate stay in "keeplock" longer than necessary, or pretending not to hear someone locked in a cell asking for toilet paper or other necessary items. Lombardo (1981/1989) noted the practice of putting an inmate in "keeplock" on a Friday even without a supportable charge because the disciplinary committee would not meet until the following Monday to release the inmate, the use of profanity toward inmates even in front of families, not notifying an inmate of a visitor, and losing passes.

Kauffman (1988) notes that during the time period she studied, officers sometimes flushed cell toilets to aggravate inmates, dumped good food into the garbage, withheld toilet paper or matches, made up "tips" reporting contraband in a cell that resulted in a shakedown, scratched artwork, and in other innumerable informal ways made the targeted inmate's life miserable.

Because prisoners are in a position of need, having to ask for things as simple as permission to go to the bathroom, officers have the power to make inmates feel even more dependent than necessary and humiliated because of their dependency. The relative powerlessness of the officers in relation to their superiors, the administration, and society in general creates a situation where some take advantage of their only power—that over the inmate.

Even more so than police, C.O.s work every day with large numbers of men or women who simply do not like—indeed, sometimes hate—the correctional officer for no other reason than the uniform he or she is wearing. There is always the potential of injury from an unprovoked attack, while subduing an inmate, while breaking up a fight, or from being taken hostage. Officers will say this last possibility is never far from their minds and may affect to a certain extent their supervision of inmates, since it is potentially dangerous to be personally disliked.

On the other hand, on a day-to-day basis inmates are not that much different from anyone else; some are friendly, some are funny, and some are good conversationalists. A comfortable alliance is sometimes formed between the guards and the guarded, especially in work settings, that is not unlike a foreman–employee relationship. This strange combination of familiarity and fear results in a pervasive feeling of distrust. Officers insist that "you can be friendly with inmates, but you can never trust them." Mature officers learn to live with this basic inconsistency and are able to differentiate situations in which rules must be followed from those in which rules can be relaxed. Younger and less perceptive officers either take on a defensive attitude of extreme distrust or are manipulated by inmates because they are not able to tell the difference between goodwill and gaming. In the accompanying quotes, the concept of the gulf between the status of guard and guarded is the theme.

QUOTE

I never shake hands with an inmate. . . . They neither are nor ought to be viewed as equals.

George Beto, administrator of Texas prison system, 1962–1972, quoted in Dilulio, 1987: 177.

. . . the Sergeant had succeeded in making me feel even more isolated from the world that existed outside the prison walls. I was no longer so proud to be an American. I was just a convict without rights. . . .

Victor Hassine, inmate, 1996: 52.

Because legitimate power is so unevenly distributed between the keepers and the kept, left to its own inertia abuses of that power will inevitably creep into any prison without diligent and sensitive oversight.

Patrick McManus, state correctional official, reported in Martin, D., 1993: 333.

General Conduct and the "Good Officer"

Historically, correctional officers have been described as role models for inmates. In reference to an early and idealistic view of who should be hired and for what reasons, one author writes that this was a "pursuit of men with 'special gifts of personality and character' capable of achieving the moral transformation of their fellow men merely by the exercise of 'personal influence'" (Hawkins, cited in Crouch, 1980: 55). This was, by and large, probably a false dream, but it has always been true that no one else in corrections has more day-to-day contact with inmates. For this reason, it is important to look at the types of individuals hired to fill correctional officer positions and how they respond to the environment of the prison.

Officers, of course, are individuals, and they respond differently to the demands and job pressures of corrections. Officers fall into various adaptational types: some are violence-prone, using the role of correctional officer to act out an authoritarian role; another type serves time in prison much the same way as the inmates do, avoiding trouble and hoping that nothing goes wrong on their shift; and other officers seek to enlarge their job description and perceive their role as including counseling and helping the inmate rather than merely locking doors and signing passes. This type of officer has been called the *human service officer* and incorporates the tasks of providing goods and services, acting as a referral agent or advocate, and helping with institutional adjustment problems (Johnson, 1996/2002).

Not surprisingly, C.O.s and inmates tend to agree on a description of a good officer. A good officer is described as one who treats all inmates fairly with no favoritism, but who does not always follow rules to the letter. Discretion is used judicially; when a good officer makes a decision to bypass rules, all involved tend to agree that it is the right decision. A good officer is not quick to use force, nor afraid of force if it becomes necessary. A good officer treats inmates in a professional manner and gives them the respect they deserve as human beings. A good officer will treat the inmate in the way anyone would like to be treated; if the inmate abuses the officer, then that inmate earns different treatment, but it is through formal channels, not informal. In some cases such an officer will go far outside regular duties to aid an inmate who is sincerely in need; however, he or she can detect game playing and cannot be manipulated. These traits—consistency, fairness, and flexibility—are confirmed as valuable by research (Johnson, 1987: 139). Although many officers in prisons reach this ideal, the trend today seems to be a less honorable approach to the position because of the pressures described below (Conover, 2000).

Recent changes have taken away much of the service functions that C.O.s used to perform. Lombardo (1997), in his update of an older study, found that in the ten years that ensued since his first study, much of the ability of C.O.s to grant favors had been taken away. For instance, telephones in the yard eliminated the need for C.O.s to run interference for inmates and get them a pass to make a phone call. This situation increased the autonomy of inmates, but it reduced the ability of the C.O.s to develop helping relationships with inmates or, to put a more negative interpretation on their loss, it reduced their ability to create debts from the inmate—favors owed in return for favors given. C.O.s have much less discretion today, and practically every decision that, in the past, had been made by a C.O. is now made by sergeants and specialized officers. C.O.s feel less responsible and, one might argue, act less responsibly because of this feeling.

Like police, correctional officers feel that court decisions and administrative goals have not supported their needs and have sacrificed their safety to meet inmates' demands. One result of this feeling that superiors and society do not protect their interests is an individualistic response to the ethical issues that may come up in the course of the job. The following presents a fairly negative view of the correctional officer's ethical position (Carroll, cited in Crouch, 1980: 318):

> [T]he officers are not working for the inmates, they are working for themselves. Unable to secure compliance with their directives by the enforcement of a set of impersonal rules, they seek to secure compliance by means of friendships, overlooking infractions, and providing highly desired information to inmates. Their behavior is not so much a repudiation of the goal of custodial control as it is an attempt to maintain order, and at the same time to protect themselves, in the face of institutional changes that have made order more difficult to maintain and their position more vulnerable.

Correctional officers report much stress, and stress-related illnesses such as hypertension are common, as well as social problems such as alcoholism and divorce. Some reports indicate that these problems exist in higher numbers with correctional officers than with police officers. Correctional officers feel criticized and even scorned by many, and it is little wonder that they adapt to their role by such means, yet it is important to understand the consequences of such a position. Kauffman (1988: 222) talked to officers who reported that they had lost their morality in the prison. These officers experienced anguish at the change that was wrought in them by the prison environment:

> Initially, many attempted to avoid engaging in behavior injurious to inmates. . . . As their involvement in the prison world grew and their ability to abstain from morally questionable actions within the prison declined, they attempted to neutralize their own feelings of guilt by regarding prisons as separate moral realms with their own distinct set of moral standards or by viewing inmates as individuals outside the protection of moral laws. When such efforts failed, they shut their minds to what others were doing and to what they were doing themselves.

Without a strong moral and ethical code, correctional officers may find themselves drifting into relativistic egoism: what benefits the individual is considered acceptable, despite long-term effects or inconsistencies with their role and their personal value system. The result is feelings of disillusionment and anomie, and the side effects can be serious dissatisfaction and depression. To maintain a sense of morality in an inherently coercive environment is no easy task, yet a strong set of individual ethics is probably the best defense against being changed by the negative environment of the prison.

Use of Force

The use of force is a legal and sometimes necessary element of correctional supervision, and most observers say that the serious abuse that occurred in prisons in the past simply does not occur today. For instance, "tune-ups" in the

Texas prisons involved "verbal humiliation, profanity, shoves, kicks, and head and body slaps"; "ass-whipping," and using blackjacks and batons to inflict injury. Severe beatings were reserved for those few inmates who attacked staff members (Crouch and Marquart, 1989: 78). Murton (1976) described a litany of abuses that occurred in Arkansas prison farms, including the "Tucker telephone" an electrical device that was attached to the genitals of inmates and used to deliver severe shocks as a form of torture (see accompanying quote). These uses of force are not pervasive today; however, there are still reports that force is used as an extralegal punishment against unruly or aggressive inmates.

QUOTE

[L]ashing an inmate ten times a day with the "hide," a five-foot leather strap capable of maiming. This official method of discipline was augmented by such illegal but customary techniques as inserting needles under the fingernails, crushing knuckles and testicles with pliers, hitting the inmate with a club, blackjack, or "anything you can lay your hands on," kicking inmates in the groin, mouth, or testicles—and, of course, use of the infamous "Tucker Telephone."

Murton, T. *The Dilemma of Prison Reform* (New York: Irvington Publications, 1976): 147.

Ironically, the reduction of official oppression in the late 1970s and 1980s opened the door to gangs and inmate cliques who filled the power vacuum and used violence to get what they wanted. Inmates in the 1980s had less to fear from guards, but more to fear from each other as racial gangs and other powerful cliques or individuals solidified their control over prison black markets. There was a time in the 1970s and 1980s when officers described some prisons as "out of control." There were prisons where guards were afraid to walk into living units, and inmates literally controlled some parts of the prison. In Rhode Island, for instance, officers, who felt betrayed by the courts and management, in effect, gave up guarding. Carroll tracked the changes that occurred during the 1970s in Rhode Island and described how the events there were quite similar to those of Texas in the 1980s, and other states when court decisions upset the balance of power (Carroll, 1998). Taylor (1993) documented similar changes in the Mississippi system.

The "golden years" of prison depend on one's perspective. Glenn (2001), a retired prison warden, described the Texas prison system in the early 1960s as "fair" and "just," arguing that the allegations of abuse by guards and building tenders was slander (2001: 24). He then describes the forms of punishment used. The "rail" was a two by four turned on its side. An inmate found guilty of a minor offense was required to stand on the rail for a period of four hours; if he fell off, the time would start again. If an inmate didn't pick enough cotton, he would be made to stand on a barrel for four or five hours. Up to four inmates might be placed on a single barrel and if one fell off, the time would start again for them all. Other inmates would have their hands raised above their head and handcuffed to the bars in the inmate mess hall; their feet would be handcuffed too. They might be hanging all night (2001: 25-26).

He also described a situation where an inmate tried to escape, was shot, and then was hung on the front gate, bleeding, for the field hoe squads to see as they came back in from the fields. This was described by Glenn as an "effective . . . object lesson" rather than brutality (2001: 44). Glenn also described a prison captain who played a "game" with inmates who he believed weren't working hard enough on the hoe squad. He would have them tied and stripped, and then he would lower his pants and threaten to sodomize them. The author does not profess to know whether this captain ever carried out the threat (2001: 69).

According to observers, this type of official violence has been drastically reduced or even eliminated entirely. Less pervasive violence, however, continues. As with the use of force in law enforcement, policy definitions of *necessary force* are vague. This may mean that the resort to violence is the absolute last alternative available, or it may mean that force is used when it is the most convenient way to get something accomplished (Morris and Morris, cited in Crouch, 1980: 253). During the course of a fistfight or a struggle with an inmate, officers react to violence instinctively—that is, without much rational thought as to whether a blow is necessary or gratuitous.

Evidence that beatings still exist can be found in court cases. For instance, in *Hudson v. McMillian* (503 U.S. 1 [1992]) the Supreme Court dealt with a case involving an inmate who had been forced to sit in a chair while two officers hit him in the head and chest area, with a lieutenant looking on. The state argued that since there was no "serious injury," there was no constitutional violation, since cruel and unusual punishment had to involve serious injury. Although some justices agreed with this logic, the majority held that injuries need not be serious for a constitutional violation to occur if they stemmed from such abuse at the hands of correctional officers.

Some uses of force may result in death. Nine Florida guards were indicted in 1999 for the murder of an inmate. The inmate died from injuries including broken ribs, swollen testicles, and innumerable cuts and bruises. He was on death row for killing a prison guard in a botched escape attempt in 1983. Prosecutors alleged he was killed because he was planning to go to the media with allegations of widespread abuse in the prison. Accused guards insisted he killed himself by flinging himself against the concrete wall of his cell; or, alternatively, that he was killed by other guards (Cox, 2000). The first three officers who were tried were acquitted in February of 2002 (Three Guards. . . , 2002).

C.O.s may view such beatings as utilitarian in that they serve as warnings to all inmates that they will receive similar treatment if they attack C.O.s; thus, the action protects all officers to some extent from inmate aggression. Officers might also defend the action on retributive grounds, since the inmate would probably not be punished for the attack through legal channels. However, these retaliations always represent the most brutal and inhumane aspects of incarceration and damage the integrity of all correctional professionals.

Bowker (1980) and other authors describe the victimization of inmates by correctional officers, including psychological torture, racial discrimination, and severe physical abuse. The explanations for why this type of behavior on the part of officers exists include the officers' pervasive sense of fear and the C.O. subculture that tolerates if not encourages such victimization. Crouch and Marquart (1989) and Crouch (1986) also discuss the use of violence as a rite of passage for the correctional officer, a way to prove oneself as a competent officer. Baro (1995) describes a more systemic brutality in the Hawaii prison system that eventually led to an investigation by the U.S. Attorney General's office.

The use in federal prisons of Special Operations and Response Teams SORT teams—the prison version of Special Weapons and Tactical Teams SWAT teams—is a new wrinkle in the use of force in prison. These officers, who respond to incidents in full riot gear, which makes them look like a mixture of a professional football team, astronauts, and toxic waste disposal experts, epitomize depersonalized violence—they are so fully padded, helmeted, and hooded that they can hardly feel pain, and they come in such numbers that the individual inmate is immediately overwhelmed. This approach is touted as actually preventing official brutality and minimizing the injuries that can occur to inmates and officers alike when there is an altercation. The highly trained team members subdue an inmate before he can strike any blows; they are so swift that the inmate is stripped, handcuffed, and picked up and carried away in a matter of minutes. These teams also exist in state prisons.

The very depersonalization of such teams leads to worries about abuse. In the same way an inmate can be subdued, stripped, and moved by the team, they can also take him down a flight of stairs, with his head hanging and hitting every step. Their masks give them the anonymity that was not available to officers in the "old days," when inmates were just called into the captain's office for a "tune up." In fact, in some prisons it is a practice not to let it be known which officers are on the team—because of the hatred that prisoners feel for team members.

It should be noted that prison brutality is not a uniquely American phenomena. The United Kingdom, Australia, and other countries have had their own scandals concerning abuse of prisoners. The Bathurst riots, for instance, in New South Wales, in the 1970s initiated a Commission inquiry and report. The report included a scathing commentary on the prison management's efforts to cover up the widespread practice of "bashing intractables" upon entry to the prison and for the most trivial of rule infractions (Findlay, 1982).

Corruption

McCarthy (1991, 1995) and Souryal (1999) discuss the major types of corruption engaged in by correctional officers and other officials in institutional corrections. Categories include theft, trafficking, embezzlement, and misuse of authority. Under misuse of authority McCarthy details the following:

- Accepting gratuities for special consideration for legitimate purposes
- Accepting gratuities for protection of illicit activities
- Mistreatment/harassment or extortion of inmates
- Mismanagement (e.g., prison industries)
- Miscellaneous abuses

Souryal (1999), in another typology, describes the types of corruption as falling into the following categories: arbitrary use of power (treating workers or inmates preferentially or in a biased fashion), oppression, failure to demonstrate compassion/caring, and abusing authority for personal gain (extortion, smuggling, theft).

Periodically, news stories will describe officers who committed illegal, and/or unethical acts. For instance, four state prison guards faced felony bribery charges after they agreed to launder money for inmates. One received $60,000 with the understanding that he would get $10,000 for his services (A.P., 2000: A3). In 1990, wide-scale corruption involving smuggling drugs into Florida's Martin Correctional Institution resulted in fifteen arrests of corrections officers (Houston, 1999: 360). Carroll (1998) presents other examples where investigations uncovered abuses including sexual abuse of inmates, brutality, and bribery at the highest levels of corrections departments.

As discussed earlier, Tom Murton uncovered a web of corrupt practices in Arkansas in the early 1970s. His experience was fictionalized to some extent in the movie *Brubaker*, but the worst aspects of prisoner abuse shown in the movie were real. An associate superintendent from a prison in Pennsylvania testified before an investigative committee of the state legislature after a four-day riot in which inmates and officers were savagely beaten (cited in Hassine, 1996: 149–152; also see Murton and Hyams, 1969). His testimony detailed the widespread corrupt practices of many of the officers and supervisors in the prison, including the following:

- An officer was beaten up by other officers in the prison.
- An officer was caught smuggling in contraband (sneakers, coffee, chewing gum, letters, etc.) for inmates.
- An officer was caught attempting to deliver methamphetamine.
- An officer allowed an inmate into restricted housing, where he beat another inmate for two hours.
- An officer raped an inmate.
- A female officer sent an inmate money and personal items, visited an inmate at another institution, and wrote letters to inmates.
- A staff member appeared at work under the influence of cocaine.
- An instructor was found with a box of ammunition and alcoholic beverages in his van at the rear gate of the prison.
- An activities director embezzled funds from the inmate Jaycees and Lifers association.
- An officer engaged an inmate in a fistfight in the dayroom over losing a bet with the inmate.
- An instructor smeared peanut butter into a black inmate's hair, put flour and jelly in other inmates' hair, rubbed an onion in the face of another, conducted a mock hanging off a steam pipe dressed as a Ku Klux Klan member, and abused others verbally—his actions were directed only to African-American inmates.

- A labor foreman purposely slammed on his brakes and flipped an inmate over the hood of his truck.
- A food service supervisor allowed a food fight in the kitchen.
- An officer engaged in horseplay—punching and wrestling an inmate.
- An officer was investigated for shoplifting.

More recently, Corcoran prison guards in California were accused of setting up gladiator-type fights between inmates, and encouraging or allowing prisoner rapes. One former guard testified that a "loudmouth" prisoner was placed with a prison rapist known as the "Booty Bandit" (Arax, 1999a; 1999b). Other guards were accused of an unlawful use of force by shooting an inmate during one of the gladiator fights. Eventually, several guards received federal indictments and were tried for the killing, as well as the other acts of oppression. They were acquitted even though former guards and other experts supported the inmate's allegations (Guards Acquitted. . . . , 2000). Some argue that the officer union "tainted" the jury pool by running television ads before the jury selection that showed officers as tough, brave, and underappreciated. The television ads, with the tagline of "Corcoran officers: They walk the toughest beat in the state," aired only in the Fresno area where the trial was held (Lewis, 1999).

Questionable practices are engaged in by individuals in every level of the prison structure. In Texas, Andy "James" Collins, an ex-director of the Department of Corrections was investigated for his business association with a Canadian company that made VitaPro—a vegetable-based protein substance that evidently tasted bad and created digestive problems for some people. It was discovered that (a) the state prison system had warehouses full of this product because inmates wouldn't eat it and the state was locked into a contract that mandated a certain number of pounds of it had to be bought every month; (b) the contract, which was worth millions, had not been approved by the Board of Criminal Justice, an overseer body, because of a loophole that allowed products for prison industry to avoid the bidding and approval process, yet the only relationship this product had to prison industry was that prisoners repackaged the stuff and sent it to other prisons; and (c) the director, immediately upon leaving his job in 1996, started as a thousand-dollar-per-day consultant with the same company. In 2001, he and the director of that company were finally convicted by a federal jury on charges of bribery, conspiracy and money laundering. The case is on appeal.

A Florida news article reported that prison guards were more than twice as likely as police officers to violate state standards of conduct. An analysis of the state records for disciplinary actions showed that from January 1998 to June 1999, 769 corrections officers (29.6 per 1,000) were brought up on disciplinary charges, including sexual assault, shoplifting, and excessive force. During the same period 559 law enforcement officers from city, county and state police forces were sanctioned (14.0 per 1,000) (Kleindienst, 1999). What can be made of this statistic? Perhaps nothing, but if it is true that correctional officers have a higher pattern of misconduct, then it would be important to identify the cause and remedy the situation. It may be that there is less of a culture of professionalism, it may be hiring incentives and standards, or it may be that training is lacking the component of ethics. One would expect that state corrections departments would want to know and understand the reasons why officers misbehave.

Corruption exists in prisons today, and it will probably continue to exist, but there are measures that can be used to address the existence of corruption. Correctional managers should generate a strong anti-corruption policy (obviously, managers should not be engaging in corrupt practices themselves). Such a policy would include proactive measures such as mechanisms to investigate and detect wrongdoing, reduce opportunities for corruption, screen employees using state-of-the-art psychological tools, improve working conditions, and provide good role models in the form of supervisors and administrators who follow the Code of Ethics presented earlier in this chapter (McCarthy, 1991). By most accounts, law enforcement seems to be ahead of corrections in ethics training for its officers.

The "trickle down" theory of ethical management is that officers will treat inmates the way they perceive they are being treated—with fairness, compassion, respect. Or with less than fairness, respect and compassion if that is the way they felt they are treated by management. It becomes easier to justify unethical actions if one feels victimized (Houston, 1999; Souryal, 1999). Furthermore, staff who are coerced to do unethical or illegal actions by management are more likely to behave in unethical and illegal ways by their own initiative.

Loyalty and Whistle blowing

There are many similarities between police and correctional staff in use-of-force abuses, the code of silence, and feelings of isolation. There are also differences. The most striking difference between the two jobs is that C.O.s must deal with the same people daily in a closed, oppressive environment. Police officers have freedom of movement and can avoid peers or citizen troublemakers to a certain extent, but C.O.s have no such luxury. If a C.O. fears an inmate, he or she must still face him or her every day. If a C.O. violates the correctional subcultural code, the sanctions are felt perhaps even more acutely than by police officers, because one must work closely with other C.O.s all day long. Whereas police officers cite the importance of being able to trust other officers as backups in violent situations, one could make the argument that C.O.s need to trust each other more completely, more implicitly, and more frequently, given that violence in some institutions is pervasive and unprovoked, and the C.O. carries no weapon. An officer described to Kauffman (1988: 207) the result of violating peer trust:

> If an incident went down, there was no one to cover my back. That's a very important lesson to learn. You need your back covered and my back wasn't covered there at all. And at one point I was in fear of being set up by guards. I was put in dangerous situations purposely. That really happened to me.

Fear of violating the code of silence is one reason that officers do not report wrongdoing. Loyalty is another. C.O.s feel a strong *esprit de corps* that is similar to the previously discussed loyalty among police. This positive loyalty also results in covering for other officers and not testifying or reporting offenses.

McCarthy (1991) discusses types of corrupt behaviors in a prison, including theft, trafficking in contraband, embezzlement, and misuse of authority. These offenses are known yet unreported by other correctional officers because of loyalty and subcultural prohibitions against "ratting."

A pattern of complicity also prevents reporting. New officers cannot possibly follow all the many rules and regulations that exist in a prison and still adequately deal with inmates on a day-to-day basis. Before long, they find themselves involved in activity that could result in disciplinary action. Because others are usually aware of this activity and do not inform supervisors, an implicit conspiracy of silence develops so that no one is turned in for anything because each of the others who might witness this wrongdoing has engaged in behavior that could also be sanctioned (Lombardo, 1981: 79).

Hamm (1989) discusses whistle blowing in corrections. He presents examples where correctional professionals did come forward. The examples included instances of norm violations including injustice, inefficiency, or ineffectiveness, fairness, and incompetence. It may be a person or a policy that was the object of whistle blowing. He also points out that whistleblowers sometimes are pursuing self-interest or personal goals by informing. At times, there are minimal costs; however, in instances where the individual goes against the subculture, there may be serious consequences.

A rabble-rouser or whistleblower can be defined as someone who finds it impossible to live with knowledge of corruption without doing something about it—usually creating a scandal that exposes the corruption. The term has negative connotations, but it actually describes someone who is typically responding to a higher ethical code than those whose behavior is exposed. Tom Murton found his career dramatically altered when he was hired by the Arkansas Department of Correction as the director of corrections. Upon arriving in the Arkansas system he discovered abuses and inhumane conditions, described later in several writings and immortalized in the movie *Brubaker*. The Supreme Court case of *Holt v. Sarver*, 442 F.2d 304 (8th Cir. 1971), also documented the abuses. In addition to extreme physical treatment, including the *Tucker Telephone*—an electrical apparatus used to shock inmates—Murton had information that there were hundred of inmates listed as escapees who had evidently disappeared. Acting on the information of one informant, he dug up (on the grounds of the prison) two bodies that had injuries exactly as the inmate described—one had been decapitated, and one had a crushed skull. Opposing testimony at the legislative hearing called in response to his investigation proposed that the bodies were from an old church cemetery. Instead of pursuing the matter further and digging up more bodies or testing them in any way for age and other identifying marks, state officials fired Murton and threatened him with prosecution as a graverobber (Murton, 1976).

Jail Officers

Very little has been written about jail officers. Jail officers may be sheriff deputies who must complete their assignment at the jail before they can "promote" to street patrol. Sometimes jail officers are street deputies who are transferred back to the jail for punishment. In other situations, jail officers are not

American Jail Association Code of Ethics for Jail Officers

As an officer employed in a detention/correctional capacity, I swear (or affirm) to be a good citizen and a credit to my community, state, and nation at all times. I will abstain from all questionable behavior which might bring disrepute to the agency for which I work, my family, my community, and my associates. My lifestyle will be above and beyond reproach and I will constantly strive to set an example of a professional who performs his/her duties according to the laws of our country, state, and community and the policies, procedures, written and verbal orders, and regulations of the agency for which I work.

On the job I promise to:

Keep the institution secure so as to safeguard my community and the lives of the staff, inmates, and visitors on the premises.

Work with each individual firmly and fairly without regard to rank, status, or condition.

Maintain a positive demeanor when confronted with stressful situations of scorn, ridicule, danger and/or chaos.

Report either in writing or by word of mouth to the proper authorities those things which should be reported, and keep silent about matters which are to remain confidential according to the laws and rules of the agency and government.

Manage and supervise the inmates in an evenhanded and courteous manner.

Refrain at all times from becoming personally involved in the lives of the inmates and their families.

Treat all visitors to the jail with politeness and respect and do my utmost to ensure that they observe the jail regulations.

Take advantage of all education and training opportunities designed to assist me to become a more competent officer.

Communicate with people in or outside of the jail, whether by phone, written word, or word of mouth, in such a way so as not to reflect in a negative manner upon my agency.

Contribute to a jail environment which will keep the inmate involved in activities designed to improve his/her attitude and character.

Support all activities of a professional nature through membership and participation that will continue to elevate the status of those who operate our nation's jails.

Do my best through word and deed to present an image to the public at large of a jail professional, committed to progress for an improved and enlightened criminal justice system.

SOURCE: American Jail Association. Reprinted with permission.

deputies, and have a separate title and pay scale (usually lower). In all these situations, the tasks and skills associated with managing jail inmates are discounted or ignored. There is a need for greater recognition of the profession of jail officer; the position should not merely be a dreaded rite-of-passage assignment, a punishment, or a stepping-stone to deputy status, since the body

---

Jail Guards Taunt Prisoner Dying of Cocaine Overdose

FORT PIERCE, FLA.—A man who swallowed cocaine when he was arrested died after jailers ignored his pleas for help and taunted him in a three-hour ordeal captured on video by a jail surveillance camera.

Two sheriff's deputies were later fired, and five others disciplined.

Anderson Tate moaned, thrashed and chanted prayers for more than three hours while bound to a chair Dec. 3 at the St. Lucie County Jail. Jail employees and deputies walked past him, and one made fun of him.

"I don't want to die. I'm burning up," he said on the footage released Wednesday. "I'm 300 degrees. I've got too much cocaine in my system."

State prosecutors are investigating and will decide whether to bring criminal charges against the officers. . . .

Tate is black; six of the officers are white, and the other is Hispanic . . .

Tate had been pulled over for not having a license plate and driving without a valid license. He apparently swallowed some cocaine he was carrying when he was arrested but initially refused medical treatment, said St. Lucie County Undersheriff Dennis Williams.

One of the fired deputies taunted Tate, clapping and stomping his feet to the beat of Tate's chants and fanning him with a clipboard when he said he was burning up, Williams said.

Jail officials didn't become alarmed until the 22-year-old man went into convulsions and stopped breathing. Tate died about 11 hours later at a hospital.

Rubin said a jail nurse checked on Tate three times.

Williams called the officers' behavior unacceptable. Deputies told investigators that they knew something wasn't right but that everyone assumed someone else was taking charge, the undersheriff said.

SOURCE: Associated Press. *Austin American-Statesman,* February, 8, 1997: A16. Reprinted with permission.

---

of knowledge required to do the job well is different from that which a street deputy needs. Recently, there has been an attempt to professionalize the image of jail officers, starting again with a code of ethics. See the "American Jail Association Code of Ethics for Jail Officers."

Arguably, the job of jail officer is even more difficult than that of correctional officer because jail officers must deal with a transitory population rather than a fairly stable one. Offenders come into jail intoxicated, suffer from undiagnosed epilepsy or other diseases, may suffer overdoses (as in the chilling account in the box above), and may be suicidal. Visitation is more frequent, and family issues are more problematic in jails than prisons. The constant activity and chaotic environment of a jail often create unique ethical dilemmas. One can also find the same type of unethical behavior that one finds with police and correctional officers—jail officers can be uncaring and insensitive to human needs. Then again, some jail officers follow the **human service model** described on page 325.

Farkas (1999), in a study of 125 county correctional officers, found that many officers expressed support for rehabilitation. For instance, more than 70 percent disagreed with the statement "rehabilitative programs are a waste of time and money." These officers were not naïve; they also overwhelmingly agreed that you couldn't trust an inmate (84 percent), and that a personal relationship with an inmate invited corruption (95 percent). Furthermore, she found that older officers expressed greater support for a counseling orientation, consistent with Toch and Klofas (1982). Female officers were more likely to express both high agreement with counseling principles and a punitive approach. However, work variables were more influential than individual characteristics (i.e., shift, contact hours, job satisfaction, role conflict, etc.), although some of the relationships are a bit puzzling. For instance, high job satisfaction correlated with less support for a counseling role and less agreement with harsher conditions. High job satisfaction correlated with a desire for greater social distance from inmates. Whether these findings can be applied to a prison guard sample is debatable, but it does seem clear that there are differences between officers and these differences aren't always simply limited to age, race, and sex. These differences have obvious relevance to whether unethical behaviors are likely.

TREATMENT STAFF

Treatment specialists have their own ethical dilemmas. Although hired by the state, many feel their loyalties lie with the offender. Prison psychologists may be privy to information or confessions that they feel bound to hold in confidence, even though the security of the prison may be jeopardized. The professional goal of all treatment specialists is to help the client. This may be fundamentally inconsistent with the prison (or jail) environment, which emphasizes punishment. Making the decision as to whether the individual is cured also involves mixed loyalties. Any treatment necessarily involves risk. How much risk one is willing to take depends on whether the public should be protected at all costs, in which case few people would be released, or whether one feels that the public must risk possible victimization in order to give offenders a chance to prove themselves.

Another dilemma is the administration of treatment programs. If a program has potential, someone must make decisions on who gets into it. Ideally, one would want similar people in the treatment program and in a control group. However, it is sometimes hard to justify withholding the program from some people who may sincerely wish to participate. Laypersons have difficulty understanding the concepts of random sampling and control groups. Pressure sometimes exists to admit anyone who sincerely wants a chance to participate, despite what this might do to experimental design.

Another, more basic issue is the ethics of providing treatment to people who do not want it. In particular, psychiatrists and psychologists have to reconcile their professional ethics in two fields, corrections and psychiatry, and at times this is hard to do. Psychiatrists in corrections, for instance, feel at times that they are being used for social control rather than treatment. Disruptive inmates, although needing treatment, pose security risks to prison officials, so intervention, especially chemotherapy, often takes the form of control rather than treatment.

QUOTE

[discussing an inmate who was not violent, but was extremely talkative, loud, and inclined to discuss his delusions]

As it was, John's illness needed to be controlled, not because he was unhappy with it, but because those around him found it objectionable. What can the psychiatrist do in cases like this? He has the uneasy task of respecting "his" patient's wishes, of listening to the demands of the prison guards to keep the patient from disturbing the peace, of obeying the orders from the prison bureaucracy to treat the patient, of heeding the request from the other inmates to do something to quiet "the crazy guy . . . or else," and last but not least, of paying attention to his own needs to do his best and to obtain a modicum of job satisfaction. Practically all of these demands are antithetical.

Arboleda-Florez, 1983: 52.

The practice of using antipsychotic drugs is especially problematic for treatment professionals. Although the Supreme Court has determined that the administration of such drugs to unwilling inmates is not unconstitutional, the practice must be scrutinized and held to due-process protections in order to uphold professional ethical standards. Some allege that psychotropic drugs are used to control inmates, rather than for legitimate treatment purposes. There are pervasive stories from ex-inmates of inmates being maintained on high dosages of drugs during their prison stay. The problem is that once released, they may experience withdrawal and have no assistance from community mental health facilities because of governmental cutbacks in services (Martin, 1993).

QUOTE

A little-acknowledged aspect of chemical straitjackets is the direct threat they pose to law-abiding society . . . A violent man at Lompoc who was nearing the end of a ten-year-sentence was kept heavily dosed with antipsychotic drugs. . . . When his sentence was finished, the guards walked him to the front gate and shoved him out into the free world—no halfway house, no parole—and I doubt he went off to a psychiatrist and got a prescription to continue on psychotropic drugs. I've often wondered what happened when he regained his physical momentum after ten years of suppression by disabling chemicals. . . .

Martin, D. *Committing Journalism: The Prison Writings of Red Hog* (New York: Norton, 1993): 225–227. Article originally appeared in the *San Francisco Chronicle.*

Psychologists have their own ethical code, and some principles seem especially relevant to corrections. For instance, under the principle of responsibility, psychologists are instructed to prevent the distortion, misuse, or suppression of their psychological findings by the institution or agency by which they are employed. This obviously affects institutional psychologists, who may feel that their findings are compromised by custody concerns. For instance, something confessed to in a counseling session may be used in parole reports to prevent release, findings may be used to block transfer, behavior brought out in psychological testing may be punished, and so on ("Ethical Principles," 1981: 633).

Other principles involve the treatment of clients: "In their professional roles, psychologists avoid any action that will violate or diminish the legal and civil rights of clients or of others who may be affected by their actions" ("Ethical Principles," 1981: 634). This principle may be applicable to certain treatment programs in prison that restrict inmates' liberty or choice—for instance, some of the behavior modification programs have been questioned legally and ethically. Many treatment professionals think that behavior modification has been subverted by the prison environment. Although it is effective in inducing behavioral change, some professionals feel uneasy participating in a punishment-oriented program in an environment that is already one of deprivation. The coercive power inherent in the prison setting creates the potential for unethical practices by treatment personnel. The fact that prisoners are captive audiences makes them attractive subjects for experimentation of all kinds. Most programs ask for volunteers rather than force participation, but in a prison environment the assumption is always there that release is tied to compliance, so what may appear as voluntary action may be the result of no choice at all.

The psychologist's or psychiatrist's responsibility to innocent victims is being scrutinized more closely today. What is the ethical responsibility of a counselor when an offender threatens future violence toward a particular victim? As in the legal profession, confidentiality is an issue for psychologists. As their ethical principles state:

> Psychologists have a primary obligation to respect the confidentiality of information obtained from persons in the course of their work as psychologists. They reveal such information to others only with the consent of the person or the person's legal representative, except in those unusual circumstances in which not to do so would result in clear danger to the person or to others. Where appropriate, psychologists inform their clients of the legal limits of confidentiality. ("Ethical Principles," 1981: 636)

Some psychiatrists find it hard to be associated with something as damaging as prison and feel a moral resistance to involvement with prison treatment efforts, given the negative effects that are inevitable. As Thomas (quoted in Tanay, 1982: 386) writes:

> The length of sentences and the nature of maximum-security prisons combine to damage the personalities of the prisoners to such a degree as to make it especially difficult for them to function as autonomous and independent individuals in a free society following their release. I believe that whenever a man serves three or more years in a maximum security prison, the experience will usually have a lasting deleterious effect on his personality.

Even for those who feel comfortable working in prison, treatment and security concerns clash in many instances. The treatment professional must choose between two value systems. To emphasize security concerns puts the psychiatrist or counselor in a role of a custodian with professional training used only to better control inmate behavior. To emphasize treatment concerns puts the professional in an antagonistic role *vis-à-vis* the security staff, and they may find themselves in situations where these concerns directly conflict. For instance, if the superintendent demands to see a client's file to support a disciplinary committee's decision, should the psychiatrist surrender the information that was given in confidence? In answer to this dilemma, the psychiatrist or psychologist should probably have never allowed the inmate to assume that information regarding rule infractions or potential wrongdoing could ever be confidential. However, if inmates believe that counselors and psychologists can offer no confidentiality protections, then is there any possibility of a trusting relationship? The issues that confront treatment personnel in prison seem to always involve the conflicting goals of punishment and treatment.

Although religion has always had a role in corrections, the separation of church and state has relegated religion to a separate element, unsanctioned while not necessarily unsupported by prison officials. This may change since faith-based programs have been supported and encouraged by the White House. Prison Fellowship Ministries, Inc., a Washington, D.C., group headed by Watergate figure Charles Colson, is one such prison program. The program is Christ-centered, biblically rooted, and values-based, and emphasizes family, community, and Jesus Christ. Inmates volunteer for the program (Ward, 1996).

A recent evaluation by the state of Texas Criminal Justice Policy Council showed that prison inmates who completed a religion-based program were less likely to commit new crimes. The program was The Innerchange Freedom Initiative introduced in 1997. The study tracked 177 offenders who were released from the program and compared them to a control group that met the selection criteria but did not participate. Only 8 percent of program participants returned to prison, compared to 20 percent for the control group during the two-year study period (Criminal Justice Policy Council, 2003).

The existence of such programs in prison raises several issues. Some argue that such programs violate the separation of church and state and are an unconstitutional violation of freedom of religion. If the program offers hope for early release or other advantages, Muslims or those following other religions, may participate only if they also compromise their faith.

MANAGEMENT ISSUES

Administrators are removed from day-to-day contact with inmates, but their power over decision making may actually be greater than that of line staff. Administrators emphasize the goal of control—that is, keeping the organization out of the newspapers and minimizing negative publicity. Because of this emphasis, administrators may be faced with difficult choices. For instance, in prisons or jails all treatment programs using outside people are potential security risks. An easy solution would be to prohibit all outsiders from entering the prison. Obviously, few prison administrators are this stringent in their control, but the choice may be made in specific instances to limit entry based on convenience and security. The decision to limit entry could probably be justified under a utilitarian framework, but other ethical systems may not support it.

Another dilemma that decision makers face is the balance between needs and costs. If inmates' programming is sparse, clothing is minimal, or medical care is inadequate, or if officers' safety and efficiency are compromised because too few are employed or too much overtime is required, a decision maker must, at some point, determine priorities. Obviously, administrators often have no choice since they can work only within the budget given. However, situations do arise in governmental agencies where workers are told there is no money in the budget for needed items such as office supplies and equipment or overtime pay, yet at the same time administrators manage to find the money to order expensive new office furniture or go on expensive training weekends. This discrepancy between what administrators say and what workers see is demoralizing to those who try to make do with increasingly smaller budgets. Moral leadership is exhibited by those administrators who share the sacrifices. Ethical decisions for administrators arise when budget allocations are made, when program futures are decided, and when rules and procedures are developed.

Barrier et al. (1999) discussed an ethics training program with correctional officers, and part of the training involved having the officers identify important elements of an ethics code. Many of the elements involved had to do with practices of management rather than officers:

- Treating all staff fairly and impartially
- Promoting based on true merit
- Showing no prejudice
- Leading by example
- Developing a mission statement that is clear in every way
- Reducing the negative tone of a code of ethics and making a list of dos, not don'ts
- Creating a culture that promotes performance, not seniority
- Soliciting staff input on new policies
- Being respectful
- Letting the word out that upper management cares about ethics

Correctional Management and the Courts

Administrators have found themselves forced to change after prisoners' rights suits have resulted in court mandates to change. The implementation of court-ordered changes has often been halting and superficial, showing that compliance to the letter of a court ruling may be different from compliance to the spirit of one. Is this response to court-ordered change an ethical one? *Cruz v. Beto* (Civil

No. 71-H-1371 [S.D. Tex. 1976]) was a case dealing with the actions of administrators in the Texas system in response to a particularly active prisoners' rights attorney who was taking on cases *pro bono* that challenged the practices of the Texas Department of Corrections. First, the director barred her from all prisons in the state, and then, when forced to allow her back into the prison because the ban was an unconstitutional infringement on the inmates' right to legal assistance, transferred all inmates who were her clients to one unit, deprived them of good behavior points that were necessary for higher security classifications and favorable parole decisions, and evidently subjected the inmates to a barrage of pressure indicating that if they dropped her as their lawyer they would have all privileges reinstated. Not surprisingly, the court took a dim view of these actions. What ethical system would justify such behavior?

Administrators have also found themselves in the position of testifying in court about conditions or the actions of their employees. Their testimony may be perjured to protect themselves or others; in this situation, their ethical dilemma is similar to that of police officers testifying about undercover activities. However, an issue more specific to administrators is pleading ignorance of activities for which they arguably should be held responsible.

Individuals are often forced to make a choice between their career and challenging unethical or illegal practices. For administrators, this dilemma may appear more often since their scope of knowledge is broader than that of line staff. Often the career path of an administrator, with its investment of time and energy and the mandate to be a "company man," creates an immersion in bureaucratic thinking to the point that an individual loses sight of ethical issues. For instance, protecting the department or the director from scandal or litigation becomes more important than analyzing the behavior that created the potential for scandal in the first place. If decision making becomes influenced solely by short-term gains or avoidance of scandal, then decisions may be unsupported by the ethical systems discussed previously.

Another issue for correctional managers is what to do when faced with a worker alleging sexual harassment. The type of behavior defined as constituting a **hostile work environment** was common when women first entered as officers in prisons for males. Female officers reported behavior such as C.O.s making sexual references and disparaging comments to them in front of inmates, "setting them up" by having inmates masturbate when they were sent down the tier, putting up posters with naked women and sexual messages, and even more serious behaviors such as assaults and attempted rapes. Today, the behavior that women experience is usually not so blatant, but some workers still experience problems. When a correctional manager is approached by a female subordinate who is being subjected to a work environment where other officers or workers conduct themselves in a manner that makes her uncomfortable, there is a tendency to encourage her to handle it herself and not rock the boat. All administrators fear negative publicity and lawsuits, and if a problem such as sexual harassment can be swept under the rug, there is a great temptation to do so. Even ethical administrators face conflicting duties. They have a duty to the organization (to keep from having to defend it against a lawsuit), but also to the employee (to help the employee undertake the best course of action), and that might be to pursue charges.

Possible ethical resolutions to the problem might be to talk to the individuals involved, punish the wrongdoers, or encourage the complainant to pursue internal or external sanctions. Obviously, administrators and managers themselves should take pains to avoid behavior that may be misconstrued as sexual coercion or be perceived by their employees as offensive. Managers have a higher duty than co-workers to set a tone for an office free from sexual innuendo that may lead to a description of the workplace as a hostile work environment. They have an ethical and legal affirmative duty to stop sexual humor, inappropriate touching, and inappropriate behavior before there is a complaint.

Administrators are in a difficult position when officers under their command have been accused of (and are guilty of) wrongs against inmates or probationers or parolees, such as brutality or harassment. If the administrator supports the officer (publicly or privately), he or she is in effect condoning that behavior and allowing it to continue. If the administrator exposes the officer and subjects him or her to punishment, then there is a possibility that the administrator will lose the trust and allegiance of other officers who feel betrayed. Of course, the ideal situation would be one where everyone involved would not condone such behavior and would resolve it satisfactorily. Realistically, this is usually not the case. Probably the best an administrator can do is to make clear to all what will not be tolerated and to serve as a role model; when wrongdoing is exposed, to treat the individuals involved fairly, with due process and offering them an opportunity to change; and if sanctions are deemed necessary, to administer them fairly and without favoritism.

It should be noted that in cases of a pattern of corruption, whether it be brutality or other kinds, it is hard to make the argument of ignorance. Prisons are smaller than small towns, and like a small town, there are no secrets unless one is willfully ignorant of them. Top administrators often have an outward orientation because their role is to communicate with legislators, the central office, and the community; however, a good administrator never ignores his or her own backyard. MBWA (Management by Walking Around), and having a good sense of what is happening in the institution has always been the mark of a good administrator and is also the best defense against having the institution end up on the front page of the newspaper.

Correctional Management and Unions

Unions have so far been seen by researchers as a resistant force to rehabilitation, and only concerned with individual benefits for members rather than the mission or goal of corrections. Unions provide legal assistance to officers in personnel and legal attacks, and often support officers who, many would argue, have no business working in corrections. In California, for instance, unions have provided legal assistance to officers who have been accused of assaulting inmates, having sex with inmates, giving drugs to inmates, and setting up gladiator fights between inmates (Josi and Sechrest, 1998: 161). Governor Davis attempted to direct $4 million to the correctional officer union for the officers' defense fund. In effect, the public would have ended up paying for both the prosecution of errant officers and their defense costs, as well as their salary. When senators discovered the plan, criticism was so strong that the administration cancelled the funding, although the officers' union still received the money to be used for other things, and officers obtained the pay raise and other concessions demanded in contract negotiations (Salladay, 1999).

Unions have been very successful in protecting and improving the position of the correctional officer. There is no doubt that states where unions are active are those states where correctional officers receive better pay and working conditions. In the latest budget cuts in California, only corrections has so far escaped proposed cuts, and some observers contend that this has more to do with the strength of the correctional officers' union than Californians' desire to take money away from health services and education and give it to prisons.

Cross-Sex Supervision

Cross-sex supervision is emerging as a volatile issue in the management of prisons. In the seventeenth and eighteenth century female prisoners were housed together in jails, with predictable results. Women were raped, sexually exploited and sold themselves for food and other goods. With the development of the Walnut Street Jail and penitentiaries, women were separated from male inmates, but still guarded by men, and sexual exploitation continued. Various scandals and exposes of prostitution rings led to women's reform groups pressuring legislatures to build completely separate institutions for women in the late 1800s and early 1900s. Finally, women were guarded by women, although men often held the highest administrative positions in these institutions.

This pattern continued until the mid-1970s when female officers challenged state prison systems' hiring patterns that barred them from working in institutions for men. Female officers had a very constricted career path in corrections when they were only allowed in institutions for women. Few could get promoted, and they often had to move great distances to the only facility in the state for women even if a prison for men was in their hometown. States resisted assigning women to prisons for men because of a fear that they would be victimized, that they would have less control over the inmates, and that they would "sexually excite" the inmates, leading to disruption in the institution.

In *Dothard v. Rawlinson* (433 U.S. 321, 97 S.Ct. 2720, 53 L.Ed. 2d 786 [1977]), the Supreme Court agreed with these fears, but only because the Alabama prison where Diane Rawlinson wanted to work had such high levels of violence that it was already under a federal monitor. The dictum of this case convinced many state systems that, despite the holding that Rawlinson could be prohibited from the Alabama prison, in most situations, women would have to be allowed in. And so they were, and early evaluations showed that they did their job about as well as male officers (Zimmer, 1986; Zupan, 1992). Inmates tended to appreciate the presence of women, although evaluations indicated inmates had concerns over privacy and the ability of female officers to protect them. Male officers were much more antagonistic toward their presence.

Today about 20 percent of the state correctional officer force and thirty percent of the federal correctional officer force are women. Women work in prisons for men in forty-six states (Reichel, 1997: 379). There is great variability, however, in how many women work in prisons for men. In some states only about 1 percent of the force in prisons for men are women, while in others the percentage is closer to 10 percent (Reichel, 1997: 379). Criticism of female officers in prisons for men has centered on the fact that they tend to be weaker and less able to protect themselves, that they may be subject to intimidation or seduction from inmates, and that they create sexual tension in the prison. Male inmates express mixed views regarding female officers. Understandably, they object to having women watch them take showers or go to the bathroom. Some also complain that women engender desire and fantasies. However, male inmates also report appreciating the presence of women who seem to care more than male officers and are able to treat them with respect.

Another type of problem occurs when the actions of female C.O.s may be misinterpreted by male inmates. Even if the female C.O. is merely expressing a professional interest in the inmate, or when she performs her job in a manner that is more interactive than that of male C.O.s, a male inmate may see the female C.O. as desiring a personal relationship. Female C.O.s must learn to interact with male inmates in such ways as to make it clear that they do not desire personal involvement. Of course, there are also situations where romantic relationships do develop—between female C.O.s and male inmates, between male C.O.s and female inmates, and between C.O.s and inmates of the same sex. These are always against institutional rules, unethical, and in many states, illegal.

The ironic effect of these court cases and the entry of women into prisons for men was that male officers were no longer barred from working in prisons for women. In the early 1980s, fairly small percentages of male officers could be found in prisons for women, and they were restricted to public places. Now, male officers are assigned to all posts inside prisons for women, including sleeping and shower areas. In some states, over half of the total guard force in women's prisons are men. Thus, male officers again are in positions of power over women and again, abuses are occurring. An increasing number of incidents where male officers have coerced female prisoners to have sex or, in some cases, sexually assaulted them, have been substantiated.

Amnesty International (1999) condemned the practice of allowing male officers to guard female inmates and cited many court cases across the nation that resulted in officers being fired or indicted and convicted of sexual assault or misfeasance. Sex between an officer and inmate is always coercive because of the vast power differential between the two parties. A recent lawsuit filed on behalf of female inmates in New York alleges a pattern of sexual abuse by officers at Albion Correctional facility and across the state. Further, the suit claims that the Department of Correctional Services cannot "prevent and remedy sexual misconduct. . . ." There are also allegations that female inmates who complained about sexual harassment and abuse were subject to transfer, solitary confinement, or disciplinary charges. In 2002, an officer was convicted of third-degree rape; the female inmate had an abortion after she learned she was pregnant (Craig, 2003).

It is clear that the reality of cross-sex supervision has created a major problem for administrators. Observers note that widespread abuse could not occur with either the tacit consent or clear negligence of administration because in the instances of documented abuse, the perpetrator often had multiple victims and/or there had been inmate reports of harassment. Management's task is to eliminate or minimize the incidents of officers sexually abusing or exploiting inmates. Selection, training, and supervision are the key elements in protecting inmates. Some states are considering reducing and restricting job assignments of male officers in women's institutions. Officer unions have been resistant to such solutions, and there will be court actions regarding management decisions to bar men from women's institutions. Any generalized rule barring men from supervising women is an insult to men because it implies that they cannot control themselves. However, if incidents continue and departments are unable or unwilling to employ selection criteria, training, oversight, and discipline to minimize or eliminate them, then removing the opportunity for such conduct may be the last resort.

CONCLUSION

In this chapter we have touched on some of the ethical issues that correctional personnel face. These individuals have much in common with other criminal justice practitioners, especially in the area of discretion, but they are also in a unique position in that they hold power over the most basic aspects of life for confined inmates. This position allows correctional officers either to intensify the humiliation that incarcerated offenders feel or to make the prison experience more tolerable for those who serve time. The difficult decisions for correctional officers arise from the personal relationships that develop with inmates, the trust that is sometimes betrayed, the favors that seem harmless, and the coercive environment that makes violence normal and caring abnormal. Correctional treatment personnel have their own problems in resolving conflicts between loyalty toward clients and toward the system. To be in a helping profession in a system geared for punishment is a difficult challenge for anyone, and the temptation to retreat into bureaucratic compliance is ever present.

Although this chapter has discussed officers mistreating inmates and correctional professionals engaging in other unethical conduct, we do not mean to imply that criminal justice workers are blatantly or pervasively unethical. Arguably, the criminal justice system operates only as well as it does because of the caring, committed, honest people who choose it as a career.

REVIEW QUESTIONS

1. Describe the C.O. subculture.
2. Describe the formal ethical code for correctional personnel.
3. Choose three ethical issues of C.O.s and analyze them by using the ethical frameworks.
4. Discuss the differences between guarding jail inmates and guarding state prison inmates.
5. What are the two interests that treatment staff have to balance? Give examples.
6. Choose and discuss three ethical issues of managers.

ETHICAL DILEMMAS

Situation 1

You are a prison guard supervising a tier. One of the inmates comes to you and asks a favor. Because he is a troublemaker, his mail privileges have been taken away. He wants you to mail a letter for him. You figure it's not such a big deal; besides, you know he could make your job easier by keeping the other inmates on the tier in line. What would you tell him?

Situation 2

As a new C.O. you soon realize that there is a great deal of corruption and graft taking place in the prison. Guards routinely bring in contraband for inmates in return for money, food bought for the inmates' mess hall finds its way into the trunks of staff cars, and money is being siphoned from inmate accounts. You are not sure how far up the corruption goes. Would you keep your mouth shut? They're just inmates, anyway. Would you go to your supervisors? What if, in exposing the corruption, you implicated yourself? What if you implicated a friend?

Situation 3

You are a prison psychologist, and during the course of your counseling session with one drug offender, he confessed he has been using drugs. Obviously, this is a serious violation of prison rules. Should you report him? What if he told you of an impending escape plan?

SUGGESTED READINGS

Conover, T. 2000. *New Jack: Guarding Sing Sing.* New York: Random House.

Crouch, B. (Ed.). 1980. *Keepers: Prison Guards and Contemporary Corrections.* Springfield, IL: Charles C. Thomas.

Johnson, R. 2002. *Hard Time: Understanding and Reforming the Prison.* Pacific Grove, CA: Brooks/Cole.

Kauffman, K. 1988. *Prison Officers and Their World.* Cambridge, MA: Harvard University Press.

Martin, D. 1993. *Committing Journalism: The Prison Writings of Red Hog.* New York: Norton.

Pollock, J. 2003. *Prisons and Prison Life: Costs and Consequences.* Los Angeles, CA: Roxbury.

13

Corrections in
the Community

Key Terms

community corrections
net widening
cynicism
punitive law enforcer
welfare/therapeutic worker

passive time server enforcer
peacemaking corrections
stigmatization
Victim Satisfaction model

Chapter Objectives

- Understand the concept of community corrections.
- Understand the ethical issues that might face probation and parole officers.
- Understand the concept of peacemaking corrections and restorative justice.

In the last chapter we focused on institutional corrections; however, the majority of offenders are on some form of community supervision—either probation or parole. The correctional professionals who supervise offenders in the community have slightly different ethical issues than those who work in an institution.

THE CONCEPT
OF COMMUNITY CORRECTIONS

Community corrections has a more positive and helpful image than does institutional corrections. However, even in this subsystem of the criminal justice system, the ideals of justice and care become diluted by bureaucratic mismanagement and personal agendas. Professionals in community corrections do not have the same power as police or correctional officers to use physical force, but they do have a great deal of non-physical power over the clients they control. Their authority and power can be used wisely and ethically or can become subverted to personal ends.

The concept of community corrections is supported by the ethics of care. It promotes meeting the needs of the offender and the victim (through restitution). Although a prison sentence is basically a rejection or banishment; community supervision promotes the concept of acceptance and integration with the community. Even parole, coming after a prison sentence, originally operated with the philosophy of reintegration. Utilitarianism also supports community corrections since the benefit to the community by not banishing the offender to prison is both financial and emotional. Even a retributive philosophy can support community corrections because some crimes are simply not serious enough to justify a prison sentence. Souryal (1992: 356; italics in original) writes that community corrections "signifies moral concern for the individual, one that is consistent with the natural law ethics of 'dignity of man,' the constitutional ethics of individualized treatment and *perhaps* the religious ethics of redemption."

Souryal (1996a) also discussed the "mystique" of probation. He described John Augustus, the so-called grandfather of probation, as personifying the concepts of probation, including the belief in redemption. Other principles that are consistent with the mystique include honesty, fidelity and obligation, justice, public service, and self control.

Typically, **community corrections** is a term that encompasses halfway houses, work release centers, probation, parole, and any other intermediate sanctions, such as electronic monitoring—either as a condition of probation or as a sentence in itself. Jails are somewhat of a hybrid. They are located in the community, but also share many characteristics of institutional corrections. We considered jail officers in the last chapter because the dilemmas that they face *vis-à-vis* whistleblowing, the officer subculture, and the use of coercive force against inmates are more similar to correctional officers than the issues that face probation and parole officers.

Probation and parole sentences involve supervision, but also usually require meeting some other conditions. Some of these conditions pose special issues of privacy, liberty, and impact on others. Electronic monitoring programs, usually using ankle bracelets and a telephone, raise issues of privacy. Such sanctions are said to blur the line between the offender and his or her family. Electronic monitoring sometimes involves a camera connected to the telephone. When the offender calls into a monitoring station, the monitor can see past the offender into the home. Is this a violation of family members' privacy, or do we consider it a consent entry? In general, probation and parole entails consent for warrantless searches, but is it really consent when the option is prison? And, if the offender is said to give consent, how does that affect family members?

Some contend that we are needlessly "widening the net" of corrections and putting more and more people on some form of correctional supervision. Further, the use of surveillance techniques against offender populations is spilling over into other contexts. For instance, drug testing started with probationers and now seems to be common in the workplace. Other forms of surveillance start with correctional populations, but then become accepted practices in other applications. For instance, metal detectors are used now in a number of settings, and some workplaces use a polygraph, monitor employees' calls, use video cameras, track e-mails, and in other ways apply the surveillance practices created for lawbreakers to the rest of us (Staples, 1997).

The use of alcohol programs and threat of punitive sanctions raise issues of personal liberty and freedom. Since alcohol is a legal substance, should we punish convicted felons for drinking while on probation? The argument is that convicted felons do not have to accept conditions of probation that prohibit alcohol—they could choose prison—but is that a legitimate choice? Further, while such conditions may make sense for those convicted of driving while intoxicated, do the technical conditions of "no alcohol" make sense for a burglar who did not attempt to explain or defend his actions by claiming to be drunk at the moment of the crime?

The danger of intermediate sanctions is that because they are typically so innocuous, they are used more frequently for offenders who may not have received any formal system response in years past. Unfortunately, what sometimes happens is that the offender, once in the system, fails because of technical violations and becomes more and more immersed in the system. This problem of **net widening** is not only problematic from an ethical stand, but also for purely pragmatic reasons of cost. Can we foresee a time when a large portion of the population is on some type of governmental monitoring status? Some say it is already here. We may be happy to note that tax monies may not be burdened by such monitoring, since the trend to charge offenders supervision fees is growing. Still, other than providing employment for the legions of criminal justice students who are graduating from colleges and universities, are there good reasons for the dramatic expansion of the net of corrections?

PROBATION AND PAROLE OFFICERS

Formal ethical guidelines for probation and parole officers are provided by the A.C.A. code, as well as their own ethics codes (see, the box on page 352). Probation and parole officers are considered more professional than correctional officers: they typically have at least a bachelor's degree if not a graduate degree, they are subject to fewer organizational controls in the form of rule books and policies, and they have a great deal of discretion. The formal ethics of the profession is summarized by the ideal of service—to the community and to the offender. In fact, whether to emphasize offenders' needs over community needs, or vice versa, is at the heart of a number of different ethical dilemmas for the probation and parole officer. Other ethical issues are more similar to those encountered in the other subsystems discussed; they primarily revolve around decisions to substitute personal values and goals for organizational values. In the next several sections we will touch on some of the themes of previous chapters—the use of discretion, officer subcultures, and relationships with clients.

Use of Discretion

Discretion in probation exists at the point of sentencing: Probation officers make recommendations to judges concerning sentences. Discretion also exists during supervision, as probation officers decide when to file violation reports, decide what recommendation to make to the judge during revocation hearings, and make numerous decisions along the way regarding the people on their caseload. Parole board members or their designees make decisions regarding release, and parole officers have the same discretion in managing their caseload that probation officers do. What are the criteria used for these decisions?

Federal Probation Officers' Association Code of Ethics

As a Federal Probation Officer, I am dedicated to rendering professional service to the courts, the parole authorities, and the community at large in effecting the social adjustment of the offender.

I will conduct my personal life with decorum, will neither accept nor grant favors in connection with my office, and will put loyalty to moral principles above personal consideration.

I will uphold the law with dignity and with complete awareness of the prestige and stature of the judicial system of which I am a part. I will be ever cognizant of my responsibility to the community which I serve.

I will strive to be objective in the performance of my duties, respect the inalienable rights of all persons, appreciate the inherent worth of the individual, and hold inviolate those confidences which can be reposed in me.

I will cooperate with my fellow workers and related agencies and will continually attempt to improve my professional standards through the seeking of knowledge and understanding.

I recognize my office as a symbol of public faith and I accept it as a public trust to be held as long as I am true to the ethics of the Federal Probation Service. I will constantly strive to achieve these objectives and ideals, dedicating myself to my chosen profession.

SOURCE: Adopted September 1960. Federal Probation Officers' Association, Washington, D.C. Revised March 1993. The Federal Probation Pretrial Officers Association. Reprinted with permission. All rights reserved.

Usually, the risk to the public is the primary factor, but other considerations also intrude. Some of these other considerations are ethical; some might not be. How would one evaluate the criteria of race, crime, family ties, the crowding in institutions, the status of the victim, the judge's preference, or the publicity of the crime? Are these ethical criteria?

QUERY

Probation officers' dilemmas—What would you do?
- A judge directed me to change my negative recommendation for probation to a favorable recommendation.
- I found out that my supervisor changed a negative recommendation I had given to a positive recommendation.
- A judge instructed us that if we can convince female defendants to get Norplant (a birth control device) he will waive court costs and fines.

Probation officers write presentence reports to help judges decide sentences, but research has found that there may be errors in the information presented and that some officers are not as thorough as others in gathering information. This may not make much difference if it is true, as some have found, that probation officers' recommendations and judges' decisions are almost completely determined by the current offense and prior record (White-head, 1991).

Probation and parole officers have the authority and power to recommend revocation. This power is also limited because probation and parole officers' recommendations can be ignored by the judge or parole hearing officer. Yet the implicit power an officer has over the individuals on his or her caseload must be recognized as an important element of the role, not to be taken lightly or misused.

Some practices in decision making are clearly unethical and illegal. Peter Maas's (1983) book, *Marie,* details a scheme in Tennessee that involved "selling" paroles to convicts. However, other situations are perhaps more difficult to judge as unethical or not. In a controversy in Texas, ex-parole board members were found to have sold their services as "parole consultants" to inmates and inmates' families in order to help them obtain a favorable release decision. Although the practice evidently was not against any state law and those who participated described their help as simply explaining the process and helping the inmate prepare a presentation to the board, many viewed it as unethical. There is at least the possibility that what the inmate was buying was an ex-parole board member's influence. The situation was brought to light when a serial killer was arrested for yet another murder while out on parole. When how he obtained parole was investigated, it was discovered that one of these ex-parole board members/"parole consultants" had been hired by the inmate. Whether that had anything to do with a favorable parole decision will never be known, but many allege there is at least the appearance of impropriety in the arrangement, and steps were taken to eliminate the practice.

Any time government officials go into the private sector and trade on their status as ex-officials, we feel uncomfortable. There are specific laws against influence peddling at some levels of government, reflecting this discomfort. In some situations, the possibility of private gain may influence how the official performs his or her job while in office, as in the case of military officers who make decisions on contracts with private vendors and then end up in highly paid, visible positions with the company immediately upon retirement. In other instances, the ability to provide an open door, inside information, or favorable decisions is considered unfair when used only for those who are willing to pay, as in the case of ex-White House staff members who sell their services as consultants to foreign countries or corporations, or those with family connections to the White House who are paid by those seeking presidential pardons.

Probation/Parole Officer Subculture

The subculture of probation and parole officers has never been as extensively documented as that of police and correctional officers. Due to differences between these professions, the subculture of the former is not as pervasive or strong as that of the latter. On one hand, probation and parole officers do not feel as isolated as police or correctional officers do. They experience no stigmatization, they have normal working hours, they do not wear a depersonalizing uniform, and they have a less obviously coercive relationship with their clients. These factors reduce the need for a subculture.

On the other hand, one can probably identify some norms that might be found in any probation or parole office. First, there is a norm of **cynicism** toward clients. The subculture promotes the idea that clients are inept, deviant, and irredeemable. Probation and parole professionals who express positive attitudes toward clients' capacity for change are kidded as naive and guileless. Second, there is a pervasive subcultural norm of lethargy or minimal work output. This norm is supported by the view that officers are underpaid and overworked. Third, a norm of individualism can be identified. This relates to the idea that while parole and probation officers may seek opinions from other professionals in the office, there is an unspoken rule that each runs his or her own caseload; to offer unsolicited opinions about decisions another person makes about his or her client violates this norm of autonomy.

Although there does not seem to be the "blue curtain of secrecy" to the same extent as found in policing, there is no doubt a norm against informing on colleagues for unethical or illegal behaviors. This relates somewhat to the norm of individualism, but is also part of the pervasive occupational subculture against informing on colleagues. Probation and parole officers may see and hear unethical behaviors and not feel comfortable in coming forward with such information. If they work in an office where the norm against exposing such wrongdoing is strong, they may indeed suffer similar sanctions as police and correctional officers for exposing others' wrongdoing.

There also seems to be the same management tendency that is seen in law enforcement to hide or ignore wrongdoing on the part of individual officers. This may be a misguided utilitarianism in managers who are attempting to protect the organization from public scandal, or it may be simply self-interested egoism from managers who fear that the blame will be directed to them. For whatever reason, there seems to be a pervasive tendency to ignore officers who are obviously unable or unwilling to do the job. Some officers even point out that those who are arrested themselves for DWI or other crimes continue to work as probation and parole officers. If this is true, it seems ironic that the supervisors have so little moral authority over the supervised.

Probation and parole officers have been described as adopting different roles on the job. Recall that police have been described by the watchman, caretaker, and law enforcer typology. In the same way, probation and parole officers have been described by their orientation to the job and individual adaptation to organizational goals. For instance, Souryal (1992) summarizes other literature in his description of the following types: the punitive law enforcer, the welfare/therapeutic practitioner, the passive time server, and the combined model.

Different ethical issues can be discussed in relation to each of these types. For instance, the **punitive law enforcer** may need to examine his or her use of authority. This officer may have a tendency to use illegal threats and violate the due-process protections that each client deserves. The **welfare/therapeutic worker** may need to think about natural law rights of privacy and autonomy. These officers have a tendency to infringe on clients' privacy more because of their mindset that they are helping the client (and indeed, they might be), but the client may prefer less help and more privacy. The **passive time server** needs to be aware of ethical formalism and concerns of duty. All of us may have some tendency to be a time server in our respective professions. It is important to continue to take personal inventories and ask whether we are still putting in a "day's work for a day's pay."

As is the case for many of the other criminal justice professionals we have discussed in this book, parole and probation officers often have a great deal of flexibility in their day. They leave the office to make field contacts; they often "trade" weekdays for weekend days, since weekends are more conducive to home visits. This flexibility is necessary if they are to do the job, but some abuse it and use the freedom to accomplish personal tasks or spend time at home. Some offices have attempted to prevent this behavior by instituting measures such as time clocks and strict controls on movements, but these controls are inconsistent with professionalism and not conducive to the nature of the task. Other offices develop norms that accept unethical practices and lethargy. Once this occurs, it becomes a difficult pattern to change. If it is already present, a single officer will have a hard time not falling into the pattern. If all officers feel overwhelmed by their caseloads and the relative lack of power they have to do anything about failure, then the result may be that they throw up their hands and adopt a "who cares?" attitude. If the supervisor does not exhibit a commitment to the goal of the organization, does not encourage workers, treats certain officers with favoritism, or seems more concerned with his or her personal career than with the needs of the office, then there is an inevitable deterioration of morale.

QUERY

Probation officers' dilemmas—What would you do?

- One morning a fellow officer was meeting with a probationer. This officer was yelling profanities and was very rude to this probationer, for whatever reasons.
- A close colleague at work was dating a probationer and they were planning to move in together. The close colleague told me about it.
- I took a supervisor's job and one of the officers I supervised didn't do anything—all day. Read magazines at her desk. The thing was, I was told I couldn't fire her. She had already been transferred around, and now I was stuck with her.
- In one office I worked, there was an officer who took naps in the afternoon. It was well known. He would close his door and lie down on the floor. After a couple hours he would open his door again and go on. No one did anything about it.

Whitehead (1991) discusses workers' frustration over incompetents being promoted, low wages, and high caseloads that lead to burnout. Souryal (1992) notes that low pay, a public view that probation and parole are ineffective, and the politicization of parole and probation are factors in professionals' feeling that their role is ambiguous, contradictory, and politically vulnerable. Disillusionment becomes almost inevitable. Although these issues exist in many organizations, they are especially problematic in a profession that requires a great deal of emotional investment on the part of the practitioner. If the organization does not encourage and support good workers, then it is no wonder that what develops is an informal subculture that encourages minimum effort and treats organizational goals with sarcasm and cynicism.

Caseload Supervision

Discretion exists not only at the recommendation to release stage, but also throughout supervision. Officers do not make the decision to revoke, but they do make the decision to file a violation report and make a recommendation to the judge or the parole hearing examiner as to whether to continue on supervision status with perhaps new conditions, or revocation and a prison sentence. Many do not submit violation reports automatically upon discovery of every offender infraction. In this way they are like police officers who practice selective enforcement of the laws. And, like police officers, some of their criteria for decision making are ethical and some are not. Also, like police officers, many report ethical dilemmas when the law doesn't seem to be able to take into account social realities, such as poverty.

The discretion to decide when to write a violation report is a powerful element in the control the officer has over the offender, but it obviously can be a difficult decision to make sometimes. If the officer excuses serious violations (e.g., possessing a firearm or continuing drug use), and the decision to do so is based on personal favoritism, fear, or bribery, then that officer is putting the community at risk unethically. Those situations in which the officer sincerely believes the offender made a mistake, has extraordinary excuses for such misbehavior, and is a good risk still present a danger to the community. Is the decision any more ethical because of the officer's belief in the offender? Would it be more ethical to conduct oneself "by the book" and always submit violation reports when the offender committed any violation, including a purely technical one?

Probation and parole officers are presented with other dilemmas in their supervision of offenders. For instance, the offender often acquires a job without the employer's knowledge of his or her previous criminality. Is it the duty of the officer to inform the employer and thereby imperil the continued employment of the offender? What about when offenders become personally involved with others and refuse to tell them about their past history? Does the probation or parole officer have a duty to the unwary party? Recently, the issue of confidentiality *vis-à-vis* AIDS has emerged. If the probation or parole officer knows or suspects that the offender is HIV positive and the offender begins an intimate relationship with someone, does the officer have a duty to warn the other party? Most states protect the confidentiality of victims of AIDS, and in these cases the officer has a legal duty *not* to disclose. This issue is extremely problematic: The rights of the offender, the rights of unwary innocents, and the responsibilities of society are not well sorted out at this point.

QUERY

Probation officers' dilemmas—What would you do?

- I had a cousin on probation for his second DWI. No one in the family knows he is on probation. At a family gathering I see the probationer drinking (more than one drink).
- A friend from high school had a boyfriend on probation. The boyfriend had violated his conditions of probation and an M.T.R.P. (Motion to Revoke Probation) was filed in his case. The girlfriend wanted me to give her confidential information out of his file.
- I was having dinner at a nice restaurant and the manager on duty happened to be on my caseload and offered me a free dinner and gave me basketball tickets to five games.

What is the probation or parole officer's responsibility to the offender's family? If they are unwilling to help the offender and perhaps fear his or her presence, should the officer find a reason for revocation? Again, these questions revolve around competing loyalties to public and client. The correctional professional must balance these interests in every decision, and the decisions are often not easy to make.

Very similar to the police officer, at times the probation officer's role as a family member, or friend, conflicts with the professional role. Family members and/or friends may expect special treatment or expect that the officer will use his or her powers for unethical purposes. These are always difficult dilemmas because family and friends may not be sympathetic to the individual's ethical responsibilities to the organization and to society at large. Probation and parole officers are likely to have overlapping circles of acquaintances and family connections with those on their caseloads, especially in small towns. Confidentiality and favoritism are issues that come up frequently.

The officer also has to contend with the issue of gratuities. Again, similar to the police officer, probation or parole officers may be offered special treatment, material goods, or other items of value because of their profession. In most cases, the situation is even more clearly unethical for probation and parole officers because the gift is offered by a client over whom decisions are made, as opposed to police officers who may or may not ever be in a position to make a decision regarding a restaurant or convenience store manager. Probation departments have clear rules against any "business relationships" with probationers, and this makes sense, but probation officers in very small towns ask, "How can I avoid a business relationship with a client when the only coffee shop in town is run by one of my clients? Am I never to go there during the years he is on probation?" In the same manner as police, some probation and parole officers feel that the gifts offered are given in the spirit of gratitude or generosity and not to influence decision making.

QUERY

Probation officers' dilemmas—What would you do?

- I discovered that the applicant was an illegal alien but had a family of four with a baby who was born with a defect. His wife did not work and he was the sole provider of the family. The dilemma was that if INS was contacted, the individual would be deported while his family stayed with no support.
- Do I not collect fees from a client who is a single mother with three children because it would come out of her budget and mean she must neglect the needs of her children, or do I collect the fees and disregard the problems the client is struggling with, and alienate the client more?

Because probationers may appear to be similar to the probation or parole officer in socioeconomic status, family background, lifestyle, or personal value systems, there is a greater tendency to feel affinity and friendship for some clients. Some probation officers have been known to have clients baby-sit for them, to rent a room in their house, or to socialize with them and their families. Obviously, these personal relationships hinder the ability to perform one's official function as a protector of the community and enforcer for the legal system. Personal relationships of any type—romantic, platonic, or financial—are simply not appropriate or ethical for the probation and parole professional.

Corruption

No doubt there are some probation recommendations based on bribery or favoritism, or decisions not to violate based on unethical criteria. Sexual coercion of clients may exist. Urinalysis testing may be subverted by some corrupt scheme to switch test results. One should not be surprised if these practices exist, although they are not widespread and many people will complete their careers and retire without having heard about or being involved in any of them. However, it would be a wise approach to consider what one would do in a situation similar to the dilemmas described in this section, or similar to any of the others in this book.

Corrupt practices exist because honest people allow them to. Organizations experience corruption because they do not support and nurture ethical workers. Hopefully, the increasing professionalism of each of the subsystems of the criminal justice system will create a situation in which "rabble-rousers" don't have to lose careers and suffer subcultural sanctions because of standing up for what is ethical.

PAROLE

We have been discussing probation and parole officers simultaneously in the sections above, but there are some important distinctions between the two. First, parolees are perceived to be more of a threat to the community, and so the supervision role of parole officers is emphasized much more strongly than in probation where supervision has been balanced with a service/counseling emphasis. Further, the offenders are usually older and have a longer criminal record, so the relationship between supervisor and client might be different. It is certainly true that the problems faced by parolees are quite different than those probationers face.

It is estimated that roughly 600,000 prisoners are re-entering our communities each year (King and Mauer, 2002: 3). In fact, the number of releasees has increased in recent years. There was an increase of 8.4 percent in the number of individuals released from 1998 and 2000 (B.J.S.a, 2002: 7). Most of them have the same low levels of education and vocational skills that they had going into prison and have not had access to many, if any, rehabilitative programs in prison. Further, many of the new releasees will be those who *maxed out*—meaning they completed their entire sentence with no requirements to be supervised (Talbot, 2003).

Many of them return to prison—in fact, according to a recent Justice Department study, 67 percent of released inmates were charged with at least one serious crime within three years. The study tracked 272,111 released inmates in fifteen states. Other study findings indicated that the recidivism rate of offenders is worse than twenty years ago, not better, despite longer sentences imposed. Men were more likely to recidivate than women (68 percent compared to 57 percent); African Americans were more likely to recidivate than whites (73 percent compared to 63 percent), and young people under eighteen were more likely to recidivate than older offenders forty-five and over (80 percent compared to 45 percent). Offenders with the highest recidivism rates included car thieves, those convicted of receipt of stolen property, burglars, and those convicted of robbery (Murphy, 2002).

The fact is that our incarceration rates, currently one of the highest in the world, have had a tremendously negative impact on communities. Whole neighborhoods are affected when a large percentage of their population are sent away for years at a time. Generational effects are obvious; we know that children of inmates are six times as likely to be delinquent. More subtle effects exist as well. The economy and social fabric of a community is also affected when large numbers of young people are removed (Mauer and Chesney-Lind, 2002). Community corrections professionals have some amount of power in this scenario—they can make release recommendations and affect revocation rates. They can help offenders with re-entry problems or they can blindly enforce every bureaucratic rule.

Recall that under ethical formalism, to be an ethical professional one must do one's duty. What is the parole officer's duty? Some officers feel that they have met their ethical duty by explaining the rules to a parolee and then catching them if they "mess up." Others see a more expanded role wherein the officer has some duty to help the offender readjust to society. This may involve taking some responsibility for counseling the offender, referring him or her to services, acting as a troubleshooter or mediator in conflict with family or others, and acting as an advocate in obtaining help. In other words, this officer takes a proactive approach to the parolee's success. Is filing a violation report a success (because the offender was caught) or a failure (because the offender did not succeed)?

A NEW PARADIGM OF CORRECTIONS?

The high incarceration rate of this country has made a few people rich and others economically comfortable because of strong unions and/or white-collar jobs in corrections. Many more people have found poorly paid jobs keeping prisoners inside the bars. A huge network of profitable enterprise has sprung up because of the corrections industry. At the American Correctional Association meeting, delegates are enticed to a huge ballroom or conference hall filled from front to back with vendors. Participants pick up freebies of pens, water bottles, candy, and other items while they look at prison wares—everything from riot batons to stainless steel stools are displayed. The fact is that the field of corrections is big business, and it supports a huge number of ancillary businesses. We have become so inured to the concept of deprivation of liberty that it is hard to think of a different approach—but there might be one.

A relatively recent philosophical approach to crime and punishment has been called *restorative justice* or **peacemaking corrections.** Reichel (1997) briefly describes the origins of the movement during the development of restitution and community service sentences in the 1970s. Although these innovative sentences were originally touted as rehabilitative, as rehabilitative goals lost favor with public sentiment, rationales and justifications were redefined, and, instead of rehabilitation, restoration or reparation (for the victim) became the philosophical rationale behind such programs (Bazemore and Maloney, 1994).

Whether restitution was individual (with compensation paid directly to the victim) or symbolic (where the community benefited from the offender's labor or payments), the idea was to restore the victim to his or her condition before the victimization event, or if the victim was not easily identifiable, to produce a measurable positive effect for the community. For instance, Bazemore and Maloney (1994) discuss one program where community service offenders helped rebuild a town ravaged by a tornado. There are five goals of the approach:

1. The service meets a clearly defined and obvious need.

2. Service should symbolically link offender and victim, or offender and his or her community.

3. Offenders should be viewed as resources, and outcome measures are directed to the work itself (rather than the offender's behavior).

4. Offenders should be involved in planning and executing the projects.

5. Included should be a sense of accomplishment, closure, and community recognition. (adapted from Bazemore and Maloney, 1994: 27)

The historical origins of and analogies to restorative justice can be found throughout recorded history; early laws demanded victim compensation, and reparation has a much longer history than does penal servitude. Many advocates (cf. Umbreit, 1994; Umbreit and Carey, 1995; van Ness and Heetderks Strong, 1997) now believe that restorative justice quite appropriately places the emphasis back onto the victims, but can also be life affirming and positive for the offender as well. The key is in finding a method of restoration that is meaningful and somehow related to the offense instead of merely punitive labor—such as the infamous rock pile—which is devoid of worth to the victim, the offender, or society.

There are strong similarities and overlap between restorative justice and the peacekeeping model of corrections. Peacemaking corrections offers a similar approach of care and of *wholesight*, or looking at what needs to be done with both the heart and the head (Braswell and Gold, 2002). Both approaches are consistent with the ethics of care and might be considered a "feminine" model of justice because of the emphasis on needs rather than retribution.

One wonders what meaning and impact a restorative justice program might have on the offender. If one can assume that a retributive, punitive orientation results in an offender's perception of unfairness (through denial of victim, denial of injury, or a belief that a more serious victimization was visited upon the offender), then it is interesting to speculate that perhaps the offender would not be able to generate the rationalizations and excuses for his or her behavior if involved in a restorative justice program that focuses attention on the injuries of the victim and does not involve stigma, banishment, or exclusion for the offender.

Peacemaking circles or *healing circles* are one model of this type of correctional approach. In these circles, adapted from Native American and indigenous cultures interventions, the offender meets with the victims, his or her family, and other interested parties. The goal is to find some resolution to the problem; but the problem may not be simply the offender's wrongdoing; it could be the victim's behavior, or the family's failings. The orientation is acceptance of the person and rejection of the behavior (Umbreit, Coates and Vos, 2002).

Reintegrative Shaming versus Stigmatizing Shaming

As mentioned in an earlier chapter, there are a number of punishments inflicted on offenders today that incorporate the concept of shame. Judges have made those convicted of DWI use special license plates, sex offenders have had to put signs on their house, and offenders have had to confess and seek the forgiveness of their community by publishing an advertisement or making a public appearance of some kind.

These types of shaming punishments hark back to the stocks and pillory when punishment was effective arguably more because of the community scorn, rather than the physical pain involved. Some believe that it is not a useful or helpful trend; for instance, one A.C.L.U. spokesperson called such punishments "gratuitous humiliation that serves no social purpose" (cited in Book,

1999: 653). Whitman (1998) argues that the use of such penalties are contrary to a sense of dignity; and create an "ugly complicity" between the state and the community by setting the scene for "lynch justice."

There is even some question as to whether such punishments are legal because some state laws demand that probation conditions have a "rehabilitative function." In general, however, judges have imposed these punishments without much serious challenge. Legally, they seem to be acceptable, but what about ethically?

The major issue seems to be whether such shaming conditions are reintegrative or stigmatizing. Braithwaite (2000) is the most well-known spokesperson for reintegrative shaming. He argues that shame is different from guilt because it comes from one's beliefs about how one's community feels about the crime. He argues that societies that don't have shame attached to certain crimes have a lot of that type of crime. Thus, what is necessary to reduce crime is a return to the concept of shame.

According to Braithwaite (2000), **stigmatization** is disrespectful shaming. In punishments where the offender is treated as a bad person rather than someone who has done a bad act, the society is rejecting the individual, which leads the individual to reject society. He points out that some African societies that use reintegrative shaming have low crime rates, as does Japan, which uses techniques of reintegrative shaming for delinquents. The difference is that these cultures do not reject the individual; rather, they reject only the behavior. Individuals continue to feel a part of their family, school, neighborhood, and community. Stigmatizing punishments lead to oppositional subcultures; reintegrative interventions do not.

It is not a coincidence that communities that are more integrated and have stronger social ties have less crime. These communities are much more likely to be able to employ the concept of reintegrative shaming on its members and, thereby, control them. The corollary to this, of course, is that if one feels disenfranchised from society, then shaming will not work at all (Karp, 1998).

QUOTE

Key values of restorative justice are healing rather than hurting, respectful dialogue, making amends, caring and participatory community, taking responsibility, remorse, apology, and forgiveness.

Braithwaite, 2000: 300.

Karp (1998) provides an interesting perspective as to why restorative justice and reintegrative shaming interventions have received positive responses. The public may not feel that probation or other forms of alternative sanctions have the same moral condemnation that prison does; and, therefore, they cheapen or lesson the moral blame of the offender. Shaming penalties, however, emphasize the individual's responsibility to the victim and society. There is a strong dose of morality and redemption in such programs, and the public seems to respond to that.

Karp also emphasizes the difference between stigmatizing and reintegrative shaming. He points out that most of the shaming punishments that have been reported, such as sex offenders being required to post signs on their doors, are stigmatizing shaming punishments. They may lead to unintended results, such as the offender being victimized by the community through vigilante justice. This is what Whitman (1998) finds problematic and distasteful about such punishments. Recall that he saw the state as setting the scene for "lynch justice" and, in fact, such punishments have led to the community victimizing offenders. Megan's Laws that require registration of sex offenders and allow publication of such lists are questioned by some who point out that such laws have led to cases where an offender or his family have been attacked and, in some cases, actually driven from the community. Although one's response might be, "So what, he is a sex offender!" it should be noted that in some states, all sex crimes are included and this may mean a man who was convicted of statutory rape when he was eighteen because his girlfriend was sixteen. Further, the family members are also stigmatized and, arguably, they are innocent of wrongdoing.

Stigmatizing shaming punishments are ineffective with those who are already "on the margins" of society anyway. Reintegrative shaming uses whatever "community" the offender has, whether that be a family, workplace, neighbors, or school, to instill the shame that can lead to changing behavior. However, it may work only with those types of offenders who do feel a part of a community. These interventions are most common with juveniles and less serious offenders.

Ethical Issues in Restorative Justice

This approach to the problem of crime seems to be a healthy alternative to prison. There are some issues, however, that might be discussed. First, because such interventions are seen as so benign, they have the potential to create "net widening," further enlarging the scope of corrections over the citizenry (Roach, 2000). There are also questions of due process and whether restorative justice meets the traditional goals of crime prevention (Dzur and Wertheimer, 2002).

Another issue is the potential privacy issues of both the offender and other members that are involved. One of the strengths of restorative justice interventions is the inclusion of a number of parties, including the offender's family, co-workers, friends, as well as the victim and the victim's support group. But what if some individuals important to the process choose not to participate? In fact, even schools have trouble getting parents to involve themselves in their children's progress. It is entirely possible that a juvenile, otherwise qualified for a program, would not be able to participate because of an unwillingness of family members. Does this mean that the juvenile would be punished for having uncaring or unwilling parents?

It may be that parents are caring, but choose not to allow the state to intervene in what is considered "private" family business. Parents and relatives may point out that they have not broken any laws and the state cannot tell them what to do. Even when the process is seen as a positive intervention, whenever state actors are involved, there is a potential of coercion and some people react strongly to that.

Restorative justice programs are looked upon with favor by victim's rights groups because of the idea of restoration and restitution for victims. What happens, however, when victims aren't as harmed as offenders have needs? The approach is oriented to meeting the needs of victims and offenders, and in some cases, it may be that the offender is needier. Would a victim reject such an approach? Should the victim be able to veto this approach and demand traditional punishment? Is it possible for a victim to be too vindictive?

One example of an interesting program that can be labeled restorative is the Texas mediation program. This program allows the family members of homicide victims to meet with the killer, even if the killer is on death row. Such meetings are preceded by months of counseling by trained volunteers for both the offender and the victims. The counselors decide when both parties are ready to meet, and the meeting doesn't take place if the victim is seen as too emotionally fragile or too retaliatory; or if the offender is seen as too manipulative or doesn't admit culpability.

In one mediation session, a woman and her teenage granddaughter met with the killer of the woman's daughter and young girl's mother. The father and brothers refused to participate, but the mother and daughter wanted to see and talk to their loved one's killer. The daughter was only five years old when the killing took place, and she wanted to learn more about how her mother died and to see the man who did it. The offender turned out to be a man who had killed the victim when he was fifteen. His childhood was marked by sexual abuse, physical abuse, and abandonment. He and another teenager were high on "speedballs" (cocaine and methamphetamine) when they were picked up by the young mother after their car broke down. They raped and killed her. In prison, he got to know the family of a cellmate who eventually adopted him. The family evidently had been instrumental in changing his life and outlook and his goal for participating was to tell them how sorry he was for the crime and ask forgiveness.

The mediation between the women and young man continued for most of one day. The counselor guided the discussion. He told them what he remembered from the crime, and they told him about the dead woman. At the end of the day, the two women hugged the murderer and had a picture taken with his arms around their shoulders (Nowell, 2001). While not all, or even most, mediations end with the victims and offenders hugging, this story is amazing in the illustration of the power of humans to move beyond anger, hate, and grief to some type of solace and forgiveness. The women experienced a good deal of negative reaction from their family members for participating and, especially, for having their picture taken with him. From their point of view, the experience left them with something more than they had before—they had some glimpse of their loved one in her final hours, and some reassurance that the offender was not an inhumane monster.

It should be noted that victims' rights groups tend to be cautious about restorative justice programs in general because of the focus on offenders. The anger that victims feel at the offender and the system that ignores their needs leaves little room for forgiveness. Most groups advocate harsher punishments, not restorative justice; they discuss "rights" rather than "needs" and, thus, draw their moral legitimacy from retribution rather than the ethics of care. However, there are other sources that also argue that forgiveness and restorative justice are just as beneficial to the victim as the offender (Morris, 2000).

There is an emerging perspective that indicates the pendulum has swung too far in making the victim feel a part of the process. The **Victim Satisfaction model** (Stickels, 2003) proposes that Packer's models of due process or crime control have given way to victim satisfaction. That is, the system and its actors (specifically, prosecutors) attempt to appease the victim in all decisions from charging to plea bargaining. This creates a situation wherein the criminal justice system becomes, in effect, a civil system with the victim as plaintiff and the prosecutor a plaintiff's attorney. The implications are diverse and include cost-benefit issues (is it worth prosecuting some cases?) and also justice (does the victim's perspective of just resolution always equal an objective view of a just resolution?). This emerging perspective is contrary to the more established perspective that the system "forgets" the crime victim and is solely focused on the offender.

Does a murderer ever deserve forgiveness? Did the women in the mediation program forgive the offender or simply recognize his humanity? We can't say that the family members who can't forgive are wrong, so is there ever a good in forgiveness? These questions are at the heart of restorative justice and probably explain why it has, thus far, been limited largely to nonserious property crimes and with juvenile offenders. The questions posed, however, are at the very heart of any discussion of justice and ones we've asked in prior chapters. Specifically, do criminals ever deserve forgiveness?

QUERY

Would you want to meet with the murderer of a loved one? What would you want to ask him or her? Would you be able to forgive?

CONCLUSION

In this chapter we looked at two approaches to community corrections. The first was to explore the traditional forms of community corrections; specifically, probation and parole. We looked at the ethical issues of these professionals in the same way that other criminal justice professionals were considered in previous chapters. The second approach was to explore a new paradigm of justice called restorative justice. In this model, rights are replaced with needs, and punishment is replaced with restoration. It is a fairly new idea in corrections, and the concepts are still being formed. However, it presents important questions about how to best meet the ends of justice.

REVIEW QUESTIONS

1. Describe the probation officer subculture.
2. Discuss ethical issues for probation and parole officers.
3. Describe the principles of restorative justice and contrast them with traditional models of justice.
4. Distinguish between reintegrative shaming and stigmatizing shaming.
5. Explain whether the ethical systems would support restorative justice programs.

ETHICAL DILEMMAS

Situation 1

You are a probation officer and have a specialized sex-offender caseload. The judge disagrees with a recommendation for a prison sentence and places an offender on probation. This man was convicted of molesting his four-year-old niece. One of the conditions of his probation is that he notify you whenever he is around children. He becomes engaged and moves in with a woman who has three children under the age of twelve. You believe that the man is not repentant and that there is a good chance he will molest these children. Although the woman knows his criminal history, she does not seem to care and, in fact, allows him to baby-sit the young girls. The judge has indicated that he will not entertain new conditions or a revocation unless there is evidence of a crime, but you understand from the offender's counselor that he continues to be sexually aroused by children. What can you do?

Situation 2

You are a probation officer with a DWI probationer that had not been reporting for any of the court-sanctioned programs and a Motion to Revoke was supposed to be filed. However, a very high-ranking administrator in your office told you to not file the M.T.R., nor take any negative actions, as this person was a personal friend, and, anyway, he wasn't a "serious criminal."

Situation 3

You are a parole officer who has a single mother with three hyperactive, attention-deficit-disorder young children on your caseload. She receives no support from her ex-husband. Her mother wants nothing to do with her or the children, as the mother believes "God is punishing her." She works as a topless dancer but hates it. She continues dancing because it pays the bills so well. In an effort to deal with stress, you know she smokes marijuana on a fairly regular basis. Obviously, this is a violation of probation. However, if you file a violation report on her, she will go back to prison. You know she is doing the best she can with her kids, is very involved with their school, and they are strongly bonded to her. You worry about what will happen to the kids. What would you do?

SUGGESTED READINGS

Braithwaite, J. 2000. "Shame and Criminal Justice." *Canadian Journal of Criminology* 42, 3: 281–301.

Braswell, M., B. McCarthy and B. McCarthy. 2002. *Justice, Crime, and Ethics.* Cincinnati, OH: Anderson.

Mauer, M., M. Chesney-Lind. and T. Clear. 2002. *Invisible Punishment: The Collateral Consequences of Mass Imprisonment.* New York: The Sentencing Project.

Van Ness, D., and K. Heetderks Strong 1997. *Restoring Justice.* Cincinnati, OH: Anderson.

14

Criminal Justice Policy

Making Ethical Choices in Troubled Times

Key Terms

ideology

explication

imperative principle

utilitarian principle

generalization principle

Chapter Objectives

- Become familiar with the ways that paradigms and ideologies shape our beliefs about crime and how to control criminals.
- Understand that the fundamental nature of crime control in a democracy includes respect for individual liberties.
- Understand how criminal justice policies are formed by belief systems.
- Know the elements of good, ethical leadership.
- Review procedures for individual ethical decision making.

In this book we have explored ethical issues in each of the subsystems of the criminal justice system. We have discovered certain themes that run through each of the subsystems—the ethical use of authority, power, force, and discretion; subcultural barriers to ethical decision making; and the importance of ethical leadership. In this final chapter we will reiterate these themes. We start with a discussion of how ideologies (albeit somewhat stereotypical) have the power to shape our thinking about crime and social control.

POLICY MAKING IN CRIMINAL JUSTICE

Professionals in criminal justice are called upon to enforce laws and also to implement policies. Policy making is undertaken by the executive and legislative branches of the government, as well as by agencies in the criminal justice system. Policies can be formal or informal. They have tremendous influence on people's lives. For instance, the policy of *zero tolerance* in the war on drugs has meant that many individuals have become entangled in the criminal justice system. If laws are the skeleton of the system, then policies are the muscles—they influence the way that the laws are enforced.

Policies sometimes have more to do with belief systems than with empirical reality. In the next section we present an extended discussion of liberalism and conservatism. Although these descriptions are stereotypical, they are so powerful in our thought processes and so often used that a great deal of meaning is transmitted by their use. The label of *liberal* or *conservative* communicates definitional elements about what is right and wrong and good and bad in social control that, if not universally agreed upon, at least provide a basis of comparison.

Ideologies of Liberalism and Conservatism

An **ideology** is "a set of general and abstract beliefs or assumptions about the correct or proper state of things, particularly with respect to the moral order and political arrangements, which serve to shape one's positions on specific issues" (Hornum and Stavish, 1978: 143). Two opposing ideologies regarding crime and criminals are the liberal versus the conservative view. Both the liberal perspective and the conservative perspective are primarily operating under the consensus paradigm in that they accept the basic definitions of crime as given by law.

The Liberal Perspective The liberal perspective explains criminal behavior and deviance through reference to psychological, social, or biological causation. Because individuals are seen as influenced by factors outside their control, they are not completely culpable for their crimes. Rather, explanations are developed to explain behavior, including psychological, sociological, and other definitions of "why" behavior occurs.

In policing, the liberal perspective is manifested by attempts of police departments to make themselves more accessible to the community, and departmental approval for informal means of resolving disputes. Innovations such as neighborhood or community policing, team policing, and youth groups attempt to help the police understand and empathize with certain groups they come into contact with. The liberal ideology would endorse police officers as a positive social control tool in their provision of services to the community that would, in turn, influence pro-social values. For instance, *officer friendly* programs in schools not only teach bicycle safety tips but also give the message that the police officer is a friend and that the child should look up to him or her as a role model. "Storefront" police stations transmit the message that the police are a part of the community, and neighborhood policing allows the police officer to become involved in non–crime issues in the community, creating and cementing relational ties to the community that is being policed.

In courts, the liberal perspective is seen in individualized justice—the preference to consider the offender rather than the offense. This would involve the acceptance of reasons or rationales for unlawful behavior. For instance, the burglar who had lost his job and had bills to pay, the enraged wife who killed her husband because he left her for another woman, or the ghetto youth whose father turned him onto drugs would all have their individual backgrounds considered in decisions regarding responsibility and punishment. The liberal perspective perceives that law cannot easily label and set punishment for wrongdoing because human behavior is complex, not categorical. Thus, the courts, and their human representatives in the legal system, must use discretion to administer individual justice.

In corrections, the liberal ideology supports most correctional programming. Attempts to make criminals more like us, by vocational training, education, and social skills training, are based on the idea that the criminal could change given a different environment, different influences, or solutions to problems such as illiteracy or addiction. Correctional programs target biological problems (addiction), social problems (negative role models), or psychological problems (weak ego state), and all are based on the assumption that if the problem is corrected, the criminal would no longer commit crime.

The liberal perspective may identify as unethical any treatment of the offender by the system that does not take into account individual factors. For instance, it would be considered unethical to ignore the fact that an individual was coerced into an illegal action. It would be unethical to ignore a prisoner's need for special attention or medical care. It would be unethical to prosecute a very young offender in the same way that one would a more culpable older offender. It would be unethical to ignore evidence that an individual was mentally ill when committing an offense. Basically, the liberal perspective is concerned when the law tries to uphold some unrealistic standard of objective justice, since that is not possible.

The Conservative Perspective The conservative perspective, in general, agrees with the liberal that the legal code is a true representation of society's morals and values, but differs in the perception of the offender. Rather than influenced by forces beyond their control, offenders are seen as persons who freely choose actions and must be held accountable for them. Public safety is paramount and victims deserve more care and attention than offenders. Thus, if some technical rules are violated in order to get an offender off the street, then that is an acceptable cost for protecting innocent victims.

The conservative perspective views the police as enforcers of society's morality, and any attempts to weaken that role are to be resisted. Court restrictions against police power or police actions should be limited because criminals must be caught and punished in whatever way is most effective. Police are seen as becoming "soft" or bureaucratized in recent years, and there may be a wistful element in the popularity of such fictional characters as Dirty Harry, who bypass due process to get criminals off the streets.

In the conservative perspective, courts are the worst threat to society, because they allow criminals to go free. Only the most punitively oriented judges achieve conservative approval, and the majority of judges are seen as do-gooders who do not give criminals the prison sentences they deserve. Conservatives believe the death penalty is justified and not used often enough. Criminals are believed to have too many rights and victims none in the court system.

Under the conservative perspective, correctional facilities have too many programs; these programs only coddle the criminals and teach them that they will be rewarded and excused for criminal behavior. Old-fashioned punishments, such as chain gangs and rock piles, are seen as appropriate and worthy. Although prisons should satisfy basic needs, anything beyond what is absolutely necessary for survival is considered a luxury and decreases the effectiveness of prison as a deterrent.

The conservative concern for ethics involves criminal justice practitioners who may use their powers of discretion too freely. It is unethical to let criminals off because of courtroom deals or because of some error in the proceedings. It is unethical for police to ignore wrongdoing when it is done by informants, especially if it is someone who will continue the behavior. It is unethical for criminal justice practitioners to give special privileges to criminals because of status or money—for instance, to give special favors to mobsters in prison. Whenever the system is less than objective in handing out punishment, the conservatives' concern for ethics is aroused, and that would also include disparate sentencing based on offender characteristics. For instance, it is unethical if two defendants had committed the same crime for one defendant to get more years in prison than the other due to different circumstances.

Smith (1982: 137) uses the terms *right* and *left* instead of our terms *conservative* and *liberal,* and presents additional definitional elements of the two ideologies. If disorder is feared, social control becomes more acceptable. The left's concern for justice includes distributive justice, and that is why offenders' backgrounds are considered in the equation. For the right, the paramount value is order—an ordered society based on a pervasive and binding morality—and the paramount danger is disorder—social, moral, and political. For the left, the paramount value is justice—a just society based on a fair and equitable distribution of power, wealth, prestige, and privilege—and the paramount evil is injustice.

Smith (1982) and others associate the liberal (or left) viewpoint with due process. However, the liberal ideology does not necessarily or even logically imply a due-process position. The liberal support of treatment implies that one may go beyond what even conservative, retributive ends would dictate. Of course, these descriptions are fairly simplistic. Most people hate to be labeled as conservative or liberal, probably because it denies the presence of more complicated views of humanity and human relationships. Despite the obvious generalizations apparent in these characterizations, however, they can be detected in news coverage or political speeches and are useful to understand the development of policy. The conservative position is obviously more popular today than the liberal perspective, which might explain the greater emphasis on accountability and punitiveness in discussions about crime and social control.

Braswell and Whitehead (1999) urge putting aside these two viewpoints in favor of a different approach. They point to dangerous practices when one presents research from one point of view or the other. The liberal approach is represented by Braswell and Whitehead by those who present prison research in a light that denies the possibility that prisons do have any effect on crime, or that they might actually help offenders. The conservative approach is represented by those who view prisons as a management issue with no recognition or concern for the social, racial, and economic factors that so obviously play a part in the way prisons are used in society today. Conservatives point to research that shows the public favors incarceration and the death penalty; liberals point to research that shows that when the public is offered alternatives, the answers change. Both sides are dishonest, even if unconsciously, in presenting research that is less than the truth, unbalanced, and biased. Braswell and Whitehead (1999) argue for *whole sight,* meaning using one's heart as well as head to understand and present research findings.

Myths and Reality in Criminal Justice

What we believe about crime and criminals is partially influenced by our ideology, as described above, but it also is influenced by what we know about crime—or what we think we know. Several excellent sources now debunk some of the more standard myths in criminal justice. Walker (1985) was one of the first to address fundamental beliefs that influenced criminal justice policy—for example, that belief that more police patrols would reduce crime has little, if any, empirical support. He also addressed fundamental beliefs that support liberal ideology—for example, the belief that education reduces crime is refuted by studies that show no effect. Some of Walker's findings and use of empirical evidence may be criticized, but the approach of a skeptic is a necessary one if we want to avoid complacency and policy making influenced by unsupported truisms.

Others have continued this inquiry. For instance, Kappeler, Blumberg, and Potter (2000) present in their work a series of myths that influence criminal justice policy—the myth of crime waves, the myth of child abduction, the myth of the drug crisis, the myth of equal justice, the myth of the utility of punishment, and the myth of a lenient criminal justice system. Bohm (1996) also discusses myths—crime is a bad social problem, the criminal justice system enforces all laws, crime is primarily violent, and crime is increasing—and their influence on criminal justice policy. He also explains their function: they offer identities (good guy, bad guy), they aid comprehension by creating order out of the bombardment of information we experience today, and they help to form common bonds and reinforce a sense of community.

These sources show us that what we think we know is not necessarily accurate. If our beliefs about what should be done with criminals are based on the myth that the system is lenient and/or the myth that crime is increasing, then we are operating under faulty assumptions. How do these myths develop? The media and government are obvious participants in creating and perpetuating false perceptions, but social science bears a great deal of responsibility, as well. This book has not dealt with ethics in criminal justice research, and there are obvious issues relevant to the development and testing of hypotheses in this area.

Criminal Justice Researchers—Participants in Myth Making?

The argument that social science can never be truly objective has been discussed in a variety of venues (Roberg, 1981). A social scientist is influenced by his or her value system, ideology, and perception of reality. What questions to ask may be more important than the answers one finds. Individual perceptions will always somewhat influence the research process; however, if hypothesis construction and methodology are tainted by special interest groups or political agendas, then one must question any results that emerge from such research.

In one study of criminal-justice researchers' experiences with ethical dilemmas, it was found that the most common ethical dilemma was perceived pressure to study a certain topic, issue, or question, and/or pressure to influence the findings (Longmire, 1983). False research findings may occur because of laziness, incompetence, or political pressure. Recent exposés in the medical research field have called into question what we think we know about such things as heart disease; unethical researchers in criminal justice may also affect what we think we know about crime and criminals.

In addition to outside pressures that influence the selection of a research question or prompt improper influence over, improper use of, or outright falsification of research findings, other dilemmas in research exist, including the following:

- Protection of subject confidentiality
- Negative effects of the research on the client (e.g., the Milgram experiment and the Zimbardo experiment are the two best-known examples of research that had tremendously negative effects on subjects) and issues of privacy for subjects
- Deception of subjects in terms of what they will experience or the true focus of the research
- Obtaining informed voluntary consent
- Withholding benefits or services to subjects for the purpose of research
- Use of research findings—either misinterpretation or overreaching, otherwise illegal, or unethical treatment based on findings

The interaction among ideology, knowledge acquisition, and policy formation is complicated. Policies may originate in ideology and then become supported by research, or research may influence a shift of ideology. The danger is that individual decision making may be subverted by myths and that individual ethics may be the victim of misguided ideologies.

ETHICAL LEADERSHIP

In order to have an ethical organization, there must be ethical administrators and managers. They are responsible not only for their personal conduct but also for the actions of those they supervise. In other countries and cultures, this responsibility seems to be more pronounced than in the United States. For instance, when the Falkland War occurred, the foreign minister in Great Britain resigned. He did so because the situation happened on "his watch." Even though he did nothing personally blameworthy, and he was not negligent in his duties and in all respects performed his job competently, he held himself personally responsible because he failed to know of and therefore warn or prepare for the threat that Argentina presented. Contrast this with the attitude of the captain of the *Exxon Valdez,* responsible for the largest oil spill in history, who professed innocence because he wasn't the one on the bridge at the time of the incident, or Darryl Gates, the Los Angeles police chief, who, even after the Christopher Commission described a widespread management lapse, insisted that the problem of brutal officers was an individual problem and not one for which he should be held responsible.

Of course, the explanation that one was unaware of wrongful behavior has been used by the highest office in the country, as well as other excuses for why one shouldn't be held responsible for one's behavior. Thus, it should not be surprising that it is frequently heard from administrators when faced with the wrongdoing of their subordinates. There seem to be so few of those who are willing to take responsibility for their actions that when someone does say, "I did it, I'm responsible, and I'm sorry," it comes as such a refreshing surprise that they sometimes are excused from punishment simply because they came forward.

What does it mean to be an ethical leader? Obviously, one first needs to be sure that one is not engaged in unethical and corrupt behaviors oneself. Unfortunately, we have many recent examples where leaders cannot pass even this first test. In addition, one has to take responsibility for the larger role responsibilities of a leader position. Standards applied to public administrators can be helpful to this discussion. The American Society for Public Administration (1979) has promulgated standards that can be applied to all administrators if they aspire to be good leaders. The standards include the following:

- *Responsibility and accountability:* Measures of quality service delivery should be developed and implemented to enable the administrator to identify strengths and weaknesses.

- *Commitment:* Leaders should be dedicated and enthusiastic about the role of the organization, as well as have a commitment to the law, codes, regulations, and professional standards of behavior.

- *Responsiveness:* Leaders should be sensitive to changing circumstances and evolving demands and needs of the public. Good leadership exhibits flexibility in the face of social change.

- *Knowledge and skills:* Technology is dynamic, and leadership must keep abreast of better ways of accomplishing its mission, as well as possess the understanding to interpret data that are relevant to the mission of the organization. Training—both upon entry and in-service—is a necessity in order to have an effective workforce.

- *Conflicts of interest:* Since there will always be conflicts, the administrator should be sensitive to them, especially when personal needs conflict with organizational needs.

- *Professional ethics:* Administrators should practice self-reflection and continually check their decision making against some ethical standard.

Administrators and managers do not necessarily ensure an organization free from corruption merely by avoiding engagement of corrupt practices themselves; they must take affirmative steps to encourage ethical actions. Issues that could be examined in a discussion of ethical leadership include the practice of recruitment, training, discipline and reward structures, and evaluation of performance. Souryal (1992: 307) offers advice to leaders who would like to advance ethical decision making and emphasizes the importance of organizational support for ethical actions. Ethical leaders should do the following:

- Create an environment that is conducive to dignified treatment on the job.
- Increase ethical awareness among the ranks through formal and informal socialization.

- Avoid deception and manipulation in the way officers are assigned, rewarded, or promoted.
- Allow for openness and the free flow of unclassified information.
- Foster a sense of shared values and incorporate such values in the subculture of the agency.
- Demonstrate an obligation to honesty, fairness, and decency by example.
- Discuss the issue of corruption publicly, expose corrupt behavior, and reward ethical behavior.

Metz (1990) offers a similar set of advice. He proposes that ethical administrators do this:

- Establish realistic goals and objectives.
- Provide ethical leadership (meaning set a moral tone by actions).
- Establish formal written codes of ethics.
- Provide a whistleblowing mechanism.
- Discipline violators of ethical standards.
- Train all personnel in ethics.

The common administrative reaction to unethical practices is to institute even more rules covering a greater range of behavior. As discussed in previous chapters, extensive rules seem to be present in inverse proportion to high ethical standards; what often occurs is as more rules are written, more creative ways are found to get around them. Rules are not ethical standards, and without a commitment and belief in the legitimacy of the rules, there is no way that more rules will affect the ethics of an organization.

When top leaders take responsibility for their subordinates' behavior, they will lead and administer with greater awareness, interaction, and responsibility. Because of this responsibility, a supervisor or administrator must be concerned with how the workplace treats the worker, how the worker views the mission, and how the public views the organization. Concern for one's public image may be shared by ethical leaders and egoistic bureaucrats, but the first group has a sincere desire to understand the public's complaints and respond to them, and the second group is concerned solely with protecting the image of the organization—a stand that may mean whistleblowers are punished rather than appreciated for bringing problems out in the open.

A strong ethical leader would have a personal relationship with subordinates—without showing favoritism. This personal relationship is the building block of modeling, identification, and persuasive authority. Strong leadership involves caring and commitment to the organization. A strong leader is someone who is connected with others but also has a larger vision, if you will, of goals and mission. Delattre (1989b) discusses a realistic idealist—it's possible he would also be content with the phrase *an idealistic realist*. What he was referring to was the capacity for good leaders to understand social realities but to avoid cynicism in the face of such social realities—for instance, in the use of force, a realistic idealist would understand that force is necessary at times but attempt every alternative means to protect all human life, including the offender's life. Leaders must never lose sight of the organizational mission; for public servants, this means public service. Souryal also describes ethical leaders as those with "a mental state that is characterized by vision, enlightened reasoning, and moral responsibility" (1992: 186).

Good leaders must recognize and relay the idea that public service applies to all, not just a favored few. Criminals are also part of the public that the criminal justice system serves. This means that they deserve the same civility, protections, and services as the rest of us unless such is prohibited by law or personal safety is threatened. When the protections represented by our Bill of Rights and democratic process become reserved for certain groups, the rights of all are threatened.

INDIVIDUAL DECISION MAKING

In these final sections, we revisit the question discussed in the first several chapters of this book—how to make an ethical decision. John Rawls (1957) presents a somewhat abstract procedure for deciding moral issues. He explains that moral principles can be developed through inductive logic. The method to discover these moral principles is through the considered moral judgments of a number of cases by a number of moral judges. These individuals would have the following characteristics:

- They would possess common sense—they would not intellectualize the problem but apply common reason to arrive at a resolution.
- They would have open minds.
- They would know their own emotions.
- They would have a sympathetic knowledge of humans.

The cases given them to decide would be such that the judges would not be harmed or benefited in any way by their decision in order to ensure neutrality. The cases would present real conflicts of interest, but conflicts that were not too difficult and that were likely to present themselves in ordinary life. The judges would be presented with all relevant facts in the matter so that they could make a reasoned judgment. The judgments should be certain, and they should be stable; that is, other judges at other times should also arrive at the same judgments. Finally, the judgments should be intuitive. The reason for this is that ethical principles are to be derived from a series of judgments, and if judges were already using predetermined rules, there would be no way to derive general rules from the judgments. Rawls (1957: 180) describes the procedure in the following way:

> Up to this point I have defined, first a class of competent judges, and, second, a class of considered judgments. If competent judges are those persons most likely to make correct decisions, then we should take care to abstract those judgments of theirs which, from the conditions and circumstances under which they are made, are most likely to be correct.

The next step is to formulate an explication of the total range of judgments. An **explication** is a set of principles described as follows (Rawls, 1957: 182):

> [I]f any competent man were to apply them intelligently and consistently to the same cases under review, his judgments, made systematically nonintuitive by the explicit and conscious use of the principles, would be, nevertheless identical, case by case, with the considered judgments of the group of competent judges.

These explications must be written in ordinary language, be written in the form of principles, and be comprehensive in solving the range of moral judgments. In other words, common principles are extrapolated from the decisions of the moral judges, and these common principles are then used by the rest of us in decision making (Rawls, 1957).

Obviously, Rawls's proposal is more rhetorical device than useful tool for deciding ethical issues. However, the basic premise of this exercise is to discover common principles that can be used to decide moral questions. This is fundamental to any logical solution to moral dilemmas. The ethical systems we have discussed throughout this book present principles similar to the explications Rawls seeks through moral judges. Another principle that one can derive from Rawls' discussion is that only neutral judges can come to some objective and fair moral principles. These principles can also be found in more pragmatic guidelines for use in decision making. A method proposed by Laura Nash (1981) helps individuals make business decisions, and these same questions seem applicable to those situations faced by criminal justice professionals (see box).

How to Make an Ethical Decision

1. Have you defined the problem accurately?
2. How would you define the problem if you stood on the other side of the fence?
3. How did the situation occur in the first place?
4. To whom and to what do you give your loyalty as a person and as a member of the corporation?
5. What is your intention in making this decision?
6. How does this intention compare with the probable result?
7. Whom could your decision or action injure?
8. Can you discuss the problem with the affected parties before you make your decision?
9. Are you confident that your position will be as valid over a long period of time as it seems now?
10. Could you disclose without qualms your decision or action to your boss, your CEO, the board of directors, your family, your society as a whole?
11. What is the symbolic potential of your action if understood? If misunderstood?
12. Under what conditions would you allow exceptions to your stand?

SOURCE: Nash, 1981: 81.

Although Nash's guidelines are obviously directed to business decisions, they have applicability to other fields. Basically, the questions are designed to lead individuals to analyze their behavior and its implications. There is an assumption that exposure of unethical conduct will make the individual feel uneasy. To some extent, there is an assumption that a commonly agreed-upon definition of right and wrong exists. The general principles that can be drawn from these questions are obvious. First, we are interested in attaining all the facts of the situation; this includes the effects of the decision on oneself and others. It is important to understand hidden motivations and indirect effects. Second, the concept of scrutiny works well to evaluate the decision taken; one must be comfortable with public disclosure. Along with this concept goes the notion that others should be able to make the same decision and have it judged acceptable. Finally, the concept of rationale or reason implies that the individual decision is based on a larger set of moral or ethical principles.

Let us apply these guidelines to a criminal justice example. If a police officer were confronted with an opportunity to accept some type of gratuity, either a dinner or a more expensive present, the officer should first evaluate all facts. Is anything expected in return? Is the gift really a gift, or a payment for some service? Would the officer be comfortable if others knew of the gift or gratuity? Could the officer reconcile the decision to take the gratuity with a larger set of moral principles, such as the Law Enforcement Code of Ethics?

Krogstand and Robertson (1979) describe three principles of ethical decision making. The first is the **imperative principle,** which directs a decision maker to act according to a specific, unbending rule. The second is the **utilitarian principle,** which determines the ethics of conduct by the good or bad consequences of the action. The third is the **generalization principle,** which is based on this question: "What would happen if all similar persons acted this way under similar circumstances?" These should sound familiar because they are, respectively, religious or absolutist ethics, utilitarianism, and ethical formalism. Ethical frameworks, if recognized, can be a great aid in individual decision making. If one is familiar with these ethical principles, then any specific dilemma can be analyzed using an ethical framework as a guideline.

To question one's general ethical behavior, take the challenging self-survey in the box on the next page. The boxed set of questions takes a general approach to evaluating one's ethics. It comes from the American Society for Public Administration (1979: 22–23) but has been adapted where necessary to apply to those who work in the criminal justice field.

Close and Meier (1995: 130) provide a set of questions more specific to criminal justice professionals and sensitive to the due-process protections that are often discarded in a decision to commit an unethical act. They propose that the individual decision maker should ask the following questions:

1. Does the action violate another person's constitutional rights, including the right of due process?
2. Does the action involve treating another person only as a means to an end?
3. Is the action under consideration illegal?

Ethics Self-Survey

1. Do I confront difficult ethical decisions directly and attempt to think through the alternatives and the principles involved? Am I inclined to make decisions on grounds of convenience, expediency, pressure, impulse, or inertia?
2. Do I systematically review my behavior as an administrator and question whether what I do is consistent with my professional values?
3. If someone asked me to explain my professional ethics, what would I say?
4. Have my values and ethics changed since I began working as a public administrator? If so, why and how have they changed? What are the primary influences that have changed my thinking?
5. Looking ahead to the remainder of my career, are there particular areas of my ethical conduct to which I would like to pay closer attention?
6. Do I ever find myself in situations in which providing equitable treatment to clients, members of my organization, or members of other organizations creates ethical conflicts? How do I handle such dilemmas? Can I perceive any consistent pattern in my behavior?
7. Where do my professional loyalties ultimately lie? With the Constitution? The law? My organization? My superiors? My clients? The general public? Do I feel torn by these loyalties? How do I deal with the conflicts?
8. Do I ever confront situations in which I feel that it is unfair to treat everyone in the same way? How do I determine what to do in those cases? How do I decide what is fair?
9. When I am responsible for some activity that turns out to be inappropriate or undesirable, do I accept full responsibility for it? Why? How?
10. Do I ever dismiss criticism of my actions with the explanation that I am only "following orders"? Do I accept any responsibility for what happens in these circumstances?

SOURCE: Adapted from American Society of Public Administrators, 1979: 22–23.

---

4. Do you predict that your action will produce more bad than good for all persons affected?

5. Does the action violate department procedure or professional duty?

The simplest formulation of questions on which to base an ethical decision is as follows:

1. Does it affect others?

2. Does it hurt others?

3. Would I want it done if I were on the other side?

4. Would I be proud of the decision?

These four simple questions may be sufficient to address most ethical dilemmas.

In Chapter 2, the ethics of virtue was discussed. Part of this ethical framework is the idea that one's character is most relevant to ethical decision making. That is, good character comprises virtues such as honesty, trustworthiness, and generosity. Bad character, obviously, would be the absence or opposite of these traits. If one has a bad character, then one is unlikely to perceive ethical dilemmas, since one will go through life in essence an egoist, making choices influenced by one's negative character traits. If one has a good character, then one does not perceive ethical dilemmas in some situations either, since it is second nature for one to do the honorable thing, whether it be not to steal or tell the truth or whatever. Most people in the criminal justice field (or indeed any profession) have basically good characters; some do not.

In some situations, however, even those who have formed habits of honesty, truthfulness, and integrity are sincerely perplexed as to the correct course of behavior. These situations occur because the behavior choice seems so innocuous or trivial (e.g., whether to accept free coffee) or seems so difficult (e.g., when a partner or friend wants you to cover up something they did wrong). In these instances where basically good people have trouble deciding what to do, the ethical frameworks provided in this volume might help them analyze their choices. It must also be accepted that in some dilemmas, there are going to be costs involved when making the right decision. For instance, an officer who knows it is his duty to provide evidence against his brother-in-law who is a major drug dealer may lose his wife's love and, in the process, his children's. There is no assurance that "doing the right thing" will not come at a high cost. The ethical person may not necessarily be a happy person.

In any organization, there are those who will almost always make ethical choices, those who will usually make unethical ones, and those who can be influenced one way or the other. The best course of action is to identify those in the second group and encourage them to find other employment or at least remove them from temptation. Then organizational leaders must create an atmosphere for the third group that encourages ethical decision making. This can be done by promoting ethical administrators, rewarding morally courageous behavior, and providing clear and powerful organizational policies that emphasize worthwhile goals and honest means.

For criminal justice practitioners, ethical decisions arise from the exercise of discretion and the use of power. In criminal justice we must wrestle with questions of responsibility and excuse, the limits of the state's right to control the individual, the ethical use of force, and the appropriate use of discretion. Although professionals and practitioners may get bogged down with day-to-day problems and bureaucratic agendas may cause them to lose sight of larger goals, foremost in their minds should be the true scope and meaning of the power inherent in the criminal justice system. It is people who make a *justice* system *just* or corrupt.

To protect citizenry from any misuse and abuse of power, personnel in the criminal justice system must have a strong professional identity. There is a continuing debate over whether police officers can be described as professionals; there is even more debate over whether correctional officers can be described as such. These arguments miss a central point. Whether one calls the men and women who wear these uniforms professionals, practitioners, or some other term, the fact is that they have immense power over other people's lives. This power must be recognized for what it is and held as a sacred trust.

Criminal justice professionals are public servants and, as such, should aspire to a higher standard of behavior. They have a duty to the citizenry they serve, but even more than that, they must possess the moral and ethical sense to prevent the power inherent in their positions from being used for tyranny. Education isn't enough. Learning a body of knowledge and acquiring essential skills do not give individuals the moral sense necessary to use those skills wisely. Witness the recurring scandals involving lawyers and business professionals—a highly educated group does not necessarily mean that the group is free from corruption.

The greatest protection against corruption of power is a belief in and commitment to the democratic process and all it entails. If one desires a career in criminal justice, one must ask these questions: Do I love the Constitution? Do I believe in the Bill of Rights? and Do I truly believe in the sanctity and natural right of due process? (See the accompanying box of the Bill of Rights and other amendments.) If the individual views these as impediments, nuisances, or as irrelevant, then that person should not be a public servant.

Criminal justice practitioners find themselves faced with ethical choices when balancing friendship against institutional integrity—that is, when friends and colleagues engage in inappropriate or illegal behavior or rule breaking. There are also ethical choices to be made when balancing client (offender) needs against bureaucratic efficiency and institutional goals. Ethics are at issue when the individual professional has personal goals or biases that conflict with fair and impartial treatment of the public and the clients served. The inappropriate use of discretion occurs when the professional uses unethical criteria to resolve decisions.

In conclusion, the individual should become aware of the implications of day-to-day choices—sharpen his or her ethical antennae, so to speak. Small decisions become larger life positions in a slow, cumulative way. When faced with a choice of behavior, one should first examine all possible solutions to the problem and be aware of the direct and indirect effects of each response. Often, ethical issues arise and are not recognized for what they are. The individual may limit analysis of a problem to finding a short-term solution or making a quick decision, in which case the larger issues or the situation's ethical implications are never addressed. It becomes easy to rationalize unethical behavior in this way by the explanation that it only happened once, or it was the easiest way, or there was no intention to do wrong.

Then one should determine whether any solutions would be viewed as unacceptable if made public, and for what reason. If an individual would be uncomfortable talking about an action, then chances are it is questionable. Too often, unethical decisions are protected by a shroud of secrecy, and then the secrecy is defended by pleading institutional or agency confidentiality. On an individual level, unethical behavior is almost always hidden, and further unethical behavior may follow to cover up what has already been done. Probably the best signal that something is wrong is when a person hesitates to make it public knowledge.

The Bill of Rights Plus Selected Amendments

Article I. Congress shall make no law respecting an establishment of religion, or prohibiting the free exercise thereof; or abridging the freedom of speech, or of the press; or the right of the people peaceably to assemble, and to petition the Government for a redress of grievance.

Article II. A well regulated militia, being necessary to the security of a free State, the right of the people to keep and bear arms, shall not be infringed.

Article III. No Soldier shall, in time of peace be quartered in any house, without the consent of the owner, nor in time of war, but in a manner to be prescribed by law.

Article IV. The right of the people to be secure in their persons, houses, papers, and effects, against unreasonable searches and seizures, shall not be violated, and no warrants shall issue, but upon probable cause, supported by oath or affirmation, and particularly describing the place to be searched, and the persons or things to be seized.

Article V. No person shall be held to answer for a capital, or otherwise infamous crime, unless on a presentment or indictment of a Grand Jury, except in cases arising in the land or naval forces, or in the militia, when in actual service in time of war or public danger; nor shall any person be subject for the same offense to be twice put in jeopardy of life or limb; nor shall be compelled in any criminal case to be a witness against himself, nor be deprived of life, liberty, or property, without due process of law; nor shall private property be taken for public use, without just compensation.

Article VI. In all criminal prosecutions, the accused shall enjoy the right to a speedy and public trial, by an impartial jury of the State and district wherein the crime shall have been committed, which district shall have been previously ascertained by law, and to be informed of the nature and cause of the accusation; to be confronted with the witnesses against him; to have compulsory process for obtaining witnesses in his favor, and to have the assistance of counsel for his defense.

Article VII. In Suits at common law, where the value in controversy shall exceed twenty dollars, the right of trial by jury shall be preserved, and no fact tried by a jury, shall be otherwise reexamined in any Court of the United States, than according to the rules of the common law.

Article VIII. Excessive bail shall not be required, nor excessive fines imposed, nor cruel and unusual punishments inflicted.

Article IX. The enumeration in the Constitution, of certain rights, shall not be construed to deny or disparage others retained by the people.

Article X. The powers not delegated to the United States by the Constitution, nor prohibited by it to the States, are reserved to the States respectively, or to the people.

Article XIII. Section 1. Neither the slavery nor involuntary servitude, except as a punishment for crime whereof the party shall have been duly convicted shall exist within the United States, or any place subject to their jurisdiction. Section 2. Congress shall have power to enforce this article by appropriate legislation.

continued

The Bill of Rights Plus Selected Amendments (continued)

Article XIV. Section 1. All persons born or naturalized to the United States, and subject to the jurisdiction thereof, are citizens of the United States and of the State wherein they reside. No State shall make or enforce any law which shall abridge the privileges or immunities of citizens of the United States; nor shall any State deprive any person of life, liberty, or property, without due process of law; nor deny to any person within its jurisdiction the equal protection of the laws. . . .

Article XV. Section 1. The right of citizens of the United States to vote shall not be denied or abridged by the United States or by any State on account of race, color, or previous condition of servitude. . . .

Article XIX. The right of citizens of the United States to vote shall not be denied or abridged by the United States or by any State on account of sex. . . .

Finally, the individual must be able to reconcile the decision with his or her personal set of values or ethical system. Hopefully, the ethical concepts, discussions, and issues we have presented in this book have helped clarify these decision processes. When one has to make a difficult decision about a moral issue, although one has recourse to value systems passed on by family and advice and counsel from friends and colleagues, ultimately the decision made should be one for which the individual is willing to take responsibility.

WHY BE ETHICAL?

After completing a class on ethics that involved detailed explanations and applications of the ethical systems discussed in this book, an individual responded with the question, "Why should we?" The student was really asking why anyone should be ethical or moral. There is a long version and a short version of the answer to this question. The short answer was what was given by another class member: "So you can sleep at night."

The long version is that philosophers down through the ages have examined, debated, and analyzed this same question. The ethical systems can be seen as not only answering the question, "What is good?" but also the question, "Why be good?" Under ethical formalism, the answer is that the world works better, and it is rational to do one's duty and live up to the categorical imperative. Under utilitarianism, the answer is that it is better for everyone, including the individual, to do what benefits the majority. Under the ethics of care, the answer is that we naturally and instinctively have the capacity to care and to be concerned about others. Each of the other frameworks also provides answers. One dominant theme emerges from all the ethical systems—that we are connected to each other in fundamental and emotional ways. The golden rule, the universalism principle under the categorical imperative, rule utilitarianism, and even enlightened egoism recognize this connection. The theme running through the ethical systems is empathy and caring for one another. The reason we should act ethically can be explained rationally (ethical formalism and utilitarianism) or intuitively (ethics of care and religion).

A similar question was asked by Tyler (1990) in a book titled *Why People Obey the Law*. The answers found in his research may shed light on this discussion. He found that people obey the law not because of fear of being punished but rather because of a fundamental belief in the goodness of law. If they believe that the system is fair, that their rights are protected, and that they are treated with dignity and respect, then they typically believe in and abide by the law. Arguably, the converse is that if people *do not* hold these beliefs, then they have no normative controls on their behavior and the only thing left is deterrence. Tyler's findings present an interesting commentary on what effect the criminal justice system has on citizens. One obvious conclusion is that unethical behavior that ignores rights by criminal justice professionals creates the very criminality that one is trying to prevent.

Professional ethics is merely an application of moral systems to a particular set of questions or a specific environment. The basis of all professional ethical codes is the same: to be a good professional, one must be a good person. Many of the ethical choices one will make throughout the course of a career are easy: no one needs to tell a police officer that bribery is wrong, or correctional officers that hitting a shackled and helpless inmate is wrong. These actions occur because individuals have chosen to take the path of least resistance, pursue personal interests over organizational values, or succumb to emotions such as fear and anger. For those choices that are truly difficult, people of goodwill, using rationality and sensitivity, can apply any ethical system and come up with an ethical solution. It may not be one that everyone will agree upon, but it will allow the individual to make the decision public and will allow the person to be satisfied that his or her choice was based on ethics rather than egoism.

Two of the greatest dangers in criminal justice are cynicism and burnout. Cynical leadership, cynical instructors, and overwhelming evidence that we live in an imperfect world create the all-too-common occurrence of workers who are cynical, who are burned out, and who have abandoned the ideals that led them to the profession in the first place. As mentioned before, ethical leaders should be able to transmit a vision and be committed to the mission of the organization, but many administrators and managers exhibit only pessimistic cynicism over the potential for change, the worth of humanity, and the importance of doing what is right.

How does one avoid cynicism and burnout? First, one can begin by adopting realistic goals before entering the profession. A police officer cannot expect to save the world, and a treatment professional should not expect to find success with every client. A more realistic career goal might be a resolution to do one's best and to always follow the law. Second, find and nurture a network of mentors and colleagues that promotes ethical values. In every department that has a corruption scandal, there are also those who have managed to avoid participating in such activity.

Cynical people are contagious, and cynicism breeds rationalizations for committing unethical behavior—from leaving work early or falsifying overtime records to violating the rights of suspects. Third, seek self-fulfillment and personal enrichment. This could be higher education, reading self-help books, attending church, joining interest clubs, participating in charitable activities, volunteering to coach community sport teams, or becoming involved in the PTA. Note that such activities all have the element of communication and interaction with others. Such activities promote connectedness with the community at large and counteract the negativity that pervades the criminal justice field. Unfortunately, criminal justice professionals see humanity at its worst, and there is a great need to see the best of the human spirit as well.

REVISITING "MEANS–END" THINKING IN TIMES OF TROUBLE

In the last edition of this book, cynicism and burnout were identified as factors leading to unethical practices in the criminal justice system. Today, there is a third–fear. The World Trade Center attack and other assaults on American targets around the world have created a sense of vulnerability and fear. The response to this fear has been to reduce civil liberties. In earlier editions, we discussed the "means–end" thinking that was used to justify skirting due-process requirements and laws in order to catch criminals and protect the public. Noble-cause corruption describes *testilying* as acceptable if it puts a criminal behind bars. Intimidation is justified as long as it gets a confession. Beating a prisoner is justified by the fact that he must be taught a lesson. Racial profiling is unfortunate for young black men, but it catches drug dealers. This "end justifying the means" thinking is insidious—even more so now that that threat is so much greater. Fear, unfortunately, leads to bad decisions. Fear causes police officers and correctional officers to use illegal force. Fear caused this country to incarcerate tens of thousands of citizens during WWII whose only crime was being born of Asian descent. Fear causes a country's leaders to trample the rights of those who are feared.

The immediate federal response to the World Trade Center was the Patriot Act, which allows federal agencies to spy on Americans without probable cause or even reasonable suspicion. It also allows authorities to share information obtained via search warrants obtained through the Foreign Intelligence Surveillance Act, which does not require probable cause, with criminal prosecutors. The Patriot Act also allows deportation for anyone who supports financially a "terrorist organization," but the definition is so ambiguous that it might be used if a person contributed humanitarian aid. The Patriot Act also required all Arab-born citizens to report to immigration offices around the country to be interviewed and registered under the National Security Entry–Exit Registration system. There is enough rising anxiety among the Arab community that volunteers take information from registrants as they go into the federal buildings—in case they don't come back out again (Wood, 2003).

The Patriot Act was passed swiftly, with little debate. Later proposals have been more scrutinized, but debate is still framed as those who are against such "protections" must be unpatriotic. The Total Information Awareness pilot program is a program proposed by the government to collect voluminous amounts of information about citizens through the Internet. Although some are not concerned about this privacy invasion, others are very concerned about the growing surveillance allowed legally and the potential invasion of privacy (Kravets, 2003; Moss and Fessenden, 2002). Another proposal—"Operation TIPS"—encouraged citizens to spy on each other and proposed an official identity card. This program, at least, was roundly rejected by both political parties (Cole, 2002).

QUOTE

We're protecting freedom and democracy, but unfortunately freedom and democracy have to be sacrificed.

Jethro Eisenstein—New York Lawyer quoted in Moss and Fessenden, 2002: A 18.

Since 9/11 we have detained thousands of noncitizens for months without charging them. Some argued that those held in Guantanamo Bay without charging or trial were "enemy combatants" and not deserving of liberties ensured by the Constitution, but now we are doing the same to citizens (Cole, 2002). There are disturbing analogies to the WWII detainment of 110,000 Americans of Japanese ancestry. We now have secret detentions and secret proceedings—concepts that have been an anathema to the concepts of democracy and liberty. It is indeed ironic that those who sought the freedoms that this country holds up as the essence of its strength and tradition have found that these freedoms and liberties do not apply to them because of the color of their skin or their national heritage (Cole, 2002).

QUOTE

Political liberty, which is one of the greatest gifts a people can acquire for themselves, is threatened when social order is threatened. It is dismaying to see how ready many people are to turn to strong leaders in hopes that they will end, by adopting strong measure, the disorder that has been the product of failed or fragile commitments. Drug abuse, street crime, and political corruption are the expression of unfettered choices. To end them, rulers, with the warm support of the people, will often adopt measures that threaten true political freedom. The kind of culture that can maintain reasonable human commitments takes centuries to create but only a few generations to destroy.

James Q. Wilson, cited in Cole, 2002: 234

Although the quote above is discussing the sacrifice of due process in the drug war and crime control, it has incredible relevance to the issues of terrorism. How do we meet the threat of terrorists? It is important to look around the world to see how other countries have managed their fear. It is interesting that many European countries that have a longer history of dealing with terrorism have embraced the concept of international human rights. The premise is that some acts are never justified. No end is so important that governments can succumb to slavery, genocide, or torture. No situation ever justifies sexism, racism, murder, rape, or intimidation (Paul and Elder, 2003).

The Universal Declaration of Human Rights mandates thirty articles. They include the following:

- All humans are born free and equal in dignity and rights.
- Everyone has the right to life, liberty, and security of person.
- No one shall be held in slavery or servitude.
- No one shall be subjected to torture or to cruel, inhuman, or degrading treatment or punishment.
- Everyone has the right to a standard of living adequate for the health and well being of himself and of his family.
- Everyone has the right to education.
- Everyone has the right to freedom of peaceful assembly and association.
- Everyone is entitled to all the rights and freedoms set forth in this Declaration, without distinction of any kinds, such as race, color, sex, language, religion, political or other opinion, national or social origin, property, birth, or status.
- All are equal before the law and are entitled, without any discrimination, to equal protection of the law.

Even though over 130 countries have adopted the declaration, virtually every country in the world violates one or several of these principles. The United States hasn't even ratified the Treaty. As this book is written, newspaper editorials debate whether or not international law allows torture of Afghanistani or Iraqi captives. United States officials freely admit tactics just short of physical torture, including deprivation of food, sleep, light, and medical care. The argument is that the "end" of finding out information is more important than the "means" of how to obtain it. As always, the problem with this type of thinking is that one can never know the effects or costs of one's actions. "Means" that can be justified only by the intent to achieve a good "end" may not even accomplish that. This generation of Middle Eastern children may identify the United States only as an aggressor. Our actions, misunderstood, could create many times more terrorists than the number we are trying to control today. In this country, those of Arab descent who came here for freedom now find that their heritage denies them that precious gift. In our haste to protect ourselves, we may lose the very thing that defines this country and, not incidentally, germinate the seeds of future destruction in the children who watch their fathers being taken away.

In an earlier section in this chapter, we discussed the "checks" one can apply to individual decision making that allows one to determine whether the choice will stand the test of public exposure and time. The individual rights approach—and a commitment that these rights are so important that they can never be subverted no matter what the cause—would prevent the "end justifies the means" type of thinking that we might someday look back upon with regret.

CONCLUSION

In this chapter we took a last look at ethical decision making. We process information based on our perceptions and this tendency is just as true of researchers and writers as it is of anyone else. Liberal and conservative thinking tends to narrow one's focus and impede a balanced view of the world. The most important factor in having ethical organizations is ethical leaders. The most important factors in making ethical decisions is to follow the steps of ethical reasoning and not succumb to fear.

REVIEW QUESTIONS

1. Select the most difficult ethical dilemma in the previous chapters and try to answer it again, using the questions posed by Laura Nash.
2. Now select an ethical or moral dilemma from your own life and try to solve it by using any guidelines derived from this book. Be explicit about the procedure that you used to arrive at a decision and about the decision itself.
3. Write a code of ethics for yourself.

ETHICAL DILEMMAS

Situation 1

You obtain a job as a probation officer upon graduation and quickly realize that several probation officers in your office engage in offensive racial humor and sexist remarks. They swear at clients and act inappropriately toward the female secretaries. One has been making suggestive comments to you, and you dread getting caught alone with him in the coffee room. You don't want to make waves because you have been there only a month, but what can you do?

Situation 2

You are a criminal justice student and have become friendly with another student named Joe. You are both nearing graduation, and Joe has told you that he will start work as a constable in a small town. The problem is that you believe Joe is a bigot and a bully who shows entirely too much interest in guns. He brags about how he's going to "teach people a lesson" and that he can match anyone in "firepower." You truly believe that someone is going to get hurt. What can you do?

Situation 3

You are a new police officer and are talking with other officers before roll call. The group is loudly and energetically proposing various gruesome torture techniques to get Al Qaeda operatives to talk. There is some amount of hyperbole in the discussion, but also the sincere belief that torture is justified by the circumstances. How do you feel about this position? If you object to torture, would you make your position known?

SUGGESTED READING

Alderson, J. 1998. *Principled Policing: Protecting the Public with Integrity.* Winchester, MA: Waterside Press.

Braswell, M., B. McCarthy, and B. McCarthy. 2002. *Justice, Crime and Ethics.* Cincinnati, OH: Anderson Press.

Kappeler, V., M. Blumberg, and G. Potter. 2000. *The Mythology of Crime and Justice.* Prospect Heights, IL: Waveland Press.

Glossary

act utilitarianism type of utilitarianism that determines goodness of a particular act by measuring the utility for all, but only on that specific act and without regard for future actions

age of reason legal age at which a person is said to have the capacity to reason and thus to understand the consequences of her or his action

appeal a legal motion objecting to the judgment based on error in the proceedings

applied ethics study of ethics applied to a specific profession or subject

authority the ability to influence or command based on one's position

bad-apple argument explanation of police deviance that points to bad individuals that use position for corrupt purposes

baksheesh bribe

blue curtain of secrecy refers to a police department or other organization where the members refuse to inform on each other and will cover up the wrongdoing of individual members

bureaucratic justice concept referring to the goal of efficiency over justice; policy of assuming guilt and moving cases through the system quickly with the least amount of work

civil disobedience voluntary, nonviolent disobedience of established laws based on moral beliefs

civilian review model one type of deviance control that utilizes an external investigative body and external determination of sanctions

code of silence law enforcement subcultural prohibition against informing on a fellow officer

cognitive dissonance psychological term referring to the discomfort that is created when behavior and attitude or belief are inconsistent; the inclination is to change one or the other to achieve congruence

community corrections probation, parole, or other community-based correctional alternatives

commutative justice component of justice concerned with the fairness of contracts and business relations

conflict paradigm the idea that groups in society have fundamental differences and that the powerful control societal elements

consensus paradigm the idea that most people have similar beliefs, values, and goals and that society reflects the majority view

correctional officer   guard in a prison or jail

corrective justice   component of justice concerned with punishments and sanctions

crime   violation of a law

cruel and unusual punishment   as defined by the Eighth Amendment, any punishment that is disproportional or gratuitous

culpability   blameworthiness

cultural relativism   idea that many values and behaviors differ from culture to culture and are functional to the culture that holds them

cynicism   attitude of negativity, distrust, and lack of hope

deontological ethical system   study of duty or moral obligation emphasizing the intent of the actor or goodwill as the element of morality; character of the person (as in virtue-based ethics) or consequences of the action (as in utilitarianism) are not seen as important

Dirty Harry problem   taken from the movie, this idea proposes the dilemma wherein a bad action might result in a good end, i.e., inflicting torture to get important information

discretion   the power to make a decision or a choice

discrimination   treating an individual or group differently based on categorical factors, i.e., their membership in a group

distributive justice   component of justice concerned with the allocation of the goods and burdens of society

due process   constitutionally mandated (Fifth and Fourteenth Amendments) procedural steps designed to eliminate error in any governmental deprivation of protected liberty, life, or property; that is, right to a neutral hearing body, presentation of evidence, cross-examination and confrontation of accusers, appeal, and so on

duties   required behaviors or actions

egoism   ethical system that claims that good results from pursuing self-interest (see also psychological egoism)

enlightened egoism   concept that egoism may look altruistic, since it is one's long-term best interest to help others (since, then, they will help oneself)

equality   the state of even measures or values

ethical dilemmas   a decision that is difficult to make either because the right course of action is not clear or the right course of action carries some negative consequences

ethical formalism   ethical system espoused by Kant that depends on duty; holds that the only thing truly good is a goodwill, and what is good is that which conforms to the categorical imperative

ethical system   systematic ordering of moral principles, also called moral theory or moral philosophy

ethics of care   ethical system that defines good as meeting needs and preserving and enriching relationships

ethics of virtue   ethical system that bases ethics largely on character and possession of virtues

ethics   study of what constitutes good or bad conduct

exclusionary rule   court-created rule of evidence that excludes evidence obtained through illegal means

expiation   atonement

explication   explanation

fairness   the quality of just measures

force   physical coercion

general deterrence   what is done to an individual to prevent others from committing crimes

generalization principle   philosophical principle that states one must do something when one would want others to do the action as well, or not do something that one would not want others to do

graft   use of position for dishonest gain

grass eaters   term used for police officers who passively accept and take advantage of opportunities of corruption

gratuities   gifts given because of occupation or role of the recipient

group think psychological term referring to the tendency of a group that works together and develops a common mind-set to agree on ideas that are problematic or even irrational, using objective evaluation

guidelines suggested or preferred behavioral rules

halo effect psychological term referring to the tendency to believe a person who is an expert in one area is knowledgeable about other areas as well; giving greater weight to opinion because of irrelevant expertise

hostile work environment term that comes from sexual harassment litigation; an environment that is so permeated with sexual tension, has such a sexually charged atmosphere, or where other elements combine to make the workplace too uncomfortable to work

human service model concept or description of a correctional officer who sees the position as an opportunity to help individuals change through a caring and sensitive administration of the rules and offering oneself as a role model of mature coping

hypothetical imperatives a statement of contingent demand (if I want something, then I must work for it) contrasted with the categorical imperative, which states that one must conform to the imperative with no "ifs"

ideology organized and integrated set of ideas or beliefs

impartiality without bias or special regard

imperative principle philosophical principle that states one must do something just because it is the right thing to do

imperfect duties general moral values that do not specify acts; for instance, to be charitable

incapacitation to make incapable; in corrections, to hold someone for any length of time in order to prevent him or her from committing a crime

informants individuals who give information to police, usually in return for money or reduced sentences

Innocence Project(s) legal teams across the country that are reviewing cases of death-row offenders to determine whether or not they are innocent and on death row in error

integrity testing various means of testing the honesty of workers through the presentation of corrupt opportunities

intent the most culpable mental state; indicates the decision and capacity to carry out an action

internal affairs model one type of deviance control that utilizes an internal investigation and internal sanctions

judgments decisions of value

just deserts model model of punishment advocated by von Hirsh that states that the only appropriate punishment is proportional to the seriousness of the crime and rejects treatment as a correctional policy related to sentencing

justice model model of punishment advocated by Fogel that is similar to the just deserts model and states that treatment can be made available but should not influence sentence

justice the quality of being just, impartial, or fair; the principle or ideal of just dealing or right action

knowing the second most culpable mental state; indicates that one knows what one is doing

Kohlberg's moral stages the idea that moral development is hierarchical; each developmental stage is described as moving from pure egoism to a higher moral stage that leads to altruism

laws written rules of society that come with sanctions

legal moralism a justification for law; law protects and enforces society's morals

meat eaters term used for police officers who actively seek out and take advantage of opportunities of corruption

mechanical solidarity Durkheim's concept of societal solidarity as arising from similarities among its members

meta-ethics discipline investigating the meaning of ethical terms

modeling   learning theory concept that people learn behaviors, values, and attitudes through relationships; they identify with another person and want to be like that other person and so pattern their behavior, expressions, and beliefs after that person; transitory to the extent that the relationship is transitory

moral pluralism   the concept that there are many competing moral truths

moral rules   rules that define right or wrong behavior that come from each ethical system

morals   judgments of good and bad conduct

natural law   concept that there are laws of nature such as gravity; such laws are discovered by reason but exist apart from humankind; natural laws also govern morality and human nature

natural right   the concept that one has certain rights just by virtue of being born

negligence   the least culpable mental state; indicates that one should have known the risk inherent in the action that caused a harm

net widening   concept that refers to the situation where a community alternative that is designed to be used as a diversion from prison is used, instead, for minor offenders who might not have received any sanction; therefore the total effect is not diversion, but increasing the number of people under the corrections umbrella

new rehabilitationists   current thinkers who argue that rehabilitation was never completely ineffective and should be given a chance to work

noble-cause corruption   concept that police officers may lie or commit illegal or unethical acts for a good end, i.e., to catch a criminal

normative ethics   study of what is right and wrong in particular situations

opinions   attitudes or judgments not subject to proof

organic solidarity   Durkheim's concept of societal solidarity as arising from differences among people, as exemplified by the division of labor

passive time server enforcer   type of probation officer who merely "gets by" doing the least amount of work

paternalism   the concept that government protects people from themselves, i.e., through seat belt, helmet, and speeding laws

peacemaking corrections   paradigm or approach that eschews retribution and instead looks to make all parties whole, both victim and offender

persuasion   the ability to influence or direct through skillful argument

pluralist paradigm   the concept that there are many groups in society and that they form allegiances and coalitions in a dynamic exchange of power

pluralistic ignorance   idea that in any occupational subculture or group of people, the vocal minority appear to represent the beliefs of the majority and the majority believe that they do, but when polled, private beliefs are different and opposite from what the majority believe everyone believes; for instance, prison correctional officers privately believe in more treatment principles than what they express or what they believe others agree with

power   authority combined with potential force

predeterminers   inherent factors that affect outcomes

prevention   justification for punishment that states the person will be deterred, incapacitated, or reformed through the punishment

principle of double effect   philosophical principle that states that an action can be considered good if it is for a good end, results in a bad consequence and a good consequence, but only the good consequence was intended

principle of forfeiture   states that one gives up one's right to be treated under the principles of respect for persons to the extent that one has abrogated someone else's rights; for instance, self-defense is acceptable according to the principle of forfeiture

principle of the golden mean
Aristotle's concept of moderation, that one should not err toward excess or deficiency; associated with the ethics of virtue

procedural justice   component of justice that concerns the steps taken (due process) to reach a determination of guilt and punishment

professional ethics   study of ethics for a specific profession or all professionals

psychological egoism   concept that humans naturally and inherently seek self-interest, and that they can do nothing else because it is their nature

public servants   professionals or workers who are paid from public monies and have duties to the public

punishment   pain inflicted on an individual by a legitimate authority after a determination of a wrong

punitive law enforcer   type of probation officer who emphasizes the supervision aspect of the role

reciprocity   relationship between a guard and prisoner that is based on the prisoner doing favors for the guard and then the guard owing the prisoner for such favors

recklessness   a more culpable mental state than negligence; indicates one knew of a risk and performed a behavior that resulted in a harm

regulations   rules that do not carry the same weight as laws but may involve sanctions

reinforcements   rewards

reintegrative shaming   type of shaming that involves rejecting only the behavior, not the individual, the argument is that it depends on the connection between the individual and his or her community and can be a powerful tool to control behavior

religious ethics   ethical system that is based on religious concepts of good and evil; what is good is that which is God's will

repressive law   Durkheim's view that law controls behavior that is different from the norm (related to mechanical solidarity)

restitutive law   Durkheim's view that law resolves conflicts between equals, as in commutative justice (related to organic solidarity)

restorative justice   new paradigm that emphasizes repairing the harm of a crime and making all parties whole

retribution   justification for punishment that states the person deserves punishment because of the harm done to another

retributive justice   component of justice that concerns the determination and methods of punishments

rights-based model   approach of law enforcement that emphasizes human and natural rights of the citizenry over crime control

rule utilitarianism   type of utilitarianism that determines the goodness of an action by measuring the utility of that action when made into a rule for behavior

shadow jury   tool used by trial consultants; group selected to match characteristics of real jury who are then used to test trial tactics to see how they will react

situational ethics   philosophical position that although there are a few universal truths, different situations call for different responses; therefore some action can be right or wrong depending on situational factors

situational model   approach of legal ethics that is similar to situational ethics, an action may be considered good or bad depending on situational factors

social contract theory   concept developed by Hobbes, Rousseau, and Locke, the state of nature is a "war of all against all"; in which life is nasty, brutish, and short; to protect being victimized by those who are stronger, each member gives up some liberties in return for protections; the contract is between society, which promises protection, and the individual, who promises to abide by laws and punishments if laws are broken

social contract   see social contract theory

specific deterrence   what is done to an individual to prevent that person from committing another crime

standards   guidelines or model behavior to follow

stigmatization   concept that what we do to an offender will change the way society treats the person even after the formal punishment is over

stigmatizing shaming   type of shaming that involves demeaning and rejecting the individual; the argument is that it invites more deviant behavior

street justice   idea that police may resolve disputes or situations by informal means

substantive justice   concept of just deserts; appropriate amount of punishment for the crime

superogatories   actions that are commendable but not considered moral duties required to be a moral person

systems model   a more absolute approach to legal ethics that views wrong actions as wrong all the time

teleological ethical system   study of ends; a teleological system is one concerned with the consequences or ends of an action to determine goodness

three strikes law   sentencing laws which provide for a much longer term of imprisonment for an offender facing a conviction for a third felony

treatment   what an individual is subjected to with the express purposes of changing his or her behavior in a positive way

utilitarian principle   philosophical principle that states one must do something when it benefits the majority

utilitarianism   ethical system that claims that the greatest good is that which results in the greatest happiness for the greatest number; major proponents are Bentham and Mill (*see also* act utilitarianism and rule utilitarianism)

values   measures of worth or priority

victim precipitation   concept related to victim's participation in the criminal act; victim plays a role and is not a passive object to the criminal's action; precipitation can range from instigating the victimization to merely making it possible, i.e., being an attractive target

Victim Satisfaction model   new approach that argues that the criminal justice system has now become too oriented to satisfying the victim instead of pursuing justice; the prosecutor in this view becomes merely a plaintiff's attorney rather than an officer of the court

victim-compensation programs   government program that provides funds to crime victims

victimology   study of victims

wedding-cake illustration   schemata of the justice system illustrating that a few cases get a lot of attention, but that the bulk of cases (on the bottom) are processed with few resources and little attention

welfare/therapeutic worker enforcer   type of probation officer who emphasizes the counseling aspect of the role

wholesight   a term that means to think with your heart as well as your head

zero tolerance policy   approach using full enforcement of the law for all offenses, no matter how minor

Bibliography

Adams, V. 1981. "How to Keep 'Em Honest." *Psychology Today* November: 52–53.

Albert, E. T. Denise, and S. Peterfreund. 1984. *Great Traditions in Ethics.* Belmont, CA: Wadsworth.

Alderson, J. 1998. *Principled Policing: Protecting the Public with Integrity.* Winchester, MA: Waterside Press.

Allen, H., and C. Simonsen. 1986. *Corrections in America: An Introduction.* New York: Macmillan.

American Bar Association. 1986. *Informal Opinions, Committee on Ethics and Professional Responsibility.* Chicago: American Bar Association.

American Society for Public Administration. 1979. *Professional Standards and Ethics: A Workbook for Public Administrators.* Washington, DC: American Society for Public Administration.

Amnesty International. 1999. *"Not Part of My Sentence": Violations of the Human Rights of Women in Custody.* London, England: Amnesty International.

Anderson, C. 1989. "DNA Evidence Questioned." *American Bar Association Journal* October: 18–19.

Anderson, P. and L. T. Winfree. 1987. *Expert Witnesses: Criminologists in the Courtroom.* Albany, NY: SUNY Press.

Arafat, I: and K. McCahery. 1978. "The Relationship Between Lawyers and Their Clients." In *Essays on the Theory and Practice of Criminal Justice,* ed. R. Rich, 193–219. Washington, DC: University Press.

Arax, M. 1999a. "Ex Guard Tells of Brutality, Code of Silence at Corcoran." *Los Angeles Times,* July 6, 1999.

Arax, M. 1999b. "Ex-Guard Says 4 Men Set Up Rape of Inmate." *Los Angeles Times,* October 14, 1999.

Arboleda-Florez, J. 1983. "The Ethics of Psychiatry in Prison Society." *Canadian Journal of Criminology* 25(1): 47–54.

Arbuthnot, J. 1984. "Moral Reasoning Development Programmes in Prison: Cognitive-Developmental and Critical Reasoning Approaches." *Journal of Moral Education* 13(2): 112–113.

Arbuthnot, J., and D. Gordon. 1988. "Crime and Cognition: Community Applications of Sociomoral Reasoning Development." *Criminal Justice and Behavior* 15(3): 379–393.

Armstrong, K. November 11 2002, and M. Possley. 2002. "The Verdict: Dishonor." *Chicago Tribune* Reports. Retrieved November 11, 2002, from http://www.ishipress.com/ dishonor.htm

Aronson, R. 1977. "Toward a Rational Resolution of Ethical Dilemmas in the Criminal Justice System." In *Criminal Justice Planning and Development,* ed. A. Cohn, 57–71. Beverly Hills, CA: Sage.

Associated Press. 2000. "Prison Guards Suspected of Money Laundering." *Austin American-Statesman.* January 27, 2000, B3.

Associated Press. 2002. "U.S. Supreme Court Could Make Miranda Warnings Thing of the Past." Cnn.Com, posted December 1, 2002, retrieved December 2, 2002, from http://www. cnn.com/2002/LAW/12/01/ scotus.police.questioning.ap/ index.html.

Attorney General's Commission on Pornography. 1986. *Final Report.* Washington, DC: U.S. Government Printing Office.

Aubert, V. 1969. *Sociology of Law.* London: Penguin.

Auerhahn, K. 1999. "Selective Incapacitation and the Problem of Prediction." *Criminology* 37, 4: 705–734.

Austin, J., and J. Irwin. 2001. *It's About Time: America's Imprisonment Binge.* Belmont, CA: Wadsworth.

Axtman K. "Bungles in Texas Crime Lab Stir Doubt over DNA," *Christian Science Monitor,* 18 April 2003. Retrieved 4/21/03 from: http://www.csmonitor.com/2003/ 0418/p03s01-usgn.html.

Babwin, D. 2001. "In Chicago, Allegations Plague Police Department," *Austin American-Statesman,* Sunday, April 22, 2001, A26.

Baelz, Peter. 1977. *Ethics and Beliefs.* New York: Seabury Press.

Baker, M. 1985. *Cops.* NYC: Pocket Books.

Barker, T. 1983. "Rookie Police Officers' Perceptions of Police Occupational Deviance." *Police Studies* 6: 30–40.

Barker, T., and D. Carter. 1991. "Police Lies and Perjury: A Motivation-Based Taxonomy." In *Police Deviance,* 2d ed., eds. T. Barker and D. Carter. Cincinnati, OH: Anderson.

Barker, T., and D. Carter. 1999. "Fluffing Up the Evidence and Covering Your Ass: Some Conceptual Notes on Police Lying." In *Policing Perspectives,* eds. L. Gaines and G. Cordner, 342–351. Los Angeles: Roxbury.

Baro, A. 1995. "Tolerating Illegal Use of Force Against Inmates." In *Morality in Criminal Justice,* eds. D. Close and N. Meier, 380–396. Belmont, CA: Wadsworth.

Barrier, G., M. Stohr, C. Hemmons, and R. Marsh. 1999. "A Practical User's Guide: Idaho's Method for Implementing Ethical Behavior in a Correctional Setting." *Corrections Compendium* 24, 4 (April):1–3.

Barry, Vincent. 1985. *Applying Ethics: A Text with Readings.* Belmont, CA: Wadsworth.

Bartollas, C., and S. Miller. 2001. *Juvenile Justice in America.* Upper Saddle River, NJ: Prentice-Hall.

Bazemore, G., and D. Maloney. 1994. "Rehabilitating Community Service Toward Restorative Service Sanctions in a Balanced Justice System." *Federal Probation* 58(1): 24–35.

Beauchamp, T. 1982. *Philosophical Ethics.* New York: McGraw-Hill.

Beccaria, C. 1977. *On Crimes and Punishment,* 6th ed. Trans. Henry Paolucci. Indianapolis, IN: Bobbs-Merrill.

Bedau, H. 1991. "How to Argue About the Death Penalty." *Israel Law Review* 25: 466–480.

Bedau, H. 1982. "Prisoners' Rights." *Criminal Justice Ethics* 1(1): 26–41.

Bentham, J. 1970. "The Rationale of Punishment." In *Ethical Choice: A Case Study Approach,* eds. R. Beck and J. Orr. New York: Free Press (original work published 1843).

Blumberg, A. 1969. "The Practice of Law as a Confidence Game." In *Sociology of Law,* ed. V. Aubert, 321-331. London: Penguin.

Bohm, R. 1996. "Crime, Criminal, and Crime Control Policy Myths." In *Justice, Crime, and Ethics,* eds. M. Braswell, B. McCarthy, and B. McCarthy, 341–363. Cincinnati, OH: Anderson.

Book, A. 1999. "Shame on You: An Analysis of Modern Shame Punishment as an Alternative to Incarceration." *William and Mary Law Review* 40, 2: 653–683.

Borchert, D., and D. Stewart. 1986. *Exploring Ethics.* New York: Macmillan.

Bossard, A. 1981. "Police Ethics and International Police Cooperation." In *The Social Basis of Criminal Justice: Ethical Issues for the 80's,* eds. F. Schamalleger and R. Gustafson, 23–38. Washington, DC: University Press.

Bourge, C. 2002. "Sparks Fly Over Private v. Public Prisons." UPI. Retrieved February 21, 2002, from www.upi./com/view. cfm?storyID=20022002-064851-41221.

Bowie, N. 1985. *Making Ethical Decisions.* New York: McGraw-Hill.

Bowker, L. 1980. *Prison Victimization.* New York: Elsevier

Boyer, P. 2001. "Bad Cops." *The New Yorker.* May 21, 2001. Retrieved on January 17, 2003, from http://www/ newyorker.com/printable/?fact/ 010521fa_FACT.

Boyce, W., and L. Jensen. 1978. *Moral Reasoning: A Psychological–Philosophical Integration.* Lincoln: University of Nebraska Press.

Braithwaite, J. 2000. "Shame and Criminal Justice." *Canadian Journal of Criminology* 42, (3): 281–301.

Braswell, M. 1996/2002. "Ethics, Crime, and Justice: An Introductory Note to Students." In *Justice, Crime, and Ethics,* eds. M. Braswell, B. McCarthy, and B. McCarthy, 3–9. Cincinnati, OH: Anderson.

Braswell, M., and J. Gold. 2002. "Peacemaking, Justice, and Ethics." In *Justice, Crime, and Ethics,* eds. M. Braswell, B. McCarthy, and B. McCarthy, 25–43. Cincinnati, OH: Anderson.

Braswell, M., B. McCarthy, and B. McCarthy. 2002. *Justice, Crime and Ethics.* Cincinnati, OH: Anderson.

Braswell, M., and J. Whitehead. 1999. "Seeking the Truth: An Alternative to Conservative and Liberal Thinking in Criminology. *Criminal Justice Review* 24, (3): 50–63.

Brown, M. 1981. *Working the Street.* New York: Russell Sage Foundation.

Bureau of Justice Statistics. 1992. *Prosecutors in State Courts, 1990.* Washington, DC: U.S. Department of Justice.

Bureau of Justice Statistics. 2002a. *Prisoners in 2001.* Washington, DC: U.S. Department of Justice.

Bureau of Justice Statistics. 2002b. *Capital Punishment, 2001.* Washington, DC: U.S. Department of Justice.

Buttell, F. 2002. "Exploring Levels of Moral Development Among Sex Offenders Participating in Community-Based Treatment." *Journal of Offender Rehabilitation.* 34 (4): 85–95.

Callahan, Daniel. 1982. "Applied Ethics in Criminal Justice." *Criminal Justice Ethics* 1(1): 1, 64.

Cao, L., J. Frank, F. Cullen. 1996. "Race, Community Context and Confidence in the Police." *Am. J. of Police* 15, 1: 3–22.

Carroll, L. 1998. *Lawful Order: A Case Study of Correctional Crisis and Reform.* New York: Garland Press.

Carter, D. 1999. "Drug Use and Drug-Related Corruption of Police Officers." In *Policing Perspectives,* eds. L. Gaines and G. Cordner. 311–324. Los Angeles: Roxbury.

Casey, R. 1996. "Cop Wins One Million in Whistleblower Appeal." In *The Ethics Roll Call* (Fall) 4(6).

Chevigny, P. 1995 *The Edge of the Knife: Police Violence in the Americas.* New York: The New Press.

Clinard, M. 1985. "Illegal Corporate Behavior." In *Exploring Crime,* ed. J. Sheley, 205–218. Belmont, CA: Wadsworth.

Close, D., and N. Meier. 1995. *Morality in Criminal Justice.* Belmont, CA: Wadsworth.

CNN.Com. 2001. Florida Judge Hears Motions in Child Murder Case. CNN.Com Law Center. Posted February 23, 2001. Retrieved on February 6, 2003, from http://www.cnn.com/2001/law/02/23/child.killer.hearing/

Cohen, E. 2002. "Pure Legal Advocates and Moral Agents Revisited: A Reply to Memory and Rose." *Criminal Justice Ethics* 21 (1): 39–55.

Cohen, E. 1991. "Pure Legal Advocates and Moral Agents: Two Concepts of a Lawyer in an Adversary System." In *Justice, Crime, and Ethics,* eds. M. Braswell, B. McCarthy, and B. McCarthy, 123–163. Cincinnati, OH: Anderson.

Cohen, H. 1983. "Searching Police Ethics." *Teaching Philosophy* 6(3): 231–242.

Cohen, H. 1985. "A Dilemma for Discretion." In *Police Ethics: Hard Choices in Law Enforcement,* eds. W. Heffernan and T. Stroup, 69–83. New York: John Jay Press

Cohen, H. 1986. "Exploiting Police Authority." *Criminal Justice Ethics* 5(2): 23–31.

Cohen, H. 1987. "Overstepping Police Authority." *Criminal Justice Ethics* (Summer/Fall): 52–60.

Cohen, H, and M. Feldberg. 1991. *Power and Restraint: The Moral Dimension of Police Work.* New York: Praeger.

Cohen, R. 2001. "How They Sleep at Night: DAs Turned Defenders Talk About Their Work." *American Lawyer: The Legal Intelligencer* (April 9, 2001).

Cole, G. 1970. "The Decision to Prosecute." *Law and Society Review* 4 (February.): 313–343.

Cole, D. 1999. *No Equal Justice.* New York: The Free Press.

Cole, D. 2002. "Trading Liberty for Security after September 11." Foreign Policy in Focus Policy Report." Retrieved August 29, 2002, from http://www.foreignpolicy-infocus.org/papers/post9-11_body.html

Cole, D., and J. Lamberth. 2001. "The Fallacy of Racial Profiling." *New York Times,* May 13, A19.

Columbia Law School. 2002. "A Broken System, Part II: Why There Is so Much Error in Capital Cases, and What Can Be Done About it." Columbia Law School Publications. Retrieved February 11, 2002, from http://www.law.columbia.edu/brokensystem2/exe_summary.html

Commission on Accreditation for Law Enforcement Agencies. 1994. *Standards for Law Enforcement Agencies.* Fairfax, VA: CALEA.

Conover, T. 2000 *New Jack: Guarding SingSing* NYC: Random House.

Copelin, L. 2003. "Oden Leaving Office to Join Law Firm." *Austin American-Statesman,* February. 14, 2003: A8.

Corey, G., M. Corey, and P. Callanan. 1988. *Issues and Ethics in Helping Professions.* Pacific Grove, CA: Brooks/Cole.

Corrections Digest. 2002. "Capital Sentences Dip 21% to 20-Year Low." *Corrections Digest* 33 (1) 4–5.

Cox, D. 2000. "Grand Jury Inquiry Into Death of Inmate Extended." *Sun-Sentinel,* January 5, 2000.

Craig, G. 2003. "Suit Alleges Rampant Female-Inmate Abuse." *Democrat and Chronicle.* Retrieved January 30, 2003, from http://www.rochesterdandc.com/news/forprint/0129story2_news.shtml.

Crank, J. 1998. *Understanding Police Culture.* Cincinnati, OH: Anderson.

Crank, J. 2003. *Imagining Justice.* Cincinnati, OH: Anderson.

Crank, J., and M. Caldero. 2000. *Police Ethics: The Corruption of Noble Cause.* Cincinnati, OH: Anderson.

Criminal Justice Newsletter. 2002. "Supreme Court Declines Case on Juvenile Death Penalty." *Criminal Justice Newsletter* 32, 19: 2–4.

Criminal Justice Policy Council 2003. Initial Process and Outcome Evaluation of the Inner Change Freedom Initiative. Available from Website: www.cjpc.state.tx.us

Crouch, B. 1986/1995. "Guard Work in Transition." In *The Dilemmas of Corrections,* 3d. Edition eds. K. Haas and G. Alpert, 183–203. Prospect Heights, IL: Waveland Press.

Crouch, B. 1980. *Keepers: Prison Guards and Contemporary Corrections.* Springfield, IL: Charles C. Thomas.

Crouch, B., and J. Marquart. 1989. *An Appeal to Justice: Litigated Reform in Texas Prisons.* Austin: University of Texas Press.

Curry, M. 2002. "Faulty Drug Cases Draw Police Inquiry." *Dallas Morning News,* February 21, 2002, 25A

Daley, R. 1984. *Prince of the City.* New York: Berkley.

Daly, K. 1989. "Criminal Justice Ideologies and Practices in Different Voices: Some Feminist Questions About Justice." *International Journal of the Sociology of Law* (17): 1–18.

Davis, M. 1991. "Do Cops Really Need a Code of Ethics?" *Criminal Justice Ethics* 10(2): 14–28.

Davis, M., and F. Elliston. 1986. *Ethics and the Legal Profession.* Buffalo: Prometheus Books.

Dawson, J. 1992. "Prosecutors in State Courts." *Bureau of Justice Statistics Bulletin.* Washington DC: U.S. Department of Justice.

Delaney, H. 1990. "Toward a Police Professional Ethic." In *Ethics in Criminal Justice,* ed. F. Schmalleger, 78–95. Bristol, IN: Wyndham Hall Press.

Delattre, E. 1989a. *Character and Cops: Ethics in Policing.* Washington, DC: American Enterprise Institute for Public Policy Research.

Delattre, E. 1989b. "Ethics in Public Service: Higher Standards and Double Standards." *Criminal Justice Ethics* 8(2): 79–83.

Dershowitz, A. 1994. *The Abuse Excuse and Other Cop-Outs, Sob Stories, and*

Evasions of Responsibility. Boston: Little, Brown and Company.

Dershowitz, A. 1982. *The Best Defense.* New York City. Vintage Books.

Deutsch, L. 2001. "L.A. Police Corruption Probe Set to Wrap Up." San Jose Mercury News. Retrieved 11/12/01 from http://www.mercurycenter.com/ premium/local/docs/rampart08.htm.

Dilulio, J. 1987. *Governing Prisons: A Comparative Study of Correctional Management.* New York: Free Press.

Dix. G. When Government Deception Goes Too Far, *Texas Lawyer* 7(31) (1991): 12–13.

Donn J. "Ex. Agents say FBI Over Looked Informants Violent Crimes," *Austin American Statesman,* 2 March 2003, A 16.

Dorschner, J. 1989. "The Dark Side of the Force." In *Critical Issues in Policing,* 2d ed., 254–274. Prospect Heights, IL: Waveland.

Douglass, J. 1981. "Prosecutorial Ethics." In *The Social Basis of Criminal Justice: Ethical Issues for the 80's* eds. F. Schmalleger and R. Gustafson, 109–171. Washington, DC: University Press.

Dror, Y. 1969. "Law and Social Change." In *Sociology of Law,* ed. V. Aubert, 90–100. London: Penguin.

Dunningham, C., and C. Norris. 1999. "The Detective, the Snout, and the Audit Commission: The Real Costs in Using Informants." *Howard Journal of Criminal Justice* 38 (1): 67–87.

Durkheim, E. 1969. "Types of Law in Relation to Types of Social Solidarity." In *Sociology of Law,* ed. V. Aubert, 17–29. London: Penguin.

Dzur, A., and A. Wertheimer. 2002. "Forgiveness and Public Deliberation: The Practice of Restorative Justice." *Criminal Justice Ethics.* 21 (1): 3–20.

Elias, R. 1986. *The Politics of Victimization.* New York: Oxford University Press.

Ellis, L., and A. Pontius. 1989. *The Frontal-Limbic-Reticular Network and Variations in Pro-antisociality: A Neurological Based Model of Moral Reasoning and Criminality.* Reno, NV: Paper presented at the 1989 ASC conference.

Elliston, F. 1986. "The Ethics of Ethics Tests for Lawyers." In *Ethics and the Legal Profession,* eds. M. Davis and F. Elliston, 50–61. Buffalo, NY: Prometheus Books.

Elliston, F., and M. Feldberg. 1985. *Moral Issues in Police Work.* Totawa, NJ: Rowman & Allanheld.

"Ethical Principles for Psychologists." 1981. *American Psychologist* 36 (June): 633–638.

Ewin, R. 1990. "Loyalty and the Police." *Criminal Justice Ethics* 9(2): 3–15.

Farkas, M. 1999. "Correctional Officer Attitudes Toward Inmates and Working with Inmates in a 'Get Tough' Era." *Journal of Criminal Justice* 27, 6: 495–506.

"FBI, Media Could Face Lawsuit in Jewell Case." *Austin American-Statesman,* October 27, 1996: A1, A8.

Fecteau, L. 1999. "Private Prisons Warned." *Albuquerque Journal.* http://www. albqjournal.com/news/2news08-27-99. html.

Feibleman, J. 1985. *Justice, Law and Culture.* Boston: Martinus Nijhoff.

Feinberg, J., and H. Gross. 1977. *Justice: Selected Readings.* Princeton, NJ: Princeton University Press.

Felkenes, G. 1987. "Ethics in the Graduate Criminal Justice Curriculum." *Teaching Philosophy* 10(1): 23–36.

Felkenes, G. 1984. "Attitudes of Police Officers Towards Their Professional Ethics." *Journal of Criminal Justice* (12): 211–220.

Feuer, A. 2000. Ex Officer Details Surge of Rage as He Began Attack on Louima. *New York Times.* Retrieved on February 18, 2000, from http://www. nytimes.com/yr/mo/day/news/ national/regional/ny-louima. html.

Findlay, M. 1982. "Bathurst — Riots, Bashings and Cover Up." In *The State of the Prison.* M. Findlay, 21–41. Australia: Mitchell College Printery.

Fink, P. 1977. *Moral Philosophy.* Encino, CA: Dickinson.

Fishman, E. 1994. "'Falling Back' on Natural Law and Prudence; A Reply to Souryal and Potts." *Journal of Criminal Justice Education.* 5(2): 189–203.

Fishbein, D. 2000. *Biobehavioral Perspectives on Criminology.* Belmont, CA: Wadsmorth.

Fitzgerald, G. 1989. Report of a Commission of Inquiry Pursuant to Orders in Council. Brisbane: Goprint Publishers. (Cited in T. Prenzler and C. Ronken, 2001.)

Flanagan, D., and K. Jackson. 1987. "Justice, Care, and Gender: The Kohlberg–Gilligan Debate Revisited." *Ethics* (97): 622–637.

Fletcher, G. 1993. *Loyalty: An Essay on the Morality of Relationships.* NYC: Oxford University Press.

Fogel, David. 1975. *We Are the Living Proof.* Cincinnati OH: Anderson.

Fogel, D, and J. Hudson. 1981. *Justice as Fairness.* Cincinnati OH: Anderson.

Fogelson, R. 1977. *Big City Police.* Cambridge, MA: Harvard University Press.

Foot, P. 1982. "Moral Relativism." In *Relativism: Cognitive and Moral,* eds. J. Meiland and M. Krausz, 152–167. Notre Dame, IN: University of Notre Dame Press.

Fountain, J. 2001. "Former Top Chicago Detective Admits to Leading Theft Ring." *New York Times,* October 26, 2001, A16.

Freedman, M. 1986. "Professional Responsibility of the Criminal Defense Lawyer: The Three Hardest Questions." In *Ethics and the Legal Profession,* eds. M. Davis and F. Elliston, 328–339. Buffalo, NY: Prometheus Books.

Fried, C. 1986. "The Lawyer as Friend." In *Ethics and the Legal Profession,* eds. M. Davis and F. Elliston, 132–157. Buffalo, NY: Prometheus Books.

Fuller, L. 1969. *The Morality of Law.* New Haven, CT: Yale University Press.

Gallup Poll (2001). *Gallup Poll Online,* Jan. 4, 2002: Retrieved February 20, 2003, from http://www.gallup.com/ polltopics/hnsty_ethcs.asp.Jan4,2002.

Galston, W. 1980. *Justice and the Human Good.* Chicago: University of Chicago Press.

Garland, D. 1990. *Punishment and Modern Society.* Chicago: University of Chicago Press.

Gavaghan, M., K. Arnold, and J. Gibbs. 1983. "Moral Judgement in Delinquents and Nondelinquents: Recognition versus Production Measures." *The Journal of Psychology* (114): 267–274.

Geis, G., A. Mobley, and D. Shichor. 1999. "Private Prisons, Criminological Research and Conflict of Interest." *Crime and Delinquency* 45 (3): 372–388.

Gershman, B. 1991. "Why Prosecutors Misbehave." In *Justice, Crime, and Ethics,* eds. M. Braswell, B. McCarthy, and B. McCarthy, 163–177. Cincinnati OH: Anderson.

Getlin, J. 2002a. "Officer Refuses to Arrest Homeless." *Austin American-Statesman,* November. 30, 2002: A8.

Getlin, J. 2002b. "DA Suggests Overturning Convictions in Jogger Case." *Austin American-Statesman,* December. 6, 2002: A16.

Gibbs, J., K. Arnold, H. Ahlborn, and F. Cheesman. 1984. "Facilitation of Sociomoral Reasoning in Delinquents." *Journal of Consulting and Clinical Psychology* 52(1): 37–45.

Gilligan, C. 1982. *In a Different Voice: Psychological Theory and Women's Development.* Cambridge, MA: Harvard University Press.

Gilligan, C. 1987. "Moral Orientation and Moral Development." In *Women and Moral Theory,* eds. E. F. Kittay and D. Meyers, 19–37. Totawa, NJ: Rowman, Littlefield.

Glendon, M. 1994. *A Nation Under Lawyers.* New York: Farrar, Straus and Giroux.

Glenn, L. 2001. *Texas Prisons: The Largest Hotel Chain in Texas.* Austin, TX: Eakin Press.

Glover, S., and M. Lait. 2000. "71 More Cases May Be Voided Due to Rampart," *Los Angels Times,* Retrieved on April, 20, 2000, from www.latimes.com/news/state/reports/rampart/lat_rampart000418.html

Government Accounting Office (G.A.O.). 1996. *Private and Public Prisons —*
Studies Comparing Operational Costs and/or Quality of Service. Washington DC: U.S. Government Printing Office.

"Guards Acquitted of Staging Gladiator Fights." 2002. *New York Times,* June 10, 2002, A16.

Golab, J. 2000. "L.A. Confidential." *Salon.Com.* Retrieved on January 17, 2003, from http://dir.salon.com/news/feature/2000/24/rampart/index.http.

Gold, J., M. Braswell, and B. McCarthy. 1991. "Criminal Justice Ethics: A Survey of Philosophical Theories." In *Justice, Crime, and Ethics,* eds. M. Braswell, B. McCarthy, and B. McCarthy, 3–25. Cincinnati OH: Anderson.

Greene, J. 1999. Zero Tolerance: A Case Study of Police Policies and Practices in New York City." *Crime and Delinquency* 45 (2): 171–187.

Greene, J. 2001. "Bailing Out Private Jails." *American Prospect* 12 (16): 23–27.

Greenwood, P. 1982. *Selective Incapacitation.* Santa Monica, CA: Rand Institute.

Grossi, E., and B. Berg. 1991. "Stress and Job Dissatisfaction Among Correctional Officers: An Unexpected Finding." *International Journal of Offender Therapy and Comparative Criminology,* 35 (1): 79–110.

Hafetz, D. 2002. "Their Innocence Proved, Men Sue." *Austin American-Statesman,* November 8, 2002: B1.

Hall, M. 2002. "Death Isn't Fair." *Texas Monthly,* December: 124–167.

Hamm, M. 1995. *The Abandoned Ones.* Boston, MA: Northeastern Press.

Hamm, M. 1989. "Whistleblowing in Corrections," *Sociological Viewpoints* 5 (1): 35–45

Harper, J. 1992. "Local Judge on Hot Seat Over Conduct." *Houston Post,* July 6: A9.

Harris, C. 1986. *Applying Moral Theories.* Belmont, CA: Wadsworth.

Hartman, V. 2001. "Implementing an Asset Forfeiture Program." *FBI Law Enforcement Bulletin,* 70 (1): 1–7.

Hassine, V. 1996. *Life Without Parole: Living in Prison Today.* Los Angeles: Roxbury.

Heffernan, W., and J. Kleinig. 2000. *From Social Justice to Criminal Justice: Poverty and the Administration of Criminal Law.* NY: Oxford Univ. Press.

Heffernan, W., and T. Stroup. 1985. *Police Ethics: Hard Choices in Law Enforcement.* New York: John Jay Press.

Heidensohn, F. 1986. "Models of Justice: Portia or Persephone? Some Thoughts on Equality, Fairness and Gender in the Field of Criminal Justice." *International Journal of the Sociology of Law* (14): 287–298.

Hentoff, N. 1999. "Serpico: Nothing Has Changed." *Village Voice.com.* Retrieved November 4, 1999, from http://www.villagevoice.com/issues/9944/hentoff.shtml

Herbert, B. 2002. "In Tulia, Justice Has Gone into Hiding," *Austin American Statesman,* August 13, 2002, A9.

Herbert, B. 2003. "Truth Has Been Told About Tulia, But story isn't over yet," *Austin American Statesman,* 29 April 2003, A9.

Hersh, F. 1979. *Developing Moral Growth: From Piaget to Kohlberg.* New York: Longman.

Hickey, J., and P. Scharf. 1980. *Toward a Just Correctional System.* San Francisco: Jossey-Bass.

Hinman, L. 1998. *Ethics: A Pluralistic Approach to Moral Theory.* 2d ed. Ft. Worth, TX: Harcourt Brace College Publishing.

Hockstuder, L. 2003. "Texas to Toss Drug Convictions Against 38 People," *Washington Post,* 2 April 2003, A 03.

Hofer, P., K. Blackwell, R. B. Ruback. 1999. "The Effect of Federal Sentencing Guidelines on Inter-Judge Sentencing Disparity." *Journal of Criminal Law and Criminology* 90 (1): 239–321.

Holmes, M. 2000. "Minority Threat and Police Brutality: Determinants of Civil Rights Criminal Complaints in U.S. Municipalities." *Criminology* 38 (2): 343–36.

Hook, S. 1977. "Social Protest and Civil Disobedience." In *Moral Philosophy,* ed. S. Hook, 122–130. Encino, CA: Dickinson.

Hook, M. 2001. "How and Why the System Is Failing Victims with Mental Impairments." *Crime Victims Report,* 4 (6): 81–82.

Hopfe, L. 1983. *Religions of the World.* New York: Macmillan.

Hornum, F., and F. Stavish. 1978. "Criminology Theory and Ideology: Four Analytical Perspectives in the Study of Crime and the Criminal Justice System." In *Essays on the Theory and Practice of Criminal Justice,* ed. R. Rich, 143–161. Washington, DC: University Press.

Houston, J. 1999. *Correctional Management: Functions, Skills, and Systems.* Chicago: Nelson-Hall Publishers.

Human Rights Watch. 1998. *Shielded from Justice; Police Brutality and Accountability in the U.S.* NY: Human Rights Watch.

Hunter, R. 1999. "Officer Opinions on Police Misconduct." *Journal of Contemporary Criminal Justice* 15, 2: 155–170.

Huspek, M., R. Martinez, and L. Jiminez. 2001. "Violations of Human Civil Rights on the U.S.–Mexico Border, 1997–1997: A Report." In *Notable Selections in Criminal Criminology and Criminal Justice,* eds. D. Baker and R. Davin, 183–202. Guilford, CT: McGraw-Hill/Dushkin.

Jablon, R. 2000. "L.A. Confronts Police Scandal That May Cost Tens of Millions." *Austin American-Statesman,* February 19, 2000: A18.

Jaccoby, J., L. Mellon, and W. Smith. 1980. *Policy and Prosecution.* Washington, DC: Bureau of Social Science Research.

Jenson, E., and J. Gerber, 1996. "The Civil Forfeiture of Assets and the War on Drugs: Expanding Criminal Sanctions While Reducing Due Process Protection." *Crime and Delinquency* 42(3): 421–434.

Johnson, C., and G. Copus. 1981. "Law Enforcement Ethics: A Theoretical

Analysis." In *The Social Basis of Criminal Justice: Ethical Issues for the 80's,* eds. F. Schmalleger and R. Gustafson, 39–83. Washington, DC: University Press.

Johnson, D. 1982. "Morality and Police Harm." In *Ethics, Public Policy, and Criminal Justice,* eds. F. Elliston and N. Bowie, 79–92. Cambridge, MA: Oelgeschlager, Gunn and Hain.

Johnson, Leslie. 1982. "Frustration: The Mold of Judicial Philosophy." *Criminal Justice Ethics* 1(1): 20–26.

Johnson, R. 1987/1996/2002. *Hard Time: Understanding and Reforming the Prison.* Belmont, CA: Wadsworth Publishing Co.

Johnson, R. 1991. "A Life for a Life? Opinion and Debate." In *Justice, Crime, and Ethics,* eds. M. Braswell, B. McCarthy, and B. McCarthy, 199–210. Cincinnati, OH: Anderson.

Johnston, M. 1995. "Police Corruption." In *Morality in Criminal Justice,* eds. D. Close and N. Meier. Belmont, CA: Wadsworth.

Josi, D., and D. Sechrest. 1998. *The Changing Career of the Correctional Officer: Policy Implications for the 21st Century.* Boston: Butterworth-Heinemann.

Kamisar, Y., W. LeFave, and J. Israel. 1980. *Modern Criminal Procedure: Cases, Comments, and Questions.* St. Paul, MN: West Publishing.

Kania, R. 1988. "Police Acceptance of Gratuities." *Criminal Justice Ethics* 7(2): 37–49.

Kania, R. 1999. "The Ethics of the Death Penalty." *The Justice Professional* 12: 145–157.

Kant, I. 1949. *Critique of Practical Reason,* trans. Lewis White Beck. Chicago: University of Chicago Press.

Kant, I. 1981. "Ethical Duties to Others: Truthfulness." In *Lectures on Ethics,* ed. L. Infield, 224–232. Indianapolis: Hackett.

Kaplan, M. 1976. *Justice, Human Nature and Political Obligation.* New York: Free Press.

Kappeler, V., M. Blumberg, and Potter, G. 2000. *The Mythology of Crime and Justice.* Prospect Heights, IL: Waveland.

Kappeler, V., and G. Potter. 1996. *The Mythology of Crime and Justice.* Prospect Heights, IL: Waveland.

Kappeler, V., K. Sluder, and G. Alpert. 1984/1994. *Forces of Deviance: Understanding the Dark Side of Policing.* Prospect Heights, IL: Waveland.

Karmen, A. 1984. *Crime Victims: An Introduction to Victimology.* Pacific Grove, CA: Brooks/Cole.

Karp, D. 1998. "The Judicial and Judicious Use of Shame Penalties." *Crime and Delinquency* 44 (2): 277–295.

Kauffman, K. 1988. *Prison Officers and Their World.* Cambridge, MA: Harvard University Press.

Kessler, G. 1992. *Voices of Wisdom: A Multicultural Philosophy Reader.* Belmont, CA: Wadsworth.

King, R., and M. Mauer. 2002. *State Sentencing and Corrections Policy in an Era of Fiscal Restraint.* Washington, DC: Sentencing Project.

King, R., and M. Mauer. 2001. *Aging Behind Bars: Three Strikes Seven Years Later.* Washington DC: Sentencing Project.

King, R., M. Mauer, and T. Huling. 2003. *Big Prisons, Small Towns: Prison Economics in Rural America.* Washington, DC: The Sentencing Project.

Kittel, N. 1990. "Criminal Defense Attorneys: Bottom of the Legal Profession's Class." In *Ethics in Criminal Justice,* ed. F. Schmalleger, 42–62. Bristol, IN: Wyndam Hall Press.

Kleindienst, L. 1999. "Florida Prison Guards Twice as Likely as Police to Commit Violations." *Sun-Sentinel,* August 25, 1999.

Kleinig, J. 1999. "Human Dignity and Human Rights: An Emerging Concern in Police Practice." In *Human Dignity and Police: Ethics and Integrity in Police Work,* ed. G. Lynch, 8–4. Springfield, IL: Charles C. Thomas.

Kleining, J. 1996. *Handled with Discretion.* Lanham, MD: Rowman and Littlefield.

Kleinig, J. 1986. "The Conscientious Advocate and Client Perjury." *Criminal Justice Ethics* 5(2): 3–15.

Klockars, C., and S. Mastrofski 1991. *Thinking About Police.* New York: McGraw-Hill.

Klockars, C. 1983. "The Dirty Harry Problem." In *Thinking About Police: Contemporary Readings,* ed. C. Klockars and S. Mastrofski, 428–438. New York: McGraw-Hill.

Klockars, C. 1984. "Blue Lies and Police Placebos." *American Behavioral Scientist* 27(4): 529–544.

Klockars, C., S. Ivkovich, W. Harver, and M. Haberfeld. 2000. *The Measurement of Police Integrity? NIJ Research in Brief.* Washington, DC: U.S. Dept of Justice.

Knudten, M. 1978. "The Prosecutor's Role in Plea Bargaining: Reasons Related to Actions." In *Essays on the Theory and Practice of Criminal Justice,* ed. R. Rich, 275–295. Washington, DC: University Press.

Kohlberg, L. 1984. *The Psychology of Moral Development.* San Francisco: Harper & Row.

Kohlberg, L. 1983. *Essays in Moral Development, Vol. 2. The Psychology of Moral Development.* New York: Harper & Row.

Kohlberg, L. 1976. "Moral Stages and Moralization." In *Moral Development and Behavior: Theory, Research and Social Issues,* ed. T. Lickona, 31–53. New York: Holt, Rinehart and Winston.

Kohlberg, L., and D. Candel, 1984. "The Relationship of Moral Judgment to Moral Action." In *The Psychology of Moral Development,* ed. L. Kohlberg, 498–582. San Francisco: Harper & Row.

Kottak, C. 1974. *Anthropology: The Exploration of Human Diversity.* New York: Random House.

Kramer, R. 1982. "The Debate Over the Definition of Crime: Paradigms, Value Judgments, and Criminological Work."
In *Ethics, Public Policy and Criminal Justice,* eds. F. Elliston and N. Bowie, 33–59. Cambridge, MA: Oelgeschlager, Gunn and Hain.

Kraska, P., and V. Kappeler. 1995. "To Serve and Pursue: Exploring Police Sexual Violence Against Women." *Justice Quarterly* 12 (1): 85–111.

Kraus, C. 1994. "Poll Finds a Lack of Faith in the Police." *New York Times,* June 19, at A1.

Kravets, D. 2003. "ACLU: Privacy Rights Diminished." *Salon.com.* Retrieved January, 16, 2003 from http://www.salon.com/tech/wire/2003/01/16/aclu/index.http.

Krisberg, B. 1975. *Crime and Privilege: Toward a New Criminology.* Englewood Cliffs, NJ: Prentice-Hall.

Krogstand, J., and J. Robertson. 1979. "Moral Principles for Ethical Conduct." *Management Horizons* 10(1): 13–24.

Kronenwerter, M. 1993. *Capital Punishment: A Reference Handbook.* Santa Barbara, CA: ABC–CLIO.

Lait, M., and S. Glover. 2000. "LAPD Chief Calls for Mass Dismissal of Tainted Cases." *LATimes.com* Retrieved February, 1, 2000, from http://www.latimes.com/news/state/200000127/t000008518.http.

Laitinen, A. 2002. *Corruption of the Police: Is it Not at all a Problem in Finland?* Presented at ACJS, Anaheim, CA, March 2002.

Langford, T. 1997. "Company Defends Its Jailers Conduct." *Austin American-Statesman,* August 22, B3.

Leahy, R. 1981. "Parental Practices and the Development of Moral Judgment and Self Image Disparity During Adolescence." *Developmental Psychology* 17(5): 580–594.

LeDuff, C. 2002. "Los Angeles Police Chief Faces a Huge Challenge." *New York Times,* Retrieved October, 25, 2002, from http://www.nytimes.com/2002/10/24/national/24GANG.html.

Leiser, B. 1986. *Liberty, Justice and Morals.* New York: Macmillan.

Levine, C., L. Kohlberg, and A. Hewer. 1985. "The Current Formulation of Kohlberg's Theory and Response to Critics." *Human Development* (28): 94–100.

Levy, C. 2003a. "Prison Company's Courtship Provokes New York's Scrutiny." *Nytimes.com*. Retrieved on February, 20, 2003, from http://www.nytimes.com/2003/02/17/nyregion/17PRIS.http.

Levy, C. 2003b. "Prison Company Faces Fine on Gaps in Lobbying Records." *NYTimes.com*. Retrieved on February, 10, 2003, from http://www.nytimes.com/2003/02/06/nyregion/06LEGI.html.

Lewis, D. 1998. *Guilty by Reason of Insanity*. New York City: Ivy Books.

Lewis, M. 1999. "Corcoran Guards Launch Ads." *Fresno Bee*, September 17, 1999, A1.

Lickona, T. 1976. *Moral Development and Behavior: Theory, Research and Social Issues*. New York: Holt, Rinehart and Winston.

Liptak, A. "Houston DNA lab worst in country, experts say," *Austin American Statesman*, 11 March 2003, B1.

Lombardo, L. 1989. *Guards Imprisoned: Correctional Officers at Work*. Cincinnati, OH: Anderson.

Lombardo, Lucien. 1981. *Guards Imprisoned: Correctional Officers at Work*. New York: Elsevier.

Lombardo, Lucien. 1997. "Guards Imprisoned: Correctional Officers at Work." In *Correctional Contexts*, eds. J. Marquart and J. Sorensen, 189–203. Los Angeles: Roxbury.

Longmire, D. 1983. "Ethical Dilemmas in the Research Setting." *Criminology* 21(3): 333–348.

Louthan, W. 1985. "The Politics of Discretionary Justice Among Criminal Justice Agencies." In *Discretion, Justice, and Democracy: A Public Policy Perspective*, eds. C. Pinkele and W. Louthan, 13–19. Ames: Iowa State University Press.

Lucas, J. 1980. *On Justice*. Oxford: Oxford University Press.

Lutwak, N., and J. Hennessy. 1985. "Interpreting Measures of Moral Development to Individuals." *Measurement and Evaluation in Counseling and Development* 18 (1): 26–31.

Lynch, G. 1999. *Human Dignity and the Police: Ethics and Integrity in Police Work*. Springfield, IL: Charles C. Thomas.

Maas, P. 1973. *Serpico*. New York: Viking Press.

Maas, P. 1983. *Marie*. New York: Random House.

MacIntyre, A. 1999. *Dependent Rational Animals: Why Human Beings Need the Virtues*. Chicago, IL: Open Ct.

MacIntyre, A. 1991. *After Virtue*. South Bend, IN: University of Notre Dame Press.

Macintyre, S., and T. Prenzler 1999. "The Influence of Gratuities and Personal Relationships on Police Use of Discretion." *Policing and Society* 9: 181–201.

Mackie, J. L. 1977. *Ethics: Inventing Right and Wrong*. New York: Penguin.

Mackie, J. L. 1982. "Morality and the Retributive Emotions." *Criminal Justice Ethics* 1(1): 3–10.

Maestri, W. 1982. *Basic Ethics for the Health Care Professional*. Washington, DC: University Press.

Malloy, E. 1982. *The Ethics of Law Enforcement and Criminal Punishment*. Lanham, NY: University Press.

Manning, P. 1997. *Policework*. 2d ed. Prospect Heights, IL: Waveland Press.

Manning, P., and L. Redlinger. 1991. "Invitational Edges." In *Thinking About Police: Contemporary Readings*, ed. C. Klockars and S. Mastrofski, 398–413. New York: McGraw-Hill.

Mappes, T. 1982. *Social Ethics*. New York: McGraw-Hill.

Margolis, J. 1971. *Values and Conduct*. New York: Oxford University Press.

Marks, F., F. Raymond, and D. Cathcart. 1986. "Discipline Within the Legal Profession." In *Ethics and the Legal Profession*, eds. M. Davis and F. Elliston, 62–105. Buffalo, NY: Prometheus Books.

Marquart, J., and J. Roebuck. 1986. "Prison Guards and Snitches." In *The Dilemmas of Corrections: Contemporary Readings,* eds. K. Haus and G. Alpert, 158–176. Prospect Heights, IL: Waveland.

Martin, D. 1993. *Committing Journalism: The Writings of Red Hog.* New York: Norton.

Martinelli, T. 2000. *Combating the Charge of Deliberate Indifference Through Police Ethics Training and a Comprehensive Risk Management Policy.* Presented at the 2000 Annual Meeting of the Academy of Criminal Justice Sciences, New Orleans, LA.

Marx, Gary. 1992. "Under-the-Covers Undercover Investigations: Some Reflections on the State's Use of Deception." *Criminal Justice Ethics* 11(1): 13–25.

Marx, G. 1991. "The New Police Undercover Work" In Thinking About Police: *Contemporary Readings,* ed. C. Klockars and S. Mastrofski, 240–258. New York: McGraw-Hill.

Marx, G. 1985a. "Police Undercover Work: Ethical Deception or Deceptive Ethics?" In *Police Ethics: Hard Choices in Law Enforcement,* eds. W. Heffernan and T. Stroup, 83–117. New York: John Jay Press.

Marx, G. 1985b. "Who Really Gets Stung? Some Issues Raised by the New Police Undercover Work." In *Moral Issues in Police Work,* eds. F. Elliston and M. Feldberg, 99–129. Totawa, NJ: Rowman & Allanheld.

Matthews, J., and R. Marshall. 1981. "Some Constraints on Ethical Behavior in Criminal Justice Organizations." In *The Social Basis of Criminal Justice: Ethical Issues for the 80's,* eds. F. Schmalleger and R. Gustafson, 9–22. Washington, DC: University Press.

Mauer, M., M. Chesney-Lind, and T. Clear. 2002. *Invisible Punishment: The Collateral Consequences of Mass Imprisonment.* New York: The Sentencing Project.

McAnany, P. 1981. "Justice in Search of Fairness." In *Justice as Fairness,* eds. D. Fogel and J. Hudson, 22–51. Cincinnati, OH: Anderson.

McCarthy, B. 1991. "Keeping an Eye on the Keeper: Prison Corruption and Its Control." In *Justice, Crime, and Ethics,* eds. M. Braswell, B. McCarthy, and B. McCarthy, 239–253. Cincinnati, OH: Anderson.

McCarthy, B. 1995. "Patterns of Prison Corruption." In *Morality in Criminal Justice,* eds. D. Close and N. Meier, 280–285. Belmont, CA: Wadsworth.

Memory, J., and C. Rose. 2002. "The Attorney as Moral Agent: A Critique of Cohen." *Criminal Justice Ethics* 21, 1: 28–39.

Messner, S., and R. Rosenfeld. 1994. *Crime and the American Dream.* Belmont, CA: Wadsworth Publishing Company.

Metz, H. 1990. "An Ethical Model for Law Enforcement Administrators." In *Ethics in Criminal Justice,* ed. F. Schmalleger, 95–103. Bristol, IN: Wyndam Hall Press.

Milgram, S. 1963. "Behavioral Study of Obedience." *Journal of Abnormal and Social Psychology* 67: 371–378.

Miller, K., and M. Radelet. 1993. *Executing the Mentally Ill.* Newbury Park, CA: Sage.

Mitchell, J., and S. Banks. 1996. "Once Again, Americans Fall into Racial Rut." *Austin American-Statesman,* February 9, 1996.

Mitford, J. 1971. *Kind and Usual Punishment.* New York: Vintage Books.

Mobley, A., and G. Geis. 2002. "The Corrections Corporation of America a.k.a. The Prison Realty Trust, Inc." In *Justice Crime and Ethics,* eds. M. Braswell, B. McCarthy and B. McCarthy, 329–349. Cincinnati, OH: Anderson.

Moore, M. 1997. *Police Integrity: Public Service without Honor.* NIJ: U.S. Dept of Justice.

Mores, T. 2002. "Police Misconduct: A Global Problem." *Crime and Justice International,* January: 9–10, 24–26.

Morris, R. 2000. *Stories of Transformative Justice.* Toronto, Ontario: Canadian Scholars Press.

Moss, M., and F. Fessenden, 2002. "War Against Terrorism Stirs a Battle over Privacy." *Austin American-Statesman,* December 11: A17–19.

Muir, W. 1977. *Police: Streetcorner Politicians.* Chicago: University of Chicago Press.

Murphy, C. 2002. "Monitor Gives DC Police Mixed Review," *Washington Post,* Retrieved on August 8, 2002, from www.washingtonpost.com/wp-dyn/articles/A52807-2002Aug6.http.

Murphy, J. 1985/1995. *Punishment and Rehabilitation.* Belmont, CA: Wadsworth

Murphy, K. 2002. "States Get Grants to Help Ex-Offenders." *Stateline.org.* Retrieved July 17, 2002, from, www.stateline.org/story.do?storyID=248888.

Murphy, P., and D. Caplan. 1989. "Conditions that Breed Corruption." In *Critical Issues in Policing,* eds. R. Dunham and G. Alpert, 304–324. Prospect Heights, IL: Waveland.

Murphy, P., and K. Moran. 1981. "The Continuing Cycle of Systemic Police Corruption." In *The Social Basis of Criminal Justice: Ethical Issues for the 80's,* eds. F. Schmalleger and R. Gustafson, 87–101. Washington, DC: University Press.

Murton, T. 1976. *The Dilemma of Prison Reform.* New York: Irvington.

Murton, T., and Hyams, J. 1969. *Accomplices to the Crime: The Arkansas Prison Scandal.* New York: Grove.

Nash, L. 1981. "Ethics Without the Sermon." *Harvard Business Review,* November–December: 81.

National Institute of Justice. 1992. "Community Policing in the 1990s." *National Institute of Justice Research Bulletin,* August: 2–9.

Nelson, J. 2000. *Police Brutality.* NY: W.W. Norton and Co.

Nettler, G. 1978. *Explaining Crime.* New York: McGraw-Hill.

Newman, G. 1978. *The Punishment Response.* New York: J. B. Lippincott.

Neyroud, P., and A. Beckley. 2001. *Policing, Ethics and Human Rights.* Devon, England: Willan Publishing.

Noddings, N. 1986. *Caring: A Feminine Approach to Ethics and Moral Education.* Berkeley: University of California Press.

Nowell, S. 2001. "Face to Face." *Houston Press,* September 27 to October 3, 2001.

Office of Juvenile Justice and Delinquency Prevention (O.J.J.D.P.). 2001. *National Report Series Bulletin: Law Enforcement and Juvenile Crime,* December 2001. Washington, DC: Department of Justice.

Ogle, R. 1999. "Prison Privatization: An Environmental Catch 22." *Justice Quarterly* 14 (3): 579–600.

Packer, H. 1968. *The Limits of the Criminal Sanction.* Stanford, CA: Stanford University Press.

Papke, D. 1986. "The Legal Profession and Its Ethical Responsibilities: A History." In *Ethics and the Legal Profession,* eds. M. Davis and F. Elliston, 29–49. Buffalo, NY: Prometheus.

Parenti, C. 1999. *Lockdown America: Police and Prisons in the Age of Crisis.* New York City: Verso (New Left Books).

Pasztor, D. 2003. "Laywer, Ex-judges Fear Texas About to Kill an Innocent Man." *Austin American Statesman,* March 6, 2003: A1, A11.

Pasztor, D. "Rejected Appeals leave Inmate with Execution Date a Day Away," *Austin American Statesman,* 11 March 2003, A1.

Paul, R., and L. Elder. 2003. *Ethical Reasoning. The Foundation for Critical Thinking.* Retrieved February 11, 2003 from www.criticalthinking.com.

Payne, D. 2002. *Police Liability: Lawsuits Against the Police.* Durham, NC: Carolina Academic Press.

Pearson, F. 2002. "The Effects of Behavioral/Cognitive-Behavioral Programs on Recidivism. *Crime and Delinquency* 48 (3): 476–497.

Pellicotti, Joseph. 1990. "Ethics and the Criminal Defense: A Client's Desire to Testify Untruthfully." In *Ethics and Criminal Justice,* ed. F. Schmalleger, 67–78. Bristol, IN: Wyndam Hall Press.

Pepinsky, H. 1999. "Peacemaking Criminology and Social Justice." In *Social Justice/Criminal Justice,* ed. B. Arrigo, 51–69. Belmont, CA: Wadsworth.

Perez, E. 2001. "For Profit Prison Firm Wackenhut Tries to Break Shackles to Growth." *Wall Street Journal.* Retrieved May 15, 2001, from www.msnbc. com/news/570728.asp?cpi=1.

Piller, C., and R. Mejia. 2003. "FBI's Bullet Analysis Method Is Flawed, Studies Suggest." *Austin American-Statesman,* February 4, 2003: A8.

Plohetski, T. 2002. "Hearing Resumes Today for Fired Austin Officer." *Austin American-Statesman,* November 18, 2002: B3.

Pinkele, C., and W. Louthan. 1985. *Discretion, Justice and Democracy: A Public Policy Perspective.* Ames: Iowa State University Press.

Platt, A. 1977. *The Child Savers.* Chicago: University of Chicago Press.

Postema, G. 1986. "Moral Responsibility in Professional Ethics." In *Ethics and the Legal Profession,* eds. M. Davis and F. Elliston, 158–179. Buffalo, NY: Prometheus.

Power, C., and L. Kohlberg. 1980. "Faith, Morality, and Ego Development." In *Toward Moral and Religious Maturity,* eds. J. Fowler and C. Bursselmans, 311–372. Morristown, NJ: Silver Burdett.

Pranis, K. 2001. "Sodexho to End Support for Right Wing Lobby." News Release. Retrieved April 20, 2001, from www.nomoreprisons.org.

Prenzler, T. 2000. "Civilian Oversight of Police: A Test of Capture Theory." *British Journal of Criminology* 40: 659–674.

Prenzler, T. 1995. "Police Gratuities: What the Public Thinks." *Criminal Justice Ethics* 14 (1): 15–26.

Prenzler, T., A. Harrison, and A. Ede. 1996. The Royal Commission into the NSW Police Service. *Current Affairs Bulletin,* April/May: 4–13.

Prenzler, T., and J. Ransley. 2002. *Police Reform: Building Integrity.* Sydney, Australia: Hawkins Press.

Prenzler, T., and C. Ronken. 2001a. "Police Integrity Testing in Australia." *Criminal Justice* 1, 2: 319–342.

Prenzler, T., and C. Ronken. 2001b. "Models of Police Oversight: A

Critique." *Policing and Society* 11: 151–180.

Prior, W. 1991. "Aristotle's Nicomanchean Ethics." In *From Virtue and Knowledge: An Introduction to Ancient Greek Ethics,* ed. W. Prior, 144–193. New York: Routledge, Kegan Paul.

Quinney, R. 1969. *Crime and Justice in America.* New York: Little, Brown.

Quinney, R. 1974. *Critique of the Legal Order.* New York: Little, Brown.

Radelet, M., H. Bedau, and C. Putnam. 1992. *In Spite of Innocence: Erroneous Convictions in Capital Cases.* Boston: Northeastern University Press.

Raphael, D. 1980. *Justice and Liberty.* London: Athlone Press.

Rawls, J. 1957. "Outline of a Decision Procedure for Ethics." *Philosophical Review* (66): 177–197.

Rawls, J. 1971. *A Theory of Justice.* Cambridge, MA: Belknap Press.

Reasons, C. 1973. "The Politicalization of Crime, the Criminal and the Criminologist." *Journal of Criminal Law, Criminology and Police Science* 64 (March): 471–477.

Reichel, P. 1997. *Corrections.* Minneapolis: West.

Reiman, J. 1990. *Justice and Modern Moral Philosophy.* New Haven, CT: Yale University Press.

Report of the Commission on Obscenity and Pornography. 1970. *Final Report.* New York: Random House.

Reuss-Ianni, E. 1983. *Two Cultures of Policing: Street Cops and Management Cops.* New Brunswick, NJ: Transaction Books.

Rich, R. 1978. *Essays on the Theory and Practice of Criminal Justice.* Washington, DC: University Press.

Riddle, A. 2001. "Recent Murder Trial Sparks Debate." *ABC News.* Retrieved on May 21, 2001, from http:// dailynews.yahoo.com/h/ap/ 20010518/vs/young_killers/.http.

Rimer, S. 2000. "Lawyer Sabotaged Case of a Client on Death Row." *New York Times,* Nov. 24, 2000. Retrieved on

November, 11, 2002, from http://www.againstdp.org/sabotage.http.

Roach, K. 2000. "Changing Punishment at the Turn of the Century: Restorative Justice on the Rise." *Canadian Journal of Criminology* 42 (3): 249–269.

Roberg, K. 1981. "Management Research in Criminal Justice: Exploring Ethical Issues." *Journal of Criminal Justice* (9): 41–49.

Robinson, C. 2003. "Perry Wants Review of Convictions in 1999 Sting," *Houston Chronicle,* 14 May 2003, A02.

Roth, A., and J. Roth. 1989. *Devil's Advocates: The Unnatural History of Lawyers.* Berkeley, CA: Nolo Press.

Rothbart, M., D. Hanley, and M. Albert. 1986. "Differences in Moral Reasoning." *Sex Roles* 15, 11/12: 645–653.

Rothlein, S. 1999. "Policy Agency Efforts to Prevent Abuses." In *Human Dignity and the Police: Ethics and Integrity in Police Work,* ed. G. Lynch, 15–27. Springfield, IL: Charles C. Thomas.

Ryan, J. 2002. "The Appearance of Ethics." *Austin American-Statesman,* November 16, 2002: A11.

Salladay, R. 1999. "Prison Guard Union, Davis Cozy Pairing," *San Francisco Examiner,* September 14, 1999: B3.

San Antonio Express News. 2002. "Lawyers Should Not Aid, Abet Wrongdoers." *San Antonio Express News,* December 29, 2002, 2H.

Scheingold, S. 1984. *The Politics of Law and Order.* New York: Longman.

Schoeman, F. 1986. "Undercover Operations: Some Moral Questions About S.804." *Criminal Justice Ethics* 5(2): 16–22.

Schoeman, F. 1985. "Privacy and Police Undercover Work." In *Police Ethics: Hard Choices in Law Enforcement,* eds. W. Heffernan and T. Stroup, 133–153. New York: John Jay Press.

Schoeman, F. 1982. "Friendship and Testimonial Privileges." In *Ethics, Public Policy and Criminal Justice,* eds. F. Elliston

and N. Bowie, 257–272. Cambridge, MA: Oelgeschlager, Gunn and Hain.

Sellin, T. 1970. "The Conflict of Conduct Norms." In *The Sociology of Crime and Delinquency,* eds. M. Wolfgang, L. Savitz, and N. Johnston, 186–189. New York: Wiley.

Serrano, R., and R. Ostrow. 2000. "Probe of FBI Lab Reviews 3,000 Cases — Affects None." *LATimes.com.* Retrieved August 21, 2000, from http://www.latimes.com/news/front/20000817/t0000077169.http.

Sheley, J. 1985. *Exploring Crime.* Belmont, CA: Wadsworth.

Sherman, L. 1985a. "Becoming Bent: Moral Careers of Corrupt Policemen." In *Moral Issues in Police Work,* eds. F. Elliston and M. Feldberg, 253–273. Totawa, NJ: Rowman & Allanheld.

Sherman, L. 1985b. "Equity Against Truth: Value Choices in Deceptive Investigations." In *Police Ethics: Hard Choices in Law Enforcement,* eds. W. Heffernan and T. Stroup, 117–133. New York: John Jay Press.

Sherman, Lawrence. 1982. "Learning Police Ethics." *Criminal Justice Ethics* 1(1): 10–19.

Sherman, L. 1981. *The Teaching of Ethics in Criminology and Criminal Justice.* Washington, DC: Joint Commission on Criminology and Criminal Justice Education and Standards, LEAA.

Silberman, M. 1995. *A World of Violence: Corrections in America.* Belmont, CA: Wadsworth.

Skolnick, J. 1982. "Deception by Police." *Criminal Justice Ethics* 1(2): 40–54.

Skolnick, J., and J. Fyfe. 1993. *Above the Law: Police and the Excessive Use of Force.* New York: The Free Press.

Skolnick, J., and R. Leo. 1992. "Ideology and the Ethics of Crime Control." *Criminal Justice Ethics* 11 (1): 3–13.

Smith, D. 1982. "Ideology and the Ethics of Economic Crime Control." In *Ethics, Public Policy and Criminal Justice,* eds. F. Elliston and N. Bowie, 133–156. Cambridge, MA: Oelgeschlager, Gunn and Hain.

Smith, S., and R. Meyer. 1987. *Law, Behavior, and Mental Health.* New York: New York University Press.

Sniffen, M. 1997. "FBI Suspends Agent Whose Charges Led to Critical Report." *Austin American-Statesman,* January 28, 1997: A5.

Solomon, A. 1999. "Wackenhut Detention Ordeal." *Village Voice.* Retrieved on March 5, 1999, from http://www.villagevoice.com/features/9935/solomon.html.

Souryal, S. 1999a. "Corruption of Prison Personnel." In *Prison and Jail Administration: Practice and Theory,* eds. P. Carlson and J. Garrett, 171–177. Gaithersburg, MD: Aspen Publishing.

Souryal, S. 1999b. "Personal Loyalty to Superiors in Criminal Justice Agencies." *Justice Quarterly* 16 (4): 871–906.

Souryal, S. 1996a. "Probation as Good Faith." *Texas Probation* 11 (3): 1–6.

Souryal, S. 1996b. "Personal Loyalty to Superiors in Public Service." *Criminal Justice Ethics,* Summer/Fall: 44–62.

Souryal, Sam. 1992. *Ethics in Criminal Justice: In Search of the Truth.* Cincinnati, OH: Anderson.

Souryal, S., and Potts, D. 1996. "What Am I Supposed to Fall Back On? Cultural Literacy in Criminal Justice Ethics." *Journal of Criminal Justice Education* (4): 15–41.

Sowers, C. 2001. "Lawyers Seek Panel to Investigate When Innocents Sent to Prison." *The Arizona Republic.* Retrieved on November 12, 2001, from http://www.arizonarepublic.com/arizona/articles/1112innocence12.html.

Spader, D. 1984. "Rule of Law v. Rule of Man: The Search for the Golden Zigzag Between Conflicting Fundamental Values." *Journal of Criminal Justice* 12: 379–394.

Spence, G. 1989. *With Justice for None.* New York: Penguin.

Stace, W. 1995. "Ethical Relativity and Ethical Absolutism." In *Morality and Criminal Justice,* eds. D. Close and

N. Meier, 25–32. Cincinnati, OH: Anderson.

Staples, W. 1997. *The Culture of Surveillance.* New York: St. Martin's.

Stefanic, M. 1981. "Police Ethics in a Changing Society." *The Police Chief,* May: 62–64.

Sterba, J. 1980. *The Demands of Justice.* Notre Dame, IN: University of Notre Dame Press.

Sterngold, J. 2000. "Los Angeles Police Admit a Vast Management Lapse." *New York Times,* March 2, 2000: A14.

Stickels, J. 2003. *The Victim Satisfaction Model in Criminal Justice.* Ph.D. dissertation from University of Texas.

Stitt, B., and G. James. 1985. "Entrapment: An Ethical Analysis." In *Moral Issues in Police Work,* eds. F. Elliston and M. Feldberg, 129–147. Totawa, NJ: Rowman and Allanheld.

Stover, R. 1989. *Making It and Breaking It: The Fate of Public Interest Commitment During Law School,* ed. H. Erlanger. Urbana: University of Illinois Press.

Stuntz, W. 2002. "Terrorism, Federalism, and Police Misconduct." *Harvard Journal of Law and Public Policy* 25 (2): 665–680.

Sutton, L. 1991. "Getting Around the Fourth Amendment." In *Thinking About Police: Contemporary Readings,* ed. C. Klockars and S. Mastrofski, 433–446. New York: McGraw-Hill.

Sykes, G. 1996. "How Much Is Our Credibility Worth?" *The Ethics Roll Call* 3(1) (1996): 5.

Sykes, G. 1989. "The Functional Nature of Police Reform: The Myth of Controlling the Police." In *Critical Issues in Policing,* eds. R. Dunham and G. Alpert, 292–304. Prospect Heights, IL: Waveland.

Sykes, G. 1980. "The Defects of Total Power." In *Keepers: Prison Guards and Contemporary Corrections,* ed. B. Crouch. Springfield, IL: Charles C. Thomas.

Talbot, M. 2003. "Catch and Release." *The Atlantic online.* Retrieved Junuary 23, 2003, from http://www.thatlantic.com/

cgi-bin/send.cgi?page=http%2A//
www.theatlantic.com/issues/.

Talvi, S. 2002. "The Other War." *The Nation,* December 24, 2002.

Tanay, E. 1982. "Psychiatry and the Prison System." *Journal of Forensic Sciences* 27(2): 385–392.

Tanner, R. 2002. "Central Park Case Puts Focus on Confessions." *Austin American-Statesman,* December 7, 2002: A9.

Tarnoff, S. 2001. "Hard Line on a White Lie." *ABA Journal* 87: 32–33.

Taylor, W. 1993. *Brokered Justice: Race Politics and Mississippi Prisons 1798–1992.* Columbus: Ohio State University Press.

Teepin, T. 1996. "For Private Prisons, Crime Does Pay." *Austin American-Statesman.* December 12, 1996: A15.

Texas Criminal Justice Policy Council. 2003. *Overview of the Innerchange Freedom Initiative: The Faith Based Prison Program Within the TDCJ.* February 2003. Austin, TX: Criminal Justice Policy Council (available through Web site).

Thoma, S. 1986. "Estimating Gender Differences in the Comprehension and Preference of Moral Issues." *Developmental Review* (6): 165–180.

Thompson, D. 1980. "Paternalism in Medicine, Law and Public Policy." In *Ethics Teaching in Higher Education,* eds. D. Callahan and S. Bok, 3–20. Hastings, NY: Hastings Center.

"Three Guards Acquitted." 2002. *New York Times,* February 16, 2002: A13.

Toch, H. 1977. *Living in Prison.* New York: Free Press.

Toch, H., and J. Klofas. 1982. "Alienation and Desire for Job Enrichment Among C.O.s," *Federal Probation* 46: 35–47.

Tonry, M., L. Ohlin, and D. Farrington. 1991. *Human Development and Criminal Behavior.* New York: Springer Verlag.

Tyler, T. 1990. *Why People Obey the Law.* New Haven, CT: Yale University Press.

Umbreit, M. 1994. *Victim Meets Offender: The Impact of Restorative Justice and*

Mediation. Monsey, NY: Criminal Justice Press.

Umbreit, M., and M. Carey. 1995. "Restorative Justice Implications for Organizational Change." *Federal Probation* 59(1): 47–54.

Umbreit, M., R. Coates, and B. Vos. 2002. "Peacemaking Circles in Minnesota: An Exploratory Study." *Crime Victims Report* 5 (6): 81–82.

Uniform Crime Reports. 1998. *Crime in the United States.* Washington, DC: Department of Justice.

Van Maanen, J. 1978. "The Asshole." In *Policing: A View From the Street,* eds. P. Manning and J. van Maanen, 221–240. Santa Monica, CA: Goodyear Publishing Company.

Van Natta, D. 2003. "Blurry Line Marks Banned, Acceptable in Interrogations," *Austin American Statesman,* March 2003, A13.

Van Ness, D., and K. Heetderks Strong. 1997. *Restoring Justice.* Cincinnati, OH: Anderson.

von Hirsch, A. 1985. *Past or Future Crimes.* New Brunswick, NJ: Rutgers University Press.

von Hirsch, A. 1976. *Doing Justice.* New York: Hill and Wang.

von Hirsch, A., and L. Maher. 1992. "Can Penal Rehabilitation Be Revived?" *Criminal Justice Ethics* 11 (1): 25–31.

Walker, L. 1986. "Sex Difference in the Development of Moral Reasoning." *Child Development* 57: 522–526.

Walker, S. 2001. *Police Accountability: The Role of Citizen Oversight.* Belmont, CA: Wadsworth Publishing.

Walker, S. 1985. *Sense and Nonsense About Crime.* Monterey, CA: Brooks/Cole.

Walker, S., C. Spohn, M. Delone. 2000. *The Color of Justice.* Belmont, CA: Wadsworth.

Walsh, A. 2001. *Biosocial Criminology: Introduction and Integration.* Cincinnati, OH: Anderson.

Walsh, A. 1995. *Biosociology: An Emerging Paradigm.* Trenton, NY: Praeger Publishing.

Ward, G. 2001. "C.C.A. Majority Shareholder to Sell Stocks." *Tennessean.* Retrieved May 23, 2001, from www.tennessean.com/business/archives/01/04/05094888.shtml?Element_ID=50948.

Ward, M. 1996. "State Approves Faith-Based Pre-Release Program for Texas Inmates." *Austin American-Statesman,* November 16, 1996: B12.

Weber, D. 1987. "Still in Good Standing. The Crisis in Attorney Discipline." *American Bar Association Journal,* November: 58–63.

Weitzer, R. 1999. "Citizens' Perceptions of Police Misconduct: Race and Neighborhood Context," Justice Quarterly 16 (4): 819–846.

Whitehead, J. 1991. "Ethical Issues in Probation and Parole." In *Justice, Crime, and Ethics,* eds. M. Braswell, B. McCarthy, and B. McCarthy, 253–273. Cincinnati, OH: Anderson.

Whitman, J. 1998. "What Is Wrong with Inflicting Shame Sanctions?" *Yale Law Journal* 197 (4): 1055–1092.

Wiley, L. 1988. "Moral Education in a Correctional Setting: Reaching the Goal by a Different Road." *Journal of Offender Services and Rehabilitation* 12 (2): 161–174.

Williams, Gregory. 1984. *The Law and Politics of Police Discretion.* Westport, CT: Greenwood.

Wilson, J. Q. 1976. *Varieties of Police Behavior.* New York: Atheneum.

Wilson, J.Q. 1993. *The Moral Sense.* NYC: The Free Press.

Wood, D. 2003. "Registration for Arabs Draws Fire." *FindLaw.com.* Retrieved February 10, 2003, from http://news.findlaw.com/csmonitor/s/20030206/06feb2003104706.http.

Wood, J. 1997. *Royal Commission into the New South Wales Police Service, Final Report.* Sydney: Government of the State of N.S.W. (Cited in T. Prenzler and C. Ronken, 2001.)

Worral, J. 2001. "Addicted to Drug War: The Role of Civil Asset Forfeiture as a Budgetary Necessity in Contemporary Law Enforcement." *Journal of Criminal Justice* 29 (3): 171–187.

Wozencraft, Kim. 1990. *Rush.* New York: Random House.

Wren, T. 1985. "Whistle-blowing and Loyalty to One's Friends." In *Police Ethics: Hard Choices in Law Enforcement,* eds. W. Heffernan and T. Stroup, 25–47. New York: John Jay Press.

Zimmer, L. 1986. *Women Guarding Men.* Chicago: University of Chicago Press.

Zimring, F., G. Hawkins, and S. Kamin. 2001. *Punishment and Democracy: Three Strikes and You're Out in California.* Oxford: Oxford University Press.

Zupan, L. 1992. "The Progress of Women Correctional Officers in All-Male Prisons." In *The Changing Roles of Women in the Criminal Justice System,* ed. I. Moyer, 323–343. Prospect Heights, IL: Waveland.

Name Index

Subject Index

Table of Cases